Criminology

W9-DDS-218

CRIMINOLOGY

THIRD EDITION

Piers Beirne
UNIVERSITY OF SOUTHERN MAINE

James Messerschmidt
UNIVERSITY OF SOUTHERN MAINE

Westview
PRESS

A Member of the Perseus Books Group

For our students, who continue to
teach us how little we know

All rights reserved. Printed in the United States of America. No part of this publication may be reproduced or transmitted in any form or by any means, electronic or mechanical, including photocopy, recording, or any information storage and retrieval system, without permission in writing from the publisher.

Copyright © 2000 by Westview Press, A Member of the Perseus Books Group

Published in 2000 in the United States of America by Westview Press, 5500 Central Avenue, Boulder, Colorado 80301-2877, and in the United Kingdom by Westview Press, 12 Hid's Copse Road, Cumnor Hill, Oxford OX2 9JJ

Find us on the World Wide Web at www.westviewpress.com

Library of Congress Cataloging-in-Publication Data
Beirne, Piers.
  Criminology / Piers Beirne, James Messerschmidt.—3rd ed.
    p. cm.
  Includes bibliographical references and index.
  ISBN 0-8133-6655-0
  1. Criminology. I. Messerschmidt, James W. II. Title.
HV6025.B43 1999
364—dc21
                                                                99-41263
                                                                CIP

Designed by Heather Hutchison

The paper used in this publication meets the requirements of the American National Standard for Permanence of Paper for Printed Library Materials Z39.48-1984.

10   9   8   7   6   5   4   3   2   1

Brief Table of Contents

Detailed Table of Contents

Tables, Figures, and Boxes

Figures

Preface to the Third Edition

In this third edition of *Criminology*, we have tinkered with the original organization of chapters so that the structure of the book has an added coherence and a tighter feel. Where necessary, we have revised certain sections of the book, adding material in some cases and subtracting it in others. New and up-to-date empirical data are presented throughout the book, and we discuss types of crime, such as animal abuse and interpersonal violence in the workplace, that we did not address in the previous editions. In addition, several theories are discussed here for the first time, including routine activities; self-control; control balance; and revised strain theory.

The aim of *Criminology* is to introduce the basic aspects of modern criminology to undergraduate students. This is no easy task in such a diverse discipline. All textbook authors have to make a number of hard choices. This book very much reflects our teaching experience in the undergraduate criminology program at the University of Southern Maine, where our 200-level course in criminology both surveys the major areas of the discipline and provides an introduction to more specialized, upper-level courses in criminology. We have attempted both to strike a balance between depth of analysis and breadth of coverage and to make the book comprehensive in its presentation of the sociological aspects of criminology. Although we aim to survey all the major aspects of the field, we especially emphasize the importance of historical, feminist, and comparative perspectives on crime.

This book is divided into four parts. Part One (Chapters 1–2) focuses on two surprisingly difficult questions: What is crime? How can we measure crime? Chapter 1 outlines the two major ways in which popular discourse about crime is articulated—through the mass media and through the pronouncements of the moral entrepreneurs of social problems—and summarizes the key elements of crime as a legal category. The chapter stresses the importance of sociological definitions of crime and introduces the three key sociological concepts of criminology: crime, criminal law, and criminalization. Chapter 2 outlines the major sources of crime data. These include both official crime data (the FBI's *Uniform Crime Reports*, the *National Crime Victimization Survey*, and records of various federal agencies) and unofficial crime data (self-report studies, participant observation, biographies, and comparative and historical data). We stress here that crime data can never represent criminal behavior objectively because there are inherent biases in the way that all data are conceived and constructed. Data do not speak for themselves! How crime data are explained, therefore, depends both on criminologists' concepts of crime and on the assumptions underlying their theories of crime. The importance of this point will become clear as the contents of the book unfold.

Part Two (Chapters 3–8) is a systematic guide to modern criminological theory and its historical development. Theories about crime can be greatly misunderstood by wrenching them from the context of the era in which they were conceived; therefore, the six chapters in Part Two unfold chronologically, with respect both to the contents of each chapter and to the position of each chapter in relation to the other five. We believe that all theories, including those popular today, should at first be understood historically. One virtue of this belief is the humbling discovery that our understanding of crime has advanced only very little beyond that of theorists of a century ago. In describing each theory, we try to show why it arose when it did, what theories it supplanted or modified, how it was understood and criticized by its competitors, and how it contributes to our understanding of crime today.

Part Three (Chapters 9–14) provides an introduction to various types of crime. Typologies of crime can be constructed in an infinite variety of ways. We have chosen a sociological typology that combines (1) those crimes usually defined in the legal codes and (2) those crimes outside the criminal law that have received much attention in the sociological and criminological literature. Because crime is found in every social institution, the chapters in Part Three offer a comprehensive understanding of the nature, extent, types, and costs of crime found not only in the street but also in the family, the workplace, and the state. In these chapters, we rely heavily on research done in the United States, but we also include material from other countries, such as Canada and Britain.

Part Four (Chapters 15–16) tries to synthesize some of the main themes of Part Two and Part Three. Here we offer the rudiments of a critical sociological perspective on the relationship between crime and structured social inequality. In Chapter 15 we examine the influence of four major forms of social inequality—class, gender, race, and age—on patterns of crime and victimization in the United States. In Chapter 16 we show how the understanding of crime in the United States can be greatly enhanced by examining crime in other societies. We outline the key concepts and sources of data in comparative criminology and assess the merits of various cross-national generalizations about crime and crime rates.

We have avoided the common division in criminology textbooks between crime and corrections by altogether omitting the usual lengthy descriptions of the criminal justice system. Our focus in this book is not criminal justice but crime, and we have tried to discuss the complexity of the latter in the depth we believe it warrants. However, various aspects of social control (criminalization, labeling, police practices, comparative penal policies, and so on) naturally press their claims for attention, and we explore them here especially when they affect the links between crime and structured social inequality.

CHAPTER PREVIEWS AND CHAPTER REVIEWS

Each chapter begins with a *chapter preview* of the main themes that follow. Included in the preview is a list of *key terms* that you should be especially aware of as you read through the chapter. These terms are highlighted in the text and then followed immediately by a definition to help you understand them more easily. At the end of each chapter, a *chapter review* outlines the major points that have been discussed.

QUESTIONS FOR CLASS DISCUSSION AND SUGGESTIONS FOR FURTHER STUDY

Each chapter review is followed by several *questions for classroom discussion*. These questions are followed by a list of *suggested readings* that will be helpful for essays or term papers. Each of these suggested readings is then followed by several *websites* that offer additional information on specific crimes and theories.

WEBSITES

Because the Internet is an important source of information for criminology, we recommend that students explore the websites that we have listed at the end of each chapter. The use of these websites will allow students to expand and update their horizons somewhat beyond the information and analysis presented in any given chapter. For instance, if a student is curious about recent data on workplace deaths and injuries, s/he can point the web browser to the site provided at the end of the chapter, search for the federal and state legislation governing workplace safety, and thereby begin to compile a report on the topic. Indeed, most government agencies maintain websites, and many activist organizations devote resources to their own websites.

REFERENCES AND GLOSSARY

After the main text, there is a comprehensive, alphabetical list of *references* cited in the book. In the body of the text, you will find the references cited in the following way: (Smith, 1999:21). This example begins with the last name of the author (Smith), then gives the year the material was published or written (1999), and ends with the page number of the citation (21). In the *glossary* students will find brief definitions of all of the key terms used in the book.

A NOTE ON CHAUVINIST LANGUAGE

In writing this textbook, we have been especially sensitive to chauvinist language, which creates the impression that one particular group—gender, race, country, species, and so on—is superior to another. For example, we do not use "he," "his," or "him" when referring to people in general because these terms effectively exclude women. Similarly, we do not refer to the United States as "America," because the latter term should properly be reserved to signify the entire Western Hemisphere—North, Central, and South America.

Piers Beirne
James Messerschmidt

Acknowledgments

A book such as this inevitably incurs many debts. First and foremost, we thank our many students, who forced us to clarify our ideas and who provided us with critical comments during our classroom presentations of the material. During the gestation period of this third edition, very competent and usually cheerful research assistance was provided by Debra Bruns, Charlene Leavitt, Cara Neary, and Cheryl Palmer.

Our colleagues in the Department of Criminology at the University of Southern Maine have contributed tremendously to this book with their time, their wisdom, their energy, and, thank goodness, their good humor. In these respects it is hard to imagine two finer colleagues than Kimberly Cook and Sandra Wachholz. Thanks, too, to Rosemary Miller, without whose help and calm sanity this book would never have been completed so smoothly. Many colleagues at other institutions were kind enough to read portions of the manuscript. Their comments have undoubtedly turned it into a far better book than it otherwise would have been. In this regard, we are indebted to Stuart Henry, Eastern Michigan University; Dana Britton, Dianne Carmody, Travis Eaton, William Alex Pridemore, SUNY–Albany; Eleanor Miller, the University of Wisconsin–Milwaukee; Joseph E. Jacoby, Bowling Green State University; J. William Spencer, Purdue University; Sandra Emory, University of New Mexico; Edna Erez, Kent State University; Pat Murphy, SUNY–Geneseo; Julius Debro, University of Washington; Polly F. Radosh, Western Illinois University; Mary T. Texeira, California State University–San Bernardino; Karen F. Parker, University of Florida; Kathleen Casey Jordan, Western Connecticut State University; and Alan Block, Pennsylvania State University.

A textbook such as this could not have been written without the constant support of the staff of the Interlibrary Loan Services at USM's Glickman Library; R. Carr Ross, Barbara Stevens, Cassandra Fitzherbert, and David Vardeman have our heartfelt gratitude for their professional expertise and unfailing patience.

Finally, for their enthusiasm and editorial skills we wish to thank the staff at Westview, especially Adina Popescu, Tom Kulesa, Leo Wiegman, Andrew Day, Michelle Schayes, Julie Tesser, Kevin W. Perizzolo, and David Toole.

P. B.
J. M.

Preview

Chapter 1 introduces:
- the distorted images of crime projected by the mass media
- how crime as a sociological problem differs from crime as a social problem
- three of the key concepts of criminology: "crime," "criminal law," and "criminalization"
- various sociological definitions of crime, including crime as a breach of conduct norms, crime as social harm, crime as a violation of human rights, and crime as a form of deviance

Key Terms

conduct norms　　　　　　　　human rights
crime　　　　　　　　　　　　social control
criminalization　　　　　　　social problem
criminal justice system　　　sociological problem
criminal law　　　　　　　　the state
deviance

1.1　IMAGES OF CRIME

Our focus in this book is **crime**. What is crime? How much crime is there? How can we explain it? Even before reading this book, you probably have opinions about the causes of crime, its harmful effects, and how best to control it. We all hold strong opinions about crime. But you will learn here that crime is a difficult phenomenon to explain. Nowhere in this book will you be offered any neat and tidy answers. There are none!

Whatever the depth of your own opinions about crime, it is widely seen as one of the leading social problems today. Many people are genuinely fearful of crime. On TV, in everyday conversation, and in our worst nightmares, our fears are constantly fueled by images of crime, especially violent crime.

Crime as a Social Problem

Thirty years ago the National Commission on the Causes and Prevention of Violence made the following bleak predictions about the quality of life in large cities in the near future (1970:38–39):

High-rise apartment buildings and residential compounds protected by private guards and security devices will be fortified cells for upper-middle and high-income populations living at prime locations in the city.

Suburban neighborhoods, geographically far removed from the central city, will be protected mainly by economic homogeneity and by distance from population groups with the highest propensities to commit crimes.

Lacking a sharp change in federal and state policies, ownership of guns will be almost universal in the suburbs, homes will be fortified by an array of devices from window grills to electronic surveillance equipment, armed citizen volunteers in cars will supplement inadequate police patrols in neighborhoods closer to the central city, and extreme left-wing and right-wing groups will have tremendous armories of weapons that could be brought into play without any provocation.

High-speed, patrolled expressways will be sanitized corridors connecting safe areas, and private automobiles, taxicabs, and commercial vehicles will be equipped routinely with unbreakable glass, light armor, and other security features. Inside garages or valet parking will be available at safe buildings in or near the central city. Armed guards will ride shotgun on all forms of public transportation.

Streets and residential neighborhoods in the central city will be unsafe in differing degrees, and the ghetto slum neighborhoods will be places of terror with widespread crime, perhaps entirely out of police control during nighttime hours. Armed guards will protect all public facilities such as schools, libraries, and playgrounds in these areas.

Between the unsafe, deteriorating central city on the one hand and the network of safe, prosperous areas and sanitized corridors on the other, there will be, not unnaturally, intensifying hatred and deepening division. Violence will increase further, and the defensive response of the affluent will become still more elaborate.

Because of our great fear of crime, the Commission warned, we are in danger of closeting ourselves in anticrime fortresses. To a certain extent the Commission's terrifying images of life in large U.S. cities have not been contradicted, at least not in the minds of the public or, as we will soon see, in the messages conveyed by the media.

It seems that we live in a society whose obsession with crime reaches into almost every corner of our public and private lives. Candidates for political office campaign on the promise of restoring law and order to the nation's streets. Elections are sometimes decided in favor of the candidate with a hard-line approach to the detection and punishment of criminals. But there is a widespread feeling that crime and violence are rapidly spinning out of control and are quite unaffected by police intervention. Neighborhood crime watch programs and groups like the Guardian Angels have prospered across the country. First created in the 1970s to assist in road traffic management, video surveillance systems have at the turn of the millennium been rapidly extended to public transport, city streets, the workplace, stores, the approaches to public buildings, and sports stadiums (Vitalis, 1998). Opinion polls (such as Gallup, 1997:21) show that the public believes both that crime is by far the most important problem facing this country today and that the greatest problem facing the nation's public schools is not an absence of academic excellence but a lack of student discipline.

Research shows consistently that the relatively powerless sections of the community—such as the elderly, females, and racial minorities—experience the greatest fear of crime and suffer the greatest psychological trauma from its effects (e.g., Bennett and Flavin, 1994; Madriz, 1997; and see Chapter 9.2). Indeed, a National Institute of Justice study estimates that when one includes such factors as pain, suffering, and the reduced quality of life, the cost of crime in the United States is $450 billion annually (Miller, Cohen, and Wiersma, 1996:1; and see Butterfield, 1996). This colossal figure, which does not even include the costs associated with many forms of white-collar crime and drug-related crimes, is nearly double the size of the U.S. Defense Department's total annual budget! Though criminologists may debate whether fears of crime accurately reflect the likelihood of victimization, it is true that the rate of violent crime, especially homicide, is considerably higher in the United States than in any other technologically developed country. In short, to most citizens crime is the leading **social problem** in the United States today.

But what are "social problems"? How are they defined as problems, by whom, and for what reasons?

We must stress that there is no objective set of social conditions whose harmful effects necessarily make them social problems. As Herbert Blumer once wrote, a social problem

Fear of crime: In 1970 the National Commission on the Causes and Prevention of Violence predicted that before very long most private homes in the United States would be protected by an array of security devices. Current trends support the prediction. What might the rococo style of the otherwise unwelcoming steel gate in this photo reveal about the homeowners who erected it? (Courtesy of Cathy Cheney)

must be understood primarily in terms of how it is defined and conceived in society (1971:300; and see Sasson, 1995). What is regarded as a social problem thus varies over time—child abuse, for example, has been seen as a full-blown problem only quite recently (see Chapter 9.2). Social problems also vary from person to person or group to group. For example, some people regard social inequality as a social problem; others see it as a virtue that encourages competition and economic responsibility. Some people regard the use of animals in laboratory experiments as a necessary step in the elimination of disease among humans; others see this as unjustified abuse of our fellow creatures.

Several factors determine whether given circumstances are defined as a social problem. These factors include the pressure tactics of private interest groups (for instance, the American Medical Association, the National Rifle Association, Mothers Against Drunk Driving, and so on) and the professional utterances of public officials such as politicians, judges, police and correctional officers, and, on occasion, those engaged in teaching, writing, and research in the social sciences, including criminology (Jamrozik and Nocella, 1998:64–75). Nowadays, concerns about some problems are conveyed to the public

Dick Locker's View, Chicago Tribune, 1998

largely through the mass media—TV in particular, but also newspapers, the Internet, advertising, movies, videos, and so on. Mass media are the most influential mechanisms for creating public agreement about social problems. Observe some of the images of crime portrayed in the mass media.

Crime in the Mass Media

Each of us already has a great deal of information about crime. We know, for example, that some areas of cities are safer than others. We know that it is dangerous to leave infants unattended, front doors unbolted, cars unlocked, and bicycles unchained. We routinely process such knowledge, and we take defensive action accordingly.

We know, or at least we think we know, what sorts of people are likely to commit a crime. Each of us has an image of the typical criminal—a sick, degenerate, violent person who preys on the innocent and the vulnerable. But crime is a difficult phenomenon to explain, given that our obsession with it is seldom based on rational reflection. Far from it. In modern societies like the United States, everyday images of crime tend to be filtered through the self-interested and often distorted lenses of the mass media.

Reflect for a moment on some of the typical images of crime routinely conveyed to us by the mass media. The media construct two predominant images of crime and criminality: the amount of crime and the most common types of crime.

Prime-crime TV: The mass media routinely produce stereotypical images of crime for popular consumption, such as this scene from the television series *NYPD Blue*.

Concerning images of the amount of crime, it is important to note that crime consumes an enormous chunk of dramatic and informational space in the media. According to media researchers (Graber, 1980:26; UCLA, 1998), 33 percent of the total TV program time in the United States is devoted to crime or law-enforcement shows, with a concentration at prime time. Among the most popular prime-time crime TV shows are *NYPD Blue, Homicide, Law and Order,* and *Walker, Texas Ranger.* Many topical TV shows (such as *ER*) also regularly concern crime, as do such documentaries as *Unsolved Mysteries, 48 Hours, 60 Minutes,* and *Dateline.* New "reality-based" shows—some featuring talk-show interaction among police officers or even audience participation—include *COPS, Real Stories of the Highway Patrol,* and *America's Most Wanted* (Cavender and Bond-Maupin, 1993; Cavender, 1998). Besides the content of TV shows, TV news and newspapers also conveniently convey to us images of the amount of crime. A high percentage of stories in the evening and late-night local news programs concerns crime, as do their lead items. Indeed, it has been found that crime and justice topics occupy 10–13 percent of all national TV news, 20 percent of local TV news, and as much as 25 percent of all newspaper news space (Surette, 1998:67).

Concerning images of the most common type of crime, it is important to recognize that the media are preoccupied with violent crime rather than other forms of crime. Thus, nearly all the prime-time crime shows mentioned previously address violent crime exclusively. According to a violence index used by researcher George Gerbner for the years 1967 to 1987, approximately 80 percent of all TV programs contained violence (Liebert and Sprafkin, 1988:116–119). In addition, at least 90 percent of children's cartoon shows contain violence. Although the definition of violence in Gerbner's index may seem overly broad to some (it includes violence in humorous situations, for example), the fact remains that violence, however defined, is the staple of the crime-related TV diet. In the news, as well, there is a strong bias toward coverage of murder, sexual crimes, and other forms of violence, often coupled with drug abuse (Ericson, Baranek, and Chan, 1989; Surette, 1998:67–68; Welch, Fenwick, and Roberts, 1998).

Moreover, the mass media episodically channel viewer attention toward particular sorts of immoral or criminal behavior. Examples of moral panics aided by the media include the white slavers of the Progressive Era, sex fiends in the 1940s, communists in the 1950s, serial murderers during the 1980s (see Chapter 2.1), youth crime in the 1990s (Baer and Chambliss, 1997), and the ever-present druggie. As Philip Jenkins (1988:1) warns:

> If we relied solely on the evidence of the mass media, we might well believe that, a particular form of immoral or criminal behavior becomes so dangerous every few years as almost to threaten the foundations of society. . . . These panics are important in their own right for what they reveal about social concerns and prejudices often based on xenophobia and anti-immigrant prejudice.

At this point, let us comment briefly on the typical images of crime conveyed by the mass media:

First, the enormous volume of crime-related items in the media creates the mistaken image of a society with an enormous amount of violent crime. Though for the moment we leave open the question of how much crime there is in the United States, we should stress that the volume of crime in the media (in TV shows and news items) bears scant relation to what is reported in official crime data such as the FBI's *Uniform Crime Reports* (see Chapter 2.1). Graber (1980:39) found in the *Chicago Tribune,* for example, that although murder constitutes only 0.2 percent of all crimes recorded by the police, it composes 26.2 percent of all newspaper entries about crime. Moreover, sometimes when the media accurately depict the volume of violent crime, they distort its seriousness. For example, one study has found that 84 percent of prime-time TV shows contain at least one episode of sexual harassment, which perhaps accurately reflects the commonplace nature of this violent crime (Grauerholz and King, 1997). But the depiction of sexual harassment in the media tends to reflect several myths, including the view that it is not a serious offense and that its victims can often remedy the situation themselves (pp. 142–143). Another study shows that *Time* and *Newsweek* cover stories misrepresent the problem of crime as primarily a problem of urban African Americans (Barlow, 1998).

Second, the media have created the misleading impression that crime rates increased consistently during the last decade. From the 1940s to the present, the percentage of total TV program time devoted to crime-related shows has persistently increased; however, according to official crime data, the violent crime rate fell sharply in the 1980s and 1990s (see Chapter 2.1). Also, white-collar crimes are the least likely crimes to be reported on TV (Ericson, Baranek, and Chan, 1991:247; Chermak, 1994:574).

Third, the media distort the incidence of nonviolent crime. Thus, whereas nonviolent crimes like theft compose 47 percent of all crimes reported to the police, such crimes constitute only 4 percent of all crime items in newspapers (Graber, 1980; and see Chapter 2.1).

We should not be too surprised that the mass media's images of crime are almost never objective. After all, the mass media depend for their existence on reporting—or creating—the apparently unusual. When social life is routine and orderly, there is little news. Media executives know full well that nothing sells like violence. To maximize their audience, the media feature unusual events rather than representative events; they emphasize the sensational rather than the mundane. But the media's distorted images of crime do not, of course, teach us much about the true nature of crime. To learn about this we must obtain a clearer idea of what crime actually is. In other words, we need a working definition of "crime."

1.2 CRIME, CRIMINAL LAW, AND CRIMINALIZATION

The question "What is crime?" is a surprisingly difficult one to answer. Consider, for example, the events discussed in the book *Captain Kidd and the War Against the Pirates* (Ritchie, 1986).

During the early 1690s the soon-to-be-infamous Captain William Kidd was an obscure naval pirate who was based in New York and who operated in the Caribbean. In 1695 he obtained a commission as a privateer, which allowed him to engage essentially in the same piratical activities, but this time with the economic support and moral blessings of the King and of some of the most powerful families in England. Kidd's commission directed him to sail to the Indian Ocean and to end the practices of pirates from the North American colonies who were plundering British East India Company ships. For attacking and capturing one or more pirate ships and bringing some pirates to trial, Kidd, as well as the King and all the backers of the scheme, would earn a handsome profit. But for doing roughly what he had been commissioned to do, Kidd did not earn the fame and fortune to which he believed he was legally entitled. In 1701, in London, Kidd was tried on charges of murder and multiple conspiracies, convicted after a farcical trial, sentenced to death by hanging, and—after a false start when the hangman's rope broke and the unfortunate Kidd lay stunned on the ground—he was duly executed. During his trial and execution—a dramatic time when convicts were expected to repent their sins, beg the indulgence of the Lord, and warn the many onlookers not to tread in their sinful footsteps—Kidd protested his innocence.

Kidd had been caught in the complicated and rapidly changing web of maritime trade and British imperialism of the late seventeenth century. Although there was little evidence that he had engaged in (illegal) piracy rather than (legal) privateering—and therefore British authorities had no proper reason to prosecute him—Kidd's activities in the Red Sea against the French and against the Dutch East India Company ensnared him in a larger movement that would find him a convenient symbol for a much broader problem, even though Kidd was never very successful either as a pirate or as a privateer.

Kidd was squeezed by the coincidence of two forces. On the one hand, there were thriving British companies such as the East India Company that needed order and regularity on the high seas for the profitable expansion of their commerce. On the other hand, there were the administrative and military apparatuses of the British state that, after tremendous expansion as a result of various European wars, could not tolerate maverick and unpredictable challenges to their power. Privateering, or legalized piracy, was therefore doomed. Kidd's activities as a privateer commissioned by royalty and by the rich were suddenly renamed piracy.

This story is a good example of how difficult it is to pinpoint the precise nature of crime. Clearly, Kidd's actions were defined as piracy rather than national heroics largely because of the changing fortunes of British imperialism. It is also clear that nothing in the nature of Kidd's actions was inherently criminal.

What, then, is crime? As a historical phenomenon, the concept of crime is of fairly recent origin. Prior to the eighteenth century, both in western Europe and in colonial North America, most offenses—when not handled privately—were typically the domain either of canon law (religious law) or of civil law (especially the law of torts). **Criminal law** did not yet exist. Moreover, what constitutes crime varies from one culture to another. Thus anthropologists have been unable to find any behavior that is universally defined as crime (see Chapter 16.3). For example, although all known societies have a concept of murder, few societies define the act of murder in exactly the same way. Given such variation, it is nearly impossible for criminologists to agree either on a precise definition of crime or even on the definition of an act as seemingly simple to define as murder. Many sociologists and historians suggest that there is nothing in the nature of any behavior that makes it inherently criminal, because even what counts as crime changes over time within the same culture (see Chapter 7.3).

How, then, should crime be defined? Serious debate among criminologists about the proper definition of crime can be traced to the publication of a report initiated in 1933 by New York's Bureau of Social Hygiene (Michael and Adler, 1971). Written by lawyer Jerome Michael and philosopher Mortimer Adler, this report stressed that great confusion will arise unless criminologists can agree on a precise definition of crime. Only if crime is defined clearly and precisely will it be possible to distinguish criminal behavior from noncriminal behavior: "The most precise and least ambiguous definition of crime is that which defines it as behavior which is prohibited by the criminal code. It follows that a criminal is a person who has behaved in some way prohibited by the criminal law" (pp. 2–3).

Following Michael and Adler's argument, Paul Tappan claimed that crime is an intentional act in violation of the criminal law (statutory and case law), committed without defense or excuse, and penalized by the state as a felony or misdemeanor (Tappan, 1947:100). In this view, therefore, crime is a legalistic category of behavior.

Let us examine some of the major aspects of the legalistic definition of crime.

Crime as a Legal Category

The preceding legalistic definition of crime contains several elements whose formal origins can be traced to the English common law (customary law) of the twelfth century. First and foremost, a crime must be forbidden by criminal law. So, too, criminal law must provide punishment for a crime—a basic principle expressed in the English common law doctrine *nullum crimen sine lege, nulla poena sine lege* (no crime without law, no punishment without law). The formal purpose of criminal law is to protect members of the public from the wrongdoing of others. Rules of criminal law can be found either in statutory law (enacted by legislatures) or in common law (enacted from judicial decisions and based on a principle known as *stare decisis*). Criminal law is distinguished from civil law—such as tort law and contract law—which deals with private wrongs. Whereas a violation of civil law leaves a defendant open to civil suit, a violation of criminal law potentially places a defendant at the point of entry into the **criminal justice system**.

The criminal law categorizes crime in two ways. First, crimes are either *mala in se* or *mala prohibita*. This old and somewhat artificial distinction refers to the apparent differences between "acts that are evil in themselves" *(mala in se)* and "acts that are prohibited" *(mala prohibita)*. Lawyers take this distinction to mean that crimes *mala in se* are acts so inherently wrong that they are universally considered evil, whereas crimes *mala prohibita,* the list of which changes over time, are acts prohibited by statute. Second, the criminal law distinguishes between felonies and misdemeanors. Although these two categories of crime are often separated by procedural differences, the most important difference is that felonies are punishable either by death or by imprisonment in a state penitentiary for a term of not less than one year, whereas misdemeanors are punishable either by fine or by a term in a local jail of less than one year.

A second element of a crime is that it must be a voluntary illegal act or omission (an *actus reus,* some examples of which are given in Chapter 2 [Figure 2.1]). This means that no one can be prosecuted for bad or evil thoughts—although words (such as incitement to riot) can sometimes constitute a criminal act—and that failure to act (omission) can be criminal in situations where there is a legal duty to act. Leaving the scene of a traffic accident and failing to file an annual tax return with the Internal Revenue Service are examples of crimes by omission.

Culpability for a crime depends on a defendant's mental state, variously known as criminal intent or *mens rea.* According to the American Law Institute's *Model Penal Code* (§2.02), one is not guilty of an offense unless one acted with purpose to do the forbidden act, or with knowledge of the nature of the act, or with recklessness or negligence. In some cases intent can be transferred, as, for example, when A intends to shoot B but misses and kills C.

To legal scholars the precise meaning of the term "intent" is often quite elusive. For example, certain categories of individuals are judged legally incapable of forming intent: juveniles under the age of fourteen and those certified as insane or severely retarded. Moreover, in cases of strict liability, intent is not a necessary requirement of guilt. Examples of strict liability offenses include felony murder (a murder committed during a serious felony like rape or arson) and statutory rape (sexual intercourse with a juvenile, which usually means under sixteen years of age).

An act or omission is not a crime if a defendant has a socially legitimate *justification* for doing it or if s/he lacks the criminal responsibility required by the element of *mens rea.* The defense of justification can be raised in three instances: duress, necessity, and duty. The defense of duress is typically limited to homicides. Thus a killing may be justified if an individual reasonably believes that he or she is about to be killed or seriously harmed by another. The defense of necessity is available to defendants who are somehow threatened by natural circumstances over which they have no control, but this defense can be used only when there was no other reasonable course of action available. For example, one would not be guilty of vandalism if, trapped inside a burning department store, one smashed a window in order to escape. The defense of duty is typically raised by public authorities such as police officers. Many killings by police officers in the line of duty are therefore termed "justifiable homicides." This defense is also available in the United States to teachers who use "reasonable" discipline in schools.

Finally, an act or omission may not be a crime if one lacks the necessary criminal responsibility, a condition that negates *mens rea* in several ways and that includes the controversial pleas of entrapment and insanity. The defense of entrapment is intended to discourage the state from creating a crime where none would otherwise have existed. According to the *Model Penal Code* (§2.13), entrapment occurs when police methods entice an average law-abiding citizen to commit a crime. The defense of insanity differs from all other defenses in that, if the plea is successful, in most jurisdictions the defendant is neither acquitted nor released but found "not guilty by reason of insanity." In some states defendants may be found "guilty but mentally ill," in which case they are confined to mental institutions until "cured," at which point they must finish their sentences in prison. This verdict almost always results in the commitment of defendants to mental institutions, often for a longer period than if they had been found guilty of the crime and sentenced to prison. In the United States the majority of states base the legal criteria of insanity on the definition contained in the *Model Penal Code* (§4.01):

1. A person is not responsible for criminal conduct if at the time of such conduct, as a result of mental disease or defect, he lacks substantial capacity to appreciate the criminality (wrongfulness) of his conduct, or to conform his conduct to the requirements of law.
2. The terms "mental disease" or "defect" do not include an abnormality manifested only by repeated criminal or otherwise antisocial conduct.

A key element of the legalistic definition of crime—*mens rea*—is based on the assumption that crime is behavior engaged in by individuals who are capable of exercising free will. As you progress through Part Two (Criminological Theory) and Part Three (Types of Crime) of this book, you will learn that such an assumption cannot be used to explain crime. Rather, we will suggest that the actions of individuals are, in varying degrees, influenced by their position in society.

At this point we would do well to ask, Why it is that for most nonsociological purposes crime is usually defined as behavior that violates criminal law? To put this question another way, Why is it that criminal law usually defines criminal behavior? As soon as we ask (dangerously circular!) questions such as these, we should realize that criminology cannot be confined to the study of criminal behavior because the concept of criminal behavior depends for its meaning on the concept of criminal law.

A few introductory words about the role of criminal law in the process of **criminalization** are now appropriate.

Law and State

Sociologically, the ideas and institutions of law vary greatly from one culture to another. Negatively, this means that law is not necessarily what some lawmakers or zealots claim that it is. Law is not an earthly expression of the will of God. It may not represent the interests of "the people." It has no necessary connection with justice. Law is above all else a social phenomenon created by members of society under specific historical conditions. Law has not always existed in the past; it might not exist in the future.

The great bulk of research in sociology and anthropology reveals that law originated with the emergence of social inequality and, specifically, that it accompanied the transition from stateless societies to state societies. Law has not always existed because not all human societies have been characterized by social inequality. Indeed, until approximately 10,000 years ago, hunting and gathering societies were the dominant form of social organization, and these societies had egalitarian social, economic, and political relations. In these small-scale societies (about fifty members), property was communally owned, there were no social classes, and there was no organized state or societal ruler. Even in horticultural societies, which emerged after hunting and gathering societies, social relations were highly egalitarian, significant differences in wealth and power did not occur, and their leaders typically had no coercive powers over others (O'Kelly and Carney, 1986:37). Neither in hunting and gathering societies nor in horticultural societies did a state exist, and a common morality was maintained by the authority of custom rather than by the rule of law (Diamond, 1973). Within these stateless societies, offenses and conflicts were managed informally in a variety of nonlegal ways such as self-help, avoidance, negotiation, settlement by a third party, and toleration (Black, 1989:74–77; and see Durkheim's analysis in Chapter 4.2).

Not until the development of agricultural societies—wherein economic productivity was expanded by new techniques such as the plow, fertilization, and irrigation—did class inequalities become prevalent. Increased productivity permitted new lifestyles that were not devoted solely to economic survival and subsistence. In some agricultural societies— such as in Greece by the fourth century B.C.—class relations developed in which slaves did most of the productive labor and slave owners dominated and appropriated the economic surplus. In other agricultural societies—such as those of medieval Europe— peasants made up most of the population, but the monarch, the nobles, and the church owned most of the land, which they obtained through military might and conquest. In both slave and feudal agricultural societies, a particular class controlled and appropriated the economic surplus, creating significant social inequalities.

An important feature of agricultural societies was the rise of states and legal systems. **The state** may be defined as the central political institution of a given society. Its major apparatuses are the government (legislature and executive), the legal system, the military, and a variety of public bureaucracies for the collection of taxes, the management of public health, the maintenance of law and order, and so on. The legal system is both a state apparatus and, through its constitutional and administrative branches, the chief mechanism for defining the sphere of state activities.

Rules of law have a variety of sources, such as superstition, divine oracles, religion, prophecy, charismatic leadership, court cases, and legislatures. Law differs from other rules of behavior—habit, convention, tradition and custom—by its coercive nature and by the professional enforcement of its codes. Law's coercive nature can be expressed in shame, ridicule, censure, ostracism, imprisonment, torture, terror, and death. Law's professional interpreters and enforcers can comprise witches and wizards, kings and queens, popes and rabbis, village elders, chiefs, prophets, military warlords, federal judges, and state legislators, among others.

As a social phenomenon, law is a state form of **social control.** As such, its object is to manufacture conformity and to suppress what the state defines as **deviance.** In his classic book *The Behavior of Law*, Donald Black (1976:2) defined law as governmental social control and suggested that there are four basic styles of law, each corresponding to a broader style of social control: penal, compensatory, therapeutic, and conciliatory (p. 46). Each style defines deviant behavior in its own way, with its own logic, methods, and language.

In the penal style of social control, for example, the problem is to establish guilt when an offender has violated a prohibition, and the solution is punishment. Black argues that the quantity and the style of law in a given society both vary inversely with certain factors, such as the power of other forms of social control and the levels of social inequality. When other forms of social control—family ties, religion, and so on—are weak, for example, the power and the extent of law will be relatively strong (Black, 1976,6–7, 107–111). More-over, following the lengthy conflict tradition in the sociology and anthropology of law (see Chapter 7.3), Black argues that law varies directly with social inequality. That is, the societies with the most law are those with the most social inequality.

Many criminologists argue that the relationship between social inequality and crime is especially evident in the process of criminalization. We turn now to this important concept.

Law and Criminalization

The term "criminalization" refers to the process whereby criminal law is selectively applied to social behavior. This threefold process involves (1) the enactment of legislation that outlaws certain types of behavior; (2) the surveillance and the policing of that behavior; and (3) if detected, the punishment of that behavior. The study of criminalization is therefore an indispensable part of the study of crime, and in this book we offer frequent examples of this process.

The criminalization process in Western industrialized societies is heatedly debated by criminologists (Lowman, Menzies, and Palys, 1987). Argument rages over three wide-ranging questions. First, how did the criminalization process contribute to the rise of Western industrialized societies when they first emerged during the seventeenth century? Second, is criminalization today a neutral process or does it generally serve the interests of the powerful? Third, does criminalization contribute to the maintenance of specific forms of contemporary social inequality (by class, gender, race, and age)?

The answers to these questions fall at or in between two extremes. One extreme claims that since its inception on a large scale (during the eighteenth century), the criminalization process has on the whole contributed to the rise of modern society in rational and humane ways. The other extreme suggests that criminalization has operated, in more or less subtle ways, as an instrument to defend the interests of powerful new social classes (for example, the capitalist class) and to undermine the interests of the powerless.

Our general view of criminalization, and thus also of criminal law itself, is that it tends to reflect the interests of the powerful. We will therefore often look at the ways in which the criminalization process maintains unequal social relationships between the powerful and the powerless—especially in the areas of class, gender, race, and age. Nevertheless, we do not view this tendency dogmatically. Sometimes, criminalization is a direct product of power struggles and inevitably reflects the political strengths of specific power groups. At other times, it is connected to power struggles only marginally. At still other times, it appears to transcend power struggles altogether.

1.3 SOCIOLOGICAL DEFINITIONS OF CRIME

Neither the simple images of crime manufactured by the media and the moral entrepreneurs of social problems nor the definition of crime as a legal category can grasp the complex social realities of crime. The purpose of criminology is to chip away at stereotypical or value-laden images of crime and then to try to explain what remains.

The academic discipline of criminology has a lengthy intellectual history. As we outline in Chapter 3, the origins of modern criminology can be traced to the rise of the classical (1760–1820) and the positivist (1820–1890) schools of thought, both of which, in certain key respects, flourish today. The term "criminology" derives from the Latin word *crimen,* meaning "judgment," "accusation," or "offense." Though the word "criminologist" appeared in Britain in the 1850s, "criminology" itself was first used to define the academic study of crime by the Italian sociologist Raffaele Garofalo in 1885 (Beirne, 1993:233–238). Establishing itself as a respectable academic discipline in the United States during the Progressive Era (1890–1915), criminology has since become an interdisciplinary field. Though most criminologists today are drawn from sociology, its many practitioners also come from such varied disciplines as political science, law, economics, history, anthropology, psychology, biology, and geography.

We now explore four sociological definitions of crime used by criminologists:

1. crime as a violation of conduct norms
2. crime as a social harm
3. crime as a violation of human rights
4. crime as a form of deviance

Crime as a Violation of Conduct Norms

In his influential book *Culture Conflict and Crime,* Thorsten Sellin complained that "criminology as traditionally conceived is a bastard science grown out of public preoccupation with a plague" (1938:3). Sellin believed that it was unscientific for criminologists to base their studies on what the public happened to regard as a plague or (as we described above) a social problem. In studying the causes of phenomena, scientists should study objective facts as they occur in their natural states rather than as they are seen by the subjective concerns of the public, the government, powerful social groups, and the criminal law. Sellin was especially concerned that criminologists should not accept Michael and Adler's argument that the basic unit of study should be the behavior prohibited by criminal law. As Sellin stated: "The unqualified acceptance of the legal definitions of the basic units or elements of criminological inquiry violates a fundamental criterion of science. The scientist must have freedom to define his own terms, based on the intrinsic character of his material and designating properties in that material which are assumed to be universal" (p. 23).

Sellin contended that the basic units of criminological research should be **conduct norms**. For every person there are normal (right) and abnormal (wrong) forms of conduct—and the norm depends on the social values of the group that formulates it. Such norms are the rules that govern appropriate behavior. Sellin insisted that there are different types of conduct norms, including custom, tradition, ethics, religion, and rules of criminal law. Conduct norms are found wherever social groups are found. Conduct norms are not created by any one normative group; they are not confined within political boundaries; and they are not necessarily embodied in law. Sellin concluded therefore that a scientific criminology should focus on the violation of all forms of conduct norm and on the study of abnormal conduct in general. Crime is but one form of conduct norm, distinguished from others in that it violates the conduct norms specifically defined by the criminal law.

Sellin's rejection of the legalistic definition of crime and his advice about the proper subject matter of criminology are very important. Clearly, criminologists would be foolish to limit their studies simply to what the criminal law happens to forbid. Imagine, for example, how difficult it would be to study trends in the crime of marijuana use in a state where pot was constantly criminalized and decriminalized according to the whims of legislative and public opinion.

Sellin's advice has yet to exert much influence among criminologists, partly because they would be overwhelmed if they studied violations of all forms of conduct norm. However, Sellin's recommendation moves us to ask a question of much relevance to criminological research: Why are violations of one particular form of conduct regarded as crime and not others?

Crime as a Social Harm

A direct outgrowth of the debate between Michael and Adler and Sellin over the concept of crime is the important position articulated by Edwin Sutherland in his 1949 book *White Collar Crime*. Sutherland was angry that many white-collar offenses were processed as civil violations rather than as crimes. He argued:

> The essential characteristic of crime is that it is behavior which is prohibited by the State as an injury to the State and against which the State may react, at least as a last resort, by punishment. The two abstract criteria generally regarded by legal scholars as necessary elements in a definition of crime are legal description of an act as socially harmful and legal provision of a penalty for the act. (1983:46)

To Sutherland it is clearly unfair that white-collar offenders—for example, those found in civil suits to have violated regulatory laws such as the Sherman Antitrust Act or to have engaged in deceptive advertising—are not stigmatized as criminals. The behavior of white-collar offenders meets the two characteristics of his definition of crime: Their behavior is socially harmful, and they are punished for it (by fines). Because white-collar "offenses" are in fact crimes (however such behavior is defined by the state), Sutherland argues that they should be studied by criminologists. Sutherland's perspective on white-collar offenses has had great influence in criminology (see Chapters 4.4 and 12). At this point, however, we should stress that Sutherland's perspective is not opposed to the legalistic definition of crime. Rather, he suggests that criminologists should use an expanded definition of crime based on behavior prohibited either by criminal or regulatory law.

Whereas Sutherland argues that any illegalities that cause social harm should be criminalized, some criminologists (such as Reiman, 1995; Michalowski, 1985; Bohm, 1993) urge that any behavior should be criminalized if it causes social harm or analogous social injury. For Michalowski, for example, the concept of analogous social injury refers to "legally permissible acts or sets of conditions whose consequences are similar to those of illegal acts" (1985:317). This extension of Sutherland's position has far-reaching implications. Under this view, crimes might include any violent or untimely death; illness or disease; deprivation of adequate food, clothing, shelter, or medical care; and the reduction or elimination of the opportunity for individuals to participate effectively in the political decisionmaking processes that affect their lives (p. 318). Consider the following examples of events that are not regarded as crimes by the U.S. legal system:

- The American Cancer Society estimates that 175,000 cancer deaths were caused by tobacco use in 1998 (ACS, "Cancer Facts & Figures," 1998).
- Each year in the United States more than 200,000 citizens are injured or killed owing to negligence by doctors (Jesilow, Pontell, and Geis, 1993:19).
- Each year in the United States approximately 6,000 workers are killed in job-related accidents, as many as 100,000 die because of exposure to dangerous substances, at least 10 million suffer injuries at work (at least 3 million of which are serious), and 390,000 workers contract new cases of job-related diseases (see Chapter 13.2).

Given the definition of crime as analogous social injury, it seems fair to conclude that such facts justify criminal prosecution of an undetermined number of tobacco manufacturers and distributors, surgeons, and industrial employers. Sociologically, expanded definitions of crime that include both social harm and analogous social injury are therefore fitting correctives to the biased values underlying the legalistic definition of crime. Of course, these expanded definitions leave themselves open to the objection that what counts as social harm or as analogous social injury is as value-laden a category as criminal law.

Crime as a Violation of Human Rights

In response to the biased values enshrined in criminal law, some criminologists have suggested that crime should be defined as any behavior that violates **human rights**. In this view, all people have certain natural and inalienable rights (to life, liberty, happiness, and so on) that derive simply from their status as human beings. Violations of these rights, the argument continues, provide criminology with a more objective unit of analysis than does the legalistic definition of crime. This definition of crime means that criminologists must include the findings of Amnesty International within their studies. Amnesty International (1998), a recipient of the Nobel Peace Prize, noted that today in the United States

- there is a widespread and persistent pattern of police brutality and endemic physical violence directed against prisoners;
- the death penalty is used arbitrarily and unfairly and in racist ways;
- asylum seekers are often wrongly incarcerated; and
- arms are routinely exported to governments and armed groups that use them for purposes of torture and murder.

An impassioned plea that crime be defined in terms of human rights has been made by Herman and Julia Schwendinger (1975). They argued that to define crime according to human rights is a valuable humanistic approach to the problem of crime. For the Schwendingers there are two sorts of human rights: those personal rights that are absolutely essential to life (such as the right to good health) and those rights essential to a dignified human existence (freedom of movement, free speech, a good education, employment, the right to unionize, a certain standard of housing, and so on). The Schwendingers also argue that anything that causes a social injury should be considered a crime. Examples of social injury include imperialism, sexism, racism, and poverty. They have even suggested that some governments should be considered criminal if they do nothing to alleviate poverty:

> Isn't it time to raise serious questions about the assumptions underlying the definition of the field of criminology, when a man who steals a paltry sum can be called a criminal while agents of the State can, with impunity, legally reward men who destroy food so that price levels can be maintained whilst a sizable portion of the population suffers from malnutrition? (p. 137)

The Schwendingers remind us that criminology is an inherently political activity. Inevitably, we make political choices when we decide what to identify as crime. Whose side are we on in the struggle between the powerful and the powerless? Is it important that we be objective in our studies? Can we ever be objective? The suggestion that violations of human rights should be the basis of criminology is an admirable one, not least because it highlights such important questions as these. Moreover, the concept of human rights—as a category of social injury that seems to vary neither across cultures nor over time—seems to offer criminology a broader and more objective definition of crime than does the concept of crime as a legal category. Specifically, the concept of human rights opens up for analysis the obvious fact that legal categories themselves might sometimes be criminal: laws that forbid freedom of speech, that limit opposition to political parties, and so on.

However, a major problem with the human rights approach is that what constitutes a right is, like the content of criminal law, culturally quite variable. In societies such as the United States, human rights tend to be defined in individualistic terms—the rights of individuals to do certain things. Yet in societies such as Canada and several in western Europe and elsewhere, rights tend to be defined in more social terms: the right to employment and to minimum standards of housing, health, and education. Given these differences of definition, it is difficult indeed to agree on which violations of which rights should constitute crime.

Moreover, the emphasis by criminologists on human rights tends to obscure the fact that the rights of animals to a natural and peaceable existence are frequently violated by

What is crime? Few areas of social life are more contested than those that are, or that might be, subject to legal, ethical, and moral censure. In this scene, demonstrators are protesting police racism and other social harms, many forms of which are routinely excluded from censure.

humans. Since the middle of the nineteenth century, and even earlier, some animal rights have been recognized and secured both in state anti-cruelty laws and in federal legislation. Laws currently in force in the United States include the Animal Welfare Act (1966, as amended), the Endangered Species Act (1969), the Marine Mammal Protection Act (1972), and the Improved Standards for Laboratory Animals Act (1985). But quite apart from the legal and/or illegal atrocities routinely committed against them in factory farms, rodeos, circuses, zoos, and commercial laboratories, animals are abused by humans both in domestic households and in their wild or natural habitats. Violations of animal rights, we believe, are also crimes that must be investigated by criminologists.

Crime as a Form of Deviance

In the early 1960s, during a period of widespread social unrest, the study of crime was indelibly influenced by sociological theories of deviance. Deviance may be defined as any social behavior or social characteristic that departs from the conventional norms and standards of a community or society and for which the deviant is sanctioned. Examples of deviant social behavior include witchcraft, bank robbery, picking one's nose in public, mental illness, homosexuality, stuttering, sadomasochism, and murder. Examples of deviant social characteristics are extremes of height and weight, aggressiveness, laziness, and ugliness.

Several aspects of deviance shed light on the study of crime. Even from the preceding short list, it is clear, first, that the variety of deviant practices and deviant social characteristics is in principle infinite. What constitutes deviance varies from era to era and from society to society. What we call homosexuality, for example, was often regarded in classical Greece as a conforming social practice rather than as deviance. Moreover, within the same society at a given time the perception of deviance varies by class, gender, race, and age. Second, deviance is commonplace. Each of us has committed a deviant act at one time or another. Some of us commit many deviant acts in the course of a single day! Third, all deviant behavior is potentially subject to sanction. Deviant behavior can be subject to positive sanctions (such as winning a Nobel prize for discovering penicillin) or to negative sanctions (social censure for picking one's nose in public). Fourth, the norms and standards violated by deviant acts are quite diverse. They can originate in religion, political belief, etiquette, fashion, and criminal law. Of course, not all deviant acts are criminal acts (and vice versa).

The deviance perspective implies that there is nothing in the nature of any act that identifies it as deviant. Rather, deviance is in the eye of the beholder. This implication raises several important sociological questions for the study of crime. Although we explore these questions in greater depth later (Chapter 7.3; and see Sumner, 1994:197–198), certain ones are worth mentioning here.

1.   Who defines behavior as deviant, how, and why?
2.   What are the consequences for an individual whose deviant behavior is subject to sanction?
3.   Why are some deviant practices defined as criminal but not others?

1.4   ASSESSMENT: TOWARD AN ECLECTIC DEFINITION OF CRIME

This book views crime as a **sociological problem** and surveys the various sociological approaches to crime that we term criminology. To focus on crime as a sociological problem is to explain how patterns of crime arise from the interplay of political, economic, social, and ideological structures in society. In other words, we devote scant attention to explanations of crime that ignore the importance of such factors and that reduce its causes to the level of the individual. In pure form, examples of such reductionism are found, for example, in those biological explanations of crime that emphasize the links between criminality and the physical constitution of the individual, as well as in psychological explanations that focus on the links between crime and such conditions as defective character, loose morals, and so on. This book, then, focuses purposefully on the sociological questions uppermost in modern criminology.

The chief task of criminology is to understand crime as a sociological problem. Yet, we have seen already that criminologists disagree about the best sociological definition of crime. This disagreement stems partly, we believe, from a mistaken search for a universal definition of crime that can be applied to all cultures, places, and times.

We hold to no fixed or dogmatic position concerning the definition of crime. Sometimes we agree with the way in which criminal law defines crime; at other times we simply question its adequacy. Occasionally we prefer and use other definitions of crime. For example, because we believe that nonhuman animals have the right to be considered "beings" or "persons," we consider animal abuse to be among the crimes of interpersonal violence that we discuss in Chapter 3. Again, in Chapter 9.1–9.2 we point out that many women are victimized every year by the act of forcible rape defined by criminal law; but we also acknowledge that the traditional criminal law definition of rape (sexual intercourse obtained through the threat or actual use of physical violence) ignores acts that could be defined as rape, such as forms of nonphysical sexual coercion—for example, the male (either heterosexual or homosexual) who informs his economically dependent mate: "If you don't put out, I'll leave you!"

In Chapter 13.2 we go considerably beyond the legalistic definition of crime (including both criminal and regulatory law), arguing that corporate crime is any illegal and/or socially injurious act of intent or indifference that occurs for the purpose of furthering corporate goals and that physically and/or economically abuses individuals in the United States or abroad. Finally, our definition of political crime (see Chapter 14) is somewhat broader than the legalistic definition, in that it includes not only crimes committed against the state but also crimes committed by the state. In the latter we include both domestic political crimes (unlawful or unethical acts committed by state officials and state agencies inside the United States) and international political crimes (violations of domestic and international law by state officials and agencies outside the United States).

REVIEW

This chapter introduced the different images of crime found in the discourses of social-problem movements, the mass media, and sociology. The major task of the chapter was to learn about the three key sociological concepts of criminology: crime, criminal law, and criminalization.

Images of Crime

1. Crime has become one of the leading social problems in the United States. But there is no objective set of social conditions whose perceived harmful effects necessarily make these conditions social problems. What is regarded as a social problem varies over time and across cultures. What is defined as a social problem depends on numerous factors, including the activities of moral entrepreneurs.

2. Mass media have become the most influential mechanisms for organizing public sentiment so that a certain social condition is perceived as a social problem.

3. Mass media routinely provide distorted information about the amount of crime, the most common types of crime, and who typically commits crimes.

Crime, Criminal Law, and Criminalization

1. The term "criminalization" refers to the process whereby criminal law is selectively applied to social behavior. The sociological study of criminal law is therefore an integral part of criminology. Specifically, the criminalization process involves the enactment of

legislation that outlaws certain types of behavior. It also provides for the surveillance, policing, and, if detected, punishment of that behavior.

2. Criminal law distinguishes between crimes *mala in se* and *mala prohibita* and between felonies and misdemeanors. To constitute a crime, behavior must be prohibited by law, must be voluntary, and must coincide with a defendant's mental state. An act or omission is not a crime if a defendant is justified in doing (or not doing) it, or if s/he lacks the criminal responsibility required by *mens rea*.

3. Not all societies have had law. Law originated with the emergence of social inequality and accompanied the transition from stateless to state societies. The distinguishing features of law are its coercive nature, its reliance on a professional staff, and its use as a state form of social control.

4. In this book, the general view of the criminalization process, and thus also of criminal law, is that it tends to reflect the interests of the powerful (in terms of class, gender, race, and age).

Sociological Definitions of Crime

1. This book views crime as a sociological problem. It surveys the various sociological approaches to crime found in the discipline of criminology. To focus on crime as a sociological problem is to explain how patterns of crime arise from the interplay of political, economic, social, and ideological forces in society.

2. The question "What is crime?" is difficult to answer because there is little agreement about the defining sociological characteristics of crime. Criminologists use a variety of sociological definitions of crime, including crime as a violation of conduct norms, crime as a social harm, crime as a violation of human rights, and crime as a form of deviance.

3. This book uses an eclectic definition of crime.

QUESTIONS FOR CLASS DISCUSSION

1. Consider the facts in the following short story about cannibalism among a group of cave (speluncean) explorers caught in a life-threatening situation in the Commonwealth of "Newgarth." The story is adapted from a fictitious law case created by legal philosopher Lon Fuller (1949, excerpted in Schur, 1968:19–20). Although "The Case of the Speluncean Explorers" is fictitious, it is probably based on an actual case of cannibalism at sea in 1884 and on the bizarre trial that resulted from it in England (Simpson, 1984).

The Case of the Speluncean Explorers.   Five members of an amateur cave-exploring society were trapped inside a deep and isolated cave following a landslide. After some time, through the efforts of relatives and the cave-exploring society, rescuers located the cave only to encounter repeated obstacles to removing the trapped men. At great monetary expense and the cost of ten rescuers' lives (in a subsequent landslide), the rescue operation finally succeeded thirty-two days after the men entered the cave. On the twentieth day, communication between the rescuers and the trapped explorers had been established, when it was discovered that the latter had with them in the cave a radio transmitter-receiver. At that time, the trapped men asked for medical advice as to whether they could live without food (there was none in the cave) for the time engineers had determined would be required to rescue them. A physicians committee at the rescue site stated that they could not. When the trapped men later inquired if they could survive by consuming the flesh of one of their number, the reply (reluctant) was in the affirmative. But the explorers could get no guidance at all (from the physicians or from any clergyman or judge) when they went on to ask about the advisability of casting lots to determine who should be killed and eaten.

When the men were finally released, the rescuers learned that on the twenty-third day one of them, Whetmore, had been killed and eaten by the other four. Although originally it had been Whetmore's idea (at first resisted by his companions) that such an act might be necessary for survival, and also that a casting of lots would be the fairest means of selection, just before the dice were cast, Whetmore changed his mind. His companions disallowed this sudden switch, however, and cast the dice for him, after obtaining his agreement that this procedure was fair; he lost and was put to death and eaten by the others.

After they had recuperated, the four survivors were charged with Whetmore's murder.

Having read the facts in "The Case of the Speluncean Explorers," you should also know that Newgarth law commands, "Whoever shall willfully take the life of another shall be punished by death." In this case the defendants were charged with the crime of murder, convicted, and sentenced to death.

Assume that the defendants appealed the verdict and the sentence in "The Case of the Speluncean Explorers," and that you are a member of the appeals court. How would you decide the appeal? Are the defendants guilty of murder? What defense is available to them, if any? If their conviction in the lower court is upheld, would you recommend executive clemency (a pardon)?

2. The American Cancer Society estimates that in 1998 175,000 cancer deaths were caused by tobacco use (ACS, "Cancer Facts & Figures," 1998). Do you think tobacco manufacturers and distributors should be prosecuted for murder?

3. According to criminologist Ray Surette (1998:68), "criminals tend to be of two types in the news media: violent predators or professional businessmen and bureaucrats. Furthermore . . . they tend to be slightly older (twenty to thirty years old) than reflected in official arrest statistics." How would you interpret such evidence? How would you interpret the following demographic profiles of crime victims, as reported in TV news in Tallahassee, Florida—32 percent were white females; 12 percent, Hispanic females; 11 percent, black males; 6 percent, black females; 3 percent, Hispanic males; 10 percent, other (Chiricos, Eschholz, and Gertz, 1997:354)?

FOR FURTHER STUDY

Readings

Amnesty International. 1998. *USA–Rights for All.* London: Amnesty International Secretariat.
Lanier, Mark M., and Stuart Henry. 1998. *Essential Criminology.* Boulder, Colo.: Westview Press.
Vold, George B., Thomas J. Bernard, and Jeffrey B. Snipes. 1998. *Theoretical Criminology.* New York: Oxford University Press.

Websites

1. <http://www.journalism.org>: This site is sponsored by the Project for Excellence in Journalism and is affiliated with the Columbia University Graduate School of Journalism. It reports results from a national study on local TV news programs and identifies the "Bad Habits" (or "six ways stations undercut their stories") of TV news broadcasting.
2. <http://www.law.cornell.edu/topics/state_statutes.html>: This site provides links to each state's laws, including criminal codes and procedures and rules of evidence, in the United States.
3. <http://www.igc.apc.org/amnesty/home.html>: This is a site for Amnesty International, USA. It includes a general statement about the organization: its history, mission, and current activities. Especially interesting is the "Human Rights Quiz," which students may want to take; it is located at <www.igc.apc.org/amnesty/quiz.html>.

Preview

Chapter 2 introduces:
- the major sources of official crime data
- the major sources of unofficial crime data
- the idea that crime data do not have a factual, objective existence independent of concepts about crime

Key Terms

concepts	statistics
crime rate	theories
methodology	unofficial crime data
official crime data	victimization surveys

Chapter 2 outlines the major sources of crime data; precisely what such data tell us about specific types of crime is analyzed in later chapters (especially Chapters 9–14).

Criminologists usually distinguish between **official crime data** and **unofficial crime data**. Official crime data are the data collected by the government and its official agencies, such as the Federal Bureau of Investigation and the Department of Justice. Unofficial crime data are the nongovernmental data usually collected by private or independent agencies and researchers. Thus, the sources and the types of unofficial crime data are quite varied. In distinguishing between official and unofficial sources of crime data, we do not imply that one data source is in principle better than another—although in practice this is often true. Rather, official and unofficial crime data typically construct crime differently.

The majority of crime data is presented in the form of statistics. The term **statistics** derives from the seventeenth-century English term "state-istics," which referred to state data about births, marriages, and deaths. Because contemporary statistical data are so extensively used for social purposes, we tend to be lulled into thinking that they represent objective facts. However, neither statistics nor data nor facts can ever be entirely free of the biases inherent in how they are constructed. The implications of this critical point will soon become clear.

2.1   CAUTION: DATA DO NOT SPEAK FOR THEMSELVES!

In the following pages we describe the major sources of data for studying crime today. But before we describe these data we must discuss how they are influenced by **concepts** and **theories**.

In the early nineteenth century, when official crime data were first systematically recorded, positivist criminologists like Adophe Quetelet believed that crime could be observed directly by using the procedures of the natural sciences (see Chapter 3.2). In this view, crime—like rocks, plants, and insects—exists in a natural state independent of the concepts and the theories of the criminologist. Positivist criminology is based on the idea that the collection of data about human beings follows the same scientific procedures as the collection of data in the natural sciences. This view, however, greatly distorts the process of scientific investigation. Why this is so can be understood by an analogy with astronomy.

Suppose that two astronomers are examining the surface of the moon through a telescope. Suppose also that one of the astronomers is peering into her telescope in the year 1500 (in essence, pre-Copernicus) and the other in the year 1900 (namely, post-Copernicus). Would the two astronomers see the same thing? It can be argued that both astronomers would see the same image projected by the moon: a roundish, bright, yellowish object in the sky. But beyond the optico-chemical level of sensory perception, would our two astronomers really "see" the same image? The answer is probably "no." The astronomers would see lunar data in terms of (1) their respective concepts of "the moon," of "optics," and so on, and of (2) their theories of planetary motion. The early sixteenth-century astronomer would see a roundish, bright, yellowish object *that moves in orbit around the earth.* The twentieth-century astronomer, relying on modern theories of astronomy, would see a roundish, bright, yellowish object that not only moves in orbit around the earth *but that has a certain alignment with the earth and the sun.* Astronomers' perceptions of lunar images, in other words, are structured by their respective astronomical concepts and theories.

This example demonstrates that data are not objective facts that exist independently of the concepts and the theories of those who observe them. Data do not speak for themselves!

Let us apply this heavenly insight to the world of crime. When we study crime it would be wrong to believe that we can simply observe, measure, and collect the facts and nothing but the facts about crime. We do not—indeed cannot—collect facts about crime through direct observation. What constitutes a fact about crime depends on our concepts and theories of crime. Crime data, like all other data, are structured by concepts and theories. What count as crime data are therefore very much open to debate.

In Chapter 1.2, we noted that the recognition of certain behavioral data (such as killing someone) as crime depends on the concept of crime that is accepted as authoritative. According to the legalistic concept of crime, for example, murder is limited to those killings that are contrary to rules of criminal law. Thus if a police officer kills someone, the killing is not murder, according to criminal law, if it is reasonable under the circumstances and if it occurs in the lawful execution of police duties. Another concept of crime, such as human rights (a concept that is itself quite variable), yields very different crime data. Thus, to some proponents of human rights (but not to those who favor the legalistic concept of crime), murder might also include negligent surgery, many worker deaths caused by employer neglect of safety conditions, cigarette-induced deaths resulting from the commercial activities of tobacco companies, and the like.

A further example of the concept- and theory-laden character of crime comes from the criminologist Ian Taylor (1983:91), who disagrees with

> the widespread view of homicide as a highly "factual" offense, thought to be evidenced by the existence of a corpse. Homicide is thought amongst experts to have a very high degree of "reportability" (in that very few homicides are thought to be unobserved or unpunished). On both counts, there is room for skepticism. . . . There are good reasons for questioning the meaning of coroners' reports in cases of nonnatural death, and there are increasingly strong reasons for questioning whether the deaths that occur among the terminally ill, or amongst old people in care, especially in institutional settings, are absolutely unaided. Perhaps most routinely of all, there is good evidence to suggest that many more of the deaths occurring in road traffic "accidents" involving criminal negligence should be appearing in homicide statistics at present.

2.2   OFFICIAL CRIME DATA

The publication of national crime statistics was pioneered in France in 1827 (see Chapter 3.2), but not until a century later, in 1927, was a committee on Uniform Crime Records established in the United States. Three years later, in 1930, after some bureaucratic wrangling between the FBI and the Bureau of the Census, the FBI began to publish its *Uniform Crime Reports*. In January 1930, 400 cities representing 20 million inhabitants in 43 states began to participate in the *Uniform Crime Reports* (or *UCR*) program.

The *UCR* has been published under congressional mandate each year since 1930. It is popularly regarded as the most reliable set of crime data in the United States. Our immediate task is to examine what the *UCR* measures and then to assess how reliable the data actually are.

Police Data: *Uniform Crime Reports*

The *UCR* is compiled each year in Washington, D.C., by FBI statisticians. The FBI receives data from crime reports submitted voluntarily by more than 16,000 state, county, and city law enforcement agencies. In 1997 these agencies had jurisdiction over 254 million U.S. inhabitants, or 97 percent of the total population. The coverage is 90 percent in cities outside metropolitan areas and 87 percent in rural areas.

The meaning of much *UCR* data hinges on a distinction drawn by the FBI between "Index Crimes" and "Non-Index Crimes." The *UCR* provides diverse statistical information about eight Index ("Part I") Crimes but much scantier information about twenty-one Non-Index ("Part II") Crimes. The FBI also presents data on hate crimes, including the number of hate crime offenses and their motivation (see Figure 2.1). The FBI regards Index Crimes as the most serious crimes: murder and nonnegligent manslaughter; forcible rape; robbery; aggravated assault; burglary; larceny-theft; motor vehicle theft; and arson (see Figure 2.2 for definitions of these offenses). Non-Index Crimes include simple assault; forgery and counterfeiting; fraud; embezzlement; buying, receiving, and possessing stolen property; carrying and possessing weapons; prostitution and commercialized vice; sex offenses (except forcible rape and prostitution); drug abuse violations; gambling; offenses against family and children; driving under the influence; liquor law offenses; drunkenness; disorderly conduct; vagrancy; all other offenses (except traffic); suspicion; curfew and loitering law violations; and runaway persons under eighteen.

In addition to the FBI's view that Index Crimes are more serious than Non-Index Crimes (a subject to which we return in a moment), *UCR* crime data are distinguished by their source. Data about Index Crimes derive from information that comes to the attention of police departments, which in turn usually derives from reports of crime to the police by members of the public. For Non-Index Crimes data are limited to cases involving actual police arrests.

The *UCR* focuses primarily on crime trends of the eight Index Crimes. In this regard the *UCR* tabulates:

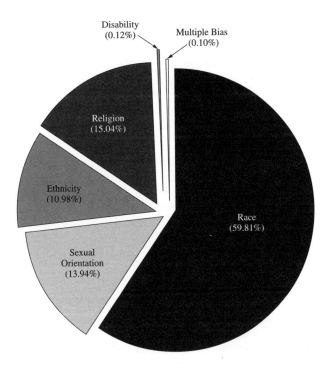

FIGURE 2.1   Hate Crimes, 1997

NOTE: According to the FBI, a hate crime is a crime commited against a person, property, or society that is motivated, in whole or in part, by the offender's bias against a race, religion, ethnic/national origin group, sexual-orientation group, or sexual/mental disability.

SOURCE: Federal Bureau of Investigation, 1998, p. 61.

1. the number of offenses
2. the offense rate per 100,000 population
3. the percentage change from the previous year
4. the offense rate by region (for example, South, North, Northeast, Midwest)
5. the nature of the offense (age, gender, and race of offenders and victims)
6. the arrest (or clearance) rates for the offense

The *UCR* displays the following information: relative frequency of the Index Crimes; changes in the number and in the rate of Index Crimes (see Figure 2.3); the distribution of each Index Crime in the Index Crime rate (see Figure 2.4); and the respective crime rates of the four regions (see Figure 2.5), of individual states, and of cities and towns of varying size. In addition, the *UCR* provides data about arrest trends by state, city, and suburban and rural areas; as well as about police employment by region, state, cities, suburban and rural counties, and universities and colleges.

FIGURE 2.2   *Uniform Crime Reports*—Index (Part I) Crime Definitions

- **Murder and Nonnegligent Manslaughter:**   the willfull (nonnegligent) killing of one human being by another.
- **Forcible Rape:**   the carnal knowledge of a female forcibly and against her will. (Attempts are included, but statutory rape [without force] and other sex offenses are not.)
- **Robbery:**   the taking of or attempting to take anything of value from the care, custody, or control of a person or persons by force or by threat of force or violence and/or by putting the victim in fear.
- **Aggravated assault:**   the unlawful attack by one person upon another for the purpose of inflicting severe or aggravated bodily injury. (This type of assault is usually accompanied by the use of a weapon, and it includes attempts.)
- **Burglary:**   the unlawful entry of a structure to commit a felony or theft. (Three subdivisions include forcible entry, unlawful entry where no force is used, and attempted forcible entry.)
- **Larceny-theft:**   the unlawful taking, carrying, leading, or riding away of property from the possession or constructive possession of another. (Included are shoplifting, pocket-picking, purse-snatching, thefts from motor vehicles, thefts or motor vehicle parts and accessories, bicycle thefts, and so forth, in which no force, violence, or fraud occurs.)
- **Motor Vehicle Theft:**   the theft or attempted theft of a motor vehicle. (Included are the stealing of automobiles, trucks, buses, motorcycles, motorscooters, and snowmobiles.)
- **Arson:**   any willful burning or malicious burning or attempt to burn, with or without intent to defraud, a dwelling house, public building, motor vehicle or aircraft, personal property of another. . . . (Excluded are fires of suspicious or unknown origin.)

SOURCE: Federal Bureau of Investigation, 1998, adapted from pp. 15–64.

Now that we have introduced the concept, and because of its importance, let us pause briefly to explain exactly what is meant by a **crime rate**. To understand this concept, let us talk in terms of "percentages" and "rates." A percentage is simply a proportion (or "rate"), a number per 100 (*centum* is Latin for 100).

A basic reason for using percentages is that they give us a feel for proportion. This feel is actually an implicit comparison with other known proportions. For instance, how are we to interpret the results of a survey reporting that 2,000 persons in California and 500 persons in Maine are afraid of crime? Does this mean that persons in California are four times more fearful of crime than persons in Maine? To answer the latter question requires a common scale—a proportion or rate of those surveyed. A percentage is the most commonly used scale to establish the rate of people in both states who report that they are afraid of crime. Thus, 90 percent translates easily into nine of ten. But when we want to know something such as the prevalence of crime relative to the population, the rate is extremely low.

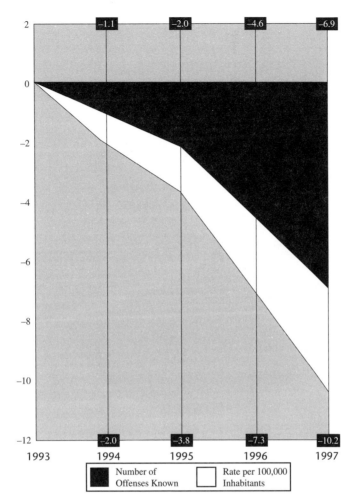

FIGURE 2.3   Crime Index Total, 1993–1997

SOURCE: Federal Bureau of Investigation, 1998, p. 8.

The foregoing can be illustrated by studying an example of an actual homicide rate. In Table 2.1 you can see the number of homicides and also the homicide rates per 100,000 inhabitants reported in the *UCR* for 1996 and 1997, when the population was an estimated 267,777,941. Given that the number of homicides in 1997 was 18,209, the homicide rate per 100,000 population was 6.8. This homicide rate for 1997 is calculated as follows:

$$\frac{18{,}209 \times 100{,}000}{267{,}777{,}941} = 6.8$$

Moreover, if the homicide rate in 1997 was 6.8, and if in 1996 it was 7.4, then there was a decline of 0.6 homicides per 100,000 people between 1996 and 1997. Thus the homicide rate in 1997 was 8.1 percent less than the 1996 rate:

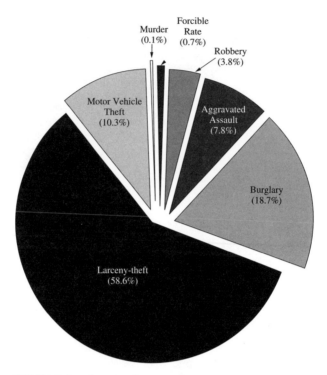

FIGURE 2.4   The Distribution of Crime Index Offenses, 1997

SOURCE: Federal Bureau of Investigation, 1998, p. 9.

TABLE 2.1   Homicide Rate Trend, 1996–1997

	Number of Homicides	Rate per 100,000 Inhabitants
1996	19,645	7.4
1997	18,209	6.8
Percent change	−7.3	−8.1

SOURCE: *Federal Bureau of Investigation*, 1998, p. 15.

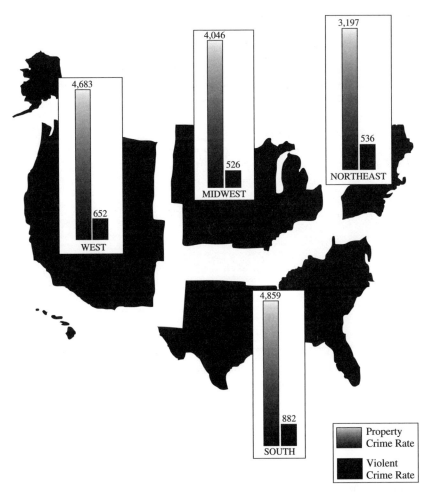

FIGURE 2.5   Regional Violent and Property Crime Rates per 100,000 Inhabitants, 1997

SOURCE: Federal Bureau of Investigation, 1998, p. 10.

$$\frac{0.6}{7.4} \times 100 = 8.1 \text{ percent}$$

Before examining the actual reliability of the crime data provided by the *UCR,* we emphasize how important the *UCR* program is as a source of crime data. In the words of the FBI itself:

While the Program's primary objective is to generate a reliable set of criminal statistics for use in law enforcement administration, operation, and management, its data have over the years become one of the country's leading social indicators. The American public looks to the Uniform Crime Reports for information on fluctuations in the

---

BOX 2.1   MURDER IN THE UNITED STATES, 1997

In 1997 the *UCR* reported 18,210 murders—a rate of 6.8 murders per 100,000 population. Although the annual number and rate of murders have decreased since 1993, many of the patterns and characteristics of murder victims have remained about the same:

- Three-fourths of the victims were male.
- Whites and African Americans each made up about 48 percent of murder victims.
- One in eight murder victims was under age eighteen.
- Firearms were used in about 70 percent of murders.
- The murder rate was highest in the South and lowest in the Northeast.
- The murder rate was higher in metropolitan cities than in smaller cities and rural areas.

(Source: Federal Bureau of Investigation, *Uniform Crime Reports*, 1997, 1998.)

---

level of crime, while criminologists, sociologists, legislators, municipal planners, the media, and other students of criminal justice use the statistics for varied research and planning purposes. (*UCR,* 1998:1)

Assessment

Criminologists often debate the question of how well the *UCR* measures the crime rate. Answers to this question tend to be twofold. First, some critics claim that although the *UCR* does a commendable job of measuring the crime rate, it could do even better with more sophisticated or more sensitive "methodological" techniques. **Methodology** involves the techniques of measurement used to collect and manipulate empirical data. Two examples of methodological techniques are opinion polls and statistical analyses.

Second, other critics claim that because of various "conceptual" biases in its methodological techniques, the *UCR* does not and cannot measure "the crime rate" very accurately. A concept involves an idea that describes a property of an empirical datum or a relation among empirical data. A **concept** is usually a part of a theory that is used to generate hypotheses. The United States is an example of a concept; some of the properties of the concept of the United States are sovereignty, fifty states, part of North America, and so on.

There are numerous methodological criticisms of the *UCR*. These are five of the most important ones:

1. There is an unknown, but probably massive, amount of crime that goes unreported to the police and that, therefore, never shows up in the *UCR*. This unknown component is often termed "the dark figure" of crime. Methodologi-

cally, as we shall see, the size of the dark figure of crime can to a certain extent be estimated with the use of victimization surveys and self-report studies.

2. Because participation in the *UCR* program is voluntary, not all police departments send crime reports to the FBI. Consequently, the FBI attempts to estimate crime rates in such jurisdictions. It is, of course, difficult to assess the precise accuracy of their estimates.

3. The *UCR* does not include federal crimes (such as blackmail), an omission that tends to underestimate the crime rate.

4. In any single criminal event, only the most serious crime reported to the police is included in the *UCR*. This is known as the "hierarchy rule." For example, if an armed man breaks into a person's home (burglary or criminal trespass), forces a woman inside to engage in sexual intercourse with him (rape), kills her (murder), and escapes with some of her belongings (robbery), only the murder is reflected in the *UCR*. Arguably, this understates the volume of crime.

5. The *UCR*'s Crime Index Total actually misrepresents the crime rate in any given year. It is an FBI composite figure for public and media consumption arrived at by combining the totals of each of the eight Index Crimes in any given year. The Crime Index Total misleads because no attempt is made to distinguish offenses by severity. Thus, if in any given year the actual number of the other six offenses (as well as population size) had remained the same, with an accompanying decrease of 3,000 larcenies and an increase of 3,000 homicides, the Crime Index Total would show that the crime rate had remained constant. Yet it is somewhat disingenuous to claim that a decrease in the number of larcenies (many of which involve theft of $50 or less) somehow cancels out an identical increase in the number of homicides and equals a constant crime rate. Clearly, larceny and homicide should not carry the same weight.

In addition to methodological criticisms of the *UCR,* there are three major conceptual criticisms of its status as a document that claims to measure the crime rate. Perhaps the first and most obvious conceptual criticism is that the *UCR* records only legally defined categories of crime (see Chapter 1.2). It must be stressed that *UCR* categories of crime are not scientific or objective categories–they reflect the biases enshrined in the rules of criminal law and in the values of legislatures and the judicial system. Given one's personal viewpoints, *UCR*'s biases may seem either good or bad or indifferent. But biases they undoubtedly are.

The ramifications of such biases are examined in greater detail in Section 2.3 of this chapter. But consider a simple example of *UCR*'s vulnerability to this sort of criticism. If you believe crime is less a violation of law than it is a breach of human rights, for example, then the *UCR* does not and cannot measure what constitutes crime. Whether or not they are defined as such in criminal law, if sexism and racism are crimes, the *UCR*–which generally counts neither of these as crimes–does a poor job of measuring crime.

A second conceptual criticism of the *UCR* is that the composition of the Crime Index imparts a distorted image of the seriousness of crime. Recall that the Index includes murder, rape, robbery, aggravated assault, burglary, larceny, motor vehicle theft, and arson. The FBI apparently includes these eight crimes in the Index because they occur in large numbers and because the public regards them as the most serious crimes. But these two reasons are rather flimsy. There is considerable agreement that murder, rape, robbery, aggravated assault, and arson are very serious crimes and that they should be recorded as serious crimes in the Index. Yet why are all burglaries, larcenies, and motor vehicle thefts sufficiently serious to warrant inclusion in the Index? How is it that the theft of a bicycle (a larceny) is recorded as a serious crime but child abuse is not? Moreover, with the exception of larceny, the crimes recorded in the greatest numbers (for instance, fraud, drug abuse violations, driving under the influence) are actually Non-Index Crimes.

The FBI is also frequently accused of omitting a variety of serious crimes from the Index. With the exception of arson, all Index Crimes are typically committed by members of relatively powerless sections of society. White-collar, corporate, and political crimes—which the public increasingly views as serious crimes—committed by members of the more powerful sections of society are Non-Index offenses to which the FBI gives relatively little attention. Why the FBI omits these latter crimes from the Index is a matter of broad speculation, including at least these possibilities:

1. The FBI recognizes the fact that crimes typically or exclusively committed by the powerful are difficult to detect, often covered up, and seldom reported to the police (see Chapter 13.2).
2. The FBI is insensitive to the plight of the powerless.
3. The FBI is politically biased in favor of the powerful (see Chapter 14.2).

The third conceptual criticism of the *UCR* takes several forms. However, most of these cluster around an intriguing question: Does the *UCR* actually measure criminal behavior (whether defined in terms of legal categories or human rights) or, instead, the bureaucratic activities of official agencies such as the police and the FBI? (Kitsuse and Cicourel, 1963; Erikson, 1966; Cicourel, 1968).

There are countless factors that influence how official crime statistics are socially constructed. Consider only the situation of the police. Quite apart from a change in actual criminal behavior, official crime statistics can be altered by changes in police reporting procedures; by improved or faster technological assistance; by changes in relations between the police and the citizenry; by crusades against particular crimes; by an increase in the ratio of police officers to population; and even by simple manipulation of crime reports. On this last point, we must stress that all police agencies are faced with two contradictory pressures in the representation of their activities to the FBI, to the media, and to the public:

1. It is in the best interests of police departments to ensure that officially recorded crime rates are low, thereby suggesting that the police are successfully doing their job of fighting crime.
2. It is in the best interests of police departments to ensure that officially recorded crime rates are high, thereby allowing the police to ask for higher budgets and more personnel.

All police departments operate at some point between these two pressures. The precise situation of any given police department depends on many factors, including levels of criminal activity, the honesty of police chiefs, local and national politics, media crusades, and pressure from the public.

Some time ago, sociologists John Kitsuse and Aaron Cicourel (1963) suggested that criminologists should be concerned chiefly with how crime rates are constructed by official agencies. Rather than searching for some mythical crime rate independent of how it is socially constructed, criminologists should examine the bureaucratic practices of agencies that record crime. The starting point of criminology, their argument implies, is understanding the behavior of those who define, classify, and record certain behavior as crime (see Chapter 14.3).

If we apply this method to the process by which criminal behavior enters the *UCR,* we find that for a crime report to enter as a datum in the *UCR,* at least five events must occur:

1. Someone must perceive an event or behavior as a crime.
2. Somehow the crime must come to the attention of the police, either through police observation, which is rare, or through a report from a victim, through a confession, or through detective work.
3. The police must agree that a crime has occurred.
4. The police must code the crime on the proper *UCR* form and submit it to the FBI.
5. The FBI must include the crime in the *UCR.*

Each of these events is subject to enormous social interpretation and negotiation. The facts in these events, in other words, do not speak for themselves; each event is socially constructed.

A dramatic example of how crime rates may reflect official activity more than they reflect criminal behavior is provided by Philip Jenkins's (1988; 1994) controversial research

---

BOX 2.2   MANIPULATING THE *UCR*

"Senior police officials around the nation are concerned that the sharp drop in crime in recent years has produced pressure on police departments to show ever-decreasing crime statistics and might be behind incidents in several cities in which commanders have manipulated crime data.

"So far this year, there have been charges of falsely reporting crime statistics in Philadelphia, New York, Atlanta and Boca Raton, Fla., resulting in the resignation or demotion of high-ranking police commanders.

"Experts say they believe these incidents do not mean that the nationwide drop in crime since 1992 is illusory. But they are beginning to question whether politicians seeking office, the news media and the public should attach so much importance to the annual, and sometimes monthly, release of the latest crime figures." (*New York Times*, August 3, 1998, p. A1)

on serial murders. Jenkins was initially puzzled by the substantial and well-publicized increase in the serial murder rate that apparently occurred between 1983 and 1985. According to Jenkins, it was the mass media that first presented the volume of serial murders in the United States as an "epidemic" unknown in other societies. The epidemic was often tied to the growth of the pornography industry, whose sexually explicit materials allegedly tended to arouse the aggressive nature of certain individuals who had been abused as children. Harrowing TV interviews with convicted serial killers—Ted Bundy, Edmund Kemper, and Henry Lee Lucas—added fuel to media fires. Jenkins quoted a Justice Department claim that as many as 4,000 Americans a year, half of them under the age of eighteen, are murdered by serial killers.

Jenkins suggested that although serial murder may well represent a growing and heinous menace to society, the mass media and Justice Department officials have grossly inflated their estimates of the annual total of serial murders. According to Jenkins's analysis—which amounts to the best and most complete identification of serial killers in the United States in this century—serial killers account for no more than 350–400 murders each year.

How, then, is it possible to distort and exaggerate *UCR* homicide data? What motives prompt such distortions? Jenkins described the bureaucratic *UCR* process that makes homicide data especially susceptible to manipulation. Whenever a murder is committed, the police department of jurisdiction is required to complete a lengthy *UCR* report and submit it to the FBI; the deadline for submission is the first five days of the month after the crime is reported. But the police must also

submit a supplementary homicide report, addressing topics like characteristics of the victim and offender; weapon; relationship of victim to offender; circumstances surrounding death; and so on. "Offenders" can be single, multiple or unknown. At this early stage, the police might well know neither the offender, a motive, nor the exact circumstances of the death. All these would thus be recorded as unknown.

Weeks or months later, the situation might well change, and the correct procedure would be for the department to submit a new report to amend the first. Here, though, there is enormous room for cutting corners. The death has been notified, and whether a further correction is submitted depends on many factors. A conscientious officer in a professional department with an efficient record system would very probably notify the reporting center that the murder was no longer "unsolved" or "motiveless," especially in an area where murder was a rare crime. Other officers in other departments might well feel that they have more important things to do than to submit a revised version of a form they have already completed. This would in fact represent a third form on a single case.

The chance of follow-up information being supplied will depend on a number of factors: the frequency of murder in the community; the importance given to record-keeping by a particular chief or supervisor; the organizational structure of the department (for instance, whether records and data are the responsibility of a full-time unit or of an individual); and the professional standards of the department. The vast majority of departments are likely to record the simple fact of a murder being committed; only some will provide the results of subsequent investigations, though these are crucial to developing any kind of national statistical profile of American homicide. (Jenkins, 1988:4)

The result of this bureaucratic process is that for many cases of homicide, even though an offender and a motive were subsequently discovered, the FBI will have only a "motiveless/offender unknown" entry in their records. In 1966 the *UCR* recorded 11,000 murders in the United States; of these, 644 (5.9 percent) were "motiveless." In 1982 there were 23,000 murders, with 4,118 (17.8 percent) "motiveless." By 1984 the motiveless category had risen to 22 percent (Jenkins, 1988:4). As Jenkins described it, there was an alarming tendency on the part of the media and the U.S. Department of Justice to assume that all or most motiveless murders were the work of serial killers.

Why would the Justice Department continue with this fabrication? Jenkins admitted that he opposes the idea of a conspiracy whereby the Justice Department is seen as responsible for creating the illusion of an epidemic of serial murders. Nevertheless, he claimed, the serial murder "epidemic" served certain organizational goals of the Justice Department. Although some FBI officials placed the number of serial murders at several hundred rather than several thousand, the orthodoxy of the latter figure was never properly contradicted by the FBI. Why not? According to Jenkins (1988:5), the serial murder "epidemic" was used as a justification for a new Violent Criminal Apprehension Program at a new center for the study of violent crime at the FBI Academy in Quantico, Virginia.

Jenkins's account of this transformation of "unsolved" homicide data into data about serial murders is a dramatic example of the way in which crime data are socially constructed. Of equal interest, and perhaps even more compelling, are the ways in which crime data are routinely constructed by the public and the police.

In this respect consider the findings of Donald Black's well-known study (1970; and see Bridges and Crutchfield, 1988; Klinger, 1994) of members of the public who report crimes to the police. Whether or not police agree that a crime has occurred and, if so, whether they formally record it as a crime are outcomes preceded by complicated processes of social interpretation and negotiation. Black investigated these processes in his study of routine police work in predominantly blue-collar residential areas of Boston, Chicago, and Washington, D.C. He noted that after a victim or an observer of a crime (a complainant) has reported the crime to the police, there are five conditions that influence whether or not a crime is actually accepted and formally recorded as a crime by the police.

The Legal Seriousness of the Crime.   The police are more likely to write a crime report if the crime is a felony rather than a misdemeanor. In Black's study, 72 percent of felonies but only 53 percent of misdemeanors were written up as reports. "It remains noteworthy," wrote Black, "that the police officially disregard one-fourth of the felonies they handle in encounters with complainants" (1970:738).

The Complainant's Preferences.   When called to the scene of a crime the police are extremely dependent on a complainant's definition of the situation. Does the complainant want the police to take official action? Does the complainant want the matter settled informally and outside official channels? Is the complainant indifferent as to further action? Black found that the police almost always agree with a complainant's preference for informal action. In situations where a complainant wished official police action, the police complied in 84 percent of felony situations and 64 percent of misdemeanor situations.

The Relational Distance.   How seriously the police regard a complainant depends partly on the relational distance between the victim and the alleged offender. The social relationship between a crime victim and an offender can be of three types: (1) fellow family members; (2) friends, neighbors, or acquaintances; and (3) strangers. Black found that when a complainant expresses a preference for official action, the police are least likely to comply in type (1), more likely in type (2), and most likely in type (3). Black also found that relational distance is often more important than the legal seriousness of the crime: "The police are more likely to give official recognition to a misdemeanor involving strangers . . . than to a felony involving friends, neighbors, or acquaintances" (p. 740).

The Complainant's Deference.   Not surprisingly, Black found that the more deference or respect shown police by a complainant, in both felony and misdemeanor situations, the more likely they are to file an official crime report. As Black puts it: "Official crime rates and the justice done through police detection of criminal offenders, therefore, reflect the politeness of victims" (p. 744).

The Complainant's Status.   Do the police discriminate in favor of complainants of high social status? In trying to answer this question, Black considered both social class and race as aspects of status. For class, Black found that the police tend to discriminate in favor of white-collar complainants in felony situations. Thus, the higher a complainant's social status, the more likely it is that police will respond to a complaint that a crime has been committed.

For race, however, Black found it almost impossible to reach a solid conclusion about discrimination because most crime is intra-racial (for instance, whites tend to commit crimes against whites, blacks against blacks, Hispanics against Hispanics, and so on). Suppose, for example, that the police tend to respond more often to a white complainant than to a black complainant. It is hard to know whether this response is discriminatory because, given that whites tend to commit crimes against whites more often than against minorities, in favoring a white complainant the police would also be more likely to be pursuing a white offender. Similarly, if the police are less likely to respond to a black complainant, they are more likely to be discriminating in favor of a black offender.

In response to some of the criticisms of the *UCR*, the FBI, in conjunction with state and local law enforcement agencies, has been developing a new supplementary reporting system in the last decade. This is known as the National Incident-Based Reporting System (NIBRS). Though the NIBRS is not yet fully operational, it is a computerized system that collects data on both offender and victim characteristics on each single crime incident and arrest within twenty-two offense categories: arson; assault; bribery; burglary/breaking and entering; counterfeiting/forgery; destruction/damage/vandalism of property; drug offenses; embezzlement; extortion/blackmail; fraud; gambling; homicide; kidnapping; larceny; motor vehicle theft; pornography; prostitution; robbery; forcible sex offenses; non-forcible sex offenses; stolen property; and weapons law violations. Besides these "Group A" offenses, the NIBRS also collects data on eleven "Group B" offenses: bad checks; curfew/loitering/vagrancy violations; disorderly conduct; DUI; drunkenness; non-violent family offenses; liquor law violations; "Peeping Tom" offenses; runaway; trespass; and all other offenses. Agencies participating in the NIBRS also submit quarterly Hate Crime Reports to the FBI, the first results of which can be seen in Figure 2.1.

Welcome though these new data are, none of them can avoid the simple fact that they, too, are partial data based on reports of crime to the police. By definition, they ignore the unreported "dark figure" of crime. We turn now to a second source of official crime data. These are the victimization surveys of the *National Crime Victimization Survey*.

Victimization Data: *National Crime Victimization Survey*

We have seen that the unreported "dark figure" of crime represents a large question mark in the statistical data of the *UCR*. We have implied that the actual size of the dark figure is unknowable and that there is no good reason to suppose either that it is constant from year to year or that it has a fixed ratio with reported crime. Moreover, because the volume of crime reported in the *UCR* depends as much on police activity as it does on the actual amount of criminal activity, the size of the dark figure of crime is, in principle, infinite. Simply put, there is as much officially recorded crime as the criminal law defines, as the public reports, and as the police accept.

During the past twenty-five years, criminologists in the United States and abroad (see Chapter 16.2) have increasingly turned to victimization surveys to understand more about the volume and the rate of crime. **Victimization surveys** examine representative samples of a general population in an attempt to discern what crimes have been experienced in a given period. Although smaller victimization surveys have been conducted occasionally by individual researchers, a victimization survey of a large national sample of U.S. households has been conducted by the Bureau of Justice Statistics each year since 1972. This is the *National Crime Victimization Survey* (NCVS).

The *NCVS* is based on a representative sample of about 45,000 households. The entire sample is interviewed twice each year (on a rotational basis) for three years. In person and by way of computer-assisted telephones, interviewers ask the sample's 94,000 household residents age twelve and over for a history of the crimes committed against them in the previous year. One of the intended advantages of the *NCVS* over the *UCR* is the former's ability to discover information about crimes not reported to the police or, in other words, about the "dark figure" of crime. The crimes examined by the *NCVS* include rape and sexual assault; robbery; assault; robbery or assault resulting in personal injury; personal theft; burglary; household larceny; and motor vehicle theft.

The *NCVS* surveys are not designed as a substitute for the *UCR* program but as a complement to it. Indeed, direct comparisons of *NCVS* and *UCR* data are of dubious value because the sources from which they derive are quite different. Whereas crime rates in the *UCR* derive from reports of incidents of crime to the police, the rates in the *NCVS* derive from reports of victimizations to survey interviewers. In other words, *NCVS* data are based on individuals actually victimized; *UCR* data are based on reported criminal acts. Because their sources of data differ, the *UCR* and the *NCVS* tend to tell us rather different things about crime.

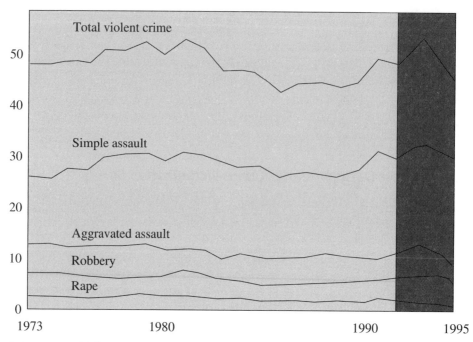

FIGURE 2.6   Violent Crime Rates, 1973–1995 (National Crime Victimization Survey)
NOTES: Victimization rate per 1,000 persons age 12 or older.
Violent crime includes murder, rape, robbery, and aggravated and simple assault.
SOURCE: Bureau of Justice Statistics, 1997a, 1.

Some of the main findings of the *NCVS* (Bureau of Justice Statistics, 1998; and see Figure 2.6, Figure 2.7, and Figure 2.8) are:

- Only 39 percent of all *NCVS* crimes were reported to the police. Only 50 percent of violent victimizations, 41 percent of all households, and 30 percent of personal thefts were reported. The highest proportion of reported crimes was for motor vehicle thefts (92 percent), the lowest for personal larceny without contact (15 percent).
- The *NCVS* property and violent crimes rates for 1997 were the lowest recorded since the survey began in 1973.
- In 1997 males had significantly higher victimization rates than females for all violent crimes except rape/sexual assault. Males were twice as likely to experience robbery and aggravated assault. African Americans had higher violent victimization rates than whites or other races.
- In about half of all violent victimizations, the victim knew the offender.
- Females and African Americans were more likely to report a crime to police than were males and whites.
- The decreasing victimization trends during 1993–1997 were experienced about equally both by males and females and by different racial and income groups.

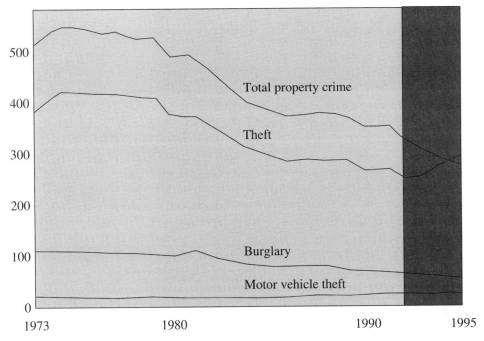

FIGURE 2.7   Property Crime Rates, 1973–1995 (National Crime Victimization Survey)

NOTES: Victimization rate per 1,000 households.
SOURCE: Bureau of Justice Statistics, 1997a, 4.

- Between 1993 and 1997 Hispanic households experienced a greater decrease in the rate of property crime victimization than did non-Hispanic households.

Assessment

The *NCVS* was originally devised to yield a better idea of the size of the dark figure of crime unreported in the *UCR*. In this task it has been reasonably successful: *NCVS* data document that a massive amount of crime goes unreported to the police. Additionally, despite consistent increases in the rates of *UCR* Index Crimes during the 1980s and early 1990s, *NCVS* data reveal that victimization rates remained remarkably stable during the same period. In the past few years they have declined to all-time measured lows.

But the *NCVS* surveys are not without their limitations. There are three problems in the *NCVS* in particular: underreporting to interviewers, response bias, and time-in-sample bias (Sparks, 1981).

1. Although victimization surveys always reveal more crime than that recorded in police-based documents such as the *UCR,* the *NCVS* also understates the crime rate. For example, because many crimes are often somewhat insignificant to their victims, they tend to be forgotten. The tendency to forget increases as the time between the crime and an *NCVS* interview increases. Reflect, too, on how

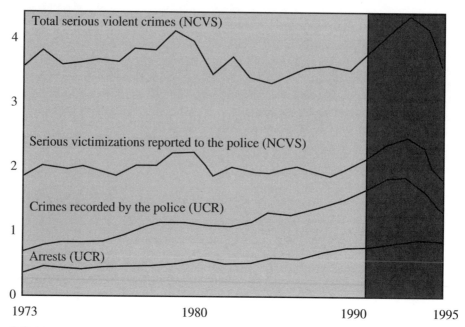

FIGURE 2.8   Four Measures of Serious Violent Crimes, 1973–1995

NOTES: Offenses in millions.

Total serious violent crime (NCVS): The number of murders recorded by police plus the number of rapes, robberies, and aggravated assaults from the victimization survey, whether or not they were reported to the police.

Serious victimizations reported to the police (NCVS): The number of murders recorded by police plus the number of rapes, robberies, and aggravated assaults that victims said were reported to the police, as measured by the victimization survey.

Crimes recorded by the police (UCR): The number of murders, forcible rapes, robberies, and aggravated assaults in the Uniform Crime Reports of the FBI, excluding those that involved victims under age 12.

Arrests (UCR): The number of persons arrested for murder, forcible rape, robbery, or aggravated assault as reported by law enforcement agencies to the FBI.

SOURCE: Bureau of Justice Statistics, 1997a, 2.

reluctant a female interviewee will be to report her victimization to a telephone interviewer if her abuser is within earshot of the telephone or if her telephone line is shared with another party—as sometimes happens, especially in rural areas.

2. The rate of underreporting is distributed unevenly throughout the class structure. Irrespective of actual victimization, whites are more likely than blacks to report having been victimized, as are college graduates compared with those with less education.

3. *NCVS* respondents are supposed to be interviewed every six months for a total of seven interviews. As interviewee participation in the *NCVS* increases, their reported victimization rates decrease consistently. This decrease may arise be-

cause respondents, having been made more aware of victimization simply by exposure to interviewers' questions, take greater precautions against victimization. The reported victimization rates of often-interviewed participants also might fall because respondents are less cooperative and less candid in later interviews.

In light of these problems, the Bureau of Justice Statistics has made several important changes to the *NCVS*. Since 1992 the redesigned *NCVS* includes a new strategy for improving the accuracy of victimization-incident recall and for expanding the scope of crimes covered (including vandalism). The new *NCVS* also includes a strategy for dealing with changing victimization rates over a longer period of time (a longitudinal design), so as to permit analysis of such issues as:

- whether crime victimization is a factor in the geographic mobility of respondents
- long-term health and economic consequences of victimization
- victim contacts with the criminal justice system over an extended period of time
- the characteristics of victims, including victims who experience one-time, periodic, or relatively continuous victimization, together with such factors as the type of crime and victim (or offender characteristics) that vary across these different temporal patterns
- the degree to which respondents in one year also account for victimizations in other years

Federal Agencies and Corporate Crime

Neither the *UCR* nor the *NCVS* contains data about corporate crime. Though we discuss corporate crime at some length in Chapter 13.2, it is worth mentioning here that important sources of official data about corporate crime are the deliberations of various federal agencies and regulatory bodies such as the Environmental Protection Agency and the Occupational Safety and Health Administration.

Corporate violations become known to these agencies in many ways, including consumer complaints, government investigations, congressional committees, and complaints made by corporate competitors. However, it is important to realize that the amount of corporate misconduct not reported in the documents of federal agencies is enormous. Such data thus suffer from some of the same problems encountered by police-based data.

2.3 UNOFFICIAL CRIME DATA

In addition to the three sources of official crime data just described, there are several unofficial (that is, nongovernmental) sources of crime data: self-reports, biographies, participant observation, and comparative and historical data. We shall refer often to these data sources in this book.

BOX 2.3   SOURCES OF CORPORATE CRIME DATA

Among the federal agencies from which information about corporate crime can be gathered are:

- for financial violations, the Securities and Exchange Commission
- for environmental violations, the Environmental Protection Agency
- for labor violations, the Equal Employment Opportunity Commission, the Occupational Safety and Health Administration, the National Labor Relations Board, and the Wage and Hour Division of the Department of Labor
- for manufacturing violations, the Consumer Product Safety Commission, the National Highway Traffic Safety Administration, and the Food and Drug Administration
- for unfair trade practices, the Federal Trade Commission
- for administrative violations, U.S. federal courts

In addition, some data about transnational corporate crime are contained in the reports and activities of a variety of international agencies, such as the World Health Organization (see Chapter 16).

Self-Report Data

Given that the volume of crime is always underestimated by official crime statistics such as the police-based *UCR* and the victim-based *NCVS,* criminologists have long felt that a more complete picture of criminal activity can be had by using offender-based data. One way in which criminologists have sought to obtain offender-based data is the self-report questionnaire. In self-report studies, researchers distribute questionnaires to respondents and ask them to admit anonymously whether they have committed certain offenses and, if so, how often.

Austin Porterfield, in his study of delinquency among male and female Texas college students (1946), was probably the first person to use a self-report questionnaire. Porterfield found no significant difference between the delinquent involvement of the students and that of a group of youths who had been processed by the juvenile court. At the same time, however, he found a significant difference in court appearances between the two groups and discovered that this differential grew out of both the powerlessness of the court children—who were overwhelmingly of low socioeconomic status—and the social disruption of their families.

Following Porterfield's pioneering research, numerous self-report studies have shown that police-based data seriously underestimate the criminal activity of certain segments of the population. Thus, whereas police-based data show that those who commit crimes in the United States are disproportionately young, male, and black, self-report findings have typically found far less differences among offenders, especially in terms of their social class (Weis, 1976; Tittle, Villemez, and Smith, 1978).

For example, in the course of his self-report study of middle-class delinquency, Joseph Weis found that "the often-cited 1:6 ratio of male to female arrestees is twice as large as the mean ratio of 1:2.56 self-reported participants in delinquent behavior" (1976:23). However, Weis also discovered large gender differences in the prevalence (the proportion of a given population that commits crime), incidence (the rate at which a given criminal population commits crime), and seriousness of delinquent involvement: Young males are more often involved than are young females in the most serious offenses. A large-scale, international self-report study has also found that in thirteen Western countries boys commit more offenses than girls (Junger-Tas, 1994:374–375).

Critics point out that self-report studies have several methodological defects (Elliott and Ageton, 1980:96). First, self-reports are vulnerable to exaggeration by respondents. Young males, especially, often exaggerate the extent of their delinquency. They do this even on anonymous questionnaires. Second, some respondents do not remember their delinquent involvements, especially their more trivial offenses. Third, until quite recently most of the items on self-report questionnaires concerned relatively minor offenses. They tended to ignore the more serious offenses involving violence. Fourth, in many self-report studies the respondents have not been drawn from a representative sample of the population but from a group easily accessible to researchers, such as high school or college students. Each of these problems casts doubt on the findings of self-report studies.

Certain problems of self-report research have been addressed explicitly in a study by Delbert Elliott and Suzanne Ageton (1983; and see Farrington, 1989; Paternoster and Brame, 1997); using the National Youth Survey, they examined the delinquency of 2,375 youths, ages 11–17. The methodology of their study was far more sensitive to the problems of measuring crime through self-report studies than were previous studies. Among other things, Elliott and Ageton found that:

> middle-class youth (both sexes) are less likely to be involved in serious offenses than are working- or lower-class youth. Further, even when they are involved in serious crimes, middle-class youth commit fewer offenses than do working- and lower-class youth. There are substantial class differences in both the prevalence and incidence of serious crime.
>
>   When the focus is shifted from serious offenses to delinquent acts in general, there are few significant class differences in the proportions of youth reporting one or more delinquent acts. The frequency at which delinquent acts are committed does vary by class for males, however. Middle-class males commit substantially fewer delinquent acts each year than do working- and lower-class males. Females of all classes have relatively low rates of offending compared to working- and lower-class males, but there is no consistent pattern of class differences in female incidence rates. (p. 165)

The interpretation of these findings is open to considerable debate. It is one thing to show empirically that males, blacks, and members of the lower class tend to commit serious crimes more often than do females, whites, and members of the middle and upper classes. But it is quite another matter to explain why this is so.

BOX 2.4   BIOGRAPHIES OF CRIME

Well-known biographies in the literature of criminology include:

- Edwin Sutherland, *The Professional Thief* (1937; see Chapter 5.4), based on the recollections of Broadway Jones, alias Chic Conwell, a professional thief, ex-drug addict, and ex-convict from Philadelphia who worked for twenty years as a pimp, pickpocket, shoplifter, and confidence man.
- Carl Klockars, *The Professional Fence* (1974; see Chapter 10.2), based on Vincent Swaggi's story of his life as a fence (one who receives and sells stolen goods); the book discusses the methods Swaggi used to obtain stolen goods for as little money as possible, as well as the elaborate rationalizations he developed to justify his career as a fence.
- William Chambliss, *Box Man* (King and Chambliss, 1984), an account of Harry King's career as a boxman (safe cracker), his philosophy of life, and his lavish consumerism.
- Darrell Steffensmeier, *The Fence* (1986), based on Sam Goodman's life as a fence; Goodman used his antique shop as a front to deal in stolen merchandise. In the book, Goodman discusses the relationships among fences, thieves, customers, and criminal justice personnel, and the skills required to perform fencing activities.
- Laurie Taylor, *In the Underworld* (1984), written after Taylor was introduced to the London underworld by John McVicar, an infamous gangster of the 1960s who, while in prison, graduated with a degree in sociology from the United Kingdom's Open University.
- Stuart Hills, *Tragic Magic* (Hills and Santiago, 1992), records the escapades of recovering addict Ron Santiago, a forty-two-year-old black male of Cuban ancestry. Set in New York, this is a harrowing and engrossing story of robberies, burglaries, drugs, and prison.

Biographical Data

Another source of data about criminal activity is criminals' personal accounts of their activities (see Cromwell, 1996). This data source was popularized in the 1920s and 1930s by Chicago criminologists who encouraged researchers to mix with the people they were studying (see Chapter 5.2).

Although one must be most cautious in generalizing from the experiences of one criminal to an entire segment of society, biographies of criminals can be a fertile source for further investigation. Each of the studies shown in Box 2.4 adds relevant information to our stock of knowledge about the social world of the professional criminal.

Participant Observation

Participant observation is a form of field research that focuses on observing people in their natural settings and doing so as unobtrusively as possible. It is especially useful for observing the behavior of people who, for one reason or another, usually resist the participa-

---

BOX 2.5   PARTICIPANT OBSERVATION STUDIES

Among the many participant observation studies in criminology and the sociology of deviance are:

- William Foote Whyte, *Streetcorner Society* (1943). Seeking to build a sociology based on observed interpersonal events (p. 358), Whyte lived for three years in Cornerville, where he ate, drank, played, and talked intimately with members of a slum neighborhood. He concluded that the slum community of street-corner boys was highly organized, a fact invisible to conventional outsiders who could see only its disorganized and aimless lifestyles.
- Ned Polsky, *Hustlers, Beats, and Others* (1967). Polsky exposed the techniques of poolroom hustling by engaging in participant observation as a hustler's opponent, a hustler's backer, and as a hustler himself.
- Laud Humphreys, *Tearoom Trade* (1970). Humphreys' account of impersonal homosexual encounters in public facilities was the result of field research, during the course of which he gained entry into the subculture by posing as a lookout.
- Jason Ditton, *Part-Time Crime* (1977a; see Chapter 13.1).The English criminologist Ditton went undercover as a dispatch operative, observing the routine fiddles to which sales operatives in Wellbread's Bakery were prone.
- Jack Douglas and Paul Rasmussen, *The Nude Beach* (1977). Douglas and Rasmussen observed the complicated interaction among bathers on a nude beach in La Jolla, California.
- Marc Reisner, *Game Wars* (1991). Reisner takes us inside the underworld of Cajun alligator poachers and ivory importers, focusing on the dangerous investigations of undercover U.S. Fish and Wildlife game warden Dave Hall.

---

tion of outsiders in their social world. Examples of such people include members of criminal syndicates such as Hell's Angels and paramilitary survivalists. Ideally, participant observation requires that the subjects of study are unaware that the observer is in fact an observer.

Each of the studies in Box 2.5 is a good example of how to gather information about criminal or deviant activities by the method of participant observation. Each study produced data available only to participants.

But the actual practice of participant observation is plagued with difficult questions. Some questions concern objectivity. For example, how can one study something objectively if one is a part of what one studies? Other questions concern ethics. Where is the dividing line between the appropriate gathering of data about human subjects and the invasion of their right to privacy? Does the researcher have an ethical obligation to report a crime when he or she witnesses one? Thus both Humphreys' (1970) research on homosexual encounters and Douglas and Rasmussen's (1977) observation of nudists have been attacked for being unethical. Still other questions concern danger. What happens if the researcher is detected by her subjects?

Largely because of the effect of questions such as these, neither courts of law nor university institutional review boards have looked with much favor on participant observation studies. Indeed, in a tragic example of what Patricia and Peter Adler (1998:xiv) refer to as "the Dark Ages" for ethnographers, Rik Scarce, a graduate sociology student at Washington State University, served six months in prison in the early 1990s for contempt of court for refusing to reveal information about the activities of a group of radical environmentalists and animal rights activists with whom he had mixed in the course of his research.

But there are now some signs that this oppressive atmosphere is about to be seriously challenged. Jeff Ferrell (1993), for example, has engaged in a fascinating study of the "creative law-breaking" of urban hip-hop graffiti writers in Denver. Moreover, twelve authors have just contributed new research to an edited volume of participation observation studies ("edgework") (Ferrell and Hamm, 1998). These studies include encounters with street gangs; the homeless; paramilitary units; sex work and gender work; drug subcultures; and sky divers and motorcyclists.

Comparative and Historical Data

The great French sociologist Émile Durkheim (1984:157) once remarked that comparative sociology is not a special branch of sociology, it is sociology itself. So it is, too, with criminology. Comparative criminology is an indispensable aspect of criminological inquiry and a rich source of data for its theories.

The focus of comparative criminology is the systematic comparison of crime in two or more societies (see Chapter 16). Comparative studies allow us to compare present crime rates in the United States, for example, with those in other cultures, places, and times. Does the United States have a higher homicide rate, for instance, than Japan, Canada, or England? If it does, why? In Figure 2.9 you may compare the homicide rates of selected U.S. and European cities. Note, for example, that between 1995 and 1997 New York City had a homicide rate of 16.8 per 100,000, compared with rates of 2.1 in London and 1.7 in Rome. Comparative criminology also enables us to examine the effectiveness of social and government policies toward crime. Thus, to what extent does gun control legislation affect the number of murders in which firearms are used?

Comparative crime data, like other crime data, have both official and unofficial sources. Official comparative crime data derive from the activities and reports of national governments and government agencies. Such data can be found in the reports of international agencies such as the United Nations, the World Court, the World Health Organization, and the International Police Organization (Interpol). Some organizations, such as the United Nations, the Dutch Ministry of Justice, and the British Home Office, also sponsor and conduct cross-national victimization surveys. Unofficial comparative crime data can be gleaned from the reports and findings of such private organizations as Amnesty International, Doctors Without Borders, and Human Rights Watch. These data are often especially useful for documenting crimes committed by governments or by the military against their own populations.

As we will see in some depth in Chapter 16, the use of national crime data for cross-national purposes is not without difficulty. Crime data are not items that can simply be pried

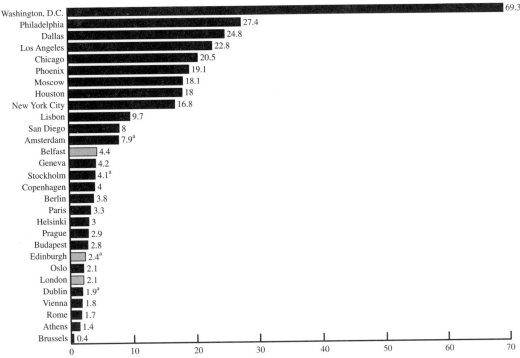

FIGURE 2.9   Homicide Rates per 100,000 Population in Selected European and U.S. Cities, 1995–1997

[a] 1994–1996.

SOURCE: Adapted from Home Office Research and Statistics Directorate, 1998.

loose from one culture and compared with those of another. Societies differ in how they define crime, for example, making simple comparisons of crime rates a hazardous activity, and in the degree of seriousness with which they regard certain types of crime.

Other types of comparative study can be based on historical data. The diverse sources of historical data include official statistics (on crime, prison populations, health, and so on), court records, books, newspapers, journals, pamphlets, plays, and oral histories. Historical data help us examine the past in order to understand how we have arrived at the present. Ideally, they allow us to make generalizations about crime that stand outside the peculiarities of any given era. Historical studies of crime are therefore implicitly comparative. Douglas Hay's (1975) study of crime and criminal law in eighteenth-century England, for example, revealed that in societies where the criminal justice system is based on terror—in this case, execution for the most petty of offenses—a national police force might be quite unnecessary. Occasionally, historical studies of crime are also cross-cultural. A good example of a study that is both historical and cross-cultural is *The Politics of Crime and Conflict* by Ted Robert Gurr, Peter Grabosky, and Roger Hula (1977). This study revealed that the relationship between public policies and crime rates in Calcutta, London, Stockholm, and Sydney during a 150-year period was in many ways strikingly similar, despite the enormous social, economic, and political differences among these disparate cities.

2.4   ASSESSMENT

In this chapter we have described the major sources of data for studying crime. We must stress again that crime data can never represent criminal behavior, however defined, in a neutral or unbiased way. Data do not speak for themselves! A particular crime rate identified and measured by official crime data, for example, very much depends on the legalistic concepts that guide the process of measurement. We do not, of course, mean by this that criminologists intentionally distort data to suit their own purposes. Rather, we mean that data are identified and defined by concepts, and that criminologists naturally differ in the concepts of crime they hold appropriate for the study of crime.

This is an important point. As you read the contents of this book, you will learn that how criminologists explain or interpret crime data depends both on their concepts of crime and on the assumptions underlying their theories of crime. **Theories** are sets of assumptions, mediated by concepts, that guide the interpretation of data. Theories try to explain both regularities and irregularities in data. In exactly the same way that what constitutes crime data depends on any given concept of crime, so, too, how we explain crime data depends on the assumptions of our theories.

REVIEW

This chapter has outlined the major sources of data available to criminologists. Official crime data are published by the state and by state agencies. In the United States such publications include the *Uniform Crime Reports* (*UCR*), the *National Crime Victimization Survey* (*NCVS*), and diverse federal records of corporate crime. Unofficial crime data include self-report data, biographical data, participant observation, and comparative and historical data. In this chapter you learned, however, that crime data can *never* represent criminal behavior in a neutral or unbiased way. We now review the major points of the chapter.

Caution: Data Do Not Speak for Themselves!

1. Data are not objective facts that exist independently of the concepts and theories of those who observe them. Data can never represent criminal behavior in a neutral or unbiased way.

2. Data are identified and defined by concepts, about whose appropriateness criminologists naturally differ in their perceptions. In exactly the same way that what constitutes crime data depends on any given concept of crime, so, too, how we explain crime data depends, to a certain extent, on the assumptions of our theories.

Official Crime Data

1. The *UCR* distinguishes between eight Index Crimes (Part I) and twenty-one Non-Index Crimes (Part II). Data about Index Crimes derive from reports to the police. Data about Non-Index Crimes derive from police arrests.

2. The *UCR* annually tabulates data about the number and rate of crimes; crime trends by year and region; the age, sex, and race of offenders and victims; and offense clearance rates.

3. Criticisms of the *UCR* are either methodological or conceptual. Among the latter is the limitation that the *UCR* records only legally defined categories of crime. Ultimately, we cannot be sure whether the *UCR* measures criminal behavior or the bureaucratic activities of official agencies. Whether or not police officers accept a crime report depends on the legal seriousness of the crime, the complainant's preferences, the relational distance between victim and offender, and the complainant's deference and social status.

4. The *NCVS* is based on reports of victimizations. It is designed to complement the *UCR*, but comparisons between the *NCVS* and the *UCR* are of dubious value because each tool attempts to measure different entities.

5. The *NCVS* indicates that only 39 percent of all crimes are reported to the police, that females and black males are among the most victimized groups in the population, and that nearly one-third of all households suffer some form of victimization annually.

6. Problems with *NCVS* data include underreporting to interviewers, response bias, and time-in-sample bias.

7. Neither the *UCR* nor the *NCVS* contains any data about corporate crime. However, various federal agencies and regulatory bodies are important sources of such data.

Unofficial Crime Data

1. Self-report data are offender-based data obtained from questionnaires. These data tend to show that middle-class youth commit as much crime as working-class youth, but that there are large gender differences in the prevalence, incidence, and seriousness of crime. Critics of self-report studies argue that self-report data suffer from exaggeration by young males, from biases due to the failure of some interviewees to recall delinquency, and from a concentration on relatively minor juvenile offenses.

2. Biographical data are accounts of personal activities given by criminals to criminologists. Biographies can be a fertile source for further investigation but are notoriously resistant to generalization.

3. Participant observation is a form of field research. Its goal is to observe people as unobtrusively as possible in their natural settings. Its actual practice is plagued with difficult questions, including the problem of where to place a dividing line between the appropriate gathering of data about human subjects and the invasion of their right to privacy.

4. Comparative and historical data are closely related. Comparative data derive chiefly from the activities and reports of national governments and such international agencies as the United Nations, the World Health Organization, and Interpol. Such data are typically used to compare crime in two or more countries at one point in time. Historical data derive

from a great diversity of sources and allow us to generalize about crime free from the peculiarities of any given era. Occasionally, historical data are also cross-cultural.

QUESTIONS FOR CLASS DISCUSSION

1. Which do the *Uniform Crime Reports* measure: activities of offenders or activities of the police?

2. Do victimization surveys help us understand the true extent of the dark figure of crime?

3. Can crime data ever represent objective facts?

Web Exercise. This exercise asks you to compare police-based crime rates in different parts of the United States. First, find the most recent *Uniform Crime Reports* on the Internet. You can do this by going to <http://www.fbi.gov/ucr/ucreports.htm>. (Be sure you have Adobe Acrobat Reader running at the same time.) Then, select one type of crime in any two cities—for instance, robbery in Boston and San Francisco. Students should produce two printed pages with statistics from a table entitled "Offenses Known to the Police [time frame], Cities over 1,000,000 in Population." Which city had more reported robbery? Did the robbery rates in either city change from one year to the next? What factors might explain differences in the two cities' robbery rates?

FOR FURTHER STUDY

Readings

Ferrell, Jeff, and Mark S. Hamm, eds. 1998. *Ethnography at the Edge: Crime, Deviance, and Field Research*. Boston: Northeastern University Press.

Greek, Cecil, and Deborah B. Henry. 1997. Criminal Justice Resources on the Internet. *Journal of Criminal Justice Education* 8 (1): 91–99.

Jenkins, Philip. 1994. *Using Murder: The Social Construction of Serial Homicide*. New York: Aldine de Gruyter.

Websites

1. <http://www.fbi.gov/ucr/ucreports.htm>: This site provides open access to the *Uniform Crime Reports*, the major official data source from the U.S. government. In order to access the tables in this site, users must also run Adobe Acrobat Reader (AAR) software because the tables are arranged in PDF files and are not accessible through standard web browser software. Downloading AAR is quick: simply click on the icon provided at this website, register for the software (which is free), and follow directions. You must run the AAR software concurrently with the web browser on your computer in order to read the tables. You will be prompted to "save" the data; after saving them, go over to the Adobe window and open the file you just saved. For efficiency, save the Adobe software in the root directory of your hard drive rather than under "windows."

2. <http://www.usdoj.gov/05publications/05_3.html>: This is a link from the U.S. Department of Justice (DOJ) homepage. It offers access to a variety of governmental reports issued by the DOJ,

including the *National Crime Victimization Surveys*. Go to the Bureau of Justice Statistics site and select "publications." This will lead you to the *NCVS*.

3. <http://www.nibrs.search.org>: This is the homepage for the National Incident-Based Reporting System project from the U.S. government. It is an alternative to the *UCR*, taking into consideration many of the *UCR*'s weaknesses. There is a set of links to all fifty states, updating readers on each state's activities with the NIBRS. Students may examine their own state's involvement with the NIBRS here.

4. <http://broadway.vera.org/pub/ocjsites.html>: This is a link from the Vera Institute of Justice, compiling eighteen different sources of crime data. It also allows users to specify a particular sort of data. For example, national data and specific state data are both available; the American Bar Association is linked here, as are the Federal Bureau of Prisons and the Office for Victims of Crime.

Criminological Theory

The Origins of Criminological Theory

Preview

Chapter 3 introduces:
- the origins of modern criminological theory
- the key writings of the early criminologists

Key Terms

born criminality	positivism
classical criminology	positivist criminology
dangerous classes	social mechanics
Enlightenment	utilitarianism
neoclassical criminology	

The ideas and concepts of the first criminologists originated in response to a variety of social conditions. These conditions included the legal and penal practices of the era and the concerns of government and influential sections of European society regarding the perceived dangers posed by the "dangerous classes."

We do not assess directly the merits of these writings here. Worthwhile though this task is, our chief focus is on the background and social context of the era in which modern criminology began.

3.1 THE ENLIGHTENMENT AND CLASSICAL CRIMINOLOGY

The origins of modern criminological theory can be traced to the writings of **Enlightenment** philosophers in the second half of the eighteenth century. To understand why these writings arose when they did we begin with the notorious case of Jean Calas, a prosperous French cloth merchant who was wrongly convicted and then executed in 1762 for the murder of his son. The sentence of execution required that Calas

> in a chemise, with head and feet bare, will be taken in a cart, from the palace prison to the Cathedral. There, kneeling in front of the main door, holding in his hands a torch of yellow wax weighing two pounds, he must make the *amende honorable,* asking pardon of God, of the King, and of justice. Then the executioner should take him in the cart to the Place Saint Georges, where upon a scaffold his arms, legs, thighs, and loins will be broken and crushed. Finally, the prisoner should be placed upon a wheel, with his face turned to the sky, alive and in pain, and repent for his said crimes and misdeeds, all the while imploring God for his life, thereby to serve as an example and to instill terror in the wicked. (quoted in Beirne, 1993:11–12).

The Enlightenment theorists opposed Calas's execution and all other punishments like it. They objected to the form of the punishment because it was cruel and inhumane. They also disagreed with prevailing views of the relation between crime and punishment. At this time, in much of Europe, crime was defined as that which opposed the Word of God as it was revealed in the dogma of Roman Catholicism. Serious crimes were often seen to result from a pact made by individual sinners with supernatural forces such as the devil, demons, and evil spirits. Catholic doctrine held that the role of lawful authorities was to eradicate the devil from the body of the condemned so that others would not be infected with their sins. The application of physical pain took a great variety of forms and was widely used both as a method of punishment and as a form of inquisition to es-

---

BOX 3.1   ANIMALS ON TRIAL

Even nonhuman animals were occasionally subjected to judicial irrationalities. Indeed, there is much evidence that until about 1800 in Europe and colonial America pigs, horses, and a variety of other species were formally prosecuted in criminal courts for crimes and, if convicted, were executed with the full majesty of the law. One such example is the public execution in 1386 of an infanticidal sow in the French city of Falaise. Having been duly tried in a court of law presided over by a judge with counsel attending, the sow was dressed in human clothes, mutilated in the head and hind legs, and executed in the public square by an official hangman on whom had been bestowed a pair of new gloves befitting the solemnity of the occasion (Beirne, 1994).

---

tablish the innocence or guilt of the accused. Michael Kunze (1987:260) offers an example of this process; he describes the barbarous forms of inquisition used to extract confessions of witchcraft from members of a peasant family in seventeenth-century Germany. Kunze reports that only after she was left dangling upside down in midair, her hands bound behind her back and fastened to a rope that ran over a pulley connected to the ceiling, did Agnes Pappenheimer (a girl of ten) confess that she and her mother were both witches.

Throughout Europe those accused of crimes were overwhelmingly poor and enjoyed little or no protection from legal systems unashamedly designed to serve monarch, government, church, and men of property. In England, for example, even as late as 1820, there were as many as 200 capital offenses, the great majority for crimes against property. During these judicial dark ages, the precise punishments for many crimes were not even contained in the legal codes. The enormous discretionary powers of judges were exercised arbitrarily and were often open to bribery and corruption.

The Enlightenment's reforming spirit emerged in France in the middle of the eighteenth century and grew into a widespread philosophical and humanist movement. The movement believed that reason and experience, rather than faith and superstition, must replace the excesses and corruption of feudal societies. The Enlightenment's demands were guided by several new doctrines, one of the most important of which was the doctrine of the social contract. The Enlightenment's chief theorists included Voltaire, Montesquieu, Helvétius, Rousseau, and Diderot in France; Kant in Germany; and Ferguson, Adam Smith, and Hume in Scotland.

The doctrine of the social contract was an attempt to avoid Thomas Hobbes's (1588–1679) belief that society was based on the nasty and brutish fact of *bellum omnium contra omnes* (the war of all against all)—all citizens pursuing their own narrow self-interests. How then could government be justified? What was the role of law in such a society? Enlightenment philosophers responded to such questions by asserting that society was held together by a contract between citizens and property owners. The fulfillment of this contract required a governmental authority. Only with such a contract could society exist. Citizens must surrender some measure of their individuality so that the government can enact and enforce laws in the interests of the common good; the government, in return,

This engraving of *"Justice"* appeared at the beginning of a 1765 edition of Beccaria's *Of Crimes and Punishments*. It was probably completed by Beccaria himself in the same year. Notice that *Justice* herself recoils from the executioner's offering of three decapitated heads. Instead she gazes approvingly at various instruments of labor, of measurement and of detention.

must agree to protect the common good but not to invade the natural, inviolable liberties and rights of individual citizens. The lives of the citizenry were to be regulated and protected not by theology but by "the rule of law." This utilitarianism view further asserted that those who challenged the social contract, those who decided to break its rules, and those who pursued harmful pleasures and wickedness were liable to be punished for their misdeeds.

Some writers at this time also began to protest the specific barbarities and inequities characteristic of feudal systems of justice, like the continued use of capital punishment. This **"classical criminology"** was part of the broad Enlightenment movement. We now examine the writings of the two most influential classical theorists: Cesare Bonesana Beccaria (1738–1794) and Jeremy Bentham (1748–1832).

Beccaria: *Of Crimes and Punishments* (1764)

At first glance it could not have been suspected that Cesare Beccaria's *Of Crimes and Punishments* (1764) would become so influential. Little of his book was original. Its proposals for reform borrowed heavily from the existing humanist and rationalist texts of Enlightenment philosophers. Even the idea for his book was suggested to Beccaria by his friend Pietro Verri. Beccaria knew very little about criminal law and punishment when he began to write *Of Crimes and Punishments,* and his ideas were developed only after long discussions and much prodding by Pietro and Pietro's brother, Alessandro. The finished product consisted less of reasoned arguments for reform than of a controversial program of reform. Because of Beccaria's singular and continuing importance in the history of criminology, we quote major points from *Of Crimes and Punishments* at length:

2. The Origin of Punishments, and the Right to Punish.   No man ever freely sacrificed a portion of his personal liberty merely in behalf of the common good. That chimera exists only in romances. If it were possible, every one of us would prefer that the compacts binding others did not bind us; every man tends to make himself the center of his whole world. . . .

Laws are the conditions under which independent and isolated men united to form a society. Weary of living in a continual state of war, and of enjoying a liberty rendered useless by the uncertainty of preserving it, they sacrificed a part so that they might enjoy the rest of it in peace and safety. The sum of all these portions of liberty sacrificed by each for his own good constitutes the sovereignty of a nation, and their legitimate depositary and administrator is the sovereign. But merely to have established this deposit was not enough; it had to be defended against private usurpations by individuals each of whom always tries not only to withdraw his own share but also to usurp for himself that of others. Some tangible motives had to be introduced, therefore, to prevent the despotic spirit, which is in every man, from plunging the laws of society into its original chaos. These tangible motives are the punishments established against the infractors of the laws. . . .

It was, thus, necessity that forced men to give up part of their personal liberty, and it is certain . . . that each is willing to place in the public fund only the least possible portion, no more than suffices to induce others to defend it. The aggregate of these least possible portions constitutes the right to punish; all that exceeds this is abuse and not justice. . . . (pp. 11–13)

6. Imprisonment.   Detention in prison is a punishment which, unlike every other, must of necessity precede conviction for crime, but this distinctive character does not remove the other which is essential—namely, that only the law determines the cases in which a man is to suffer punishment. (p. 19)

12. Torture.   A cruelty consecrated by the practice of most nations is torture of the accused during his trial. . . .

No man can be called *guilty* before a judge has sentenced him, nor can society deprive him of protection before it has been decided that he has in fact violated the conditions under which such protection was accorded him. . . . (p. 30)

16. The Death Penalty.   It is not the intensity of punishment that has the greatest effect on the human spirit, but its duration, for our sensibility is more easily and more permanently affected by slight but repeated impressions than by a powerful but momentary action. . . .

The death penalty becomes for the majority a spectacle and for some others an object of compassion mixed with disdain; these two sentiments rather than the salutary fear which the laws pretend to inspire occupy the spirits of the spectators. But in moderate and prolonged punishments the dominant sentiment is the latter, because it is the only one. (pp. 46–47)

19. Promptness.   The more promptly and the more closely punishment follows upon the commission of a crime, the more just and useful will it be. . . . (p. 55)

20. The Certainty of Punishment.   One of the greatest curbs on crimes is not the cruelty of punishments, but their infallibility, and consequently, the vigilance of magistrates, and that severity of an inexorable judge which, to be a useful virtue, must be accompanied by a mild legislation. The certainty of punishment, even if it be moderate, will always make a stronger impression than the fear of another which is more terrible but combined with the hope of impunity. (p. 58)

23. Proportion Between Crimes and Punishments.   It is to the common interest not only that crimes not be committed, but also that they be less frequent in proportion to the harm they cause society. Therefore, the obstacles that deter men from committing crimes should be stronger in proportion as they are contrary to the public good, and as the inducements to commit them are stronger. There must, therefore, be a proper proportion between crimes and punishments. . . . (p. 62)

24. The Measure of Crimes.   The true measure of crimes is . . . the *harm done to society*. . . . (p. 64)

41. How to Prevent Crimes.   It is better to prevent crimes than to punish them. This is the ultimate end of every good legislation, which, to use the general terms for assessing the good and evils of life, is the art of leading men to the greatest possible happiness or to the least possible unhappiness. . . .

Do you want to prevent crimes? See to it that the laws are clear and simple and that the entire force of a nation is united in their defense, and that no part of it is employed to destroy them. See to it that the laws favor not so much classes of men as men themselves. See to it that men fear the laws and fear nothing else. For fear of the laws is salutary, but fatal and fertile for crimes is one man's fear of another. . . .

Do you want to prevent crimes? See to it that enlightenment accompanies liberty. . . . (pp. 93–95)

We must stress that the image of crime and punishment in Beccaria's book is not one based exclusively on a single assumption about human nature. Borrowing liberally from the emerging determinism of the Glaswegian philosopher Francis Hutcheson, Beccaria believed—as did many others of his era—that human action was based on both free will and determinism. Indeed, attached to his humanism was Beccaria's attempt to apply to the study of crime and punishment some of the deterministic principles found in natural science, mathematics, probability theory, and the early forms of psychology. This project

Beccaria termed the "science of man." From the perspective of this new science Beccaria identified some of the causes of crime as "tyranny," "inequality of wealth," and "poverty."

In Beccaria's recommendations are the seeds of policies present in criminal justice systems around the world today, including the system in the United States. His book was the first widely read text to urge that the machinery of criminal justice use rules of due process; that sentencing policies reflect the harm inflicted on society by a given crime (essentially, that punishment "fit" the crime); and that punishment be prompt, certain, and contain a measure of deterrence. His major recommendations can be summarized as follows:

- The right of governments to punish offenders derives from a contractual obligation among its citizens not to pursue their self-interest at the expense of others.
- Punishment must be constituted by uniform and enlightened legislation.
- Imprisonment must replace torture and capital punishment as the standard form of punishment.
- Punishment must fit the crime. It must be prompt and certain, and its duration must reflect only the gravity of the offense and the social harm it caused.

Of Crimes and Punishments had a great impact on much of Europe and colonial America. Part of Beccaria's fame doubtless derived from the fact that in 1766 his book was condemned for its extreme rationalism and placed on the *Index Prohibitorum* (the Papal Index of forbidden books) by the Catholic Church. Beccaria's influence was most visible in the new classical legal codes of Austria, Denmark, France, Poland, Prussia, Russia, and Sweden. In the fledgling United States of America, the Constitution embraced Beccarian principles, as did the Bill of Rights. Beccaria's ideas were widely quoted by Thomas Jefferson, John Adams, and others. Upon reading *Of Crimes and Punishments,* English reformer Jeremy Bentham was driven to declare: "Oh! my master, first evangelist of Reason . . . you who have made so many useful excursions into the path of utility, what is there left to do?—Never to turn aside from that path" (cited in Paolucci, 1963:x-xi). These words bring us to the other pillar of classical criminology, Jeremy Bentham, and to his writings on punishment and prisons.

Bentham: Punishment and the Panopticon

Jeremy Bentham (1748–1832) was a gifted and passionate young man who graduated from Oxford University at the age of twelve and who later became a law student in London. Bentham never practiced law but instead became the prolific author of numerous texts on moral philosophy, punishment, jurisprudence, prison reform, and the police. A keen critic of the British constitution, and even more so of the U.S. Constitution, he traveled extensively throughout Europe and corresponded frequently with many leading intellectuals and political figures of his day.

Although much in his writings was original, Bentham owed intellectual debts to Beccaria, inevitably, and also to Scottish philosopher David Hume (1711–1776). Bentham was inspired by Beccaria to campaign for a rational, humane, and codified system of law.

Jeremy Bentham (1748–1832): Jeremy Bentham was one of the chief architects of the "inspection house" known as the Panopticon. In his will, he bequeathed his original manuscripts to the University College of London on the condition that the administrators there embalm his body and put it on permanent display for all to see. This is a photograph of Bentham in his wooden and glass box. There is no more perfect irony in the history of criminology! (Photo by Piers Beirne, with permission)

However, whereas Beccaria had simply compiled a list of humane reforms to the barbaric practices of criminal justice, Bentham intended to place these reforms on a solid philosophical foundation. While a law student, Bentham first read Hume's moral philosophy and was greatly impressed by it. Hume argued that the basic quality of moral action was its tendency to produce happiness—but that, as social beings with free will, members of a society derive pleasure from the happiness of others. Thus individual members of society should pursue not only their own pleasure but that of others. He argued that the happiness, pleasures, and security of individuals are the sole ends that laws should protect and promote. This utilitarian principle—the greatest happiness to the greatest number—became the cornerstone of Bentham's writings. We now turn to his campaign to reform punishment and prisons.

Punishment.   In the theory of punishment outlined in his 1780 book *Introduction to the Principles of Morals and Legislation,* Bentham (1973:152–203) assumed that potential criminals consciously calculate the profits and losses that arise from committing a crime. Similarly, he suggested, lawmakers should calculate the measures required to prevent and punish crimes. Bentham argued that in promoting the law of utility, legislators should prevent mischiefs such as crimes by means of various sanctions, including punishment. Crimes, Bentham argued, could be prevented either through positive sanctions (rewards) or negative sanctions (punishment).

However, Bentham urged that punishment should not be inflicted at all in certain circumstances (1973:170–178):

- where it is *groundless*—where, on balance, the act itself is not really mischievous
- where it is *inefficacious*—where it cannot act so as to prevent the mischief
- where it is *unprofitable,* or too *expensive*—where the cost of the punishment outweighs the cost of the harm it seeks to prevent
- where it is *needless*—where the mischief may be prevented, or cease of itself, without punishment

Bentham argued that when punishment is worthwhile, legislators should follow four rules of utility in calculating the proportion (balance) between crime and punishment. First, the ultimate goal is the prevention of all crime. To achieve this goal, legislators should ensure that the pleasure derived from any crime should always be just outweighed by the pain inflicted by the punishment for its commission. Second, a person about to commit a crime should be persuaded by the very threat of punishment either not to commit that crime at all or to commit a lesser offense. Third, a person who has actually decided to commit a crime should be persuaded by the threat of punishment to do no more mischief than is necessary. In no case should punishment for a crime be more than is necessary to prevent its occurrence. Fourth, legislators should try to prevent crime as cheaply as possible.

The Panopticon. In criminology, Bentham is most famous for the invention of his macabre Inspection-House, otherwise known as the Panopticon (Greek, meaning "all see-

BOX 3.2 THE PANOPTICON

The objectives of the Panopticon were to punish the incorrigible, guard the insane, reform the vicious, confine suspects, employ the idle, maintain the helpless, cure the sick, and offer training in any branch of industry and education. These objectives therefore embraced not only prisons but also workhouses for the poor, factories, madhouses, hospitals, and schools. Bentham believed that the ingenious architectural principles of the Panopticon would enable morals to be reformed and "health preserved; industry invigorated; instruction diffused; public burdens lightened; Economy seated as it were upon a rock; the Gordian knot of the Poor-Laws not cut but untied—all by a simple idea in Architecture!" (1971, I:i).

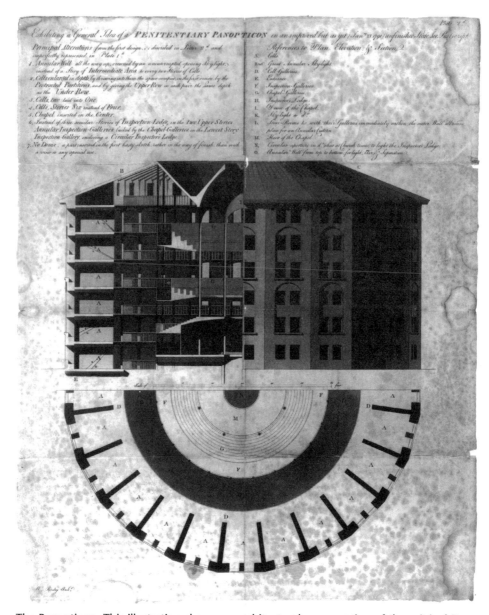

The Panopticon: This illustration shows an architectural cross-section of the original Benthamite Panopticon. It depicts the central guard tower, in which the guards remained hidden from view, and the individual cells in which inmates were exposed for inspection at any time of the day or night. University College London Library.

ing"). Bentham (1971, I:i–vii) wrote that the principles of his Panopticon represented an unequaled power of mind over mind. The Panopticon was explicitly created to be an engine of power that would discipline all of society.

We should remember that until the late eighteenth century, prisons were crudely designed and not intended for prolonged incarceration. Their uses were limited to holding-institutions for torture before trial, for debtors, for confinement prior to execution, and (especially in England and France) for the period between conviction and transportation to a penal colony. Bentham argued that the prison must be transformed from its position as one among many marginal and temporary institutions within the system of criminal justice to its permanent center. His plan for a penitentiary Panopticon began with a three-storied circular or polygonal building (Bentham, 1971, III:5–33). The circumference of the building contained the prisoners' cells, which were divided from one another by partitions in the form of radii issuing from the circumference toward the center. The prisoners were thus isolated from one another. At the building's center was a three-storied central tower, the Inspectors' Lodge for the prison guards. Because the tower's windows were draped with blinds, the prisoners were unable to see the inspectors. The prisoners were to be seen without seeing, subject to "uninterrupted exposure to invisible inspection" (pp. 88). Moreover, Bentham planned for the Panopticon to be built at a strategic location in a metropolitan area—a visible reminder to free citizens of the foolishness of their wrongdoing.

To these architectural principles Bentham added a strict regimen of visits by prisoners to the prison chapel for moral and religious instruction. Every minute of the prisoners' day was subject to discipline, order, and isolation in order to encourage self-reflection and moral reformation of character. Bentham's plans included rules for a crushing uniformity: in the segregation of inmates by sex and class; in diet, clothing, and bedding; in the ventilation, shading, cooling, and airing of cells; in the health, cleanliness, and exercise of prisoners; in the precise distribution of time; and in forms of punishment. The prison governor was charged with ensuring that all prisoners were taught some marketable skill; the profits from what the prisoners produced through a system of contract labor were to contribute to the financial management of the prison. Bentham also offered suggestions for the conduct of prisoners' lives after prison: Their release was made conditional on "acceptance by a bondsman" (payment of bail) and on successful fulfillment of apprenticeship in a worthy trade or occupation.

At first, Bentham's innovative plans were praised; they were debated in Parliament, and in 1794 several sites in England were purchased for the construction of his penitentiary houses. But no Benthamite Panopticon was ever completed in England, partly because, according to some (Phillipson, 1975:129–130), King George III opposed it and Parliament deemed it too expensive. Moreover, no pure Benthamite Panopticon was built in continental Europe—despite a frenzied program of prison construction between 1780 and 1840—and the two Panopticons undertaken in the United States (one in Pennsylvania, the other in Illinois) were eventually abandoned as impractical.

Bentham's writings on crime and criminal justice were ignored and forgotten in the fifty years after his death. However, Bentham's lasting influence lay less in the actual implementation of his architectural plans than in the widespread acceptance of his principles of punishment and prison.

Toward the Disciplinary Society

Significant questions remain about the nature of the reforms initiated by classical writers such as Beccaria and Bentham. How progressive was classical criminology? Whose interests did its ideas serve? Why did the proposals of Beccaria and Bentham gain widespread acceptance?

The origins of modern criminology begin with the writings of Beccaria and Bentham. Clearly, their ideas about penal reform gained official attention and were implemented in practice. But ideas about penal reform are rarely implemented simply because they are believed to be better somehow than those of their competitors; they are implemented also because they tend to serve certain interests and to achieve certain aims. Doubtless, the humanism of the classical writers commanded a measure of respect among most, if not all, sections of society in Europe and in the United States. The insistence that law must be subject to rules of due process, for example, was a progressive idea, as was a revolutionary, if rather primitive, belief in the scientific study of society that implicitly placed the classical writers at odds with the Catholic Church and all those who believed that free will is the basis of human action.

At the same time, Beccaria and Bentham also championed ideas that were very conservative even for their era. Though Beccaria's *Of Crimes and Punishments* was a plea for the supremacy of law rather than of religion and superstition, his proposed legal and administrative solutions to the problem of crime left untouched the social conditions in which it occurred. Bentham planned to extend Beccaria's proposals far beyond the criminal justice system. His Panopticon was to be an engine of regulation whose architectural principles would be used for the design not only of prisons but also of factories, hospitals, and schools (see Garland, 1997; Mathiesen, 1997). The ultimate aim, then, of classical criminology was not to lessen punishment but to make it more efficient and to ensure that its principles applied to everyone.

3.2   THE EMERGENCE OF POSITIVIST CRIMINOLOGY

The second source of modern criminology was **positivism**, which is a method of analysis based on the collection of observable scientific facts. Its aim is to uncover, to explain, and to predict the ways in which observable facts occur in uniform patterns. Positivist analysis can thus be applied to such things as the movement of stars through the heavens, the fertility of rabbits, and, indeed, to the entire subject matter of natural sciences such as physics, chemistry, and biology. Thus, the term **positivist criminology** is used generally to refer to the search for uniformities in the area of crime and criminal justice. Table 3.1 compares the major principles of classical criminology and positivist criminology.

Positivist criminology emerged in the writings and observations of various European authors in the nineteenth century. One of its forerunners was phrenology, whose founders were the Germans Franz Joseph Gall (1758–1828) and his pupil John Gaspar Spurzheim (1776–1832). This movement focused on the psychiatric concern with relationships between the organic structure of the brain, illness, and social behavior. But the phrenologists never regarded crime or criminals as the focus of their studies.

As a self-conscious effort to apply positivist principles to the study of crime, positivist criminology began with the ideas of French and Belgian statisticians in the 1820s. These

TABLE 3.1 Classical and Positivist Criminology—A Comparison

Classical Criminology	*Positivist Criminology*
1. The focus of criminological study should be the administration of justice and especially, the prevention of crime.	1. The focus of criminological study should be the criminal and the causes of crime.
2. Human action is based on free will, the "motivation" for which can be determined by psychological factors.	2. Human action is largely deterministic.
3. Crime is an action voluntarily engaged in by free-willed individuals; their motivation can be determined by psychological and social factors.	3. Crime is an action into which individuals are propelled by social, economic, and "mental" forces largely outside their control.
4. The punishment should fit the crime.	4. The punishment should fit the criminal.

ideas responded to a perceived crisis in classical criminology, and it is to this crisis that we now turn.

The Crisis of Classicism: The Dangerous Classes

The emergence of positivist criminology in early nineteenth-century France was an important response to changes in the system of criminal justice that occurred between the middle of the eighteenth and the beginning of the nineteenth centuries.

On one side of this transformation were the barbaric practices of feudal society, especially in France. At the center of the new system was a network of institutions of confinement ushered in by classical writers such as Beccaria and Bentham. These institutions had been created to control and to oversee the entire population of society and to operate on their inmates with the same monotonous precision as schools, barracks, and monasteries. Their expanding inventory included hospitals, workhouses, asylums, reformatories, houses of correction, and prisons. Their official aim was moral reformation through the deprivation of liberty and the prevention of crime through deterrence. Their "delinquent" and "pathological" inmates included syphilitics, alcoholics, idiots and eccentrics, vagabonds, immigrants, prostitutes, and petty and professional criminals. Inaugurated in 1810, the French prison system was based on a complex classification of inmates and included military prisons, debtors' prisons, agricultural colonies, transportation, and the galleys. These components operated in concert with a new criminal code, a professional police force *(gendarmerie)*, a system of passport and identity cards, and an extensive network of paid informers and spies (Foucault, 1979:280; Stead, 1983:47–48).

Positivist criminology itself emerged from the convergence of two areas of government activity in France. From the criminal justice system, criminology acquired a secure position of status, financial support, and, because of its pronouncements about the social distribution and causes of crime, considerable interest among the citizenry. From the statistical movement, criminology acquired its intellectual orientation and the recognition by the scientific community of its methods of analysis. During the Restoration (1814–1830), the activities of the criminal justice system and the statistical movement had a common concern: the failure of the new institutions of confinement (such as prisons) to regulate the conduct of the **dangerous classes**—a derogatory term used by law-abiding citizens to describe those members of the working classes, the unemployed, and the unemployable who seemed to pose a threat to law and order.

Criminals, especially thieves, formed a large part of the dangerous classes. That the expanding network of prisons had significantly failed to control the criminal activities of the dangerous classes was apparent in at least three ways (Beirne, 1987a:1144–1148). First, there was the growing presence in urban areas of large numbers of poor, unemployed, and working-class thieves whose desperate conditions were immortalized in such works as Victor Hugo's *Les Misérables* and Charles Dickens's *Oliver Twist*. For example, Paris, despite a doubling of its population between 1800 and 1850, remained structurally intact. It is not difficult to imagine how quickly this population explosion manifested itself in the incidence of infant mortality and related social problems of accommodation, food supplies, unemployment, public order, and crime. It has been estimated that in 1800 the only source of income for 30,000 Parisians was robbery; Balzac's *Code des gens honnêtes* recorded that twenty years later there were 20,000 professional criminals and as many as 120,000 "rogues" in Paris (Chevalier, 1973:448).

Second, the continued presence of the dangerous classes led to widespread fear of criminality. Reports of crime were widely circulated by newspapers and government inquiries—and eagerly devoured by their audiences. During certain winters of cold and destitution, the fear of crime turned to panic and terror. This widespread fear of crime was heightened by working-class insurrections, and it quickly became an unquestioned tenet of middle-class thought that crime and revolution were symptoms of the same disease (Tombs, 1980:214).

Third, after 1815, increases in the official crime rate lent support to fearful public opinion. For example, in that year a sudden increase was recorded in felony offenses, primarily in theft and disturbances of public order (Wright, 1983:48–50; Duesterberg, 1979:29–31). Between 1813 and 1820, the number of convictions in the criminal tribunals nearly doubled. Even more telling was the fact that many members of the dangerous classes were continually shuttled back and forth between incarceration and free society. This process was apparent in rising rates of recidivism, which implied that prisons were failing in their duty to reform the moral character of their inmates and that deterrence itself was a failure. In 1820 it was already understood that the prisons, "far from transforming criminals into citizens, serve only to manufacture new criminals and drive existing criminals ever deeper into criminality" (Foucault, 1980:40).

The failure of the new system of prisons to regulate the conduct of the dangerous classes stimulated considerable statistical research into their lives, which, both inside and outside prison, were examined by government investigators and independent researchers from the public health movement. One question was central: "Should (or could) the prisoners be returned to society and, if so, how?" (Petit, 1984:137). It was soon obvious that this question could not be answered with information derived solely from prison conditions. Inquiry broadened, therefore, to consider the larger population that passed through the criminal justice system. In 1825 the French government commissioned the first national statistical tables on crime, the annual *Compte général* (General Account). These tables were first published in 1827, immediately after a winter during which crime and death rates both increased and public fear and terror were the major themes of police reports and newspaper articles throughout Paris (Chevalier, 1973:3). The *Compte* reported the annual number of known and prosecuted crimes against persons and property, whether the accused (if prosecuted) were acquitted or convicted, and the punishments awarded. It also recorded the time of year when the offenses were committed and the age, sex, occupation, and educational status of both accused and convicted.

The French government reasoned that the hard facts in the *Compte's* tables could be used to understand the causes of crime and how to ameliorate them. These hopes were echoed by a group of social statisticians who were busy collecting data on such items as births, marriages, and deaths. Among this group was André-Michel Guerry, who in 1829 produced a one-page sheet of three maps that allowed the reader to see some elementary relationships between property crimes and personal crimes. But the most influential member was the young Belgian astronomer Adolphe Quetelet (1796–1874). Quetelet's account of the "social mechanics of crime" is the place to begin an examination of the development of positivist analysis in criminology.

Quetelet's Social Mechanics of Crime

Quetelet was a brilliant student of astronomy and mathematics at the University of Ghent in Belgium. In 1823, during a visit to Paris, he learned of the potential for applying algebra, geometry, and the principles of astronomy to the understanding of social conditions. Quetelet soon turned his attention to crime and crime rates. In his book *Research on the Propensity for Crime at Different Ages,* published in 1831, Quetelet stressed that **social mechanics** could never pretend to discover laws verifiable for all individuals. But he argued that the phenomena of crime—when observed on a large scale using such statistical records as the *Compte*—obeyed the same law-like regularities as did physical phenomena. In his early writings, Quetelet attempted to show that the law-like regularity existing in the heavens and the world of nature also existed in society.

From the astonishing regularity in French crime rates between 1826 and 1829, Quetelet inferred that the ratio of unknown crimes to recorded crimes was in practice constant (see Table 3.2). He also noted constancy in the annual number of accused (tried) and convicted and in the ratios of accused to convicted, of accused to inhabitants, and of crimes against persons to crimes against property. Furthermore, Quetelet noted regularities in the number of accused who failed to appear in the courts, in the number of convictions in different types of courts, and in the number of convicts sentenced to death, imprisonment, or forced labor. Quetelet found even the different methods of murder to be constant from one year to another.

From the apparent constancy of crime rates recorded in the *Compte*, Quetelet inferred that, even if individuals have free will, criminal behavior obeys scientific laws of the same sort as those that govern the motion of inanimate objects like stars. The disproportionate presence of certain categories of people in the *Compte* between 1826 and 1829 also indicated to Quetelet that young males, the poor, and those without jobs or in lowly occupations

TABLE 3.2   The Constancy of Crime, France, 1826–1829

Year Accused	Accused (Tried)	Accused of Crimes Against		Disposition	
		Persons	Property	Guilty	% Guilty
1826	6,988	1,907	5,081	4,348	62
1827	6,929	1,911	5,018	4,236	61
1828	7,396	1,844	5,552	4,551	61
1829	7,373	1,791	5,582	4,475	61
Totals	28,686	7,453	21,233	17,610	61

SOURCE: Quetelet, 1984: 20, amended.

had a greater propensity (or probability) than did others to commit crimes and to be convicted of them.

Quetelet reasoned that the many causes of crime could be divided into three types: (1) accidental causes such as wars, famines, and natural disasters; (2) variable causes such as free will and personality that can oscillate between greater or smaller limits; and (3) constant causes such as age, gender, occupation, and religion. Moreover, because he saw crime as a constant and inevitable feature of social organization, Quetelet further claimed that society itself caused crime (Quetelet, 1842:6, 108): "Every social state presupposes, then, a certain number and a certain order of crimes, these being merely the necessary consequences of its organization. . . . *Society prepares crime, and the guilty are only the instruments by which it is executed.*"

Quetelet's placement of criminal behavior in a formal structure of causality was a remarkable advance over the unsystematic speculations of his contemporaries. Flying in the face of the theory that criminals freely chose to engage in wickedness, Quetelet's intuition that society somehow caused crime marked a profound theoretical departure from the crude realism of public opinion and classical criminology.

However, in the early 1840s, Quetelet began to contrast virtues of the average law-abiding citizen with the criminality of vagabonds, vagrants, "primitives," "gypsies," "inferior classes," certain races with "inferior moral stock," and persons of low moral character. Eventually, he came to believe that unhealthy morality was manifest in biological defects and that those with such defects had high criminal propensities. Crime, he concluded, was "a pestilential germ . . . contagious . . . [sometimes] hereditary" (Quetelet, 1848: 214–215).

3.3   CRIMINAL ANTHROPOLOGY: LOMBROSO'S "BORN CRIMINAL"

Into this climate the notion of the "born criminal" was first introduced, in 1876, by Italian army physician Cesare Lombroso (1835–1909), in his book *Criminal Man*. Between 1852 and 1856, as a medical student and after studying anatomy and pathology, Lombroso became concerned about Italy's high incidence of such diseases as cretinism and pellagra.

When he began to study delinquents in the 1860s, Lombroso was convinced that only a scientific criminology (anthropometry) could avoid classical criminology's superstitious belief in free will.

Lombroso's *Criminal Man* (1876)

The major sources of the claims in *Criminal Man* derived from a diverse positivist landscape that included the new prominence of the scientific method in social investigations, the claim by statisticians that science was objective and therefore factual and free of values, and the evolutionism of Charles Darwin's *Origin of Species*. According to Lombroso's own account of his intellectual development, he began to realize gradually that the only scientific criminology was one based on an analysis of the individual criminal. This he realized after a series of revelations, one of which came during his postmortem examination of the convicted thief Vilella:

> On [Vilella's] death one cold grey November morning, I was deputed to make the *postmortem,* and on laying open the skull I found on the occipital part, exactly on the spot where a spine is found in the normal skull, a distinct depression which I named *median occipital fossa,* because of its situation precisely in the middle of the occiput as in inferior animals, especially rodents. . . .
>
>   This was not merely an idea by a revelation. At the sight of that skull, I seemed to see all of a sudden, lighted up as a vast plain under a flaming sky, the problem of the nature of the criminal—an atavistic being who reproduces in his person the ferocious instincts of primitive humanity and the inferior animals. Thus were explained anatomically the enormous jaws, high cheek-bones, prominent superciliary arches, solitary lines in the palms, extreme size of the orbits, handle-shaped or sessile ears found in criminals, savages, and apes, insensibility to pain, extremely acute sight, tattooing, excessive idleness, love of orgies, and the irresistible craving for evil for its own sake, the desire not only to extinguish life in the victim, but to mutilate the corpse, tear its flesh, and drink its blood. (Quoted in Lombroso-Ferrero, 1972:xxiv-xxv)

The arguments of *Criminal Man* stemmed from Lombroso's autopsies of sixty-six male delinquents in Italian anatomical museums. He examined several aspects of the skulls of these corpses and found them to be similar to those of insane persons examined in his clinic, to those of "blacks" in the United States, to those of the Mongolian races, and above all, to those of "prehistoric man." Lombroso also studied the physiognomy of 832 living Italian delinquents. This second group of delinquents included both males and females selected from among the "most notorious and depraved" Italian criminals. Of this group, 390 of its members were compared with 868 Italian soldiers and 90 "lunatics." From these data Lombroso (1876) concluded that

> many of the characteristics found in savages, and among the coloured races, are also to be found in habitual delinquents. They have in common, for example, thinning hair, lack of strength and weight, low cranial capacity, receding foreheads, highly

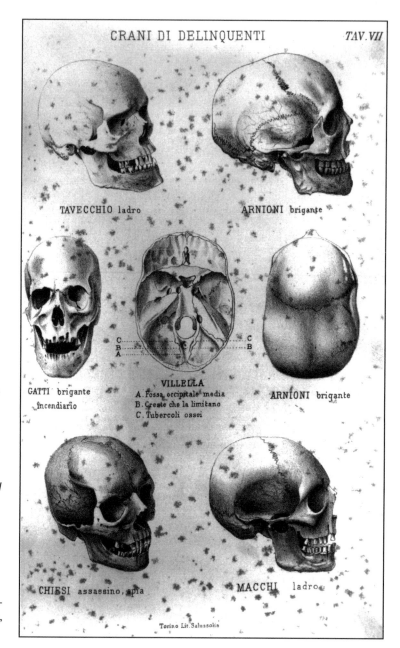

CRANI DI DELINQUENTI   *TAV. VII*

TAVECCHIO ladro   ARNIONI brigante

GATTI brigante   VILLELLA   ARNIONI brigante
incendiario   A. Fossa occipitale media
                 B. Creste che la limitano
                 C. Tubercoli ossei

CHIESI assassino, spia   MACCHI ladro

Torino Lit. Salussolia

Skulls of criminals, from Cesare Lombroso, L'Uomo delinquente, 1876: These skulls were collected by the Italian army doctor Cesare Lombroso (1836–1909) and reproduced in his book *Criminal Man*. Lombroso believed that the signs of criminality are manifest in certain bodily deformities and in physical and mental illnesses.

SOURCE: (Lilly Library, Indiana University, Bloomington, Indiana)

developed frontal sinuses . . . darker skin, thicker, curly hair, large or handle-shaped ears, a great analogy between the two sexes . . . indolence . . . facile superstition . . . and finally the relative concept of the divinity and morals.

Lombroso's discoveries of the **born criminal** established his new school as an academic science. With the publication of its own journal and key supporting texts by Ferri ([1884] 1917) and Garofalo (1885), the *scuola positiva* formed an identifiable program.

Although challenged by classical lawyers and by some socialists, Lombrosianism dominated public discussion of crime in Italy. Its reputation quickly extended beyond Italy to Germany, Russia, and France. Lombrosian findings were tested in the late 1880s and early 1890s and received favorably by several converts in France (Duesterberg, 1979:319–321), the United States (Rafter, 1992), and elsewhere.

Tarde's Criticisms of the "Born Criminal"

Enthusiasm for Lombroso's concept of the "born criminal" was not universal. Criticisms of the concept were led by French sociologist Gabriel Tarde (1843–1904) and by a coalition of lawyers and anthropologists, including Topinard, Manouvrier, and Lacassagne; criticisms were also made by criminologists in the United States, such as Frances Kellor, although somewhat later than those in Europe (see Chapter 4.1).

Three influential criticisms of the "born criminal" were put forward by Gabriel Tarde. First, he argued that there was no agreement about the characteristics of born criminals. In their anatomy, physiology, and pathology, born criminals were a mass of contradictory evidence. For example, one of Lombroso's disciples, Marro, had compared 456 "malefactors" with 1,765 "honest" persons; he reported that criminals' cranial capacity, stature, and weight were sometimes greater than average and sometimes less (Tarde, 1890:220). The anthropologist Topinard reported that pictures of criminals collected by Lombroso reminded him of photos of his own friends!

Second, Tarde showed that one of the born criminal's key attributes—moral atavism (embracing lunacy, degeneracy, and epilepsy)—was absent in many cases. He noted that the Italian provinces registering the highest rates of bodily illnesses and deformities typical of degeneracy were in fact the most moral provinces—in northern Italy. Moreover, in the provinces with the highest crime rates—in southern Italy—the inhabitants had excellent health. "Does this mean," Tarde joked, "that degeneracy constitutes the best condition for the increase of morality?" (p. 237).

Third, Tarde attempted to shift the evidence from one field to another. He suggested, for example, that variations in crime rates in different areas of his native France were caused not by different concentrations of born or habitual criminals but by local variations in the incidence of such factors as poverty and alcoholism. Another example of this tactic was Tarde's attempt to reinterpret the finding that born criminals often indulged in the practice of tattooing.

However, Tarde's criticisms offered no alternative explanation of habitual criminality. Indeed, Tarde believed that individual criminals were sometimes abnormal, inferior, and degenerate beings. Tarde's contributions were his empirical criticisms suggesting that not all criminals were born to their misdeeds. His efforts led not to the complete defeat of Lombrosianism in France but to a serious decline in its intellectual influence.

In turn, the attempt to rescue the causal purity of the notion of the born criminal increasingly led Lombroso to a thoroughly eclectic notion of causality in which an infinite number of factors could predispose someone to criminality. Indeed, in one of his last major statements, Lombroso said that "[e]very crime has its origin in a multiplicity of causes, often intertwined and confused, each of which we must . . . investigate singly" (1918:1). These expanded causes included such factors as climate, temperature, age, poverty, occupation, race, and gender.

Lombroso also retreated from his claim that all criminals were atavistic beings. A new classificatory system recognized a variety of criminal types: the born, the epileptic, the criminaloid, the occasional, the passionate, and the female. Regarding the latter, Lombroso began with the idea that although female criminality increases with the advance of civilization and education, most women are not criminal (Lombroso and Ferrero, 1895:1–102) because women are both physically more "conservative" and socially more "withdrawn." Women are physically conservative—and, therefore, physically less ferocious than men—because of "the immobility of the ovule compared with the zoosperm" (p. 109); and they are socially withdrawn because they bear the larger share of child rearing and thus necessarily lead a more sedentary life. The physical characteristics of female criminals, such as prostitutes, tend to resemble those of male criminals. Extending this paternalistic logic, Lombroso argued that because most female criminals have their crimes suggested to them by men, the best deterrent to female criminality lies in an appeal to women's natural vanity—by threatening, for instance, to cut off their hair.

Goring's *The English Convict* (1913)

Lombrosianism exercised little influence in England, but it was there that the most heralded refutation of it occurred: Charles Goring's (1913) *The English Convict: A Statistical Study.* In the history of criminology few books have commanded such high esteem. The eminent statistician Karl Pearson, for example, suggested that "it is not too much to say that in the early chapters of Goring's work he clears out of the way forever the tangled and exuberant growths of the Lombrosian School" (1919:xviii).

The English Convict combined the focal concerns of three hitherto more or less separate areas of activity. First, it continued the English tradition of prison research pursued by medical doctors such as J. Bruce Thomson, David Nicolson, and John Baker. This tradition involved the empirical calculation of "criminal propensities," often couched in the language and rhetoric of psychiatry: What mental and psychological factors distinguished prisoners from the law-abiding citizenry? Second, *The English Convict* extended the work of the British statistical movement. From the 1830s onward, the primary mission of many statisticians had been the quantification of social facts in order to address a wide range of controversial issues having to do with public health, child labor, factory conditions, education, and crime. Goring's contribution to these two traditions was the application of innovative statistical techniques to the study of criminals.

Goring's work was also strongly influenced by a third tradition, one that began with the publication of Darwin's *Origin of Species* in 1859 and that, in the 1890s, culminated in the findings of evolutionary and mathematical zoologists such as Francis Galton and W. F. R. Weldon. Galton's (1889) work on ancestral resemblance in sweet peas, for example, had shown that peas of a certain type, weight, and genetic structure tended to pass on their specific characteristics to their progeny. Weldon (1894–1895) found in his research on shrimps and crabs that creatures with deviant organs, such as long carapaces, tended to die early. Such findings led to the belief that the content of social action was itself inherited and that those with a genealogically deviant inheritance would be unable to adapt adequately to social life.

Straddling these three traditions was the desire of the professional middle class to stem the political and economic decline of the British Empire through rejuvenation of the phys-

BOX 3.3 THE SCIENCE OF EUGENICS

The basic assumption of the eugenists was that the distribution of social, moral, and intellectual qualities could be discerned in humans with the same procedures used to identify the distribution of physical qualities in the world of nature. Francis Galton pioneered the view that in any nation the natural human talents that compose "civic worth" are distributed according to certain statistical laws. Galton assumed further that the distribution of worth was spread throughout society and that its presence or absence was manifest in such indicators as wealth and pathologies, respectively. In *Hereditary Genius* (1869), Galton argued—seeking retrospective confirmation from his cousin's *Origin of Species*—that it was almost exclusively the "naturally" worthy who achieved social prominence; conversely, the naturally "worthless" never succeeded in rising above their lowly positions, and this despite all government or private supports.

ical stock and moral character of the British people. One platform in this social and political agenda was eugenics (Greek: good genes). It was hoped that eugenist principles could be used to eliminate a broad spectrum of social undesirables, including the physically unfit, alcoholics, the very poor, the morally and mentally depraved, and habitual criminals.

Eugenist proposals were of two sorts. Positive eugenics suggested that the middle and upper classes should be provided with incentives to intermarry and produce offspring, on the grounds that ordinarily only in these strata were intelligent and hardworking citizens found. Negative eugenics demanded that social undesirables (such as habitual criminals) should be isolated, sterilized, or occasionally castrated, because their useless offspring were a drain on national resources.

These diverse traditions merged in Goring's *The English Convict*. In 1903, Charles Goring, a junior medical officer in the English prison service, was made coordinator of a government-sponsored project to test the factual reality of the concept of born criminals. Goring's tests involved three phases: (1) a statistical analysis to determine the presence of thirty-seven Lombrosian characteristics in the criminal population, a group represented by 2,348 male convicts; (2) a comparison of the findings in the first phase with the characteristics of the "noncriminal public," represented by control groups including a company of soldiers, English and Scottish undergraduate students, and the staff and inmates of two separate hospitals; and (3) an analysis of the general physique of criminals. Goring (1913:173) concluded that in "the present investigation we have exhaustively compared . . . criminals as a class, with the law-abiding public. . . . *No evidence has emerged confirming the existence of a physical criminal type, such as Lombroso and his disciples have described—our inevitable conclusion must be that there is no such thing as a physical criminal type.*"

However, Goring did report that most criminals were physically inferior (in height and weight) to the general population. He reasoned that such differences could be explained perhaps by the process of "selection"; for example, those with inferior physiques were less likely to avoid arrest, given that the police were appointed only from among those with superior physiques. However, Goring suggested further that "this physical inferiority, although originating in and fostered by selection, may tend with time to become an inbred characteristic of the criminal classes, just as, with the passage of generations, the upper classes of the noncriminal community have become differentiated in physique from those lower on the social scale" (p. 200).

By the early twentieth century, most European criminologists distinguished firmly between biological and sociological causes of crime. Although most eugenists dismissed altogether the relevance of sociological factors, Goring nevertheless engaged in an analysis of the relative importance of several "adverse environmental conditions"—including employment, education, family life, and social class—and of mental defectiveness and heredity upon the recidivism of convicts and the types of their crimes. In this second line of analysis Goring assumed that sociological factors, on the one hand, and mental capacities and heredity, on the other, were independent of each other. For Goring it followed that to measure the effect of one factor, the effect of others must be controlled or eliminated. He therefore assumed that maladaptive, deviant, or defective qualities of individuals in a given species were not influenced by social environment. "Our interim conclusion," he argued "is that, relative to its origin in the constitution of the malefactor, and especially in his mentally defective constitution, crime in this country is only to a trifling extent (if to any) the product of social inequality, of adverse environment, or of other manifestations of what may be comprehensively termed the 'force of circumstances'" (p. 288).

Goring also noted that as many as 68 percent of the male offspring of criminals became criminal themselves. Was this the result of the genetic inheritance of criminal propensities or of the influence of one's family? Controlling for the influence of family contagion—by eliminating it from his calculations—Goring found the intensity of the inherited factor in criminality to be extremely significant and the intensity of family contagion to be almost negligible. "Criminality," Goring concluded, is inherited "at much the same rate as are other pathological conditions in man. . . . The influence of inheritance, and of mental defectiveness [are] by far the most significant factors we have been able to discover in the aetiology of crime" (p. 368).

In sum, *The English Convict* failed to refute Lombroso's concept of the born criminal. Indeed, Lombroso's concept of **born criminality** still had fervent followers in the United States even in the 1930s (Rafter, 1997; and see Chapter 5.1). Goring's dubious achievement was simply to replace Lombroso's atavistic criminal with one born with inferior weight, stature, and mental capacity.

3.4   NEOCLASSICAL CRIMINOLOGY

Thus far we have described the origins of the two most influential forms of modern criminology, classicism and positivism. These two versions of criminology competed strongly for legislative and popular attention throughout Europe and North America. Yet in combination they produced unworkable dilemmas for the machinery of criminal justice.

Penal Dilemmas

Classical and positivist criminology harbored fundamental differences of perspective on four key points (see Table 3.1). Especially after the rise of Lombrosianism in the mid-

1870s, the classicists and the positivists engaged in heated, bitter, and prolonged dispute. The outcome of this dispute—the precise contours of which varied from one country to another—had great significance for assumptions about criminal responsibility and the objectives and styles of punishment. In short, the intractable differences between classical and positivist criminologies, far from being confined to an academic arena, caused practical penal dilemmas whose resolution entailed a series of compromises agreed upon by the major institutions of criminal justice.

The serious implications of the conflict between the classicists and the positivists was best understood by Gabriel Tarde. In his 1890 book *Penal Philosophy,* Tarde (1912:chaps. 1–2) took issue with the debate between the classicists and the positivists over the respective merits of free will and determinism. Neither doctrine, he argued, was justified either theoretically or practically. The doctrine of free will held that the individual, uninfluenced by any external factors, chose to do one thing rather than another with complete freedom and foresight. This position was clearly absurd, Tarde indicated, given the obvious truth of the positivist insight that crime varied according to such factors as gender, age, and socioeconomic position. The doctrine of determinism had arisen, Tarde continued, largely as a reaction to the exaggerated free-willed individualism of the classicists. Determinism viewed the individual as a machine incapable of free choice. But Tarde replied that quite apart from such factors as gender, age, and socioeconomic position, individuals were authentic beings who somehow were the "authors" of their actions. Tarde therefore concluded that neither doctrine was adequate as a basis for a coherent system of penal responsibility.

Tarde attacked certain effects classicism had on the style of criminal justice. First, he denied that free will as such should be the basis of criminal responsibility. Individuals should be held accountable for their actions whether or not they exercise free will. Every individual, Tarde asserted, has unique psychological, social, and familial characteristics. Therefore, the basis of criminal liability and the relation between liability and punishment should be a combination of the social harm caused by accountable offenders and the offenders' unique personal characteristics. Second, Tarde objected to many classical legal reforms as impractical. If individuals had unique characteristics, they should not be subjected to uniformity of treatment by the criminal justice system. Legal distinctions should be made, for example, between men and women, children and adults, violent offenders and property offenders, first-time offenders and habitual criminals, and the sane and the insane.

Tarde also attacked the positivists, chiefly because their determinism greatly contributed to the ineffectiveness of the criminal justice system. If the positivists' concept of the criminal was accepted as the basis of criminal law, Tarde believed, only two unacceptable strategies would be available for dealing with criminals: either complete forgiveness of a crime or extermination of the criminal. Clearly, if the actions of criminals were "caused" by factors outside their control, rehabilitation was not a practical possibility—certainly not in the case of "born criminals." The influence of determinism was found in the increasing laxity with which prosecutors, judges, and juries treated criminals. Such leniency was apparent in the judicial tendency to reduce criminal charges from felonies to misdemeanors, which artificially reduced the crime rate and, in its turn, caused more than a threefold increase in the number of misdemeanors.

The key dilemma facing judges, legislators, and the criminal justice system, then, was this: How can justice be administered on a coherent and systematic basis? How can the partial truths of classicism and positivism be recognized without accepting the most dangerous implications of their respective extremes?

Neoclassical Compromises

The typical response of the criminal justice system to these two critical questions was doctrinal and procedural compromise. The compromise—devised roughly between 1880 and 1920, and led by Tarde and his pupil Raymond Saleilles (1911)—is known as neoclassicism. In effect, **neoclassical criminology** has become the basis of criminal responsibility and punishment in most Western countries.

The exact terms of the neoclassical compromise between classicism and positivism varied from one country to another; nonetheless, wherever it was instituted the compromise had and has six general features (Garland, 1985:chap. 3; Beirne, 1993:170–174):

1. The concept of *character* replaced the extremes of free will and determinism as the source of criminality. An offender's character was open to analysis by experts from the fields of law, medicine, psychiatry, probation, criminology, and social work. Because the links between character and crime can be influenced by an infinite variety of factors, crime should be understood through multi-causal (multifactorial) analysis.

2. There should be an *equivalence* between the seriousness of crime and the degree of punishment pronounced. Punishment should be exemplary but not vengeful.

3. *Imprisonment* must be the normal method of punishment, and a variety of penitentiary systems should be employed. The criminally insane and the recidivists should be segregated from other prisoners. There should be increased use of visitation and probation.

4. The treatment of the criminal character should not be uniform but *individualized.* Specific treatment, both in prison and during post-release programs, should be administered to offenders according to the nature and the degree of an individual's incorrigibility of character.

5. Every punishment should include a measure of *deterrence* for future miscreants. Deterrence is unworkable only for the insane.

6. The *death penalty* should be abolished for nearly all crimes.

3.5   ASSESSMENT

Classicism and positivism have been regarded as the two great systems of early criminological theory. In some ways they were quite different enterprises. Each identified a different object of analysis for criminology: the one, the application of criminal law; the other, the criminal. Each provided a different focus on punishment: Classical criminology demanded that punishment fit the social harm caused by the crime, whereas positivist criminology demanded that punishment fit the criminal. At the same time, as we already suggested above, both were part of the same broad movement to apply scientific principles to the study of society. However, whereas Beccaria's criminology (and classicism in general) held that human action is based simultaneously on both free will and determinism, the positivists of the next century insisted that crime and criminality are determined, patterned, and regular events in which an individual's will is more or less irrelevant.

As the remaining chapters of Part Two argue, the intellectual history of modern criminology is largely one of positivism's triumph over classicism. So thoroughgoing has been this triumph that even neoclassical criminology—which emerged as a compromise to the extremes of both classicism and positivism—has developed in positivist terms. Most criminological theory is modeled on the positivist methods of the natural sciences. Thus criminal behavior tends to be viewed rather like the behavior of billiard balls (they move, predictably, according to certain laws of motion): The subject of criminology—the criminal—behaves according to certain sociological, historical, psychological, or economic laws. Most crime policies, likewise, are based on the assumption that individuals can be redirected toward lawful behavior, given changes in the sociological, historical, psychological, and economic causes that propel an individual into crime. The appeal of positivism in criminology is overwhelming.

But there have been mounting signs, in the last decade or so, that the fortresses of criminological positivism are not impregnable. Put simply, if positivist criminology has accurately identified the causes of crime, why do state anticrime policies repeatedly fail? Reflecting the pessimism that seems the obvious answer to this question (anticrime policies fail because we have failed to grasp the true causes of crime), criminologist James Q. Wilson (1985:51; and see Gottfredson and Hirschi, 1990) has gone so far as to suggest that we should perhaps abandon altogether the search for the causes of crime. As policymakers, he reasons, all that criminologists can do today is devise anticrime policies that assume that potential criminals are rational actors who weigh the costs and benefits of engaging in crime. Wilson therefore asks us to return to the rational calculus of classical criminology. Let us devise policies that deter free-willed actors from committing crimes.

Wilson's plea for the prudent use of the classical criminology of Bentham and Beccaria returns us to the beginning of this chapter. Although no modern criminological research adopts the pure model of free-willed classicism, many studies have appeared recently that focus on the deterrent effect of punishment. Although we cannot explore the complicated issues associated with deterrence in this book, we note the significant influence of classical deterrence in current research on topics as diverse as the death penalty for murder (Bailey and Peterson, 1987); the impact of gun control on violent crime (Kleck, 1997:351–381); and drinking and driving (Ross, 1992). We conclude by noting further that not one of the studies found sufficient evidence to support the view that specific legislation deters criminal behavior.

REVIEW

This chapter introduced the earliest theories of modern criminology, each of which has had a great impact on the subsequent development of criminological theory. Each theory defines certain ways that criminologists understand crime today.

Classical Criminology

1. Classicism was the first form of modern criminology. It began as part of the Enlightenment's opposition to barbarism and arbitrariness in the criminal justice system.

2. Its principles are based in the belief that social action is influenced by both free will and determination.

3. The principles of utilitarianism were developed by Bentham. His views on punishment and imprisonment were widely accepted in theory if not always in practice. Bentham is best remembered for his model prison, the Panopticon.

The Emergence of Positivist Criminology

1. Positivist criminology began in France in the 1820s as a response to a breakdown in the classical penal system, chiefly evident in the failure of the new systems of incarceration to regulate the conduct of the dangerous classes. Positivist criminology was (and is) based on the belief that criminal behavior is as regular, patterned, and predictable as is behavior in the world of nature and that it should be examined with the scientific method.

2. The most influential form of early positivism was Quetelet's social mechanics of crime, which derived from the convergence of the concerns of criminal justice, astronomy, and statistics.

3. Quetelet's criminology employed natural science methods to identify the constancy of crime rates, criminal propensities, and the causes of crime.

4. Although his criminology was in some respects far in advance of his time, Quetelet ultimately believed that crime had biological causes.

Criminal Anthropology: Lombroso's "Born Criminal"

1. In 1876, Lombroso popularized the concept of the born criminal in his book *Criminal Man*. This biological concept radically opposed the supposed free-willed individual of classicism.

2. Lombroso believed that born criminals have primitive features that distinguish them from the law-abiding citizenry.

3. The crusade against Lombrosianism was led by Tarde, whose critical endeavors in the 1880s and 1890s caused a decline in the influence of Lombrosianism throughout much of Europe.

4. Goring's *The English Convict* (1913) tried to disentangle the respective influences of heredity and social environment on the activities of criminals. Goring's analysis of the physical features of English convicts, and his comparisons between them and control samples of nonconvict populations, led him to reject decisively Lombroso's concept of born criminality. Through assumptions derived from eugenics, Goring also found that English criminals engaged in crime because of alleged mental deficiencies rather than for sociological reasons. This finding was quite compatible with Lombrosianism.

Neoclassical Criminology

1. By the 1890s it was clear that a serious dilemma faced the machinery of criminal justice. Conflict between the classical and the positivist schools created a dangerous vacuum in penal policies.

2. The neoclassical school of criminology attempted to fill this vacuum with a coherent system of criminal responsibility based on accountability, individualization of punishment, and treatment programs.

3. Neoclassical criminology was led by Tarde and Saleilles. Although the exact terms of the compromise between classicism and positivism varied from one country to another, today its general outlines remain the dominant features of most Western systems of criminal justice.

QUESTIONS FOR CLASS DISCUSSION

Refer again to the grisly execution of Jean Calas in France in 1762, recounted at the beginning of this chapter. Less than a century later, in the 1830s, a very different penal style is visible in rules for the House of Young Prisoners in Paris. Some of these rules were as follows (cited in Foucault, 1979:6–7):

Art[icle] 17.   The prisoners' day will begin at six in the morning in winter and at five in summer. They will work for nine hours a day throughout the year. Two hours a day will be devoted to instruction. Work and the day will end at nine o'clock in winter and at eight in summer.

Art. 18. Rising.   At the first drum-roll, the prisoners must rise and dress in silence, as the supervisor opens the cell doors. At the second drum-roll, they must be dressed and make their beds. At the third, they must line up and proceed to the chapel for morning prayer. There is a five-minute interval between each drum-roll.

Art. 19.   The prayers are conducted by the chaplain and followed by a moral or religious reading. This exercise must not last more than half an hour.

Art. 20. Work.   At a quarter to six in the summer, a quarter to seven in winter, the prisoners go down to the courtyard where they must wash their hands and faces, and receive their first ration of bread. Immediately afterwards, they form into work-teams and go off to work, which must begin at six in summer and seven in winter.

Art. 21. Meal.   At ten o'clock the prisoners leave their work and go to the refectory; they wash their hands in their courtyards and assemble in divisions. After the dinner, there is recreation until twenty minutes to eleven.

Art. 22. School.   At twenty minutes to eleven, at the drum-roll, the prisoners form into ranks, and proceed in divisions to the school. The class lasts two hours and consists alternately of reading, writing, drawing and arithmetic.

Art. 23.   At twenty minutes to one, the prisoners leave the school, in divisions, and return to their courtyards for recreation. At five minutes to one, at the drum-roll, they form into work-teams. . . .

Art. 28.   At half-past seven in summer, half-past eight in winter, the prisoners must be back in their cells after the washing of hands and the inspection of clothes in the courtyard; at the first drum-roll, they must undress, and at the second get into bed. The cell doors are closed and the supervisors go the rounds in the corridors, to ensure order and silence.

1. What are the major differences between the assumptions of the two styles of punishment characterized respectively by the execution of Calas (in 1762) and by the rules for the House of Young Prisoners in Paris (circa 1837)?

2. This transformation of penal styles largely reflects changing theories on the causes of crime. Describe the broad transformation in such theories between the Enlightenment and Goring's *The English Convict* (1913).

3. Is one penal style more "humane" than the other?

4. What do these different penal styles imply about the possibility of the treatment and correction of criminals?

FOR FURTHER STUDY

Readings

Beirne, Piers. 1993. *Inventing Criminology*. Albany: State University of New York Press.
Hacking, Ian. 1990. *The Taming of Chance*. Cambridge University Press.
Valier, Claire. 1998. True Crime Stories: Scientific Methods of Criminal Investigation, Criminology, and Historiography. *British Journal of Criminology* 38 (1): 88–105.

Websites

1. <www.wsu.edu:8080/_dee/ENLIGHT/ENLCONT.HTM>: Provides a history of the European Enlightenment as an intellectual and scientific revolution. Offers more detail on Descartes, Rousseau, and the philosophes.
2. <www.geocities.com/_sociorealm/crime4.htm>: Provides an extensive set of links to discussions of criminological theories, with selections for classical and positivist theories.
3. <www.essential.org/dpic>: This is the site for the Death Penalty Information Center. Capital punishment was and remains one of the key points of debate between classical and positivist criminologists.

4

The Emergence of Sociological Criminology

Preview

Chapter 4 introduces:
- the major strands in the emergence of sociological criminology: Tarde's social psychology, Durkheimian sociology, and classical Marxism
- the criminological theories of Gabriel Tarde, Émile Durkheim, Karl Marx, and Friedrich Engels

Key Terms

communism	repressive law
ideology	restitutive law
imitation	social classes
mode of production	social solidarity

4.1   TOWARD A SOCIAL PSYCHOLOGY OF CRIME: GABRIEL TARDE

In Chapter 3 we learned that French criminologist Gabriel Tarde believed that rising rates of recidivism were one of the most serious aspects of criminality. Departing from public opinion, Tarde did not think these rates could be explained by the criminality of Lombroso's born criminals (see Chapter 3.3). Attempting to devise a social theory of crime that would explain more about the incidence and causes of criminality than did the notion of born criminals, Tarde began with the concept of "imitation."

Imitation and Crime

Tarde reasoned that crime—like all other social phenomena—was influenced by the processes of **imitation.** Imitation is a mental process that he defined as "the powerful, generally unconscious, always partly mysterious, action by means of which we account for all the phenomena of society" (Tarde, 1912:322). Imitation applies to the different psychological states and beliefs of individuals. It is a process in which individuals behave as if they were in a trance, as in sleepwalking. According to Tarde, the process of imitation always operates in a social context. Socially and historically it is present in the growth of cities, in national institutions, and even in international warfare. Imitation cuts across all social, racial, and religious boundaries. It infiltrates all aspects of social life, from art to architecture and from music to militarism. It produces both good and evil. It encourages crime.

Tarde (1903:331–338) argued that crime originates in the "higher ranks" and descends to the "lowest ranks." The masses are typically tied through imitative bondage to the ideas and fancies of their social superiors. Drunkenness, smoking, moral offenses, political assassination, arson, and even vagabondage are, according to Tarde, crimes that originated with the feudal nobility and were transmitted, through imitation, to the masses. Criminal propensities therefore typically travel downward and outward—from the powerful to the powerless, from urban centers to rural areas.

Why, then, despite a common exposure to the same set of imitative processes, do some people commit crimes and others do not? Tarde claimed that some people are born with psychological qualities that predispose them to crime. Those born with vicious dispositions, for example, are more likely to become violent. To the presence of predisposing qualities, Tarde added the necessary component of "a special kind of fever" (1912:261). This fever he variously described as a fermentation, an agitation, and a disturbance.

Despite his preference for an individualistic or psychological theory of crime, Tarde consistently identified two sociological factors that in practice had causal status in his criminology. First, he isolated urbanism as the greatest arena for the spread of crime through imitation. He showed that cities have the highest rate of homicide motivated by greed; it is there where murderer and victim are likely to be utter strangers, and where recidivism is most pronounced. Urban life encourages the greatest decadence in customs: the formation of political sects, increasing rates of assassination, murder and suicide, crimes against children and crimes by children, rape, and vandalism.

For Tarde a second cause of crime was the violence fostered by mass collective behavior. Such violence exemplifies the processes of imitation and is closely tied to the impersonal social relations of modern urban life.

Collective Behavior and Crime

Tarde's analysis of collective behavior reveals a frantic dislike of any body of people larger than a small and orderly gathering. For example, he suggested that "the crowd, even among the most civilized populations, is always a savage or a faun, still worse, an impulsive and maniacal beast, a plaything of its instincts and unconscious habits, occasionally an animal of a lower order" (Tarde, 1892:358). Tarde often used such concepts as somnambulism (sleepwalking), paroxysm (a fit), and mental contagion (imitation) to explain the abnormality and the dangerousness of crowds in late nineteenth-century France. In his writings on collective behavior, Tarde tended to equate mob violence with organized activities of the French working class (such as strikes). "The conduct of a crowd," Tarde declared, "largely depends on the social origin of its members, on their profession, class or caste" (pp. 372–373). Moreover, "Urban crowds are those whose contagion achieves the highest degree of speed and intensity . . . their members . . . drawn from those detached from family and tradition" (p. 373). Appalled by events such as a strike by mill workers in his native region of Périgord, by anarchist uprisings in 1871 (the "Paris Commune"), and by a wave of bombings, Tarde (1893) asserted that the emotional turbulence of crowd behavior was perfectly expressed in the deluded actions of striking workers, rioters, and revolutionary political movements.

Certain prejudices Tarde shared with sociologist Émile Durkheim. Before considering Durkheim's analysis of crime, we briefly assess Tarde's contribution to the development of criminology.

Public execution in Paris, May 1, 1871: This photograph depicts the execution of sixty-two police officers by the communards of the Paris Commune during the civil war between the Third Republic and the Paris Commune. Events such as this aggravated the French public's fears of crime and fostered the analysis of mob behavior by Gabriel Tarde.

Assessment

Tarde's criminology was an intriguing attempt to place both the sociological and the psychological dimensions of life into a unitary perspective. In his own era, Tarde's perspective was of enormous influence. His social psychology of crime forged a compromise between the classical and positivist schools of criminology. His theories on the causes of crime anticipated and influenced later developments in criminology (see Sasson, 1995:105; Zimring and Hawkins, 1997:132). Tarde's concept of imitation, and his theories about urban life and crowd behavior, for example, explicitly influenced certain of the most important theoretical developments in criminology in the United States—among them the Chicago school of criminology (see Chapter 5.2), Merton's theory of anomie (see Chapter 5.3), Sutherland's theory of differential association (see Chapter 5.4), and subcultural perspectives on delinquency (see Chapter 6).

4.2   TOWARD A SOCIOLOGY OF LAW AND CRIME: ÉMILE DURKHEIM

Émile Durkheim (1858–1917) was one of the founders of sociological criminology, and his analyses of crime and punishment exert a powerful influence in the world of criminol-

How is social order possible? A late-nineteenth-century French industrial scene

ogy today. Durkheim was a prodigious scholar whose innovative concepts and arguments spanned a great diversity of topics. The breadth of his interests is best seen in the titles of his major books: *The Division of Labor in Society* (1893), *The Rules of Sociological Method* (1894), *Suicide* (1897), *Professional Ethics and Civil Morals* (1900), and *The Elementary Forms of Religious Life* (1912).

Durkheim's writings on law and crime have had tremendous intellectual influence on the development of criminology. In much of his sociology, Durkheim tried to answer the difficult questions about how order and stability could be restored to France as it made the disruptive transition from a preindustrial social structure to modern and more complex forms of social organization in the nineteenth century: What are the preconditions of an ordered, stable, and moral society? What conditions produce social disorder? A logical consequence of Durkheim's search for the sources of social order was a concern with situations in which order and stability seemed to be lacking and which were manifest in such "pathologies" as crime and deviance.

Before outlining Durkheim's writings on law and crime, we emphasize a theme that spanned his entire work—a sociological method. For Durkheim, societies can be analyzed properly only through the scientific method of positivism. Like Quetelet's social mechanics (see Chapter 3.2), Durkheim's positivism involved a search for law-like regularities in social behavior. Unlike Tarde, Durkheim insisted that generalizations about social behavior can be made independently of individual variations in free will, psychological state, and motivation.

Durkheim's positivist method stemmed from his insistence that "the first and most basic rule is *to consider social facts as things*" (1982:60). Durkheim's chief intention here was to distinguish sociology from such sciences as biology, politics, and psychology by making the "social fact" its object of study. But for Durkheim social facts were not to be confused with the psychic phenomena that exist only in individual consciousness; in reality, although we are often victims of the illusion that we act with free will, our actions are usually imposed on us externally. Durkheim defined social facts as "manners of acting, thinking and feeling external to the individual, which are invested with a coercive power by virtue of which they exercise control over him" (p. 52). Social facts are thus obligatory and coercive. They have this character not because they are practiced by many people but because they are practiced collectively. "Social phenomena," Durkheim wrote, should thus "be considered in themselves, detached from the conscious beings who form their own mental representations of them" (p. 70).

For Durkheim, then, social phenomena (such as law and crime) have an objective existence of their own and exist quite independently of the individuals who experience them. This is a crucial insight, as we shall learn.

Law and Social Solidarity

Durkheim analyzed law in many of his writings. His most extended treatment occurs in *The Division of Labor* (1893). Here he tried to find the sources of social order ("social solidarity") in modern industrial societies and to determine the changes they undergo during evolution from lower to higher stages of civilization.

Durkheim argued that social development lies along a continuum, with primitive societies of "mechanical solidarity" at one end and modern societies of "organic solidarity" at the other. Mechanical solidarity is typical of simple societies with only a limited role specialization or division of labor. Members of such societies are quite similar to each other in their ways of acting, thinking, and feeling. They live within a shared consensus of beliefs and values—the "collective conscience"—in which collective life dominates and replaces individualism. During the course of social evolution, as roles within the division of labor became more specialized, **social solidarity** is transformed from a mechanical to an organic basis. Organic solidarity is thus typical of societies with an advanced division of labor and with members who have diffuse ways of acting, thinking, and feeling. Individualism dominates and replaces collective life. The cohesion of such societies derives from complex patterns of interdependence among the members and is based on the morals of different occupational categories and also on increasing respect for individual differences.

In his search for the sources of social order, Durkheim realized that social solidarity, which is abstract and internal to consciousness, does not lend itself to exact observation or precise measurement. Thus, to classify and compare the different forms of social solidarity he believed that it was necessary to use another, more visible aspect of social life that varies directly with solidarity. Durkheim argued that "to arrive at this classification, as well as this comparison, we must therefore substitute for this internal datum, which escapes us, an external one which symbolizes it, and then study the former through the latter" (p. 24). That visible symbol, he asserted, is law.

Durkheim never explicitly defined the essential qualities of law. But he implied that law differs from other forms of social regulation (including custom, ritual, ceremony, and professional obligation) because it alone exercises an organized pressure on individuals to conform to its commands. This pressure appears in the form of sanctions. To classify the different types of law, which themselves correspond to the different types of social solidarity, Durkheim reasoned that one must only classify different types of sanctions. Two forms of legal sanction correspond to the two forms of social solidarity: repressive sanctions and restitutive sanctions, which Durkheim termed respectively repressive law and restitutive law.

Durkheim held that **repressive law** is found chiefly in societies of mechanical solidarity. It is religious in origin and largely identical with penal and criminal law. The violation of repressive law results in the use of repressive sanctions. These sanctions consist in inflicting suffering or loss on individuals for having offended the strong sentiments of the collective conscience. Because repressive sanctions tend to be enforced by the whole of society, no special or organized institution (lawyers, courts, police, and so forth) is needed to enforce them. Durkheim provided numerous examples to show that the vast majority of the commands of ancient legal systems—such as the last four books of the Pentateuch (Exodus, Leviticus, Numbers, and Deuteronomy)—are solely directed to sentiments offended by crimes.

During the evolution from mechanical to organic solidarity, Durkheim argued, the volume of penal law in legal systems declines relative to other forms of law. He noted that certain crimes, such as those offending sexual and traditional sentiments, have nowadays almost disappeared (1984:109–110). With the decline of collective sentiments and the growth of individualism, repressive law is gradually ousted by **restitutive law.** This law consists not in the infliction of pain but in *"restoring the previous state of affairs, reestablishing relationships . . . disturbed from their normal form"* (p. 29). Restitutive law, growing continually in volume and intensity, results not from breaches of the collective conscience but from conflicts among different occupational groups (for example, guilds, unions, and professional associations). Its violation involves enforcement of the status quo ante (previously existing state of affairs). Moreover, in contrast to repressive law, restitutive law is specialized through its two basic forms: Positive law reflects the cooperation required in a complex division of labor and includes contract, administrative, domestic, and commercial legislation. Negative law involves the rules between persons and objects that enjoin others not to interfere in certain proprietary rights of the owner and includes property and tort legislation.

The Nature of Crime

Durkheim's analysis of relationships between law and sanctions was a critical tool for understanding social solidarity. In pursuing the latter goal he was led to analyze the nature of crime. As a sociologist, Durkheim rejected definitions of crime based on legalistic criteria. Such criteria—as well as criteria based on notions such as evil, social harm, violations of justice, and so forth—he regarded as inadequate for a scientific sociology.

What, then, is crime? To begin, no action is intrinsically or universally criminal. For Durkheim, the common denominator of all crimes is that they are "acts repressed by prescribed punishments" (1984:31). This is what distinguishes a crime from a minor offense such as a tort or a breach of etiquette. In societies of mechanical solidarity an act is defined as criminal because of the universal social reaction that condemns it. As Durkheim argued in *The Division of Labor:* "An act is criminal when it offends the strong, well-defined states of the collective consciousness. . . . We should not say that an act offends the common consciousness because it is criminal, but that it is criminal because it offends that consciousness" (pp.:39–40). From this it seemed to follow that to investigate the nature of crime one must examine the nature of punishment.

What functions, then, does punishment serve? Central to Durkheim's criminology is his linking of crime and punishment. Thus: "If our definition of crime is exact it must account for all the characteristics of . . . punishment" (1984:44). Durkheim defined punishment as "a reaction of passionate feeling, graduated in intensity, which society exerts through the mediation of an organized body over those of its members who have violated certain rules of conduct" (p. 52).

Durkheim rejected popular beliefs that the function of punishment is simply revenge, deterrence, or the reformation of the character of criminals. The true function of punishment is to maintain and strengthen social solidarity. Each time a crime is committed, the subsequent condemnation of it by penal law reaffirms the values of the collective conscience or the shared consensus of a community's beliefs and values. In this way "honest people" are convinced of the moral righteousness of their conformity to law and of the "inferiority" of criminals. With great insight, Durkheim therefore concluded that "punishment is above all intended to have its effect upon honest people" (p. 63).

Durkheim made three specific claims about the nature of crime: (a) crime is normal; (b) crime is inevitable; and (c) crime is useful.

Crime Is Normal. Durkheim caused considerable outrage by claiming that crime is a normal phenomenon, as normal as birth and marriage. Durkheim's discussion of this seemingly unusual claim is found in his 1894 book *The Rules of Sociological Method* (1982:85–107), in which he tried to restructure "the fundamental facts of criminology." Durkheim's starting point—like the starting point of his sociology in general—was his concept of the social fact: "*A social fact is normal for a given social type, viewed at a given phase of its development, when it occurs in the average society of that species, considered at the corresponding phase of its evolution*" (p. 97; emphasis in original).

In other words, in a given social context and against the background of a given level of social development, the very generality of social facts indicates that they must be normal phenomena. At any given moment society has a "normal" or statistically average volume of births, for example, or of marriages and deaths. For Durkheim, it is only statistical deviations from such averages that are abnormal. Because crime is a social fact, Durkheim complained that criminologists err in seeing it only as a pathological or morbid phenomenon. Generally, crime should not be viewed as deviance or as sickness—what is abnormal to the biologist or to the pathologist is not necessarily so to the sociologist.

For Durkheim, then, crime as such is rarely abnormal. Crime occurs in all societies, is tied closely to the facts of collective life, and its volume tends to increase as societies evolve from lower to higher phases. However, he was careful to add that although crime is a normal social fact, in a given context its rate might be abnormal.

Crime Is Inevitable.   To begin with, Durkheim admitted that his idea about the normality of crime surprised him. Eventually, he reasoned that no society can ever be entirely rid of crime. To illustrate this point, Durkheim asked that we imagine a community of saints in a perfect and exemplary monastery: "In it crime as such will be unknown, but faults that appear venial to the ordinary person will arouse the same scandal as does normal crime in ordinary consciences" (1982:100). Moreover, universal and absolute conformity to rules is impossible because each member of society faces variation in "the immediate physical environment, . . . hereditary antecedents, . . . [and] social influences" (p. 100). Crime is therefore inevitable. Even if all the actions regarded as criminal at one moment suddenly disappeared, new forms of crime would be created at once.

Crime Is Useful.   Durkheim first claimed that crime is normal and inevitable in *The Division of Labor*. But in *The Rules of Sociological Method* he took the argument a stage further in suggesting that "to classify crime among the phenomena of normal sociology is not merely to declare that it is an inevitable though regrettable phenomenon arising from the incorrigible weakness of man; it is to assert that it is a factor in public health, an integrative element in any healthy society" (1982:98).

Besides claiming that crime is normal and inevitable, Durkheim thus argued that crime is useful because crime is indispensable to the normal evolution of law and morality. Indeed, if crime is not a sickness, then punishment cannot be its remedy. The nature of crime and punishment must therefore lie somewhere else than in the area of wrongdoing and its correction. If there were no crimes—if there was no deviation from social norms—Durkheim reasoned, then the collective conscience would have reached an intensity, an authoritarianism, unparalleled in history. In other words, a society with "no crime" must be an extremely repressive one.

For Durkheim, crime is useful because often it is a symptom of individual originality and a preparation for changes in law and morality. He cited the fate of Socrates as an example of crime's utility. Socrates (470–399 B.C.), perhaps the most original of all Greek philosophers, committed the "crime" of independent thought. Having been convicted of not believing in the official gods of the Athenian state and of corrupting the minds of the young, Socrates committed suicide by drinking hemlock. Durkheim suggested that "Socrates' crime served to prepare the way for a new morality and a new faith—one the Athenians . . . needed [inasmuch as] the traditions by which they had hitherto lived no longer corresponded to the conditions of their existence" (1982:102). Today's criminal may be tomorrow's philosopher!

Anomie, Egoism, and Crime

Durkheim applied his sociological insights to the analysis of two specific forms of deviance—suicide and homicide. First, he tried to show that suicide—usually regarded as the supreme act of individual deviance—has profoundly sociological rather than psychological or biological causes. Indeed, Durkheim (1951:299) claimed that variations in suicide rates can be explained only sociologically. His general concern was to show that the suicide rate of any society depended on the type and extent of social organization and integration. In any society each social group "really has a collective inclination for the act, quite its own, and the source of all individual inclination, rather than their result. It is made up of the currents of egoism, altruism or anomie running through the society under consideration. . . . These tendencies of the whole social body, by affecting individuals, cause them to commit suicide" (p. 299–300).

Durkheim's explanation of varying suicide rates hinges on four types of suicide:

- *Egoistic suicide* (p. 152–216) results from a weakening of the bonds between an individual and society. It is a special type of suicide caused by excessive individualism. It recedes only with the sort of increase in collective sentiments produced by wars and political crises. Social groups prone to egoistic suicide include Protestants (whose religious beliefs foster individualism), the unmarried, the childless, and the widowed.
- *Altruistic suicide* (p. 217–240) results when individuals have insufficient inner strength to resist the demands of a social group into which they are overly integrated. Examples include Hindu widows, who place themselves next to their husbands on their funeral pyre, and slaves, who are expected to die with their masters.
- *Anomic suicide* (p. 241–276) results from a sudden crisis in economic or familial life. Thus in situations such as sudden impoverishment or unexpected riches, or immediately after family members are divorced, there is an abrupt change in expectations that causes massive personal or social upheaval. In the aftermath of these situations, those who cannot adjust to their suddenly altered position become more suicide-prone (and see Chapter 5.3).
- *Individualized suicide* (p. 277–294) has particularized characteristics, either in the mental state that leads to the act or in the way it is achieved. These characteristics include melancholy, passion, and irritation, though these might also have social causes.

In addition to suicide, Durkheim (1958) analyzed the offense of homicide. He suggested that civilized peoples always consider three broad moral attitudes as duties—respect for life, respect for property, and the honor of others. In primitive societies, homicide is the most serious breach of moral duty because it is viewed as an offense against the whole of society, against what is sacred. Offenses against individual property or individual honor are seen as far less serious than offenses against the social order as a whole—sometimes they are not considered offenses at all. In ancient Greece, Rome, and Judea, for example, victims of crimes other than homicide had to pursue their own redress and could allow the guilty party to pay a sum of money as a form of satisfaction.

Durkheim suggested that during social evolution, and especially with the onset of Christianity, something of a reversal occurs in the hierarchical order of these duties. With the growth of modern societies, collective sentiments generally are reduced in intensity and the sentiments centering on the individual achieve prominence. Homicide therefore remains the supremely forbidden act because it violates the individual. Given that homicide is so abhorred, Durkheim (1958:112–115) claimed that homicide rates tend to decline relative to the advance of civilization. At the same time, rates of other offenses against the individual, whether against person or property, tend to increase.

Durkheim was confident that homicide rates decreased with modernization because of the growth of the "cult of the individual" (namely, the great respect afforded the person by public opinion). But Durkheim knew that this explanation was too general: "The decline in the rate of homicide at the present day has not come about because respect for the human person acts as a brake on the motives for murder or on the stimulants to murder, but because these motives and these stimulants grow fewer in number and have less intensity" (p. 117).

How, then, does one explain cases in which the general rule about declining homicide rates does not apply? To explain counterexamples, Durkheim introduced statistical evidence showing how other variables—including rural/urban differences, wars, religious membership, political crises, and state power—influence homicide rates. For example, he argued that Catholic countries tend to have higher homicide rates than Protestant ones because the latter's religious beliefs are more individualistic and, therefore, promote greater respect for the sanctity of individual life (pp. 118–119).

The Evolution of Punishment

In his 1901 essay "Two Laws of Penal Evolution," Durkheim offered a sophisticated theory of the history of punishment, returning squarely to his earlier concern with law and crime in *The Division of Labor.* This final theory on the sources of punishment, and of changes in its justifications and forms, was a marked improvement on earlier analyses. Indeed, in his entire criminology it was only here that Durkheim considered that political factors sometimes influence the way in which certain behavior is defined as criminal.

In the essay, Durkheim modified his earlier argument to suggest that forms of punishment have varied historically in two ways, quantitatively and qualitatively. Each form is governed by a separate law, one quantitative in scope, the other qualitative.

Durkheim's first law contains two propositions. First, societies are more or less advanced according to their level of social complexity or to the intensity of their division of labor. Here Durkheim repeated his argument that less developed societies are dominated by repressive laws and barbaric forms of punishment, especially capital punishment. In such societies punishment is severe because most crimes are seen as religious violations that threaten the collective conscience. The second proposition concerns absolutist forms of political power: the exercise of governmental power without checks and balances. This authoritarian form of power (hypercentralization) exists in different types of society, early and modern, but occurs only when it is seen as a right: "Such was the state of the criminal law until the middle of the eighteenth century. There then occurred, throughout Europe, the protest to which Beccaria gave his name" (1983:113).

BOX 4.1 DURKHEIM'S TWO LAWS OF PENAL EVOLUTION

Law 1: The intensity of punishment is greater the more closely societies approximate to a less developed type—and the more the central power assumes an absolute character.

Law 2: Deprivations of liberty, and of liberty alone, varying in time according to the seriousness of the crime, tend to become more and more the normal means of social control.

Durkheim's first law implies that with social development the severity of punishment generally declines. This decline occurs not because authorities become more lenient but because the type of crime changes. In less developed societies, crime is seen as a threat to collective life, and, therefore, punishment is severe; in more developed societies, crime is seen as a threat to individuals only, and punishment is correspondingly less severe. However, by identifying the importance of the relationship between state power and punishment, Durkheim could now explain certain factual counterexamples to his earlier analysis. For example, he now claimed, interestingly, that in societies dominated by political absolutism, crimes retain a primarily sacrilegious character (1983:120–129). In other words, authoritarian societies act punitively and repressively not because they are not socially developed but because their organs of political power regard crime religiously—as an attack on the social order as a whole.

Durkheim's second law refers to qualitative changes in punishment. Durkheim illustrated the workings of the second law with examples from ancient Greece and modern France. He established that the death penalty had disappeared completely from some legal codes and had been taken over by incarceration. Durkheim explained this change by arguing that there is no need for incarceration in less developed societies. There a crime affects the entire community, and, because responsibility for it is communal, all members of the community ensure that the offender does not escape before trial. However, with the disintegration of ancient societies—after which crime became more of an offense against an individual rather than society as a whole—some method of pretrial detention was needed to ensure that offenders were held accountable.

Thus Durkheim advanced the brilliant argument that the prison emerged from changing forms of crime. But he realized this explanation was incomplete: "To explain an institution, it is not enough to establish that when it appeared it served some useful end; for just because it was desirable it does not follow that it was possible" (1983:117). Hence Durkheim proceeded to explain the growth of the prison in terms of his first law concerning the less repressive nature of punishment. Prisons arose because of the transformation in criminal responsibility from a collective to an individual basis. Some of the first prisons were "hole[s], in the form of a pit where the condemned wallow in refuse and vermin" (p. 119). But prisons, responding to the changed basis of criminal responsibility, gradually became milder, reflecting the general decline in the severity of punishment. As punishment as a whole became less severe, these new prisons became the typical form of punishment in developed societies.

Durkheim therefore concluded that "the qualitative changes in punishment are in part dependent on the simultaneous quantitative changes it undergoes" (p. 120). His two laws of penal evolution thus turn out to be interdependent. The very facts that bring about changes in the bases of criminal responsibility in early societies also create the apparent need for widespread use of imprisonment in modern societies!

Assessment

Quite aside from the power and scope of its analysis of crime, Durkheim's criminology has exerted tremendous influence on the development of sociological criminology. This influence has been most obvious in the writings of the Chicago school of criminology (see Chapter 5.2), Merton's theory of anomie and social structure (see Chapter 5.3), and

Hirschi's theory of control and crime (see Chapter 6.3). Moreover, criminologists today continue to draw on Durkheim's insights.

More than anyone before him, Durkheim identified the sociological links among crime, law, punishment, and social organization. He showed that in any given society the amount and the types of crime relate directly to the basic ways in which that society is organized. And societies, he insisted, should be understood historically. Durkheim also suggested that crime must be explained sociologically rather than in terms of an individual's psychological state or biological nature. Sociologically, crime is a normal and inevitable feature of social organization. Its functions lie not only in the area of sanctions but also in the creation and enforcement of solidarity.

Criticisms of Durkheim's criminology tend to focus on two questions. Did he correctly describe the historical transformation in styles of punishment? How did his own personal and political agenda influence the propositions set forth in his various theories?

The first question has been debated largely in terms of whether or not the facts of the evolution of punishment fit Durkheim's theory of crime. In a well-known study that examined legal evolution in fifty-one societies, Schwartz and Miller (1964; see also Garland, 1990:chap. 2) concluded that in simple societies restitutive law is more common than penal sanctions (Vold, Bernard, and Snipes, 1998:135; and see Foucault, 1979:3–69). This conclusion contradicts Durkheim's account of the evolution from repressive to restitutive sanctions. Therefore, it is reasonable to conclude that

> Durkheim may have derived his idea [of the evolution of punishment] from the fact that punishments in European societies were becoming much less severe at the time, due to the reforms introduced by Beccaria and other classical theorists. But the extremely harsh punishments that had been imposed prior to those reforms were not associated with simple, undeveloped societies, but rather with absolute monarchies. (Vold, Bernard, and Snipes, 1998:134–135)

Durkheim is also frequently criticized for the biases that allegedly entered his sociological method in general and his criminology in particular. Durkheim has thus been scolded because his preoccupation with the sources of social order apparently led him to neglect the sources and expressions of social conflict. It is indeed true that Durkheim's criminology is based on certain assumptions: for example, that law tends to stem from and reflect widely held social values; that crime is a breach of these shared values; and that an examination of the political factors that influence the definition of certain actions as criminal is not necessary. A sustained disagreement with such assumptions was an important theme in the works of Marx and Engels. We now turn to their writings about the relationships between law, on the one hand, and power and domination on the other.

4.3 CLASSICAL MARXISM: MARX AND ENGELS ON STATE, LAW, AND CRIME

An introduction to the emergence of sociological criminology would be seriously incomplete without an analysis of the perspectives of the authors of classical Marxism: Karl Marx (1818–1883) and his colleague and friend Friedrich Engels (1820–1895). Before outlining the various claims Marx and Engels made concerning the nature of crime, we consider briefly certain key concepts of their writings.

Key Concepts of Marxism

The development of Marxian theory can be traced to Marx and Engels's initial acceptance, subsequent rejection, and ultimate transcendence of early nineteenth-century German idealist philosophy. In his very first writings in the 1840s, Marx strongly opposed the idea that history and social change reflect such idealist factors as God, the intellect, reason, the spirit, and the progress of civilization. Marx gradually developed a materialist concept of historical change. His materialism combined the ideas of English political economists (such as Malthus, Ricardo, Bentham, and Say) and French socialists (including Saint-Simon, Lassalle, and Fourier), forging them into a new theory termed "historical materialism."

Marxism is based on the concept that although human beings make their own history, they do not do so entirely as they choose. "The history of all hitherto existing society," Marx and Engels famously declared, "is the history of class struggles" (1969a:108). During such struggles social classes actively create and recreate the conditions of their existence. At the same time, the very existence of social classes means that members of a society cannot live exactly as they would choose. Social classes, therefore, also constrain social relationships. Class position is an important determinant of such basic life events as social mobility, consciousness, level and types of education and income, leisure patterns, and (as we see later) the likelihood of incarceration.

What, then, did Marx and Engels understand by the term "social classes"? To grasp this term properly we begin with their concept of **mode of production**, which Marx analyzes carefully in his lengthy book *Capital* (1868). Analytically, the concept "mode of production" entails two major elements: the means of production and the social relations of production.

"Means of production" refers to specific types of technology, capital, labor, tools, machinery and equipment, monetary systems, and land. In combination, these items are the necessary raw materials for producing commodities. All these materials, combined in different ways, are required to produce commodities as different as bicycles and criminology textbooks. They are subject to almost infinite variety. Commodities such as reading materials, for example, can be produced on stone tablets, papyrus, parchment, biodegradable paper, and computer diskettes. Commodities can also be produced, exchanged, and sold on a small or a large scale and by capital-intensive or labor-intensive means.

"Social relations of production" refers to the many ways in which members of a society relate both to the possession (legal or otherwise) of the means of production and also to the distribution of the commodities that result from the process of production. For example, the productive process can occur in the institutional context of private or communal relationships; it can occur at home, in fields, or in factories; its participants can be slaves, free laborers, white-collar workers, bankers, landed gentry, industrialists, or state bureaucrats. The productive process can be more or less influenced by gender. It can be unaffected by or be dominated by political authority.

The means of production and the social relations of production, in combination, compose a mode of production. In their theory of history, Marx and Engels identified several distinct modes of production: primitive communal, slave, feudal, Asiatic, capitalist, socialist, and communist. Engels usually, but Marx almost never, saw such modes of production as definite stages through which all societies evolved. Several modes of production can exist in one society. For example, until at least the Civil War in the 1860s, slave, feudal, and capitalist modes of production all coexisted in the United States. Again, during the 1920s, feudal, capitalist, and socialist modes of production all coexisted in the USSR. However, in any given society, one mode of production tends to dominate and lend its character to other aspects of social relationships (Marx, 1973:106–107).

Any given society, depending on its dominant mode of production, has typical **social classes**. Under capitalism—Marx's primary focus—typical classes include the lumpenproletariat (the perennially unemployed, those "unfit" for work), the working class (skilled and unskilled workers), the middle class, and the capitalist class (those who own capital: industrialists, financiers, commercial speculators, and landlords). In capitalist societies the basic **class** struggle is between the capitalist class (bourgeoisie) and the working class (proletariat). The economic site of this particular struggle is the productive process; the struggle occurs over the distribution of the fruits of this process. The capitalist class, on the one hand, strives to maximize profit from the unpaid labor of the working class. Its income lies in rent, interest, and industrial profit. The working class, on the other hand, strives to maximize wages. It attempts to do so by reducing the length of the working day, by compelling employers to pay higher wages, and by wresting from the capitalist class such concessions as health insurance, work-safety regulations, and job security. The goals of the capitalist class and the working class are thus mutually exclusive. Typically, the one maximizes its return from the productive process at the expense of the other.

For Marx and Engels, then, social classes are determined chiefly by their economic position within a given mode of production. The relationships between different classes are rarely fixed; they vary according to changes in the political and economic power of one side or another. However, in Marxian analysis the basic source of conflict in capitalist societies is between those who own the means of production and those who have no source of income other than their labor. This exploitive situation is inherently unstable and, Marx and Engels asserted, tends to lead towards socialism. Under socialism the means of production are socialized and class struggles begin to evaporate.

We note here the great importance of political power to the maintenance, development, or rupture of a mode of production and the class relationships associated with it. Maintenance of class relationships ultimately depends on coercion. Sometimes this coercion is quite naked; usually it is a subtler process. The relationship between economic position and political power—and, indeed, between economic position and many other aspects of social life—Marx often depicted in terms of the metaphorical "base and superstructure." He once described the relationship between economy and politics in the following terms:

In the social production of their life, men enter into definite relations that are indispensable and independent of their will, relations of production which correspond to a definite stage of development of their material productive forces. The sum total of these relations of production constitutes the economic structure of society, the real foundation, on which rises a legal and political superstructure and to which correspond definite forms of social consciousness. The mode of production of material life conditions the social, political and intellectual life process in general. It is not the consciousness of men that determines their being, but, on the contrary, their social being that determines their consciousness. (1969c:503–504)

The mode of production thus conditions the life process in general. It does so with a mechanism Marx and Engels term "ideology." **Ideology** has several meanings in their writings. First, it refers to any set of structured beliefs, values, and ideas. Examples include bourgeois ideology, proletarian ideology, and legal ideology. Bourgeois ideology, for example, refers to beliefs and values—such as thriftiness and respect for private property—typically held by bourgeois (capitalist) classes. In capitalist society, the ideas of the capitalist class tend to be the ruling ideas.

Second, ideology refers sometimes to a set of mistaken or false beliefs. "Ideology is a process," wrote Engels, "accomplished by the so-called thinker consciously, it is true, but with a false consciousness" (1970d:496). Marx often attacked religious beliefs ("the opium of the masses"), not only because he believed they alienated people from each other but also because religious beliefs wrongly assumed the existence of God. In the same context, Marx sometimes contrasted ideology with science: Ideology is false belief; science is correct belief.

Finally, and most difficult, the term "ideology" refers to a set of beliefs that both reflect social reality and simultaneously distort it. To help understand this dual process think of a straight stick standing upright in a pool of water. In this situation the image conveys the appearance that the stick is bent. Thus the image is both a reflection of physical matter (governed by the laws of optics) and a distortion of it (the stick is not actually bent). This final meaning of ideology, then, refers to a process whereby beliefs, deriving from real social relationships, hide or mask the precise nature of such relationships. Certain ideas, such as those associated with justice, fulfill the ideological function of masking from exploited classes the nature of their oppression and its precise source.

This final meaning of ideology was especially important for Marx and Engels's analysis of state and law. Here the institutions and doctrines of state and law play a key role in the dominance of bourgeois ideology.

State and Law

Marx and Engels used the term "state" to refer broadly to the organs of political authority and to the ideological processes that underpin the legitimacy of this authority, including the standing army, police, bureaucracy, clergy, and judicature. Generally, Marx and Engels saw the state both as a product of society at a certain level of development and as an institution that seemingly stands above society. However, this apparent ability to stand above society and represent itself as neutral and independent of class struggles is in fact an ideological distortion, inasmuch as the state and its various components are actually manipulated by the dominant class.

The state thus has a class character. In capitalist societies the state is typically a weapon or instrument manipulated by the capitalist classes, though Marx realized that state activities are not always so simple. For example, in one analysis of French politics, Marx described how the French state represented the interests of millions of smallholding peasants

(1969b:478). In this scenario, the state is a prize actively pursued by contestants in the class struggle.

Law is a crucial component of the state apparatus. In class societies law is endowed by Marx and Engels with several functions (Cain and Hunt, 1979:144–152). First, law tends to reflect and promote the interest of the dominant class in private property. It does so by promoting and protecting all private property, thereby obscuring the fact that the vast majority of property is owned by only a tiny fraction of the population. Law fulfills this function through constitutions, statutory and case law, and, with support from agencies of the criminal justice system, by enforcing compliance with its commandments. Second, law operates as a central mechanism of bourgeois ideology. Through such notions as "justice" and "fair play," law promulgates the idea that it is independent of economic and political interests and that it can mediate conflicts in the interests of the whole society. But in class societies law cannot do this: To apply law fairly and equally in a society of inequality is merely to perpetuate inequality. Legal doctrines such as "the rule of law" and "equality before the law" are thus no more than fictions designed to lull the populace into believing that law truly does stand above society as an impartial arbiter. Finally, law acts as a repressive apparatus. Typically, this function is activated when the legal system represses the working class and its organized political movements.

Criminalization as a Violation of Rights

In certain of Marx's writings the process of criminalization was described somewhat moralistically as a violation by the state of some natural or inalienable human rights. Thus, in commenting on a decrease in the official crime rate in Britain between 1855 and 1858, Marx complained:

> This apparent decrease of crime, however, since 1854, is to be exclusively attributed to some technical changes in British jurisdiction; to the Juvenile Offenders' Act . . . and to the Criminal Justice Act of 1855, which authorizes the Police Magistrates to pass sentences for short periods, with the consent of the prisoners. Violations of the law are generally the offspring of economical agencies beyond the control of the legislator . . . [but] it depends to some degree on official society to stamp certain violations of its rules as crimes or as transgressions only. This difference of nomenclature, so far from being indifferent, decides on the fate of thousands of men, and the moral tone of society. (Quoted in Cain and Hunt, 1979:189)

In one of his very first articles—written in 1842 when he was a radical journalist in Prussia—Marx attacked censorship laws because they violated real freedom of expression (1975a:131). By "real" freedom Marx meant not only freedom to do certain things but also freedom not to be exploited by others. In another 1842 article—which led him eventually to study economic relationships—Marx (1975b) discussed a Prussian law, enacted by the Rhineland Assembly, on the theft of wood. Despite a serious shortage of firewood and a depression in the local wine industry, this draconian law made it a criminal offense for anyone to collect and pilfer fallen wood in private forests. Marx attacked this law as a blatant undermining of what had been a customary right of the Rhenish peasantry since the sixteenth century.

Crime and Demoralization

There is another way in which Marxian writings argued that criminalization violates rights. Many of Marx and Engels's writings analyzed the capitalist mode of production, and it is difficult not to believe that they thought capitalist production was unjust (Young, 1978). Thus Marx wrote in the *New York Daily Tribune,* commenting on the lot of the Irish peasantry: "There must be something rotten in the core of a social system that increases its wealth without diminishing its misery, and increases in crimes even more rapidly than in numbers" (1859). For Marx, the social system associated with capitalist production was unjust partly because it permitted others (namely, capitalists) to profit from workers' labors.

It is a simple matter of historical record that from the birth of industrialization to the time when Engels wrote *Condition of the Working Class in England* (1845), British capitalism spawned gruesome living and working conditions for the mass of the population. Sometimes these conditions led to competition among members of the working class, and hence to crime (Engels, 1975a:442). In Marxian analysis these conditions led to massive demoralization. This psychological condition, in its turn, led either to crime or to rebellion.

The linking of crime and demoralization is a vivid and recurring theme in many of Marx and Engels's more polemical passages. Thus Engels wrote that the working class is

> cast out and ignored by the class in power, morally as well as physically and mentally. The only provision made for them is the law, which fastens upon them when they become obnoxious to the bourgeoisie. Like the dullest of brutes, they are treated to but one form of education, the whip, in the shape of force, not convincing but intimidating. There is, therefore, no cause for surprise if the workers, treated as brutes, actually become such. (1975b:411–412)

In another passage, Engels (pp. 421–422) blamed the appalling conditions at home and at work for the criminality of the working class in Manchester. These conditions produced demoralization that, in turn, fostered widespread "drunkenness, sexual irregularities, brutality, and disregard for the rights of property" (p. 421). Engels also suggested a different form that demoralization might take: "True, there are, within the working class, numbers too moral to steal even when reduced to the utmost extremity, and these starve or commit suicide; . . . numbers of the poor [actually] kill themselves to avoid the misery from which they see no other means of escape" (p. 412).

Crime and Primitive Rebellion

One alternative to demoralization was rebellion. In *Capital* (1868), Marx documented the rebellion of the British working class against the harsh emergence of industrial capitalism. As a class, British workers first manifested opposition to the bourgeoisie by resisting the

A Manchester cotton mill in the mid-nineteenth century:
In his book *The Condition of the Working Class in England in 1844,* Friedrich Engels (1820–1895) described how the gruesome living conditions in Manchester and other industrial towns so demoralized the working class that they were led to commit crime.

introduction of machinery; the Luddites even smashed it or attempted to assassinate manufacturers. "Theft," said Engels "was the most primitive form of protest" (1975b: 502–503).

Although Marx and Engels identified certain working-class crime as rebellion, they did not look on it favorably. Doubtless they shared with their contemporaries a puritan assessment of the activities of the dangerous class (see Chapter 3.2). In addition, Marx and Engels condemned such forms of rebellion as having no value for working-class revolutionary consciousness. Thus Engels lamented that working-class crime is "the earliest, crudest, and least fruitful form of this rebellion" (p. 502). Elsewhere, Marx and Engels analyzed the class allies upon which the working class could realistically depend for the growth of its revolutionary movement. Within that context, they complained: "The 'dangerous class,' the social scum, that passively rotting mass thrown off by the lowest layers of the old society, may, here and there, be swept into the movement by a proletarian revolution; its conditions of life, however, prepare it far more for the part of a bribed tool of reactionary intrigue" (1848:118).

Assessment

Marx and Engels's writings are an important part of the development of sociological criminology. Their writings, like Durkheim's, have endured among criminologists because

BOX 4.2   CRIME AND COMMUNISM

In Marxian writings the longest description of the nature of crime in communist society is given by Engels:

Present-day society, which breeds hostility between the individual man and everyone else, thus produces a social war of all against all which inevitably in individual cases, notably among uneducated people, assumes a brutal, barbarously violent form—that of crime. In order to protect itself against crime, against direct acts of violence, society requires an extensive, complicated system of administrative and judicial bodies which requires an immense labor force. In communist society this would likewise be vastly simplified, and precisely because . . . the administrative body in this society would have to manage not merely individual aspects of social life, but the whole of social life, in all its various activities, in all its aspects. We eliminate the contradiction between the individual man and all others, we counterpose social peace to social war, we put the axe to the *root* of crime—and thereby render the greatest, by far the greatest, part of the present activity of the administrative and judicial bodies superfluous. . . . Advancing civilization moderates violent outbreaks of passion even in our present-day society, which is on a war footing; how much more will this be the case in communist, peaceful society! Crimes against property cease of their own accord where everyone receives what he needs to satisfy his natural and spiritual urges, where social gradations and distinctions cease to exist. Justice concerned with criminal cases ceases of itself, that dealing with civil cases, which are almost all rooted in property relations or at least in such relations as arise from the situation of social war, likewise disappears; conflicts can then be only rare exceptions, whereas they are now the natural result of general hostility, and will be easily settled by arbitrators. The activities of the administrative bodies at present have likewise their source in the continual social war—the police and the entire administration do nothing else but see to it that the war remains concealed and indirect and does not erupt into open violence, into crimes . . . It is vastly more easy to administer a communist society rather than a competitive one. (1975b:248–249)

they offer a radical, sociological approach to crime in capitalist societies. Crime, in their view, is not caused by moral or biological defects in individuals but by fundamental defects in a society's social organization.

Marx and Engels saw crime, as Durkheim did, as an inevitable feature of existing social organization. Unlike Durkheim, they believed that crime is inevitable because it is an expression of basic social and class inequalities. Working-class crime, especially, results from demoralization and occasionally turns to primitive rebellion. The extent of crime and its forms, they suggested, should be understood in the context of the specific state, legal system, and class relationships associated with a given mode of production. Yet Marx and Engels did not explain crime simply by reference to economic factors. They clearly understood that crime involves a political process whereby the state criminalizes certain conduct and in so doing often reflects the interests not of society as a whole but of certain groups within it. Crime, Marx and Engels sometimes suggested, was a form of rebellion against this process. This idea was taken up by criminologists in the 1970s and 1980s (see Chapters 7.3, 7.4, 8.4).

Marx and Engels never seriously addressed certain basic questions about the nature of crime. Why, for example, are some actions defined as criminal but others are not? Because they did not consider this definitional question, Marx and Engels, like most of their Victorian contemporaries, tended to accept that crime is a violation of moral or good conduct. In arguing, therefore, that the lumpenproletariat and the unskilled working class engage in the great bulk of this conduct, they generally ignored the different types of crime committed by different classes. Finally, the writings of Marx and Engels contain no analysis of the links between crime and other forms of social inequality (see Chapter 15).

REVIEW

This chapter outlined the early forms of sociological criminology, which derived many theories and concepts from problems identified in the basic social organization of societies. This linking of crime and social organization was, and is, the key feature of sociological criminology. These ideas indelibly imprinted the subsequent development of criminological theory.

Toward a Social Psychology of Crime: Gabriel Tarde

1. Tarde developed a theory about the causes of crime that attempted to combine individualistic and sociological concepts. He was the leading critic of such biological theories of crime as Lombrosianism.

2. Tarde applied the concept of imitation to crime, thereby suggesting that, in addition to the importance of sociological factors, individual mental states contributed to the growth of crime.

3. Influenced by the growth of socialist and anarchist insurrections in France, Tarde pinpointed the imitative behavior of crowds and mobs as one of the leading causes of violence in modern societies.

Toward a Sociology of Law and Crime: Émile Durkheim

1. Émile Durkheim was one of the founders of sociological criminology. His writings were an extremely successful attempt to integrate a theory of crime with a theory of law. His analysis of crime and punishment exerts great influence on modern criminology.

2. Durkheim's sociological method was based on the idea that societies can be fully understood only by the scientific method of positivism. Like Quetelet's social mechanics, Durkheim's criminology attempted to find regularities in criminal behavior.

3. Durkheim's criminology began with the belief that types of law and types of social solidarity were intimately connected. Mechanical solidarity is associated with repressive law; organic solidarity is associated with restitutive law. During the evolution from mechanical to organic solidarity, the volume of repressive law declines relative to other forms

of law. This is one way of explaining the broad transformation in penal strategies that accompanied the Enlightenment and classical criminology (see Chapter 3.1).

4. Durkheim argued that the function of punishment is to maintain and strengthen social solidarity rather than to repress crime. Crime is a normal, inevitable, and useful form of social activity. Detailed analyses of crime in Durkheim's works concentrate on suicide and homicide. Both of these crimes testify to the sociological causes of crime and, especially, to the effects of anomie and egoism on them.

5. Durkheim argued that forms of punishment have varied in history according to two laws. Quantitatively, punishment has tended to be more repressive the less developed the society and the more absolute the power of the central authority. Qualitatively, the more developed the society, the more imprisonment tends to become its dominant form of social control.

Classical Marxism: Marx and Engels on State, Law, and Crime

1. Marx and Engels's writings on state, law, and crime were set in the context of their sociological analysis of modern capitalist societies.

2. The key concepts of Marx and Engels's sociology are social classes, mode of production, means of production, social relations of production, and ideology. The articulation of these concepts defines the movement of social relationships throughout history, although their primary concern was with relationships in capitalist societies.

3. Marx and Engels generally insisted that the institutions of state and law, and the doctrines that emerge from them, serve the interests of the dominant economic class. The state arises from class struggles and gives the false appearance of independence from social classes. Law is endowed with several functions: It defends and enforces existing property relationships, and in class societies it does so in the context of unequal ownership of property; it acts as an ideological mechanism, promoting respect for private property; and in moments of acute class struggle, it acts as a mechanism of repression.

4. Marx and Engels offered a view of crime and capitalism that differed greatly from the social contract and free-will theorists of the Enlightenment. They defined crime in three ways: as a violation by the state of natural or human rights, as a result of the demoralization caused by the gruesome conditions of industrial capitalism, and as a form of primitive rebellion.

5. Marx and Engels tentatively believed that with the abolition of private property and with the disappearance of the class character of the state, crimes would almost disappear under **communism**.

QUESTIONS FOR CLASS DISCUSSION

1. Is crime normal?

2. Is crime inevitable?

3. Can you describe the social organization of a future society in which crime has disappeared entirely?

FOR FURTHER STUDY

Readings

Garland, David. 1990. *Punishment and Modern Society*. Chicago: University of Chicago Press.

Greenberg, David F., ed. 1993. *Crime and Capitalism: Readings in Marxist Criminology*. 2d ed. Palo Alto, Calif.: Mayfield.

Websites

1. <http://eddie.cso.uiuc.edu/Durkheim>: This site provides readers with biographical and academic summaries of Durkheim's work. Also listed is information about how to join an e-mail discussion list related to Durkheim.
2. <http://www.spu.edu/~hawk/marxh.html>: This site provides summaries of Marx's and Engels's writings, including *The Communist Manifesto*. There is also a useful link to "contemporary Marxism" for those who wish to explore the current state of Marxism.
3. <http://www.runet.edu/_Iridiner/DSS/DEADSOC.HTML>: This is a website funded by the American Sociological Association, the National Science Foundation, and Radford University. It offers biographical information and summaries of the work of many of the key nineteenth-century and early twentieth-century sociologists in Europe and the United States.

5

The Emergence of Criminology in the United States

Preview

Chapter 5 introduces:

- certain key themes and prejudices of the diverse analyses of crime that prospered in the United States before 1915
- the social factors that contributed to the emergence of criminology in the United States
- the innovative methods and concepts of the Chicago school of social ecology, culminating in the findings of Shaw and McKay's *Juvenile Delinquency and Urban Areas* (1942)
- Merton's theory of "anomie," which offers a sociological explanation for the high rates of deviance and crime in the United States
- the contributions of Edwin Sutherland—in particular, his theories of differential association and differential social organization, and his books *The Professional Thief* (1937) and *White Collar Crime* (1949)

Key Terms

anomie	social disorganization
Chicago school of criminology	social ecology
differential association	white-collar crime

Chapters 3 and 4 introduced the most influential theories of crime fashionable in much of Europe at the dawn of the twentieth century. These theories are important not only because they acted as stepping-stones in the historical development of modern criminology but also because they exert a powerful influence on the ways in which we understand crime today.

Moreover, this historical introduction to criminological theory should provide a valuable lesson in intellectual humility: the sobering realization that our understanding of crime has not advanced much beyond that of theories put forward over 100 years ago. Yet this dubious progress is not peculiar to the discipline of criminology. Taken as a whole, the social sciences have been notoriously unsuccessful in putting forward any confirmed generalization on social behavior! Criminology, then, shares its "failure" with other social sciences.

In this chapter, we continue our historical introduction by moving from Europe to the United States. We begin with certain of the diverse explanations of crime favored before 1915, just prior to the growth and professionalization of criminology in the United States.

5.1 THE EARLY HISTORY OF CRIMINOLOGY IN THE UNITED STATES, 1895–1915

Prior to the emergence of the **Chicago school of sociology** in the decade after 1915, the study of crime had few institutional facilities with which to develop a systematic intellectual content. It is therefore hard to isolate a precise event or idea that marked the first appearance of a criminology indigenous to the United States.

Following the end of the Civil War in 1865, there appeared a multitude of published opinions concerning crime. These were voiced in amateurish ways by persons with vested interests in crime and criminality: prison reformers, medical doctors, psychiatrists, journalists, politicians, social reformers, philanthropists, and moral crusaders. Some treatises were enlightened for their era (Walker, 1980:11–34; Dumm, 1987:65–86).This is not to suggest that proposals by the Pennsylvania Quakers for the "humanitarian" reform of prisons and punishment, for example, were enlightened in an absolute sense; they were enlightened only when compared with alternative proposals of the same era. Indeed, it is highly debatable whether the humanitarian basis of the modern penitentiary marks a real advance over preclassical forms of punishment (see Chapter 3.1).

The ideological leanings of these early works have been usefully charted by Boostrom (1974). Behind these works, he suggested, lay four basic beliefs that paved the way for the development of a criminology whose focus would become the "correction of criminals" (pp. 2–3):

1. . . . The idea that crime is an alien phenomenon in American society. Crime was claimed to be a phenomenon principally associated with alien, non-WASP groups. Crime was also seen as associated with the growth of urban-industrial centers stimulated by technological progress.
2. . . . The effort of correctional reformers to dissociate their ideas and panaceas from those of radical groups such as socialists.
3. . . . The effort to differentiate progressive correctional reform ideas from the perspective of Social Darwinism. Correctional reformers lobbied for creative government intervention (the positive state) to solve social problems while conservative Social Darwinists argued for the limitation of government to reactive police powers.
4. . . . The establishment of the idea that the solution of the crime problem in modern society would require social support for special "scientific" expertise and intervention.

Intellectually, the vast majority of writings on crime in the United States, up to and including the turn of the twentieth century, took the nature of crime and criminality entirely for granted. Crime was pathological activity unquestioningly committed by criminals. Sociological questions about the nature and possible normality of crime were neither raised nor, it seems, even recognized as part of serious inquiry. Moreover, the understanding of crime, and especially of its causes, tended to be combined with the explanatory framework of whatever concepts seemed appropriate to the problems at hand. And these concepts tended to be borrowed piecemeal from those of European phrenology, medicine, and psychiatry. Biological concepts were especially in fashion; and Darwinism, degeneracy, imbecility, moral insanity, and, especially, Lombrosianism—all exerted powerful influences on the public mind (Fink, 1938; Rafter 1988, 1992). Indeed, long after its apparent discredit in Europe, Lombrosianism retained a powerful hold on the U.S. public's imagination.

The multifactorial thrust of much criminology of this era is exemplified by the work of Chicago sociologist Frances Kellor. Although Kellor's studies were unusual in that they addressed female criminality, her perspective conventionally combined Lombrosianism, psychology, and environmental sociology in the search for a scientific criminal sociology. In the 1890s, for example, Kellor visited female penitentiaries and workhouses to assess

BOX 5.1 THE RISE OF SOCIOLOGY IN THE UNITED STATES, 1890–1910

Three major factors fostered the intellectual and institutional rise of sociology in the United States (Schwendinger and Schwendinger, 1974; Ross, 1991; and Camic and Xie, 1994):

1. The Progressive Era (1890–1910)—a combination of secular and Christian (especially Protestant) reform movements inspired by the professional middle classes (lawyers, doctors, teachers, and so on) and designed to improve the lot of the poor in the wake of the problems associated with the ill effects of industrialization and urbanization.
2. The rapid expansion of the university system in the United States and the institutionalization of the social sciences and of statistics at elite universities (Columbia, Johns Hopkins, Yale, Harvard, Chicago) between the mid-1870s and 1915. The first course in sociology probably was offered in 1876 by Sumner; the first book on sociology was Lester Ward's *Dynamic Sociology* (1883). The first book on criminology to use sociology specifically as one of its multifactorial perspectives was probably Kellor's *Experimental Sociology* (1901).
3. The government's recognition, between 1865 and 1905, of new academic associations—including the American Social Science Association, the American Economic Association, the American Historical Association, the American Sociological Society—for the professional security and advancement of the social science community.

how well Lombroso's concept of "born criminality" applied to women. Aided by a mobile laboratory, Kellor (1899) compared twenty-one physical and psychological characteristics of sixty-one female criminals with fifty-five students. Regarding physical differences, although she largely disagreed with the assertions of the learned Italian doctor, Kellor concluded that female inmates were differentiated among themselves: "immoral women," such as prostitutes, were found "mentally and physically . . . more defective than the criminal" (p. 543). Kellor also stressed the importance of sociological factors—including age, marital status, nationality, religion, occupation, and class origin—in understanding female criminality. For Kellor, these social and economic factors were almost always more critical than biological forces. For example, she found prostitution largely caused not by some innate female depravity but by limited economic circumstances. Kellor's multifactorialism led her to conclude that some women are criminal because of natural immorality, others because of domestic infelicity, and still others because of poor education; female recidivists tended to have "degenerate habits which enthrall them" (pp. 678–679).

In an important respect, all early studies of crime in the United States shared a common interest: their concern to correct and reform "criminals." Despite their paternalistic thrust, it was reformist motives that eventually led commentators on crime to become part of a wider and more recognized movement for the development of social science and, especially, sociology.

Criminology itself emerged from the Progressive Era's general concern with the alleviation of social problems. Criminology's position in universities across the United States

Ellis Island official questioning an Italian immigrant: In the 1920s and 1930s, sociologists and criminologists in Chicago studied the many ways in which immigrants adapted to the strains and stresses of social life in the United States.

derived from its inclusion within the movement for the expansion of sociology, and its voice was actively promoted by such professional associations as the National Prison Association and the National Conference of Charities and Corrections (later, of Social Work). This voice was enhanced in 1909 at a conference in Chicago, with the founding of the American Institute of Criminal Law and Criminology and of the *Journal of Criminal Law and Criminology*. Between 1895 (the year Max Nordau's *Degeneration* was published) and 1915 (when John Gillin's *Social Pathology* was published), the vague subject matter of criminology was transformed by a deluge of empirical studies addressing the criminality of immigrants, of the dangerous classes, and of "Negroes." Intellectually, these studies involved a selective reliance on sociological perspectives that excluded everything in the realm of theoretical speculation. This was not the time, or so it must have seemed, to speculate on grandiose sociological questions—What is society? How is social order possible? Is crime "normal"?—even if they were asked by criminologists such as Cooley in the United States and Durkheim in Europe. Instead, there was a new emphasis on such empirical social categories as poverty, alcoholism, and family upbringing (Rafter, 1988); each of these categories was seen as a potential factor in criminality in a continually expanding and, in principle, endless chain of causality. Typically, the various links in the causal chain were tied to the criminality of social, economic, political, and religious "outsiders": immigrants, persons of color, heretics, lunatics and imbeciles, the undeserving poor, the feebleminded, the naturally unfit, and others.

Titillated by the mass media and designed for popular consumption, pronouncements of criminologists on the causes of crime were naturally assured a large public audience. The focus on the individual as the appropriate object of study and on the legitimate goal of reforming the criminal character through the individualization of punishment assured criminologists of considerable financial support by both state and private agencies. By the end of World War I, criminology had gained a measure of support from the academic and scientific communities because of several criminology texts (for example, Parmalee, 1918) that urged the use of scientific principles as a basic method.

As a part of the movement for social reform, and as a fledgling member of the academic community, criminology was now charted on a respectable course. Next we consider the development of the Chicago school of social ecology, the first U.S. "school" of criminology.

5.2   CRIME AND SOCIAL ECOLOGY

By the term **social ecology** (or human ecology), we refer to a type of research that examines (1) different geographical areas within cities, communities, and neighborhoods and (2) the area concentrations, regularities, and patterns of social life in such fields as work/leisure, health/sickness, and conformity/deviance. In this section we outline the ecological approach to crime practiced by the **Chicago school of criminology** between the mid-1920s and early 1940s.

Introduction to the Chicago School of Criminology

In Chapter 4 we identified two explanatory frameworks instrumental in the development of sociological criminology. First, a sociopsychological explanation focused on the individual and, specifically, on the ways in which society cultivates the latent tendencies of those individuals psychologically predisposed to crime (see Chapter 4.1). Second, a sociological explanation focused on the patterned and regular ways in which social structures themselves exert pressures on certain groups, making them more prone to commit crimes (see Chapter 4.2). The investigations of the Chicago school of criminology included both these frameworks. Broadly, the Chicago school's work in the field of crime investigated: (1) the life histories of juvenile delinquents, interpreted both through personal accounts of their delinquent acts and with the aid of sociopsychological and, occasionally, clinical techniques, and (2) the geographical and social distribution of delinquents and delinquency rates. Many members of the Chicago school came from a common background that can be summarized as rural or small town, midwestern, Christian in upbringing, and reform-oriented or even liberal in its political views; their investigations therefore led directly to policies for social reform.

The Chicago school was part of the post-Progressive Era social science movement, many aspects of which evolved at the University of Chicago. Between 1915 and the early

1940s, sociological research in the United States was dominated by various academic disciplines at the University of Chicago, especially those of political science and sociology. This domination resulted from several factors, chief among them the nature of the city of Chicago itself. By the 1920s and 1930s, slightly more than a century after its founding, Chicago had changed beyond all recognition. From a small town of little more than two square miles and 200 inhabitants, Chicago expanded to become the second-largest industrial metropolis in the United States, with a corporate area of 211 square miles and a population of over 3.3 million. The city extended some twenty-five miles along Lake Michigan and from eight to ten miles inland. During this expansion, tremendous changes occurred in the social composition of many neighborhoods in the city. These changes were especially visible in neighborhoods in and adjacent to the central business district and in areas of rapid industrial growth. "About the only thing that could be thought beautiful about . . . Chicago," a Chicago sociologist commented pointedly, "was fresh and lively Lake Michigan" (Faris, 1970: 21). To journalists, social reformers, and sociologists, the ever-changing and fascinating patterns of daily life in Chicago were a barometer of the human condition itself. German sociologist Max Weber, visiting the city in 1904, found it "incredible and compared it to a man whose skin had been peeled off and whose intestines were seen at work" (Bulmer, 1984: xvi).

In this stimulating atmosphere, many creative scholars combined their talents and applied their energies to a sociological analysis of the harsh consequences of "urbanism," and especially to those problems generated by living in the inner city. Prominent among them were such famous names as W. I. Thomas, Ernest Burgess, Robert Park, and George Herbert Mead. Affiliated with the department of sociology—as graduate students, teachers, and quasi-independent researchers under the leadership of Park and Burgess—were such criminologists as William Healy, Frederick Thrasher, Paul Cressey, John Landesco, Clifford Shaw, and Henry McKay (Bennett, 1981: 104–210).

The Chicago school brought to its research on urbanism innovative, vigorous, and eclectic methods of analysis. In the history of empirical research, these methods fell, chronologically, midway between (although curiously unrelated to) investigations that relied on large social surveys and those that employed scientific measurement techniques. Members of the Chicago school used a dazzling array of methodological techniques in their research. Their quantitative methods included advanced statistical analyses. Their qualitative techniques included the use of life-history documents, case studies, investigative journalism, media materials, in-depth interviews, and participant observation. Above all, Chicago sociologists believed in following Park's recommendation to get their feet wet with real research (Bulmer, 1984: 108); they took great pride in conducting research in "the open," or in "the field" (on the streets, in opium dens, in brothels, and in parks), rather than in laboratories, faculty offices, or libraries.

In effect, the Chicago school believed firmly that the new methodological techniques of fieldwork would provide the basis for a factual, theory-free analysis of society. In this they agreed with French moral statisticians, such as Quetelet, that "facts speak for themselves" quite independently of theoretical interpretation (see Chapter 3.2). However, the Chicago school's "facts" did not speak for themselves. Behind their facts lay the guiding hand of an important theoretical assumption: that the social ecology of urbanism could proceed within the same framework as the ecological study of plant and animal life. This assumption was present, sometimes beneath the surface and sometimes quite overtly, in numerous writings of the Chicago school—from the early research of Park (1915) and Burgess (1925) on urban spatial analysis to Shaw and McKay's famous *Juvenile Delinquency and Urban Areas* (1942). The assumption was used to help describe how industrial and commercial expansion invades and disturbs the "metabolism" of "natural areas" (local communities) in the city. The guiding ecological assumption of the Chicago school has been described effectively by Vold, Bernard, and Snipes:

> The term ecology, as it is used today, is often linked to the idea of protecting the natural environment. In its original meaning, however, it is a branch of biology in which plants and animals are studied in their relationships to each other and to their natural habitat. Plant life and animal life are seen as an intricately complicated whole, a web of life in which each part depends on almost every other part for some aspect of its existence. Organisms in their natural habitat exist in an ongoing balance of nature, a dynamic equilibrium in which each individual must struggle to survive. Ecologists study this web of interrelationships and interdependencies in an attempt to discover the forces that define the activities of each part. (1998: 140)

After World War I (1914–1918), Chicago sociologists turned their ecological attentions to a variety of social problems. Exacerbated by the severe hardships of the Great Depression, by Prohibition, and by the well-publicized rise of gangland warfare and union racketeering, crime itself came to be seen as a major social problem. Crime, therefore, was one of the chief topics studied by members of the Chicago school. For example, W. I. Thomas and Florian Znaniecki's *The Polish Peasant in Europe and America* (1918–1920) used personal documents and life histories to examine how hard it was for immigrants to adjust to life in America. W. I. Thomas's *The Unadjusted Girl* (1923) collected information from 3,000 interviews to establish that all social behavior, including that of female delinquency, apparently derived from one or all of four motives or "wishes": the wish for new experience, for security, for response, and for recognition. As such, implied Thomas, delinquency and lawful activity were merely "functional alternatives" directed to the satisfaction of the same goals. *The Unadjusted Girl* marked a rare concern among criminologists with the "criminality" of young females. However, feminists find scant value in Thomas's book; the analysis is thoroughly sexist (females are entirely incidental to Thomas's concern with the four "wishes"). Thrasher's *The Gang* (1927) strongly implied that, although there are many gang types, delinquent gang activity represented a normal part of the process of adjustment between adolescence and adulthood. Delinquency, Thrasher found, was the best method of adjustment available to adolescents in deprived inner-city areas.

Clifford Shaw contributed two directions of research to the Chicago school before completing his famous *Juvenile Delinquency and Urban Areas* with Henry McKay in 1942. First, in his book *Delinquency Areas,* Shaw (et al., 1929) argued that the physical destruction and social deterioration of inner-city areas led to the disintegration of the community and, ultimately, to the loss of the community's ability to police itself. Social disorganization, in other words, caused increases in juvenile delinquency.

Second, Shaw showed how seemingly important it was for a researcher to listen to delinquents' own definitions of their activities. Why did juveniles, according to their own explanations, engage in delinquency? To answer this question Shaw collected more than 200 life histories of juvenile delinquents. In 1930, Shaw published *The Jack-Roller,* a widely read account of "a delinquent boy's own story." This book was followed by *The Natural History of a Delinquent Career* (1939), a book that contradicted the public condemnation of a convicted rapist and armed robber widely depicted as a brute and a beast. Instead, insisted Shaw, this felon should be understood in terms of the values transmitted to him by numerous juvenile institutions and by his economically insecure and disorganized community in Chicago. Finally, we note *Brothers in Crime* (Shaw, McKay, and McDonald, 1938), an in-depth study of the social backgrounds, criminal careers, and personality characteristics of the five Martin brothers, children of foreign-born immigrants. This book was a sympathetic view of five "criminal careers" that had been determined by the cultural conflict into which immigrant families were thrust by poverty, lack of education, and the aggravating effects of such control agencies as juvenile institutions.

This sort of criminology was very different from much that had preceded it. Members of the Chicago school did not assume that those who committed crimes were malicious miscreants. On the contrary, they believed delinquents were normal juveniles in abnormal environments. In this, the Chicago school made considerable progress over the opinionated explanations of their predecessors.

We turn now to what was, in some respects, the greatest achievement of the Chicago school's contribution to criminology—Shaw and McKay's book *Juvenile Delinquency and Urban Areas* (1942).

Shaw and McKay's Juvenile Delinquency and Urban Areas (1942)

Juvenile Delinquency and Urban Areas applied to the city of Chicago the detailed statistical analyses pioneered a century earlier by Quetelet and Guerry (see Chapter 3.2). Its sophisticated analyses tried to untangle the links among the dynamics of urban growth, community problems, and rates of juvenile delinquency. Among the crucial questions about juvenile delinquency that Shaw and McKay sought to explore were:

1. Do juvenile delinquency rates and adult crime rates vary together in different types of cities?
2. Do rates of juvenile delinquency correlate with the rates of juvenile recidivism; with the economic, social, and cultural characteristics of local communities; and with patterns of immigration?
3. How do economic and social conditions influence the development of juvenile delinquency as a cultural tradition in certain neighborhoods?
4. How can juvenile delinquency be prevented and treated?

Shaw and McKay approached these questions in four stages. First, they identified various physical and social demographic changes in Chicago neighborhoods. On the one hand, the physical changes comprised such factors as the growth of the central business district and the invasion of traditional local communities in the course of industrial and commercial expansion. With this expansion, Chicago landlords typically failed to repair rented dwellings in surrounding areas because of expectations that rising property prices—caused by the increased demand of industry and commerce for scarce land—would eventually yield fat profits. As a result, "zones of transition" surrounding the central business district and the industrial developments of Chicago were subject to increasing physical deterioration that, in turn, was manifest in the number of substandard and dangerous buildings that survived in the zone of transition.

On the other hand, the changes in Chicago's social composition derived largely from the fact that from the 1880s to the 1930s the population in Chicago's zone of transition was in relative decline while the population in its expanding suburbs was increasing. Employing census data, Shaw and McKay (pp. 32–42) found that a disproportionate number of those in professional and clerical occupations resided in the affluent suburbs, far from the central business district and industrial development. Correspondingly, a disproportionate number of industrial workers and the poor were concentrated in areas of physical deterioration. These deteriorated areas also contained the greatest number of families on welfare.

In combination, the physical and social changes in Chicago led to a far-reaching geographic segregation of the population. Shaw and McKay discovered further that patterns of immigration were part of a related process of economic and occupational segregation. The native white population not only enjoyed the highest economic status but tended to live in comfortable suburban houses; the residents of deteriorated zones of transition tended to have the lowest economic status. This latter group included: (1) white European immigrants (especially from Czechoslovakia, Germany, Greece, Italy, Ireland, Poland, and Russia) and (2) African Americans, many of whom were "internal immigrants" who had migrated to Chicago from rural areas. Each immigrant group tended to be concentrated in a particular section of Chicago, although African American families were more dispersed throughout the deteriorated neighborhoods than were European immigrants. Upon arrival in the "New World," each impoverished immigrant group tended to be pushed into the areas of lowest economic status. Eventually, however, most groups (but not African Americans, Latinos, and Native Americans) worked their way to the suburbs; their places in the deteriorated neighborhoods were simply filled by subsequent arrivals. To paraphrase the jargon of social ecology: As industry and commerce extend their habitat, the metabolism of existing natural areas is dominated or destroyed; surviving areas, in succession, are organically reconstituted as part of another natural area. Shaw and McKay (p. 42) inferred that this complicated process led to differential rates of delinquents.

In the second stage, Shaw and McKay focused on the distribution of delinquency in Chicago. The juveniles in their data were of three types:

1. alleged male juvenile delinquents (namely, those under seventeen) brought before the Juvenile Court of Cook County
2. juveniles actually committed to correctional institutions
3. all boys dealt with by the juvenile police probation officers

Although the objection could be made that these three types represented only a sample of those apprehended rather than of all juvenile delinquents, this sample was larger than any previous study. Moreover, the data were compiled from different periods of time: (1) 9,860 alleged Chicago juvenile delinquents for the period 1934–1940; (2) 8,411 for

1927–1933; (3) 8,141 for 1917–1923; and (4) 8,056 for 1900–1906. Their use of time-series data, Shaw and McKay reasoned, permitted comparisons of delinquency rates not only in the same area for different periods but also in other areas, some of which had undergone great sociodemographic changes and some of which had remained relatively stable.

Their findings, displayed with spectacular diagrams and shaded maps, were most revealing. Using a series of spot maps that located the homes of all the delinquent boys reported in their data, Shaw and McKay showed that certain areas of Chicago had large concentrations of juvenile delinquents, whereas in other areas the delinquents were greatly dispersed. The areas of heaviest concentration were generally those near the central business district or those within or near areas zoned for industry and commerce.

Shaw and McKay divided the map of Chicago into 140 units, each approximately one square mile in size. They then computed delinquency rates for each unit (a delinquency rate was the number of delinquent boys in any given unit expressed as a percentage of the total of boys in that unit). Significantly, the units with the highest delinquency rates were found to be those near the central business district and those adjacent to areas zoned for industry or commerce.

Shaw and McKay showed further that delinquency rates throughout Chicago varied in a strikingly uniform pattern (see the zone maps in Figure 5.1): The center of the city had the highest delinquency rates and the units at the extreme periphery the lowest; in between, the rates decreased regularly the farther away from the center. This finding—that delinquency rates actually declined as one moved from the center to the periphery of the delinquency zones in Chicago—is analyzed in greater detail later in this section.

In the third stage of their approach, Shaw and McKay showed that juvenile delinquency was not an isolated social problem. Analyses revealed that, area by area, juvenile delinquency rates were strongly correlated with such other community problems as high rates of school truancy (p. 90), young adult offenders (pp. 93–99), infant mortality (pp. 99–101), tuberculosis (pp. 101–104), and mental disorders (pp. 104–106). In other words, Shaw and McKay found that areas in Chicago with certain social problems also tended to have higher rates of juvenile delinquency. Moreover, these same areas had the highest juvenile recidivism rates and relatively more delinquents who were later arrested as adults (pp. 138–139).

Shaw and McKay stressed that their correlational analyses should not be confused with causal analysis. The high correlation between delinquency rates and certain sociodemographic characteristics of Chicago neighborhoods did not mean that these characteristics cause delinquency. For example, Shaw and McKay saw that although the proportion of the foreign-born and the African American population was higher in areas with high delinquency rates, this did not mean that the delinquency rates of these populations were higher because they were foreign-born or African American. They were higher, in part, because the high turnover of immigrant populations caused a withdrawal of residents' identification with their community and, correspondingly, a lack of pride in their neighborhood. Curiously, areas with high delinquency rates continued to have high rates irrespective of which groups inhabited them. Thus between 1884 and 1930, eight inner-city Chicago areas underwent no changes in delinquency rates relative to other areas, despite the fact that the dominant population in these eight areas changed from Germans, Irish, English/Scots,

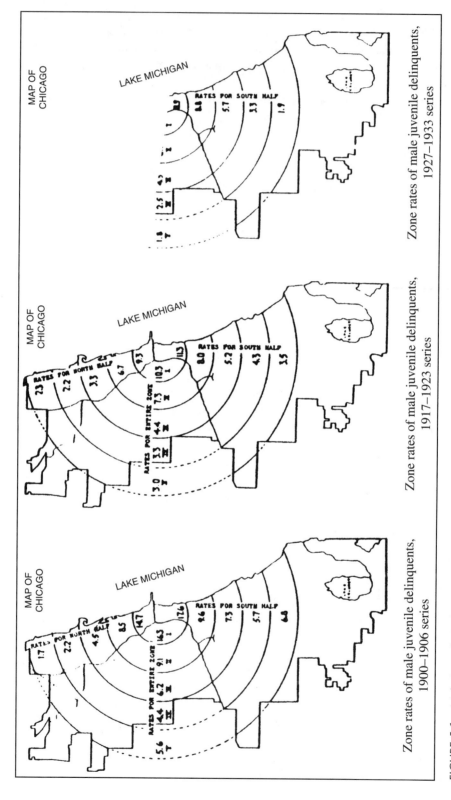

FIGURE 5.1   Male Juvenile Delinquency Rates, Chicago, 1900–1933
SOURCE: Adapted from Shaw and McKay, 1969: 69.

and Scandinavians to Italians, Poles, and Slavs (pp. 156–157). This stability in delinquency rates, in the face of changing ethnic compositions, meant that "the delinquency-producing factors are inherent in the community" (p. 315). The explanation of delinquency, Shaw and McKay promisingly insisted, must be

> in the first place, in the field of the more subtle human relationships and social values which comprise the social world of the child in the family and community. These more distinctively human situations, which seem to be directly related to delinquent conduct, are, in turn, products of larger economic and social processes characterizing the history and growth of the city and of the local communities which comprise it.

Fourth and finally, Shaw and McKay tried to extend the importance of the relationship between "social values" and "larger economic and social processes" to the causes of juvenile delinquency. In areas with low delinquency rates (i.e., generally middle-class areas and those with high economic status), on the one hand, Shaw and McKay suggested that there was a general consensus about conventional values and attitudes toward such things as the welfare of children, the desirability of education, constructive leisure-time activities, and conformity to law. In such middle-class areas, moreover, respect for social values was expressed and cultivated by a variety of voluntary social control organizations such as parent-teacher associations, women's clubs, service clubs, churches, and neighborhood centers. Children who lived in such environments tended to be insulated from direct contact with deviant forms of adult behavior and, in general, were "exposed to and participate[d] in a significant way in one mode of life only" (p. 171). In areas with high delinquency rates (generally, working-class areas and those with low economic status), on the other hand, there was found to be wide diversity in norms and standards of behavior. This diversity resulted from the different cultural beliefs and practices of migrant groups and unassimilated immigrant groups, and also from the moral values of predatory youth gangs and organized crime. Concerning these areas, Shaw and McKay summarized:

> Moral values range from those that are strictly conventional to those in direct opposition to conventionality as symbolized by the family, the church, and other institutions common to our general society. The deviant values are symbolized by groups and institutions ranging from adult criminal gangs engaged in theft and the marketing of stolen goods . . . to quasi-legitimate businesses and the rackets through which partial or complete control of legitimate business is sometimes exercised. . . . Thus, within the same community theft may be defined as right and proper in some groups and as immoral, improper, and undesirable in others. In some groups wealth and prestige are secured through acts of skill and courage in the delinquent or criminal world, while in neighboring groups any attempt to achieve distinction in this manner would result in extreme disapprobation. Two conflicting systems of economic activity here present roughly equivalent opportunities for employment and for promotion. (pp. 171–172)

For Shaw and McKay, in other words, areas with high delinquency rates were those whose children were exposed to (1) conflicting sets of moral values, (2) adult role models whose material success derived from participation in criminal activities, and (3) a social tradition of delinquency that was a hallmark of the life of the local community. Boys constantly surrounded by this social milieu were thus exposed routinely to delinquent lifestyles. However, the mere existence of criminal organizations did not explain why some boys were tempted to join and others were not. So, what causes juvenile delinquency?

In their conclusion, Shaw and McKay attempted to answer this question. Once again, they emphasized that the major difference between Chicago areas with high and low rates of officially recorded delinquency was that the former tended to be more impoverished and the latter more affluent. Despite this difference, boys in all areas of Chicago—both rich and poor—were "exposed [in school and elsewhere] to the luxury values and success patterns of our culture" (p. 319). However, success by legitimate means was difficult to achieve for boys in low-income areas because they usually lacked the opportunities and skills required to be successful. Boys from low-income families thus calculated that the best way to achieve success lay in acts of delinquency and crime. Juvenile delinquency is therefore rational activity, and delinquent boys are by no means necessarily disorganized, maladjusted, or antisocial. As Shaw and McKay explained:

> In the low-income areas, where there is the greatest deprivation and frustration, where, in the history of the city, immigrant and migrant groups have brought together the widest variety of divergent cultural traditions and institutions, and where there exists the greatest disparity between the social values to which the people aspire and the availability of facilities for acquiring these values in conventional ways, the development of crime as an organized way of life is most marked. Crime, in this situation, may be regarded as one of the means employed by people to acquire, or to attempt to acquire, the economic and social values generally idealized in our culture, which persons in other circumstances acquire by conventional means. (p. 319)

Assessment

Shaw and McKay's findings in their famous study have had enormous influence on criminology, as has the methodological legacy of the Chicago school in general. Doubtless a tribute to their signal importance, the method and findings of *Juvenile Delinquency and Urban Areas* have been reinterpreted endlessly by successive generations of criminologists.

Now let us consider several criticisms, both empirical and theoretical, of Shaw and McKay's work. First, consider the relationship between the source of their data and their finding that rates of juvenile delinquency tend to be highest in the low-income and working-class neighborhoods of cities. These data came from records of such official agencies as juvenile courts and juvenile probation officers. Though Shaw and McKay (p. 44) realized that many juveniles commit serious offenses that go undetected or for which they are not apprehended, they did not acknowledge that crime rates are not pre-given, objective facts. Crime rates are always socially constructed (see Chapter 2). Delinquency rates, for example, reflect not only the illegalities of juveniles but also the reporting activity of the public and the decision to accept an act as an offense by a police officer. Delinquency is so often found in working-class areas because working-class adolescents are more likely than others to have their offenses reported to the police, and, if their offenses are reported, they are more likely to be arrested, to enter the criminal justice system, and to leave it as officially defined delinquents.

Moreover, recent self-report studies and victimization surveys show that although lower-class neighborhoods contain a disproportionate amount of violent crime, delinquency as a whole is not concentrated among working-class adolescents. Status offenses and property crimes, in particular, are far more evenly distributed throughout the class structure.

Second, consider that Shaw and McKay's data on delinquency distribution derived from the residences of juveniles who entered the criminal justice system. Subsequent research on urban social spaces, beginning with Newman's *Defensible Space* (1973), has demonstrated the critical importance of the locations where crimes are committed (see Chapter 8.1) rather than the residences of those who commit them—a fact of obvious importance in the case of white-collar, organized, and political crimes (see Chapters 12, 13, and 14).

Third, consider Shaw and McKay's claim that delinquency rates remained stable despite great changes in the social composition of Chicago neighborhoods. If we ignore such factors as class bias in the construction of delinquency rates, it is possible that this claim was true for the specific period investigated (namely, 1906–1940). Yet, there is no good reason to suppose, as Shaw and McKay did, that delinquency rates will be stable in other places and times (Lander, 1954). Indeed, it is likely that in Chicago itself delinquency rates after 1945 did not conform to the pattern predicted for them by Shaw and McKay (Bursik, 1984). Ultimately, we cannot be sure of the exact meaning of any claim about the stability of socially constructed crime rates. Does such a claim mean that the rate of actual illegalities remained stable? Does it mean, instead, that the actions of police officers remained constant? In posing these questions we are forced to raise anew a central question of the discussion in Chapter 2: What, precisely, do crime rates measure?

Theoretical criticisms of *Juvenile Delinquency and Urban Areas* tend to object that its findings are empiricist. Shaw and McKay believed mistakenly that their findings were strictly factual (essentially, that they existed independently of theoretical assumptions); actually their findings were deeply structured by theoretical assumptions that lurked below the surface of their argument.

Recall that social ecologists tend to see urban development as a process in which areas of industrial and commercial expansion interfere with the metabolism of adjacent areas. Certain natural areas of transition—undergoing invasion, dominance, and succession—have high delinquency rates. As *Juvenile Delinquency and Urban Areas* attempted to show, this interference was manifest in the growth of juvenile delinquency and in other indices of social disorganization in inner-city neighborhoods. However, Shaw and McKay also believed that, like the processes of change in plants and animal life, the surrounding areas eventually would return to a harmonious state of equilibrium through the mechanisms of natural selection and symbiosis. It was hypothesized that when and if immigrants acquired the skills required for survival in a hostile environment, they would move up the social ladder and then move out to the suburbs. When this move did not happen in Chicago, Shaw and McKay reasoned that it was because the inner-city areas lacked sufficient community controls to restore their natural state. The sources of disorganization thus lay with the residents rather than with the profit-seeking decisions of industrialists.

However, quite aside from the difficulties of applying concepts about change in plant life to processes of change in social life, the concept **social disorganization** remains unclear. Though Shaw and McKay were quite aware of the great diversity of lifestyles in Chicago, they nevertheless tended to start with an image of conventional lifestyles; then they described those that deviated from convention as disorganized and, occasionally, as socially pathological. Sociologically, however, societies and communities can never be disorganized as such. Disorganization is a label that is always conceived of, explicitly or implicitly, in relation to some theoretically conceived yardstick of organization. Sometimes this conception is quite explicit (such as when someone says that unregulated industrial expansion is immoral because it destroys the communality of residential neighborhoods, or that, compared with the orderly lifestyles of the residents of Chicago's fashionable Gold Coast, life in the slums is disorganized). Sometimes, the concept of social organization is implicit only. Shaw and McKay assumed implicitly, and wrongly so, that the lifestyles and values of those in natural areas of transition were disorganized. Ultimately, Shaw and McKay assumed that juvenile delinquency was necessarily disorganized or deviant activity.

Moreover, their causal chain leading to delinquency suffered from theoretical confusion. Shaw and McKay made no attempt to follow through on the implications of their original insight—that industrial expansion, neighborhood destruction in zones of transition, and juvenile delinquency might be parts of the same causative process (Bursik and Grasmick, 1993; Sampson and Wilson, 1995). In other words, although they correctly identified the socially harmful effects of unregulated industrial and commercial expansion on community life, they instead argued that these effects were generated by a breakdown in the values of the affected communities. For Shaw and McKay it was not dilapidated housing, overcrowding, poor hygiene, and inadequate leisure facilities (all effects of unregulated urban growth) that caused delinquency. Delinquency was caused by a breakdown in the values of the delinquents, in those of their families, and in those of their communities as a whole. Their analysis failed to view delinquency and capital movements as anything other than aspects of a temporary, coincidental process.

In the next section we outline a theory of crime and deviance that in certain ways appears as a marked advance on the school of social ecology: Merton's 1938 theory of social structure and anomie. Merton emphasized, or so it seemed, what Chicago criminologists generally had ignored—a theoretical explanation that linked deviance and crime to the class structure.

5.3 SOCIAL STRUCTURE, ANOMIE, AND DEVIANCE

It is hard to exaggerate the importance of Robert Merton's 1938 article "Social Structure and Anomie." Strongly opposed to biological and individualistic explanations of deviance and crime, Merton focused on the rates of such conduct. In developing this focus, Merton relied on Durkheim's concept of **anomie** (see Chapter 4.2) to explain how and why "some social structures exert a definite pressure upon certain persons in the society to engage in nonconforming rather than conforming conduct" (1969:255). But whereas Durkheim had stressed that anomic states arise from unregulated human desires, Merton pinpointed the importance of the relationship between means and goals.

Merton's central hypothesis was that, sociologically, deviant behavior is a symptom of a specific sort of social disorganization: a lack of fit between culturally prescribed aspirations and socially structured avenues for achieving them. Though his essay could in principle be applied to several different societies, it is clear that Merton had in mind chiefly the United States and, especially, the goals enshrined in the "American Dream" (for more, see Chapter 8.3).

Merton's argument began with two important elements of social and cultural structures. The first element is made up of the culturally defined goals that are held out as legitimate objectives for all members of a society. These goals are "the things worth striving for." The second element is made up of the regulations, controls, and procedures for moving toward goals, which are termed institutionalized means or norms. A well-regulated, or stable, society has a balanced equilibrium between means and goals. In a stable society, both means and goals are accepted by everyone and are available to all. Social integration occurs effectively when individuals are socialized into accepting that they will be rewarded for the occasional sacrifice of conforming to institutionalized means and when they actually compete for rewards through legitimate means. Malintegrated, or unstable, societies stress the goals without stressing the means, or vice versa. In some societies, institutionalized means are not integrated with important social values. In societies such as the United States, provisions for making the means of achieving the goals available to all are insufficient.

Certain means, such as vivisection or medical experimentation, although perhaps technically more efficient in achieving goals, are sometimes unacceptable. Yet people often turn to technically more efficient means if other institutionalized means are unavailable. The more widespread the practice of using noninstitutionalized means, the more a society destabilizes or, put another way, the more widespread becomes anomie.

Competitive sports illustrate the processes that lead to anomie. If success in sports is construed as "winning the game at all costs" rather than as winning by the rules, the use of illegitimate but technically more efficient means is more attractive to participants. As Merton put it:

> The star of the opposing football team is surreptitiously slugged; the wrestler incapacitates his opponent through ingenious but illicit techniques; university alumni covertly subsidize "students" whose talents are confined to the athletic field. The emphasis on the goal has so attenuated the satisfactions deriving from sheer participation in the competitive activity that only a successful outcome provides gratification. Through the same process, tension generated by the desire to win in a poker game is relieved by successfully dealing one's self four aces or, when the cult of success has truly flowered, by sagaciously shuffling the cards in a game of solitaire. (p. 259)

Moreover, Merton suggested that if "concern shifts exclusively to the outcome of competition, then those who perennially suffer defeat may, understandably enough, work for a change in the rules of the game" (p. 257). Merton believed that the United States is a society in which great emphasis is placed upon certain success-goals without a corresponding emphasis upon institutionalized means.

This lack of fit occurs in three ways. First, as in competitive sports, means are often elevated to ends (for example, money is commonly viewed as an end in itself rather than as a means to achieve a goal); moreover, its acquisition is a goal that can never be met. People in all income brackets want more money, and when they get more of it, they want still more. In other words, the goals of the American Dream are beyond nearly everyone's reach. Second, the lot of the multitudes who never achieve success-goals is made doubly worse because they not only fail to succeed but tend to endure penalties for such "failure." Through the socializing agencies of family, school, and peer groups we are bombarded constantly with such slogans as, "There is no such word as 'fail'"; "Never be a quitter"; and "You can make it if you try." Coupled with this pressure to maintain lofty goals, there are very real penalties paid by those who draw in or reduce their ambitions. The cultural manifesto, Merton argued, is clear: Never quit, never stop trying, never lower your horizons.

Merton never fully articulates the third description of the lack of fit between means and goals in the United States, although at several points it reaches the surface of his argument. Merton hints (p. 263) that because of a maldistribution of power certain segments of the population—such as individuals in the lower social strata—are continually denied access to legitimate, institutionalized means. Despite such slogans as "Anyone can be president" or "Work hard and you will be rewarded with monetary success," these goals are almost impossible to achieve for those at the bottom or at the margins of society. Tragically, failure tends to be defined as a consequence not of social inequality but of individual ineptitude or lack of ambition.

Merton's scenario of the American Dream contemplates a society that is egalitarian in its ideology but unequal in terms of the availability of the means of achieving success-goals. U.S. society, therefore, is imperfect and badly integrated; its social and cultural structures inevitably produce strain and tension.

Merton's Typology of Modes of Individual Adaptation

What are the consequences of this strain on the individual? Merton identified five different responses to the strains and tensions of social life in the United States (see Table 5.1): conformity, innovation, ritualism, retreatism, and rebellion. We stress that Merton did not conceive of these responses as psychological conditions but as structural responses to the strain of anomie. The ways in which individuals respond to anomie in part vary, in Merton's formulation, according to their position in the class structure.

I. Conformity.   Conformity is the most common practice. Although Merton did not explain why the majority of the members of society typically conform, he suggested that "were this not so, the stability and continuity of the society could not be maintained" (p. 264). However, Merton was concerned chiefly with the four deviant adaptations to the tensions generated by the gap between means and ends.

II. Innovation.   The combination of a cultural emphasis on success-goals and the rigidity of the U.S. class structure, Merton insisted, produces an innovative deviant adaptation.

TABLE 5.1   A Typology of Modes of Individual Adaptation

Modes of Adaptation	Culture Goals	Institutionalized Means
I Conformity	+	+
II Innovation	+	−
III Ritualism	−	+
IV Retreatism	−	−
V Rebellion	±	±

NOTE: + signifies acceptance, − signifies rejection, ± signifies rejection of prevailing values and substitution of new values.
SOURCE: Merton, 1969: 263.

Innovation is the most common deviant response and the most important for criminology. Innovation is deviant behavior that uses illegitimate means to achieve socially acceptable goals. Many crimes against property (such as burglaries, robberies, and larcenies) are clear examples of innovative acts. Because innovative responses are distributed throughout the U.S. class structure, there is, Merton suggested, no simple correlation between crime and poverty (pp. 269–271). The pressures to succeed operate at all points in the class structure; innovative deviance occurs throughout the social structure—from robber barons and white-collar criminals to common criminals in the lower social strata. However, Merton continued, innovative deviance in the United States is concentrated largely in the skilled and unskilled working class. It is there, more than at any other class location, that the gap between goals (which all are urged to achieve) and means is most acute.

In his theory of innovative deviance, Merton assumed that innovators are persons who have been improperly socialized. Had they been socialized properly—had they internalized the need to follow institutionalized norms—their behavior would, by definition, be conformist. An alternative for those who have fully internalized the institutionalized values but who still crave the impossible-to-achieve aspirations of the American Dream is a dogged involvement with institutionalized norms at the expense of success-goals. This alternative Merton terms "ritualism."

III. Ritualism.   Merton defined ritualism as "the abandoning or scaling down of the lofty cultural goals of great pecuniary success and rapid social mobility to the point where one's aspirations can be satisfied" (pp. 273–274). It is the response of conformist bureaucrats who "take no chances." Ritualism is expressed in such clichés as, "I'm not sticking my neck out" and "Aim low and you'll never be disappointed." Ritualism is practiced most often by members of the lower middle class, where "parents typically exert continuous pressure upon children to abide by the moral mandates of society, and where the social climb upwards is less likely to meet with success than among the upper middle class" (p. 275).

IV. Retreatism.   Retreatism is an adaptation (or maladaptation) that relinquishes culturally prescribed goals and does not conform to institutionalized means. It is an escape mechanism that often arises when, after having internalized the importance of following legitimate means toward acceptable goals, an individual suffers repeated failure in goal achievement and is unable to resort to proscribed means. Retreatists constitute the "true aliens": they are "in the society but not of it" (p. 277). They include psychotics, autistics, pariahs, outcasts, vagrants, vagabonds, tramps, chronic drunkards, and drug addicts. The retreatist adaptation, Merton insists, is by and large a private and isolated response rather than a public one.

V. Rebellion.   Rebellion involves alienation from legitimate means and values. In contrast to retreatism, rebellion is a collective activity. For a rebellious disposition to be transformed into organized political action, legitimate means and values must be viewed as arbitrary or mythical, loyalty to them must be withdrawn, and an allegiance must be developed to new groups possessed of a new myth. The new myth has two functions. First, it must identify the source of large-scale frustration in society itself rather than in the individual. Second, it must be directed to the founding of a society with closer links between merit, effort, and reward (pp. 279–281). The precise mix of these criteria, Merton could have added, is subject to almost infinite variety and includes anarchists, communists, and the Ku Klux Klan.

Assessment

Merton's analysis of the pressures and strains in the United States and of the way in which they lead to different deviant responses, including crime, is a brilliant polemic against those who believe that the causes of crime are found in such individualistic factors as defective personality or malformed biology. It is also a solid indictment of the rampant social inequality endemic to U.S. society (Sumner, 1994:120–121). Merton's argument about strain and anomie remains one of the most powerful sociological explanations of deviance and crime. As we learn in the remainder of this chapter, Merton's analysis has substantially influenced theories of delinquent subcultures (see Chapter 8.3).

However, several criticisms must be made of Merton's analysis of the relations between social structure, anomie, and deviance. First, crucial parts of his argument hinge on unstated and unproven assumptions. For example, it is questionable whether acceptance of middle-class norms and values in U.S. society is as widespread as Merton depicts. Accepted by whom? For what reason? Are middle-class norms and values in Manhattan the same as those in rural Wisconsin? Again, Merton's argument that deviance is a response to structural strain assumes that no form of deviant activity has authenticity in its own right. Yet some deviant activities are engaged in for no apparent reason other than the fact that they are enjoyable.

Second, although Merton's analysis focuses on the psychic effects of strain on individuals at different points in the class structure, there is no indication of the structural causes of strain. Of course, we should not criticize Merton for not outlining something he never intended to examine—but this remains an important omission in his theory of social structure and anomie. It is especially important if we are concerned with issues of social policy and crime. If crime is caused by tensions and strain generated by a society that, for most people, routinely fails to deliver the promises of the American Dream, then how can crime be reduced? Should structural strain be seen as the starting point of a chain of causation that ends in crime and deviance? What are the causes of strain? Can nonconformist conduct be reduced by psychiatric counseling or prescription pills?

Third, recall that Merton's analysis was directed explicitly to success-oriented societies like the United States. In such societies, the structural strain that produces nonconformist responses, and that culminates in anomie, derives from the gap between the availability of means and the ideology of equal opportunity. Strain is most intense for those with the least opportunity to partake in the promises of the American Dream (namely, lower-class individuals). Merton therefore suggests that nonconformist conduct (essentially, crime and deviance) is concentrated in the lower class. But this conclusion is at best tentative and, at worst, false. It is true that crimes of lower-class individuals are far more likely to be detected by the police and to lead to arrest (see Chapter 15.1). Yet only in this limited sense is the (property) crime rate of the lower class greater than that of other classes. This does not mean, however, that the actual volume of crime committed by the lower class is greater than that of other classes. Indeed, if the strains of life really operate as suggested, then Merton is left with the problem of explaining why it is that most members of society engage in law-abiding activities far more than in deviance. To a certain extent, this very issue was the focus of the criminology of Merton's contemporary, Edwin Sutherland.

5.4   THE CRIMINOLOGY OF EDWIN SUTHERLAND

No introduction to modern criminology is complete without recognizing the enduring contributions made by sociologist Edwin Sutherland (1883–1950). He was raised in Nebraska and Kansas; his mother was active in Christian service; and his father was a Baptist minister and historian (Geis and Goff, 1983:xxi–xxiii). By his own account, Sutherland began an academic career with primary training in political economy and political science and a major interest in the study of labor problems (1956:13–14). In 1906, Sutherland took a course in criminology at the University of Chicago, where the basic textbook was Henderson's *Dependent, Neglected, and Delinquent Classes* (1893). Then, as a sociologist at the University of Illinois, Sutherland taught courses in criminology. In 1921 he began serious work in criminology by drafting an overview of the field. This led, in 1924, to the first reasonably systematic textbook in U.S. criminology, Sutherland's cautious yet progressive *Criminology*. Here, Sutherland claimed that the criminologist should not assume the correctness of such popular and legal categories as "crime," "criminality," and "crime rates." Instead, he argued, sociology should provide the primary perspective of criminology, the focus of which should be both law and crime.

Sutherland's sociological interest in such questions as "What is crime?" and "What is the relationship between crime and law?" was apparent throughout the main body of his work from the mid-1920s to the late 1940s. In what follows we divide his sociological criminology into four areas: differential association; differential social organization; his book *The Professional Thief;* and white-collar crime.

Differential Association

In the early editions of *Criminology*, Sutherland stressed that the causes of crime were in principle infinite. However, his belief in multicausality weakened as further study convinced him to integrate existing findings about the causes of crime into a general theory of crime. In this regard Sutherland was greatly influenced by the pessimistic although, he largely agreed (Schuessler, 1973:230), correct findings of a widely read report released by the Rockefeller-funded Bureau of Social Hygiene in New York City. The report's most damning accusation (Michael and Adler, 1971) was that criminology in the United States was entirely lacking in scientific generalizations about the causes of crime. What Sutherland termed the theory (or "principle") of **differential association** resulted from his ambitious search for a general theory of the causes of crime.

The specific content of Sutherland's theory of differential association derived from Tarde's theory of imitation (see Chapter 4.1), from the Chicago school's concept of social disorganization, and from George Herbert Mead and W. I. Thomas's sociopsychological emphasis on the importance of meanings in social interaction. Although we do not address social psychology as such, it is worth quoting Vold and Bernard and Snipe's summary of the elements in Mead's theory that influenced Sutherland's theory of differential association:

> In Mead's theory a cognitive factor—"meanings"—determines behavior. Mead then argued that people construct relatively permanent "definitions" of their situation out of the meanings they derive from particular experiences. That is, they generalize the meanings they have derived from particular situations, and form a relatively set way of looking at things. It is because of these different "definitions" that different people in different situations may act in very different ways. To cite an old example, two brothers may grow up in identical terrible situations, but one may become a drug lord while the other becomes a priest. (1998:185–186)

Sutherland meant for the theory of differential association to explain both the process by which a given person learns to engage in crime and also the content of what is learned.

The theory of differential association can be summarized as follows (Sutherland, 1947:6–8). First, criminal behavior is learned, like all other behavior, within intimate personal groups in an interactive process of communication. This means that criminality is not inherited biologically. Second, the learning of criminal behavior includes instruction in the techniques of crime and in the motivational values favorable to committing it. These values are learned from definitions that state whether legal codes are favorable or unfavorable. The principle of differential association asserts that a person becomes criminal when definitions favorable to the violation of law exceed the definitions unfavorable to violation, and when contacts with criminal patterns outweigh contacts with anticriminal patterns. Exposure to such definitions and contacts varies in frequency, duration, priority, and intensity. Finally, wrote Sutherland:

> While criminal behavior is an expression of general needs and values, it is not explained by those general needs and values, since noncriminal behavior is an expression of the same needs and values. Thieves generally steal in order to secure money, but likewise honest laborers work in order to secure money. The attempts by many scholars to explain criminal behavior by general drives and values, such as the happiness principle, striving for social status, the money motive, or frustration, have

been and must continue to be futile since they explain lawful behavior as completely as they explain criminal behavior. (p. 8)

Sutherland's theory has great appeal because its basic argument seems to offer a precise sociological explanation of why some people engage in crime and others do not. Persons commit crime because they have associated, socially and culturally, more (in frequency, duration, priority, and intensity) with procriminal patterns than with anticriminal patterns. Crime is thus a deviant action that is learned by normal persons who have been influenced by a specific cultural process.

Sutherland's theory of differential association has been, and continues to be, one of the most fertile causal accounts of crime. One of its great strengths is that it is a general theory that seeks to account for both criminal and noncriminal behavior. Analysis of criminal behavior is found especially in theories about the causal relationships between crime and subcultural ideas and values (see Chapter 6); theories of noncriminal behavior—specifically addressing the question, "Why do so many people not commit crimes?"—have focused on the behavioral processes of control and learning (see Chapter 7.1 and 7.2).

The theory of differential association has gained tremendous respect among criminologists, though it has also generated substantial controversy (Costello, 1997; Matsueda, 1997; Bernard and Snipes, 1996). Sutherland's collaborator, Donald Cressey, has argued persuasively that some of this controversy is quite unwarranted (Sutherland and Cressey, 1970:78–87). For instance, certain critics suggested mistakenly that the theory of differential association fails to realize that not all persons who associate with criminals actually become criminals themselves. Indeed, a careful reading of "Proposition # 6" in Sutherland's theory suggests that it is not mere association with criminals and criminal patterns that causes crime. In fact, Sutherland fully realized that associating with criminals was not a sufficient condition for engaging in crime. Persons commit crime, Sutherland stressed, "because of an excess of definitions favorable to violation of law over definitions unfavorable to violation of law" (1947:6–7).

Some critics have suggested that Sutherland's theory does not apply to some sorts of crime, especially crimes, such as heroin addiction contracted in a hospital (Lindesmith, 1947), that involve no social milieu of procriminal associations). Gaylord and Galliher report that at one point Sutherland himself did not feel that "his theory could account for 'adventitious' crimes, criminal acts that were accidental, casual, or trivial in nature" (1988:151). But, they counter perceptively: "It is unclear what these adjectives mean when applied to crimes. Is one to believe that Sutherland thought that they were accidental in the sense that they did not have causes? Or that they were engaged in by nonprofessional criminals? Or by persons lacking a criminal identity?" (p. 151).

Behind the repeated misreadings of its basic terms lie three serious problems with the explanatory adequacy of differential association theory. First, the terms of the theory are so deliberately abstract that testing them has proven extremely difficult. How, for example, can we actually measure an "excess" of definitions favorable to violation of law over definitions unfavorable to violation of law? What, precisely, are "associations" with "criminal patterns"? Should such associations include the influence of deep-rooted, socially harmful tendencies like racism and sexism—some of which have even been expressed in law and espoused by government officials and law enforcement officers?

Questions such as these reveal clearly that the terms of Sutherland's theory are insufficiently precise.

Second, the actual causal chain in Sutherland's theory arguably rests on a tautology. Logically, if we assume that human beings are not automata, then to say that crime is engaged in by persons who are motivated to engage in it or who learn to engage in it is not to say very much at all.

Third, the premises of Sutherland's theory are highly controversial. The image of the social actor postulated by Sutherland is that of an empty vessel with no history, no beliefs, no preferences, and no capacity for choice. Into this vessel Sutherland sought to pour "pro-" and "anti-" criminal tendencies. If (for some unstated reason) there is an excess of procriminal tendencies poured into this human vessel, then, the theory of differential association suggests, the vessel engages in crime. Because of this rigid determinism the theory cannot explain why certain persons associate more with procriminal patterns than with anticriminal patterns. Yet this must certainly be incorporated into any theory that seeks to generalize about the causes of crime.

Sutherland was aware that his theory of differential association was seriously incomplete. He knew that individuals differed in their responses to procriminal patterns and that, therefore, elements of social psychology relating to differences in personality traits must be included in a revised version of the theory (Sutherland, 1956:25–29; Sutherland and Cressey, [1949] 1970:83–87). He also knew that it was one thing to explain why a particular individual engages in crime but quite another to explain why some social groups have higher or lower crime rates than others. Eventually, Sutherland gave some indications of the direction in which he would have addressed this latter difficulty concerning his theory of differential association. These indications are found in his concept of "differential social organization" (or "differential group organization"). Because criminologists (including Cressey in Sutherland and Cressey, [1949] 1970:87–91) are tempted to read more coherence into this concept than Sutherland himself could give it, we proceed with considerable caution.

Differential Social (Dis)Organization

Although his theory of differential association seemed to apply to the criminal behavior of individuals, Sutherland was also concerned with the question of why crime tended to be concentrated among certain groups in society. In his recollection of the development of the theory of differential association, Sutherland referred to the importance of three questions:

> One of these questions was, Negroes [sic], young-adult males, and city dwellers all have relatively high crime rates: What do these three groups have in common that places them in this position? Another question was, Even if feebleminded persons have a high crime rate, why do they commit crimes? It is not feeblemindedness as such, for some feebleminded persons do not commit crimes. Later I raised another question which became even more important in my search for generalizations. Crime rates have a high correlation with poverty if considered by areas of a city but a low correlation if considered chronologically in relation to the business cycle; this obvi-

ously means that poverty as such is not an important cause of crime. How are the varying associations between crime and poverty explained? (1956:15)

Sutherland (1947:8–9, 69–80) began to examine these sociological questions, albeit tentatively, in the context of his last version of differential association. Although almost wholly unintegrated, Sutherland's argument was that social organization in the United States had moved from a simple to a more complex and differentiated type as a result of the industrial revolution. At the same time there had been a relaxation in the uniformity of social control. Traditional social controls, such as those exercised uniformly within the family and local community and by religion, were increasingly challenged by the rise of economic and political individualism, increased social mobility, and material acquisitiveness. In the United States this process of social disorganization or, more accurately, reorganization (p. 75) had been exacerbated by successive waves of immigration and had resulted in culture conflict between different communities. Crime was one expression of this conflict. Crime rates would be higher in communities that lacked traditional social controls and that contained some social groups organized for criminal behavior. Crime was also, therefore, an expression of such differential social organization.

Through these incoherent remarks, Sutherland was trying to convey the idea that differential social organization explains the origin of crime and that differential association explains its transmission from one person to another. A final twist appeared in Sutherland's last major book, *White Collar Crime* (1949), in which he attempted, briefly and tantalizingly, to integrate his incoherent combination of differential association and differential social (dis)organization with Merton's concept of anomie:

Differential association is a hypothetical explanation of crime from the point of view of the process by which a person is initiated into crime. Social disorganization is a hypothetical explanation of crime from the point of view of the society. These two hypotheses are consistent with each other and one is the counterpart of the other. Both apply to ordinary crime as well as to **white-collar crime**.

Social disorganization may be either of two types: anomie, or the lack of standards which direct the behavior of members of a society in general or in specific areas of behavior; or the organization within a society of groups which are in conflict with reference to specified practices. Briefly stated, social disorganization may appear in the form of lack of standards or conflict of standards. (1983:255)

The Professional Thief (1937)

Sutherland's interest in the varying associations between crime and economic position led him to explore the crimes of those whose social position had little to do with poverty. This interest was expressed in his research on professional thieves and on white-collar crime.

Sutherland's book *The Professional Thief* was based on the recollections of Broadway Jones, alias "Chic Conwell," a professional thief, ex-drug addict, and ex-con from Philadelphia (or perhaps Boston) who had worked for twenty years as a pimp, pickpocket, shoplifter, and confidence man. Although most of the book was actually written by Conwell, Sutherland edited it for publication and wrote two interpretive chapters. Conwell's recollections provide a fascinating glimpse into the underworld of professional thieves and include details about criminal *argot* (slang); the roles of members in the mob (criminal group); rackets; the fix (techniques of avoiding conviction and/or doing time in prison); and thieves' images of the police, the law, and society at large. According to Conwell, the work habits of professional thieves are very similar to the practices of those engaged in lawful business activities:

> Professional stealing as a business is much like any other business. The conversation among thieves in a police station, prison, or hangout is concerned principally with their business, and it is no different in that respect from the conversation of monument salesmen in their meetings. Business possibilities, conditions, and returns are the foremost subjects of conversation, and just as the salesman learns of fertile territory, new methods, new laws which affect the business, so does the thief.
>
> It involves as much hard work as any other business. There is little thrill about it. . . . It is no more thrilling than the work of the factory slave. (Sutherland, 1937:140)

Sutherland's *The Professional Thief* is a classic in the history of criminology for two critical reasons. First, it provides an image of crime that is a decided alternative to the stereotypical picture of disreputable activities engaged in by poorer members of the working class. Indeed, Sutherland's portrayal of crime in this book points to the considerable skills and abilities needed to be a professional thief and to the code of ethics extant among professional thieves. This is a far cry from the popular image of criminals as mentally defective personalities or as biologically deformed individuals. In addition, it shows that the world of professional thievery is a fairly exclusive club, one to which all the learning principles of differential association fully apply. Second, the analysis in *The Professional Thief* carries through to its logical conclusion the Chicago school's theory that criminologists should investigate criminality "in the flesh" and "on the street" rather than in the comfort of their armchairs.

White Collar Crime (1949)

We have seen how Sutherland (1949) argued that socially injurious acts (such as white-collar offenses) should be part of the proper subject matter of criminology regardless of how such acts are defined in legal terms (see Chapter 1.2). In this section we outline the findings of Sutherland's courageous book *White Collar Crime* (1949). This book amplified certain of his concerns in *The Professional Thief* and extended the scope of differential association theory to "white-collar crime," a term that Sutherland coined. It was Sutherland's last major venture in criminology, and it was to be his most important contribution.

Sutherland had become distressed, at least since the mid-1930s, that criminology had devoted nearly all its energies to analyzing the crimes of the poor (Geis and Goff, 1983). In the opening sentence of *White Collar Crime*, he remarked dryly that "criminal statistics show unequivocally that crime, as popularly understood and officially measured, has a high

BOX 5.2 THE PROFESSION OF THEFT

According to Sutherland's analysis of Conwell's depiction of the professional thief, the profession of theft has five basic features: technical skill, status, consensus, differential association, and organization (Sutherland, 1937:197–228):

1. **Technical Skill.** Like bricklayers, lawyers, and physicians, professional thieves have a stock of abilities and skills. Wits, front, speaking ability, manual dexterity, and specialization are all needed to plan and execute crimes, to dispose of stolen goods, and to fix those cases in which arrests occur.
2. **Status.** Like other professionals, the professional thief occupies a certain status based on such factors as ability, knowledge, dress, manners, wealth, and power. Professional thieves therefore often show contempt toward amateur, small-time, and "snatch-and-grab" thieves.
3. **Consensus.** Professional thieves usually share similar values that aid them in their criminal careers. Their reactions to certain things, including such things as prospective victims and squealing on other thieves, tend to be similar. "These reactions are like the 'clinical intuitions,'" Sutherland diagnosed, "which different physicians form of a patient or different lawyers form of a juryman on quick inspection" (p. 202).
4. **Differential Association.** For reasons of security and safety, professional thieves often maintain a barrier between themselves and all others. They tend to associate chiefly with members of their own professional group. The group defines its own members because only professional thieves are received into it.
5. **Organization.** Because technical skills, status, consensus, and differential association form a core of knowledge informally shared by thieves in a network of cooperation, professional theft is organized crime (essentially, crime that is organized).

incidence in the lower socioeconomic class and a low incidence in the upper socioeconomic class" (Sutherland, 1983:3). Sutherland complained that official statistics of crime, most case studies, and Shaw and McKay-inspired analyses based thereon gave a distorted picture of the social distribution of criminality. These statistics and studies wrongly implied, for example, that poverty was the chief cause of crime. Yet Sutherland felt sure, from his preliminary studies of embezzlers and of the diverse crimes committed by large U.S. corporations, that criminality was far from being the preserve of the poor. Just as much as the poor, if not more so, it was the rich who committed crimes. In this attempt to reverse the familiar object of U.S. criminology—away from the crimes of the poor and toward those of the rich—lay the heart of Sutherland's revelations in *White Collar Crime*.

Sutherland defined **white-collar crime** as "a crime committed by a person of respectability and high social status in the course of his occupation" (1983:7). His studies of white-collar crime had two main thrusts, neither of which had been explored adequately before his description of them. The first was an estimate of the extent of white-collar crime, the second a theoretical explanation of the causes of white-collar crime.

The thesis of Sutherland's *White Collar Crime* is that persons of the upper socioeconomic class engage in much criminal behavior. His exposé of white-collar crime included a battery of staggering statistics provided by U.S. government agencies. For example, according to the U.S. Comptroller of the Currency, 75 percent of all banks that had been examined had violated banking laws. According to the Federal Trade Commission, commercial bribery was a prevalent and common practice of many industries. "The financial cost of white-collar crime," Sutherland estimated from the sparse data available prior to his study, "is probably several times as great as the financial cost of all the crimes which are customarily regarded as the 'crime problem'" (1983:9). However, the bulk of Sutherland's data in *White Collar Crime* consisted of decisions of federal, state, and municipal courts and administrative commissions involving the seventy largest manufacturing, mining, and mercantile corporations in the United States. Among the worst corporate offenders were such giants as American Sugar Refining; American Tobacco; Armour; DuPont; Ford; General Electric; General Motors; Gimbel; A&P; International Harvester; Loew's; Montgomery Ward; National Steel; Procter and Gamble; Sears, Roebuck; U.S. Steel; Warner Brothers; Westinghouse Electric; and Woolworth. Sutherland reported in painstaking detail that in the preceding twenty years

> each of the 70 large corporations has 1 or more decisions against it, with a maximum of 50. The total number of decisions is 980, and the average per corporation is 14.0. Sixty corporations have decisions against them for restraint of trade, 53 for infringement, 44 for unfair labor practices, 43 for miscellaneous offenses, 28 for misrepresentation in advertising, and 26 for rebates. (p. 15)

Of the seventy largest industrial and commercial U.S. corporations, 97.1 percent were recidivists in that they had two or more decisions against them. In addition, Sutherland also revealed that the Federal Trade Commission, by order of Congress, reported that during the 1914–1918 and 1939–1945 world wars many corporations had violated wartime regulations (p. 174–191). These violations included price regulation abuse, overcharging and fraudulent profiteering in war-related materials, tax evasion, restraint of trade, illegal maintenance of competitive positions, violations of embargoes and neutrality, and even treason (for example, illegally revealing classified information to the enemy). As Sutherland concluded: "The large corporations in time of war, when Western civilization was endangered, did not sacrifice their own interests and participate wholeheartedly in a national policy, but instead they attempted to use this emergency as an opportunity for extraordinary enrichment of themselves at the expense of others" (p. 191).

With these data Sutherland demonstrated that in order to maximize their profits, U.S. corporations routinely committed crimes against consumers, competitors, stockholders and other investors, inventors, employees, and the state itself. Corporations tended to commit more crimes the greater their age, the larger their size, and the more their economic position was monopolistic, anti-union, and dependent on advertising (pp. 258–263).

Sutherland complained vigorously that the criminal behavior of the lower socioeconomic class differs from the criminal behavior of white-collar and corporate offenders chiefly in the respective ways that society deals with them. The former are typically processed by the criminal justice system, the latter by quasi-judicial review boards and administrative agencies. The typical outcome for the former is prison, but for the latter it is a warning, an order to desist, or a fine (see Chapter 12). Indeed, these very different outcomes tend to hide the criminal nature of white-collar crime from the public, from the press, and from criminologists themselves.

We note also that in his explanation of white-collar crime, Sutherland preferred to ignore almost entirely both the economic form that this crime typically took and also the ways in which economic cycles (such as the Great Depression of the 1930s) stimulated economic and other abuses by the powerful. Sutherland attempted to explain the causes of white-collar crime in terms of his earlier general theory of crime. "The significant thing about white-collar crime," he emphasized, "is that it is not associated with poverty or with social and personal pathologies which accompany poverty" (1983:7). Because he had shown how white-collar crimes often occur, he believed that a general theory linking crime, poverty, and the latter's related pathologies was entirely invalid. The only factors common to the crimes of the rich and the poor, he theorized, were differential social organization and differential association (pp. 240–257).

Differential social organization fosters white-collar crime because it underpins the anomic ideology that free enterprise should not be regulated by government. Because of this ideology, neither the U.S. government nor the community is well organized to counter white-collar and corporate crime. Differential association fosters the transmission of white-collar crime because profit-seeking corporations rapidly mimic the techniques of their successful competitors and because specific techniques of violating the law are passed from one executive to another. These techniques are themselves part of a widespread corporate ideology favorable to violation of law, an ideology exemplified by such maxims as, "We are not in business for our health" and "Business is business."

Assessment

Sutherland was a pioneer who contributed immeasurably to the development of criminology. His questioning of the basic subject matter of criminology—and its extension to social harms not always perceived, defined, or processed as crimes—was a valuable insight inadequately appreciated by many criminologists even today. His search for a general theory of crime was one of the first attempts by a criminologist to make explicit the ever-present role of sociological theory in all studies of crime. These two contributions guided Sutherland's search for the factual revelations in his books *The Professional Thief* and *White Collar Crime*, both milestones in criminology. As we shall learn, Sutherland's theoretical focus on the origin (differential social organization) and on the transmission (differential association) of criminal values was soon to influence new lines of inquiry in criminology, including the analysis of delinquent subcultures (see Chapter 6.1 and 6.2) and of the processes of control (see Chapter 7.1) and learning (Chapter 7.2).

REVIEW

This chapter outlined the early forms of criminological theory in the United States. The institutional position of criminology in the United States was dramatically transformed during the Progressive Era (circa 1890–1910). Before the Progressive Era, criminology was conducted in an unorganized and amateurish way; afterward, it found a secure and well-founded base in the universities. U.S. criminology rapidly gained global dominance, although its domination of criminological theory has created some hardship for the development of comparative criminology (see Chapter 16).

The Early History of Criminology in the United States, 1895–1915

1. Intellectually, the vast majority of pre–1900 writings on crime took the nature of crime and criminality entirely for granted.

2. In addition to native concern with the crimes of immigrants, blacks, and other outsiders, early writings on crime borrowed piecemeal from European concepts of crime, especially those connected with biology.

3. Criminology emerged generally from the Progressive Era's (1890–1910) social reformism. It depended specifically on the support of the social science movement, the rise of various professional associations, and mass media stimulation of public interest in its pronouncements on the causes of crime. Gradually, criminology admitted the relevance of social factors to its investigations.

Crime and Social Ecology

1. Initially, sociological criminology in the United States was almost exclusively identified with the perspective of social ecology developed by the Chicago school from 1920 onward. Chicago was an important site of the progressive movement, and the city naturally lent itself to the study of social problems, including crime.

2. The Chicago school adopted and spread several innovative research techniques, including both quantitative and qualitative methods. The latter involved life-history documents, case studies, investigative journalism, media materials, in-depth interviews, and participant observation. These methods, it was believed, would produce objective, value-free knowledge.

3. Shaw and McKay's *Juvenile Delinquency and Urban Areas* (1942) concluded that many social problems, including juvenile delinquency, were concentrated in zones of transition populated by white lower-class immigrants and by blacks. This concentration was correlated with such factors as rates of adult crime, school truancy, disease, and mental disorders, and it remained highly stable despite resident turnover in the zones of transition. Certain of these problems, it was felt, could be alleviated by a change in the local community's values.

4. The Chicago school has been extremely influential in the development of sociological criminology. Nevertheless, it has been criticized for its factual errors and its empiricist theory.

Social Structure, Anomie, and Deviance

1. This section examined Merton's influential article "Social Structure and Anomie" (1938). Merton's analysis of deviance and crime in part developed from the work of Durkheim and the Chicago school.

2. Merton argued that certain societies, like the United States, are unstable because they fail to provide adequate means for achieving socially approved goals.

3. Failure to achieve socially approved goals leads to various structural responses: conformity, innovation, ritualism, retreatism, and rebellion.

4. Because it is based on various unproven assumptions, the validity of Merton's analysis of deviance is somewhat suspect.

The Criminology of Edwin Sutherland

1. Sutherland tried to combine an explicit sociological theory of crime with detailed empirical analyses. Significantly, he attempted to extend the proper subject matter of criminology beyond state-defined categories of social injury.

2. Sutherland's general theory of differential association attempted to explain both conformity and deviation. It held that a person engages in crime because of an excess of definitions favorable to violation of law over definitions unfavorable to violation of law. Crime is thus learned behavior. By merging social disorganization theory with differential association theory, Sutherland attempted, largely unsuccessfully, to explain the origins of crime and its cultural transmission.

3. In *The Professional Thief* (1937) and *White Collar Crime* (1949), Sutherland pioneered analyses of certain crimes not often considered crimes either by the public or by criminologists, and often not processed as crimes by the criminal justice system. The first book examined the crimes and cultural world of professional thieves; the second book examined the occupational crimes routinely committed by white-collar executives in large corporations. Sutherland explained the transmission and persistence of these crimes with the theory of differential association.

4. Sutherland's theories of the causes of crime have proven very difficult to test, largely because their content is imprecise and their scope is so general. Yet they remain the starting point for much analysis of crime today.

QUESTIONS FOR CLASS DISCUSSION

1. In the late 1920s, lawyer Jerome Michael and philosopher Mortimer Adler were commissioned by Columbia University Law School and by the Bureau of Social Hygiene in New York City to write a report on the desirability of establishing an institute of criminology in the United States. In their lengthy final report, Michael and Adler scrutinized the scientific status of existing criminology and concluded that "the work of criminologists has not resulted in scientific knowledge of the phenomena of crime" (1971:54). Do you agree with this claim?

2. Was Shaw and McKay's *Juvenile Delinquency and Urban Areas* (1942) scientific? How does a scientific explanation of crime differ from other types of explanation, such as a religious one? Are sociological and scientific explanations of the same sort? Can we understand the causes of social behavior (for example, crime) in the same way that natural scientists, such as biologists and physicists, understand the behavior of animals and inanimate objects?

3. When Shaw and McKay pinpointed the links between juvenile delinquency and the social organization of Chicago neighborhoods, were these links causative or correlational?

4. Does Merton's typology of deviance actually explain variations in crime rates?

5. Discuss the following (Sutherland, 1947:7–8): "The attempts by many scholars to explain criminal behavior by general drives and values—such as the happiness principle, striving for social status, the money motive, or frustration—have been and continue to be futile since they explain lawful behavior as completely as they explain criminal behavior. They are similar to respiration, which is necessary for any behavior but which does not differentiate criminal from noncriminal behavior."

6. Why does the mass media not cover white-collar crime as much as it does some other types of crime, such as violent crime?

FOR FURTHER STUDY

Readings

Costello, Barbara. 1997. On the Logical Adequacy of Cultural Deviance Theories. *Theoretical Criminology* 1 (4): 403–429.

Gaylord, Mark S., and John F. Galliher. 1988. *The Criminology of Edwin Sutherland.* New Brunswick, N.J.: Rutgers University Press.

Rafter, Nicole Hahn. 1997. Psychopathy and the Evolution of Criminological Knowledge. *Theoretical Criminology* 1 (2): 235–259.

Sumner, Colin. 1994. *The Sociology of Deviance: An Obituary.* New York: Continuum.

Websites

1. <http://www.sad.ch/sid/forschung/anomieresearch.html>: This site summarizes current research on anomie, as well as its application. Students should be able to see clearly how a given theoretical perspective influences a particular social policy.

2. <http://www.seweb.uci.edu/overview.html>: This is an overview of the study of social ecology provided by the School of Social Ecology at the University of California at Irvine. It traces the foundations of the ecological approach within sociology.

Delinquent Subcultures and Subcultures of Delinquency

Preview

Chapter 6 introduces:

- the ways in which—beginning in the mid-1950s—criminologists have attempted to explain the origins, beliefs, and activities of male, lower-class, delinquent subcultures
- explanations of violent delinquent subcultures
- the anti-positivist theory of David Matza, which argues that delinquents are not nearly so committed to their activities as subcultural theorists have supposed
- social control theory as an explanation of delinquency

Key Terms

containment theory	social control
control theory	status frustration
drift	subculture
middle-class measuring rod	techniques of neutralization
reaction formation	

6.1   DELINQUENT SUBCULTURES

Chapter 5 examined Merton's (1938) theory of anomie and Sutherland's (1947) theory of differential association. Following the 1939–1945 war hiatus, these two theories exercised enormous influence over criminology. During the 1950s many criminologists examined the subcultural settings in which deviant values coexist with dominant social values. These subcultural theorists took their theoretical perspectives directly from the earlier writings of Merton and Sutherland. The central question of the subcultural theorists repeated Durkheim's question: Given the widespread persistence of deviance, what functions do deviant values serve for those who subscribe to them? This section outlines the key answers given to this question.

As research on delinquent subcultures developed during the 1950s, it gradually recognized the importance of a variable never properly examined by the Chicago school—the influence of social class. We begin our outline of subcultural theory with Albert Cohen's book *Delinquent Boys* (1955).

A. K. Cohen's *Delinquent Boys* (1955)

Cohen's *Delinquent Boys* begins with the premise that juvenile delinquency is a major practicable problem of every sizable American community. All attempts to control delinquency had failed, Cohen argued, because none had accurately identified its causes. Cohen (pp. 32–33) stressed that the Chicago school had overemphasized the social disorganization of the zones of transition (see Chapter 5.2) and that these areas were not nearly so lacking in community spirit as researchers such as Shaw and McKay had imagined.

Moreover, Cohen was critical of Mertonian anomie theory (see Chapter 5.3; and Cohen, 1965) because it had failed to come to grips with the content of juvenile gangs. Cohen believed further that Merton had ignored the fact that delinquent gangs do not simply use deviant means to achieve culturally approved goals. Far from it, he insisted, delinquent gangs often seem to engage in violence simply for "the hell of it" (1955:35–36). And Sutherland's theory of differential association, too, failed to explain why some juveniles join gangs and others do not (see Chapter 5.4). Moreover, Cohen felt that Sutherland had taken for granted the existence of juvenile gangs and had failed to ask certain questions: Where do gangs come from? What are their origins? Why do delinquent gangs exist in some social settings but not in others?

About Sutherland, with whom he had done graduate study at Indiana, Cohen recorded his feeling that the theory of differential association

> has to do with how people come to acquire the delinquent or criminal culture through a process of association. But, I asked, Where does it come from? How do you explain the existence of the culture? . . . But [Sutherland] didn't think that was much of a question. Somewhere he said, actually he wrote it too, that the southern practice of dropping the r's is explained by the southern practice of dropping the r's—that's all you have to know—which incidentally is wrong. It sounds on the face of it that it might say something but the point is, some speech practices become extinct, others spread and you get novelties linguistically. Some catch on, others don't. So it really wasn't a very good answer. (quoted in Laub, 1983:189)

For Cohen, then, existing theories in criminology did not explain much about delinquent behavior. No theory had seriously examined the values and beliefs of juvenile gang members and the nature and causes of their activities. Why do some juveniles, and not others, join delinquent gangs? Why do gangs do what they do? Why do gangs persist in urban neighborhoods?

Cohen's *Delinquent Boys* tried to answer such questions by beginning with the idea that the world of juvenile delinquents is enveloped in a **subculture**. Although the term "subculture" had been in use among anthropologists at least since the 1870s, it was Cohen who first applied it to the study of delinquency (Wolfgang and Ferracuti, 1967:95–99). "Culture," for Cohen, refers to the knowledge, beliefs, values, codes, tastes, and prejudices that persist in the social relations people have regularly in their interactions with each other. A subculture, then, is a set of beliefs (and so forth) that differs in some way from the main or dominant culture. Taking part in delinquent acts is a major aspect of delinquent subcultures. As Cohen himself defined it, a delinquent subculture is "a way of life that has somehow become traditional among certain groups in American society. These groups are the boys' gangs that flourish most conspicuously in the 'delinquency neighborhoods' of our larger American cities" (1955:13).

Cohen reasoned that a good theory of delinquent subcultures must explain the existence of the six subcultural characteristics displayed in Box 6.1. But it must also explain *why* subcultures typically flourish *where* they do in the class structure.

Cohen argued that subcultures exist because they provide a solution to certain problems of adjustment shared by a group of individuals. Why, then, is the delinquent subculture found mostly in working-class environments? In his explanation, Cohen began with the

BOX 6.1   A. K. COHEN'S SUBCULTURE OF DELINQUENT BOYS

According to Cohen (1955:24–28), the subculture of delinquent boys has six major characteristics in the United States:

1. Its activities are *nonutilitarian, malicious,* and *negativistic:* Gang members are nonutilitarian because, for example, they sometimes steal simply for the hell of it; they are malicious because they take delight in others' discomfort, in terrorizing "good" children, and in flouting teachers and their rules (such as, defecating on a teacher's desk); and they are negativistic because their delinquent conduct is right by the standards of the subculture precisely because it is wrong by conventional standards.
2. *Versatility:* Gang members rarely specialize in types of delinquent acts as do adult criminals and solitary delinquents.
3. *Short-run hedonism:* Gang members have little interest in long-run goals, a fact that reflects their lower-class origins. Typically, they "hang around," "chew the fat," and "wait for something to turn up."
4. *Group autonomy:* Gang members are intensely loyal to their own gang, very hostile to others, and resist even the efforts of their families to control them.
5. *Working-class membership:* Although cautious about relying on official crime statistics, Cohen nevertheless agrees that juvenile delinquency—especially the juvenile subculture—is overwhelmingly concentrated in the working class.
6. *Male:* Although Cohen recognized the existence of female gangs and of solitary delinquency engaged in by females, he agreed with official statistics showing that delinquent subcultures are masculine dominated (see Chapter 15.2).

position of the family unit in the local community. He noted that, although the boundaries between working-class and middle-class families are sometimes indistinct, nevertheless, child-rearing practices do vary between different classes. Crucially, all children are not equally well prepared to satisfy the standards by which U.S. society evaluates their passage to adulthood. Working-class parents, for example, place less emphasis than do middle-class parents on development of analytical skills, education, self-denying discipline, and long-term planning for adult status and career; they place more emphasis on physical prowess in groups and learning through "having fun." However, because *all* children are evaluated by middle-class standards, some children are doomed to be seen as failures in middle-class terms.

The prevailing middle-class standards (the **middle-class measuring rod**) by which all children are evaluated, especially in schools, include: ambition; individual responsibility; outstanding achievement, especially academic or athletic; industry and thrift; foresight; manners, courtesy, and personality; control of physical aggression; constructive leisure; and respect for property (1955:88–91). Because middle-class children tend to acquire these skills from their parents and peers far more than do working-class children, most adolescent failures are drawn from the working class. Above all, it is in the school—that supremely middle-class institution—that working-class boys fail. Failure in school often results in **status frustration**, which causes feelings of "guilt, self-recrimination, anxiety, and self-hatred" (p. 126). Because the working-class boy finds himself at the bottom of the status hierarchy, he is now in the market for a solution (p. 119).

According to Cohen it is within the working-class delinquent subculture that the otherwise-unadjusted working-class boy finds a solution to his lack of status in middle-class life. The delinquent subculture, therefore, operates as an "adjustment mechanism" for many working-class adolescents. Adjustment occurs through a process of **reaction formation**, in which the academic success typically denied working-class boys is contemptuously redefined as the "bookish knowledge" of "sissies," whereas "street knowledge," which is learned from friends in the delinquent gang, is regarded as superior to other forms of knowledge. In general, the virtues of the working-class gang include the practices regarded by the middle class as vices: nonutilitarian, malicious, and negativistic activities. The gang confers a much-needed high status on members who practice these activities; this status is typically denied working-class adolescents when they participate in an alien middle-class world.

Additionally, Cohen addressed two further problems about delinquency that were almost completely ignored in his era and are largely so in ours: female delinquency (pp. 137–147) and middle-class delinquency (pp. 157–169).

Regarding female delinquency, Cohen suggested that because females are not socialized into being successful in the male-dominated realms of society, young females do not have the adjustment problems characteristic of male, working-class "failures." Although young females can eventually find additional satisfaction in a career, successful relationships with the opposite sex are the primary means by which they derive status. Their activities focus, therefore, on popularity with boys, dating, beautification, charm, clothes, and dancing. Although involvement in a delinquent subculture can increase the masculine status of a boy, it can only do harm to the feminine status of a girl. Cohen concluded that for a boy the delinquent response, "'wrong' though it may be and 'disreputable,' is well within the range of responses that do not threaten his identification of himself as a male" (p. 140).

Regarding middle-class delinquency, Cohen pointed out rightly that its very existence must embarrass those who argue that a poor or working-class background is the chief cause of delinquency in general. He therefore speculated that this embarrassment may stem from inadequate concepts of social class (namely, because lower-class and middle-class families may in fact be culturally closer to each other than is usually admitted, boys from both groups might be responding to the same cultural tensions). Another possibility, according to Cohen—which ties in well with other aspects of his theory—is that middle-class delinquent subcultures respond to the same tensions of gender identification as do their working-class counterparts. As Cohen argued in sociopsychological terms:

Because of the structure of the modern family and the nature of our occupational system, children of both sexes tend to form early feminine identifications. The boy, however, unlike the girl, comes later under strong social pressure to establish his masculinity, his difference from female figures. Because his mother is the object of the feminine identification which he feels is the threat to his status as a male, he tends to

"Bloods" gang member: Criminologists have traditionally ignored not only female crime but also female delinquency.

react negativistically to those conduct norms which have been associated with mother and therefore have acquired feminine significance. Since mother has been the principal agent of indoctrination of "good," respectable behavior, "goodness" comes to symbolize femininity, and engaging in "bad" behavior acquires the function of denying his femininity and therefore asserting his masculinity. This is the motivation to juvenile delinquency. (p. 164)

Consequently, Cohen reasoned that males from middle-class homes may join delinquent gangs as well.

It is appropriate now to mention three problems in Cohen's analysis. First, we note that much of the importance of Cohen's work lies in the original way in which it extended to delinquent boys an explanation of Merton's category of the rebellious deviant. At root, however, both Merton and Cohen shared the view that deviance (Merton) and delinquency (Cohen) arise as a reaction of the lower classes to their failure in middle-class terms. In this view, working-class activities, such as boys' delinquency, are wholly parasitic on middle-class practices. Indeed, what this view of delinquency ignored was precisely what the Chicago school of ecology had emphasized (at least in principle)—the importance of granting authenticity to the values of the deviants themselves. In other words, do working-class delinquents themselves regard their activities as a response to "failure"?

Second, like nearly all his contemporaries, Cohen did not refer to the importance of race in his explanations of juvenile subcultures in the United States. As Colin Sumner complains:

> No one seemed to notice the point that if the delinquent culture was so common in US cities perhaps it was not so 'sub', and few made anything of the fact that its occupants were mostly black. Their blackness, and the blackness of the so-called subculture, was completely glossed over in the theory. . . . The subculture was truly an abstraction from reality. . . . There was to be a stark awakening in the sixties; one which would render the abstraction of the subculture somewhat farcical. (1994:181)

Third, Cohen failed to provide empirical evidence that working-class delinquents accept middle-class success goals. In what sense, we are compelled to ask, does the subculture of working-class juvenile delinquency actually reject middle-class values? This question was soon addressed by other subcultural theorists, to whom we now turn.

Delinquency and Lower-Class Culture

Cohen's *Delinquent Boys* rapidly stimulated numerous responses from criminologists and a wealth of new research into the diverse origins, functions, and forms of delinquent subcultures. There follows an outline of the most influential arguments of this research.

The first major criticism of Cohen's findings was developed by Walter Miller in his article "Lower Class Culture as a Generating Milieu of Gang Delinquency" (1958). The bulk of Miller's data came from reports of daily contact with ghetto youth in a large eastern city during a three-year project into the control of juvenile delinquency. The subjects of the study were both black and white, male and female, and in early, middle, and late adolescence.

Miller suggested that adolescent members of delinquent gangs, and of other forms of "street corner society," are not psychopaths, nor are they physically or mentally defective. Far from it. Gang members are often drawn from the most "able" sections of the community. Why, then, do they commit crimes? Reasoned Miller: "The most general answer is that the commission of crimes . . . is motivated primarily by the attempt to achieve ends, states, or conditions which are valued, and to avoid those that are disvalued within their most meaningful cultural milieu" (p. 346).

For achieving these ends, gang members tend to choose the most accessible means available. Miller argued that the lower-class way of life has a set of ends, or focal concerns, that include trouble, toughness, smartness, excitement, fate, and autonomy. These focal concerns differ greatly from those of the middle classes. For example, whereas the middle class might value achievement in high school examinations, the lower class values the smartness embodied in the capacity to outfox, outwit, or con others. The distinctive focal concerns of the lower class derive from aspects of its structural position in U.S. society.

According to Miller, 40–60 percent of the United States is influenced directly by lower-class culture, and of this, 15 percent composes the "hard-core lower class group" (p. 334, n. 3). Above all, this latter group is characterized by its distinctive family unit—the female-headed household (see Chapter 15.2). The female-headed household is one that "lacks" a permanent male parent or that has no male parent involved in child care and family support.

According to Miller, the major factor that pushes lower-class boys into joining delinquent gangs is the widespread presence of female-headed households in their cultural milieu. Why is this so? Miller depicted the lower-class boy as the victim of a female web of neglect. Because he is surrounded by females, the lower-class boy suffers from acute identity crises, especially those crises associated with problems of gender-role identification (see Chapter 15.2). Miller argued that the female-headed household does not provide "a range of essential functions—psychological, educational, and others"—for the lower-class boy (p. 342). These functions, Miller concluded, are typically provided by the most accessible means available: the corner group and the gang. The focal concerns (smartness, and others) of the gang parallel those of lower-class life in general. But the gang also embraces two further concerns that in combination explain their territoriality and their positive values: (1) belonging, or adherence to the rules of the gang; and (2) status (derived from smartness, and others) *as it is defined within the cultural framework of lower-class society.*

Miller therefore reasoned that the delinquent gang functions to resolve crucial problems generated by the cultural, and especially the family, milieu of lower-class boys. But for Miller, unlike Cohen, the gang resolves these problems in its own cultural framework rather than in reaction to the cultural standards of the middle class. As an aside, we note that there is no evidence that boys in single-parent (female- or male-headed) households, for example, are more likely to be deprived emotionally or psychologically than boys in two-parent households (see Chapter 15.4).

Despite the antifeminist leanings of his argument, Miller casts serious doubt on the validity of Cohen's theory in one important respect. Recall that Cohen assumed that lower-class boys react to failure in middle-class worlds (such as school) and, as a result, seek status in the more familiar setting of the delinquent subculture. What Miller questions, quite correctly, is Cohen's assumption that the lower-class boy has no authentic values that identify gangs as good things to belong to simply because they are good things to which to belong.

Delinquency and Opportunity

Miller was part of a group of delinquency theorists (the Chicago school, Merton, and Cohen) who took the style and direction of delinquent subcultures, or gangs, very much for granted. However, this great simplification was uncovered by Richard Cloward and Lloyd Ohlin in their book *Delinquency and Opportunity* (1960). To explain why some juveniles violate conventional norms does not explain variations in the particular form of their deviant actions (such as theft, violence, drug use/abuse, and so forth). Why, for example, do some gangs allegedly focus on violence, some on theft, and still others on drug use/abuse? Following Merton's theory of anomie, Cloward and Ohlin asserted that delinquent subcultures arise because of a gap between the aspirations of lower-class youth and the pos-

TABLE 6.1   Cloward and Ohlin's Classification of Lower-Class Youth

Categories of Lower-Class Youth	Orientation of Lower-Class Youth	
	Toward Membership in Middle Class	*Toward Improvement in Economic Position*
Type I	+	+
Type II	+	−
Type III	−	+
Type IV	−	−

SOURCE: Cloward and Ohlin, 1960: 95.

sibility of their achieving those aspirations through legitimate means. However, the effects of the gap between aspirations and frustrated achievement vary from one individual to another. The direction of variation depends on two basic types of legitimate aspiration—aspirations for higher status (achieved by membership in the middle class) and for greater economic success (pp. 90–94). Table 6.1 outlines Cloward and Ohlin's four major categories of male lower-class youth.

According to Cloward and Ohlin, both Type I and Type II boys aspire to middle-class status. However, Type II boys regard a change in their reference groups as more important than greater economic success. Cloward and Ohlin agree with Cohen that when faced with frustrated opportunities for upward social mobility, boys of these two types are the ones most likely to react against middle-class values because these boys are the ones who most want to be accepted by the middle class. Type III boys, who want more economic success (namely, money) but who are neither interested in middle-class values nor in becoming middle class, seek higher status in their own cultural milieu. They want "'big cars,' 'flashy clothes,' and 'swell dames'" (p. 96). It is this group that composes the majority of delinquents. Type IV boys are street-corner boys who are not interested in social mobility in any sphere. These boys drop out, in other words, without dropping into anything else. Although they are sometimes criticized for lack of ambition, these boys rarely get into trouble with the law.

Cloward and Ohlin's astute analysis of delinquent subcultures clearly avoided an error made by Cohen. It did not assume, as Cohen's had, that the cause of most juvenile delinquency is the failure of lower-class youth to succeed in middle-class institutions such as schools. Even though they may fail, and even though they may be alienated from the school, lower-class delinquents do not become delinquent solely because of failure in school. The causative factors in delinquency are likely to be more complicated than the process suggested by Cohen. As Cloward and Ohlin indicated:

Type III youth are alienated from the school because of a conflict regarding appropriate success-goals; this conflict simply reinforces their own definitions of criteria of success [i.e., making money versus making it into the middle class]. If these youngsters subsequently become delinquent, it is chiefly because they anticipate that legitimate channels to the goals they seek will be limited or closed. (p. 97)

Finally, Cloward and Ohlin argued that the illegitimate means of achieving success are not evenly distributed within working-class communities. They identify three sorts of delinquent subculture participated in by Type III boys: (1) the criminal subculture, (2) the conflict subculture, and (3) the retreatist subculture.

The Criminal Subculture.   The legitimate aspirations of delinquency-prone boys are satisfied illegitimately in neighborhoods where a criminal subculture already exists. A criminal subculture has its own success models, learning techniques, and gradations of status (mainly by age). Its leading members are also part of the conventional culture of the community, thus lending the subculture a measure of stability and legitimacy. Its focus is the rational, albeit illegal, provision of opportunities for income through activities such as theft. In areas where no established criminal subculture is available, the typical avenue for potential delinquents is membership in either a conflict or a retreatist subculture (1960:161–171).

The Conflict Subculture.   The environs of the conflict subculture are typically poor, disorganized, transient, and unstable. The activities of the conflict subculture make it extremely visible to the media and to the public. These activities focus on interpersonal violence, gang warfare, and the physical destruction of property (pp. 171–178).

The Retreatist Subculture.   The retreatist subculture is the last avenue for boys who experience failure in both legitimate activities and also in the illegalities of the criminal and conflict subcultures. The focus of the retreatist subculture is the retreat into persistent drug use/abuse. Of course, not all lower-class youth who experience status and economic deprivation engage in drug use/abuse. But those who choose to use and abuse drugs persistently are those who either (1) experience the double failure just described or (2) cannot revise their aspirations downward, yet continue to experience the strain of frustrated opportunities (pp. 178–186).

The apparent implications of certain of the findings of Cloward and Ohlin's study were actively pursued as policy by the federal government. As Vold, Bernard, and Snipes (1998:169; and see Einstadter and Henry, 1995:168) describe:

> After Robert Kennedy, who was then attorney general of the U.S., read Cloward and Ohlin's book, he asked Lloyd Ohlin to help develop a new federal policy on juvenile delinquency. The result was the passage of the Juvenile Delinquency Prevention and Control Act of 1961, which was based on a comprehensive action program developed by Cloward and Ohlin in connection with their book. The program included improving education, creating work opportunities, organizing lower-class communities, and providing services to individuals, gangs, and families. The program was later expanded to include all lower-class people and became the basis of Lyndon Johnson's War on Poverty.

Billions of dollars were spent on the War on Poverty and other social welfare programs, but the War was eventually abandoned by President Nixon on the grounds that it showed no clear results. In fact, the reasons the program was abandoned are many and complex,

including conservative objections that government should not be in the business of eliminating social inequalities. It must be considered seriously whether the subcultural theorists, because they had failed to identify the causes of juvenile delinquency, misunderstood
the set of policies that should be implemented to contain it.

Assessment

As noted, theories of delinquent subcultures arose in the 1950s largely as an attempt to answer various questions ignored by the Chicago school. Yet, like their predecessors in the
Chicago school, the subcultural theorists continued either to ignore the delinquency of
young females or typically to view it in masculine terms. Additionally, they ignored the
delinquency of middle-class youth.

How much of an advance was the new subcultural criminology of the 1950s over the
Chicago school? As David Matza (1964:63) reported, the sociologists of delinquent subcultures provided two basic insights about delinquency. First, they showed that it typically
is not a solitary enterprise but a group activity. Second, they showed that delinquent activities, rather than being engaged in by biologically or psychologically deformed individuals, typically develop in the sociological context of particular territorial locales. Often
they develop in neighborhoods with cultural traditions associated with established gangs.

The criminology of the subcultural theorists was a real advance over earlier work in at
least two respects. First, the subcultural theorists explicitly raised what the Chicago school
left dormant: the relation between lower-class opportunities and the social and economic
inequality of the U.S. class structure. Moreover, the subcultural theorists implicitly condemned the economic inequalities, the blocked opportunities, and the strains that result
from class structure. The problem remains, however, as to whether they were correct in
concluding that benevolent social programs could contain the juvenile delinquency that
resulted from these economic conditions. Second, in some cases subcultural theory displayed considerable sensitivity to issues not previously raised. It recognized, for example,
that juvenile delinquency took a number of forms and was engaged in for a variety of
reasons.

In assessing the merits of subcultural theory, we also note that its findings provoked
widespread criticism. Certain early critics, in particular Kitsuse and Dietrick (1959), argued that Cohen, for example, overemphasized the extent to which the delinquency of
lower-class boys is a reaction to failing in middle-class terms. Perhaps most working-class
boys simply do not care about middle-class values. Do working-class boys have no authentic cultural traditions of their own? Other critics objected that the activities of delinquent gangs are utilitarian rather than nonutilitarian and far more diverse in character than
the subcultural theorists allowed. Still other critics objected that not enough emphasis had
been placed on the deviant psychological characteristics of juvenile gang leaders. For example, Lewis Yablonsky (1962) charged (without evidence) that gang leaders are typically
sociopaths.

Clarence Schrag (1962) argued that the theory of differential opportunity is too general
in the face of real world complexities. Schrag (p. 169) objected that Cloward and Ohlin's
theory fails to explain why, even in Type II and Type III communities, a substantial number of working-class boys do not join delinquent gangs. Why do some working-class boys

join gangs, but others do not? Schrag also pointed out that, especially in neighborhoods with high delinquency rates, delinquent gangs are far more diverse, more fluid, and less organized than Cloward and Ohlin maintain. Moreover, David Matza and Gresham Sykes (1961) disagreed with the subcultural theorists' portrayal of middle-class values as being centered on the Protestant ethic of hard work and abstemiousness. There are, they argued, numerous respectable subterranean values that both the middle class and the working class have in common, including the search for kicks and the identification of masculinity with toughness. In other words, Matza and Sykes questioned whether the activities of delinquent gangs really are deviant if those same activities find cultural support within the middle class.

6.2   MATZA'S *DELINQUENCY AND DRIFT* (1964)

In what at the time seemed to some criminologists a complete annihilation of subcultural explanations of delinquency, David Matza charged eloquently that subcultural theory failed altogether to understand the causes of juvenile delinquency. In his book *Delinquency and Drift,* Matza (1964:1–32) forcefully attacked the core assumptions of the lengthy positivist tradition that stretched from Quetelet's social mechanics (see Chapter 3.2) to the ideas of the subcultural theorists. At the same time, in this book, as well as in his *Becoming Deviant* (Matza, 1969) and in his writings with Gresham Sykes (Sykes and Matza, 1957; Matza and Sykes, 1961), Matza offered an alternative theory of delinquency.

The key concepts in Matza's theory of delinquency are (1) the "positive delinquent"; (2) the "subculture of delinquency"; and (3) "delinquency and drift" (neutralization, will, and preparation and desperation). To these we now turn.

The Positive Delinquent

According to Matza, positivist criminology made three explicit assumptions about crime and criminality. Each assumption, he argued, was wrong. Matza pointed out that positivist criminology assumed that the proper focus of criminological study should be the criminal rather than the criminal law. This assumption had involved a search for all sorts of motivational and socioeconomic causes of crime. However, the assumption ignored that crime is, above all, not only an action but also an infraction (namely, law breaking). In neglecting to study the legal and other institutions that define certain actions as infractions (in essence, crime and deviance), positivist criminology had "for close to a century display[ed] little concern for the essence of crime—infraction" (1964:5).

Moreover, positivist criminology had been unduly preoccupied with copying the methods of the natural sciences. Rejecting the free-will philosophies of classical criminology (see Chapter 3.1), the positivists had assumed, as a matter of faith, that all human action is determined by scientific law and that, therefore, humans are largely incapable of choice between different paths of action. "The positive delinquent does not exercise choice," Matza wrote, "his action is constrained [and he] must behave in a delinquent manner because of the determinants that have shaped him" (p. 11). Matza admitted that this approach of hard determinism, found especially in biological theories of crime, had given way in recent times to soft determinism. This modified analysis of delinquent subcultures endowed individuals with the capacity to exercise choice, but, Matza continued, advocates of soft determinism still basically believed that criminality is caused. This more subtle form of determinism is at the heart of linking crime with poverty, differential association, and the values of delinquent subcultures.

Further, argued Matza (1964:11–12), positivist criminology assumed that criminals are fundamentally different from the law-abiding citizenry. With the exception of eighteenth-century classical criminology, this assumption had been a central feature of all previous criminology. From this assumption it follows that criminals are thus constrained by a set of circumstances that simply do not apply to the law-abiding. However, Matza objected: "A reliance on differentiation, whether constitutional, personal, or sociocultural, as the key explanation of delinquency has pushed the standard-bearers of diverse theories to posit what have almost always turned out to be empirically undemonstrable differences" (p. 12).

Matza concluded that this doomed attempt to distinguish between the criminal and the law-abiding had resulted in, or perhaps paralleled, several other errors by the positivists. Because subcultural theorists had assumed that the values of delinquents differ from those of nondelinquents, for example, insufficient attention had been paid either to the values of society at large or to smaller units within it, such as the family (pp. 19–20). To study crime, Matza implied, we must look far beyond the immediate social environment where infraction is detected. Moreover, positivist criminology accounted for too much delinquency. It had been an "embarrassment of riches" that predicted far more delinquency than actually occurs. If delinquents really were as different from the law-abiding and as committed to the values of their subculture as the positivists had assumed, then

> involvement in delinquency would be more permanent and less transient, more pervasive and less intermittent than is apparently the case. Theories of delinquency yield an embarrassment of riches which seemingly go unmatched in the real world. This accounting for too much delinquency may be taken as an observable consequence of the distorted picture of the delinquent that has developed within positive criminology. (p. 22)

Matza's criticisms of the positivists' skeletal assumptions are most revealing. Matza's book *Delinquency and Drift,* however, did much more than simply criticize the explanations of subcultural theorists; as with several other texts in the emerging societal reaction and labeling perspectives (see Chapter 14.3), it also put forward an alternative image of delinquency.

The Subculture of Delinquency

The basis of Matza's alternative theory of delinquency is that *there is a subculture of delinquency but that it is not a delinquent subculture.* Matza began by saying that subcultural theorists were wrong to see the relationship between the values of a subculture of delinquency and the values of mainstream culture as one of opposition. Things are not so neat and tidy. By and large the vast majority of delinquents are children; it would therefore be surprising indeed if the subculture of delinquency were made up of children opposed strongly to the values of conventional mainstream culture. Matza believed, in other words, that juvenile delinquents are typically not very different from other juveniles and that their values are likely to be quite similar to nondelinquent youths.

These similarities between the conventional culture and the subculture of delinquency Matza termed "subterranean convergence." In many of their basic ideas the subculture of delinquency and the conventional culture converge: in cowboy masculinity, in the search for kicks and for excitement, in the Bohemian celebration of the primitive, and in the persistence of territorial sentiments in certain localities of large cities.

Matza suggested that the subculture of delinquency is of two minds regarding delinquency: One frame of mind allows and encourages its members to behave illegally and to gain prestige from doing so; the other reveals that the subculture remains basically committed to the important values of conventional culture. Both frames of mind must be examined if the subculture of delinquency is to be understood accurately. Moreover, Matza continued, conventional culture is often not quite as conventional as it is made out to be. Conventional culture is complex and many-sided. Its features consist not only of ascetic puritanism, middle-class morality, the Boy Scout oath, and the like—but also of hedonism, frivolity, and excitement (pp. 36–37).

Matza suggested that the way to understand the two-mindedness of the subculture of delinquency is to assess the posture of delinquents in a variety of circumstances (p. 40–59), especially in what he terms "the situation of apprehension" and "the situation of company." By the "situation of apprehension" Matza referred to the problem created if the subculture of delinquency and the conventional culture hold oppositional values: Delinquents will offer radical defenses of their activities when they are arrested by the police or when they are brought before a juvenile court. If the members of a subculture of delinquency are committed to their delinquent activities and values, they will feel almost no shame or guilt upon detection by authority. Yet juveniles commonly express feelings of genuine contrition on apprehension. Such feelings cannot simply be dismissed as a manipulative tactic designed to appease authority. The contrition of juveniles, Matza concluded, "cannot be ignored if we are to avoid the gross stereotype of the delinquent as a hardened gangster in miniature" (p. 41). With the exception of a few bizarre oddities—regarded by ordinary delinquents as crazy—delinquents rarely desire either to attack the values of conventional culture or to defend those of the subculture of delinquency. Moreover, if delinquents are so different from nondelinquents, why do the vast majority of them desist from delinquency at the end of their adolescence?

By "the situation of company" Matza referred to the understanding of delinquents when in the company of their peers. Matza suggested that the values of the subculture of delinquency are far more fluid and less clear than usually thought. He argued that these values are not, as such, learned formally by novice delinquents, because there is no written or formal code of delinquent values to be learned. Actually, many things are not discussed openly and must be inferred (often wrongly!) by novices from the hints and the cues of their friends. During entry into the subculture of delinquency, boys—there are very few females in Matza's *Delinquency and Drift*—suffer status anxiety about their masculinity. How can they learn the values of the subculture of delinquency without revealing that they are not yet the fully committed delinquents they believe all the other boys to be? Matza suggested that they do this by cautiously sounding out other boys about masculinity and appropriate delinquent acts. Thus: "Do I really like you? Yea, come here and such and I'll show you how much I like you." Or: "Do I think that stealing a car is a good thing? Man you a fag or something? Ain't you one of the boys?" Serious discussion of delinquency is almost always impossible for delinquents because of the anxiety it would produce about their own masculinity. Whatever the motive, Matza concluded, "the function of such remarks is to mislead the delinquent into believing that his subculture is committed to delinquency" (p. 54).

However, Matza was keenly aware that this comedy of errors cannot continue indefinitely. Most boys discover eventually, often from one close friend in whose company their anxieties can be relaxed, that almost no one is actually committed to the subculture of delinquency. They discover, in other words, that all along they were wrong to believe that delinquents are committed to their misdeeds. The importance of this eye-opening information is reinforced as juveniles become adults (as boys become "real men"). The achievement of real masculinity is marked by such new signs of status as jobs, wives, children, and mortgages. The acquisition of these "obvious" signs of masculinity allows the ex-delinquent to reject the values and activities of the subculture as "kids' stuff." Dwindling remnants of the old gang mix with the company of younger cohorts. But the great majority of members of the subculture of delinquency do not become adult criminals.

Delinquency and Drift

Recall that, against the determinism of the positivist tradition, Matza was eager to assert the presence of a certain degree of choice and free will in human action. This assertion is found in his concept of **drift**. Matza suggested that the delinquent is committed neither to the subculture of delinquency nor to the conventional culture. Instead, the delinquent chooses, more or less consciously, to drift between the one and the other, often many times in the course of a single day.

> Drift stands midway between freedom and control. Its basis is an area of the social structure in which control has been loosened [and where it is] coupled with the abortiveness of adolescent endeavor to organize an autonomous subculture. . . . The delinquent transiently exists in a limbo between convention and crime, responding in turn to the demands of each, flirting now with one, now with the other, but postponing commitment, evading decision. Thus, he drifts between criminal and conventional action. (p. 28)

Matza's theory of delinquency and drift has three components: neutralization, will, and preparation and desperation.

Neutralization is the process by which potential delinquents are freed from conventional social and moral controls, and because of which they are then able to engage in delinquency (pp. 60–62, 69–100; Sykes and Matza, 1957). With Gresham Sykes, Matza (1957) argued that most juvenile delinquents are not nearly as committed to delinquent values and activities as subcultural theorists have supposed. Indeed, precisely because they are not really opposed to mainstream values, juveniles often display feelings of shame and guilt when their delinquency is detected and exposed. To shield novice delinquents from such feelings, experienced delinquents teach them a variety of techniques to rationalize and justify their behavior. For example, they teach them to say such things as, "I didn't mean it"; "I didn't really hurt anybody"; "They had it coming to them"; "Everybody's picking on me"; "I didn't do it for myself." These techniques operate to deflect or to neutralize the disapproval of such authority figures as judges, juvenile police officers, and probation workers.

Techniques of neutralization, then, generally reduce the effectiveness of social and moral controls. They allow juveniles to engage in delinquency despite the disapproval of authority figures or of their conforming peers. At the same time, Sykes and Matza were careful to note that such techniques are not powerful enough to shield all delinquents from

---

BOX 6.2   TECHNIQUES OF NEUTRALIZATION

According to Sykes and Matza (1957:667–670), there are five basic techniques of neutralization:

1. **Denial of Responsibility.**   Insofar as the delinquent can define himself as lacking responsibility for his deviant actions, the disapproval of self or others is sharply reduced in effectiveness as a restraining influence. It may also be asserted that delinquent acts are due to forces outside of the individual and beyond his control such as unloving parents, bad companions, or a slum neighborhood.
2. **Denial of Injury.**   The delinquent frequently, and in a hazy fashion, feels that his behavior does not really cause any great harm despite the fact that it runs counter to the law.
3. **Denial of Victim.**   Even if the delinquent accepts the responsibility for his deviant actions and is willing to admit that his deviant actions involve an injury or hurt, the moral indignation of self and others may be neutralized by an insistence that the injury is not wrong in light of the circumstances. The injury, it may be claimed, is not really an injury; rather, it is a form of rightful retaliation or punishment.
4. **Condemnation of Condemners.**   The delinquent shifts the focus of attention from his own deviant acts to the motives and behavior of those who disapprove of his violations. By attacking others, the wrongfulness of his own behavior is more easily repressed or lost to view.
5. **Appeal to Higher Loyalties.**   Internal and external social controls may be neutralized by sacrificing the demands of the larger society for the demands of the small social groups to which the delinquent belongs such as the sibling pair, the gang, or the friendship clique. The conflict between the claims of friendship and the claims of law, or a similar dilemma, has of course long been recognized. If the juvenile delinquent frequently resolves his dilemma by insisting that he must "always help a buddy" or "never squeal on a friend," even when it throws him into serious difficulties with the dominant social order, his choice remains familiar to the supposedly law-abiding.

feelings of shame and guilt. Moreover, some delinquents are so isolated from the conforming world of the dominant culture that neutralization techniques are not even useful.

Matza (1964) argued that the neutralization of the values of conventional culture is insufficient to ensure that a juvenile will actually drift into delinquency. For a delinquent act to occur, the juvenile must will it. Two factors that activate the will are preparation and desperation (pp. 181–191). Preparation provides the will to repeat old infractions of law; desperation provides the will to commit new ones.

By "preparation" Matza referred to the skills a juvenile must have before committing a crime. To commit a robbery, for example, a youth must have a certain rudimentary level of strength, dexterity, speed, agility, and cunning in order to be successful. Also, a youth must not be apprehensive or "chicken" when about to violate the law; or, in the language of classical criminology, he must not be deterred by the threat of the imposition of law. Youths must believe that the police are relatively incompetent and that they are only relatively potent. In their preparation for delinquency, youths also learn that, even if their delinquency is detected, incarceration is unlikely.

By "desperation" Matza referred to what he suspected to be the primary motive in the will to delinquency: that youngsters feel they have no control over their lives. For youngsters with anxieties about their masculinity and about membership in their peer group, a mood of fatalism and desperation is the natural consequence of experiencing a lack of control. To assert control a boy cannot just do anything ("Shit, man, anybody can do that."). He must master his fate. He must make something happen. Often the subculture of delinquency stresses the importance of delinquency as a means of making things happen; sometimes it stresses the time-honored method of exploiting and conquering females. However, Matza concluded, the will to crime may be "discouraged, deterred, or diverted by countless contingencies" (p. 191).

Assessment

One means of evaluating *Delinquency and Drift* is to see it as an attempt to restore to juveniles a degree of free will denied them by the determinism of the positivist tradition. In criticizing the unwarranted determinism of positivist criminology, Matza tried to force us, instead, to appreciate the way in which deviants themselves view their activities. If certain youths consciously choose to drift between convention and delinquency, then clearly their accounts of why they drift become an essential part of explaining their actions. Deviants have voices that should be heard!

Although Matza's work has inspired few full-length studies, a notable exception is Jack Katz's (1988) phenomenological *The Seductions of Crime*. Katz believes that positivist explanations that focus on "background" correlations—like socioeconomic factors or whether criminals were dropped on their heads when they were babies—do little to help us understand what motivates criminals to commit crime. As Katz wrote:

> The statistical and correlational findings of positivist criminology provide the following irritations to inquiry: (1) whatever the validity of the hereditary, psychological, and social-ecological conditions of crime, many of those in the supposedly causal categories do not commit the crime at issue, (2) many who do commit the

crime do not fit the causal categories, and (3) what is most provocative, many who do fit the background categories and later commit the predicted crime go for long stretches without committing the crimes to which theory directs them. (pp. 3–4)

Instead, expanding upon the work of Matza, Katz argued that we need to understand the "foreground" of experience, the thrill, the magic and emotions that "seduce" persons to commit crime. Katz extended his ethnographic method to such crimes as murder, robbery, and shoplifting.

Although Katz has managed to develop Matza's insights in important ways, the question remains: Is Matza's reformulation successful, or does his reformulation merely shift the causes of delinquency from one positivist area to another—from status frustration to masculine anxiety, for example? This is a difficult question. Although Matza's basic thesis that delinquents drift between conventional and delinquent activities has been tested extensively, generally these tests have focused on the importance that Matza has attributed to **techniques of neutralization**. The tests have explored two main questions: Do techniques of neutralization come before delinquent acts? Where do delinquents stand relative to delinquent and conventional values?

Some studies (e.g., Ball, 1966) have provided limited support for Matza's concept of techniques of neutralization, whereas others (e.g., Hamlin, 1988) have found that these techniques are motives that neutralize guilt after a delinquent act. Faced with this controversy, it seems reasonable to conclude that some delinquents use techniques of neutralization before and others after their behavior has been detected and defined as deviant. For example, many people who cheat on their income tax returns rationalize their behavior beforehand by claiming, "Everyone else is cheating the IRS, and I'm stupid if I don't do it."

Carl Klockars (1974:135–161) and Darrell Steffensmeier (1986:237–249) have shown, in their biographical studies of professional fences, that certain thieves can neutralize their past *and* their future illegalities—if they are involved in a continuing criminal career—by reasoning, "I'm not hurting anyone when I steal, because insurance will always pay the loss" (and see Chapter 10.1). Listen to Sam, Steffensmeier's fence:

> I don't feel I hurt any little people 'cause most of the stuff did come out of business places and big places, which were insurance write-offs and which they will many times mark it double what it was. In a round-about way, yes, the individual is going to pay for it, like with the higher transport and that. I would not feel bad about this. It's the same as, say, chiseling on income tax. You cheat Uncle Sam, but that's not the same as cheating this here person. (1986:241)

However, such partial confirmations of Matza's thesis on the use of neutralization techniques have been challenged by Michael Hindelang (1970; 1974). In his earlier study, Hindelang (1970) obtained the confidential information of 346 boys from a middle-class section of Oakland, California. In this study Hindelang asked his subjects to record the number of times they had committed any of twenty-six offenses (including theft, drug use/abuse, fighting, sexual deviance, and truancy) in the previous year. In addition, the youngsters were asked whether they strongly disapproved, disapproved, were indifferent to, approved, or strongly approved the act. If Matza was correct, and delinquents are not committed to their misdeeds, then delinquent approval of an act should be similar to approval expressed by nondelinquents. Hindelang found that thirteen of fifteen activities he examined showed a significant association between delinquent involvement and the approval of delinquent acts. These findings clearly contradict Matza's thesis that delinquents do not differ substantively from nondelinquents in their commitment to conventional culture.

Recall Matza's point that if delinquents really were so influenced by their subculture, it would be extremely difficult to explain the fact that most members of the subculture eventually abandon their delinquency. In other words, how can we account for the maturational reform of juvenile delinquents? Why do most juvenile delinquents become conformist adults? A possible explanation of maturation is in fact precisely the one suggested by Matza himself: Most delinquents are never seriously committed to their delinquency in the first place. But as David Greenberg (1981) has argued, it is in fact unclear why most subculture carriers so soon abandon activities so highly prized within the subculture. Why do gang members eventually desist from delinquent activities? Greenberg is quick to point out that, as valuable as Matza's insight is, it opens up other nagging questions:

> Why does desistance from violen[t] offenses occur later and more slowly than [from] theft offenses? Why are some juveniles so much more extensively involved in delinquency than others? Matza's remarkable presentation of the subjective elements in delinquency must be supplemented by an analysis of the objective, structural elements in causation, if such questions are to be answered (120; and see Chapter 15.4).

According to Greenberg, then, Matza did not adequately consider the relation between social class and socioeconomic status, on the one hand, and the distribution of values on the other. Are working-class youths, for example, more likely to engage in neutralization techniques than youths from other sections of society? If so, why? Indeed, why do some youths not commit delinquent acts? Or, to ask the same question differently, why do some youths conform to positive culture but others do not? This question has been explored within the context of **control theory**, to which we now turn.

6.3 CONTROL THEORY

The concept of "social control" was pioneered by Gabriel Tarde (see Chapters 3.3 and 4.1). In the United States it was used first by sociologists (e.g., Ross, 1901) and social psychologists (e.g., Mead, 1925). Early on, "social control" was understood broadly as all institutions and processes that guarantee social order. In some writings, it was depicted as a coercive device by which the will of the powerful was imposed on society. However, during the 1940s the concept of social control was given a much narrower reading. Two aspects of this narrower view were soon adopted as guiding themes in criminology. First, social control was stripped of its critical content and declared a functional necessity that contributed to the well-being of society. Without social control, functionalists claimed, anarchy and chaos would prevail in any society. Second, the concept was narrowed to include small groups (such as families, schools, and peers). The focus here was on how these groups socialized their members.

These narrower perspectives on social control are vividly present in the studies to which we now turn. These studies proceed on the central assumption that crime is likely to occur when the social bonds between an individual and society are weakened or severed. In what follows we present the two best-known versions of control theory in criminology—Walter Reckless's (1961) containment theory and Travis Hirschi's (1969) social control (or social bonding) theory.

Containment Theory

Walter Reckless (1940:58) suggested that variation in the respective crime rates of different social groups was caused by variations in the ability to contain norm-violating behavior in the face of social change and cultural conflict. Reckless (1961:335–359) later developed this insight as **containment theory** in his book *The Crime Problem.*

Reckless developed the theory of containment largely because of a major bias he detected in existing criminological theory. To Reckless's dismay, the vast majority of theories placed too much emphasis on the process of social disorganization as the cause of crime. To correct for this misplaced emphasis, Reckless argued that crime generally is prevented, or contained, as a result of two key processes: One occurs at the level of social organization, the other at the level of individual personality.

In attempting to correct what he saw as a misplaced bias toward factors of social organization at the expense of personality factors, Reckless (1961:74–140) relied on several new empirical studies of delinquency. According to these studies (Reiss, 1951; Nye, 1958), delinquents often come from broken homes and have not been properly socialized or controlled by their families, peer groups, schools, and adult friends. These studies also found that recidivists have weak egos and personal controls and poor self-concepts, whereas "good boys" (nondelinquents) tend to come from middle-class families or from families that are stable maritally, economically, and spatially. Moreover, good boys project a good self-concept, namely, one that acts as an effective insulator against delinquency (Reckless, Dinitz, and Murray, 1956). The self-concept of good boys includes law-abiding and obedient self-evaluation together with positive responses to family life and parental (especially maternal) control. Reckless suggested that a good self-concept represents

> a favorable internalization of presumably favorable life-experiences, including an acceptance or incorporation of the proper concern which significant others have had for the person. It acts selectively on experience and holds the line against adversities (pressures), the subculture of delinquency, wrong-doing, and crime (pull), as well as discontent and frustrations (pushes). The poor self-concept is a residue of less favorable growth, the acceptance of less concern or a different concern (value-wise) of significant others. (1961:355–356)

Reckless's theory of containment is a hierarchical structure focusing on the ability of individuals to contain social and psychological conflict (1961:355–359). For Reckless, inner and outer containments occupy a position between the pressures and pulls of the social environment and the inner pushes of the individual personality (pp. 355–356). At the top of the hierarchy is a layer of social pressures that bears down on the individual. These pressures include poverty, unemployment, economic insecurity, family conflict, minority group status, lack of opportunity, and class and social inequality. At the same level is a layer of social pulls that draws individuals away from their routines and accepted patterns of life. These pulls include influential deviants ("prestige individuals"), bad company, delinquent and criminal subcultures, and propaganda such as that purveyed by the mass media.

According to Reckless, immediately surrounding the individual is a barrier of outer containment. This barrier consists of effective family living and supportive groups, and includes such factors as morality, supervision, discipline, reasonable norms and expectations, and safety valves to release tensions. If this barrier is weak, the individual is quite vulnerable to social pressures and pulls.

Inside the individual's consciousness is a barrier of inner containment. Deviance-prone individuals (essentially those with weak inner containment) are likely to possess some combination of bad self-control, weak ego, underdeveloped superego (conscience), poor self-concept, low frustration tolerance, no sense of responsibility, and inadequate goal-orientation. Inner containment is the last line of defense against internal and external pressures and pulls.

Finally, the bottom layer of the hierarchy consists of psychological pushes. These include varying degrees of hostility, aggressiveness, suggestibility, rebellion, guilt reactions, feelings of inadequacy and inferiority, sibling rivalry, and such organic difficulties as brain damage and epilepsy. According to Reckless (p. 356), certain of these psychological pushes are usually too strong for inner as well as outer containment.

Assessment

Several criticisms have been made of Reckless's theory. Some criminologists have rightly complained that important parts of his theory—such as a poor self-concept—are defined so vaguely that they are not testable (Schrag, 1962:82–89). What, precisely, is a poor self-concept? Is it, for example, the belief that one is no good? Or is it the belief that others believe that one is no good? How does one define bad company? How bad must company be for it to constitute bad company?

These difficulties notwithstanding, Reckless's containment theory fostered another, far more articulate theory of crime: Travis Hirschi's social control theory.

Social Control Theory

Travis Hirschi's *Causes of Delinquency* (1969) is a prominent landmark in the developing literature on the sociology and social psychology of **social control**. Hirschi thought that most sociological theories had failed to show that delinquency actually is caused by such factors as the strains of "sex, race, social class, neighborhood, mother's employment, the broken home, size of family, and so forth" (p. 65). Although these factors might be correlated with delinquency, Hirschi reasoned, there is no evidence they actually cause it. Instead of looking for the causes of delinquency, he argued, it is much more fruitful to look for the causes of conformity. Perhaps delinquency is merely an absence of the causes of conformity.

Hirschi therefore started with the seemingly biological proposition that most people have antisocial tendencies; however, these tendencies are actualized only if various sorts of social control are relaxed. Whether individuals are law-abiding or deviant depends on the extent of variance from the four factors that are critical in bonding them to society: (1) attachment to parents, school, and peers; (2) commitment to conventional lines of action; (3) involvement in conventional activities; and (4) belief in conventional values.

First, Hirschi theorized, juveniles will be law-abiding if they have strong attachments to positive role models or significant others—their parents, school teachers, and law-abiding friends. Weak attachments to expectations of significant others can derive from a lack of discipline by parents and teachers, poor intellectual and social skills exhibited by the juvenile, disrespect for or indifference to expectations and opinions of significant others, and differential association with juvenile delinquents.

Second, Hirschi maintained that for a system of social control to be effective, juveniles must fear punishment. He reasoned that delinquents are likely to be juveniles who, during their difficult passage to adulthood, are less committed to completing their education or achieving a high-status career. Hirschi therefore disagreed with subcultural theories that identified frustrated aspirations as the main provocation for delinquency, though he did not identify the factors that cause variance in juvenile attachment to conventional lines of action.

Third, juvenile attachments and attitudinal commitments to positive role models and to conventional goals are likely to be reflected in the juvenile's daily involvement in conventional activities. The more juveniles are involved in such conventional activities as education and school-related activities, the more they are discouraged from engaging in delinquency, and vice versa.

Fourth, Hirschi argued that belief in the goodness of certain values—such as respect for the law and for the police, and in the wrongness of such actions as juvenile delinquency—operates as a brake on delinquency. Finally, we note that Hirschi implied that all four factors (attachment, commitment, involvement, and belief) are strongly interrelated: "In general, the more closely a person is tied to conventional society in any of these ways, the more closely he is likely to be tied in the other ways. The person who is attached to conventional people is, for example, more likely to be involved in conventional activities and to accept conventional notions of desirable conduct" (p. 27).

In *Causes of Delinquency,* Hirschi attempted to test his theory empirically. His test was based on a study of school records, police records, and questionnaire responses gathered from a large sample of juveniles (stratified by race, sex, school, and grade) in the San Francisco-Oakland area in the mid-1960s. Self-report items included many questions about juvenile attitudes toward family, school, and peers. Six items in the questionnaire were meant to serve as an index of delinquency. Three questions asked whether in the last year the juvenile had stolen anything worth less than $2, worth $2–$50, and worth over $50. Three questions asked if he or she had ever "taken a car for a ride without the owner's permission," "banged up something that did not belong to you on purpose," and (not counting fights with brothers and sisters) "beaten up on anyone or hurt anyone on purpose" (p. 54).

From these data Hirschi made a variety of generalizations about the links between social control and delinquency, each of which seemed remarkably at odds with previous theories. The seven most important of these generalizations are:

1. Juveniles engage less in delinquency the more they are attached to their families.
2. Juveniles engage less in delinquency the better they perform in school.
3. The greater a youth's stake in conformity, then, irrespective of the delinquency of his or her peers, the less likely he or she is to be delinquent.
4. Members of delinquent gangs do not have cohesive or warm associations with fellow gang members.
5. The importance of techniques of neutralization in delinquency is inconclusive.
6. There is no significant causal link between delinquency and social class.
7. In the United States, no section of society encourages delinquency more than any other.

Finally, we note that Hirschi later (1983) reformulated his theory somewhat and extended its scope to focus on child socialization rather than on adolescence. In this revised version Hirschi borrowed from the Oregon Social Learning Center's treatment of families with problem children. He reported the Center's "commonsense" finding that "children must be *punished* for their misdeeds" (p. 53). Continuing forcefully to reject theories of crime that stress such factors as poverty, social class, and unemployment, Hirschi asserted that good child-rearing techniques and proper discipline are the chief ways to prevent or control juvenile delinquency. Good techniques include monitoring children, recognizing problems, and punishing misbehavior. Thus, inadequate child-rearing techniques and lax discipline are allegedly the chief factors in juvenile delinquency. These factors are especially present, Hirschi argued, among working mothers, in situations of child abuse (p. 58–65), among parents with criminal records, in large families, and in single-parent families. "The single parent (usually a woman) . . . is less able to devote time to monitoring and punishment, and is more likely to be involved in negative, abusive contacts with her children" (p. 62).

Hirschi proposed, somewhat vaguely, three policies for the control of problem children. First, child-rearing classes should be standard fare in high school so that future parents learn the rudiments of sound child-rearing techniques. Second, parents and teachers should combine their knowledge and their supervisory roles in order better to address child-rearing issues. Third, there must be appropriate governmental commitment to ensuring that families have incentives to raise law-abiding children. However, as Hirschi (1983:68) recognized, these proposals are highly controversial. For instance, should the government penalize parents (and guardians) who do not employ sound child-rearing practices? If so, how severe a penalty is appropriate? Where should the dividing line be drawn between family privacy and governmental responsibility?

Assessment

Among many criminologists the control theory of crime continues to be extremely influential. In Hirschi's version (nowadays often referred to as "social bonding" theory), especially, it is a formalized theory whose several propositions lend themselves easily to empirical tests. It is a major source of current research and, until quite recently, has consistently received empirical support from researchers (Voorhis, Cullen, Mathers, and Garner, 1988; Laub and Sampson, 1988). Moreover, it has motivated other researchers (such as Toby, 1983) to pinpoint the apparent importance of strict control—and the dire consequences of lax discipline—in institutions such as schools.

However, certain research has shown that some of Hirschi's key concepts should be refined. For example, Stephen Cernkovich and Peggy Giordano (1987:299–300; and see Wells and Rankin, 1988) complain that Hirschi's concept of attachment is too vague. What exactly is attachment? How does one measure it? They suggest that to understand the subtle dynamics of family interaction, future researchers should (1) recognize the importance of different measures of attachment—including control and supervision, identity support (during adolescent crises), caring and trust, forms and degrees of intimate communication, parental disapproval of peers, and conflict—and (2) explore the effects on delinquency of the variety of intact and broken family units—including both-parent, mother-only, father-only, father/stepmother, and mother/stepfather homes.

The relation between Hirschi's concept of conformity, on the one hand, and his other key concepts (attachment, involvement, commitment, and belief), on the other, has also been criticized strongly. As discussed earlier, Hirschi asserted that juveniles are law-abiding or conforming if they have strong attachments to their positive role models. But Hirschi's statement confuses a definition of conformity with an explanation of conformity. As Thomas Bernard wrote: "If conformity is *defined* as acts controlled by attachments, involvements, commitments, and beliefs, conformity cannot be *explained* by the same statement without simply restating the definition" (1987:417). In other words, Hirschi's reasoning appears to be circular. It is not at all clear that the concepts of control theory explain anything at all.

Other criminologists have raised serious doubts about the validity of Hirschi's findings. In his longitudinal study of 2,213 boys between 1966 and 1968, Robert Agnew (1985) found that Hirschi's theory cannot explain serious forms of juvenile crime. In other words, even if control theory can explain minor crimes such as petty theft, it does not and cannot explain why some juveniles commit very violent offenses. Some other explanation is needed of these latter offenses. Agnew also found that although at any given point in time delinquency may appear strongly correlated with Hirschi's control variables, in the long run, rather than delinquency being caused by weak social controls, delinquency itself can causally affect control! Agnew therefore concluded that "the explanatory power of Hirschi's social control theory has been exaggerated" (p. 58).

Criminologists have engaged in a heated dispute over the causal relationships indicated by theorists of control. There are essentially two sides to this dispute. According to conservatives such as Hirschi and his followers, the allegedly high and rising U.S. crime rates have been caused by the lax discipline and the cultural permissiveness of 1960s liberalism. On this view, rising crime rates have been caused by the general permissiveness of liberal parents, the decline of religious values, the collapse of order in the nation's high schools, governments that have been too generous with the poor and with welfare recipients, and criminal justice systems that are too soft on criminals. On this view the solution to the problem of crime lies in greater social control. Typical conservative policies for controlling crime include compulsory religious instruction from the elementary school upward, restoration of strict discipline (including corporal punishment) in the nation's high schools, reduction or elimination of government welfare programs in order to cultivate individual responsibility and to foster initiative among the "undeserving poor," and increased severity of penal sanctions (such as longer prison sentences and determinate sentencing).

On the other side of this dispute are the liberal critics of control theory. Elliot Currie (1997), for example, has argued that the high violent crime rates in the United States have little to do with lax social control and much to do with the logic of free economic enterprise and its unfortunate consequences. Chief among these consequences are (Currie, 1997:154):

- the progressive destruction of jobs and livelihood
- the growth of extremes of economic inequality and material deprivation
- the withdrawal of public services and supports, especially for families and children
- the erosion of informal and communal networks of mutual support, supervision, and care
- the spread of a materialistic, neglectful, and "hard" culture
- the unregulated marketing of the technology of violence
- and the weakening of social and political alternatives

Moreover, liberal critics of control theory counter that strict discipline neither deters nor controls delinquency. Stricter discipline (including corporal punishment) may actually encourage delinquency, they continue, because its use teaches children that physical force is the appropriate way to solve interpersonal problems. It is no accident, the liberal argument concludes, that the United States has both the highest rate of violent crime and the highest rate of incarceration of all industrial nations. Punitive control and high rates of violent crime are both symptoms of the same problem: The United States is a thoroughly violent society, even, ironically, in its response to violent crime. In the liberal scenario, the causes of crime must be attacked by social policies that seek alternatives to imprisonment, that foster community spirit, that create employment for the poor, and that make adequate provision for the children of poorer families.

Although we do not explicitly assess the respective merits of the conservative and liberal viewpoints—admitting that the arguments supporting them are many and complex—we conclude this assessment of social control theory by noting one basic, perhaps fatal, criticism of the conservative viewpoint. Hirschi's theory of social control derives from an assumption about human nature that is probably undemonstrable and quite likely wrong: At the moment of birth, when society has not yet imprinted its values and its controls on our social characters, we are all aggressive and naturally violent animals. In this dark and pessimistic vision, as in the biblical theory of original sin, criminal behavior is something that parents, educators, and other agents of social control must work to avoid. But as Currie complains:

Whatever one may think, on a purely philosophical level, about Hirschi's attitude toward human nature, it cannot tell us why some times, some places, and some groups are more criminal than others. In order to accomplish this, Hirschi must go on to blame a variety of changes in contemporary values and attitudes for weakening parents' capacity to quash their children's unruly impulses. (1985:187)

REVIEW

This chapter outlined subcultural perspectives on delinquency. First, we looked at the key themes emerging in the sociology of delinquent subcultures during the 1950s; this sociology was influenced strongly by earlier traditions of anomie and differential association. Second, we summarized David Matza's criticism of the positivist approach to juvenile delinquency. In his alternative formulation, Matza emphasized that juveniles consciously drift between the conventional culture and the subculture of delinquency. Third, we examined various theories that focus on the causal importance of the notion of control.

Delinquent Subcultures

1. Beginning in the 1950s, Mertonian anomie theory led directly to further examination of the cultural settings that fostered juvenile delinquency.

2. Cohen's *Delinquent Boys* (1955) suggested that delinquent boys inhabit a subculture whose activities are nonutilitarian, malicious, and negativistic. Lower-class boys (rather than middle-class boys, or girls in general) are doomed to fail in terms of middle-class standards, especially in school, and they react by participating in the creation of a delinquent subculture or by joining a bearer group of such a subculture. This reaction provides the status that the middle-class world denies them.

3. Cohen's findings were criticized by numerous scholars, including Miller (1958) and Cloward and Ohlin (1960). Miller suggested that Cohen had overemphasized the extent to which lower-class youth internalized middle-class values. Lower-class delinquent subcultures should therefore be understood in terms of the focal concerns of lower-class life, especially the female-headed household.

4. In *Delinquency and Opportunity* (1960), Cloward and Ohlin responded that earlier theorists had simplified both the reasons why lower-class youth join delinquent subcultures and the variety of such subcultures. Delinquents tend to be boys who desire greater economic success but who, uninterested in becoming middle class, seek higher status in lower-class terms. Boys generally join a criminal subculture, if available; if not, they join a conflict subculture. Boys who fail in these subcultures, or for whom they are unavailable, tend to join the retreatist subculture.

Matza's *Delinquency and Drift* (1964)

1. *Delinquency and Drift* offered powerful criticisms of the lengthy positivist tradition stretching from Quetelet's social mechanics of crime to subcultural theories of delinquency discussed in this chapter. Matza argued that this tradition teaches wrongly that all activities of juveniles are determined by social and environmental forces over which they have absolutely no control. Matza claimed, rather, that juveniles exercise rational choice over their activities, whether these are delinquent or conformist.

2. Matza stressed the existence of a subculture of delinquency that is not a delinquent subculture. Because most delinquents are children, it is not surprising that the values of the subculture of delinquency are not opposed to those of the conventional culture. For this reason most delinquents mature as conformist adults rather than adult criminals.

3. Delinquents drift in and out of delinquency and conventional behavior. They rationalize their delinquent activity by means of five main techniques of neutralization: denial of responsibility, denial of injury, denial of victim, condemnation of condemners, and appeal to higher loyalties. These techniques are supplemented by situations of preparation and desperation.

4. Matza identified serious problems in the positivist tradition. But there is little conclusive evidence that his image of a less constrained deviant is actually closer to social reality. Some critics have suggested that Matza has paid insufficient attention to constraints of social class and racial inequality.

Control Theory

1. The two major forms of control theory are containment theory and social control (or social bonding) theory. Control theory assumes that crime is likely to occur when the social bonds between an individual and society are weakened or severed.

2. Reckless's theory of containment focuses on an individual's ability to contain social and psychological conflict. Inner and outer containments occupy a position between the pressures and pulls of the social environment and the inner pushes of the individual personality. Deviance-prone individuals tend to have weak inner and outer containments that result from some combination of factors such as bad self-control, weak ego, badly developed superego, and poor self-concept.

3. Containment theory has been criticized because several of its key concepts are either too vague or immune to empirical proof.

4. Hirschi's theory of social control is based on the idea that it is better to look for the causes of conformity than for the causes of delinquency. Delinquency is an absence of the causes of conformity. Whether individuals are law-abiding or deviant depends on variation among four factors that bond them to society: (1) attachment to parents, school, and peers; (2) commitment to conventional lines of action; (3) involvement in conventional activities; and (4) belief.

5. Hirschi argued that good child-rearing techniques and proper discipline are the chief means of preventing and controlling delinquency.

6. Although it has been criticized, Hirschi's theory remains very influential today. As with containment theory, its concepts are rather vague and difficult to test.

7. The policy implications of control theory are the subject of heated debate among criminologists. Conservatives argue that stern discipline and family values are the best means of delinquency prevention; liberals reply that such discipline has never been shown to deter crime. Liberals argue that to reduce crime, we must attack its causes with policies that seek alternatives to prison, foster community spirit, create employment for the poor, and provide adequately for children of poorer families.

QUESTIONS FOR CLASS DISCUSSION

1. To what extent does Albert Cohen's *Delinquent Boys* (1955) represent a rejection of the findings of Clifford Shaw and Henry McKay's *Juvenile Delinquency and Urban Areas* (1942)?

2. How do the respective explanations of the causes of juvenile delinquency advanced by Walter Miller (1958) and by Richard Cloward and Lloyd Ohlin (1960) represent an advance over Cohen's *Delinquent Boys?*

3. Do delinquents drift?

4. Can the assumptions of David Matza's *Delinquency and Drift* accurately be described as a return to the assumptions of classical criminology?

5. Which is more important as a cause of crime: lax social control or unregulated economic activity?

FOR FURTHER STUDY

Readings

Adamson, Christopher. 1998. Tribute, Turf, Honor, and the American Street Gang. *Theoretical Criminology* 2 (1): 57–84.

Klein, Malcolm W. 1995. *The American Street Gang: Its Nature, Prevalence, and Control.* New York: Oxford University Press.

Short, James F. 1997. *Poverty, Ethnicity, and Violent Crime.* Boulder, Colo.: Westview Press.

Websites

1. <http://www.radcliff.edu/murray/data/ds0896.htm>: This site compiles several links and an extensive bibliography on juvenile delinquency research in the tradition of Sheldon and Eleanor Glueck.

2. <http://www.ocjp.ca.gov/iidpbrnch.html>: From the Office of Juvenile Justice and Delinquency Prevention, this site has useful information and links regarding official policies established to combat juvenile delinquency in the United States.

3. <http://www.ncjrs.org/ojjdp/conference/contents.html>: These are the conference proceedings from the 1998 national meeting of the Office of Juvenile Justice and Delinquency Prevention. Several current research articles written by prominent social scientists are available.

Preview

Chapter 7 introduces:

- the theoretical diversity in criminology that first appeared during the turbulent decade of the 1960s and that continues today
- five influential theories of crime: social learning theory; the labeling perspective; conflict theory; radical theory; and feminist theory

Key Terms

conflict theory   reinforcement
criminalization   secondary deviance
labeling   social constructionism
liberal feminism   social learning theory
Marxist feminism   socialist feminism
patriarchy   societal reaction
primary deviance   stigma
radical feminism

This chapter examines five theories of crime that matured during the 1960s and 1970s. In combination, these theories represent the beginnings of the extraordinary theoretical diversity that now characterizes U.S. criminology. Social learning theory developed, in part, from much of the existing criminological theory examined thus far. The **labeling** perspective and **conflict theory** have been influenced less by existing theories of crime than by various social and political movements that flourished in the 1960s; these same movements also influenced radical theory and feminist theory.

7.1   SOCIAL LEARNING THEORY

In Chapter 5.4 we examined Sutherland's focus on the origins and the transmission of delinquent values, and we learned that he stimulated new lines of inquiry, one of which is social learning theory. With Sutherland's original insight in mind, subsequent empirical studies indeed seemed to confirm that the more serious a juvenile's delinquent involvement, the more likely he or she will be to have friends who are also delinquent. This finding, however, does not explain how or why associational patterns influence delinquent involvement.

In arguing that Sutherland's theory of differential association and differential social organization cannot account for the process leading to individual criminality, Robert Burgess and Ronald Akers (1966:130) urged that criminologists try to use the genetic explanations of social behavior found in behavioral psychology. When these explanations are combined with structural explanations, such as subcultural and anomie theories, criminologists have termed them "social learning theory."

The basic premise of social learning theory is that social behavior is determined neither by inner personality drives nor by outer sociological and environmental factors. Rather, it is a cognitive process in which personality and environment engage in a continuous process of reciprocal interaction. Modern learning theory, especially the operant conditioning theory of such behavioral scientists as B. F. Skinner (1953), was pioneered in laboratory settings. Operant (or active) conditioning theory begins with the empirical fact that animal behavior is effected by its consequences, both negative and positive. Animals are easily trained to perform certain actions if they are rewarded for doing so. For example, dogs usually learn to sit following the command "Sit!" if, after every time they sit, they receive positive **reinforcement** in the form of a bone or a friendly pat from their trainer. Desired behavior, in other words, is reinforced through a process of conditioned learning that emphasizes rewards or (for dogs who do not sit on command) punishments.

However, Bandura (1973) has shown that the process of social learning would be extremely tiring and hazardous if it depended solely on rewards and punishments. Although some behavior patterns are acquired through the process of rewarding and punishing direct experience, other behavior patterns are acquired by observing the behavior of significant others (family and peer group).

Differential Reinforcement

Several criminologists have indicated the importance of learning theory as an explanatory tool for understanding crime. For example, in a direct application of Skinnerian theory, Clarence Ray Jeffery (1965) claimed that, in any given social situation, whether someone commits a crime depends largely on his or her past conditioning history, namely, whether the individual has been reinforced (or rewarded) for crime. Jeffery's theory of differential reinforcement states: "A criminal act occurs in an environment in which in the past the actor has been reinforced for behaving in this manner, and the aversive consequences attached to the behavior have been of such a nature that they do not control or prevent the response" (p. 295).

Crime is therefore a response to reinforcing stimuli. For example, the crime of robbery may produce either money or imprisonment (often both). If only money is produced, the behavior is likely to continue; if only imprisonment is produced, the aversive consequence is likely to deter the act. Thus, according to this explanation, crime depends chiefly on the process of differential reinforcement.

For Burgess and Akers (1966), social behavior (including criminal behavior) responds chiefly to a complicated network of rewards and punishments. Any given behavior is likely to continue or to increase if it is followed more by rewards than by punishments; the same behavior is likely to decrease or to end if it is followed more by punishments than by rewards. Paraphrasing Burgess and Akers, criminal behavior is actually learned in seven stages (1966:146; and see Akers, 1973:46–47; and Akers, Krohn, Lanza-Kaduce, and Radosevich, 1979:637–639):

1. Criminal behavior is learned through direct conditioning or through imitation.
2. Criminal behavior is learned both in nonsocial reinforcing situations (for example, the physical effects of drug use) or nonsocial discriminative situations and through social interaction in which the behavior of others is either for or against criminal behavior.

3. The principal component of learning criminal behavior occurs in groups that compose the individual's major source of reinforcements: peer friendship groups, the family, schools, and churches.

4. Learning criminal behavior—including specific techniques, attitudes, and avoidance procedures—depends on the effective and available reinforcers and the existing reinforcement contingencies.

5. The specific type and the frequency of learned behavior depend on the reinforcers that are effective and available, and on the norms by which these reinforcers are applied.

6. Criminal behavior is a function of norms that are discriminative for criminal behavior, the learning of which occurs when such behavior is more highly reinforced than is noncriminal behavior.

7. The strength of criminal behavior is a direct function of the amount, frequency, and probability of its reinforcement.

For Akers, all seven stages in this process must be examined. However, the central part of his theory lies in two factors that concern the learning of acts and definitions: (1) differential reinforcement and (2) positive and negative definitions (Akers, 1973:287–288; 1997:62–70). All social behavior is either strengthened by reward (positive reinforcement) and avoidance of punishment (negative reinforcement) or weakened by aversive stimuli (positive stimuli) and lack of reward (negative punishment). Whether a deviant act or a conforming act occurs depends on differential reinforcement (essentially, the cumulative effect of past and present rewards or punishments both for the act and also for alternative acts.) However, besides learning an act, a person also learns if the act is defined as good or bad. The more a person defines an act as good or as justifiable, the more likely s/he is to engage in it and the less likely s/he is to engage in alternatives. As Akers summarized: "A person participates in deviant activity then to the extent that it has been differentially reinforced over conforming behavior or defined as more desirable than conforming alternatives, or at least justified" (1973:287–288).

As with Sutherland's theory of differential association, Akers's social learning theory is intended as a general theory of crime. The broad scope of this theory is best seen in Akers's book *Deviant Behavior: A Social Learning Approach* (1973). Here Akers tries to apply social learning theory to all deviant behavior—"the principal forms of which . . . [include] drug use and addiction; homosexuality; prostitution; white-collar, professional, organized, and violent crimes; suicide; and mental illness" (p. vii). In this book Akers applies the general principles of social learning theory to each aspect of deviance: (1) how a person first engages in the deviant act, (2) how that person progresses to more frequent engagement, (3) the substantive events that reinforce the act, and (4) the content of the definitions favorable to the act.

Consider two examples of Akers's use of learning theory: suicide and drug use. Suicide presents an interesting test case for a learning theory of deviance that relies on reinforcement as the major motivating element because, without exception, the act of taking one's own life cannot be reinforced for one's future behavior (one has none!). Moreover, on the whole, U.S. culture condemns suicide, which means that there are very few definitions favorable to it. But Akers is confident that the act of suicide is based on social learning, and he offers a four-stage model as evidence (1973:245–252):

1.   People learn that suicide appears to be a solution to personal problems. Everyone knows, or learns, that some people eliminate their problems successfully by hanging themselves, jumping off bridges, and by drug overdoses. A terminal illness, the loss of a loved one, financial ruin, and existential angst are all situations in which suicide can be rationalized, justified, excused, or forgiven. These rationalizations are not defined as definitions favorable to the act of suicide, but they often operate to neutralize unfavorable definitions.

2.   People learn about specific techniques of suicide. We learn that a drug overdose (which sometimes can be interrupted after the drug is taken) is less likely to be successful than suicide by shooting. We also learn, according to Akers, that certain techniques are considered more appropriate for one sex than another: the violence of shooting, for example, is a "masculine" technique, whereas a drug overdose is more "feminine."

3.   People learn that the act of suicide receives considerable attention. Thus, some proportion of suicidal behavior is not actually intended to result in death but in attention from loved ones. Suicide resulting from previously learned nonfatal suicidal behavior is common. In some cases of suicide without prior attempts, the act of suicide derives from imitation—psychiatrists, therefore, have high rates of suicide compared with most other occupations.

4.   Whether a person tries to commit suicide again depends in part on the reaction of others. "They may increase their attention to him without necessarily solving the crises and thus reinforce further attempts, or they may reinforce his belief that there is no hope. In either case he is likely to attempt again, and one of these attempts may be fatal (p. 251)."

Another test of social learning theory was conducted by Akers et al. (1979) in a study of drug (marijuana) and alcohol use among teenagers. This study was based on a self-report questionnaire administered to 3,065 male and female teenagers attending grades 7 through 12 in seven communities in three Midwestern states. It strongly confirmed social learning theory: The probability of abstinence from drug and alcohol use decreases and the frequency of use increases when individual teenagers (1) associate more with using rather than abstaining peers and adults, (2) are more rewarded than punished for use, and (3) are exposed more to favorable than to unfavorable definitions of use (p. 639). Akers and his colleagues concluded that these three factors explained 55 percent of the differences between users of and abstainers from alcohol, and 68 percent of the differences between users of and abstainers from marijuana (p. 642). Another study (Wood et al., 1997) has claimed that criminal behavior recurs through a nonsocial learning process, that is, offenders (especially violent offenders) experience a neurophysiological sensation or "high" that reinforces their propensity to commit crime.

Finally, we note that in a more recent book Akers (1998) offered a useful personal history of the development of his theory and, at the same time, a slightly revised version of it. Here, Akers proposed a "social learning and social structure" model of crime. Figure 7.1 shows that social learning mediates the relationship between social structure (the independent variable) and criminal behavior and crime rates (the dependent variable). Although Akers acknowledges that many of the variables in this model have been tested extensively, he bemoans the fact that there has been little research on the relationship between social learning and social structure (pp. 370–371). He suggests, for example, that imitation (see Chapter 4.1) will likely turn out to be a key factor in the learning of criminal behavior. Moreover, he points to the need for more research on social learning and serious crime, such as white-collar crime, in adult samples and in many areas of noncriminal deviance, such as sexual deviance and problem drinking.

Assessment

Apart from his own sustained research and that of a small group of followers, the basic principles of Akers's social learning theory, and its explanations of why some persons commit criminal and deviant acts, have still not been tested widely or deeply.

It is probable that many criminologists shy away from social learning theory because of the ethical difficulties associated with its policy implications. If criminal tendencies, including violence, are chiefly learned, it seems to follow that they can just as easily be unlearned through behavior modification. Controversial examples of behavior modification treatment include drug-based therapy, electro-cardiac treatment, chemotherapy, and confrontational juvenile correctional programs such as Visionquest and boot camps. Although none of these strategies has proven very effective, all arouse widespread ethical controversy because they appear to foreshadow a return to the violent criminal justice system of the dark and distant past.

Social learning theory arose when the notion of deterministic causation was unfashionable in criminology. Recall, for example, the devastating challenge posed by Matza's view that delinquency is not caused by deterministic forces but that juveniles episodically drift into (and out of) delinquency (Chapter 6.3). This detachment from deterministic theories was reinforced, in turn, by the tremendous popularity of the labeling perspective, which seemed to imply that crime should not be understood as having causes at all.

7.2   THE LABELING PERSPECTIVE

During the 1960s, the legitimacy of political authority was challenged by many college students, liberal intellectuals, women's movements, and members of minority racial groups. Questions about U.S. foreign policy in Vietnam and elsewhere, about domestic civil rights, and about the stark social, economic, racial, and gender inequalities in the world's richest society quickly filtered through to sociological perspectives on crime and criminal justice. Certain radical intellectuals (such as Marcuse, 1964) argued that social inequality and injustice in the United States could be removed only by the powerless, deviant, outcast, criminal populations typically studied by criminologists. These populations, it was thought, had nothing to lose and everything to gain from a revolutionary overthrow of the existing social order. Reflecting this turbulent political climate, sociologists and

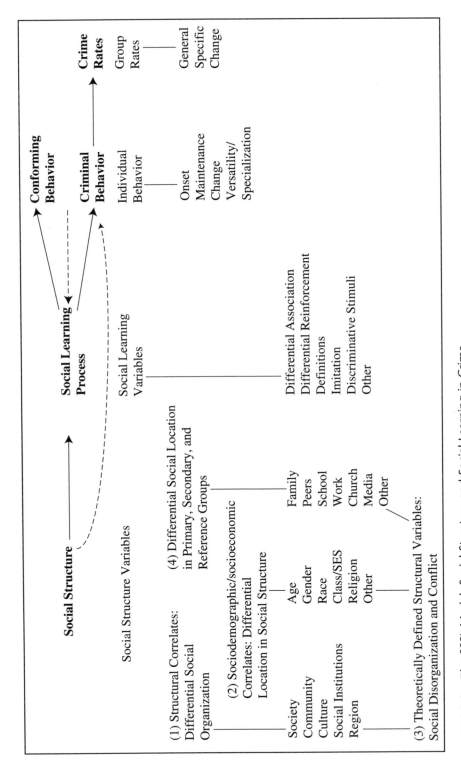

FIGURE 7.1   The SSSL Model: Social Structure and Social Learning in Crime

SOURCE: Akers, 1998: 331.

criminologists opened a Pandora's box, using a key provided by Robert S. Lynd's (1939) famous question: "Knowledge for what?" In such an inegalitarian society as the United States, why is criminology typically concerned with crimes of the powerless rather than with crimes committed by the government, by white-collar executives, and by corporations? *Who* defines certain behavior as criminal? Whose side are *we* (the "we" who study crime with detached objectivity) on?

The criminologists who first examined such politicized questions were mainly younger scholars attached to **the labeling perspective** and conflict theory. As the labeling perspective developed, its neutral posture toward deviants became a celebration of deviant activity as evidence of the virtue of social diversity. Many deviant activities began to be seen in a different and more interesting light. The "opening up" and "demystifying" implied by the concept of deviance involves a very different relationship between the deviant and the student of deviance. In coming out of their criminological closets, labeling theorists tended to see in alcoholism, criminality, and mental illness, for example, individuals who are victimized by society and who are potential rebels against its values.

It is not easy to pin down the key concepts of the labeling perspective. There is even disagreement about the term itself. The labeling perspective has also been described as societal reaction, "sociology of deviance," "social interactionism," "the neo-Chicago school," and "the new deviancy theory." For convenience, we use "the labeling perspective" for all these terms.

There are three key concepts held by a majority of those using this perspective: (1) the social meaning of deviance, (2) societal reaction, and (3) stigma.

The Social Meaning of Deviance

Following in the footsteps of the Chicago school of the 1920s and 1930s (see Chapter 5.2)—and drawing on the social psychology (phenomenology and symbolic interactionism) of George Herbert Mead, his student Herbert Blumer, and others—those researching deviance from the labeling perspective agree on the central importance of meanings in everyday life. Social reality itself is seen as an ongoing, fluid process that is constructed according to the outcome of the meanings that we attach to our interaction with others, on the one hand, and the meanings that they, on the other, attribute to us. Crime and deviance, then, are not pre-given, objective categories but negotiable statuses. Thus in interactionist or participant observation studies, the researcher participates in the social interaction of drug users, alcoholics, mental patients, and others in order to "appreciate" the meanings that those people defined as deviant attribute to their own activities. As we saw in Chapter 6.2, this was partly the view of deviance advocated by David Matza.

The emphasis on meanings takes a number of twists and turns in the labeling perspective. At one level, the labeling perspective is skeptical that our knowledge can ever be objective and value-free. Because social behavior means different things to different people, one cannot have the sort of complete knowledge about social interaction that, for example, a natural scientist may have about the movement of inanimate objects such as billiard balls. Many of the studies in the labeling tradition have thus rejected the use of the scientific method. At another level, because they do not exist in a social vacuum, the meanings, perceptions, and opinions of certain individuals or groups are taken more seriously than those of others. Therefore, although reality is socially constructed, not all members of society have an equal voice in deciding precisely how it is constructed. Taking a sympathetic cue from the way in which society devalues deviants and outsiders, the labeling perspective typically sides with the underdog and the outcast.

A well-known example of the centrality of meaning in the labeling perspective is provided by Howard Becker's book *Outsiders* (1963). Becker (pp. 46–58) argued (relying somewhat on learning theory) that marijuana users must learn to experience the meanings and effects of using marijuana if they are to get high "properly." He emphasized that social reality is constructed by the meanings embedded in everyday life. Indeed, Becker even claimed that the subjective experience of drugs is structured much more by social meanings and perceptions than by biological and pharmacological factors! If a situation is perceived and defined as real, then it is real in its consequences. Moreover, as human and social beings, each of us differs in the meaning that we attach to our own behavior and to that of others. At different times, and to different people, our behavior (such as having a tattoo) may be perceived as interesting or exotic or daring. The very same behavior may also be seen as dangerous, abnormal, sick, delinquent, or criminal. The labeling perspective insists that such perceptions are the only real difference between normal and deviant behavior.

Becker argued that it is a mistake to see deviance simply as the breaking of some agreed-upon rule. To look at deviance in this way is to ignore the fact that what counts as deviance is largely a function of the ability of groups with political power to impose their concept of right and wrong on the behavior of other groups. Because there is great diversity in the values of groups with political power there is great cross-cultural and cross-temporal variety in what officially (let alone unofficially) counts as deviance (see Chapter 16). Homosexuality, for example, is perceived as morally deviant in some cultures, but in others it is tolerated; and in still others, such as classical Greece and Rome, its practice is regarded as a positive virtue. In other words, suggested Becker, to understand deviance one must recognize that typically a given form of deviance is only statistically abnormal. As Becker argued:

> *Social groups create deviance by making the rules whose infraction constitutes deviance,* and by applying those rules to particular people and labeling them as outsiders. From this point of view, deviance is *not* a quality of the act the person commits, but rather a consequence of the application by others of rules and sanctions to an "offender." The deviant is one to whom that label has successfully been applied; deviant behavior is behavior that people so label. (p. 9, emphasis in original)

Societal Reaction

In arguing that "deviant behavior is behavior that people so label," Becker does not claim that such acts as homicide would not exist without the label that is often attached to them. Rather, he points to the important role of **societal reaction** in the designation of certain acts as deviant or criminal. For example, though the act of killing another human being can occur without societal reaction to it, whether a given killing is labeled as murder, manslaughter, accidental death, or justifiable homicide depends crucially on the meaning attributed to it by a social audience. From Becker's perspective, it follows that society itself "creates" deviance because it is society that defines it as such.

Half a century ago, Frank Tannenbaum (1938:17–18) pointed out that there is often a shift in society's reaction to delinquency and to delinquents, a process he described as the "dramatization of evil." Tannenbaum argued that the community's condemnation of delinquent behavior changes into a view of the offender as a delinquent person. Boys who vandalize school are seen as "bad boys." In attempting to understand the mechanisms of this transformation, Edwin Lemert distinguished between primary and secondary deviance.

Primary and Secondary Deviance

In his books *Social Pathology* and *Human Deviance, Social Problems, and Social Control,* Lemert (1951:75–78; 1967:40–64) used the sociopsychological concepts of primary and secondary deviation to understand the process of deviance. Lemert proposed this distinction in order to draw attention to the difference between the "original" and the "effective" causes of the deviant attributes and actions "associated with physical defects and incapacity, crime, prostitution, alcoholism, drug addiction, and mental disorders" (1967:40).

According to Lemert, **primary deviance** has many causes. It can be caused by a host of social, cultural, and psychological events. Primary deviants undergo no change in their psychological makeup or in the way they act as members of society. **Secondary deviance** is caused by the way in which society reacts to some of the people who engage in primary deviance. After they are apprehended, primary deviants suffer a variety of consequences, many of which focus on the application to them of such deviant labels as sick, cripple, criminal, insane, and so on. Such labels can have important consequences—for friendship, for job opportunities, and for self-image. Sometimes the effect of deviant labels is so powerful—either through a self-fulfilling prophecy or through the negative consequences of stigmatization—that labeled individuals are forced to reorient their lives around the label. Secondary deviants accept their new identity as a "deviant" and act in accordance with the societal reaction to their primary deviance. Secondary deviance is thus a powerful tool for explaining recidivism.

Labeling theorists do not study the causes of crime in the same way that most theories examined thus far in this book do. Indeed, labeling theorists tend to evade altogether questions of individual causation. It is clear that labeling theorists are concerned chiefly with the way society itself causes deviance. They are interested in how and why society labels certain behaviors deviant. Lemert, for example, argued that, whereas previous studies of deviance tended to rest heavily upon the idea that deviance leads to social control, "I have come to believe that the reverse idea, i.e., social control leads to deviance, is equally tenable and the potentially richer premise for studying deviance in modern society" (1967:v).

According to the labeling perspective, the response to certain behavior is the crucial element in the designation of deviance. Much of the time the process of deviance creation is a routine and humdrum affair that commands little comment by the media. This is especially so for most property crimes and many crimes against public order. The great bulk of offenders processed by the criminal justice system—those accused of public drunkenness, larceny-theft and fraud, driving under the influence, and disorderly conduct—receive almost no attention in the media (see Chapter 1.1).

Every so often, however, a society becomes engrossed in a process of public frenzy directed to certain forms of crime and deviance. Well-known examples of this intense process include the sixteenth- and seventeenth-century witch hunts in Europe and in colonial America, the moral crusade against prostitution between 1890 and 1920, the Nazi slaughter of Jews in the 1930s and 1940s, the McCarthyite search for communists in the 1950s, and the campaign against child abuse in the 1980s.

Lemert never suggested that societal reaction to primary deviance itself causes subsequent deviance, though he came very near to this position. However, the diverse ways in which society reacts to and actually creates deviance have been examined in various other studies. Consider, for example, Stanley Cohen's (1972) research on how the media, the police, and various moral entrepreneurs conspired to create a panic over the activities of two youth gangs (the Mods and the Rockers) in southern England in the mid-1960s. Since the 1970s a similar, far more controversial panic has arisen over soccer hooliganism in Britain (Redhead, 1987). In each case the media and the agencies of social control acted in such a way as to fan out of all proportion what was originally a fairly small problem. This part of the process has been termed "deviance amplification" (Wilkins, 1964).

Deviance Amplification

One well-known study illustrates the major features of the process of deviance amplification (Young, 1971). The subjects of Young's participant observation study were marijuana users in west London in the late 1960s. Young showed how the socially harmless activity of marijuana use was transformed into a social problem through the complicated web of interaction among the mass media, the public, the police, and the users themselves (see Figure 7.2).

Young described how the mass media made marijuana use a social problem through sensationalistic and lurid accounts of the lives of marijuana users. The media's portrayal of marijuana users as sick, unwashed, promiscuous weirdos completely committed to drug use was a stereotype that inflamed popular indignation during 1967. Young showed how this media pressure led police to amplify the very problem they vigilantly sought to curb. Intensive police action led to an organized defensive posture in the drug-using community. Drug users united around a shared sense of injustice concerning harsh sentences and mass media stereotypes. Drug use became a symbol of defiance against an unjust and intolerant society.

The media used the rising number of drug convictions to fan public indignation about marijuana use even further. Increased pressure was then put on the police to stamp out this new evil. Expanded police drug units ensured greater detection of marijuana users. Once again the number of drug convictions soared. The vicious cycle was firmly established.

Young's research demonstrated, then, that the police actually amplify the deviant activities they mean to control. Moreover, Gary Marx (1981) has shown that there are three types of interdependence between rule enforcers (such as police, prosecutors, and judges) and deviants that involve the possibility of deviance amplification: (1) escalation, (2) nonenforcement, and (3) covert facilitation.

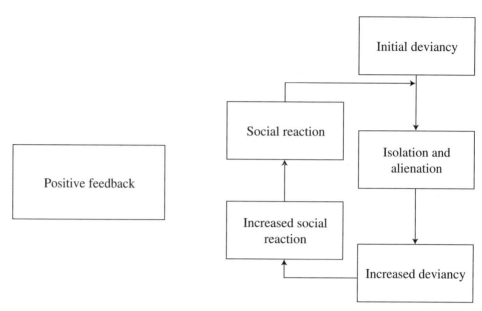

FIGURE 7.2   The Amplification of Deviance
SOURCE: Young, 1971: 34.

First, the situation of escalation can arise from initial attempts at social control. Marx pointed out, for example, that "police involvement in family conflict, crowd, and automobile chase situations can contribute to violations where none was imminent, or it can increase the seriousness of these situations" (p. 223). The mere presence of police officers at the scene of a domestic disturbance, for instance, can easily escalate a potentially dangerous situation into an overtly violent one. High-speed police vehicle chases, which sometimes result in injuries or death, can lead to manslaughter charges where none would otherwise have existed.

Second, there is the situation of nonenforcement, which is less direct than escalation. According to Marx (pp. 226–231), the nonenforcement of rules is difficult to identify because often it is hidden and illegal. Marx (p. 227) documented that police may adopt a policy of nonenforcement with respect to informants, for example, who provide information about the law breaking of others and/or help to facilitate a controlled commission of a crime, or with respect to vice entrepreneurs who agree to keep their own illegal behavior within agreed-upon limits.

Third, in a situation of covert facilitation, rule enforcers take an active role in encouraging others to break rules (pp. 231–233). The police go undercover to buy or sell illegal goods and services, for example, or the police may pose as johns in order to arrest prostitutes or try to buy drugs in order to arrest drug dealers. Or the police may use a decoy, such as a female police officer in civilian clothes, in order to create a robbery and/or assault, or they may pose as the representatives of a foreign country in order to trap unwitting members of Congress taking a bribe to secure political influence in Washington.

Stigmatization

As noted, whether or not individuals are regarded as deviant depends on societal reaction to their behavior. Moreover, partly because of this reaction to their behavior (primary deviance), some deviants are pushed into further (or secondary) deviance. This redirection of behavior occurs in a variety of ways. We now consider why societal reaction to deviance often results in, and can actually stem from, the fact that those who deviate from the norm tend to be stigmatized. Goffman related that, for the ancient Greeks, *stigma* referred to

> bodily signs designed to expose something unusual and bad about the moral status of the signifier. The signs were cut or burnt into the body and advertised that the bearer was a slave, a criminal, or a traitor—a blemished person, ritually polluted, to be avoided, especially in public places. Later, in Christian times, two layers of metaphor were added to the term: the first referred to bodily signs of holy grace that took the form of eruptive blossoms on the skin; the second, a medical allusion to this religious allusion, referred to bodily signs of physical disorder. (1963:1)

A **stigma** is therefore a sign of disgrace imposed on an individual. It is a way of spoiling a person's real identity, marking him or her as someone to be avoided. The stigmatizing process operates in numerous settings, and a stigma can be applied as a label to numerous persons: in medicine, to those with physical deformities (cripples, gimps, dwarfs, giants) or mental deviancy (weirdos, lunatics, crazies); in education, to those who achieve low grades in school (retards, dumbos, failures) or, sometimes, to those who achieve high grades (egg heads, nerds, brains); in religion, to those who do not believe in the "one and true" God (witches, heretics, pagans); and in the criminal justice system, to those convicted of crimes (excons, recidivists, career criminals). In these examples a stigma is a sign denoting someone who is disqualified, by varying degrees, from full social acceptance. It can affect self-esteem, self-concept, and future behavior. Returning to the central importance of meaning, we emphasize that a stigma can vary in the meaning that it has both to the person stigmatized and to the social audience.

What are the effects of the stigmatizing process? According to one study (Schwartz and Skolnick, 1964), the effectiveness of legal sanctions against stigmatized individuals often varies with the social position of the defendant penalized. This study showed that unskilled workers suffer much more from the stigma that goes with accusations of assault than do doctors from the effects of accusations of medical malpractice. This finding is supported by a similar study in Holland (Buikhuisen and Dijksterhuis, 1971). This study found that two groups of convicts–one convicted once for theft, the other for drunken driving–received significantly less positive responses than nonconvicts in their job applications to seventy-five large companies.

However, another study, with a somewhat different focus, found that the effects of a stigma are not quite so straightforward. In this study Terance Miethe and Richard McCorkle (1997) set out to test whether prosecutors and judges are biased in their perceptions of gang members. If the "master status" of gang members includes their stereotypical designation as "vile, dangerous, detached, and unpredictable youths" (p. 411), as it did in this study of 168 gang and 202 nongang felony cases in Las Vegas in 1993, then we would expect the criminal justice system to deal relatively harshly with gang members. The study found that the master status was at work, in that sentencing decisions for gang members were far less likely than for nongang members to be affected by other offender and offense characteristics. But the study also found that charges against the sentencing of gang members were more lenient than in nongang cases! This is so, the authors speculated, because of additional images that are attached to the master status of gang membership. For example, prosecutors may be so keen to secure convictions of gang members that they "give up more" to do so, perhaps by plea bargaining or by being more likely to dismiss cases with unreliable witnesses.

What are the different ways in which people respond to being stigmatized? How do stigmatized individuals—to pose Goffman's graphic question—"negotiate" their "spoiled identities" (1963:9)? Research addressing these two questions is inconclusive. The response to stigmatization clearly varies. Sometimes it is relatively easy for stigmatized individuals to hide or to "correct" their stigma. For example, persons with certain forms of deviant attributes, such as physical deformities or illiteracy, can seek surgical or educational remedies to reform or hide their apparent defects. However, as Goffman suggested, these strategies are not always completely successful: "Where such repair is possible, what often results is not the acquisition of fully normal status, but a transformation of self from someone with a particular blemish into someone with a record of having corrected a particular blemish" (1963:9).

The effects of a stigma also depend partly on the institutional context in which it is conferred. In his book *Asylums,* for example, Goffman (1961) reports that in "total institutions"—such as mental hospitals, where "a large number of like-situated individuals, cut off from the wider society for an appreciable period of time, together lead an enclosed, formally administered round of life" (p. xiii)—it is very difficult to shrug off the effects of a stigma. Goffman reported that in the mental institution he studied for three years (St. Elizabeth's Hospital in Washington, D.C.), whenever patients exhibited "normal" behavior, the staff often interpreted that very normalcy as a sign that they were "abnormal"! According to some research (for example, Link, Cullen, Frank, and Wozniak, 1987), former mental patients often encounter public preconceptions that they are dangerous—not on the basis of their behavior but because of the label attached to them.

It is reasonable to conclude that responses to stigmatization are associated strongly with social class and relative powerlessness. The exact nature of this association, however, is unclear. Allen Liska, for example, noted:

> Since blacks occupy a negative social status and are not well integrated into society, they are not very sensitive to official reactions of society. Labeling may have its maximum effect on people well integrated into society; hence, the effects of labeling should be maximal for first offenders, the middle-class, and whites and minimal for prior offenders, the lower class, and blacks. (1987:132–133)

However, although negative labeling arguably can be seen as affecting those with higher social status more than those with lower social status (for example, African Americans), it is also true that the former have greater resources for counteracting stigmatization. The question of whether certain social groups are better equipped to counteract the

The preconceptions of stigmatization: According to the labeling perspective, the societal reaction to deviance exacerbates problems of social isolation and exclusion.

effects of labeling returns us to another question raised by Lemert's distinction between primary and secondary deviance: Is the person on whom the label "criminal" is conferred likely to be propelled into more crime or deterred from future criminal behavior? (Paternoster and Iovanni, 1989; Hagan and Palloni, 1990)

Assessment

In recent years the amount of new empirical research on labeling has dwindled, though the labeling perspective itself remains quite influential in criminology. Its influence continues largely because it reminds us that labels like "crime" and "deviance" are applied selectively to social phenomena. Moreover, the labeling perspective has uncovered the ironic ways in which the process of societal reaction sometimes amplifies the very problems it seeks to eliminate through the stimulation of moral panics and the effects of stigmatization.

A major difficulty with the labeling perspective is that its adherents have never pursued its own ambitious agenda. If terms like "crime" and "deviance" are applied selectively to social behavior, then it is crucial to explore the criteria of selection. Such an examination would involve thoroughgoing questions about the interests served by criminal law. In his book *Controlology*, Jason Ditton therefore complained:

The total rejection of positivism by followers of the labeling perspective either had no effect at all on the institutionalized study of crime or, at best, the massive theoretical critique was distilled into an additional factor ("the reaction") to be henceforth co-opted in the unchanged rhetoric of mathematical calculation. It has always been content instead to snipe at convention from the theoretical sidelines—happy to stand on the lunatic fringe and lob distracting stories of strippers, nudists, gays, teddy boys, nutters, dwarfs, and druggies at the central juggernaut of state-sponsored criminology. (1979:5)

In this assessment Ditton bemoaned the fact that the labeling perspective never became the labeling theory. If criminal behavior really is what agents of social control define it as, then, concluded Ditton, the term "controlology," rather than "criminology," better reflects what we should be studying!

Though the labeling perspective has failed to travel as far as its logical conclusion–what Ditton refers to as "controlology"—nevertheless, its great insights continue to contribute to the development of criminology in at least two respects. First, because its emphasis on the harmful effects of labels has been widely recognized as correct, it has led, with mixed results, to certain changes in criminal justice policy. These changes embrace what Werner Einstadter and Stuart Henry (1995:220–223) have described as decriminalization, diversion, decarceration, and restitution (and see Henry and Milovanovic, 1996; Lanier and Henry, 1998:174–178; and Chapter 8.4). The changes also include the Australian-based movement towards "reintegrative shaming" and "restorative justice" (e.g., Braithwaite, 1989; Braithwaite and Pettit, 1990).

Second, because of its inclination to demystify powerful label-conferring institutions in areas such as criminal justice, mental health, and medicine, the labeling perspective nourishes a climate for the growth of "social constructionism" in criminology. **Social constructionism** encourages a healthy sociological disrespect for how knowledge of social problems like crime is phrased, manipulated, defined, and disseminated in the mass media and in other public forums (see Chapter 1.2). In criminology its influence can be found in numerous studies of how moral entrepreneurs, social movements, and the mass media mold–or ignore–the public perception of the causes, the prevalence, and the seriousness of crimes like serial murder, child abuse, drug use, prostitution, and drinking and driving (e.g. Best, 1990; Jenkins, 1994). Like that of the labeling perspective, the motto of social constructionism might be: "Question Authority!"

7.3   CONFLICT THEORY

In this section we examine conflict theory, a theory of crime that overlaps with the labeling perspective. To understand what conflict theory says about crime, criminalization, and criminal law, we review certain general ideas that conflict theorists hold about the nature of social conflict.

Conflict theory usually is approached by thinking of it in relation to its polar opposite, consensus theory. The debate over consensus and conflict theories pivots on three questions: How is social order possible? What is the nature of power? What is the nature of authority? The many answers given to these questions often hinge on the answers to certain other questions: What is human nature? What are the causes of social inequality? What is a "good" or a "just" society?

According to consensus theory, a democratic society is held together by its members' common acceptance of such basic values as virtue, honor, right, and wrong. These are the basic values on which most people agree most of the time. Because of this common agreement concerning the most important values, social order proceeds in a harmonious and predictable fashion. This means that social change occurs only very slowly, and in a nondisruptive, evolutionary fashion. In such a situation power and authority tend to be invested in persons with intellectual or moral capabilities—persons knowledgeable about and attentive to the public good and the national interest. According to conflict theory, on the other hand, there is little agreement on basic values. Society is made up of many competing groups, each with different interests. Conflict is the paradoxical feature of social order, and social change occurs in disruptive ways. Power and authority tend to be self-perpetuating domains of life that reflect deep-seated patterns of social, economic, and political inequality. In this conflict scenario, law is a weapon that the powerful use to enforce their private interests, often at the expense of the public interest.

Crime and Criminalization

The best introduction to conflict criminology is the pioneering work of Thorsten Sellin. We have already noted (Chapter 1.2) the importance of Sellin's (1938) concept of conduct norms to the continuing debate over the proper definition of crime. We now focus on another aspect of Sellin's argument in his book *Culture Conflict and Crime:* the role of conflict in understanding crime. Sellin suggested that the advance of civilization (namely, of urbanization and industrialization) vastly increases the potential for social and cultural conflict. Instead of the well-knit social fabric of less technologically developed cultures, modern society contains many competing groups, poorly defined interpersonal relationships, and, especially in cities, social anonymity. The rules (conduct norms) of such a society increasingly lack the sort of moral force possessed by the rules that grow out of deep-rooted, unified community sentiments.

For Sellin, crime was one of the many consequences of the conflicting conduct norms and social disorganization of modern society. Culture conflict exists when a person is caught between conflicting cultural rules. Two forms of cultural conflict, especially, tend to result in crime. Primary culture conflict arises when there is a clash between the norms of different cultures. This type of conflict can occur when the law of one group is extended to cover the territory of another group, or when members of one cultural group migrate to the territory of a different group (pp. 63–67, 104). Secondary culture conflict arises from the process of differentiation and inequality in the parent culture (pp. 105–107). An example of secondary culture conflict is the clash between law enforcement and the second generation of immigrant families over the rules governing views of gambling, prostitution, and liquor.

Whereas Sellin emphasized the importance of cultural conflict as a cause of crime, George Vold (1958:203–219; and see Vold, Bernard, and Snipes, 1998:236–238) pointed to the role of what he termed "group conflict" and "political organization." Vold believes

New York police captain tells members of an Irish lesbian and gay organization that they
will be arrested if they try to join a St. Patrick's Day Parade in Bronx, New York in 1999.
(AP Photo/Stephen Chernin)

that in any society people in similar social situations group together to further their interests through collective action. Groups conflict with other groups when the goals of one
can be achieved only at the expense of others: "The prohibitionist wishes to outlaw the
manufacture and sale of alcoholic beverages; the distillers and brewers wish unrestricted
opportunity to make and sell a product for which there is a genuine economic demand"
(1958:208). In turn, distillers and brewers face competition over goals from other groups,
such as trade unionists (who want to raise wages and improve working conditions) and environmentalists (who do not want distillery chemicals to pollute the atmosphere, the soil,
or the land). Environmentalists, in turn, face competition from groups who claim that economic progress should not be restricted by undue government interference. In a democratic society, Vold continued, each of the many interest groups attempts to secure its own
interests by lobbying the legislature to enact laws in its favor. Groups that muster the
greatest number of votes effectively enact new laws that enforce their interests and that, at
the same time, curb the behavior and goals of competing groups. In other words:

The whole political process of law making, law breaking, and law enforcement becomes a direct reflection of deep-seated and fundamental conflicts between interest

groups and their more general struggles for the control of the police power of the state. Those who produce legislative majorities win control over the police power and dominate the policies that decide who is likely to be involved in violation of the law. (p. 209)

For Vold, therefore, crime is behavior committed by minority groups whose regular actions and goals have not been secured by legislative process. Juvenile delinquency, for example, is minority behavior unacceptable to the more powerful adult world. Those who reject the majority view tend to be criminalized. Because patterns of **criminalization** reflect the different degrees of political power wielded by different social groups, Vold argued that much crime should be understood as having a political nature. This is obviously the case for crimes that result, for instance, from political revolution and social protest movements. But it is also true for other, less obvious cases, such as the clash of interests between management and workers and the struggle of racial minorities and women to secure their interests in racist and sexist societies. Vold concluded: "There are many situations in which criminality is the normal, natural response of normal, natural human beings struggling in understandably normal and natural situations for the maintenance of the way of life to which they stand committed" (p. 218).

Vold's focus on the role of power in the process of criminalization was expanded by the influential contributions to conflict theory of Richard Quinney (1970; 1977; Quinney and Wildeman, 1977). Quinney applied his theoretical perspective on the social reality of crime to a variety of situations: the religious and political foundations of criminal law; the behavior of judges, the judiciary, and the police; and such diverse conduct as that defined by the laws of theft, antitrust laws, food and drug laws, sexual psychopath laws, and legislation protecting morality and public order.

Austin Turk has also made influential contributions to conflict theories of crime, especially in his book *Criminality and Legal Order* (1969). Turk's theory is most insightful in showing how conflict theorists understand the process of criminalization. Turk's complicated argument begins with the assumption that the social order of modern societies is based on the relationships of conflict and domination between authorities and subjects (1969:32–34). Authorities are those who make the most important legal decisions about the social order; subjects are those who have little or no influence on the process of decisionmaking or on its substantive content. Slum dwellers, for example, have virtually no control over decisions affecting their life chances in such vital areas as tenancy and welfare. Conflicts between authorities and subjects occur over a wide range of social and cultural norms. Law is a crucial mechanism for resolving (essentially, treating but not curing) many conflicts over acceptable values and behavior. Criminalization is the process by which authorities, for any reason, confer an illegal status on certain behaviors of subjects (resisters). Authorities are either first-line (police) or higher-level enforcers (prosecutors, trial court judges, and appellate court judges).

Turk's theory of criminalization is designed to answer two questions (pp. 64–75): Under what circumstances do subjects become criminals? When are subjects dealt with harshly? Turk's answer to these questions has three parts. First, the more significant a law is to authorities, the more likely it is that resisters will be criminalized. This scenario, of course, assumes that the various enforcers agree to waive their respective discretionary powers not to arrest, not to prosecute, and not to find mitigating circumstances.

BOX 7.1   RICHARD QUINNEY'S CONFLICT THEORY OF CRIME

In his book *The Social Reality of Crime,* Richard Quinney (1970:15–25) stated the six propositions of his conflict theory of crime:

1. The defining quality of crime lies in the definition of crime rather than in criminal behavior as such. This definition is applied by legislators, police, prosecutors, and judges; it is always applied in the context of a society characterized by diversity, conflict, coercion, and change. Society is divided along political lines rather than being an entity based on consensus and stability. Persons become criminal when others define their behavior as criminal.
2. Criminal definitions exist because the interests of some segments (or groups) of society are in conflict with the interests of others. Segments with greater power can have their definitions formulated in law and imposed on those with lesser power. According to Quinney, the greater the degree of social conflict, the more likely it is that the powerful will criminalize the behavior of powerless groups that conflict with their interests.
3. The content of laws and their application tend to reflect the interests of the powerful because the powerful typically control or manipulate members of law enforcement and judicial machinery.
4. Different societal groups typically learn to do different things. The less frequently people engage in law making and law enforcing, the more frequently their actions are defined as criminal. Moreover, increased experience with criminal definitions increases the likelihood that people will do things that are subsequently defined as criminal.
5. There are many conceptions or opinions about which actions should be criminalized. However, Quinney pointed out that the opinions of the most powerful are in fact the most powerful opinions. Through the mass media the opinions of the powerful are communicated to others as the opinions that must be obeyed.
6. The social reality of crime is a composite of the first five propositions (see Figure 7.3).

Second, Turk argued that the probability of criminalization varies according to the respective power of enforcers and resisters. Turk pointed out that "power differences between enforcers and norm resisters vary from relationships in which the enforcers are virtually all-powerful to cases where enforcers and resisters are about equal in resources, including effective organization, manpower, skills, funds, weaponry" (p. 67). One would expect perhaps that the relatively greater the power of enforcers the more likely they are to criminalize offensive behavior. Paradoxically, for Turk the probability of criminalization has a curvilinear relationship with power differences between enforcers and resisters. Turk suggested that the degree of criminalization of resisters depend largely on how threatened the enforcers feel by resisters. He argued that the greater the power of enforcers relative to

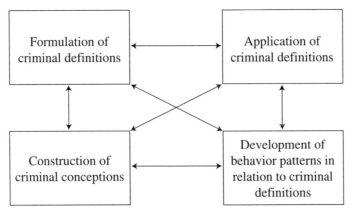

FIGURE 7.3   A Model of the Social Reality of Crime
SOURCE: Quinney, 1970: 25.

resisters, the less likely is it that conflict results in criminalization; the closer their respective amounts of power, the more likely is it that the enforcers resort to criminalization.

Finally, Turk asserted that the probability of criminalization is influenced by what he termed "the realism of conflict moves" (pp. 70–75). By this Turk means that the criminalization of resisters' activities sometimes serves the interests of neither enforcers nor resisters. Because realism depends on knowledge of what it takes to be successful in a conflict, the act of criminalization is therefore often a sign of failure. It would not be particularly astute on the part of the police, for example, if arrests created martyrs that increased the size of the opposition. By the same token, from the point of view of resisters, arrests might be very useful! Again, criminalization is less likely to occur the more sophisticated the resisters.

Criminal Law and Crime

We have seen that criminalization is one of the key concepts of conflict theory. Crime is behavior that is criminalized through the application of criminal law. For conflict theory, then, we cannot understand crime without simultaneously understanding the role of criminal law in society (see Chapter 1.3). We now examine certain ways in which conflict theorists have understood criminal law.

One of the best-known conflict accounts of criminal law is contained in William Chambliss and Robert Seidman's *Law, Order, and Power* (1971). This book contains a comprehensive application of conflict theory to (1) the creation of law, (2) the general principles of law, and (3) the implementation of law. The analysis of law is approached with the underlying assumption that "the central myth about the legal order in the U.S. is that normative structures of the written law represent the actual operation of the legal order" (p. 3). The law in the books, in other words, is not at all the same thing as the law in action. Chambliss and Seidman continued:

This myth of the operation of the law is given the lie daily. We all know today that blacks and the poor are not treated fairly or equitably by the police. We know that judges have discretion and in fact make policy (as the Supreme Court did in the school desegregation cases). We know that electoral laws have been loaded in the past in favor of the rich, and the average presidential candidate is not a poor man, that one-fifth of the senators of the United States are millionaires.

It is our contention that, far from being primarily a value-neutral framework within which conflict can be peacefully resolved, the power of the state is itself the principal prize in the perpetual conflict that is society. The legal order . . . is in fact a self-serving system to devise and maintain power and privilege. (p. 7)

As nineteenth-century philosopher Anatole France once remarked: "The majestic equality of the law allows both the rich and the poor to sleep under bridges if they so choose!"

Chambliss and Seidman's detailed analysis of the relationships between conflict, power, and the purposes of law is extended to such institutions as legislatures, appellate courts, and the police. But perhaps the most telling sections of their analysis concern appellate courts. Although many citizens see how easily the decisions of Congress can be swayed by lobbyists and special interest groups, most of us reject the idea that appellate courts are open to such persuasion. Yet Chambliss and Seidman suggested that the various inputs into the rule-making processes of the appellate courts are "necessarily biased in favor of ensuring that courts as institutions are more available to the wealthy than to the poor, and tend to produce solutions in the interests of the wealthy" (p. 113). These biases cluster around several variables, the two most important of which are (1) the selection of issues with which judges are confronted and (2) their personal characteristics and socialization (pp. 89–112).

Because most appellate cases are initiated by individual litigants, it follows that the majority of such appeals are actually brought by those with sufficient funds to afford them. Thus, most appellate cases, such as those in the area of trusts and corporate law, concern legal problems of the relatively wealthy. Conversely, legal problems of the poor rarely come to the attention of appellate courts. Nowhere is this bias reflected more than in the area of criminal law and police powers. The poor are arrested, interrogated, abused, and incarcerated more often than any other societal group (see Chapter 15.1). But the problems the poor routinely encounter throughout the criminal justice system almost never reach appellate courts. Moreover, the poor lack the funds to hire lawyers to initiate the necessary legal proceedings. Indeed, to protect themselves from the abuse of police powers, the poor must rely almost exclusively on the charitable endeavors of such groups as the American Civil Liberties Union.

For their accounts of the links between power, law, and crime, conflict criminologists have drawn examples from diverse historical periods and a variety of societies. An excellent example concerns a change in the law of theft in medieval England: the *Carrier's Case* of 1473, in which an English court in effect altered the definition of larceny in order to convict a cotton carrier of stealing the contents of several bales that he had been hired to transport.

The *Carrier's Case* is an example of the crude power and conflict that lie behind the majesty of the law. The case is important not only because it shows how judges in fact

> ## BOX 7.2   THE *CARRIER'S CASE*
>
> As reported in Jerome Hall's account of the *Carrier's Case* of 1473 (1969; and see Chambliss, 1964), the facts of the case were as follows. A "carrier" had been hired as a bailee to transport certain bales of cotton to the English port of Southampton. However, during the journey he took the bales to another place, broke them open, and took the contents. The bailee was apprehended, charged, and convicted of larceny by a majority of judges in the Court of Star Chamber.
>
> This innocent-looking case marked an important innovation in the English law of larceny. Prior to the *Carrier's Case*, the element of trespass had to be demonstrated by the prosecution in order for a defendant to be convicted of larceny. At that time, legal opinion agreed that (1) trespass was an essential element of larceny, (2) a person having possession of property could not commit a trespass upon that property, and (3) a bailee has possession (Hall, 1969:34). The common law recognized no criminal liability if a person who was legally entitled to the possession of an item later converted it to his or her own use (the rationale being that owners should protect themselves by selecting a trustworthy carrier [p. 50]). These three precedents therefore created a serious problem: Because the carrier had been legally consigned the bales, they were in his possession. There was then no legal precedent by which the carrier could be convicted of larceny! However, by clever intellectual juggling (known as a legal fiction), it was ruled that the mere opening of the bales ended the carrier's legal possession of them. In this way some of the most important English judges who were hearing the case ruled that the carrier was in fact guilty of larceny. The law of larceny was thus expanded to include this and similar factual situations.

make law but also because it shows how extralegal factors influence judges when they make law.

Hall (1969) identified various political and economic conditions that thrust themselves upon the court in the *Carrier's Case*. It is interesting to note that when the carrier was indicted for larceny no specific mention was made of the contents of the bales he had opened. Hall produced evidence, however, to show that these contents were almost certainly either wool or cloth—no ordinary commodities during the fifteenth century. Indeed, wool and cloth were the products of the most important industry in England at that time, an industry encouraged by a king deeply committed to solidifying his rule at home by gaining the economic and political support of European merchants who traded in these commodities. According to Hall, King Edward IV (the reigning monarch of England) desperately needed to regulate and elevate the standards for security and honesty in the transportation of commodities bound for foreign markets. It is therefore quite likely that the king persuaded the court to expand the law of theft even though legal precedent did not permit it to do so.

Why did the judges expand the law? According to Hall, it was a matter of simple political expediency. During the fifteenth century the court of Star Chamber, like most other judicial bodies, was subject to the political will of the king. Thus, although judges at the time of the *Carrier's Case* wanted to assert their independence from the monarch, they were politically unable to do so. The result was a legal decision dictated by political interests.

The *Carrier's Case* illustrates the conflict theorists' claim that behind the majestic impartiality of the law often lies the power of an elite or a ruling class. When the situation requires, as in the *Carrier's Case,* and in numerous other cases from antiquity forward, the criminal law's thin veneer of neutrality is readily stripped away.

Toward an Integrated Conflict Theory

Recently there has appeared a two-pronged tendency to integrate the many propositions of the conflict tradition and the empirical studies that have sought to test them. On the one hand, this integration has been furthered by a somewhat formal synthesis of the various concepts employed in existing conflict theory. Thus Edmund McGarrell and Thomas Castellano's (1991) integrative model applies ideas about structural conflict, the influence of the mass media, fear of crime, and victimization to the formulation and enforcement of criminal law. Vold, Bernard, and Snipes (1998:253–259) have also offered a unified conflict theory of crime. This theory combines an understanding of how the diverse values and actions in modern societies intersect with political and economic power to influence the enforcement of criminal law and the distribution of official crime rates. On the other hand, especially in the work of John Hagan (1989), there is a movement to integrate aspects of existing conflict theory with concepts derived from the other traditions in criminology and elsewhere.

In his book *Structural Criminology*, Hagan (1989; and see Messerschmidt, 1993:11–14) and his colleagues have developed what is variously termed "power-control theory" and "structural criminology." In his analysis of crime Hagan has combined insights from the labeling perspective, control theory, Marxism and feminism, and a criminology that recognizes the importance of the macro-level of social structure. Hagan's core claim is that the vertical relations of power (e.g., parents over children, and men over women) are more important in understanding patterns of crime and exploitation than horizontal relations (e.g., the effect of peer pressure). In his book Hagan extended this core claim to white-collar and corporate crime; sentencing and punishment; perceptions of (in)justice by different social classes and by race; and delinquency and the family.

One example of Hagan's approach was his integration of studies of labor force participation with those of household structures in order to examine why delinquency rates for males are almost universally higher than for females (1989:145–154). Hagan argued that in Western industrialized societies, an instrument-object relationship exists between parents and children. Parents are the instruments of control, the objects of which are children. This relationship shapes gender patterns. However, these power relations vary with class and gender. In particular, Hagan continued, women gain new power in the family as they enter the labor market. He identifies two family structures based on women's participation in the paid labor market: "patriarchal" and "egalitarian". In the former, the husband/father works outside the home in an authority position and the wife/mother works at home. Through socialization, daughters "focus their futures around domestic labour and consumption, as contrasted with sons who are prepared for participation in direct production" (p. 156). In the latter, the husband/father and wife/mother both work in authority positions outside the home. These egalitarian families "socially reproduce daughters who are pre-pared along with sons to join the production sphere" (p. 157).

Thus, although daughters are less delinquent than sons in both types of family because daughters are more controlled by their mothers, Hagan argued that daughters in patriarchal families are more often taught by parents to avoid risk-taking activities; in egalitarian fam-ilies both daughters and sons are taught to be open to risk-taking. It is this combination of the instrument-object relationship and the corresponding social psychology of risk-taking that affects delinquency. According to Hagan, patriarchal families are characterized by larger gender differences in delinquency: "Daughters become more like sons in their in-volvement in such forms of risk-taking as delinquency" (p. 158).

Hagan must be applauded for integrating some feminist insights into a framework for understanding girls' youth crime and for developing a theory that takes gender seriously as an explanatory variable. Though Hagan's original formulation of power-control theory seems to conclude that "mother's liberation causes daughter's crime" (Chesney-Lind, 1997:22), the theory is important because it demonstrates that gender is constructed dif-ferently in diverse family structures and social classes.

Assessment

Conflict explanations of crime, criminal law, and criminalization have been tested often and, to a certain extent, confirmed by criminologists. Confirmatory test cases include such diverse examples as laws concerning vagrancy (Chambliss, 1964), alcohol (Gusfield, 1963), drugs (Reasons, 1974; Galliher and Cross, 1983), prostitution (Roby, 1969), and bias in court decisions (Hagan, 1974; Chiricos and Waldo, 1975; Lizotte, 1978). In each case the ability of one segment of society to impose its moral view on another was a cru-cial element in the passage of a given law. We note also a study by David Jacobs and David Britt (1979) on police use of deadly force. This study addresses a crucial opera-tional component of the criminal justice system: the relationship between inequality and officially sanctioned violent death. Jacobs and Britt attempted to test the proposition that violence, or the threat of violence, is the crucial element upholding the unequal relation-ships found in nearly all societies today. Controlling for such confounding factors as the police being more likely to use violence in areas with high rates of violent crime, they found that states with the most unequal income distribution were the most likely to have the highest number of police-caused homicides. Moreover, Steven Messner (1980; and see Chapter 16.3) has shown that a variation of this conflict hypothesis applies in many soci-eties around the world. According to Messner, in a sample of 110 societies, high homicide rates were positively correlated with, and perhaps caused by, the social conflict that results from high levels of income inequality.

Finally, we note that it clearly requires a great leap of faith to assume either that law al-ways arises from conflict or that crime always expresses conflict, or that the process of criminalization always serves the interests of the powerful. Most criminologists today re-alize that arguments based on such general assumptions are seriously open to doubt. In-deed, we note that conflict theory has rarely been precise in defining such crucial terms as "power" and "conflict." What, precisely, is "conflict"? Do all conflicts involve "power"? But quite apart from whether the claims of conflict theory should be seen as confirmed, disconfirmed, or simply too abstract to be testable, its chief legacy is its introduction of a "political" dimension largely lacking in earlier criminology. We will return to this dimension in Chapter 15.

7.4   RADICAL AND FEMINIST THEORIES

Radical criminology and feminist criminology are two perspectives on crime that gained considerable importance in criminology in the 1970s and 1980s. In this section we introduce the respective theories and concepts of each perspective.

Radical Criminology

In Chapter 4.3 we outlined Marx and Engels's work on crime. As noted, neither Marx nor Engels devoted much time to the analysis of crime; however, several European socialist writers of the late nineteenth and early twentieth centuries did—attempting to apply Marxist theory to an understanding of crime. Foremost among these socialists was Willem Bonger, who published *Criminality and Economic Conditions* in 1905. Bonger reasoned that a capitalist economic system promotes egoism at the expense of altruism in all members of society and that certain people in all social classes develop a "criminal thought" from such egoism, which eventually leads to crime and to a criminal class (p. 40). All crimes—economic, sexual, political, and pathological—committed by both the economically powerless and the powerful, Bonger argued, were the result of egoism engendered by a capitalist economic system.

Not until some seventy years later was Marxist theory first applied to an understanding of crime in the United States. Instrumental in the development of this "radical criminology" were a number of criminologists, such as Herman and Julia Schwendinger (1975, 1977), William Chambliss (1975), Richard Quinney (1973a, 1973b), Tony Platt (1974), and Raymond Michalowski and Edward Bolander (1976). In Britain, Ian Taylor, Paul Walton, and Jock Young, in *The New Criminology* (1973), assembled a devastating critique of mainstream criminology and then called for a social theory capable of explaining both the wider and immediate origins of the criminal act, as well as the effect of societal reaction on criminal behavior. Although it did not develop an explicit theory of its own, this book prompted theorists in the United States to form various radical perspectives on crime during the 1970s and 1980s.

Steven Spitzer (1975) devised probably the most intriguing Marxist theory of deviance. Assuming that capitalist societies are based on class conflict and that harmony is achieved through the dominance of a specific class, Spitzer reasoned that deviants are drawn from groups who create problems for those who rule. Although these groups largely victimize and burden people in their own classes, "their problematic quality ultimately resides in their challenge to the basis and form of class rule" (p. 640). In other words, populations become problematic for those who rule when they disturb, hinder, or call into question any of the following (p. 642):

1.   capitalist modes of appropriating the product of human labor (called into question when the poor "steal" from the rich)

2. social conditions under which capitalist production takes place (questioned by those who refuse or are unable to perform wage labor)
3. patterns of distribution and consumption in capitalist society (questioned by those who use drugs for escape and transcendence rather than sociability and adjustment)
4. the process of socialization for productive and nonproductive roles (questioned by youth who refuse to be schooled or those who deny the validity of family life)
5. ideology that supports the functioning of capitalist society (questioned by proponents of alternative forms of social organization)

Spitzer argued that problem populations are created in two ways: directly, through fundamental contradictions in the capitalist economy, and indirectly, through contradictions in social control institutions. An example of the direct creation of a problem population is the inherent production of surplus labor (as technological innovation replaces workers with machines) in capitalist economies. Surplus populations are necessary for capitalism because they help support continued capital accumulation. A surplus population provides a mass labor pool that can be drawn into wage labor when necessary and that simultaneously keeps wages down by increasing competition for scarce jobs. However, this surplus population is also problematic in that it must be neutralized and controlled (since it may rebel) if capital accumulation and, therefore, profit making are to continue. Thus, members of this group become eligible for processing as deviants.

Spitzer used mass education as an indirect example of the creation of a problem population. The widespread education of youth from all social classes was developed initially to withhold large numbers of young people from the labor market until they could later be absorbed into wage labor. Yet education simultaneously provides many youth with critical insights into the oppressive character of capitalism. These insights ultimately lead to hostilities toward the system and subsequent mobilization against it (for example, by dropouts and radicals). These youth then become eligible for deviant processing.

Spitzer identified two specific and discrete problem populations: social junk and social dynamite. "Social junk" refers to those who represent a control cost—the handicapped and mentally ill—but are relatively harmless to society. Their deviant status arises from their failure or inability to participate adequately in the capitalist marketplace. "Social dynamite" refers to those with the potential to challenge capitalist relations of production and who, therefore, represent a political threat to the capitalist class. An example of social dynamite is the Communist Party.

Finally, Spitzer maintained a somewhat instrumentalist view of the state; such a view holds that the capitalist class dominates and utilizes the state as a vehicle for capital accumulation and the preservation of economic power. Thus the institutions of the state are molded in accordance with the goals of the capitalist class. Spitzer argued that the institutions of the superstructure—of which the state is part—"originate and are maintained to guarantee the interests of the capitalist class" (p. 643).

In *Class, State, and Crime,* Richard Quinney (1977) also developed a Marxist perspective on crime. He focused on four major areas. First, to understand crime we must study the development of the capitalist political economy, the forces and relations of production, the capitalist state, and the class struggle between the owners of capital and the working class. Second, we must uncover the systems of domination and repression historically used to benefit the capitalist class. Third, the forms of accommodation and resistance to capitalism by oppressed people must be revealed. Finally, the dialectical relationship of accommodation and resistance to the overall conditions of capitalist political economy must be disclosed, since it is there that we find the creation of crimes of domination and crimes of accommodation.

Quinney identified four types of crimes of domination that result from the reproduction of the capitalist system itself (pp. 50–52). "Crimes of control" include crimes by the police and the FBI, such as misdemeanors, felonies, brutality, illegal surveillance, and violation of civil liberties. "Crimes of government" involve political crime, such as Watergate and CIA assassinations of foreign political leaders. "Crimes of economic domination" consist primarily of corporate crimes ranging from price-fixing to pollution but also including the close connections between syndicated crime and criminal operations of the state. Finally, "social injuries" are harms not defined as illegal in legal codes, such as the denial of basic human rights resulting from sexism, racism, and economic exploitation.

"Crimes of accommodation" are acts of adaptation by the lower and working classes in response to the oppressive conditions of capitalism and the domination of the capitalist class (pp. 54–55). "Predatory crimes" are parasitical in nature and include such acts as burglary, robbery, and drug dealing. "Personal crimes"—such as murder, assault, and rape—are directed at other members of the lower and working classes and result from the brutalized conditions of capitalism. Finally, "crimes of resistance" are actions conducted by members of the working class that are specifically directed at the workplace—such as sabotage and machine breaking. As Quinney summarized:

> Crimes of accommodation and resistance thus range from unconscious reactions to exploitation, to conscious acts of survival within the capitalist system, to politically conscious acts of rebellion. These criminal actions, moreover, not only cover the range of meaning but also actually evolve or progress from *unconscious reaction* to *political rebellion*. Finally, the crimes may eventually reach the ultimate stage of conscious political action—*revolt*. (p. 59)

Thus, for Quinney, the crimes of domination seem to be the real societal harms, but they are not criminalized because they benefit the ruling class. Crimes of accommodation, on the other hand, range from simple adaptation to conscious political resistance. In fact, for Quinney some crimes and, therefore, criminals are admirable elements in the overall class struggle.

Quinney also took an instrumentalist view of the state, arguing that it promotes the interests of the ruling class and "is a device for controlling the exploited class, the class that labors, for the benefit of the ruling class" (pp. 44–45). Quinney maintained further that the "coercive force of the state, embodied in law and legal repression, is the traditional means of maintaining the social and economic order" (p. 45). Law then "is an instrument of the state that serves the interests of the developing capitalist ruling class" (p. 45).

Spitzer and Quinney developed their models of crime in the 1970s. In the 1980s, new models emerged. We summarize one of these, the work of William Chambliss.

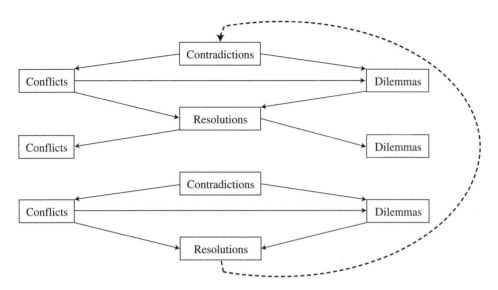

FIGURE 7.4   Structural-Contradictions Theory
SOURCE: Chambliss, 1988: 305.

William Chambliss (1988b) outlined a structural contradictions theory of crime. Chambliss argued that all historical eras and all societies, while constructing their means of survival, create contradictory forces, dilemmas, and conflicts (pp. 300–309). Under capitalism, the basic contradiction is between capital and labor. This contradiction results in worker demands for better working conditions and higher wages, even as capitalists resist these demands. The dilemma for capital, labor, and the state is how to reconcile the conflict, inasmuch as the fundamental contradiction is ignored. Resolving the conflict can result either in further conflicts—because the fundamental contradiction persists—or in an additional contradiction (as shown in Figure 7.4).

Chambliss also took a structuralist–rather than instrumentalist–position on the state. For structuralists, the state in capitalist societies takes a capitalist form not because of those who fill decisionmaking positions but because the state reflects capitalist economic relations; that is, the state is molded to fit and serve the interests of the capitalist economy regardless of those who fill its offices. For Chambliss, then, the law represents the state's response to various aspects of class struggle in a contradictory capitalist economy. Contradictions create dilemmas and conflicts—which those in state positions attempt to resolve—leaving the contradictions in place. Although Chambliss agreed with instrumentalists that the capitalist class puts pressure on the state to pass laws that serve its interests (winning most of the time), resistance and pressure from other class forces are always present. When resistance leads to open conflict, the state responds through the law.

Chambliss also identified two fundamental contradictions in a capitalist political economy that lead to crime (pp. 308–309). The first is the "wages, profits, and consumption contradiction." If, on the one hand, workers have insufficient money to purchase commodities (because capitalists do not pay them enough in wages), the economy becomes sluggish. If, on the other hand, workers are paid high wages, this cuts into profits, and there is less money for reinvestment. This inherent contradiction of capitalism culminates in crime (pp. 308–309).

In addition, Chambliss identified a "wages–labor supply contradiction." Capitalism maintains a surplus labor force that helps keep wages down and provides a supply of labor from which capital can draw whenever the demands of workers threaten profits. The demanding workers are let go, and fresh labor is brought in. However, this reserve army of labor simultaneously "forms an underclass that cannot consume but nonetheless is socialized into a system in which consumption is the necessary condition for happiness. Criminal behavior offers a solution for the underclass: what they cannot earn legitimately they can earn illegitimately" (p. 309).

In sum, the above approaches employ Marxist theory to understand the relationship between the political and economic realms of a capitalist society. These perspectives advance our understanding of why certain behaviors are criminalized by the state whereas others are not, and of how a capitalist economic system itself generates certain class patterns of crime.

Assessment

Using Marxist social theory, radicals in the 1970s and 1980s developed theories that give priority to historical and structural analyses of crime, focusing on economic relationships, class struggle, capital accumulation, and the role of the reserve army of labor.

Radical criminology is not without its critics. For some, a radical criminology grounded in Marxist theory is actually impossible, inasmuch as crime is not an explicit Marxian concept like, for example, "mode of production" or "capital accumulation." Mainstream criminologists have criticized radical criminology for being unscientific (Turk, 1979), for being moralistic (Klockars, 1979; Toby, 1979), and for being utopian (Nettler, 1978). Radicals, however, have soundly addressed all these criticisms (Beirne, 1979; Greenberg, 1981).

Some of the most useful criticisms of radical criminology have been made by radical criminologists themselves. For example, Spitzer (1980) argued that much of radical criminology is metafunctional. That is, capitalism is theorized "as 'needing' crime in order to justify its oppression of the masses" (p. 176). Radical criminologists have also identified problems with instrumental outlooks on the state. As noted, this position holds that the ruling class exercises state power directly through the manipulation of state policies. Critics have pointed out that neither the state nor the ruling class is monolithic—conflicts of interests exist both within the state and the ruling class, as well as between them (Spitzer, 1980:177; Beirne, 1979; Chambliss and Seidman, 1982).

Radical criminology has also been criticized for its one-dimensional nature. Radical criminology, it is claimed, attempts to explain all crime in economic terms. This means that other social relations, such as gender and race relations, are at best secondary to class relations. This secondariness has been challenged by feminist criminologists and is discussed in the following section.

Feminist Criminology

The feminist movement has made an important impact on the social sciences, including sociology and criminology. The term "feminist" is commonly and broadly used to refer to all those who consciously maintain that women are discriminated against because of their gender and who seek to end women's resulting subordination through social change.

Kathleen Daly and Meda Chesney-Lind (1988:108) have outlined five core elements of feminist thought that help distinguish feminism from other forms of social theory:

1. Gender is not a natural fact but a complex social, historical, and cultural product; it is related to, but not simply derived from, biological sex difference and reproduction capacities.
2. Gender and gender relations order social life and social institutions in fundamental ways.
3. Gender relations and constructs of masculinity and femininity are not symmetrical but are based on an organizing principle of men's superiority and social- and political-economic dominance over women.
4. Systems of knowledge reflect men's views of the natural and social world; the production of knowledge is gendered.
5. Women should be at the center of intellectual inquiry, not peripheral, invisible, or appendages to men.

Contemporary feminist contributions to criminology can be divided into two phases, the first extends from the late 1960s to the mid-1980s and the second from the late 1980s throughout the 1990s (Daly and Maher, 1998). We discuss the second phase in Chapter 8.4

In the first phase, feminist criminologists concentrated on criticizing criminological theory for either being gender-blind or misrepresenting women. Feminist criminologists also conducted investigations of women's experiences as offenders, victims, and workers in the criminal justice system, and they employed popular feminist theories of the time—liberal, Marxist, radical, and socialist—to explain women's and men's involvement in crime.

In the next section we briefly consider the feminist theoretical perspectives on crime that emerged in the 1970s and 1980s.

Varieties of Feminist Criminology

As Jaggar and Rothenberg (1984:83–84) point out, **liberal feminism** has its roots in the eighteenth- and nineteenth-century social ideals of liberty and equality. Liberty came to be understood as freedom from interference by the state, primarily in the private sphere. The ideal of equality required that

> each individual should be able to rise in society just as far as his or her talents permit, unhindered by restraints of law or custom. What qualities should count as talents and how they should be rewarded is to be determined by the supply and demand for those talents within a market economy. In order to guarantee that the most genuinely talented individuals are identified, it is necessary to ensure that everyone has an equal opportunity to develop his or her talents. Within the liberal tradition, therefore, equality has come to be construed as equality of opportunity. (p. 84)

The formulation of the ideals of liberty and equality created the conditions that motivated women to demand that these ideals be applied to them as well as to men. From Mary

Wollstonecraft's *A Vindication of the Rights of Women* in 1792 and John Stuart Mill's *The Subjection of Women* in 1851 to *Ms.* magazine and the publications of the National Organization for Women (NOW), the roots of women's subordination, for liberal feminists, are embedded in the denial to women of civil rights and social opportunities. Liberal feminists argue that women should receive the same rights and have the same opportunities as men. Women are oppressed because of gender discrimination, which deprives them of the same opportunities and rights that men enjoy. Consequently, women are effectively kept outside the mainstream of society (politics, business, finance, medicine, law, and so forth). Liberal feminists argue that this problem can be resolved by letting women into the mainstream. The liberal feminist program calls for state reform to bring about those changes necessary to promote women's rapid integration into the backbone of society.

One of the reasons for women's discrimination, according to liberal feminists, is gender role socialization. Liberal feminists argue that conventional family patterns structure masculine and feminine identities. Girls and women, on the one hand, are socialized to be patient, understanding, sensitive, passive, dependent, and nurturing. The female role, liberal feminists continue, centers on functions reflecting these personality traits; such functions are found specifically in the family (women's identity resides in the domestic sphere) but also in the labor market, where women take gender-specific jobs such as clerical, service, and sales-type jobs. Boys and men, on the other hand, are socialized to be self-confident, independent, bold, responsible, competitive, and aggressive. The male role reflects these traits, as a man is encouraged to find an identity in the public sphere (the workplace), thus providing money and security for "his" family. Because the role and the traits associated with femininity are defined as inferior, sexist ideologies arise that consider women to be second-class persons. Accordingly, because of the emphasis on both equality and socialization, liberal feminists have called for policies providing women with equal opportunities and androgynous socialization.

Some criminologists have used liberal feminist theory to explain the relationships between opportunity, socialization, and crime. Rita Simon (1975), for instance, argued that until the 1970s women's crime was quite limited because women's opportunities were restricted. With the rise of the second wave of the feminist movement in the 1960s and the subsequent liberated woman of the 1970s, women were provided with more opportunities to act like men. Simon alleged that this increased equality in the labor market resulted in increased opportunities for women to commit occupationally related crimes such as embezzlement. However, as we note in the assessment below, increased women's crime is made up of primarily nonoccupationally related crimes such as larceny (mostly shoplifting) and petty forms of fraud.

A more sophisticated formulation of liberal feminist opportunity theory was provided by Josephina Figueira-McDonough (1980), who theorized that similar levels of strain (resulting from high success aspirations and low legitimate opportunities) lead to similar criminal behavior patterns by both genders if they have equal knowledge of and comparable access to illegitimate means.

Liberal feminists also attempt to explain crime in terms of gender role socialization. In the 1970s several liberal feminist writers emphasized the relationship between gender role and crime. For example, Dale Hoffman-Bustamante (1973) explained how patterns of crime are related to the different role expectations of men and women and thus to gender differences in socialization patterns. Ann Oakley was more explicit, contending that "the patterns of male and female crime are tied to cultural patterns of masculinity and femininity, so that the type and the amount of crime committed by each sex express both sex-typed personality and sex-typed social role" (1972:68). Oakley saw crime as specifically masculine, which helps explain women's lower crime rate:

> Criminality and masculinity are linked because the sorts of acts associated with each have much in common. The demonstration of physical strength, a certain kind of aggressiveness, visible and external "proof" of achievement, whether legal or illegal— these are facets of the ideal male personality and also of much criminal behavior. Both male and criminal are valued by their peers for these qualities. Thus, the dividing line between what is masculine and what is criminal may at times be a thin one. (p. 72)

Oakley went on to argue that although crime may be a specific manifestation of masculinity and, therefore, predominantly male, "the sex difference has narrowed considerably in recent years, suggesting that, as some of the differences between the sex roles are reduced by the conditions of modern life, the deviance of male and female becomes more alike" (p. 70). This point was later emphasized by Adler in her book *Sisters in Crime* (1975). Adler argued that because of the women's movement, by the mid-1970s gender roles had so merged that women became more masculine and, thus, engaged in more violent crime.

Specific types of female crime have also been analyzed by liberal feminists in terms of gender role socialization. For example, Karen Rosenblum (1975:179) argued that important parallels exist between the attributes of the female gender role and prostitution, so that the latter can be interpreted simply as a consequence and extension of fundamental aspects of the former. Women are defined as sex objects—either of lust or chastity—yet are socialized to be passive sexually and also to use sex as a means to status. Consequently, "the difference between the utilization of and expectations regarding sexuality is only one of degree. The decision to become a call girl simply requires an exaggeration of one aspect of the situation experienced as a nondeviant woman" (p. 180).

Marxist feminism differs considerably from liberal feminism. Marxist feminists theorize, following Engels (1970a), that the class and gender divisions of labor together determine the social position of women and men in any society, but the gender division of labor is seen as resulting from the class division of labor. According to Marxist feminists, as private property evolved, males began to dominate all social institutions. Thus Marxist feminists view the capitalist mode of production as the basic organizing mechanism of Western societies; this mode of production determines the social relations between classes and genders. Gender and class inequalities result from property relations and the capitalist mode of production. For Marxist feminists, masculine dominance is an ideological manifestation of a class society in which women are primarily dominated by capital and only secondarily by men. The latter form of domination, however, results from the mode of production. Although most Marxist feminists examine masculine dominance and sexism in society, they comprehend the roles of men and women in relation to capital, not in relation to a separate system of masculine power and dominance. Women's labor in the home is analyzed not in terms of how it benefits men but, rather, how it provides profits for the capitalist class.

An excellent illustration of a Marxist feminist approach to crime is the work of Sheila Balkan, Ron Berger, and Janet Schmidt in their book *Crime and Deviance in America* (1980). Discussing women's crime, they argued that a capitalist mode of production "lays the foundation for a theory of women's criminality" (p. 211). In order to understand female criminality, they continued, we must understand the ideology of sexism and how it legitimates the structure of the family under capitalism. By reason of the needs of a capitalist society—in particular the reproduction of labor power—women's social position has been centered in the family, sexuality, and the home. Sexism, they argued, is an ideological result of capitalist relations that structure women's position and women's crime. Consequently, nonviolent crime by women—such as shoplifting and prostitution—reflects such conditions. Moreover, when women commit violent crimes such as murder, their victims are usually family members, relatives, or lovers. Women are also less likely to use guns and more likely to use such household implements as kitchen knives as weapons. Thus women's crime reflects their oppressed position in a capitalist economic system.

Similarly, Julia and Herman Schwendinger's (1983) Marxist feminist analysis of rape contended that the level of male violence in any society is determined primarily by class relations and the mode of production. The Schwendingers argued that societies without commodity production are gender egalitarian, women are deemed equal to men in most aspects of social life, and violence against women is almost nonexistent. When such societies begin to produce for exchange (either voluntarily or because of the imposition of colonial power), men control the production system and women are confined to the home. This new division of labor results in an increase in male authority, a decrease in women's social position, and violence against women. Hence, gender inequality and violence against women become closely tied to and rooted in the mode of production. Indeed, the Schwendingers concluded that exploitative modes of production in class societies either produce or intensify gender inequality and violence against women (p. 179).

Marxist feminism emphasizes the structural conditions of a class society (more specifically, a capitalist society) as the root cause of masculine dominance, women's special oppression, and thus crime; **radical feminism** sees masculine power and privilege as the root cause of all social relations and inequality. For radical feminists, the most important relations in any society are found in **patriarchy** (masculine control of the labor power and sexuality of women); all other relations (such as class) are secondary and derive from male–female relations. Radical feminists also assert the following (Jaggar and Rothenberg, 1984:86):

- Women were, historically, the first oppressed group.
- Women's oppression is the most widespread, existing in virtually every known society.
- Women's oppression is the deepest, in that it is the hardest form of oppression to eradicate and cannot be removed by other social changes such as the abolition of class society.

Catharine MacKinnon (1984:515), a prominent radical feminist, adds that the control of women's sexuality by men is central to masculine dominance. Sexuality, the primary social sphere of male power, entails the expropriation of women's sexuality by men, and this expropriation structures men and women as social and sexual beings within society. For MacKinnon, power is maintained over women through compulsory heterosexuality and sexual violence (rape, wife beating, sexual harassment, and pornography).

It follows that when discussing crime, radical feminists concentrate on violence against women. Certain segments of radical feminism emphasize biological determinism in their discussion of crime. For example, writing about rape, Susan Brownmiller argued that "by anatomical fiat—the inescapable construction of their genital organs—the human male was a *natural* predator and the human female served as his *natural* prey" (1975:16, emphasis added). For Brownmiller, gender inequality is the result of the anatomical and biological makeup of men and women. Male anatomy and biology provide men with the apparatus to rape women; by the very nature of their anatomy and biology, women "cannot retaliate in kind" (p. 14). Women's overall subordination and men's criminality—particularly male violence against females—result from these biological facts.

Many radical feminists disagree with Brownmiller's extreme biological determinism, arguing instead that women's victimization by men results from their social position rather than their biology. For example, Elizabeth Stanko (1985) argued in her book *Intimate Intrusions* that because of masculine dominance and female powerlessness, the "normal" male is physically aggressive and the "normal" female experiences this aggression in the form of sexual violence. For Stanko, violence against women seems to be universal across time and place: "To be a woman—in most societies, in most eras—is to experience physical and/or sexual terrorism at the hands of men" (p. 9). Thus, male violence is a reflection of the universality of male dominance and the secondary status of women. Moreover, following MacKinnon's position on sexuality, Stanko argued: "Women learn, often at a very early age, that their sexuality is not their own and that maleness can at any point intrude into it. Sexuality, then, is a form of power, and gender, as socially constructed, embodies it, not the reverse. As such, male sexual and physical prowess takes precedence over female sexual and physical autonomy" (p. 73).

According to Stanko, women, as appendages to men, are "expected to endure or alternatively have been seen as legitimate, deserving targets of male sexual and physical aggression because that is part of what men *are*. Women, as connected to men, are then violated" (p. 74). Male violence is customary in patriarchal culture; therefore, it is also customary that women endure it. Thus this ideology helps maintain male dominance and control over women. As Stanko concluded: "Forced sexuality for women is 'paradigmatic' of their existence within a social sphere of male power" (p. 75).

In short, radical feminists view the basic structure of social reality as a total system of male domination. This form of domination is constructed by men and enables them to control women's bodies and thereby to trap women as forced sexual slaves (Jaggar, 1983:270).

Finally, **socialist feminism** differs from both Marxist and radical feminism: It prioritizes neither class nor gender. Socialist feminists view both class and gender relations as interacting and co-reproducing each other in society. For socialist feminists, class and gender interact to determine the social organization of society at any particular time in history.

To understand class, socialist feminists argue that we must recognize how it is structured by gender; conversely, to understand gender requires an examination of how it is structured by class. Consequently, our overall life experiences are shaped by both class and gender relations, and the interaction of these relationships structures crime in society.

An example of a socialist feminist explanation of crime is James Messerschmidt's book *Capitalism, Patriarchy, and Crime* (1986b). Messerschmidt argued that the United States is a patriarchal capitalist society and that the interaction of patriarchy and capitalism patterns the types and seriousness of crime. This interaction creates a powerless group of women and the working and lower classes, on one hand, and, on the other, a powerful group of men and the professional-managerial (traditional middle) and capitalist classes on the other. For Messerschmidt, power constituted by both gender and class is critical to understanding crime:

> It is the powerful (in both the gender and class spheres) who do most of the damage to society, not, as is commonly supposed, the disadvantaged, poor, and subordinate. The interaction of gender and class creates positions of power and powerlessness in the gender/class hierarchy, resulting in different types and degrees of criminality and varying opportunities for engaging in them. Just as the powerful have more legitimate opportunities, so they have more illegitimate opportunities. (p. 42)

Given that men and members of the professional-managerial and capitalist classes have the most power, they have greater opportunities to engage in crime, not only more often but also in ways that are more harmful to society. Males of all social classes therefore commit more crime than females, their class position determining the type of crime they may commit (for example, lower- and working-class males have no opportunity to commit corporate crimes, whereas professional- and managerial-class males have no need to resort to conventional crimes). Low female crime rates were understood by Messerschmidt to be related to women's powerless position in the United States. Their subordinate position relegates women to fewer legitimate as well as fewer illegitimate opportunities and to fewer resources with which to engage in serious forms of crime. Thus, overall, socialist feminists argue that crime is related to the opportunities a gender/class position allows, and they attempt a simultaneous explanation of the gender and class patterns of crime.

Assessment

Feminist criminology of the 1970s and 1980s made significant contributions to the field of criminology and, as we will see in chapter 8.4, continues to flourish in the 1990s. Most concerns about first phase feminist criminology centered on the feminist theories used to explain crime. For example, liberal feminism has been criticized for its inability to "explain the emergence of gender inequality, nor can it account, other than by analogy, for effects of race and class stratification on the conditions of women's lives. Its analysis for change tends to be limited to issues of equal opportunity and individual choice" (Andersen, 1993:318).

A critique of Rita Simon's position on crime supplies another example of the kind of criticism leveled at liberal feminism. Simon (1975) argued that the women's movement has increased women's opportunities in the labor market and that this explains their increasing involvement in property crimes. But this argument ignores the fact that the sharpest increases in property crimes are found in nonoccupational theft, such as larceny (mostly shoplifting) and minor fraud (such as check and welfare fraud) (Chesney-Lind, 1997). Moreover, most female property offenders are adolescents with little or no contact with the labor market (Chesney-Lind, 1997).

The liberal feminist emphasis on gender role socialization has also been criticized. Smart argued that liberal feminism failed to place the discussion of gender roles "within a structural explanation of the social origin of those roles" (1976:69). In other words, liberal feminists did not account historically, socially, and economically for women's subordinate position in the gender division of labor and, therefore, did not explain the broader reasons for the current patterns of socialization. Smart also criticized role theory for not discussing female motivation or intent. As she pointed out: "Role theory does not explain why, even though women are socialized into primarily conforming patterns of behavior, a considerable number engage in crime" (p. 69).

Both Marxist feminism and radical feminism have been criticized for being reductionist. Marxist feminists have been faulted for reducing all social phenomena—including male and female crime—to economic conditions and for being unable to explain gender divisions and power relations between men and women. Radical feminist theory has been criticized for its view that social classes are simply an epiphenomenon of gender inequality. Moreover, a major problem with radical feminist theory is that it assumes universal female subordination. Yet anthropological research has shown that in many gathering and hunting societies, gender relations were quite equal and men did not control the labor power and sexuality of women (Reiter, 1975; Shostak, 1983). Radical feminists have also been criticized for explaining male violence against women in biological terms or as simply a reflection of masculine power and dominance. Finally, the term "patriarchy," which both radical and socialist feminists use to label masculine dominance, has been criticized for its timeless characterization of masculine power and prestige. In other words, neither radical nor socialist feminists have adequately accounted for historical changes in patriarchy and its various forms.

REVIEW

This chapter examined five influential theories of crime: social learning theory; the labeling perspective; conflict theory; and radical theory and feminist theory. Each offers a different view of the processes that culminate in crime.

Social Learning Theory

1. Social learning theory begins with the idea that social behavior is a cognitive process in which personality and environment interact reciprocally. It was pioneered in laboratory settings under the influence of B. F. Skinner's operant conditioning theory, according to which desired behavior can be reinforced by conditioned learning based on rewards and punishments.

2. Some criminologists have argued that whether individuals commit crime depends on their past conditioning history (namely, whether they have been reinforced [or rewarded] for having committed crime). Akers's social learning theory attempted to revise Sutherland's theory of differential association. Its major concepts are (1) differential reinforcement and (2) positive and negative definitions.

3. Social learning theory is a general theory of crime: It attempts to explain all crime.

4. Social learning theory has not (as yet) greatly influenced criminology, partly because it arose at a time when deterministic theories of crime were unfashionable.

The Labeling Perspective

1. The labeling perspective claims that deviance and crime are in the eye of the beholder. It is not the quality of an act that makes it deviant or criminal but the perception of it as such by a social audience. The labeling perspective is very much a creature of the social and political unrest of the 1960s.

2. Its underlying themes are a romantic attachment to the underdog, a reflexive concern with the role of the criminologist in an inegalitarian society, an opposition to scientism, and an emphasis on the importance of meanings in social interaction.

3. The distinction between primary and secondary deviance highlights how the societal reaction to deviance creates and amplifies the very behavior it seeks to control.

4. Deviance amplification also occurs through stigmatization. The stigmatizing effect of the label attached to primary deviation is one of the most important factors in secondary deviation. The handling of stigmatization requires skill and power that many individuals do not possess.

5. The labeling perspective has never been carried through to its logical conclusion. If crime and deviance are only categories conferred on behavior by agents of social control, then criminology should be reoriented "controlology."

Conflict Theory

1. Conflict theory, often contrasted with consensus theory, overlaps with the labeling perspective. Its key idea is that in order to understand crime we must also understand the interests served by criminal law. On this view, crime is a category applied to some persons after a politico-legal process of criminalization. Theoretically, then, crime and criminal law are merely different sides of the same coin.

2. According to conflict theory, crime and criminal law are the two basic aspects of the process of criminalization. It is this process that criminologists should study.

3. The most influential examples of conflict theory are Vold's theory of group conflict and crime, Quinney's theory of the social reality of crime, and Turk's theory of criminalization.

4. Chambliss and Seidman have applied many insights of conflict theory in an attempt to understand the creation of law, the general principles of law, and the implementation of law. Law typically reflects the interests of the powerful.

5. Many assumptions of conflict theory have been revealed as overly generalized. Conflict theory, as such, has been most influential in the continuing popularity of the labeling perspective and in the emergence of radical criminology.

Radical and Feminist Criminology

1. Although Marx and Engels never gave crime concerted attention, several European socialist writers, such as Willem Bonger, applied Marxist theory to crime in the late nineteenth and early twentieth centuries.

2. It was not until the 1970s that a radical criminology emerged in the United States.

3. In the 1970s and 1980s, radical criminology developed various Marxist perspectives on crime and social control.

4. These approaches use Marxist theory to understand (1) why some behavior is criminalized and other behavior is not and (2) how a capitalist economic system generates class patterns of crime.

5. Feminist criminologists have developed four major perspectives–liberal, Marxist, radical, and socialist–that have been used to explain crime. Each feminist perspective looks at gender relationships in a distinct way, asks different questions, and explains crime differently.

QUESTIONS FOR CLASS DISCUSSION

1. Can social learning theory adequately explain the causes of suicide?

2. In his book *Outsiders,* Howard Becker wrote that "deviance is *not* a quality of the act the person commits, but rather a consequence of the application by others of rules and sanctions to an 'offender'" (1963:9). Do you agree with Becker's view? Why? Why not?

3. Can crime be studied properly without simultaneously studying the process of criminalization?

4. Compare the various Marxist perspectives on crime with some of the other theories discussed in this book.

5. Choose several crimes (such as wife battering or prostitution) and show how the four feminist perspectives explain them.

FOR FURTHER STUDY

Readings

Akers, Ronald L. 1998. *Social Learning and Social Structure: A General Theory of Crime and Deviance*. Boston: Northeastern University Press.

Daly, Kathleen, and Meda Chesney-Lind. 1988. Feminism and Criminology. *Justice Quarterly* 5 (4): 101–143.

Matza, David. 1964. *Delinquency and Drift*. New York: John Wiley.

Michalowski, Raymond. 1985. *Order, Law, and Crime*. New York: Random House.

Vold, George B., Thomas J. Bernard, and Jeffrey B. Snipes. 1998. *Theoretical Criminology*. New York: Oxford University Press.

Websites

1. <http://www.aber.ac.uk/~dgc/tv07.html>: This Media and Communication Studies site compiles information regarding television viewing and violent behavior, with links to social learning theory. This site also has a link to Bandura's famous study of the "BoBo" dolls.
2. <http://www.sonoma.edu/cja/info/Edintro.html>: This site is constructed in memory of Edwin Lemert. It is a professional and personal biography of this influential criminologist.
3. <http://sun.soci.nui.edu/~critcrim/CC/cc.html>: A special issue of the *Critical Criminologist*, newsletter of the Division on Critical Criminology in the American Society of Criminology. This site provides summary essays about radical and feminist criminological perspectives.

Preview

Chapter 8 introduces:
- the theory of routine activities and crime
- two general theories of crime and deviance: the theory of self-control and the theory of control balance
- two notable revisions to Mertonian strain and anomie theory: general strain theory and institutional anomie theory
- several varieties of critical criminology, including left realism, peacemaking, postmodernism, and feminism

Key Terms

constitutive criminology
control balance
control deficit
control surplus
feminism
general theory
integrated theory
left idealism

left realism
peacemaking criminology
postmodernism
rational choice
routine activities theory
self-control theory
strain

In this chapter we outline the key aspects of several new theories in criminology. Each of these theories was developed at some point in the late 1980s or early 1990s. To a greater or lesser extent, each has been further elaborated and refined in response to scholarly criticism.

Though several of these theories embody a new movement towards "integrated" theory, the only accurate generalization that can be made about the theories discussed in this chapter is that they are extraordinarily varied in their basic assumptions about human sociality and in their substantive claims about crime. Some of them regard themselves as "general" theories of crime, that is, they attempt to explain all cases of the phenomena in their scope. Each has a somewhat different idea of the process of theory construction. Most of the theories discussed here differ from their competitors in what they identify as the causes of crime. Some of them believe that the search for the causes of crime is a futile enterprise doomed from the very outset. Moreover, critical criminology, which emerged from radical and feminist criminologies of the 1970s and 1980s, attempts to develop theoretical perspectives that contribute to the pursuit of positive social change and social justice.

8.1   ROUTINE ACTIVITIES AND CRIME

Routine activities theory reflects the fact that high crime rates have become a normal part of life in the United States (see Garland, 1999). The main features of routine activities theory derive from the insights of a number of other perspectives on crime and victimization, including the free-will basis of human action (rational choice), allegedly popularized by the eighteenth-century classical criminology of Beccaria and Bentham (Cornish and Clarke, 1986; and see Chapter 3.1); the Chicago school of ecology (see Chapter 5.2); and empirical studies showing that patterns of crime and victimization vary in time, in location, and in the social distance between offender and victim (e.g., Hindelang, 1976; Hindelang, Gottfredson, and Garofalo,1978; and see Chapter 15). The key claim of routine activities theory is that patterns of crime and victimization are the result of the everyday interaction of likely offenders, suitable targets, and guardians. The interaction of these three variables in geographical space and in time determines crime rates in modern society.

The Chemistry of Crime

According to Cohen and Felson, routine activities include any "recurrent and prevalent activities which provide for basic population and individual needs, whatever their biological or cultural origins" (1979:593). Routine activities may occur at home or away from home. Examples of these everyday activities include commuting to work and numerous events associated with providing and acquiring food and shelter, sexual outlets, leisure, learning, and childrearing.

Figure 8.1 displays the three basic ingredients in routine activities theory, which Felson provocatively terms "the chemistry for crime" (1998:52–74).

1.   There must be a suitable target. Targets may be either property or persons. Though the sociological characteristics of offenders are not a part of routine activities theory, the theory specifies four factors according to which the "suitability" of a target varies from the offender's perspective. These factors include its value, its inertia (how mobile or how easy it is to carry), its visibility, and its accessibility. Clearly, some targets, such as corner lots or public parks—called "hot spots"—are more vulnerable than others. Some targets are more suitable not only because they are worth more, for example, but also because no one is protecting them or looking out for them.

2.   There must be a target whose guardian or protector can be overcome by an offender. A suitable target may be protected either by formal guardians such as police officers or, far more likely, by ordinary citizens such as neighbors and pedestrians going about their everyday affairs. Their mere presence may deter a likely offender. Guardians also include nonhuman surveillance systems such as video security systems or burglar alarms.

3.   There must be a likely offender who may consciously plan to find a suitable target or else stumble across it. Although the specific motivation of any given offender is irrelevant to routine activities theory, offenders tend to be opportunists who may choose to commit crimes either against property or against persons. In the case of the latter, offenders are more likely to pick victims who are physically weaker or who are outnumbered or otherwise at a disadvantage.

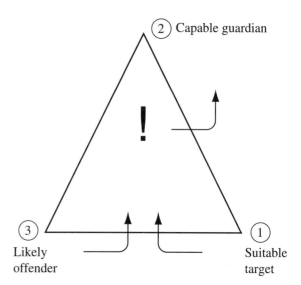

FIGURE 8.1   Dashing for the Goods
SOURCE: Felson, 1998: 53.

A Routine Activity Approach to Crime Trends

Cohen and Felson have used the microlevel assumptions described above to explain changes in crime rates in the United States in two periods: 1947–1974 and 1992–1996. Crimes in both periods were viewed as normal events that matter-of-factly accompanied modernization and business growth. For the period 1947–1974 Cohen and Felson (1979) began with the seeming paradox that during that time crime rates increased substantially even though there were, by some criteria, improvements in the economic conditions that many think are the breeding grounds of crime.

To explain this paradox they argued that some basic changes in the routine activities of the population led to an increase in the number of suitable targets and to a decrease in guardian presence; in combination, these changes produced an increase in the crime rate. They pointed out that during the period 1947–1974 there were some basic changes in the routine activities of families and household members. Thus in the decade after 1960 the percentage of the population consisting of female college students increased by 118 percent and married female labor force participation rose 31 percent. In other words, more households were empty during the day, which made them more vulnerable and, therefore, more suitable targets. Moreover, after 1960 there was a huge increase in the availability of and expenditures on durable consumer goods. Revolutions in the technology of durable consumer goods—especially electronic household appliances—made them lighter or smaller in size and, correspondingly, much easier to steal.

Felson and Cohen argued that these fundamental changes in the circulation of goods and people were reflected in changes in crime rates during the 1960s. In particular, they found that

- personal and household victimizations increased faster than business victimizations;

- shoplifting increased more rapidly than other types of thefts from businesses;
- personal offenses by strangers outpaced such offenses by nonstrangers;
- daytime residential burglaries increased more than those at night.

Felson (1997) has also used routine activities theory to explain the general decline of crime rates during the 1990s. As documented by the *UCR,* crimes reported to the police dropped by around 20 percent for robbery, burglary, and motor vehicle theft (1992–1996) and also for homicide (1993–1996). According to Felson, the major reason for the decline was a revolution in the use and movement of cash during the 1990s. Specifically, between 1990 and 1994 there was a 57 percent increase in credit card spending, from $466 to $731 billion (p. 1). With less cash in circulation, theft is far harder to accomplish successfully.

In *Crime and Everyday Life*, the latest version of routine activities theory, Felson (1998) extended his analysis to fights, drug deals, youth crime, crime linkages, and recidivism. This analysis is clearly sympathetic to the "broken windows" theory (Kelling and Coles, 1996), which suggests that, cumulatively, the presence of many minor crimes like vandalism and graffiti creates a climate for the growth of serious crime. For example, Felson identified eight ways in which, from the offender's perspective, one offense can lead to another (1998:126–127):

1. The successful property offender is inclined to party, blowing some of the money on illegal drugs or prostitutes.
2. An offender who succeeds at a crime may try it again, or try something like it.
3. With success, he may spend more time with his co-offenders; they then lead him into more crime.
4. Offenders are dangerous; hanging out with them puts the offender at risk of becoming a victim himself.
5. Just being out late and in dangerous places leads the drug offender toward more offenses and victimizations.
6. The offender may provoke others to retaliate or to attack him first.
7. Drug crimes may lead to the desire for more, or even dependency. To get money for more drugs, the drug offender may steal, rob, engage in prostitution, or perform other illegal behaviors.
8. Using drugs over time impairs judgment and ability at crime, so the offender may take more risks.

Assessment

Routine activities theory has considerable commonsense appeal. Partly as a result of this appeal, it has been widely discussed and tested and its implications have been applied as designs for local crime control. But how well it explains crime is quite uncertain. Several studies have confirmed aspects of the theory. One study, for example, found that reports of crime to police dispatchers in Minneapolis came from only 3 percent of the locations in the city (Sherman, Gartin, and Bueger, 1989), which seems to confirm the idea that some locations are hot-spots for crime. Another study reported that in the aftermath of Florida's Hurricane Andrew in 1992 the temporary absence of police briefly contributed to a rise in looting (Cromwell et. al, 1995). This finding tends to confirm the claim that the absence of capable guardians makes targets more suitable for offenders. Another study found that routine activities theory can explain male arrest rates—though not women's—for minor thefts in developed countries but that it is unable to do so in undeveloped countries (Anderson and Bennett, 1996).

However, two major doubts must be raised about the explanatory power of routine activities theory. First, as Charles Tittle (1995:14) has complained, nowhere does the theory offer criteria to determine which routine activities are relevant to which criminal activity. For example, brushing one's teeth or reading the morning newspaper are routine activities, but presumably the theory would not say that these actions are relevant to crime. Why are some routine activities relevant to the understanding of crime but not others?

Second, routine activities theory is less a theory of the causes of crime than a statement about victimization—and a rather misleading one at that, because it fails to provide much or any of the sociological context of criminogenic situations, such as how and why crime is related to class, gender, race, and age. Consider just the area of gender and crime (Schwartz and Pitts, 1995; but see Felson and Messner, 1998). In arguing, for example, that an increase in female labor force participation leads to increases in crime because more households are unguarded during the day, the theory comes dangerously close to blaming females for precipitating their own victimization. Moreover, with its emphasis on a criminology of place rather than on sociological context, routine activities theory is quite silent about the fact that women are typically most in danger not from traveling to work but from their relationships with intimate males in their own households. Is patriarchy perhaps a routine activity?

About their lack of attention to the sociological contexts of crime, Tittle (1995) has concluded appropriately that **rational choice** theories in general, including routine activities theory, resemble little more than a mechanical gearbox that transforms inputs into outputs. "Without knowing how and why the inputs take on particular values," he pointed out,

> understanding the gearbox is of limited use in explaining and predicting behavior. For example, if one is trying to understand why and how automobiles move, it may be essential to gain a knowledge of how transmissions work, for surely the automobile cannot move unless the power generated by the engine is transformed into an appropriate mode for turning the wheels. Nonetheless, it would be silly to concentrate on the transmission and the intricacies of its operation. After all, without fuel, a mechanical device to transform the fuel into physical movement, and a drive shaft, a transmission would be useless. In what sense then would understanding the internal structure of a transmission explain the movement of the car? (p. 12)

8.2   SELF-CONTROL AND CONTROL BALANCE

We now describe two theories that are intended to be general theories of crime: the theory of self-control and the theory of **control balance**. Their common focus is the concept of control (see Chapter 6.3).

Gottfredson and Hirschi's Theory of Self-Control

In recent years Travis Hirschi has radically narrowed or refocused, though not entirely abandoned, the theory of social control he presented in *Causes of Delinquency* (Hirschi, 1969, see Chapter 6.3). This change of emphasis was signaled in Michael Gottfredson and Hirschi's wide-ranging and influential book *A General Theory of Crime* (1990), in which they put forward a theory of self-control and crime.

Gottfredson and Hirschi argued that individual differences in criminal behavior are due to differences in "self-control." Finding much merit in classical criminology's emphasis on the relationships between pleasure and pain, they defined the problem of **self-control** as "the differential tendency of people to avoid criminal acts whatever the circumstances in which they find themselves" (1990:87). Low self-control coupled with opportunity increases an individual's propensity to commit crime, especially crimes involving force or fraud. High self-control effectively reduces the likelihood of committing crime. Moreover, those having high levels of self-control are significantly less likely throughout their lives to commit crime.

Clearly, this claim about the importance of self-control in the generation of crime has two crucial features: first, the characteristics of self-control and, second, the factors that promote or retard the level of self-control.

Gottfredson and Hirschi assumed that the characteristics of self-control can be derived from the nature of crime itself, of which they outlined five chief aspects (pp. 89–90):

1. Because crime offers immediate gratification of desires, people with low self-control wish to give in to their desires at once. They live in the "here and now." For this reason, those with low self-control also tend to indulge in a variety of other immediate pleasures that are not criminal. Among these other immediate pleasures are smoking, drinking, using drugs, gambling, having illegitimate children, and engaging in illicit sex.
2. Because crime is exciting, risky, and thrilling, people with low self-control tend to be adventuresome, active, and physical rather than cautious, cognitive, and verbal.
3. Because crime provides few or meager long-term benefits and because engaging in crime interferes with jobs, marriages, family, and friends, people with low self-control tend to have marriages, friendships, and job profiles that are also unstable.
4. Because crime requires little skill or planning, people without self-control need not have or need not value cognitive or academic skills.
5. Because crime often causes victims pain or discomfort, people with low self-control tend to be self-centered and indifferent to others' suffering and needs.

To these five major characteristics of crime and self-control Gottfredson and Hirschi added that for those with low self-control, crime is not an automatic occurrence (pp. 91–94). Low self-control must be coupled with an opportunity to commit crime for crime to occur. The opportunity for crime usually dictates whether any given person with low self-control actually commits a crime. Because crime is not a specialized activity, a potential criminal (in other words, a person with low self-control) will tend to commit a crime if the opportunity presents itself. Thus a rapist is more likely than a non-rapist to (mis)use drugs and to commit robberies and burglaries. Moreover, if the opportunity to commit a crime is absent, then persons with low self-control are more likely to engage in other acts that are "psychologically or theoretically equivalent to crime." Thus in areas where property is secure and guarded, persons with low self-control will tend not to commit property crimes but are more likely than non-thieves to smoke, drink, and play truant from school.

What, then, are the sources or "causes" of low self-control? Gottfredson and Hirschi argued that the major cause is ineffective child-rearing (pp. 97–98, 118–120). As such, they continued, crime can be predicted from evidence of low self-control at very early stages in life. Children without self-control are children whose parents or guardians (1) do not monitor their behavior; (2) do not recognize deviant behavior when it happens; and (3) do not punish such behavior. By the time of the age of responsibility (eight years) most, if not all, children have attained—or failed to attain—a level of self-control that will remain constant for the rest of their lives:

> All that is required to activate the system is affection for *or* investment in the child. The person who cares for the child will watch his behavior, see him doing things he should not do, and correct him. The result may be a child more capable of delaying gratification, more sensitive to the interests and desires of others, more independent, more willing to accept restraints on his activity, and more unlikely to use force or violence to attain his ends. (p. 97)

Gottfredson and Hirschi asserted that many of the conventional causes of crime are in fact not causes of crime but consequences of low self-control. Persons with low self-control sort themselves into and are sorted into circumstances that are correlated with crime. For example, consider the long-standing finding that one of the causes of delinquency is that delinquents tend to have friends who are delinquent. This finding is rejected by Gottfredson and Hirschi; they believe that young persons with low self-control are attracted to the pleasures of delinquent activities and that the delinquent gang provides the opportunity for crime.

Assessment

Hirschi, in formulating the theory of crime and self-control with Gottfredson in *A General Theory of Crime*, apparently abandoned his earlier multifaceted theory of social control in favor of a monocausal theory whose core concept is intended to explain all crime. Hirschi and Gottfredson insisted that the theory of self-control can explain such diverse behavior as delinquency, white-collar crime, and organized crime. The theory of self-control has been criticized because of this claim, among others. This never-ending search for a **general theory** is like the Holy Grail of criminology. It leaves itself open to the continuing objection that a theory that attempts to explain everything ultimately explains very little or even nothing at all.

Nevertheless, Gottfredson and Hirschi's theory of crime and self-control has led to some excitement among criminologists in the United States, and it has been subjected to considerable empirical testing (e.g., Gibbs and Giever, 1995; Burton et al., 1998; Gibbs, Giever, and Martin, 1998). The results have been mixed: Some researchers have rejected the theory; others have found that its key terms should be specified more clearly; and still others have lent it modest support. Perhaps a key reason for this mixed reception is that Gottfredson and Hirschi did not originally spell out precisely what they meant by "self-control" and by "opportunity" (see Chapter 8.3). Moreover, the theory seems to be based on a tautology. As Akers (1997; and see Hirschi and Gottfredson, 1993) has pointed out, if low self-control increases the propensity for crime, and if high propensity for crime is defined as low self-control, then what the theory says is that low self-control causes low self-control. What is needed, in short, are reliable indicators and measures of self-control that are separate both from the propensity to commit crime and from crime itself.

Let us now point to three difficulties with self-control theory that return us squarely to important themes we raised earlier in the book.

First, crime is not simply an objective fact that can be identified and categorized in the same scientific way as rocks and butterflies. Crime is not only an action by an individual, a corporation, or a government but also a definition that is imposed on behavior by some lawful authority. Whether or not an action is a crime, in other words, hinges on the attitudes and reactions of powerful others. For example, we have described (Chapter 1.2) how the seafaring activities of Captain Kidd were transformed from being the praiseworthy and patriotic enterprise of a skilled sailor into the depraved and self-seeking illegalities of a pirate. Kidd's actions were criminal only because the British government so defined them and criminalized them as such!

Second, it seems impossible to characterize all criminal behavior as involving individuals with low self-control. Indeed, most criminologists would agree that persons with high levels of self-control who practice deferred gratification are precisely the individuals who engage in the numerous types of political, white-collar, and syndicated crime! At the very least, there are many crimes that require a specific rather than a general explanation and numerous others that have nothing to do with self-control (e.g., Reed and Yeager, 1996).

Third, if crime is an individual matter of self-control, then how does one explain that some societies have much greater crime rates than others (see Chapter 4.2)? Why does the United States have a homicide rate seven to ten times higher than the rate in most European countries (see Chapter 16)? Is it because the U.S. population somehow has less self-control, or is it something to do with the nature of social organization in the United States?

We now turn to another recent exploration of the importance of the concept of "control": Charles Tittle's (1995) theory of control balance.

Tittle's Theory of Control Balance

After the great success of labeling theory in the 1960s and 1970s, the concept of deviance did not play a very large role in the theoretical development of criminology. However, with Tittle's book *Control Balance* (1995), the concept of deviance has reemerged as an innovating force in criminology. Like Gottfredson and Hirschi's (1990) theory of self-control, Tittle formulated a theory whose focus is control and whose aim is nothing less than a general explanation of its subject matter. Indeed, the subtitle of his book is *Toward a General Theory of Deviance*. Tittle's theory tries to combine aspects of numerous other theories, including differential association, anomie, Marxism/conflict, social control, labeling, rational choice, and routine activities.

Tittle stated that though what counts as deviance is subject to great variation, deviance is "any behavior that the majority of a given group regards as unacceptable or that typically evokes a collective response of a negative type" (p. 124). It is thus not the number of people who engage in an act that makes it deviant but the number of people who view it as such. Crime is merely a specialized form of deviance, one that is regarded as such by criminal law. Tittle identified six forms of deviance, distinguished by how serious they are (pp. 136–140):

1. *Predation*. Acts of direct physical violence, manipulation, or property extraction, including theft, rape, homicide, robbery, assault, fraud, and individual price gouging, as well as acts like parents' use of guilt to get a child's attention
2. *Exploitation*. Acts of indirect predation, such as corporate price-fixing, unsafe workplaces, influence peddling, and contract killings
3. *Defiance*. Acts of hostility or contempt for social norms—including vandalism, sullenness by a marital partner, and political protests—that bring the actor no obvious benefit
4. *Plunder*. Acts of autocratic behavior, ethnic cleansing, and the destruction of the environment, rarely committed with an awareness of their harmfulness
5. *Decadence*. Acts of undisciplined excess such as group sex with children, humiliating others for entertainment, sadistic torture
6. *Submission*. Acts whereby one allows oneself to be physically abused, humiliated, or sexually degraded

Tittle's theory begins by accepting the basic premise of other control theories. This premise is that the main variable in explaining individual acts of deviance or crime is control of the ability to act. The theory's central premise is that "the amount of control to which an individual is subject, relative to the amount of control he or she can exercise, determines the probability of deviance occurring as well as the type of deviance likely to occur" (p. 135).

The "amount of control to which an individual is subject, relative to the amount of control he or she can exercise" is known as the "control ratio" for that individual. Individuals are in "**control balance**" if the amount of control that they exercise is the same as the amount of control that they experience. If one controls more than one experiences control, then one has a **control surplus**. If one experiences control more than one controls, then one has a **control deficit**. Individuals with a control balance tend to conform. Those who have more control and those who have less control both tend to engage in more deviance than those in control balance—and the extent of their deviance is proportionate to how far out of balance they are. Individuals with control surpluses are likely to want to extend them; they will tend to do so by engaging in acts of exploitation, plunder, or decadence. Individuals with the smallest control surpluses are most likely to engage in exploitation, those with the largest surpluses (e.g., Nero, Howard Hughes, or Michael Jackson) are most likely to engage in decadence. Those with control deficits are likely to wish to remove them or to minimize their effects; they will tend to do so by engaging in acts of predation, defiance, or submission. Individuals with marginal control deficits are most likely to engage in acts of predation, those with the most deficits in acts of submission.

Under what conditions are individuals with an unbalanced control ratio motivated to engage in deviance? What provides the push, reason, impulse, or urge for them to deviate? Tittle said that motivating factors are of two basic sorts, one predispositional, the other situational. Predispositional factors include bodily and psychic needs; the desire for autonomy, which we all learn at a very early age; and the control ratio, which varies from one individual to another and depends on such factors as age, class, status, race, and gender. But being predisposed to deviance does not necessarily mean that deviance will happen: "For deviant motivation to emerge, those predisposed toward it by an imbalanced control ratio must comprehend, or perceive, the possibility that deviance will alter their control ratios in an advantageous way" (p. 162). The situational influences on deviant motivation include provocations, such as verbal insults and racial slurs, and challenges from or displays of weakness by others. Adolescent subcultures, for example, are acutely aware of repression and encourage their members to resist it. Tittle added a third and a fourth factor to this complex theory. The third is constraint (pp. 167–168), which refers to the probability, or perceived probability, that control will actually be exercised. Fourth, and finally, is opportunity. Clearly, one must have access to another person in order to assault them, and access to another's property in order to steal it.

Assessment

Tittle's theory of control balance is a sophisticated example of a movement now underway in criminology toward an **integrated theory** (e.g., Elliott, Huizinga, and Ageton, 1989; Hagan, 1989; Braithwaite, 1989; Vila, 1994; Bernard and Snipes, 1996; Barak, 1998). A key goal of this movement is to model the process of theory building on the natural sciences. An integrated theory seeks to be both as simple and as general as possible. The theory of control balance is clearly regarded by its author as a work in progress. Tittle himself has written that "it was unveiled like a roughly shaped clay statue with a sign saying 'bring your tools and your ideas and refine or reshape this'" (1997:99).

Some modifications to some of the key components of control balance theory have been proposed in an otherwise favorable review by John Braithwaite (1997; and see Tittle, 1997, 1999; Piquero and Hickman, 1999). Braithwaite believes that the differences between exploitation, plunder, and decadence are not clearly defined (1997:83–87). Moreover, there is perhaps no great difference between predation on the deficit side of control balance and exploitation on the surplus side. For example, predation might easily include shakedowns, bribery, extortion, and price fixing. Indeed, Braithwaite recommended that most of Tittle's categories of deviance be abandoned in favor of a simplified theory of predatory deviance. In addition, Braithwaite (p. 94; and see Braithwaite and Pettit, 1990) advanced four implications of the theory of control balance, each of which makes an important statement about what a democratic and egalitarian society would look like:

1. Societies with greater equality of control will be better off because of reduced predatory deviance and reduced withdrawal from social and political life.

2. For any level of inequality of control, control that is exercised respectfully, without humiliation or debasement, will generate less predatory deviance.

3. When control is distributed with equity and exercised with virtuous respect, acceptance of that control is desirable because, especially for men, this acceptance will defuse predatory deviance.

4. When social bonds, social support, and communities are strong, equality of control is likely to increase, as is the respect with which control is exercised and the willingness of citizens to accept equitable, virtuous, and public-regarding controls.

8.3   REVISED STRAIN THEORY

The search for a general theory of crime is also present in various revisions to strain theory. We have already discussed Merton's arguments on **strain** and anomie, and we have seen how original and important they have been in criminology (Chapter 5.3). But we have also seen that crucial parts of Merton's arguments hinge on assumptions that are unstated and unproven. For example, it is highly questionable whether the acceptance of middle-class norms and values—whatever they might be—is as widespread in the United States as Merton depicted. Moreover, though Merton's analysis focused on the psychic effects of strain on individuals at different points in the class structure, he tended to assume that strain is unidimensional in its origins and that it transfers in a rather straightforward way from the social structure to individuals.

In what follows we outline the two most influential attempts to fill in some of the gaps in Merton's original formulation. These are, respectively, Robert Agnew's "general strain theory" and Steven Messner and Richard Rosenfeld's "institutional anomie theory."

Agnew's Social-Psychological Basis for a General Strain Theory

In his article "Foundation for a General Strain Theory of Crime and Delinquency," Agnew (1992) suggested that, with suitable revisions, strain theory has a central role to play in explaining crime and delinquency. Agnew tried to develop this role with new insights from research on stress in medical sociology and psychology, on equity and justice in social psychology, and on aggression in psychology. Agnew's approach focused on the individual and his or her immediate social environment.

Whereas Merton's strain theory focused on the ways in which an individual is barred from achieving conventional goals, Agnew expanded strain theory to include the analysis of "relationships in which others present the individual with noxious or negative stimuli" (p. 49)—relationships, for example, in which an individual is not treated in the way(s) s/he would like to be. Strain may therefore result from failure either to achieve conventional goals or to escape from painful relationships.

Agnew pinpointed three chief sorts of strain (pp. 50–61). First, strain can be brought on by *failure to achieve positively-valued goals*. This failure can happen in many ways, including disjunctions between aspirations and expectations/actual achievements, disjunctions between expectations and actual achievements, and disjunctions between just/fair outcomes and actual outcomes. Adolescents may experience stress when they perceive their own position in life as unjust, for example, and as a result they may engage in delinquency in order to reduce their inputs (e.g., by playing truant) or increase the inputs of others (e.g., by being disorderly); alternatively, they may try to increase their outcomes (e.g., by theft) or reduce others' outcomes (e.g., by vandalism, theft, and assault). Some individuals may perceive their situation as so unjust that they remove themselves altogether from it (by running away or, we might add, by suicide).

Second, strain results from *the removal of positively-valued stimuli from the individual.* Examples of this situation include the loss of a boyfriend/ girlfriend, a friend's serious illness or death, and the separation of one's parents. According to Agnew, such events can lead to delinquency "as the individual tries to prevent the loss of the positive stimuli, retrieve the lost stimuli or obtain substitute stimuli, seek revenge against those responsible for the loss, or manage the negative effect caused by the loss by taking illicit drugs" (p. 58).

Third, strain occurs through *the presentation of negative stimuli.* By "negative stimuli" Agnew means such stressful life events as child abuse/neglect, criminal victimization, verbal threats and insults, and negative relations with parents, peers, and at school. Each of these events can cause an aggressive response. Negative stimuli might also include physical pain, heat, noise, and pollution, all of which may be experienced as noxious for biological reasons.

Animal abuse is an example of crime to which Agnew (1998:196–198; and see Beirne, 1999) has applied his general strain theory. He suggested that strain may lead both directly and indirectly to animal abuse, particularly to its socially unacceptable forms. The negative behavior of our companion animals, such as when they bite us or chew our possessions, may sometimes cause us to be angry. Sometimes individuals who abuse animals do so to seek revenge on an animal that has caused them stress. At times, strain resulting in abuse may occur when animals threaten crops or livestock or when endangered species halt economic development.

Some of the animal abuse that is attributed to stress is often viewed as socially acceptable. How many of us protest farmers who shoot coyotes? Who spares the mosquito that bites one's arm?

Agnew argued that animal abuse, particularly of the type that most people believe to be unacceptable, may also be fostered by strain that is not caused by animals. This type of abuse occurs, first, when we are so stressed that our awareness of how we abuse has become dulled. Here, we might have a general propensity to lash out at all other beings, including animals. Second, animals may sometimes be used as weapons by one party against another in a domestic dispute, as has become quite well documented (see Chapter 9.2).

Two further aspects of Agnew's analysis of stress and animal abuse have considerable bearing on his general strain theory. The first is that Agnew recognizes that strain may sometimes reduce the likelihood of animal abuse. To illustrate this tendency Agnew pointed out that some members of the eighteenth-century English working class were motivated out of sympathy—for creatures in similarly wretched conditions—to take part in the early anti-vivisection movement (p. 198). We might note, as does Agnew himself, that

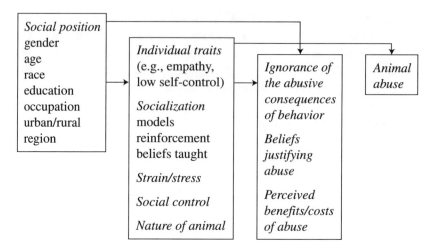

FIGURE 8.2   A Social-Psychological Model of Animal Abuse
SOURCE: Agnew, 1998: 182.

nowadays feminist members of the animal protection community stress that they and animals often have a common oppressor (i.e., men).

Second, when he brings his theory of strain to bear on animal abuse, Agnew displays his willingness to admit the relevance of numerous other factors, both sociological and psychological (see Figure 8.2). Among these other factors—which might in principle be infinite—are an individual's social position; psychological traits, like empathy; level of stress and strain; socialization; social control; and the nature of the animal under consideration. It remains to be seen whether this flexibility dilutes or strengthens the explanatory power of Agnew's general theory.

Assessment

Some key problems exist both with how best to test Agnew's theory and also with what its advantages are compared with Mertonian anomie theory. The scope of Agnew's general theory of strain and delinquency is much broader than earlier theories of anomie and strain. In particular, its reach extends far beyond the confines of social class. However, despite the narrow demographic make-up of the populations used to test his theory so far, it has gained some preliminary empirical support (Paternoster and Mazerolle, 1994; Agnew et al., 1996). For example, one study, which used data drawn from a nationally representative sample of 2,213 male public high school students, found that delinquent adolescents are more likely than nondelinquents to experience modest relief from strain's effects on anger, resentment, anxiety, and depression (Brezina, 1996). Agnew has said that at heart his theory is very simple: "If we treat people badly, they may get mad and engage in crime" (1995:315), a conclusion that is similar to Christopher Jencks's (1987:38) finding that "adolescents who are treated like dirt will react accordingly." Few criminologists are likely to disagree.

Messner and Rosenfeld's Institutional Anomie Theory

Whereas Agnew extends Merton's anomie theory by applying it at a social-psychological level, Steven Messner and Richard Rosenfeld have tried to extend it to the macro level of social organization. In their book *Crime and the American Dream*, Messner and Rosenfeld (1998) stated that the American Dream refers to "a commitment to the goal of material success, to be pursued by everyone in society, under conditions of open, individual competition" (p. 6). The American Dream contains the basic values of American culture, in particular its commitment to achievement, individualism, universalism, and the glorification of materialistic success associated with the fetish for money. Messner and Rosenfeld claim that despite how it is filtered differently through race and through gender, the American Dream is composed of values that are agreed on by a fairly high consensus of U.S. citizens.

Messner and Rosenfeld usefully extended Merton's analysis with their argument that U.S. society is unable to deliver the American Dream to a proportion of its citizens because in the United States—far more so than in other technologically-developed societies—the capitalist economy has a lopsided dominance over all other major social institutions. This dominance of the economic realm in the institutional balance of power occurs in three interrelated ways (pp. 70–76).

First, *noneconomic institutional functions and roles are devalued.* Education, for example, tends to be seen not as end in itself but as a route to a well-paying job. Also, the chief tasks of families, such as parenting and nurturing, are not highly valued. Thus, home*makers* do not have a high status; however, because of the fetish with material success, home*owners* do, and, we might add, they are even rewarded with tax breaks by the government. Second, *other social institutions are forced to accommodate to economic requirements.* For example, whereas societies like Japan and some western European countries are strongly committed to family welfare, family life in the United States is dominated by the schedules and rewards of the labor market. Moreover, both schools and government depend heavily on private financial support. Third, *economic norms penetrate most other institutional areas.* Thus "husbands and wives are 'partners' who 'manage' the household 'division of labor' in accordance with the 'marriage contract'" (p. 75). Schools are increasingly forced to be 'accountable' to taxpayers, and students are sometimes described as 'products' or even as 'raw material' for the labor market.

Messner and Rosenfeld argued that the culture and the institutional structure of the United States—its social organization, in other words—lead directly to high levels of crime (see Figure 8.3 below). Crucially, the anomic forces in U.S. society that encourage crime are not opposed by the forces of social control that are meant to be nurtured by noneconomic institutions like families and schools. Precisely because the power of capitalist economic values has devalued the prosocial messages of these noneconomic institutions, the latter are relatively powerless to create the sort of cooperative community that opposes crime. Hence anomie is exacerbated and a vicious cycle occurs. According to Messner and Rosenfeld, the resultant generalized anomie helps to explain not only the high rate of predatory crime in the United States but also white-collar and corporate crimes (and see Passas, 1990), as well as the pervasive inclination in the United States to own guns and to use them in illegal ways.

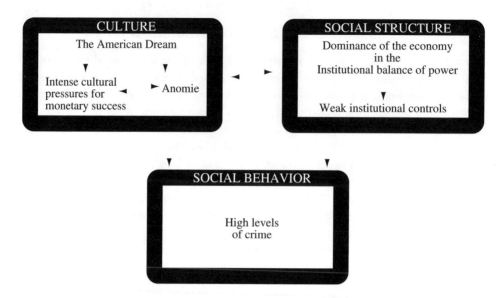

FIGURE 8.3   An Analytical Model of the Linkages Between Macrosocial Organization and Crime

SOURCE: Messner and Rosenfield, 1998: p. 77.

Assessment

Messner and Rosenfeld's account of the links between anomie, the decay of major social institutions, and the growth of crime in the United States in the 1990s has striking similarities to Durkheim's account of the same phenomena in France in the 1890s (see Chapter 4.2). Moreover, like Durkheim, Messner and Rosenfeld have responded to this crisis by searching for the causes of social order; and like Durkheim, they lament the rise of egoism, the decline of community, and the loss of faith in, or the lack of influence of, certain social institutions such as the family and the school. Messner and Rosenfeld's analysis is also similar to those conflict and Marxist explanations of crime that focus on the distorting effects on social life of the dominance of capitalist relations of production (see Chapter 4.3, 7.3, 7.4).

Messner and Rosenfeld's solution to the problem of crime entails two broad movements for social change (1998:86–108). In combination, these movements—one institutional, the other cultural—would amount to a radical restructuring of American society. The first is the rebalancing of the major social institutions so that the economy is no longer dominant—with the effect that the polity, the family, the school, and the system of social stratification are all democratized and given an egalitarian thrust. This is not a novel proposal, though it is an important one.

The second movement entails what Messner and Rosenfeld term "cultural regeneration"—a proposal that is, regrettably, found only rarely in contemporary criminology. Cultural regeneration involves a radical reappraisal of the American Dream. In order to reduce strain, money and material possessions must no longer serve as the chief gauges of social worth. Parenting, 'spousing,' teaching, learning, and serving the community must become meaningful ends in themselves. Moreover, Messner and Rosenfeld warn that such a society will have to develop a "cultural receptivity to restraints" (p. 105). By this they mean that significantly lower levels of crime are unlikely to occur unless we become less obsessed with individual rights, interests, and privileges and more concerned with collective obligations and mutual support.

8.4 CRITICAL CRIMINOLOGIES

Critical criminology developed from the radical and feminist criminology of the 1970s and 1980s and is an umbrella term for describing numerous perspectives that emerged in the mid- to late-1980s and throughout the 1990s. Although these perspectives differ in significant ways—which we outline below—critical criminologies are similar in the sense that they uniformly question the following (MacLean and Milovanovic, 1998:11):

- the usage of the legalistic definition of crime—dominant conceptions of the "violent" offender that exclude many other agents of social injuries
- prevailing usages of linear, non-dialectical notions of "causation"
- "correctional" penal policy
- the increasing investment of energy in more punitive responses to crime
- the limited attention paid to political economy in the contribution to crime
- the targeting of selected groups, informally or formally, for official police intervention
- the resistance to entertaining gross inequalities in living standards, alienating working conditions, and dilapidated communities
- the continued and often systematic practices of sexism, racism, classism (and the effects of their intersecting nature) often disguised as "neutral" categories

Critical criminologists are committed to theory construction that provides better conceptual tools for understanding "what is," and "what can be," and, in this way, contributes to the quest for positive social change and social justice (p. 15–16). In this section we briefly summarize four critical criminologies: left realism, peacemaking criminology, postmodernism, and feminism.

Left Realism

As we discuss more thoroughly in Chapter 15.1, conventional crime is predominantly an intra-class phenomenon. The conventional offender and victim are drawn from those classes—lower and working classes—that radical criminologists (see Chapter 7.4) tend to represent in their theorizing. In the mid-1980s, several radical criminologists attempted to develop a more coherent explanation of conventional crime than that offered by Marxist theory. In so doing, they advanced a critique of what they termed **left idealism**. According to this critique, left idealists argue that absolute economic deprivation (unemployment) drives people into crime and that the conventional criminal is somewhat of a rebel (Lea and Young, 1984). Indeed, some early radical criminologists of the 1970s (such as Quinney, discussed in chapter 7.4; and see Greenberg, 1981), not only depicted the conventional criminal as a rebel but also argued that the criminal class, rather than the working class, was the vanguard of the revolution.

In his critique of left idealism, Jock Young (1986:12) added that for the left idealist the conventional criminal sees through the inequitable nature of present day society, and crime itself in an attempt—however clumsy and ill-thought out—to redress this balance. From this perspective, there is little need to have complex explanations for working-class crime; its causes are obvious. To blame the poor for their criminality is to blame the victim and to point moral accusations at those whose very actions are a result of their being social casualties. The real crime on which we should focus is that of the ruling class: the police, the corporations, and the state agencies. The ruling class causes real problems for the mass of people, whereas working-class crime is minor, involving petty theft and occasional violence and having little impact on working-class communities. To this portrayal of left idealism, Lea and Young (1986:358) added that left idealists do not provide any realistic solutions for crime, other than emphasizing "changing the social order."

According to this critique of left idealism, left idealists adhere to a romantic image of the conventional criminal, make no attempt to understand the complex nature of conventional working-class crime, focus almost exclusively on the harms of the "ruling class," and ignore the development of a coherent program for curbing conventional crime.

Consequently, in the 1980s, left realists proposed the following as their program of **left realism**. First, conventional crime is a real problem for the working class. Rather than viewing crime as the result of absolute deprivation and as a form of rebellion, left realists argued that conventional crime is driven by relative deprivation as well as by reactionary, selfish, and individualistic attitudes (Lea and Young, 1984, 1986). Moreover, conventional crime has a disorganizing effect, pitting the poor against the poor. Rather than helping create a politically conscious community, conventional crime hinders working-class solidarity and thus "the ability to fight back" (1986:359). As Matthews put it, crime is not a heralded revolt but "tends to extend the fragmentation of urban life, mimic individualistic and acquisitive values, and limits public space and social and political participation"(1987:373). Because of this disorganizing effect, left realists argued that conventional crime must be examined seriously by radical criminologists.

Besides rejecting the Robin Hood image of the criminal and the need for thoughtful empirical investigations of conventional crime, left realists also argue that crime control must be taken seriously. Rather than ignoring the conventional crime problem—as left idealists allegedly do—left realists argue for a concrete crime control program. Such a program first requires an honest assessment of the state, an assessment that, according to left realists, is lacking in left idealism. For left idealists, "the state is the direct instrument of the ruling class" and its ideological and repressive institutions "exist in order to maintain capitalism" (Lea and Young, 1984:101–102). Thus, left idealists argue that reform in such a state is impossible and will most likely backfire, turning against the working class. Left realists maintain that the state "represents very largely ruling-class interests," but they argue nonetheless that gains can in fact be "wrung out of it; reforms, however difficult to achieve, are possible and, in fact, relate to the state as in essence a site of contradictory interests" (p. 103). Therefore, the possibility of a concrete crime program does in fact present itself.

Certain elements of this program were outlined by Lea and Young (1986:360–363). First, they argued for demarginalization. Lea and Young proposed that instead of marginalizing offenders in prison, we should use such measures as community service orders, victim restitution schemes, and widespread decarceration. Second, they advocated preemptive deterrence (deterring crime before it is committed) through citizen groups who cooperate with the police, as well as through evening youth patrols such as the Guardian Angels. Third, Lea and Young argued for minimal use of prisons. They suggested that prisons, and thus custodial sentences, should be used only in cases of extreme danger to the community. Fourth, they suggested that criminologists must look realistically at the circumstances of both offender and victim. Fifth, they argued that criminologists must be realistic about policing: The "police force" must be transformed into a "police service" accountable to the public. Finally, Lea and Young proposed that criminologists must be realistic about the problem of crime in the present period. Because the degree of relative deprivation has risen continually, a situation of considerable discontent exists. Yet, concurrent with this rise of deprivation and discontent, there has been no increase in working-class politics. The door is thus open for a criminal—rather than a political—response in working-class communities. Lea and Young advocated pursuing "alternative politics that harness the energies of the marginalized," helping create a "politics of crime control" that is part of other grass roots movements, and combating "the tendency of a divided and disillusioned public to move to the right" (p. 363).

In more recent work, left realists have argued that 1990s left idealism differs in form from the left idealism of the 1970s and early 1980s, which is not to say that it is any more palatable to the left realists. According to Jock Young (1997), current left idealists emphasize the biased nature of the criminal justice system, which is seen as more of a problem than crime itself. When left idealists do discuss crime, Young asserted, it is viewed simplistically as the result of poverty and/or the "war" on drugs. Moreover, Young contended that left idealists see the increased use of incarceration not as the result of crime but as the result of "a moral panic about crime, created by conservative politicians, law enforcement agencies, and the mass media. . . . The public are lambasted by these writers as if they were cultural dupes whose attitudes and opinions are a product of watching too much TV" (p. 478). Thus, according to Young, current left idealists fail to "take crime seriously."

Young also extended the left realist position that the "potent" cause of crime is relative, as opposed to absolute, deprivation:

Realist criminology points to relative deprivation in certain conditions as being the major cause of crime. That is, when people experience a level of unfairness in their allocation of resources and utilize individualistic means to attempt to right this condition, it is a reaction to the experience of injustice. One such individualistic response is "every man for himself," which is particularly prevalent in the U.S. Not surprisingly, the U.S. has the highest crime rate among advanced industrialized societies. (p. 488)

Moreover, Young argued that left realism does not simply dismiss correlations between biology and crime, because to do so is to "throw the baby out with the bath water." For example, regarding body size, Young stated the following: "It is a fact that larger, more powerful, people commit more violence than smaller people, that their male hormones correlate strongly with violence, that the well-muscled are more of a threat than the plump and un-fit. People do not, after all, cross the street at night to avoid old ladies" (p. 489). Thus Young's left realist position holds that although crime is rooted in social conditions, the biological and physical capacity to commit crime are intervening variables.

Peacemaking Criminology

One of the distinctive products of the leftist concern with realism is a renewed attempt to humanize the institutions of criminal justice. This attempt is known as **peacemaking criminology,** the eclectic theoretical basis of which lies in a loose mixture of religious hu-manism and feminism. This combination is most visible in Harold Pepinsky and Richard Quinney's edited book *Criminology as Peacemaking* (1991). At the beginning of their book Pepinsky and Quinney declare:

> The peacemaking perspective is steadily making its way into criminology. In recent years there have been proposals and programs that foster mediation, conflict resolu-tion, reconciliation, and community. They are part of an emerging criminology of peacemaking, a criminology that seeks to alleviate suffering and thereby reduce crime. This is a criminology that is based necessarily on human transformation in the achievement of peace and justice. (p. ix)

The different authors of the twenty chapters in this book address a wide variety of prac-tical issues that converge on the need to use more humane and more caring approaches to the problem of crime. Though all the authors seem to agree with other critical criminolo-gists that it is economic, political, and social inequality that foster crime, the emphasis here is less on the causes of crime than on how to resolve the conflicts of which crime is an expression. The key policies of peacemaking criminology thus involve terms like "re-sponsiveness," "reconciliation," "conflict resolution," "harmony," and "community."

Some critical criminologists have expanded the peacemaking perspective. For example, Susan Caulfield and Angela Evans have argued that at its core "peacemaking has a rever-ence for life, for the connectedness of all beings" (1997:103). To help reduce human suffer-ing, including the suffering that results from crime, Caulfield and Evans call for the crimi-nal justice system to address the "essence," rather than the "appearance," of being human:

> Much of criminology and criminal justice focuses on the appearance of a human be-ing: what they did, ascriptive characteristics, and the like. Rarely is there concern with understanding the essence of a person: how they feel, what they fear, how they see themselves in reference to the universe. We surmise, as do others, that this avoid-ance of one's essence is a part of self-defense or self-denial on the part of both indi-viduals and criminal justice. . . . Knowing only the appearance, rather than the essence of harm, how can criminal justice keep from being fragmented and in search of some form of control, no matter how illusory? (p. 105)

According to Caulfield and Evans, peacemaking criminology, through an emphasis on cooperation, compassion, and respect for all species, allows for the examination of the essence rather than the appearance. Such an ideology, they argued, will move U.S. society toward peace and justice for all.

Similarly, Hal Pepinsky has argued that peacemaking criminology allows for the construction of a "compassionate discourse" that will "heal rifts in the social fabric" and weave all societal members "back into accepted, responsible, safe social relations, rather than identifying, condemning, punishing, and separating offenders from the community" (1997:109).

Finally, Richard Quinney (1997) has maintained that current responses to crime by the criminal justice system are a form of "negative peace." That is, the purpose of the criminal justice system is to deter or process acts of crime through the threat and application of force. Thus the criminal justice system's response to crime is a form of violence in itself, which subsequently begets further violence. Quinney therefore views peacemaking criminology as part of the movement toward "positive peace," which exists when the sources of crime—such as poverty, inequality, racism, and alienation—are no longer present. As Quinney concluded:

> There can be no peace—no positive peace—without social justice. Without social justice and without peace (personal and social), there is crime. And there is, as well, the violence of criminal justice. . . . Criminal justice keeps things as they are. Social policies and programs that are positive in nature—that focus on positive peacemaking—create something new. They eliminate the structural sources of violence and crime. A critical, peacemaking criminologist is engaged in the work of positive peace. (p. 117)

Postmodernism

At its most abstract level, **postmodernism** is a reaction to the scientific rationalism and to the positivist certainty of the Enlightenment. It rejects scientific notions of "cause" just as it rejects the idea that "crime" is a simple or fixed category. Henry and Einstadter summarized some of the more common themes associated with postmodernism:

> For postmodernists there are no eternal truths; indeed, any truth claims are subject to challenge and deconstruction. The emphasis is on what postmodernists term alternative discourse and meaning. Positivism is rejected in favor of subjectivistic accounts. There is no such thing as certainty, rather uncertainty is the order of the day. In its extreme form, no explanation of a phenomenon is superior to any other, a belief which, in the view of some, leads to nihilism. (1998:417)

Henry and Einstadter went on to argue that postmodernist criminologists likewise challenge traditional (modernist) criminological "truths," yet must simultaneously reconstruct criminological discourse "along lines seen to better reflect the human condition, but always subject to change" (p. 417). Thus postmodern criminologists argue for a "replacement discourse," or a method of "talking about crime, harm, and social justice that invests energy in displacing the negative discourse which feeds structures of oppression" (p. 417).

The most thoroughgoing postmodernist position in criminology is **constitutive criminology**, an avowedly political position that seeks to get behind or to lay bare the rhetoric, the dogma, and the mystification that goes into the public discourse about crime; in other words constitutive criminology examines how crime is constituted by public discourse. The chief authors of constitutive criminology are Stuart Henry and Dragan Milovanovic (1991, 1994, 1996). For present purposes, we can strip away the complex philosophical and linguistic wrappings of their labors and reduce constitutive criminology to three major propositions.

First, crime is not simply what the criminal law says it is. Rather, crime is the ability or the power to impose one's will upon others in any particular social context: Crimes "are nothing less than moments in the expression of power, such that those who are subjected to them are denied . . . their own humanity, the power to make a difference" (1996: 116). Henry and Milovanovic thus redefined crime "in terms of the power to create harm (pain) in any context" (p.118). This redefinition of crime identifies two major forms of harm: "harms of reduction," which occur "when an offended party experiences a loss of some quality relative to their present standing," and "harms of repression," which occur "when an offended party experiences a limit or restriction preventing them from achieving a desired position or standing" (p. 103).

Second, Henry and Milovanovic rejected modernist notions of causality, arguing that crime is "discursively constructed through human processes" in which "people lose sight of the humanity and integrity of those with whom they interrelate and whom their actions and interactions affect" (pp. 170, 175). The "psycho-socio-cultural matrix" provides the "discursive medium" through which individuals construct "meaningful harms to others" (p. x). In short, some individuals become "excessive investors" in the expression of power and control, resulting in "thought processes which objectify others as separate, dehumanized entities" (p. 175).

Finally, Henry and Milovanovic constructed a policy for curbing crime. They argued that any human relationship that involves the actual or potential infliction of harm must be analyzed carefully in its discursive context, exposed, and restructured in non-harmful ways. Thus, their policy included the development of alternative "replacement discourses" (primarily in the mass media) as well as "narrative therapies" in which excessive investors are assisted in developing "liberating life narratives" (p. 224).

Constitutive criminology, then, is an attempt to go beyond "modernism" and "skeptical postmodernism" by developing an "affirmative postmodern" approach to the study of crime and its control.

Feminism

Contemporary contributions to criminology by **feminism** can be divided into two phases, the first extending from the 1970s and into much of the 1980s (see Chapter 7.4), and the second extending from the late 1980s and throughout the 1990s. In the first phase, feminist criminologists concentrated on criticizing criminological theory for being either gender-blind or for misrepresenting women. In addition, feminist criminologists conducted investigations of women's experiences as offenders, victims, and workers in the criminal justice system and employed popular feminist theories of the time—liberal, radical, Marxist, and socialist—to explain women's (and men's) involvement in crime.

In the second phase of feminist contributions to criminology, two specific directions of theorizing about women and crime have occurred (Daly and Maher, 1998). These two directions involve (1) the examination of how women are constructed in and by particular discourses such as the law and (2) the exploration of women's actual lives and how their specific problems and responses to these problems influence involvement in crime. Daly and Maher contrasted these two directions in feminist theorizing in the following way: The first "often characterizes women as effects of discourse" and the second "tends to characterize women as subjects of their own lives" (p. 4).

The work of Carol Smart (1998) is an example of what it means to examine the effects of discourse (language and symbolic representation) on women. Smart has argued that the law can be understood as a discourse that produces gender identities. In particular, Smart has shown that the law constructs both different "types of Woman" and "Woman as distinct from Man." Smart used the example of the prostitute to explain this distinction more fully: "In legal discourse the prostitute is constructed as the bad woman, but at the same time she epitomizes Woman in contradistinction to Man because she is what any woman could be and because she represents a deviousness and a licentiousness arising from her (supposedly naturally given) bodily form, while the Man remains innocuous" (p. 28).

Smart also examined how legal discourse constructs the "bad mother." Taking us back to seventeenth-century England, Smart pointed out a statute that was passed in 1623 making it illegal for a mother to kill her bastard infant. With the introduction of this new law, the burden of proving innocence was placed on the mother alone. Then in 1803 the first statute on abortion was enacted in Britain, criminalizing abortion at any stage of pregnancy. In 1882 the age of consent was raised to thirteen and in 1885 to sixteen, thus exposing young women who became pregnant—yet who were too young to marry—to legal control; and in 1913 the Mental Defective Act resulted in the incarceration of unmarried mothers on grounds of moral imbecility or feeble-mindedness. According to Smart, this set of laws established a type of woman (the bad mother) as well as Woman distinct from Man because motherhood was constructed as "natural":

> Means of avoiding motherhood were denied to women, and the inevitability of the link between sex and reproduction was established through the harsh repression of those deploying traditional means of rupturing this link. We see the rise of compulsory motherhood for any woman who was heterosexually active. The "bad mother" reinforced notions of proper motherhood and, therefore, is constructed by legal discourse as a type of woman. Yet simultaneously this legal discourse establishes the "bad mother" as Woman because "she invokes the proper place of Man." She is the problem (supposedly) because she does not have a man. (p. 30)

In contrast to Smart's postmodern feminism, the work of Meda Chesney-Lind explores women as subjects of their own lives. For example, in a study of gang members in Hawaii, she examined personal and familial characteristics, self-reported delinquency, and the gang activities of both boys and girls (Joe and Chesney-Lind, 1998). The evidence (based on interviews) revealed significant differences between boy and girl gang members. Although both boys and girls came from high-crime and economically depressed neighborhoods, 75 percent of the girls (as opposed to 55 percent of the boys) reported being victims of parental physical and/or sexual abuse. Thus although the gang provides a surrogate family role to most youth who join, this is especially so for girls who previously have been victimized by a family member. In other words, the reasons for joining a gang are not the same for girls and boys: Girls are more likely to be runaways from physical and sexual victimization at home who eventually approach a gang for solace as an alternative family. Chesney-Lind (1995, 1997) concluded that to understand female crime, it is important to focus on the "real" lives of women and girls and on how their real-life specific problems—based on gender, race, and class inequalities—and their response to these problems are related to eventual delinquent and criminal behavior. Obviously, this focus is quite different than Smart's focus on women as the effects of discourse.

In the early 1990s, feminist scholars also became interested in examining the relationship between masculinities and crime. Since then, numerous works have been published, from individually authored books (Messerschmidt, 1993, 1997; Polk, 1994; Collier, 1998) to edited volumes (Newburn and Stanko, 1994) to special academic-journal issues (Carlen and Jefferson, 1996). Like the work on girls and women by feminist criminologists, the examination of masculinities and crime has developed in two similar directions: men as effects of discourse and men as subjects of their own lives.

An example of the former is the work of Richard Collier's book *Masculinities, Crime, and Criminology* (1998). The bulk of this book describes the ways in which various types of men—lawyers, criminologists, youth offenders, mass murderers, and fathers—have been constructed by discourse. As an example, Collier explored the discursive production of the "dangerous" male child in contemporary Britain. In particular, he focused on how adolescent male offenders have been produced through discourse. Collier discussed the "rat boy" media discourse that emerged in Britain in the early 1990s due to growing concern over "what to do" with persistent adolescent male offenders. Rat boys would engage in "crime sprees" and then "hide in the maze of ventilation shafts, tunnels, and roof spaces . . . while trying to evade capture by the police"—hence, the name "rat boy" (p. 92). Various media discourses characterized these working-class boys as "monsters," "animals," "vermin," and "as beyond the social, outside society, as venal" (p. 91). According to Collier, what emerged through this characterization was an offending adolescent male who is simultaneously masculine "like other boys and yet, also appeared as other, as less than human, as *different* from other boys" (p. 91).

An example of exploring men as subjects of their own lives is the book *Crime as Structured Action* (1997) by James Messerschmidt. Here, Messerschmidt explored the relationship among masculinities as they are constructed by men differentiated through race, class, time, and social situation. As one example, Messerschmidt examined the changes in Malcolm X's masculine identity within a range of race and class contexts: a childhood in which he constantly battled for acceptance as a young man; a zoot-suit culture that embraced him without stigma as a "hipster" and "hustler"; and a spiritual and political movement that celebrated him as father, husband, and national spokesperson. Across these sites and through shifting currencies of his sense of masculine, race, and class identity, Malcolm X moved in and out of crime. Malcolm X simply appropriated crime as a resource for "doing masculinity" at a specific moment in his life, a period when gender, race, and class relations were equally significant. Thus Messerschmidt provided information about why Malcolm X "chose" crime at a certain stage of his life and how that engagement relates to his gender, race, and class position in society.

As with feminist theorizing on women and crime, then, current efforts by profeminist men maintain two tendencies: Postmodern work investigates how men and boys are constructed by discourse, whereas other efforts explore men as active agents who construct masculinities and crime in particular social contexts.

Assessment

Although critical criminology is somewhat unified (as outlined at the beginning of this section), developments during the 1980s and 1990s led to a diversity of perspectives. We discussed four of these perspectives: left realism, peacemaking, postmodernism, and feminism. Before we briefly assess these four critical criminologies, it is important to point out that because of space limitations we cannot discuss all forms of critical criminology.

Indeed, another example of critical criminology is "abolitionism." This perspective focuses on the faulty logic of using incarceration to solve the crime problem (Bianchi and Van Swaaningen, 1986; Hudson, 1997). Another is "anarchism." This approach views the state as the source of all social ills, including crime (Tifft and Sullivan, 1980; Pepinsky, 1978; Ferrell, 1997). The most recent critical perspective is "cultural criminology," which explores the relationship between "imagery, style and symbolic meaning" and "that [which is] categorized by legal and political authorities as criminal" (Ferrell and Sanders, 1995:3). Let us now return to our assessment of left realism, peacemaking, postmodernism, and feminism.

The left-realist emphasis on taking street crime seriously and constructing policy for curbing such crime represents an important contribution to criminology in general and critical criminology in particular. Nevertheless, some criminologists have criticized left realists for remaining unidimensional; that is, their concentration on "relative deprivation" is linked exclusively to social class, excluding any conceptualization of how gender and race might impact street crime. For example, given the fact that men perpetrate more street crimes and the more serious of these crimes than do women, the logic of left realism requires that we conclude that men experience more relative deprivation than do women. Thus, as Sandra Walklate (1998) has argued, left realists fail to explore how gender, race, and class interconnect with one another and how this interconnection constructs crime differently. Finally, Don Gibbons has emphasized that although it would be incorrect to view left realism as simply "old wine in new bottles," much of what "passes for realist theorizing is paralleled in viewpoints that are fairly common among mainstream criminologists" (1994:170).

Peacemaking criminology sensitizes the discipline to the importance of humanistic approaches to crime and criminal justice. It emphasizes more humane and more caring approaches to the criminal justice system. Nevertheless, although laudable in its ideology, peacemaking criminology as yet offers no blueprint for achieving a humanistic criminal justice system. In other words, how does society move from a criminal justice system based on repression to one that concentrates on cooperation, compassion, and respect for all species?

Both constitutive criminology and postmodern feminist criminology pose a challenge to "modernist" criminology, especially to the concentration of conventional criminology on the "scientific" study of crime and social control. However, important questions remain about the writings of constitutive and postmodernist criminologists: Have they simply replaced a modernist truth with a postmodernist truth? For example, from a postmodernist position, constitutive criminology is simply a discourse in itself that (possibly unintentionally) declares that it frames the "true" picture of crime.

Finally, given the failure of criminology to theorize the best predictor of crime—"maleness"—current work on masculinities and crime is a welcome corrective to this past neglect. Indeed, this work has been located by criminologists "at the edge of criminological theorizing and empirical investigation" (Walklate, 1998:87) and characterized as having "enormous intuitive appeal" (Cullen and Agnew, 1999:365). Nevertheless, this work is not without its critics. For example, Cullen and Agnew (pp. 364–365) have criticized such efforts for omitting women from the analysis, for maintaining a narrow definition of masculinity, and for not easily explaining conformity among disadvantaged men.

REVIEW

In this chapter we have introduced a variety of criminological theories that have been developed in the last decade. Each will no doubt be developed further in the next decade. Several of these theories embody a movement towards general and integrated theory, yet they are remarkably diverse in their basic assumptions about human sociality and the causes of crime.

Routine Activities and Crime

1. Crime should be understood in terms of the conjunction of the triangular relationships between likely offenders, suitable targets, and capable guardians.

2. Changes in crime rates are determined by fundamental changes of everyday patterns of life. These routine activities may occur in or outside households. Examples of routine activities include commuting to work and numerous events associated with providing and acquiring food and shelter, sexual outlets, leisure, learning, and childrearing.

3. Despite its commonsense appeal, the theory offers no formal criteria about which routine activities are relevant to understanding crime. It also fails to place criminogenic situations in their broader sociological context.

Self-Control and Control Balance

1. Gottfredson and Hirschi's theory of self-control suggests that individual differences in criminal behavior are due to differences in "self-control." Low self-control coupled with opportunity increases an individual's propensity to commit crime, especially crimes involving force or fraud.

2. The major cause of low self-control is ineffective child-rearing. The characteristics of self-control can be derived from the nature of crime itself, of which Gottfredson and Hirschi outline five chief aspects.

3. Empirical tests of self-control theory have had mixed results, with some critics characterizing its core proposition as a tautology.

4. The main premise of Tittle's theory of control balance is that the amount of control to which an individual is subject relative to the amount of control s/he can exercise determines the probability and type of deviance. The theory identifies six types of deviance: predation, exploitation, defiance, plunder, decadence, and submission.

5. Individuals are in control balance if the amount of control they exercise is the same as the amount of control they experience. If one controls more than one experiences control, then one has a control surplus. If one experiences control more than one controls, then one has a control deficit. Individuals with a control balance tend to conform. Those who have more control and those who have less control both tend to engage in more deviance.

6. Some modifications to Tittle's theory have been proposed, including simplifying it into a theory of predatory deviance.

Revised Strain Theory

1. Whereas Merton's strain theory focused on the ways in which an individual is barred from achieving conventional goals, Agnew expands strain theory to include the analysis of relationships in which others present the individual with noxious or negative stimuli.

2. Agnew's social-psychological theory pinpoints three chief sorts of strain: failure to achieve positively-valued goals; the removal of positively-valued stimuli from the individual; and the presentation of negative stimuli. Agnew has said that at heart his theory is very simple: "If we treat people badly, they may get mad and engage in crime."

3. In his analysis of animal abuse, Agnew admits the relevance of numerous other factors, both sociological and psychological. These include an individual's social position; psychological traits, like empathy; level of stress and strain; socialization; social control; and the nature of the animal under consideration.

4. Despite the narrow demographic make-up of the populations that have been used to test it so far, Agnew's theory has gained some preliminary empirical support.

5. Messner and Rosenfeld's institutional anomie theory extends Merton's theory at the macro level. They argue that the American Dream in unachievable for some because of the lopsided dominance of the capitalist economy in the institutional balance of power.

6. This dominance of the economic realm occurs in three ways: noneconomic institutional functions and roles are devalued; other social institutions are forced to accommodate to economic requirements; and economic norms penetrate most other institutional areas. In combination, and in the absence of social control and cultural counterweights, this leads to high crime rates.

7. Messner and Rosenfeld's radical solution to the problem of crime in the United States involves both a rebalancing of the major social institutions and also cultural regeneration.

Critical Criminologies

1. Since the mid-1980s, some radical criminologists have developed a left-realist approach to crime. They argue that crime and its control must be taken seriously, and they have developed a program for curbing conventional crime.

2. Peacemaking criminologists attempt to humanize the institutions of criminal justice by emphasizing cooperation, compassion, and community rather than punishment, condemnation, and separation.

3. Constitutive criminology, a type of postmodernism, challenges modernist criminology in its definition of crime, in its arguments on causation, and in its policies for curbing crime.

4. In the second phase of feminist contributions to criminology, two specific directions of theorizing have occurred: the exploration of women's and men's actual lives and an examination of how women and men are constructed in and by discourse.

QUESTIONS FOR CLASS DISCUSSION

1. What implications does the theory of routine activities have for the design of local crime control?

2. In what circumstances might individuals who are in control balance commit suicide? Is suicide evidence of low or high self-control?

3. Is the American Dream actually a nightmare?

4. How does the American Dream contribute to high crime rates?

5. Choose two or three types of crime (e.g., homicide, robbery, and employee theft) and then compare how each of the critical criminologies discussed in this chapter would explain the causes of each crime.

FOR FURTHER STUDY

Readings

Agnew, Robert. 1998. The Causes of Animal Abuse: A Social-Psychological Analysis. *Theoretical Criminology* 2 (2): 177–209.

Daly, Kathleen, and Lisa Maher, eds. 1998. *Criminology at the Crossroads: Feminist Readings in Crime and Justice*. New York: Oxford University Press.

MacLean, Brian D., and Dragan Milovanovic, eds. 1998. *Thinking Critically About Crime*. Vancouver, B.C.: Collective Press.

Reed, Gary E., and Peter Cleary Yeager. 1996. Organizational Offending and Neoclassical Offending: Challenging the Reach of a General Theory of Crime. *Criminology* 34 (3): 357–382.

Schwartz, Martin D., and Victoria L. Pitts. 1995. Exploring a Feminist Routine Activities Approach to Explaining Sexual Assault. *Justice Quarterly* 12 (1): 9–31.

Tittle, Charles R. 1995. *Control Balance: Toward a General Theory of Deviance*. Boulder, Colo.: Westview Press.

Websites

1. <http://sun.soci.niu.edu/~critcrim/>: This is the Critical Criminology Homepage of the American Society of Criminology; it has links to a wide variety of data, current statistics, legal writings, and political resources.

2. <http://www.preventingcrime.com/report>: This is a congressionally-mandated report from the University of Maryland entitled *Preventing Crime: What Works, What Doesn't, and What's Promising*. It is a good example of the relationship between theory and policy, especially rational choice and modern strain theories of crime.

3. <http://www.albany.edu/scj/jcjpc>: This is an electronic journal, the *Journal of Criminal Justice and Popular Culture*. When readers select the link to volume 3, they will find an article outlining cultural criminological theory.

PART THREE

Types of Crime

9

Interpersonal Violence

Preview

Chapter 9 introduces:
- the different types of interpersonal violence
- the nature and extent of interpersonal violence
- the varying definitions of interpersonal violence

Key Terms

aggravated assault	murder
animal abuse	professional murder
battering	rape
child abuse	serial murder
hate crimes	sexual harassment
interpersonal coercion	social coercion
manslaughter	victim precipitation
mass murder	wife rape

Interpersonal crimes of violence have affected the way many of us live. We fear the streets, fear being home alone, fear being by ourselves in the center of the city, and fear specific acts, such as murder, assault, and rape. Fear of crime clearly alters our lifestyle.

Moreover, we are particularly afraid of strangers. In 1967 the President's Commission on Law Enforcement and the Administration of Justice reported that "the fear of crimes of violence is not a simple fear of injury or death or even of all crimes of violence, but at bottom, a fear of strangers" (President's Commission, 1967:52). There is no reason to believe this has changed. Many of us assume that most violent crimes are committed on the streets by strangers. We fear most of all the random, unprovoked attack on the street by a stranger.

Much of this fear (see Chapter 1.1) is created by the mass media, for it is here that most people develop their comprehension of where, by whom, and how often violent crime is committed. Magazines, newspapers, and television focus on dramatic, violent crimes like murder; "prime-time criminals," usually strangers to their victims, commit their crimes on the street. A distorted view of crime is thus encouraged.

Indeed, most conventional crime is not violent. There are many more crimes against property than crimes of interpersonal violence. Moreover, crimes of interpersonal violence occur most frequently indoors and, therefore, are more or less invisible to the public; the perpetrators—although sometimes strangers—are usually relatives, friends, or acquaintances of the victims. This is not to say, however, that crimes of interpersonal violence in the United States are not a substantial problem. We as citizens are rightly concerned about a major social cancer: the United States—according to the best available evidence—has a higher level of interpersonal violence than any other industrialized country (Currie, 1998).

With this in mind, we turn now to a discussion of certain specific acts of interpersonal violence. We discuss the nature, extent, and types of three categories of interpersonal violence: (1) murder, assault, and rape; (2) violence in the family; and (3) violence in the workplace. These crimes are often referred to as "one-on-one" or "person-to-person" crimes because one person inflicts violence on another. Interpersonal violence therefore differs from other types of violence—such as corporate violence (see Chapter 13.2)—that inflict harm on larger numbers of people and do not entail direct face-to-face interaction.

9.1 MURDER, ASSAULT, AND RAPE

When we think of violent crimes, what commonly comes to mind are the crimes of murder, assault, and for women in particular, rape. In this section we look at the nature and extent of these three forms of interpersonal violence. We begin with a discussion of murder and assault.

Murder and Assault

Murder is defined as "the willful (nonnegligent) killing of one human being by another" (Federal Bureau of Investigation, 1998:15). Individuals also can be charged by the state with **manslaughter** for killing another person through gross negligence. The difference between murder and manslaughter is based on intent, or what is referred to as *mens rea* (a guilty mind is present in the offender)—the conscious intent of the murderer is to kill. In murder, malice is always present, although the degree of murder is based on the level of premeditation (essentially, plotting the murder in advance). Manslaughter is divided into two types, voluntary and involuntary. Voluntary manslaughter occurs when there is sudden passion arising from an immediate adequate cause. If the victim does not die but sustains serious injury, the crime is defined by the state as assault. Involuntary manslaughter results when one individual unintentionally kills another through recklessness or gross negligence, such as might happen during an automobile accident.

The most comprehensive source for determining the number of murders is the *Uniform Crime Reports (UCR),* published by the Federal Bureau of Investigation. Obviously, it is impossible to conduct victimization surveys on murder. Although it is difficult to conceal a killing from official investigation, a number of murders may be ignored, overlooked, or disregarded; coroners may err in ruling an accidental death as a murder; and some bodies simply may be hidden. Thus, although we must rely on police data as our source for determining the nature and extent of murder in the United States, this data must be viewed with some degree of skepticism.

In 1997 there were 18,209 murders in the United States. This means that approximately 7 of every 100,000 people were victims of murder (Federal Bureau of Investigation, 1998:15). Although murder is the most serious form of crime, fortunately it occurs the least often. In 1997, murder accounted for only 0.1 percent of all Index Crimes (p. 9).

Murder also occurs primarily in big cities and in the South. Generally the larger the city, the higher the violent crime rate. Moreover, studies over several decades have consistently shown a close relationship between city size and murder rates. That is, the larger the city, the higher the murder rate (Reiss and Roth, 1993).

As shown in Table 9.1, the murder rates declined from 1993 to 1997 for all regions, with the largest decreases occurring in the Northeast and the West. From 1995 to 1997, the West experienced a dramatic drop in the murder rate. Although the murder rate decreased from 1993 to 1997 regardless of city size, metropolitan cities experienced a murder rate almost twice that of smaller cities and rural counties.

The typical killing—whether in large cities or small—results from a disagreement between individuals who know each other. Approximately 50 percent of murders involve family members, friends, or acquaintances, and 14 percent involve strangers; in the remaining 36 percent the relationship between victim and offender is unknown (Federal Bureau of Investigation, 1998). Moreover, most murders involve arguments over romantic triangles, property and money, and other issues. The typical murder, then, involves family, friends, or acquaintances, who are engaged in an argument—usually over a trivial matter—that eventually leads to a killing. Consequently, according to official data as well

TABLE 9.1   Regional Murder Rate per 100,000 Residents

	1993	1994	1995	1996	1997
Region					
Northeast	8.2	7.1	6.2	5.4	4.8
Midwest	7.6	7.5	6.9	6.4	6.1
South	11.3	10.7	9.8	9.0	8.4
West	9.9	9.4	9.0	7.7	6.8
Urban character					
Metropolitan cities[a]	10.6	10.0	9.1	8.1	7.4
Smaller cities[a]	5.3	4.8	4.7	4.5	4.2
Rural counties	5.4	5.0	5.0	4.7	4.6
Number of murders and					
nonnegligent manslaughters	24,530	23,330	21,610	19,650	18,209

[a] Metropolitan cities are those in Metropolitan Statistical Areas (MSA's), and smaller cities are those outside an MSA.
SOURCE: Bureau of Justice Statistics, 1998; FBI, 1998.

as numerous studies of both large and small cities, we have more to fear from those to whom we are close than from strangers (Riedel and Zahn, 1985; Daly and Wilson, 1988; Iadicola and Shupe, 1998).

It is therefore not surprising to find that the typical murder is also related to routine social activities among family, friends, or acquaintances. Murder is most likely to occur during times when routine activities are more concentrated around the home. For example, murder occurs most often during summer vacations (July and August) and Christmas holiday seasons (December and January), which are traditionally a time when family members, neighbors, and friends are together (Federal Bureau of Investigation, 1998:16). Moreover, weekend murders are more likely to occur at home, among family members, and during the early evening hours (Messner and Tardiff, 1985:258–260).

Although the typical murder discussed thus far is characteristic of the largest proportion of murders, there are other types. For example, **professional murder** takes place when one individual kills another for personal profit. An unwritten "contract" is arranged, usually over the telephone, between people who have never met personally. The victim, or "hit," is normally unknown to the killer, as this makes it easier for the killer to "deny the victim" (Levi, 1981:52). Moreover, by conceptualizing the killing as a "business" or as "just a job," professional murderers can deny wrongfulness and thus justify their behavior even further (p. 53).

Another type of murder, **serial murder**, occurs when an individual kills a number of people over a period of time. There are two types of serial murderers. First, there are those killers who murder within the general area of their residence. An example of this type of serial murderer is John Wayne Gacy, who in 1979 murdered thirty-three young boys in or near his home and then buried them in the crawl space of his home, the attic, inside the walls, and under the patio and driveway. Another example is that of Donald Harvery, a nurse's aide in Cincinnati. In the late 1980s, Harvery systematically killed twenty-one patients to allegedly relieve them from their suffering. Second, there are murderers who kill outside the proximity of their own residences. Examples of this type are Theodore Bundy, who was found guilty of killing more than twenty women in Washington, Utah, and Colorado, and Henry Lee Lucas, who *admitted* killing 365 people in twenty-five states. According to some researchers, at least 142 of Lucas's killings have been verified (Holmes and DeBurger, 1985:30–31). A more recent example is the case of the "Unabomber," or Theodore Kaczynski who, over the course of seventeen years (1978–1995), killed three people and injured twenty-two by sending bombs through the mail. On January 22, 1998, Kaczynski plead guilty to thirteen federal bombing offenses.

There is controversy over the annual number of serial murder victims in the United States. Holmes and DeBurger (1988:19) estimated that between 3,500 and 5,000 persons are victims of serial murderers each year. As noted in Chapter 2.2, however, Philip Jenkins's (1988) investigation of FBI serial murder data revealed at most 350–400 murders associated with serial killers.

Finally, a **mass murder** is committed when an individual kills a number of people at once, rather than singly over time. An example of a mass murder is a husband/father who kills his wife and children. More recent examples are the various killings of students and teachers at schools. Some of the more well-known of these "school shootings" include:

- On February 2, 1996, in Moses Lake, Washington, Barry Loukaitus (age 14) shot and killed a teacher and two students at his junior high school.
- Eight months later, in Pearl, Mississippi, Luke Woodman (age 16) shot and killed two students in his high school.
- Two months later, in West Paducah, Kentucky, Michael Carneal (age 14) shot and killed three students in his high school.
- On March 24, 1998, in Jonesboro, Arkansas, Michael Johnson (age 13) and his accomplice, Andrew Golden (age 11), shot and killed a teacher and four students in their junior high school.
- On April 20, 1999, in Littleton, Colorado, Eric Harris (age 18) and Dylan Klebold (age 17) shot and killed a teacher, twelve students, and themselves.

Serial and mass murders are the rarest types of murder, yet they attract—as we all know—the most media attention.

The most common weapon used to commit murder in the United States is a firearm. In 1997 approximately 70 percent of all murders were committed with a firearm, 53 percent with a handgun (Federal Bureau of Investigation, 1998:16). Many people argue that because of the relationship between firearms and murder, firearms (especially handguns) should be controlled rigidly by the state. Others, in particular members of the National Rifle Association (NRA), argue that "Guns do not kill, people do."

Although the debate over firearm ownership and murder is likely to continue for some time, sociologists and criminologists have generated some interesting information that sheds light on the subject. First, the risk of death from a firearm is not uniformly distributed throughout the U.S. population: "The highest fraction of homicides committed with firearms peaks for 15–19 year olds, at 81 percent of homicides, and consistently declines relative to other weapons used as the offender age increases" (Iadicola and Shupe,

HARRIS   KLEBOLD

The school shootings: From 1997 to 1999 there were eight school shootings in the United States. One shocking example occurred on March 24, 1998, when the Jonesboro boys killed four students and a teacher at their middle school in Jonesboro, Arkansas. On April 20, 1999, the worst school shooting ever took place when two students at Columbine High School in Littleton, Colorado, killed twelve students, a teacher, and themselves.

1998:107). Second, firearm ownership varies by region, which correlates with the regional murder rates. The South has both the highest murder rate and the highest rate of firearm ownership. The Northeast, on the other hand, has the lowest murder rate and the lowest rate of firearm ownership (Federal Bureau of Investigation, 1998:16). Third, the chance of dying from a firearm wound is much higher than from assault with a knife, club, or fist. In fact, assaults with firearms are two to six times more likely to result in death than assaults with knives (Wright, Rossi, and Daly, 1983:18, 198). Fourth, increases in murder are correlated with increases in firearm ownership (Iadicola and Shupe, 1998). Fifth, because of easy availability of firearms, more accidental deaths and injuries occur.

All of this does not mean that firearms *cause* murder. However, it is obvious that households with firearms present are more likely—during a family argument, for instance—to experience a firearm death than are households without firearms. Thus, although there is scant evidence to suggest that firearm ownership deters crime (Green, 1987), by assuming it does and then purchasing guns, households actually become less, rather than more, safe and secure.

Hate groups: Hate groups like "skinhead" gangs have mobilized to perpetrate violence on people because of their race, religion, disability, ethnicity, and sexual orientation. "Skinheads" hold white supremacist views and routinely target people of color for violent attacks.

In 1958 criminologist Marvin Wolfgang coined the term "victim-precipitated murder," applying it to those murders in which "the victim is a direct, positive precipitator in the crime" (1958:252). In victim-precipitated murder, the victim is the first to display and use a deadly weapon or to strike a blow and, therefore, "the first to commence the interplay of resort to physical violence" (p. 252). For example, such a murder may involve two people having an argument during which the victim threatens the offender with a knife. Responding, the offender pulls out a gun and fires a fatal bullet. Wolfgang estimates that in one of every four murders, the victim precipitates the killing (p. 254).

A number of criminologists have questioned the thesis of **victim precipitation**, suggesting that the interaction between offender and victim actually involves challenges and provocations by *both* participants to the killing. In his research, David Luckenbill (1977) found that murder results from an "intense interchange" between offender, victim, and sometimes an audience and parallels a "character contest" wherein both offender and victim attempt to maintain "face" at the other's expense. This interchange between offender and victim takes place as follows:

1. The victim makes what the offender perceives as an offensive move, gesture, or remark.
2. The offender then retaliates with a verbal or physical challenge.

3. The victim then retaliates, creating a "working" agreement that commits both parties to a violent resolution of the conflict.

4. The battle eventually results in the death of the victim.

In 63 percent of Luckenbill's cases such an exchange between offender and victim took place (p. 179). Additional research has reported similar results, concluding that the typical murder involves both offender and victim contributing to the violent conflict (Felson and Steadman, 1983; Polk, 1994).

Although Luckenbill's theory is intriguing, it is questionable whether it is applicable to all forms of murder. Obviously, it is little help in understanding professional, serial, and mass murder. Moreover, Nancy Jurik and Peter Gregware (1992) have shown that for female-perpetrated murder, the idea of a character contest does not seem to hold in many cases, such as murder resulting from child abuse and killing in self-defense (to avoid wife beating). Thus, Luckenbill's theory may help us understand some male offender/male victim murder but is inadequate when applied to typical female offender/male victim murders. Whereas Luckenbill emphasizes a character contest, Jurik and Gregware's data on women "suggest the salience of strategic, life-saving dimensions and an imposed—rather than consensual—characterization of the violence in these homicides" (p. 196).

Aggravated assault is "an unlawful attack by one person upon another for the purpose of inflicting severe or aggravated bodily injury" (Federal Bureau of Investigation, 1998:33). Aggravated assault is usually accompanied by the use of a weapon or by other means likely to produce death or great bodily harm.

Assault and murder are closely related crimes. In fact, much of what has already been discussed regarding murder can also be applied to aggravated assault. However, there are some differences between the two crimes. The first and most obvious difference is that an assault does not result in an actual death. Although the typical assault and the typical murder are similar in most major respects, it is the existence of a dead body that creates the major difference between them. If a killing does not occur, the crime is some type of assault.

A second difference is that there are more assaults in the United States than murders. In 1997 there were approximately one million reported aggravated assaults, resulting in a rate of about 382 per 100,000 individuals (Federal Bureau of Investigation, 1998:33). This rate is more than forty times the murder rate. However, in its *National Crime Victimization Survey (NCVS),* the Department of Justice found that only 59 percent of the victims of aggravated assault reported the crime to the police (Department of Justice, 1999). Consequently, aggravated assault occurs much more often than the *UCR* data indicate. Indeed, the *NCVS* estimated that almost two million aggravated assaults occurred in 1997.

Finally, according to the *NCVS,* assaults—unlike murder—involve strangers more often (54 percent of the time) than relatives, friends, or acquaintances (Department of Justice, 1999:53). However, victims may be less likely to report assaults by people they know. Thus, it could well be that regarding the victim/offender relationship, aggravated assault is similar to murder.

Hate Crimes

A pervasive fact of life in industrialized societies is the existence of **hate crimes**, or violence perpetrated on people because of their race, religion, disability, ethnicity, or sexual orientation. In 1997, there were 8,049 hate crimes reported to the FBI, of which 4,710 were motivated by racial bias; 1,385 by religious bias; 1,102 by sexual-orientation bias; 836 by ethnicity bias; 12 by disability bias; and 4 by multiple biases (Federal Bureau of Investigation, 1998: 60). Moreover, a study of antigay and lesbian violence in eight U.S. cities—Boston, New York, Atlanta, St. Louis, Denver, Dallas, Los Angeles, and Seattle—found that among those surveyed (Berrill, 1992:20)

- 19 percent reported having been punched, hit, kicked, or beaten at least once in their lives because of their sexual orientation.
- 44 percent had been threatened with physical violence.
- 94 percent experienced some type of victimization—such as verbal abuse, physical assault, vandalized property, or being spat upon, chased, or pelted with objects.
- More than two-thirds (68 percent) of those threatened with violence and nearly half (47 percent) of those assaulted reported multiple victimizations.

A more recent report by the National Coalition of Anti-Violence Programs (1998) found that in 1997 there were 2,445 reported incidents of violence against lesbian, gay, bisexual, transgender, and HIV-positive people. This represents a 2 percent increase in hate crimes over the previous year, yet only approximately 50 percent were reported to the police. Moreover, in 1997 the number of victims who identified as lesbian or gay actually decreased 1 percent from the number in 1996. However, the number of heterosexuals reporting hate crime victimization rose 36 percent in 1997. This shows that hate crimes are crimes of perception: Victims are chosen not necessarily because they are, for example, lesbian or gay but because the perpetrator perceives them to be (p. 4).

Despite the many positive changes resulting from the civil rights movement, racism persists in the United States, expressing its extreme form in racist attacks on African Americans and other racial and ethnic minorities. During the 1970s there were increasing reports of racial violence against African Americans by white youth. In 1980, the Subcommittee on Crime of the U.S. House of Representatives investigated this violence. In its report, *Increasing Violence Against Minorities,* the Subcommittee found anti-African American attacks both by individuals (primarily young white males) and by groups such as the Ku Klux Klan. The report concluded that there "is abundant evidence of a marked increase in the incidence of criminal violence directed against minority groups" (U.S. House of Representatives, 1980:2). Today, 60 percent of hate crimes are motivated by racial bias (Federal Bureau of Investigation, 1998: 61).

Moreover, a number of skinhead gangs exist around the country. Skinheads hold extremely conservative and neo-Nazi views, and they routinely target racial and ethnic minorities and homosexuals for violent attacks. Indeed, Mark Hamm's (1993) important study *American Skinheads: The Criminology and Control of Hate Crime* reported that the defining characteristics of skinhead ideology are racism, homophobia, and anti-Semitism.

Hate crimes differ from other forms of interpersonal violence in three important ways: They are more vicious, extremely brutal, and frequently perpetrated at random on total strangers (commonly a single victim) by multiple offenders (usually groups of white working-class male teenagers) (Levin and McDevitt, 1993:11–20, and see Chapter 2.3). For hate crimes perpetrated in 1997 against specifically lesbian, gay, bisexual, transgen-

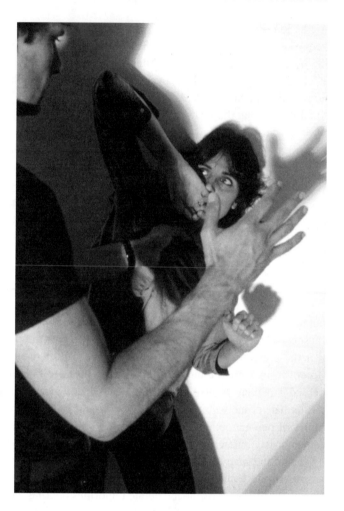

Wife rape and battering: Wife rape and battering occur much more frequently than commonly assumed. Historically, many criminologists argued that these crimes are "victim precipitated" or "victim provoked." Such arguments blame women and remove responsibility for the violence from men, the community, and society.

der, or HIV-positive people, offenders were strangers (34 percent), law enforcement officers (18 percent), landlord/neighbor (11 percent), employer/coworker (9 percent), and other (28 percent) (National Coalition of Anti-Violence Programs, 1998). Moreover, victims of hate crimes seem to face greater difficulty than many other victims in coming to terms with their victimization. This is because their victimization "is based on *who* they are, since the characteristics that elicit their victimization (e.g., race, ethnicity) often are important elements in their own identities" (Martin, 1995:305).

Why do hate crimes occur? One of the better explanations is offered by Levin and McDevitt, who have argued that this type of crime is the result in the United States of a "growing *culture of hate:* from humor and music to religion and politics, a person's group affiliation—the fact that he or she *differs from people in the in-group*—is being used more and more to provide a basis for dehumanizing and insulting that person" (1993:34). Although this "culture of hate" does not actually cause hate crimes, in a social context of growing unemployment and hard economic times, coupled with an influx of recent immigrants from Eastern Europe, Asia, Africa, and Latin America, as well as a visible gay/lesbian rights movement, a culture of hate provides "support and encouragement to those who seek to express their personal version of bigotry in some form of criminal behavior" (pp. 42–43). Indeed, Barbara Perry's research on hate groups in the United States found that such groups facilitate a negative politics of difference:

> Hate groups have mobilized in an effort to reassert a narrow, exclusive understanding of national identity. In particular, they provide a menu of ideologies which presume the hegemony of white, heterosexual, Christian male power. . . . To the extent that hate groups define their collective identity as the norm, they necessarily engage in a politics of difference which seeks to negate, exclude and repress those groups that fall outside of that norm, namely non-Whites, non-Christians, non-heterosexuals, even non-males. And they do so by invoking ideological claims to superiority and power. (1998:32)

Rape

Rape, as traditionally defined in the criminal law, is "the carnal knowledge of a female forcibly and against her will" (Federal Bureau of Investigation, 1998:25). By concentrating on "against her will," the criminal law makes it imperative that the threat or actual use of physical violence by the offender be present to constitute proof that the victim did not consent. Consequently, this traditional definition of rape actually means, in practice, sexual intercourse obtained by the threat or actual use of physical violence. Hence, the criminal law labels rape "forcible rape."

However, many scholars have argued that the traditional criminal law definition of forcible rape is inadequate, for it recognizes only one type of force—sexual intercourse obtained through the threat or actual use of physical violence. Some scholars argue that this definition does not provide for rape resulting from intimidation or pressure other than the threat or actual use of physical force. For example, a rape omitted from this traditional definition involves a woman who is coerced *economically*—"If you don't 'put out' you'll be fired"—where her overt genuine consent is absent (Box, 1983:122–127).

Moreover, some criminologists have pointed out that the traditional definition of rape does not include *all* rapes that occur through the threat or actual use of physical violence. These criminologists note that in many states the violent forcible rape of a wife is simply not considered rape. Although in 1993 wife rape became a crime in all fifty states, in thirty-three states certain exemptions from rape prosecution exist for husbands. For example, in the majority of these states a husband cannot be prosecuted for wife rape if the woman "is unable to consent because she is mentally or physically impaired, asleep, or unconscious. In these states husbands are held to a lesser standard than other assailants" (Bergen, 1998:22).

Nevertheless, because of feminist criticism, state definitions of rape have been expanded in certain ways: They are now gender neutral, meaning either men or women can be victims of rape; they cover anal and oral penetration by a penis or other objects; and they include nonforcible intercourse with someone unable to consent (e.g., unconscious, mentally incapacitated) (Koss and Cook, 1998).

Not everyone agrees with expanding the definition of rape to include "economic coercion," however. Some argue that an important distinction should be made between those who are coerced physically and those who may be coerced in other ways. For example, David Finkelhor and Kersti Ylló (1985:84–98) have argued that although labeling as rape sexual assault obtained through economic force highlights how oppressive and coercive sex is under certain circumstances, it simultaneously expands, and therefore dilutes, the meaning of the word "rape." Moreover, they have argued, it is extremely difficult to determine when force or coercion is being used in a relationship. For these two reasons, then, Finkelhor and Ylló have contended that the term "rape" should be used only for situations of actual or threatened physical force. This does not mean that other kinds of force are not employed. Indeed, Finkelhor and Ylló held that "a woman whose husband tells her he is going to humiliate her publicly if she won't perform some sexual act, for instance, may be making a more fearsome and devastating threat than a man who threatens only to push himself on his wife. We would be prepared to call this type of coercion forced sex, but not rape" (pp. 89–90).

Thus, Finkelhor and Ylló proposed that there are two types of sexual coercion in the United States but that sexual coercion, although frightening and traumatic, is clearly not, and should not be considered, rape. They distinguished "social coercion" from "interpersonal coercion." **Social coercion** occurs, for example, when women feel they should have sex with their husbands because it is their wifely "duty." Many women feel they cannot say no because they are married, or because he pays the bills, or because of religious authority. Thus, there exist social pressures on women to have sex with their husbands even if they do not want to do so. **Interpersonal coercion**, Finkelhor and Ylló's second type of sexual coercion, occurs when a woman has sex with her husband or an employer in the face of nonviolent threats. For example, a wife may have sex with her husband "to keep peace in the house," or a female employee may have sex with her boss to gain a promotion or just simply to keep a job.

Whether we agree with Finkelhor and Ylló or with the expanded definition of rape, the important point to understand is that sexual coercion can, and in fact does, occur in ways other than through the threat or actual use of physical violence.

In 1997 there were 96,122 reported forcible rapes, representing a rate of 36 per 100,000 people (Federal Bureau of Investigation, 1998:25). However we must view the police data with caution, inasmuch as the majority of rapes are not reported to the police. Indeed, Diana Russell (1990:96) found that only between 9 percent and 10 percent of rapes and attempted rapes were reported to the police. This is due not only to fear of retaliation but to "the trauma the rape victim experiences, the shame she often is made to feel, and also her likely perception that getting involved with the criminal justice system would itself be traumatic and possibly futile" (Schur, 1984:151). Moreover, because there is considerable evidence that women have a far greater chance of being raped by someone they know rather than by a stranger, this clearly affects the victim's decision to report the crime. Women who have been raped by someone they know—husband, friend, acquaintance— are the least likely to report the crime. A study of victimization data over a ten-year period found that almost 60 percent of stranger rapes, but only 45 percent of nonstranger rapes, were reported to the police (Bureau of Justice Statistics, 1985:3). Furthermore, a comparative study of stranger and acquaintance rape found that 21 percent of stranger rape victims, but only 2 percent of acquaintance rape victims, reported their victimization to the police (Koss, Dinero, Siebel, and Cox, 1988). Women raped by someone they know are

BOX 9.1 RAPE ON CAMPUS

A study of 6,000 undergraduate women and men at thirty colleges in the United States found the following (Koss and Cook, 1998):

- 27 percent of college women had experienced rape or attempted rape since the age of 14.
- In a 12-month period, 8 percent of college women experienced one or more attempted or completed rapes.
- 80 percent of the rapes or attempted rapes were committed by someone the victim knew.
- 57 percent of the rapes or attempted rapes occurred on a date.
- 25 percent of the men stated they had engaged in some type of sexual coercion since the age of 14.
- 4 percent of the men admitted engaging in legally defined rape.

Other research confirms these findings. For example, in their Canadian National Survey of sexual violence in college dating relationships, DeKeseredy and Kelly (1993) found that 45 percent of the women reported sexual abuse since leaving high school and 20 percent of the men reported having sexually victimized a female partner since high school.

Bergen (1998) pointed out that the literature on date rape suggests a positive correlation between the violence and the level of commitment and length of the relationship. In other words, the violence does not begin until "the couple has been together for a significant amount of time. This may help explain why 30 percent to 50 percent of couples who are experiencing violence have not ended their relationships" (p. 81).

Moreover, numerous researchers have shown that certain university-related male peer groups construct a pro-rape culture on college campuses (Schwartz and Dekeseredy, 1997; Benedict and Klein, 1998). For example, Patricia Yancey Martin and Robert Hummer (1998) studied a "fraternity-brother" group rape that occurred on the Florida State University campus. Their findings have shown that certain fraternities foster a pro-rape, hypermasculine culture through emphasis on brotherhood (e.g., loyalty, secrecy, alcohol as a weapon, etc.) and the commodification of women (e.g., women as bait, servers, and sexual prey). Indeed, a recent study of fraternities and pro-rape culture found that specific fraternities are places where there exists a high risk of rape on campus (Boswell and Spade, 1996). In such high-risk fraternity houses: brothers treated women as subordinates and kept them at a distance. Men in high-risk houses actively discouraged ongoing heterosexual relationships, routinely degraded women, and participated more fully in the hook-up scene; thus, the probability that women would become faceless victims was higher in these houses (p. 143).

less likely to report the crime to the police because they may feel (1) embarrassed, (2) that they should have been able to prevent the rape, (3) that they want to protect the offender, or (4) that they will not be believed (Bureau of Justice Statistics, 1985:2). Consequently, for all the preceding reasons, the number of rapes in U.S. society is much larger than statistics in the *Uniform Crime Reports* indicate. Indeed, the *National Crime Vic-*

timization Survey estimated that 311,110 forcible rapes occurred in 1997, suggesting that only approximately 30 percent of incidents were reported to the police (Department of Justice, 1999). Paralleling murder, then, rape is more likely to be committed by someone the victim knows. Women are more likely to be raped by an acquaintance or a date than by a stranger.

Some sociologists and criminologists have argued that date rapes are simply "victim-precipitated rapes." According to Menachem Amir, writing in the early 1970s, "victim-precipitated rape" occurred in

> those rape situations in which the victim actually, or so it was deemed, agreed to sexual relations but retracted before the actual act or did not react strongly enough when the suggestion was made by the offender(s). The term applies also to cases in risky situations marred with sexuality, especially when she uses what could be interpreted as indecency of language and gestures, or constitutes what could be taken as an invitation to sexual relations. (1971:266)

Amir believed that victims of rape are sometimes a "complementary partner" to their own victimization, and he concluded that about 19 percent of the rapes in his Philadelphia study were victim precipitated (1967:493; 1971:266).

A number of criminologists responded to the idea of "victim-precipitated rape," arguing that a male bias is clearly revealed in this theorizing—the male criminologists simply identifying with the rapist (Box, 1983; Schwendinger and Schwendinger, 1983). As Julia and Herman Schwendinger pointed out:

> The concept of victim precipitation can be criticized because its defining elements are exactly the same as those chosen by male supremacists, who insist that a victim's right to refuse sex can be ignored because the rapist has the right to force sexual intercourse when she is considered responsible for arousing him sexually. (1983:66)

According to some criminologists, then, the "victim-precipitated rape theorists" fail to acknowledge the victim's rights, in particular, the right to change her mind whenever she pleases. This is collusion—exactly what the rapist has done, namely, refused to recognize the victim's right to change her mind. The Schwendingers (p. 66) argued that the victim-precipitation theory of rape simply takes the rapist's judgments and rationalizations at face value—"She was asking for it," or "She did not resist strongly enough," or "She changed her mind too late"—and transforms them into a causal explanation of rape. Moreover, by shifting blame for the rape from offender to victim, these theorists divert attention from the rapist as well as from the broader macrosociological factors forming the context in which rape occurs (Box, 1983:135). Thus, although the idea of victim precipitation may be relevant to the crime of murder, it is clearly wrong to apply the concept to rape. As Box has asked: "By what stretch of the imagination do rape victims initiate the sexual assault? Do they actually start to assault sexually the persons who subsequently assault them sexually?" (p. 135).

Others have gone even further than the preceding criticisms, arguing that the idea of victim-precipitated rape is based on the pervasive myth in our society that men have a special and overwhelming "urge" or "drive" toward heterosexual intercourse. According to this myth, men have virtually an uncontrollable sexual need that, once "sparked," must find instant satisfaction, regardless of the consequences. Thus, if a woman awakens this sexual desire by engaging in provocative behavior, it is argued, the man cannot be held responsible for his behavior because the "urge" will be too strong for him to control. However, as feminist criminologist Carol Smart has responded, the "basic fallacy of the male sex-drive myth lies in the belief that rape is a spontaneous act (an immediate response to desire) and that it is a purely sexual act engaged in for the purpose of sexual satisfaction" (1976:95).

Rapists do not randomly and spontaneously assault their victims. Even Amir (1971:142) found that approximately 82 percent of rapes in his sample were either partially or entirely planned. Most stranger rapists spend time looking for women in locations most likely to be immune from surveillance, such as inside a home, an apartment, or a motor vehicle. Thus, stranger and date rape are not explosive acts, the result of sudden and uncontrollable sexual desire. Rape is an act of violent sexual domination intended to devalue and humiliate the victim. It is not an expression of sexual desire.

In the traditional definition of rape, the victims of forcible rape are always female. However, there are cases of males being forcibly raped by both males and females. When women are arrested for forcible rape, they are usually an accomplice to a man, assisting him in raping a female. This was just the case with Susanne Perrin of Oakland, California, who was forced by her husband—through repeated episodes of rape and battering—to hunt down other potential victims (Russell, 1982:280–282). However, there are also cases of women raping men without being an accomplice to a man. These types of rape are extremely uncommon and statistically insignificant.

Male rape of another male is also rare, except in prison. In prison a male's chance of being a rape victim increases. It has been estimated that in U.S. prisons approximately one of every five male inmates has been raped. And the combination of continued budget cuts, longer sentences, overcrowding, and understaffing will most likely increase its incidence (Cahill, 1985:32). Rape as an act of violent sexual domination intended to devalue and humiliate the victim is a widespread practice in male prisons. Young men in U.S. prisons must seek protection from stronger, older, and more powerful inmates, and many of them become sexual slaves to their "protectors." Others are forced into prostitution and traded for such prison commodities as cigarettes (p. 32). As Anthony Scacco concluded in his work on rape in male prisons: "In today's world the judge who sentences a young person to reform school or prison passes male rape on him as surely as the sentence. Every inmate has a very short time, once inside, to pick a 'wolf' (a tough protector) or face gang rape, becoming the 'girl' of the institution, or death" (1982:vii). Rape in male prisons is thus more than a power dynamic among men. As Don Sabo has argued: "In the muscled, violent, and tattooed world of prison rape, woman is symbolically ever-present. The prison phrase 'make a woman out of you' means that you will be raped. Rape-based relationships between prisoners are often described as relations between 'men' and 'women' and in effect conceptualized as 'master' and 'slave'" (1992:6). In other words, the social dynamics of prison rape are extremely instructive in understanding the rape of women in the larger society.

Moreover, it is quite unlikely that a male will be the victim of a rape unless he is incarcerated, and even then, once he has reached adulthood, he is virtually safe from any form of sexual assault.

Finally, the discussion above of fraternity group rape points to the fact that certain institutions—such as college campuses—may create forms of social interaction conducive to rape. Another example is the military. As Peter Iadicola and Anson Shupe have shown, throughout history rape has often been an institutionalized component of war:

> The systematic rape by soldiers of innocent women in towns and villages in the United States during the American Revolution, during the conquest and attempted genocide of native people on the North American continent, during the American Civil War, during World Wars I and II in Belgium, France, China, Germany, and during the most recent wars of our time in Korea and Vietnam, Bangladesh, Nicaragua, El Salvador, Russia and the former Yugoslavia, are just a few examples. Rape has been used to punish the enemy and as a reward for the victors. (1998:127)

9.2   INTERPERSONAL VIOLENCE IN THE FAMILY

The family is, on the one hand, a "haven in a heartless world," a place where love and security prevail. On the other hand, it is a site of conflict among its members. Unfortunately, for many this conflict turns into violence. Although considerable violence occurs among family members (as we have seen), violent crimes like murder, assault, and rape are not specific to the family and can occur outside its boundaries. In this section we focus on those types of interpersonal violence that occur only within the family setting. An accurate measure of interpersonal violence specific to the family is difficult to establish, but sociologists estimate that the problem is widespread for families throughout Western industrialized societies (Dobash and Dobash, 1979; Straus, Gelles, and Steinmetz, 1980). We discuss four types of interpersonal violence specific to the family—wife rape, battering, child abuse, and animal abuse.

Heterosexual Wife Rape and Battering

"It is within marriage," write sociologists Dobash and Dobash, "that a woman is most likely to be slapped and shoved about, severely assaulted, killed or raped" (1979:75). In fact, sociologists and criminologists have shown since 1977 that wife rape is more common than rape by dates, acquaintances, and strangers (Gelles, 1977; Hunt, 1979; Russell, 1982). Following Patricia Peacock, we define **wife rape** as "any sexual activity by a legal spouse that is performed without the consent of the other spouse" (1998:226). In the section above on rape we showed that women are more likely to be raped by someone they know. Adding to this, Russell (1990:62) argued that *any* woman could be raped by an acquaintance, friend, date (assuming the woman had one), relative, authority figure, or stranger. However, wife rape is different in the sense that *only* women who have ever been married can actually be raped by a husband or ex-husband. Thus, Russell (pp. 61–62) calculated rape and attempted rape based upon the percentage of women who had ever been married—rather than as a percentage of the entire sample—and found that "the prevalence of wife rape increases from 8 percent to 12 percent. This percentage places rape and attempted rape by husbands second only to rape and attempted rape by acquaintances" (p.

62). When Russell looked only at *completed* rapes (rather than the combination of completed and attempted rapes), she found that more women had been victimized by their husbands than by any other type of perpetrator. Although only 3 percent of the women in her sample were the victim of a completed rape by a stranger, 5 percent were the victim of a completed rape by a lover or ex-lover and 8 percent were the victim of a completed rape by a husband or ex-husband. One could therefore conclude from Russell's data that the more intimate the relationship between the victim and the offender, the greater the chance that the rape attempt will be completed.

Similarly, Finkelhor and Yllö (1985) surveyed 323 Boston-area women to determine how widespread wife rape is there. Finkelhor and Yllö (pp. 6–7) found that 10 percent of these women had experienced a rape by a husband or ex-husband, whereas only 3 percent had been raped by a stranger. In addition, another 10 percent of the women had been raped by a date. Finkelhor and Yllö concluded that "sexual assaults by intimates, including husbands, are by far the most common type of rape" (p. 7). It is estimated that 14 percent to 25 percent of married women are forced by their husbands to have sexual intercourse against their will during the course of their marriage (Bergen, 1998).

More recently, Patricia Peacock (1998) surveyed 278 women and found that 40, or 14 percent of the sample, reported at least one incident of wife rape. The following are the sexual activities in which husbands forced their wives to participate: intercourse (88 percent); perpetrator fondling victim (48 percent), victim forced to fondle perpetrator (45 percent), victim forced to perform oral sex on perpetrator (45 percent), perpetrator engaging victim in anal sex (40 percent), and perpetrator performing oral sex on victim (17 percent).

Moreover, the victims of wife rape reported not only that the rape by their husbands was frightening and brutal but that it involved humiliation, degradation, and hatred (Bergen, 1998; Peacock, 1998). In addition, they experienced physical injuries and for years suffered psychological trauma. The following are selected examples of wife rape that Finkelhor and Yllö (p. 18) found in their research:

- One woman was jumped in the dark by her husband and raped in the anus while slumped over a woodpile.
- One woman had a six-centimeter gash ripped in her vagina by a husband who was trying to "pull her vagina out."
- One woman was gang raped by her husband and a friend after they surprised her alone in a vacant apartment.
- One woman was raped at knifepoint by her estranged partner.
- One woman was forced to have sex the day after returning from gynecological surgery, causing her to hemorrhage and obliging her to return to the hospital.
- One woman was forced to have sex with her estranged husband in order for her to see her baby, whom he had kidnapped.

For most victims of wife rape, sexual assault is a common occurrence rather than an isolated episode in their marriage. Finkelhor and Yllö (1985:23) found that 50 percent of the women in their study had been assaulted twenty times or more. Peacock (1998:229) reported that 34 of the 40 women, or 85 percent, had been raped more than once by their spouse.

Women are assaulted not only by their current husbands; many are victimized by their ex-husbands. In the Russell (1990) study, 15 percent, or one in every seven, was raped by an ex-husband. The Finkelhor and Yllö (1985:205) study similarly found that 25 percent of the women had been raped by an ex-husband.

There also seems to be a close relationship between wife rape and wife beating. Studies indicate that between 30 and 50 percent of all wife beating involves some form of sexual abuse (Bergen 1998). In Russell's (1990) study, 36 percent of the women interviewed experienced some combination of beating and rape: 9 percent were primarily the victim of wife rape but were beaten also; for 22 percent of the wives, the frequency of rape and beating was approximately equal; 5 percent were primarily the victim of wife beating but were also raped. In the Finkelhor and Yllö (1985:23) study, 50 percent of the wife rape victims were battered. Moreover, battered women seem the most vulnerable of all wife rape victims to repeated rapes. As Finkelhor and Yllö found, "twice as many battered women suffered chronic rapes (twenty times or more) as the other raped women. In addition to being punching bags, the battered women were also, as one woman put it, 'masturbating machines'" (pp. 23–24). Thus, the wife batterer is more likely to be simultaneously the wife rapist.

However, this does not mean that the sexual assault of a wife cannot occur without violence—the threat or actual use of physical force. On the contrary, sexual intercourse can be coercive in other ways (social coercion and/or interpersonal coercion) as the following example illustrates:

> In my relationship I am forced to give sex because of the marriage vows. My husband has on occasion threatened to withhold money or favors—that is, permission of some sort or another—if I do not have sex with him. So I fake it. What the hell. When the kids are older I just might lay my cards on the table.

It is clear, then, that the sexual assault of a wife is not limited to battered women. It occurs as well in marriages where there is little or no physical violence (Finkelhor and Yllö, 1985:37).

This violence against women was not always illegal. Throughout the seventeenth, eighteenth, and nineteenth centuries in western Europe, it was legal for men to beat their wives, as long as the method used, and the extent of the violence, remained within certain limits (Andersen, 1993:170). For example, in eighteenth-century France the law restricted violence against wives to "blows, thumps, kicks, or punches on the back if they leave no traces." Moreover, the law did not allow for the use of "sharp-edged or crushing instruments" (p. 170). The phrase "rule of thumb" is derived from English common law, which specified that a man could beat his wife—for disciplinary reasons—as long as he used a stick no thicker than his thumb (p. 170). An ordinance, still in effect in Pennsylvania in the 1970s, prohibited a husband from beating his wife after 10:00 in the evening and on Sundays (Martin, 1982:266).

Although ideas on wife **battering** have changed considerably—it is now socially abhorred and illegal—it still occurs more frequently than most people believe. It is impossible to generate useful statistics on wife battering because the beating most likely has taken place in isolation from the community and most victims are too embarrassed to report the assault to the police, social service agency, or shelter. Therefore, in order to understand the prevalence of wife battering, we must rely on estimates provided by researchers in the field.

Estimates of the amount of wife battering in this country vary. For instance, *Time* magazine reported in 1983 that six million women are physically abused each year by their husbands, battery being the "single major cause of injury to women, more significant than auto accidents, rapes, or muggings" (1983:23). According to the National Coalition Against Domestic Violence, more than 50 percent of women will be battered in their lifetime, and every 15 seconds a woman is battered in the United States (Bergen, 1998). Sociological research has been more conservative, indicating that between 25 and 33 percent of heterosexual couples experience wife battering (Renzetti, 1992:18). However, most women battered by their husbands do not report the incident; approximately one in every ten cases is reported to the police (Davis, 1988:2). Thus, the amount of wife battering is probably higher than the above figures indicate.

Many women are beaten repeatedly over a period of years. This violence does not entail simply slapping, shoving, and pushing but intensifies into serious injuries to the victim. Women are burned, stabbed, and shot; bones and teeth are fractured; and miscarriages and severe internal injuries occur (Schechter, 1982:16; Dobash and Dobash, 1979:238).

Nevertheless, heterosexual wife battering is not uniformly distributed across society. Walter DeKeseredy and Ronald Hinch (1991:26–28) reviewed the research on wife battering and found that

- married women are more likely to be beaten than unmarried women;
- women aged 18–34 are more likely to be victimized than women of other age groups;
- low-income men are more likely to assault their wives than males in higher income groups;
- unemployed men are more likely than both employed and part-time employed men to abuse their wives.

An important question always asked by students of wife abuse is "why doesn't she leave?" In fact, most victims of battering do leave violent relationships (Schwartz, 1989). Nevertheless, Angela Browne (1995:229–30) has argued that asking "why don't battered women leave?" is based on the assumption that leaving an abusive relationship will end the violence. Indeed, studies show that battered women who leave a violent relationship may possibly experience more violence (Schwartz, 1988). Yet several researchers have answered this question, reporting that women stay in a violent relationship for a number of reasons. First, of course, is fear. The wife fears that if she leaves, the husband will find her and injure her even more severely. As Browne reported, based on interviews with battered women: "Many of the women stayed because they had tried to escape and been beaten for it, or because they believed their partner would retaliate against an attempt to leave him with further violence" (1995:232). Many women also fear for the safety of others (such as children), and they fear being without a home and losing the status of "wife" (Stanko, 1985:58). Second, most battered women do not have the material resources to survive.

The abuse of women and children: Violence against women and children in the family occurs most frequently in patriarchal households where adult men dominate and control family members. This mother and daughter were both abused by the same man.

Many are normally full-time homemakers, with few marketable skills and several children for whom to provide. Third, Browne (1995:230–232) reported "practical problems" faced by battered women in effecting a separation from an abusive relationship, such as where to live, how to obtain legal help, and how to plan for continued safety (e.g., can she go to work or will the batterer find her there and cause her further harm?). Finally, women in abusive situations adopt "coping" strategies—similar to prisoners of war—evaluating which particular method will allow survival with the least amount of violence. As Browne found in her study of battered women, "the women . . . often attempted to appease the aggressor by compliance, and to work through the relationship to obtain leniency and safety. Their primary concern during assaultive incidents was to survive. Their main concern after abusive incidents was to avoid angering the partner again" (1995:239).

However, because of the existence of shelters today, more and more women are able to leave such situations. There are more than 2,500 women's shelters and service programs in the United States offering short-term refuge for women and their children, and every state has legislation against wife battering (Bergen, 1998). Moreover, in 1994 Congress passed the Violence Against Women Act, establishing the Office in Domestic Violence within the Department of Justice and appropriating $1.5 billion to eliminate violence against women (p. 178).

Finally, wife battering is related to spouse killings. The case of O. J. Simpson serves as an example. In 1995 O. J. Simpson was found not guilty for the murders of his ex-wife Nicole Brown Simpson and her friend Ronald Goldman. However, in a subsequent civil trial, Simpson was found liable for the two deaths and ordered to pay $33.5 million in damages to the Brown and Goldman families. The heart of the civil case against Simpson was that the deaths resulted from a pattern of continued wife battering, with Goldman caught in the crime by chance. As one example of this wife battering, on New Year's Day 1989, Nicole Brown Simpson suffered a split lip, a red welt over one eye, and scratches and bruises, including a handprint on her neck. Police charged Simpson with wife battering, he pleaded no contest to the charge, and the judge found him guilty (Berry, 1998).

The case of O. J. Simpson is not unique, as husbands/boyfriends are much more likely to murder wives/girlfriends than wives/girlfriends are to murder husbands/boyfriends. According to the *Uniform Crime Reports,* in 1997 among all female murder victims, 29 percent were killed by husbands/boyfriends and 3 percent of all male murder victims were killed by wives/girlfriends (Federal Bureau of Investigation, 1998). Moreover, studies show that husbands often kill wives after lengthy periods of prolonged physical violence, yet the roles in such cases are seldom if ever reversed for wives (Dobash, Dobash, Wilson, and Daly, 1992). Husbands and wives also do not initiate similar acts of murder, as men are more likely than women to kill their spouse and children together, stalk and kill a spouse who has left them, kill their spouse as part of a planned murder-suicide, and kill their spouse in response to revelation of wifely infidelity (p. 81). Unlike husbands, wives kill their spouses after years of suffering physical violence, after all attempts for assistance have been exhausted, when they feel trapped by the violence, and because they fear for their own and/or others lives (p. 81; Browne, 1987).

Homosexual Partner Battering

Most research on battering concentrates on heterosexual relationships. However, recent studies suggest that battering is not only found in heterosexual monogamy but also occurs in other family forms, such as homosexual relationships.

Like heterosexual wife battering, homosexual partner battering is difficult to document. Therefore, we must rely on estimates. In the major work on battering in gay male relationships to date, David Island and Patrick Letellier (1991) estimated in *Men Who Beat the Men Who Love Them* that between 350,000 (10 percent) and 650,000 (20 percent) gay men per year are battered in the gay men's community. Other studies of gay male battering suggest comparable figures (Merril, 1998). Similarly, Claire Renzetti (1992:17–19) recently examined studies on battering in lesbian relationships, concluding that this type of battering is possibly comparable to heterosexual wife battering. Thus, we can conclude from recent studies of homosexual partner battering that homosexuals, like heterosexuals, frequently "aggress against their intimate partners in ways that are physically and emotionally abusive and sometimes violent" (p. 19).

Additionally, the dynamics of homosexual partner battering are similar to heterosexual wife battering. In both types, the effect of the battering is the social control of the victim. Island and Letellier concluded for battering in gay male relationships:

> The batterer tends to control and dominate the behavior, speech, decisions, thoughts, general activities, circle of friends, spending patterns, clothing choices, reading materials, and eating habits of the victim. Over time, the perpetrator increases his efforts to widen the circle of control to include more and more of the victim's life. (1991:76–77)

Similarly, an examination of battering in lesbian relationships concluded that the physical abuse was triggered by "issues of power imbalance and/or a struggle for varying levels of interdependency and autonomy in the relationship" (Lockhart, White, Causby, and Isaac, 1995:488). Both Renzetti (1992) and Hart (1986) came to similar conclusions.

Moreover, most victims of homosexual partner battering remain in abusive relationships for similar reasons as heterosexual wife battering victims (Island and Letellier, 1991; Renzetti, 1992; Lobel, 1986; Merril, 1998). Thus, overall homosexual partner battering is in many ways very similar to heterosexual wife battering.

However, there are important differences as well. For example, one difference derives from the homophobic culture we live in, whereby the abuser may threaten to reveal to others that the partner is lesbian or gay. Claire Renzetti pointed out that this practice is labeled "outing," resulting in "shunning by relatives and friends, the loss of a job, and a range of other discriminatory consequences with little or no legal recourse for victims; homophobia is indeed a powerful weapon of coercion and control" (1998:119). This is a form of abuse that does not exist in heterosexual couples, and Renzetti (1992) found that 21 percent of participants in her study had threatened to "out" their partners.

Child Abuse and Animal Abuse

Prior to the 1960s, no laws existed that criminalized child abuse—not because there was no child abuse but because it was not in the interests of medical doctors to "see" it. According to Stephen Pfohl (1984), four factors impeded the recognition of child abuse by the medical profession:

1. Physicians were unaware of the possibilities of an abuse diagnosis.
2. Many physicians were unwilling to believe that parents would abuse their own children.
3. The "norm of confidentiality" created an obstacle for an abuse diagnosis.
4. Physicians were reluctant to become involved with the criminal justice system because it was time-consuming and hindered their ability to control the consequences of such a diagnosis.

However, for a specific specialty within medicine—pediatric radiology—these four barriers, Pfohl argued, did not apply. Abuse diagnosis was in fact an ultimate consequence of their mission: Pediatric radiologists constantly viewed children's X-rays and thus observed broken bones and other abnormalities. Pediatric radiologists were also removed from direct contact with the patient's family and thus had no need to be fearful of confidentiality. Most importantly, the "discovery" of child abuse provided pediatric radiologists—working in a low-profile specialty—the possibility of greater recognition within the medical community, as well as an opportunity to coalesce with more academic segments of that community, such as psychiatrists. Thus, as Pfohl pointed out: "The organizational advantages surrounding the discovery of abuse by pediatric radiology set in motion a process of labeling abuse as deviance and legislating against it" (p. 61). Indeed, in a four-year period beginning in 1962, all fifty states passed laws against child abuse. Consequently, the "discovery" of child abuse "manifestly contributed to the advancement of humanitarian pursuits while covertly rewarding" pediatric radiology with enhanced status (p. 45).

After its discovery, public concern about child abuse increased dramatically, so that by the mid-1980s, 90 percent of the U.S. population considered it a serious national problem (Wolfe, 1985:462). Moreover, although more people today seem concerned about child abuse, the media have helped perpetuate the myth that most abuse of children—especially sexual abuse—occurs *outside* the home by day-care workers and child molesters lurking around elementary school playgrounds. However, most physical and sexual abuse of children occurs within the family (Bergen, 1998).

Among researchers in the area of child abuse there tends to be agreement that **child abuse** takes four forms—physical, sexual, emotional, and child neglect. Approximately three million cases of child abuse are reported each year, or a rate of approximately 16 per 1,000 children (Gelles, 1998). Of these cases, 21 percent entail physical abuse, 49 percent neglect, 11 percent sexual abuse, 3 percent emotional abuse; the remaining 16 percent are classified as "other" types of abuse.

Regarding specifically physical abuse, Straus and Gelles (1988)—in a nationally representative sample that considered only physical violence against children by a parent (based on whether the child was kicked, bitten, punched, beaten up, burned, or scalded, or was threatened or attacked with a knife or gun)—estimated that approximately 24 per 1,000 children are physically abused each year. Moreover, when Straus and Gelles added "hitting the child with an object" to the above list, they found that approximately 110 per 1,000 children are the victims of *serious* violence by a parent.

Although the physical abuse of children in the United States is extremely high, research indicates that child neglect is more prevalent and that its consequences are just as serious as physical abuse. Child neglect is harm resulting from a parent or guardian's inattention to a child's basic needs for health, nutrition, shelter, education, supervision, affection, and protection.

Indeed, at least twelve types of neglect have been documented in the child neglect literature (Dubowitz, Black, Starr, Zuravin, 1993:16):

- refusal or delay to provide physical health care
- refusal or delay to provide mental health care
- supervisory neglect
- custody refusal
- custody-related neglect
- abandonment/desertion

- failure to provide a stable home
- neglect of personal hygiene
- housing hazards
- inadequate housing sanitation
- nutritional neglect
- educational neglect

Although the basic needs of most children in Western industrialized societies are satisfied, a large number of children experience neglect in some or all of the areas listed above (p. 16).

There are important gender differences regarding abuse and neglect. According to the National Center on Child Abuse and Neglect (1993:29–33), females are more likely to be abused and to suffer injuries due to abuse than are males. Females experience more abuse than do males, whereas males experience more neglect than do females. For both males and females, abuse and neglect increase with age.

Both men and women commit child abuse. However, although women perform most of the child care in U.S. society, they commit only about 50 percent of the *physical* abuse and neglect of children. In other words, 50 percent of those who physically abuse and neglect children are men, who have on average little responsibility for children (Stark and Flitcraft, 1998).

Because sexual abuse has been surrounded by extreme secrecy, it is difficult to document the actual amount in the United States. Nevertheless, it is estimated that approximately 20 percent of women and 10 percent of men in the United States have been sexually abused as children (Bergen, 1998).

In *The Secret Trauma,* Diana Russell (1986) examined specifically incestuous abuse and found that 16 percent of the 930 women interviewed reported at least one experience of incest before the age of eighteen years. Of these women, 12 percent (152) had been sexually abused by a relative before their fourteenth birthday (p. 60). Thus, incestuous abuse is by no means rare.

Most incestuous abuse is committed by an adult male (usually the father) with the victim a child (usually the daughter) under the age of eighteen (Russell, 1986). Certain "typical characteristics" of incestuous assault include the following (Chesney-Lind, 1997; Herman and Hirschman, 1977):

- Approximately 70 percent of incestuous abuse victims are female.
- The majority of victims are either the oldest child or the only daughter, and the assault usually begins between the ages of six and nine.
- Incestuous abuse usually begins earlier for girls than for boys, and victimization of girls lasts longer than for boys.
- The assault commonly takes place repeatedly, lasting three years or more.
- Sexual contact is normally limited to fondling and masturbation if the victim has not reached puberty, but with older children sexual intercourse is more likely to occur.

As with other sexual assaults, the victim experiences incestuous abuse as coercive. At first—because of her young age—the victim may be unable to comprehend what is hap-

BOX 9.2   ANIMAL ABUSE

One of the most unrecognized forms of interpersonal violence is violence against nonhuman animals. **Animal abuse** has been found to be disproportionately present in situations of partner abuse, child physical abuse, child sexual abuse, and sibling abuse. Just how prevalent animal abuse might be has not yet been properly researched, though findings about how serious it is have been drawn from a variety of sources, including victimization surveys, structured interviews with battered women and abused and neglected children, and reports of animal abuse to veterinarians, animal shelters, women's shelters, and police. Almost certainly, defenseless pets are used as weapons of terror and psychological abuse by powerful members of households against vulnerable ones (Beirne, 1995, 1999; Ascione, 1998).

Most of us already know how widespread animal abuse might be from mass media reports linking animal abuse and subsequent interhuman mass murders committed by adolescent males. For example, it was reported that before the school shooting of two high school girls in 1997, the teenage murderer Luke Woodham had gruesomely tortured his own dog. Woodham repeatedly beat the dog with a club, wrapped it in garbage bags, torched it with a lighter, listened to it whimper and tossed it in a pond (*New York Times,* October 15, 1997). After describing the sight of the dog sinking beneath the surface of the pond, Woodham added "[it] was true beauty" (p. A10). In another report of a school shooting mass murder (of two classmates and both his parents) in Springfield, Oregon, in 1998, it was revealed that 15-year-old Kip Kinkel had earlier enjoyed shooting squirrels, setting off firecrackers in cats' mouths, or stuffing them down gopher holes (*Associated Press,* May 23, 1998). At a similarly anecdotal level, this "maturation link" has been claimed for a number of serial killers in the United States, including Thomas Lee Dillion, Ted Bundy, Alberto DeSalvo, and Jeffrey Dahmer.

pening. However, as she suffers the assaults over time, she eventually understands that something "different" and wrong is happening to her. She feels guilty and humiliated and blames herself for the continued assaults (Stanko, 1985:25). Many such victims not only experience fear, anxiety, depression, anger, and difficulties in school; they also run away from home (Chesney-Lind, 1997). Incestuously abused women also reveal that they remain frightened and upset years later (Kendall-Tackett and Marshall, 1998). Moreover, 60–70 percent of prostitutes report that their first sexual experience was in the home as a result of incestuous abuse (Russell, 1998). Prostitutes have informed sociologists that as victims of incestuous assault, they were first bribed by an adult family male (sex for clothes, toys, and affection, for example), only later to be forced into sexual intercourse with him (Chesney-Lind, 1997). Consequently, they learn that they can obtain commodities by making their bodies available to men.

Finally, father-daughter incestuous abuse seems to cause the most trauma. In Russell's (1986:231–232) sample, 54 percent of victims where fathers were the perpetrators reported being extremely upset by the assault(s), compared with 25 percent of victims of all other incest perpetrators combined. The following are some of the factors that may have contributed to this greater trauma (pp. 213–232):

- Fathers were more likely to impose vaginal intercourse on their daughters than were other incest perpetrators.
- Fathers sexually abused their daughters more frequently than did other incestuous relatives.
- Fathers were more likely to use physical force than were other incestuous relatives.
- In the vast majority of cases, the father was also the victim's provider.

Most father-daughter incest occurs in families maintaining traditional male-dominant and authoritarian attitudes. The fathers expect sexual, housekeeping, and child-rearing services from their wives. When this "breaks down"—because of physical and mental illness, alcoholism, and drug addiction, or simply because the wife is not "performing well"— they turn to their daughter(s). The incestuous father does not engage in these expectations himself but usually delegates that responsibility to the eldest daughter, while simultaneously perpetrating incestuous abuse upon her. As a result, this daughter may gain some power in the family, but her basic experience is "shame and guilt, isolation, and an oppressive disproportionate sense of responsibility for holding the family together, which she accomplishes in part by keeping her secret" (Breines and Gordon, 1983:526).

9.3 INTERPERSONAL VIOLENCE IN THE WORKPLACE

In Chapter 13.2 we discuss some of the environmental hazards in the workplace such as unsafe working conditions due to inadequate protection from dangerous substances. Although workplace dangers such as environmentally unsafe working conditions are of an impersonal nature, murder, assault, and, primarily for women, sexual harassment, are different, entailing violence perpetrated in a personal manner. For these reasons we discuss murder, assault, and sexual harassment as interpersonal violence rather than occupational crime.

Murder and Assault

Every year approximately 2 million people are victimized by violent crime outside the home; and the most common type of workplace violent crime is simple assault (Warchol, 1998). Each year, approximately 1.5 million simple assault victimizations occur in the workplace, followed by 395,000 aggravated assaults, and 1,000 murders (p. 1). Table 9.2 shows the number of violent victimizations by occupation, indicating that retail sales and law enforcement suffer the most occurrences of violence. Table 9.3 outlines the nature of the workplace victim–offender relationship and indicates that the majority of offenders are strangers to the victim.

Although a large majority of workplace violence occurs among strangers, personal disputes among coworkers have received the most attention by criminologists. Indeed, this type of workplace murder is classified by researchers as "murder by proxy" in which vic-

TABLE 9.2   Average Annual Number of
Violent Victimizations in the Workplace by
Occupation, 1992–1996

Retail sales	292,482
Law enforcement	240,480
Teaching	138,124
Medical	133,012
Mental health	80,711
Transportation	73,894
Private security	61,790

SOURCE: Warchol, 1998.

tims are chosen by a vengeful employee because of their association with the revenge target. The vengeful employee—usually a middle-aged white male who is "falling down"
(was recently fired or reprimanded by a boss or lost his "status" or job to younger competitors, racial minorities, women, or immigrants)—responds by "getting back" at those
seen as causing his frustration or simply being an employee at his place of work where the
painful event occurred (Fox and Levin, 1994). Tables 9.4 and 9.5 provide some additional
information on workplace murder. Table 9.4 shows that between 1992 and 1996, murder
at the workplace consistently accounted for approximately 17 percent of all deaths in the
workplace. Table 9.5 shows that most workplace murder victims, once again 1992 to
1996, were employed in retail sales.

Finally, Table 9.6 depicts workplace assaults by occupation. Law enforcement officers
suffer the largest amount of assault victimization on the job, followed by those working in
retail sales, medical health, teaching, mental health, and transportation occupations. An
additional interesting observation from Table 9.6 is that transportation workers suffer more
aggravated, but not simple, assault than those who work in medical health, teaching, and
mental health jobs. Other research on workplace assault—both simple and aggravated—
indicates that approximately 75 percent result from fistfights, 17 percent from shootings,
and 8 percent from stabbings (Neuman and Baron, 1997).

TABLE 9.3   Victim-Offender Relationship in Workplace Violence, 1992–1996

Relationship of Offender to Victim	*Percentage of Workplace Violence Victims*		
	Total	*Male*	*Female*
Total	100	100	100
Intimate	0.9	0.2[a]	2.2
Other relative	0.5	0.2[a]	1.0
Acquaintance	35.3	29.9	46.2
Stranger	59.6	65.9	47.0
Unknown	3.6	3.7	3.5

[a] Detail may not add to totals because of rounding. Fewer than 10 sample cases.
SOURCE: Warchol, 1998.

TABLE 9.4   Murder Accounts for About
17 Percent of All Deaths in the Workplace

	Total Accidents	Murder
1992	6,217	1,044
1993	6,331	1,074
1994	6,632	1,080
1995	6,275	1,036
1996	6,112	912

SOURCE: Warchol, 1998.

TABLE 9.5   Occupation of Workplace Murder Victims

Occupation of Victim	Average Annual Number
Sales	327
Executive/manager	154
Law enforcement	69
Security guard	60
Taxi driver/chauffeur	74
Truck driver[a]	25

[a] Based on 1993 and 1995–1996.
SOURCE: Warchol, 1998.

Sexual Harassment

Whereas males are mostly the victims of murder and assault at work (Fox and Levin, 1994), female workers have always been victims of sexual harassment, but it was not until the mid-1970s that sexual harassment was recognized as a social problem (Benson and Thompson, 1982:236). And it was not until 1980 that sexual harassment actually became a crime. The Equal Employment Opportunity Commission of the federal government issued guidelines in 1980 for determining sexual harassment as a violation of Title VII of the U.S. Civil Rights Act. This act was intended to prohibit discrimination on the basis of gender, and its guidelines apply to federal, state, and local government agencies as well as to private employers with fifteen or more employees. The guidelines specify that employers have an "affirmative duty" to prevent and eliminate sexual harassment on the job and that "unwelcome sexual advances, requests for sexual favors, and other verbal or physical conduct of a sexual nature" are offenses if submission is explicitly or implicitly a condition of the individual's employment. When the submission or rejection affects one's employment and/or it affects an individual's work performance by creating a working environment that is intimidating, hostile, and offensive, a violation of Title VII has also occurred (Pear, 1980:1, 20). Thus, following this definition, **sexual harassment** includes not only attempted and completed forcible rape and "interpersonal coercion" but also sexist jokes and innuendos, "accidental" collisions and fondling, and constant ogling and pinches.

TABLE 9.6   Workplace Assaults by Occupation, 1992–1996

| | Average Annual Number of Assaults | |
	Simple	Aggravated
Medical	137,500	12,800
Teaching	126,500	16,800
Mental health	79,000	15,300
Law enforcement	326,900	98,500
Transportation	45,200	17,400
Retail sales	215,700	90,700

SOURCE: Warchol, 1998.

Myths about sexual harassment—such as that it affects only a few women, that women really "ask for it," and that charges of sexual harassment are commonly false—continue to be perpetuated in U.S. society. However, studies of sexual harassment indicate the prevalence of *nonconsenting* interpersonal sexual violence in the workplace. For example, in 1981 the Merit System's Protection Board conducted a study of sexual harassment among federal employees for the Subcommittee on Investigations of the House Committee on Post Office and Civil Service (Russell, 1990:269–270). The board found (in their random sample of over 20,000 federal employees) that 42 percent of all female employees reported being sexually harassed at work. The number of sexual harassment complaints filed with the Equal Employment Opportunity Commission jumped from 5,694 cases in 1990 to 10,900 cases in the first eight months of 1993, most likely because of the national "teach-in" on sexual harassment following the confirmation hearings of Supreme Court Justice Clarence Thomas (Ingrassia, 1993:57). What this information reveals is that sexual harassment in the workplace is likely very widespread.

Why does such harassment take place? Some have argued that certain organizations maintain value systems, communicative processes, rituals, and organizational symbols that create a sexist culture at work (O'Toole and Schiffman, 1997). Many organizations use sexual metaphor in communicative processes that may be conducive to sexual harassment. For example, female employees at Stroh's Brewing Company brought a sexual harassment suit against the company, charging the Swedish Bikini Team advertising campaign in the early 1990s contributed to a sexualized work environment in which women were subjected to daily verbal and physical abuse from male employees.

Studies of sexual harassment also indicate that rape and interpersonal coercion exist within the workplace. Approximately 8 percent of all rapes occur at the workplace, and 5 percent of women victimized at work are attacked by a husband, ex-husband, boyfriend, or ex-boyfriend (Bachman, 1994). Interpersonal coercion (recalling our earlier discussion in this chapter) involves economic threats made by a male supervisor to the effect that if the female employee or possible employee does not engage in sexual intercourse with him she either will not be hired, retained, or promoted, or else will be fired, demoted, or transferred to a more unpleasant position. If we assume that the female employee or possible employee does not secretly desire sexual intercourse with the male supervisor, such threats can be very coercive. As Box has argued, "economic deprivation is a serious and expensive cost even when set beside unwelcome and undesired coitus" (1983:143). Indeed, as Barbara Gutek and Mary Koss (1997:152) have asserted, sexual harassment has similarities with incestuous abuse: The victim of incest, like the sexually harassed woman, is economically, if not emotionally, dependent on the offender. Sexual harassment is likewise humiliating, and paralleling incestuous abuse, there is motivation to keep it a secret. Finally, sexual harassment, like incestuous abuse, often continues for a long time and is experienced as an abuse of power and a betrayal of trust.

The effects on the victims of sexual harassment are severe. The majority of women report emotional stress, such as nervousness, fear, and sleeplessness, as well as interference with their job performance, and many also find it necessary to obtain psychological help (Schur, 1984:139). Moreover, victims of sexual harassment at work report higher rates of absenteeism and low productivity. Sexual harassment not only affects a victim's self-esteem but costs an average Fortune 500 company (24,000 employees or more) $6.7 million a year (Crawford, 1993:17). In addition, for those victims who refuse sexual demands their job is at stake (p. 17). Consider what happened to one woman who refused to "give at the office." The supervisor, "following rejection of his elaborate sexual advances, barraged the woman with unwarranted reprimands about job performance, refused routine supervision or task direction, which made it impossible for her to do her job, and then fired her for poor work performance" (MacKinnon, 1979:35).

This threat of job loss or actually being fired for not complying with the sexual demands of a male supervisor seems most prevalent for women in traditional male jobs (Andersen, 1988:134). For women who enter traditionally male occupations, "harassment seems to be a form of retaliation directed against women for threatening male economic and social status. In these settings, harassment expresses men's resentment of the presence of women" (p. 134).

An example of this indignation and outright hostility occurred at the Tailhook Association convention of top Navy pilots in 1991. According to a report prepared by the Pentagon Inspector General, sexual assaults at the convention "varied from victims being grabbed on the buttocks to victims being groped, pinched and fondled on their breasts, buttocks and genitals. . . . Some victims were bitten by their assailants, others were knocked to the ground and some had their clothing ripped or removed" (cited in Gordon, 1993:1). This violence against women officers, the report concluded, was "not significantly different from those at earlier meetings" and was in fact "widely condoned by the Navy's civilian and military leaders" (p. 1).

Probably the most notorious feature of the convention was the "gauntlet," in which women who attempted to walk through a hotel hallway were fondled and assaulted by approximately 200 men. In total, 117 naval officers were implicated in one or more incidents of sexual assault and other demeaning practices such as "mooning" (baring one's buttocks at women), "ballwalking" (publicly exposing one's testicles), and "sharking" (biting women on the buttocks). Finally, it should not be surprising to learn that a number of male officers wore T-shirts during the convention with "Women Are Property" and "He-man Women's Haters Club" printed on them (Gordon, 1993; Goodman, 1993).

Sexual harassment in the military: Sexual harassment occurs frequently in male-dominated occupations. As women increasingly enter such occupations, their presence is threatening to some men—it challenges notions of masculinity—and they respond by engaging in sexual harassment to "put women in their place."

More recently, a Pentagon survey of 90,000 active-duty members conducted in 1995 found that 4 percent of female soldiers reported being the victim of an actual or attempted rape within the previous twelve months (Vistica, 1996). Moreover, the same survey found the following percentages of women in each service reporting some type of sexual harassment: Marines, 64 percent; Army, 61 percent; Navy, 53 percent; and Air Force, 49 percent (p. 30). The largest sources of harassment were military coworkers (44 percent) and higher-ranking personnel (43 percent); in addition to rape, the types of sexual harassment included pressure for sexual favors (11 percent); touching, cornering (29 percent); looks, gestures (37 percent); letters, calls (12 percent); pressure for date (22 percent); teasing, jokes (44 percent); and whistles, calls (23 percent).

REVIEW

In this chapter we have discussed interpersonal crimes of violence—murder, assault, hate crimes, rape, wife and homosexual partner battering, child abuse, animal abuse, and sexual harassment. These crimes create extensive public concern and fear—and rightly so—inasmuch as the United States has the highest level of violent crime in the industrialized world. However, crimes of interpersonal violence occur most often indoors—not on the streets—and are usually committed by relatives, friends, and acquaintances of the victims.

Murder, Assault, Hate Crimes, and Rape

1. Murder is the most serious form of interpersonal violence; fortunately, it occurs the least often.

2. Murder is primarily a big-city crime and occurs most frequently in the South.

3. There is little evidence suggesting that owning a firearm is the chief cause of murder.

4. In some cases the interaction between offender and victim involves threats and retaliation by both participants to the murder.

5. There are important similarities and differences between murder and aggravated assault.

6. Hate crimes differ from other forms of interpersonal violence in that they are more vicious, excessively brutal, and frequently perpetrated at random on total strangers (commonly a single victim) by multiple offenders, and victims face great difficulty coming to terms with their victimization.

7. Rape occurs much more often in the United States than most people recognize.

8. Sociologists, criminologists, and feminists are currently debating the appropriate definition of rape.

9. Women are more likely to be raped by someone they know than by a stranger.

10. The idea of victim-precipitated rape is a myth.

11. Although there are a few reported cases of women raping men, males are relatively safe from sexual assault unless they are in prison.

12. Throughout history rape has been an institutionalized component of war.

Interpersonal Violence in the Family

1. Women of completed rapes are victimized more by their husbands than by any other type of perpetrator.

2. Victims of wife rape feel humiliated and degraded and experience psychological trauma for years afterward.

3. Between 30 and 50 percent of battered women are also raped by their husbands.

4. Wife battering was legally and socially acceptable for centuries.

5. Between 25 percent and 33 percent of wives are battered by their husbands each year.

6. Many women, because of social and economic pressures, feel they cannot leave an abusive relationship.

7. Homosexual battering—in lesbian and gay male relationships—seems to occur at a similar rate as wife battering in heterosexual relationships.

8. The dynamics of battering in lesbian and gay male relationships are similar to those in heterosexual relationships, although there are some important differences.

9. Most physical and sexual abuse of children occurs inside the family.

10. Child neglect is more prevalent than child physical abuse, and its consequences are just as serious.

11. There are important gender differences in child abuse and neglect, especially as children grow older.

12. Men and women each commit 50 percent of the physical abuse and neglect of children.

13. Incestuous abuse is by no means rare in the United States; it is usually committed by an adult male (usually the father), and the usual victim is a child under eighteen (generally a daughter).

14. Incestuously assaulted girls and women find the encounter coercive, and years later many report still being frightened and upset.

15. Father–daughter incest causes the most trauma.

16. One of the most unrecognized forms of interpersonal violence is violence against nonhuman animals.

17. Animal abuse is disproportionately present in situations of partner abuse, child abuse, and sibling abuse.

18. Some of the boys involved in school shootings have also been found to have engaged in animal abuse.

Interpersonal Violence in the Workplace

1. The most common form of interpersonal violence in the workplace is assault, and retail sales and law enforcement suffer the most victimizations.

2. The typical violent person in the workplace is a vengeful middle-aged white male.

3. Sexual harassment includes behavior ranging from sexist jokes to interpersonal coercion and rape.

4. Sexual harassment in the workplace is not uncommon in U.S. society.

5. Sexual harassment causes emotional stress and interferes with job and nonoccupational performance.

QUESTIONS FOR CLASS DISCUSSION

1. The media foster the image that most interpersonal violence occurs in the streets; as we have seen, it mostly takes place indoors. Discuss why you think the media distort the reality of interpersonal violence and why most violence occurs indoors.

2. Is there a "culture of hate" in North America? If so, what type of policy would you create to curb that culture?

3. Is the legal definition of rape too narrow, or is it satisfactory as it stands? Explain thoroughly.

4. There are clear gender differences for child abuse. Discuss why you think such gender differences exist.

5. Why are males the primary perpetrators of murder, assault, and sexual harassment in the workplace?

6. Three theories discussed in Part Two that help us understand interpersonal violence are feminist theories, control balance theory, and general strain theory. Discuss how each might explain the various crimes of interpersonal violence.

FOR FURTHER STUDY

Readings

Bergen, Racquel Kennedy, ed. 1998. *Issues in Intimate Violence.* Thousand Oaks, Calif: Sage.
Polk, Kenneth. 1994. *When Men Kill: Scenarios of Masculine Violence.* New York: Cambridge University Press.
Renzetti, Claire M. 1992. *Violent Betrayal: Partner Abuse in Lesbian Relationships.* Newbury Park, Calif: Sage.

Websites

1. <http://www.usdoj.gov/vawo>: The Department of Justice Violence Against Women Office's website provides links to federal legislation and current research on violence against women.
2. <http://www.abanet.org/domviol/home.html>: The American Bar Association's Commission on Domestic Violence provides excellent and up-to-date statistics on intimate violence. Especially useful is the "Myths vs. Facts" page where many misperceptions are clarified.
3. <http://www.igc.org/fund/workplace>: From the Family Violence Prevention Fund, this site provides links to educational and popular media sites specifically dealing with domestic violence in the workplace.
4. <http://jan.ucc.nau.edu/~pms/sash.html>: The International Coalition Against Sexual Harassment website provides useful links to the most current issues related to sexual harassment, including "facts about sexual harassment."

10

Property Crime

Preview

Chapter 10 introduces:
- what sociologists mean by property crime
- the different types of property crime
- the difference between amateur and professional property offenders
- the nature, extent, and costs of property crime

Key Terms

armed robbery	income-tax fraud
arson	larceny
automobile theft	motor vehicle theft
burglary	property crime
carjacking	robbery
check fraud	shoplifting
credit-card fraud	strong-arm robbery
fencing	

In Chapter 9 we discussed interpersonal crimes of violence. Most crime, however, is not violent but entails the taking of property. When we compare crimes of interpersonal violence with property crimes, property crimes constitute approximately 90 percent of all crimes reported to the police. Moreover, according to *National Crime Victimization Survey (NCVS)* data, property crimes make up more than 90 percent of all victimizations (Department of Justice, 1999:12).

In addition to being more frequent, property crimes differ from crimes of interpersonal violence in another significant way: Offender and victim are, in most cases, strangers. For crimes like burglary, automobile theft, and arson, usually no direct interaction between offender and victim takes place. And in those crimes where interaction does exist—such as check fraud—it is not immediately apparent that a crime has even been committed.

We define **property crime** as the unlawful damage to or taking of the property of another, regardless of whether the threat of or actual use of physical violence occurs. We discuss seven types of property crimes: robbery, burglary, shoplifting, automobile theft, fraud, fencing, and arson. While discussing each, we examine the similarities and differences between professional and amateur property offenders. Professional and amateur property offenders are similar in that each commits the same type of crime. In other words, there are both professional and amateur robbers, burglars, auto thieves, and so forth; however, professionals and amateurs differ in important ways. Professionals carefully plan and execute their crimes, using sophisticated techniques and skills. They are committed to crime as a lifestyle and tend to specialize in one particular form of property crime. Amateurs engage in crime when the opportunity arises, do not extensively plan their theft, do not always think of themselves as criminals, and do not usually specialize in one type of property crime.

10.1   ROBBERY AND BURGLARY

Our discussion of property crime begins with what most of us—including criminologists—consider to be the two most serious forms of property theft: robbery and burglary.

Robbery

Robbery is defined as the unlawful taking or attempting to take something of value from another person or persons by using some type of violent force or threat of force. Robbery is a unique crime and ranks among the most feared because it entails both threatened or actual use of violence and also loss of property to the victim. Moreover, robbery—unlike the other property crimes discussed in this chapter—is similar to interpersonal crimes of violence in another way: It involves a direct confrontation between offender and victim.

Robbery also differs in significant ways from interpersonal crimes of violence: Robberies are more likely to involve two or more offenders; the majority of robberies are committed by strangers to the victim; and robbery offenders are more likely to use weapons. Moreover, the primary motive of the robbery offender is not violence but economic gain. Thus, sociologically it is more appropriate to designate robbery a property crime and not a crime of violence. In robbery, violence is secondary to the taking of property: Violence is a means to obtain a more significant end.

In 1997 there were 497,950 robberies reported to the police, or approximately 186 per 100,000 inhabitants (Federal Bureau of Investigation, 1998:28). However, the *NCVS* (Department of Justice, 1999) disclosed that for 1997 slightly over half of all robberies were reported to the police. Consequently, the *NCVS* reported almost twice as many robberies as the police, for a total of 945,000. Although we do not have a completely accurate figure for the total robberies in a given year, it is safe to assume that the police are aware of only slightly more than half.

Many U.S. citizens feel that robbery almost always entails violence. When one thinks of robbery, what usually comes to mind is a mugging—someone physically attacked on the street and a purse or wallet stolen. However, only about one-third of all robberies involve some degree of violence resulting in an injury to the victim, and only about 12 percent of all victims are treated in the hospital (Department of Justice, 1999).

Nevertheless, the likelihood of violence occurring, and thus of an injury inflicted, is related to the type of robbery. **Strong-arm robbery** (sometimes referred to as unarmed robbery because the offender robs without the use of a weapon) is actually much more dangerous than **armed robbery** (the display of a deadly weapon to carry out the robbery). Approximately twice as many strong-arm-robbery victims, compared to armed-robbery victims, are injured (Wright, Rossi, and Daly, 1983:208). Not only are armed robberies less dangerous than strong-arm robberies, they also occur more often and are more likely to be successful (Department of Justice, 1999).

Robbery as Transaction

Robbery is similar to murder and assault in that it involves a face-to-face confrontation between offender and victim. In fact, Luckenbill (1981) went so far as to argue that robbery actually entails a "transaction" between offender and victim. From his research, Luckenbill (pp. 28–41) developed a model of robbery consisting of four stages. Each stage involves important tasks that the offender and victim execute together. In the first stage, the offender—having selected a victim—creates "copresence" with the victim by moving into striking range without causing suspicion. In other words, the robber attempts a "normal appearance" while maintaining an appropriate position for the imminent robbery. After establishing copresence—and after the offender decides and subsequently initiates the robbery—the victim determines in the second stage whether to resist, whereas the offender considers how much force, if any, is required to obtain the desired property. It is this interaction, and acknowledgment by both offender and victim, that creates a "common robbery frame" to which each, Luckenbill argued, most likely adheres. Once a common robbery frame is established, the third stage involves transfer of the property. Although transfer is in most cases under the control of the offender, several obstructions may occur: The victim may not adhere to the robbery frame; outsiders may disrupt the robbery; or the offender may not have the knowledge and skill required to complete the transfer. Assuming transfer of the property takes place, the fourth stage involves the offender's escape, such as jumping into a "getaway car" and/or containing the victim in some fashion (such as tying up the victim).

Luckenbill's work is important in that it shows robbery to be more than illegal behavior by an offender: Robbery is an interaction involving joint contributions by both offender and victim. However, although robbery involves an interaction to which both offender and victim contribute, it is hardly a simple "transaction" between equal partners as Luckenbill seems to argue. The key point in a robbery scenario is that the interaction is coercive, one party—the offender—exercising a dominant power position over the victim. "Transaction" implies "equality," yet equality does not exist between robbery victim and offender.

It is also questionable whether Luckenbill's model is applicable to all robbery types. For instance, does his model help us understand (1) robbery of banks and armored cars, (2) muggings and purse snatchings, and/or (3) robbery during a burglary? In fact, these robbery types constitute the majority of all robberies. Over 50 percent of robberies are committed against persons who as part of their employment are in charge of money and goods (for example, banks and armored cars); 20–25 percent of robberies occur in the open following a sudden attack (such as muggings and purse snatchings); 12–17 percent of robberies occur on private premises (for instance, during a burglary) (Walsh, 1986:82).

Two robber types selected by scholars for examination, and first discussed in typology form by Conklin (1972), are professional robbers and opportunist robbers. Both types can be involved in similar robbery scenarios.

Professional robbers carefully plan and execute their crimes, exhibiting greater skill than other robbery offenders and, usually, operating with accomplices (Conklin, 1972:63). Walsh (1986:74) found that when professionals operate with accomplices, they commonly are people "recommended" to them. The professional commits to robbery as a lifestyle, engages in sophisticated planning, neutralizes security, and investigates all possible escape routes (Conklin, 1972:64). Thus, professional robbers are considerably more skilled and conduct more extensive planning than other robbers.

Conklin (p. 64) identified two types of professional robbers. The first commits robbery almost exclusively. The second commits other types of crime but occasionally commits robbery with professional skill. In addition to these "solo professionals," Walsh (1986:154) found two other types of professionals—criminal syndicates that assemble teams of robbers, and independent, small, professional teams of two or three robbers.

The opportunist robber is probably the most common type of robber. Opportunists do not commit to robbery on a long-term basis as do professionals. Rather, these individuals rob infrequently, choosing such easily accessible and vulnerable victims as the elderly, public drunks, taxi drivers, and people walking alone on unlit streets. Opportunists are sometimes involved in other forms of conventional property theft, such as burglary (Conklin, 1972:68–71).

When we commonly think of "street crime" or "muggings," it is an opportunistic rob-bery that we usually contemplate. These haphazard, random, and spur-of-the-moment rob-beries generally net only small amounts of cash (Feeney, 1986).

Four of every five opportunistic robberies are the work of strangers to the victim(s) (Bureau of Justice Statistics, 1993:10). Moreover, opportunists rob their victims—more than 50 percent of the time—on the street or in some outdoor area near their own home, such as a park, a playground, or a parking lot (Feeney, 1986). Opportunistic robberies oc-cur more often in inner districts of the largest cities. As shown in Table 10.1, street/high-way robberies reported to police increase as size of city population increases. The table also shows that although street robberies increase with city size, other forms of robbery actually decrease with city size.

Robbers on Robbery

Richard Wright and Scott Decker's (1997) recent study of "active armed robbers" sheds light on the processes involved in committing the crime of armed robbery. Unlike previ-ous studies of robbery, which have focused on incarcerated offenders, these criminologists interviewed eighty-six offenders who were actively involved in robbery on the streets of St. Louis, Missouri. The interviews generated data from the robber's point of view on (1) deciding to commit robbery, (2) choosing the target, and (3) committing the offense. Re-garding the first issue, the vast majority of the offenders decided to commit robbery be-cause of deep involvement in self-indulgent activities promoted by street culture, such as gambling, alcohol use, and drug use. When faced with a pressing need for cash, these in-dividuals turned to robbery as the quickest and easiest way out of financial difficulties.

In choosing a target, most of the robbers reported that they preferred victims in close proximity to where they reside, typically preying on local criminals, especially street cor-ner drug dealers. Drug dealers are "good robbery victims" because they carry plenty of cash and are in no position to report their victimization to the police. These robbers also, of course, robbed law-abiding citizens, choosing victims who through their demeanor and dress indicate they have a supply of easily available cash. Finally, a small number of the robbers Wright and Decker interviewed victimized small commercial establishments, such as liquor stores, gas stations, taverns, and pawn shops. These businesses were chosen be-cause they also had a ready availability of cash

Finally, having settled on the particular target, the next step is to actually "pull it off," that is, commit to the robbery and carry it out. Here Wright and Decker's data correspond with Luckenbill's (1981) perspective discussed earlier. First, robbers approach the victim, announcing the robbery and allowing victims no room for negotiation by "creating an il-lusion of impending death" (Wright and Decker, 1997:96). Robbers attempt to catch vic-tims off guard and through tough talk, a fierce demeanor, and the display of a deadly weapon, they usually scare people into compliance. Once dominance over the victim is es-tablished, the robber attempts to manage the transfer of goods. Many armed robbers sim-ply order victims to "hand over the money," whereas some choose to actually search their victims. Only if victims fail to comply with demands do robbers turn to violence. As Wright and Decker explained, "faced with a recalcitrant victim, most of the offenders responded with severe but nonlethal violence in the hope of convincing the person to

TABLE 10.1 Robbery, Percentage Distribution, 1997

	Group I (55 cities, 250,000 and over; population 39,439,000)	Group II (130 cities, 100,000 to 249,999; population 19,009,000)	Group III (303 cities, 50,000 to 99,999; population 20,466,000)	Group IV (583 cities, 25,000 to 49,999; population 20,162,000)	Group V (1,372 cities, 10,000 to 24,999; population 21,638,000)	Group VI (5,067 cities, under 10,000; population 17,688,000)	County agencies (2,913 agencies; population 64,242,000)
Street/highway	58.4	50.7	46.7	38.3	34.5	28.7	31.8
Commercial house	12.5	13.6	14.9	14.7	14.4	14.3	18.3
Gas or service station	1.5	2.4	2.8	3.7	4.5	3.7	3.9
Convenience store	3.6	5.9	6.4	8.2	9.3	10.2	10.3
Residence	11.6	10.9	9.4	10.5	11.5	12.4	15.2
Bank	1.4	2.1	2.2	2.8	2.9	3.1	2.9
Miscellaneous	11.0	14.5	17.6	21.8	23.1	27.6	17.5

SOURCE: FBI, 1998, p. 31.

cooperate. Often this violence involved smacking or beating the victim about the head with a pistol" (p. 113).

Finally, the offender must escape. Most of the robbers in this study preferred to be the first to depart the robbery scene. However, before making their escape, these robbers once again make verbal threats, such as "If you come out of this alley . . . I'm gonna shoot the shit out of you" (p. 116). Such threats are designed to continue the illusion of impending death from the beginning of the robbery to its completion.

Burglary

Burglary is defined as unlawful entry of a house, business, or other structure, with the intent to commit a felony. Thus, although robbery entails theft through the threat or actual use of violence, for burglary to occur someone must actually enter a structure unlawfully with the intent to commit a felony. Moreover, burglary—like the other property crimes to be discussed in this chapter—differs from robbery in another critical way: It very seldom involves a direct, face-to-face confrontation between offender and victim.

The FBI categorizes burglary in three ways: forcible entry, unlawful entry without force, and attempted forcible entry. In 1997, 66 percent of all burglaries reported to the police involved forcible entry, 27 percent were unlawful entries without force, and 7 percent were forcible entry attempts (Federal Bureau of Investigation, 1998:41). In the same year there were 2,461,120 burglaries reported to the police, or approximately 920 per 100,000 inhabitants (Federal Bureau of Investigation, 1998:40). However, the *NCVS* (Department of Justice, 1999) reported that for 1997 only about half of all burglaries were reported to the police. Consequently, the *NCVS* reported almost twice as many burglaries occurring as did the FBI, for a total of 4.6 million. As with robbery, the police probably know about, at most, only 50 percent of all burglaries committed.

Burglars can also be classified as amateurs and professionals. Amateurs and professionals are similar in that both may burglarize houses and/or businesses and might operate alone or work with others in a team (Walsh, 1986:3–4). However, they also differ in important ways.

Amateur burglars enter a structure when they "feel the need." Their style of intrusion is extremely unsophisticated—perhaps simply breaking a window or breaking down a door. Because amateurs are more interested in volume of burglaries than in quality, very little planning is involved. Amateur burglars rarely specialize in theft of specific items but steal a variety of merchandise as opportunities arise, usually accessible goods such as televisions, stereos, VCRs, CD players, silverware, jewelry, and money (Walsh, 1986:33). Thus, amateurs are part-time burglars who engage in burglary as "only a small, episodic part of a life of crime in general" (Walsh, 1986:22).

Most amateur burglars engage in theft for personal financial gain. In Bennett and Wright's (1984) study, 46 percent of the burglars interviewed claimed they committed the offense only when they were short of money. Moreover, amateur burglars engage in burglary for subsistence or basic everyday needs, as well as to obtain money for entertainment, gambling, drinking, or drugs (p. 32).

Finally, some amateur burglars are likely to commit "opportunistic" burglaries—that is, discovering a vulnerable and attractive target while involved in other activities (lawful or

Bank robbery: Although the above bank robber looks somewhat sophisticated and professional, the majority of bank robbers use no disguises, despite the widespread use of surveillance equipment in banks.

unlawful) and immediately engaging in the burglary. However, the majority of amateurs first decide to commit a burglary—as stated previously, when they "feel the need"—next search for a suitable target, and then immediately commit the burglary when a promising target is identified (pp. 43–46; Cromwell, Olson, and Avary, 1991).

Professional burglars are specialists who employ considerable skill and planning in executing a burglary. A good example of a professional burglar is Harry King—a boxman (safecracker)—who reported to Chambliss (King and Chambliss, 1984:31–37) all the intrigues and skill required to enter a building successfully, open or "kidnap" a safe, and efficiently escape. King's activities closely followed Sutherland's model of the professional thief outlined in Chapter 5.4. King learned his trade from another professional boxman, working initially as an apprentice. He eventually made his living from burglary, engaging in extensive planning and never feeling the need to carry a weapon during a "caper." Moreover, he kept up with the latest technology applicable to his trade. According to King, it is essential for the professional to be familiar with the latest "burglary tools," such as drills and saws, and to spend time practicing and preparing for future capers (p. 35).

Professional burglars also rely on contacts with tipsters, or persons who identify possible burglary targets for the burglar. As Neal Shover pointed out in his examination of professional burglars: "A 'tipster' . . . conveys information to a burglar about certain premises or its occupants which is intended to aid him in burglarizing those premises" (1972:546). In addition to tipsters, professional burglars establish important contacts with police, attorneys, and judges. This liaison with members of the criminal justice system frequently allows professional burglars to "fix" their cases prior to committing the burglaries. King found it easy to fix cases because "the only people that really profit from theft are the fix, the judge, and the district attorney" (King and Chambliss, 1984:84). The sociological literature indicates that professional burglars commonly rely on "the fix" (Abadinsky, 1983:70–75).

Burglars on Burglary

Several researchers have interviewed active residential burglars who are not currently incarcerated (Cromwell, Olson, and Avary, 1991; Wright and Decker, 1994). The major conclusions of these studies of "burglars on burglary" include the following:

- Need for money is the primary motivation for involvement in burglary. A legitimate job, when available, does not adequately respond to the immediacy of desire of cash.
- The majority of burglars cannot compete in the labor market because they are poorly educated, unskilled, and heavy illicit drug and alcohol users.
- Burglars use their proceeds for food, shelter, and clothing, yet the greatest percentage goes toward the maintenance of a "partying" lifestyle based in illicit drug and alcohol use.
- Burglary is a means for a burglar to "be somebody" by successfully completing a dangerous act.
- Most burglars watch potential targets before committing a burglary.
- Burglars choose residences to burglarize because of "external cues"—such as the size and condition of the dwelling, and type of cars in the driveway—suggesting that there are goods worth stealing inside.
- Once a residence is chosen as a possible target, burglars employ a decision-making strategy consisting of three questions: (1) Can the residence be entered without the burglar being seen and reported? (2) Is the residence currently occupied? and (3) Can the residence be broken into easily? If the answer is "yes" to all three questions, the burglar most likely will burglarize the residence.
- Most burglaries are committed during daytime hours when victims usually are at work.
- Situational factors, such as the presence of a dog, an alarm system, and alert neighbors are the most effective deterrents to burglars.

10.2   VARIETIES OF LARCENY

In Chapter 12.1 we discuss employee theft—the taking of merchandise and job-related items from one's workplace. Our immediate concern, however, is with nonoccupational theft, or what is commonly referred to as larceny. **Larceny** is the unlawful taking of property from the possession of someone other than one's employer. A larceny does *not* involve the threat of actual use of force (robbery)—with the exception of carjacking—or

BOX 10.1 PERSISTENT PROPERTY OFFENDERS

An important question asked by criminologists is why offenders persist in committing crime. That is, even after arrest, conviction, and incarceration, many continue to engage in property crime. Why?

Kenneth Tunnell (1992), in his book *Choosing Crime,* examined this question by interviewing sixty chronic repeat property offenders. These were individuals who had committed a great number of crimes (mostly robbery and burglary) and with considerable frequency. In questioning these offenders about their motivation to continually commit property crimes, Tunnell found that 88 percent engaged in crime for "quick, easy money" to be used for living expenses and pleasurable commodities, such as illicit drugs (p. 39). In addition, many property offenders commit these crimes for a sense of accomplishment, to gain power over someone, for revenge, and simply as a sport.

This engagement in property crime primarily for money is related to their class position and, therefore, limited access to legitimate alternatives. As Tunnell found through his interviews, repetitive offenders choose "the best alternative available to them since crime often allowed them to obtain satisfaction of their immediate needs" (p. 70). Indeed, these offenders spent money as quickly as it came in and therefore had little to show for their risky criminal activity. Since the immediate need for drugs and easily consumable commodities continued, along with a lack of legitimate legal options, these offenders persisted in property crime.

An interesting aspect of this study considered whether the decision to commit crime was related to possible negative consequences of their illegal actions—getting caught. As Tunnell reported:

> Nearly all sixty reported they rarely considered the threat of capture, arrest, and imprisonment and that risk was considered a nuisance rather than a real, tangible threat. Risk-related thoughts were considered distracting from their prime objective—committing the crime. Thus, many were simply able to not think about risks and put them out of their minds (p. 100).

Thus, crime control policies based on severe penalties (such as lengthy prison sentences) that attempt to scare criminals to "go straight" do not seem to have an impact on persistent property offenders.

A more recent study of street robbers and burglars is Neal Shover's (1996) similar exploration of why property offenders persist in committing crime. Shover has shown how the class background of persistent robbers and burglars limits their legitimate occupational options and, therefore, their ultimate choices. Born into a life of poverty, lower-working-class children are prepared to accept these limited legitimate choices. After dropping out of school, many of these youth are attracted to the local street culture, making it even more difficult for them to "defer gratification" in favor of long-range goals. Shover has shown that the street culture is much too attractive because of its emphasis on "life as party":

> The hallmark of life as party is enjoyment of "good times" with minimal concern for obligations and commitments external to the person's immediate social setting. Those who pursue life as party are determined to suspend concern for serious matters in favor of enjoying the moment. . . . Life as party is enjoyed in the company of alcohol and other drugs. In bars and lounges, on street corners, or while cruising in automobiles, party pursuers celebrate and affirm values of spontaneity, independence, and resourcefulness (pp. 93–94).

The pursuit of life as party quickly exhausts one's meager financial resources. Consequently, members of the street culture oscillate in and out of financial desperation. Robbery and burglary, then, become solutions for obtaining the badly needed "fast money" to adequately participate in the party. Thus, the cycle continues, and members of the street culture become persistent property offenders.

breaking and entering (burglary). In 1997, there were 7.7 million larcenies in the United States reported to the police, or approximately 2,886 per 100,000 inhabitants (Federal Bureau of Investigation, 1998:45).

The *NCVS* does not use the term "larceny" but rather the term "theft," which refers to personal larcenies without contact, such as theft of an umbrella from a restaurant, a radio from the beach, or a bicycle from a school yard. Only 12 percent of such thefts valued at less than $50.00 were reported to the police in 1997. However, in the same year, for thefts of $250.00 or more, 56 percent were reported to the police. Thus, the greater the value of the merchandise stolen, the greater the likelihood the theft will be reported to the police. Finally, given these reporting figures, we should not be surprised to find that the *NCVS* reported more than twice as many victimizations as the *UCR:* in 1997 there were 19.7 million (Department of Justice, 1999).

New types of larceny are always being made possible by technological change. A recent example—not yet examined by sociologists and criminologists—is cellular phone number theft, which costs cellular carriers an estimated $300 million per year in unauthorized calls (Flanagan and McMenamin, 1992). A common method of stealing a cellular phone number is through "cloning," which involves altering the microchip in another cellular phone so that the phone number matches the one stolen from an authentic customer. The conversion can be accomplished with a personal computer, and cellular phone numbers are "either purchased from insiders or plucked from the airwaves with a legal device, about the size of a textbook, that can be plugged into a vehicle's cigarette lighter receptacle" (p. 189).

In this section we discuss three major types of larceny: shoplifting, motor vehicle theft, and fraud.

Shoplifting

One particular type of larceny—shoplifting—has been accorded extraordinary attention by sociologists and criminologists. **Shoplifting**—theft of property from a retail store by "customers"—accounts for approximately 25–30 percent of all business losses (Klemke, 1992:10).

One of the earliest efforts by a sociologist to study shoplifting is the classic work by Mary Owen Cameron (1964), *The Booster and the Snitch.* Cameron divided shoplifters into two types: "boosters," who steal merchandise to sell it, and "snitches," who steal for their own consumption (1964:39–60). In other words, the booster is a professional who steals for the purpose of making money; the snitch is an amateur who steals for personal use. According to Cameron, boosters—composing about 10 percent of shoplifters—possess five characteristics:

1.   Boosters work a large number of stores rather than a few large stores.
2.   Boosters employ considerable planning and skill to execute their theft.
3.   Boosters steal only expensive merchandise and, like professional robbers and burglars, sell it to a professional fence.
4.   Boosters often easily "fix" their cases if caught.
5.   Boosters employ very sophisticated methods and devices for engaging in shoplifting.

Victims of shoplifting: Not only businesses suffer losses from this crime. As consumers, we are victims, too. Forty percent of us shoplift at some point during our lives. Businesses simply raise their prices to compensate for their losses, and consumers pay for it.

These devices include "booster bloomers," garments especially designed to hold stolen merchandise, and "booster boxes," specifically designed to look like wrapped packages but that actually contain secret openings into which items can be placed quickly and easily (pp. 40–50, 56–58).

The type of professional shoplifter receiving the greatest attention has been the so-called California Pro, who shoplifts in a wide geographical area and sells large quantities of merchandise to a fence (Baumer and Rosenbaum, 1984:26). In the United States, professional shoplifters tend to operate in rings. One group allegedly has a membership as high as 1,000 and steals as much as $150 million worth of merchandise each year (p. 26).

The other 90 percent of shoplifters, according to Cameron, are snitches, or amateurs, who possess the following characteristics:

1. Snitches are "respectable" members of the community.
2. Snitches do not think of themselves as criminals.
3. Snitches have no criminal associations or connections.
4. Snitches steal from a store when the opportunity arises.
5. Snitches do not plan extensively but enter the store "prepared" to shoplift (equipped with "shopping lists," large handbags, briefcases, shopping bags, and scissors and razor blades for snipping off price tags).

Snitches simply place items in pockets or inside coats, sometimes actually wearing the stolen merchandise under their clothing, or engage in such activities as price-tag switching, whereby they pay less for merchandise (pp. 58–60). Self-report studies indicate that snitching is a fairly common activity in the United States (Baumer and Rosenbaum, 1984:18–19). About 40 percent of shoppers have shoplifted at some time.

Cameron's findings are important because they show shoplifting to be a very frequent crime and one committed not primarily by professionals, "lower-class" people, or a unique criminal element of deranged, psychologically disturbed people. Rather, shoplifting is committed by "normal" and "ordinary" individuals.

Initially, the work of Robin (1963) on patterns of department store shoplifting and of Won and Yamamoto (1968) on middle-class shoplifting confirmed the major findings published by Cameron. In the 1980s, research by Farrell and Ferrara (1985), Baumer and Rosenbaum (1984), and Meier (1983) agreed with most of the conclusions by Cameron. But Meier added that being a professional shoplifter means that one must acquire adequate training and learn "which items can be fenced, with what percentage of profit, and to whom." Meier also pointed out that snitches are more likely to switch or remove price tags or simply grab "merchandise and run from the store" (most salespeople do not run after thieves) and that many juveniles engage in considerable planning for their shoplifting escapades (p. 1499).

However, some of Cameron's findings can be questioned. For example, Lloyd Klemke's review of shoplifting literature indicated that "significant numbers of boosters who shoplift for resale also shoplift for their own use" (1992:71). Moreover, many snitches do not enter a store prepared to shoplift but, rather, their shoplifting is often a spur-of-the-moment act. One snitch interviewed by Klemke stated: "I never went into a store knowing that I was going to shoplift. I would just be walking around and then take something, makeup or candy, never thinking before that I would. Just see it. Didn't really think about it" (p. 72). Fifty-six percent of Klemke's sample of "college student shoplifters" claimed they did not plan on shoplifting prior to entering the store (p. 72).

Finally, after a careful review of the literature on shoplifting in the United States, Britain, and Australia, Murphy concluded that instead of shoplifting being a peculiar and strange activity, it is an offense that many people engage in at some time in their life and that "far from being an offense motivated by personal frustrations of whatever sort," shoplifting is "an everyday activity" (1986:58).

Motor Vehicle Theft

Motor vehicle theft is the unlawful taking or attempting to take a motor vehicle such as an automobile, van, truck, or motorcycle. In 1997 there were 1,353,707 motor vehicle thefts reported to the police, or approximately 506 per 100,000 inhabitants (Federal Bureau of Investigation, 1998:51). The estimated national loss from reported motor vehicle theft was $7.6 billion in 1992, and at the time of the theft the average value per vehicle stolen was $4,713 (p. 50).

The *NCVS* (Department of Justice, 1999) found that for 1997, 92 percent of completed motor vehicle theft victimizations were reported to the police. Not surprisingly, the *NCVS* reported a figure close to the FBI total: approximately one million motor vehicle thefts in 1997.

Most scholars have concentrated on one type of motor vehicle theft, **automobile theft**, which is probably the best reported of all property crimes (90 percent) because of (1) the high value of vehicles, (2) insurance requirements, (3) the assistance needed from police to recover stolen cars, and (4) the high probability that stolen cars will actually be located (Clarke and Harris, 1992). Also, as with robbery, burglary, and larceny, sociologists have dichotomized auto thefts into the primary types of amateur and professional. One of the earliest applications of this typology is seen in Jerome Hall's (1952:250–256) well-known book, *Theft, Law, and Society.* For Hall, most auto thieves are amateur joyriders who steal automobiles for excitement and to "show off," quickly abandoning the car after a short time. According to Hall, joyriders mostly steal cars with unlocked doors, open windows, keys in the ignition, and sometimes even the motor running.

Professional auto thieves steal automobiles in more indirect and skillful ways. According to Hall, many simply work with repair-shop employees who secure duplicate keys for the professional thief. Others steal cars advertised in newspapers by providing the owner with a "down payment," never to be heard from again. Once an automobile is stolen, many professionals work with or personally control a "chop-shop," in which a stolen automobile is stripped of all saleable accessories. These accessories are sold to dealers, repair shops and garages, and professional fences.

A more recent sociological discussion of auto theft—by McCaghy, Giordano, and Henson (1977:376–383)—has argued that Hall's typology is too simplistic for this crime. According to these sociologists, auto thieves "are a more complex lot" (p. 377), and they have suggested a typology that includes five categories: (1) joyriding, (2) short-term transportation, (3) long-term transportation, (4) commission of another crime, and (5) profit. We now examine each.

McCaghy, Giordano, and Henson agreed with Hall that joyriding auto theft signifies recreational, nonutilitarian, short-term use of cars. For the joyrider, the primary goal is not simply to obtain transportation, but rather "automobile symbolism is predominant: the car is stolen not for what it does, but for what it means" (p. 378). The second type—short-term transportation—is similar to joyriding in the sense that it clearly involves short-term use of a stolen automobile. It differs, however, in that the thief's primary interest in the car is its ability to provide transportation from one location to another—from one place in the city to another, or even from one state to another. As with joyriding, many juveniles are involved in short-term auto theft. The third type—long-term transportation—involves thieves who steal the vehicle with the intent of keeping it for long-term personal use. This type of auto thief usually steals automobiles outside his or her state of residence and, upon returning home, if not before, repaints the vehicle. Most long-term auto thieves are adults. Some auto thieves—the fourth type—steal cars to aid them in the commission of another crime, such as robbery or burglary. This fourth type represents only a small portion of all auto thefts, even though the scenario is depicted over and over again on prime-time television. Once again, the motivation is utility of the automobile. Finally, the fifth type identified by McCaghy, Giordano, and Henson is for profit, which is somewhat similar to Hall's "professional." However, for McCaghy, Giordano, and Henson, this fifth type includes a wide variety of individuals whose motive is not to keep the car but to resell it, or its parts, for profit. They identify two forms of this type: amateurs and professionals. Amateurs steal a car to strip it of easily accessible components such as batteries, tires, and a variety of engine parts. They sell these parts to friends, acquaintances, or amateur fences, or they re-equip their own cars using some of the parts. Professionals, however, are highly organized, reselling expensive stolen cars in the United States and internationally. Professionals alter the vehicle registration numbers and falsify registration papers. Many purchase expensive wrecked vehicles and their ownership documents for a very low cost. They steal an identical car (year, make, model), replacing the vehicle identification number plate with that of the wrecked vehicle and also making other minor alterations. Subsequently, the converted vehicle is sold to an unsuspecting party who registers and retitles the vehicle in his or her name, giving it a legitimate identity virtually impossible to trace to the thief. McCaghy, Giordano, and Henson argued that professionals are also involved in the chop-shop business, specializing in the sale of specific parts to fences: hoods, fenders, bumpers, grills, and other hard-to-obtain parts.

Although amateurs and professionals clearly differ in skill and quality of theft, they both consider the automobile a valuable piece of property. Auto theft for profit differs from the other types of auto theft identified by McCaghy, Giordano, and Henson—joyriding, short- and long-term transportation, and aiding in the commission of another crime—because those who commit these latter types consider the automobile either a symbol or a form of transportation.

Ronald Clarke and Patricia Harris (1992:6) have provided the most recent typology of auto theft, which includes three types:

- Thefts for temporary use, such as joyriding and short-term transportation
- Professional thefts intended to deprive the owner permanently of the vehicle, which is used for resale, for export, or for chopping
- Thefts from vehicles, such as CD players, radios, and batteries

Clarke and Harris's typology differs from those of other researchers in one basic way—it includes "theft from vehicles" as a category of auto theft.

All of the above examples of auto theft usually occur without direct contact between offender and victim. However, in the 1990s a new type of auto theft began to be discussed in the media—**carjacking**—in which the auto thief uses direct physical force to steal a car from a driver. In a carjacking, automobiles are stolen from drivers in such places as rest stops, service stations, car washes, red lights, and shopping mall parking lots.

Some facts on carjacking include (Rand, 1994):

- Carjackings account for 2 percent of auto thefts each year.
- Approximately 35,000 completed or attempted carjackings take place every year.
- Fifty-two percent of carjackings are successful.
- Victims are injured in 24 percent of completed carjackings and in 18 percent of attempted carjackings.
- Four percent of all victims of all attempted or completed carjackings suffer serious injury, such as gunshot or knife wounds, broken bones, and internal injuries.
- Offenders use a weapon in 77 percent of all attempted and completed carjackings.
- Approximately two-thirds of all carjackings occur after dark, away from the victim's home.

The most dangerous auto theft: Although carjackings are the least frequent of all types of auto theft each year, they are the most dangerous. Carjacking is a form of auto theft in which the perpetrator uses direct physical force to steal a car from the driver.

- Fifty-four percent of all completed or attempted carjackings are committed by groups of two or more offenders.

Fraud

In Chapter 12.1 and 12.2 we discuss occupational fraud and corporate financial fraud; here we focus on nonoccupationally related frauds such as **check** and **credit-card fraud** and defrauding the government. We begin with an examination of check fraud.

The crimes thus far analyzed—interpersonal crimes of violence and property crimes such as robbery, burglary, shoplifting, and motor vehicle theft—are clearly recognizable as crimes by an offender against a victim. In contrast, check fraud—deliberately deceiving someone for personal economic gain by producing a counterfeit or forged check—has "little in the criminal act or the interaction between the check passer and the person cashing the check to identify it as a crime" (Lemert, 1967:101). In other words, check fraud is not at the time of its commission easily recognizable as a crime. Indeed, this holds true for all forms of fraud discussed in this section; it is not until sometime later that the event is determined to be a crime.

Individuals can even engage in check fraud without knowing it. For instance, if someone continually writes checks against his or her account at a time when that account does not hold sufficient funds to cover the checks, the checks normally are returned with the designation "Nonsufficient Funds" (NSF), and the individual could be prosecuted for fraud. Other forms of check fraud include altering checks, forging someone else's personal checks, producing counterfeit personal and payroll checks, stealing government checks (checks rendering a salary, tax refund, pension, welfare allotment, and/or veteran benefit), and forging a signature.

Lemert's (1967:99–134) classic study of "naive" and "systematic" check forgery remains the most extensive examination of check fraud. Naive check forgers are amateurs who commit the crime only when they have an urgent need for money and who are unfamiliar with "criminal techniques" (pp. 102–105). The naive check forger, Lemert found, ordinarily has completed more years of school than the general population and works in a clerical, skilled, or professional occupation. Lemert also established that a majority of naive check forgers reside in the community in which their crimes are committed.

Systematic check forgers (pp. 109–113) view themselves as forgers, regularly employ a special technique to pass bad checks, and organize their lives around check fraud. Some systematic check forgers view their fraud as a "regular business," but most do not, engaging in it for the alleged "fast and luxurious" life (p. 110). These forgers give special attention to such details as banking hours and the best places to present checks; yet, according to Lemert, such details serve only as "guides" for the fraud. Moreover, systematic check forgers are less likely than other professional property offenders to use the "fix" because they simply have "too many bad checks outstanding and too many victims to mollify by offering restitution" (p. 111). The systematic check forger is different from other professional property offenders in another way. According to Lemert, check forgery requires neither a high degree of technical skill nor a long learning "apprenticeship"; you simply "learn as you go." However, systematic check forgery does require the ability to impersonate someone else, and therefore success is based on development of expertise in assuming fictitious roles. Finally, although the systematic check forger tends to be migratory (like other professional property offenders), most tend to work alone, avoiding contact with a network of illegitimate and legitimate people. Lemert found that some systematic check forgers work in "check passing gangs" and a few "contract out" their services, yet the majority operate on a solitary basis (pp. 112–113). These forgers manufacture or steal checks (usually personal or payroll checks) and then work alone to pass them illegally.

Lemert's discussion of check fraud identified fraudsters as migratory isolates; Tremblay (1986) found fraudsters working together in groups. Tremblay investigated check frauds and credit-card frauds (defined as the unauthorized use of a credit card for personal gain by someone other than the cardholder) related to a "check guarantee program" of a major bank, where all credit cardholders—whether customers of the bank or not—could withdraw $500 a day from any domestic branch by check if they presented their credit card to guarantee the transaction. The bank saw this program as a marketing opportunity, encouraging regular customers to use its resources while simultaneously attracting noncustomers. However, it was precisely at the introduction of this program that a wave of check and credit-card frauds began.

According to Tremblay (pp. 238–241), three major types of fraud occurred as a result of this program: check guarantee fraud, purchase credit-card fraud, and purchase check fraud. The first, check guarantee fraud, occurs when individuals "ride" a stolen credit card—or several cards—by cashing checks (also stolen) in numerous bank branches in the shortest possible time. The term "ride" refers to the total number of banks visited by fraudsters with just one credit card; "the take" is the total amount of cash withdrawals per ride. In this case, an average ride yielded a take of approximately $6,000, whereas particularly successful rides netted as much as $15,000 (p. 242). The other types of fraud discussed by Tremblay—purchase check and purchase credit-card fraud—simply entailed using stolen checks and credit cards to purchase goods from retail stores.

The overall network of fraud consisted of thieves (people who stole the checks and cards), riders (people who used the checks and cards in banks and stores), and fences (who bought the fraudulently obtained merchandise). Tremblay (p. 242) found that this overall scheme could not have operated without the following:

- Access to a stable supply of stolen checks, credit cards, and other identification items, such as stolen drivers' licenses.
- Thieves available to obtain the checks, cards, and "identification kits." Men who frequented prostitutes had their wallets stolen by them, who then sold the stolen cards to the fraudsters. Other targets were hospital employees and sports club members, because they remove their clothes during their work and leisure routines.
- False bank accounts as a means for obtaining personalized checks, which were then fraudulently used.
- Access to a complex fencing network for purchase check and purchase credit-card frauds.

Tremblay's research is important because it challenges the assumption that check fraud—and also credit-card fraud—is committed in isolation. Tremblay emphasized the links between different criminal practices and illicit markets. Indeed, other research indicates that large organized schemes account for one-half the total dollar loss due to credit-card fraud (Caminer, 1985:748).

The government is also a potential victim of fraudsters. One reason is that defrauding the government is actually limitless because of the vast number and variety of government programs. To fraudsters, the federal government is a bottomless financial pit. **Income-tax fraud**, however, is probably the most prevalent form of defrauding the government. Cheating on one's income tax is made possible in the United States because of the following:

1. the complexity of the tax codes
2. the seemingly infinite number of deductible expenses
3. the Internal Revenue Service's (IRS) reliance on a system in which taxpayers calculate their own tax bill
4. the small number of returns actually scrutinized by the IRS (Mattera, 1985:9)

Simon and Witte (1982:7–15) have identified four major forms of tax fraud. The first, "underreported wages of tax filers," refers to income earned in off-the-books activity. An example is working a second job—for which earnings are paid in cash—but filing an income-tax return only for wages earned from the first job. Another example concerns the many workers who arrange with their employer to report only a certain amount of their wages; therefore, the "portion reported allows the individual to qualify for social security, unemployment, and similar benefits, while taxes and social insurance payments are avoided on the unreported portion" (p. 7). By operating on a cash-for-labor basis, employees *and* employers avoid paying taxes because there is no record of earnings. This operation occurs in the second type of tax fraud as well—"unreported wages for nonfilers" (p. 9)—wherein people earn wages and salaries in a variety of ways but file no income-tax return for *any* portion of it. This completely off-the-books employment is not uncommon among restaurant and construction workers, as well as among providers of personal services, such as house painters and appliance repair persons. The third type of tax fraud discussed by Simon and Witte is "underreported income of the self-employed" (p. 10). Much income earned by the self-employed—from carpenters to small businesses and independent professionals—is underreported to the IRS. In fact, some businesses and professionals have been found to "use double sets of books, fake invoices, deduct fictitious expenses, and conceal assets by placing them in the names of friends, relatives, and shell corporations" (p. 10). Finally, the fourth type of tax fraud is "income of the self-employed who do not file" (p. 12). This refers to self-employed individuals—such as carpenters and independent professionals, as well as some small business persons—who file no tax return at all. However, this type of tax fraud is arguably not very prevalent for small businesses because "fixed business operations give too much exposure to the IRS to make it safe to entirely fail to file tax returns" (p. 12). Thus, businesses who cheat more commonly underreport income on their tax return.

10.3   DEALING AND DAMAGE

Fencing and arson, although property crimes, are somewhat different from robbery, burglary, and larceny. Fencing is buying and selling—or dealing in—stolen goods, and arson involves damage to property of another.

Fencing

As stated above, **fencing** is buying, selling, or dealing in stolen goods. A fence's sources of goods include robbers, burglars, shoplifters, auto thieves, fraudsters, and employee thieves (whom we examine in Chapter 12.1). Once a thief successfully steals "the goods" and does not plan to make personal use of them, he or she must dispose of the goods as quickly as possible. Some thieves engage in "self-fencing"—that is, selling the stolen goods to people who do not know the goods are stolen or selling them to consumers who are unconcerned with their origin. Many people jump at the opportunity to buy items at a discount; consequently, thieves find accessible outlets for stolen merchandise in friends, acquaintances, and on the street generally (Wright and Decker, 1994).

For example, in their interviews with burglars, Cromwell, Olsen, and Avary found that the market for stolen property is both diverse and ubiquitous, including

school teachers, social workers, plumbers, operators of small business establishments, attorneys, bail bond agents, drug dealers, systems analysts, college professors,
high school and college students, and other individuals who regularly or occasionally
purchased merchandise they knew or believed to be stolen. (1991:80)

Most of the individuals interviewed in this study reported that they bought stolen goods
for personal use—and did not resell the goods—and, technically, can be considered "receivers," rather than fences.

Some thieves, however, sell their goods to amateur fences. Stuart Henry's (1978; 1976)
work on the amateur trade in stolen goods is interesting in this regard. Henry defined amateur fencing as "the activity of regular part-time purchase of genuine quality merchandise
(usually, though not necessarily stolen) for the purpose of selling cheaply for the interest
of those involved" (1976:794). Most amateur fences *say* they participate in the trade of
stolen goods for personal economic gain. Notwithstanding, it seems that amateur fences
rarely make money. Henry (pp. 796–797) found this to be the case because amateur fences
are unlikely to come into contact with either highly valued articles or large quantities of
these items, and when they do, they find it is difficult to resell them. But more importantly,
the price charged by the fence is determined by the nature of the relationship between the
fence and the buyer. Most stolen goods go from the amateur fence to relatives and friends
who "are often given the goods and not even charged cost price," and when friends and
relatives are charged, it is rarely more than the fence actually paid for the items (p. 798).
Thus, even though amateur fencing is structured in terms of economic exchange, Henry
concluded that in actuality, the majority of deals are made for the purpose of reaffirming
established relationships. Amateur fencing provides the individual fence with "status,
prestige and reciprocal social favors" (Walsh and Poole, 1983:89). As Henry stated, "the
social content of the relations surrounding amateur exchange outweighs the material value
of the goods involved" (1976:801). Amateur trade in stolen goods becomes a means of
sustaining a network of communal relations among relatives, friends, and acquaintances.
Consequently, amateur trade in stolen goods is quite informal and even takes place in people's homes. Henry provided an example: "Whenever Jim, a shoplifter, supplied cheap
goods to Freddy, a plumber, there would be a Sunday-morning knock at the door: 'I got
some suits: Do you want them?'" (1978:18).

Many thieves, however, sell their stolen merchandise to a professional fence. For example, burglars prefer a professional fence because they can purchase large amounts of
merchandise, they tend to ask fewer questions than other buyers of stolen goods, and they
are motivated to be discreet about their business dealings (Wright and Decker, 1994:174).

Several classic studies have examined professional fencing operations in relation to
property theft. Within such literature there seems to be consensus that most professional
fences have strong ties to the legitimate business community. As Hall wrote in his book
Theft, Law, and Society, the professional fence is "an established participant" in the legitimate "economic life of society" (1952:155). Professional fences are "offshoots from legitimate businesses," frequently specialize in a chosen field, and thus are "able to evaluate
merchandise expertly and to compete generally on the basis of their special skills" (p. 157).

Marilyn Walsh (1977:15) reported that the average professional fence in her study was
"a 45–55-year-old white, male businessman. As such, he looked strikingly similar to most

managers and administrators in wholesale and retail trades." For Walsh, then, the professional fence is "strikingly dissimilar" to the thief and is "demographically a very ordinary man" (p. 15).

Finally, the most recent—and methodologically the most rigorous—study of the professional fence, by Darrell Steffensmeier, confirms that the "overwhelming majority of fences . . . are simultaneously proprietors or operators of a legitimate business which provides a cover or front for the fencing" (1986:20). "Sam Goodman," the main character of Steffensmeier's book, is a legitimate and successful businessperson who also—as part of his business—sells stolen merchandise. In Sam's view, it is very difficult for anyone to succeed in business without "chiseling" in some form or fashion; professional fencing is simply his type of chiseling.

The legitimate business identity of the professional fence covers the comings and goings of thieves, making thieves indistinguishable from customers and legitimate delivery persons (Klockars, 1974:88). In short, the evidence on fencing shows that, as Henry put it, "it is not the case that one species of actor, the 'fence,' buys stolen goods, whereas another, the 'businessman,' buys legitimate ones. Rather it demonstrates that businessmen buy cheap goods in order that they may sell at a profit; a greater or lesser proportion of their purchases may be illicit" (1977:133).

The professional fence is "in the shadow of two worlds" (the subtitle of Steffensmeier's book), providing legitimate and illegitimate goods in the business world while simultaneously buying stolen goods in the criminal world. Professional fencing is in fact indistinguishable from legitimate business activity.

There can also be a close relationship between the thief and criminal syndicates. Abadinsky (1983:64–65) reported that criminal syndicates provide vital services to thieves, such as information on the police, whom to "connect" with in the case of arrest, information on possible targets, reliable fences, financial assistance, and protection. In return, the thief offers the skill and ability required to provide "the goods" criminal syndicates are interested in.

The professional fence may develop a special relationship with the police:

> Fences are able to offer various "perks" or payoffs to the police and other legal officials. . . . In return for these perks, the police may be less zealous in responding to complaints against the fence or may sabotage an ongoing investigation. (Steffensmeier, 1986:152)

Most detectives who frequented Sam's shop were simply recipients of Sam's generosity, yet a few were "actively on the take" (p. 153).

In Klockars's (1974:104) earlier case study of the fence "Vincent Swaggi," it was found that the largest single group of his buyers was in some way connected to the criminal justice system: police officers, detectives, lawyers, judges, customs officials, insurance adjusters, and crime reporters. The relationship between Swaggi and these buyers was quite comfortable and friendly. As Klockars pointed out, "a joking atmosphere prevails, with 'What's hot today, Vince?' as a standard opening from Vincent's law enforcement customers. Although Vincent has heard that question a thousand times he always answers, 'Everything,' and laughs" (p. 104). Thus, both amateur and professional thievery, as well as amateur and professional fencing, must be understood as being embedded in a network of relations with other legitimate and illegitimate people.

Arson

Arson is the willful or malicious burning of a house, public building, motor vehicle, aircraft, or other property of another. In 1997 there were 81,753 arson offenses reported to the police, or approximately 48 per 100,000 inhabitants (Federal Bureau of Investigation, 1998:56). The vast majority of arson crimes occur in cities with populations of over one million (p. 56). However, it should be pointed out that only fires determined through investigation to have been willingly or maliciously set are classified as arsons by the FBI. Fires of suspicious or unknown origins are excluded. In addition, it is not simply in big cities but in the economically declining inner-city neighborhoods of big cities that the most common arson sites exist (Brady, 1983:4). Arson also causes more injury, death, and property loss than any other crime listed by the FBI as a felony (p. 1).

When we think of arson, what commonly comes to mind is the psychologically deranged pyromaniac we see on prime-time television. Clearly there are cases of individuals who have an "uncontrollable impulse" to start fires and who engage in this behavior for the excitement and mere "pleasure" of setting fires and watching structures burn; however, their number is indeed small when compared with other types of arsonists. Excluding pyromaniacs, four major types of arson have been identified by sociologists, police officials, and firefighters. The types are based on arsonist motives and include crime concealment, revenge, vandalism, and profit. We briefly consider each type.

Crime concealment refers to individuals setting fires to destroy evidence—for example, of a burglary, a larceny, or a murder. In such cases individuals employ arson to remove any evidence connecting the perpetrator to the crime or to prevent identification of the victim. In addition, people set fires to destroy records that contain evidence of other crimes, such as fraud and white-collar crimes like embezzlement and corporate crime.

Revenge arsons result from quarrels, hatred, and jealousy among lovers, neighbors, employees, family members and relatives, and persons motivated by racist and religious contempt. Children sometimes express resentment against siblings who receive greater attention by burning a brother's or sister's bed, and/or may indicate incest victimization by setting afire the bed in which they were victimized. Similarly, women who are the victims of physical and/or sexual abuse in the home may obtain revenge by setting afire the bed— quite possibly with the perpetrator asleep in it—as depicted in the television movie *The Burning Bed.* The church arsons that occurred in the mid-1990s are examples of arson resulting from race and religious contempt. According to the National Church Arson Task Force (1997), between 1995 and 1997 approximately 429 church arsons were committed. Of these incidents, 162 involved African American churches, more than three quarters were located in the southern United States, and the vast majority of offenders were white.

The third type of arson—vandalism—usually is associated with youths who set fires in schools, automobiles, and vacant buildings. Vacant buildings often serve as playgrounds for inner-city youths, some of whom may rationalize that a fire in such a building will not hurt anyone. Watching the building burn, as well as the fire department extinguishing it, can be "exciting" to these youth. Thus, most vandalism fires occur shortly after 3 P.M.,

Arson for profit: This type of arson frequently occurs by defrauding insurance companies. Individuals may set a structure on fire to obtain insurance coverage money or to improve the quality of the structure with the financial return on an insurance claim.

when children are generally dismissed from school (Jacobson, 1985:50). However, it is difficult to determine whether such fires are actually the result of arson. Determining criminal intent of youth is based on age and the motive behind the fire setting. If the youth is under the age of consent and there is insufficient evidence indicating malicious and willful fire setting, the youth most likely will not be labeled an arsonist (Garry, 1997).

Finally, the most costly arson—in terms of property damaged and lives lost and injured—results from profit-making ventures. There are several ways individuals can profit from arson: "stop-loss" arson—when businesses on the verge of great financial loss or even financial ruin "sell" the business to an insurance company by setting it ablaze to obtain the coverage proceeds; "property improvement or rehabilitation" arson—where property owners improve a structure or replace deteriorating furnishings from the proceeds of small fire insurance claims; "elimination of competition" arson—where a business eliminates its competition by setting it afire; and "extortion, coercion, and intimidation" arson—where criminal syndicates use the threat of arson to extort money from businesses (Jacobson, 1985:37–45). However, arguably the most lucrative and destructive form of arson-for-profit occurs when individuals purchase a particular property—usually in an economically depressed area of a city—and insure the property for more than its value. By setting the property ablaze, the owner can reap a substantial profit.

Brady's (1983) study of arson concentrated on this latter type of arson-for-profit. His research went considerably beyond an examination of individuals, connecting arson-for-profit to major banks and criminal syndicates in one particular city, Boston. Brady (pp. 6–9) showed first that there was, in the late 1970s and early 1980s, a pattern to the fires occurring in Boston—arson being demographically concentrated within certain poor Boston neighborhoods, such as Roxbury, North Dorchester, East Boston, and Jamaica Plain. Within these economically depressed areas, arson was more common in buildings owned by absentee landlords than in either owner-occupied tenements or public housing projects. Many of these privately owned buildings had been abandoned, and between 1978 and 1982 more than one-half of Boston's 3,000 arsons occurred in abandoned buildings.

Brady further showed that these buildings are not abandoned because of a "natural process of neighborhood evolution" but because of "discriminatory mortgage-lending policies of banks that deny credit to certain districts of the inner city in order to invest in more profitable suburban real estate" (p. 10). This latter practice is known as redlining, and it devastates neighborhoods by forcing small businesses to close because they cannot secure bank loans. Moreover, landlords fail to repair their buildings, eventually abandoning them, because property values decline drastically. Brady found that arson is specifically concentrated in these areas.

In addition to the foregoing, Brady (pp. 11–12) presented convincing evidence that because of redlining, banks actually foreclose on unpaid bank mortgages, resulting in their holding neglected and abandoned buildings. Clearly, this appears to represent a great financial loss for the bank. Not so, as Brady explained:

> Enter the organized crime racketeers. They offer to buy the "problem buildings," often at a price far greater than true market value, on condition that the bank write out a new mortgage for close to the full purchase price, and sometimes more, to cover the cost of "renovation." Thus, the racketeers acquire large numbers of properties with little investment of their own capital. In some cases they can further increase their "leverage" by arranging second, third or fourth mortgages whose total value far exceeds the original inflated purchase price. Backed by mortgages from a major bank, it is fairly simple to arrange insurance coverage for the buildings at a level well above the total value of the mortgages. (p. 11)

The overmortgaged and overinsured property is then set fire by criminal syndicate figures or individuals who earn a living as professional "torches." Not only do criminal syndicates gain, but so do banks, as potential losses represented by foreclosure are actually turned into profit because "the new mortgage paid by the insurance company greatly exceeds the old bad debt assumed under foreclosure" (p. 11).

An excellent example of the comfortable relationship between banks and criminal syndicates is the case of the South Boston Savings Bank (pp. 11–12). From 1970 to 1977 the bank foreclosed on 76 properties, 39 of these suffering 79 fires, or almost two fires per property. In 1978 it was discovered that some of the most notorious Boston arsonists were clients of the bank. Brady lists these shady figures as follows:

> Caroll St. Germaine, convicted arsonist and murderer (over $500,000 to 1978); Russell Tardanico, convicted arsonist (over $730,000 in 16 mortgages to 1982); George Lincoln, confessed "torch" and arsonist who turned "state's witness" in exchange for

immunity in a 1978–1979 Boston arson conspiracy trial (over $150,000 in five mort-
gages in 1978); Nicholas Shaheen, convicted arsonist (over $100,000 in five mort-
gages to 1978). (p. 12)

Brady's research shows the extent of arson-for-profit and how different types of crime
are actually linked together. In the case of arson, banks (corporate crime) are connected to
racketeers (criminal syndicates) who in turn are linked to "torches" (property crime). Indeed, we cannot understand the crime of arson—and many other crimes for that matter—
without analyzing such connections.

Similarly, Jacobson and Kasinitz (1986) have described the conviction of two South
Bronx insurance brokers and landlords. The two brokers, Bernard Gold and Eugene Bell,
together with several hired "torches" and insurance adjusters, were convicted in 1985 of
federal conspiracy charges related to fifty fires in seventeen buildings in the South Bronx.
Gold and his associates purchased buildings from banks and insurance companies for as
little as $2,500, yet insured these buildings through other companies—either based in an-
other state or another country, such as Lloyd's of London—for between $200,000 and
$500,000. What this particular case shows, according to Jacobson and Kasinitz, is the re-
lationship between insurance companies and arson, and

> how simple it can be to insure buildings for vastly more than they are worth, and how
> little attention some insurers pay to the condition of the properties they insure or to
> the track records of the landlords with whom they do business. Finally, it reminds us
> that many reputable insurance companies are reluctant to undertake their own inves-
> tigations of suspicious fires or to help law enforcement agencies pursue criminal
> charges. (p. 512)

REVIEW

This chapter examined seven different types of property crimes: robbery, burglary,
shoplifting, motor vehicle theft, fraud, fencing, and arson. These property crimes are different from crimes of interpersonal violence in certain ways:

- They occur much more frequently.
- Offender and victim are usually strangers.
- In many cases no direct interaction occurs between offender and victim.
- In some cases—as in most frauds—it is not immediately apparent that a crime
  has been committed.

Robbery and Burglary

1. Robbery is a unique property crime involving direct interaction between offender and
victim. It also entails both the threatened or actual use of physical violence and property
loss to the victim.

2. Because robbery differs from crimes of interpersonal violence in significant sociological ways, we label it a property crime.

3. Strong-arm robbery is considerably more dangerous than armed robbery.

4. Robbery can be classified both in terms of incidents and offenders. The two major types of robbery offenders are professionals and opportunists.

5. Burglars can be classified as professionals and amateurs.

6. Important information on robbery and burglary has come from interviews with criminals who are not incarcerated but are actively involved in these crimes.

7. Property offenders persist in their crimes because of their desperate economic situation and pursuit of "life as party."

Varieties of Larceny

1. One type of larceny—shoplifting—has received the most attention by criminologists.

2. There are two major types of shoplifters: boosters (professionals) and snitches (amateurs).

3. Individuals steal automobiles for joyriding, short- and long-term transportation, commission of another crime, and for profit.

4. Check fraud consists of drawing checks on insufficient funds in a checking account, forging someone else's personal checks, producing counterfeit personal and payroll checks, altering payroll checks, and stealing government checks and forging a signature.

5. Two major types of check fraud are naive forgers (amateurs) and systematic forgers (professionals).

6. Systematic forgers differ from other professional property offenders in significant ways.

7. Check and credit-card fraudsters may work alone or in groups.

8. Federal welfare programs and the Internal Revenue Service are the victims of substantial fraud.

Dealing and Damage

1. Fencing is the buying and selling of stolen goods and is conducted by both professional and amateurs.

2. The majority of amateur fences sell their goods to relatives, friends, and acquaintances—not for purposes of economic gain but to enhance established relationships.

3. Most professional fences have strong ties to the legitimate business community and are part of a loosely structured, yet mutually supportive, network of individuals involved in acquiring and distributing stolen property.

4. This network consists of thieves, fences, criminal justice personnel, criminal syndicates, goods transporters, and buyers.

5. Arson causes more injury, death, and property loss than any other of the *UCR Index* offenses.

6. There are four major types of arson: crime concealment, revenge, vandalism, and profit.

7. The most costly type of arson—in terms of property damage and lives lost and injured—results from profit-making ventures.

QUESTIONS FOR CLASS DISCUSSION

1. Identify and discuss how property crimes differ from crimes of interpersonal violence.

2. This textbook argues that robbery is a property crime. Examine that assessment of this crime and present an argument for or against its conclusion.

3. Most research on property offenders comes from incarcerated individuals. However, we presented research of "robbers on robbery" and "burglars on burglary." What are some of the advantages and disadvantages of this type of approach to gathering data on crime and criminals?

4. What are the major differences between professional and amateur property offenders?

5. Using examples, describe how "dealing" and "damage" are different from the varieties of larceny discussed.

6. Three theories discussed in Part Two that are relevant to property crime are techniques of neutralization, rational choice theory, and routine activities theory. Show how each theory might explain property crime.

FOR FURTHER STUDY

Readings

Shover, Neal. 1996. *Great Pretenders: Pursuits and Careers of Persistent Thieves.* Boulder, Colo.: Westview Press.

Steffensmeier, Darrell J. 1986. *The Fence: In the Shadow of Two Worlds.* Totowa, N.J.: Rowman & Littlefield.

Wright, Richard T., and Scott H. Decker. 1994. *Burglars on the Job: Streetlife and Residential Break-Ins.* Boston: Northeastern University Press.

Websites

1. <http://www.whitehouse.gov/fsbr/crime.html>: This site contains some general statistical information regarding conventional crime. Of particular interest to readers of this chapter are the plummeting rates of property crime graphically displayed on the relevant chart.

2. <http://www.ojp.usdoj.gov/bjs/glance/mvt.htm>: From the Department of Justice, this graphic shows the rates of motor vehicle theft declining, according to the National Crime Victimization Survey.

3. <http://www.usfa.fema.gov/napi>: From the National Arson Prevention Initiatives (NAPI), this site provides national statistics and prevention efforts in the United States. There are also links to community programs aimed at preventing arson.

4. <http://www.ftc.gov./telemarketing/links.htm>: The Federal Trade Commission has provided this site to educate users about telemarketing fraud in the United States. It contains links to useful sites from cases of such fraud in various parts of the United States.

11.1 Drug Use

History, Extent, and Nature of Drug Use

Decriminalization/Legalization

11.2 Abortion

Support for Abortion

History of Abortion

11.3 Prostitution and Pornography

Prostitution

Pornography

Preview

Chapter 11 introduces:
- what sociologists mean by public-order crimes
- the different types of public-order crimes
- the nature and extent of public-order crimes
- different perspectives on whether public-order crimes are harmful and victimize individuals and/or society

Key Terms

abortion	pornography
complaintless crimes	prostitution
decriminalization	victimless crimes
legalization	

In Chapter 9 we discussed crimes of interpersonal violence, and in Chapter 10 we examined property crime. Both of these types of crime encompass an offender and a victim, and it is relatively easy to ascertain that harm has occurred. In public-order crime—such as drug abuse, abortion, prostitution, and pornography—it is unclear whether an offender or a victim even exists, or whether a harm has occurred. In fact, it is debatable whether such activity should be identified as crime.

Some criminologists argue that victimization is a critical element of these activities. They point, for instance, to prostitutes as the harmed victims of prostitution, women as the harmed victims of pornography, and drug addicts as the harmed victims of illegal drug use. As Victoria Swigert has suggested, "Whether or not such persons consent, their lives are reduced; hence, they are the victims of these activities" (1984:97).

Ten years earlier than Swigert, Edwin Schur (1974:6) argued that to outsiders a harm may seem to have occurred, yet to insiders (or participants) no harm was perpetrated, and therefore no offender or victim exists. Indeed, as Schur explained, these are for him **victimless crimes**: "Victimless crimes are created when we attempt to ban through criminal legislation the exchange between willing partners of strongly desired goods and services. The 'offense' in such a situation, then, consists of a consensual transaction—one person gives or sells another person something he or she wants" (p. 6). Realizing that those directly involved in public-order crimes do not feel harmed or victimized and, therefore, do not report such behavior to the police, Schur eventually termed these behaviors **complaintless crimes** (1984:183).

Others do not see victimization of individuals as the important issue, arguing that the purpose of public-order laws is to legitimate a certain standard of morality. Once again, Swigert articulated this position: "Shared morals and ethics bind individuals to one another. Without these bonds, society would disintegrate. A legally enforced morality, therefore, is a necessary cost of human association" (1984:97).

According to this position, the purpose of public-order laws is to maintain a public moral order. Those who violate these laws, it is asserted, simply harm the overall social order. This position, however, fails to acknowledge that the state selectively enforces a certain type of morality. Put differently, only certain types of behavior are deemed immoral and, therefore, criminalized by the state. For example, the state "sweeps" up streetwalkers while allowing "call girls" to conduct their trade. Thus, one type of prostitution is considered immoral; another type is not.

In this chapter we discuss a variety of issues regarding how public-order laws selectively enforce morality and survey different arguments concerning harm and victimization. Although the number of public-order crimes is vast, we limit ourselves to examining four: drug use, abortion, prostitution, and pornography.

11.1   DRUG USE

Psychoactive drugs are capable of altering and affecting mental processes and states. There are numerous psychoactive drugs—alcohol, tobacco (nicotine), amphetamines, tranquilizers, marijuana, cocaine, and heroin. Space does not permit a discussion of each. Accordingly, we limit our examination to the following:

1. a historical sketch of the stated reasons why the production, distribution, and use of marijuana, cocaine, and heroin have been criminalized
2. the extent, use, and nature of the foregoing three illegal drugs today
3. the drug-crime connection
4. the decriminalization and legalization movement

History, Extent, and Nature of Drug Use

Throughout much of the 1800s, U.S. residents purchased opiates (opium, morphine, and heroin) over the counters of pharmacies, groceries, and general stores and obtained them from physicians for tranquilization and the relief of pain. In fact, opiates "were as freely accessible as aspirin is today" (Breacher, 1972:3–20).

In 1875, however, the city of San Francisco enacted an ordinance outlawing opium "dens" (smoking houses). Prior to that time Chinese laborers, working for low wages building U.S. railroads, were "free" to smoke opium as they pleased and their dens were not illegal. With the onset of the 1875–1880 depression, Chinese laborers became an obstacle to white workers' economic survival. As a result, whites organized against the opium-smoking Chinese. Consequently, the San Francisco ordinance—and several other anti-opium laws enacted in other cities—legally repressed the Chinese, thus serving the interests of the white working class (Helmer, 1975:32). Eventually (in 1909) Congress enacted the Opium Exclusion Act, thereby prohibiting importation of opium and/or its derivatives, except for medical purposes.

Similarly, in the early 1900s cocaine was widely used in the United States (it was a major ingredient of Coca-Cola). Yet racist beliefs that African Americans were especially prone to cocaine use—causing them to be particularly violent, criminal, and dangerous—grew widespread at the turn of the century (p. 47). As David Musto argued, however:

> Evidence does not suggest that cocaine caused a crime wave but rather that anticipation of black rebellion inspired white alarm. Anecdotes often told of superhuman strength, cunning, and efficiency resulting from cocaine. One of the most terrifying beliefs about cocaine was that it actually improved pistol marksmanship. Another myth, that cocaine made blacks almost unaffected by mere .32 caliber bullets, is said to have caused southern police departments to switch to .38 caliber revolvers. These fantasies characterized white fear, not the reality of cocaine's effects, and gave one more reason for the repression of blacks. (1973:7)

In addition to white fear, this association of African Americans with cocaine use and the Chinese with opium use tended to mystify the actual drug users during the early 1900s. Most persons addicted to opiates and cocaine were not African Americans and Chinese—but white, middle-aged, middle-class women. Moreover, their addiction largely resulted from "medical problems" rather than, as today, from a search for euphoria and excitement; furthermore, it was as frequent in rural areas as in urban areas (Goode, 1984:218).

Eventually, because of such racist fears, the Harrison Narcotics Act of 1914 was enacted. This act taxed those who produced, imported, dispensed, and sold opium and cocaine (and their derivatives, such as heroin) and required these individuals to register with the Treasury Department. The act was aimed primarily at regulating and controlling the traffic in narcotics. However, a series of Supreme Court decisions between 1919 and 1922 also made it illegal for physicians to prescribe narcotics to patients. Thus, it was the combination of these events and the act itself that, as Oakley Ray pointed out, took "the first step toward making it impossible for addicts to obtain their drugs legally. The result was the development of an illicit drug trade that charged users up to 50 times more than the legal retail drug price" (1983:36).

And as Erich Goode added, following passage of the Harrison Act and the Supreme Court decisions, the United States "witnessed the dramatic emergence of a criminal class of addicts—a *criminal class that had not existed previously.* The link between addiction and crime—the view that the addict was by definition a criminal—was forged. The law itself created a new class of criminals" (1984:221).

Not only was a criminal class of opiate and cocaine users created by the Harrison Act and the Supreme Court decisions (this new class was composed primarily of lower- and working-class individuals; middle-class women turned to legal drugs, such as tranquilizers [Goode, 1984:221]), but those who inhaled marijuana also became victims of the law. Although marijuana was smoked for years by U.S. citizens and was not considered a social problem, all of a sudden in the 1930s it began to receive considerable attention. As with the Chinese during the 1875–1880 depression, Mexicans during the depression of the 1930s were seen as a threat to white survival because they worked for lower pay. As a result, whites began to link marijuana use with the "degenerate and violent Mexican" and called for legal intervention. Politicians, police, and prosecutors likewise "protested constantly to the federal government about the Mexicans' use of the weed" (Musto, 1973:220). Thus, by the summer of 1936 it became obvious that the only way to appease whites in the Southwest was to enact some type of federal legislation (p. 225). The result was the 1937 Marijuana Tax Act, which regulated importation and use of marijuana and, as its own product, created a criminal class of marijuana users (Helmer, 1975:79). The possession of marijuana became a criminal act in exactly the same way as possession of opiates and cocaine did—not because of a thorough examination of the effects of marijuana on human behavior but because of racist attitudes toward minorities thought to be its typical users (Goode, 1984:231).

By 1951, not only was an illegal drug market and a drug-using subculture firmly established in the United States, but Congress was well on its way to repressing that subculture. In that year it enacted the Boggs Amendment to the Harrison Act, which introduced a law-and-order stance on illegal drug use (including marijuana) by instituting minimum mandatory sentences and prohibiting suspended sentences and probation for second offenses (Ray, 1983:38). In addition, numerous laws enacted since then have continued to increase existing controls over the production, distribution, possession, and sale of what had been judged to be illegal drugs. Thus, behavior previously considered legitimate and legal was subsequently outlawed, the end result being the creation of a new class of criminals.

Eventually, the Comprehensive Drug Abuse, Prevention, and Control Act of 1970 repealed, replaced, and/or updated all pre-existing laws dealing with "dangerous drugs." This law placed all drugs controlled by the act under federal jurisdiction (by the Justice Department rather than the Treasury Department), regardless of involvement in interstate commerce. The law did not, however, "eliminate state regulations; it just makes clear that federal enforcement and prosecution is possible in any illegal activity involving the controlled drugs" (Ray, 1983:40). In addition, the law determined once and for all which drugs in circulation were to be considered dangerous, as well as who would make up the criminal class of drug users. As Graham (1975:107–122) argued in his analysis of the events leading to passage of the 1970 act, its original intent was to control the distribution and use of *all* dangerous drugs. Nevertheless, after considerable lobbying by the pharmaceutical industry, the act concentrated exclusively on drugs imported and/or produced easily by individuals (such as marijuana and heroin). Dangerous drugs produced by pharmaceutical manufacturers (such as amphetamines and tranquilizers like Valium and Librium) were not controlled, even though considerable congressional testimony indicated their use to be more widespread, incapacitating, dangerous, and socially disrupting than narcotic use.

In the 1980s, the United States witnessed new efforts by the federal government to control illegal drugs. Congress enacted the Comprehensive Crime Control Act of 1984 and the Anti-Drug Abuse Act of 1986. Each law strengthened existing drug statutes. In the 1980s, Congress also created the federal position of "drug czar," appointed by the president to oversee policies for marijuana, heroin, and cocaine.

The National Household Survey on Drug Abuse, published annually by the U.S. Department of Health and Human Services, provides data of illicit drug use. This survey is a nationally representative sample of the U.S. population (noninstitutionalized) age twelve years and older. According to its most recent report (U.S. Department of Health and Human Services, 1997:1):

- In 1996, an estimated 13 million Americans were current illicit drug users. The number of current illicit drug users was at its highest level in 1979, when there were 25 million.
- Following a significant increase from 1992 to 1995, between 1995 and 1996 there was a decrease in the rate of past month illicit drug use among youths age 12–17. The rate was 5.2 percent in 1992, 10.9 percent in 1995, and 9.0 percent in 1996. The decrease between 1995 and 1996 occurred in the younger part of this age group, those age 12–15 years.
- For those age 18–25 years, the rate of past month illicit drug use increased from 13.3 percent in 1994 to 15.6 percent in 1996. The rate of past month cocaine use also increased in this age group during this period, from 1.2 percent to 2.0 percent.
- There are an estimated 2.4 million people who started using marijuana in 1995. This was about the same number as in 1994. The annual number of marijuana initiates rose between 1991 and 1994.
- The overall number of current cocaine users did not change significantly between 1995 and 1996 (1.45 million in 1995 and 1.75 in 1996). This is down from a peak of 5.7 million in 1985. Nevertheless, there were still an estimated 652,000 Americans who used cocaine for the first time in 1995.
- There were an estimated 141,000 new heroin users in 1995, and there has been an increasing trend in new heroin use since 1992. A large proportion of these new users were smoking, snorting, or sniffing heroin, and most were under age 26. The estimated number of past month heroin users increased from 68,000 in 1993 to 216,000 in 1996.

Let us examine each of the three most widely used illegal drugs.

Cocaine is the second most widely used illegal drug in the United States and is extracted from the leaves of the Latin American coca plant. It is a stimulant that produces a euphoric reaction. Most users snort cocaine, which consists of drawing the cocaine powder high into the nasal passages. This allows for rapid absorption into the bloodstream and subsequently the brain, leaving the user with a powerful, but brief, high.

Many people ingest "traditional" cocaine, but more and more people in the 1980s and 1990s, especially teenagers, have turned to "crack." This type of cocaine is very potent and became widely available in 1985 and 1986. Crack cocaine hydrochloride powder is transformed into a base state for smoking. The powder is mixed with baking soda or ammonia and water, dried, broken into small "rocks," and then packaged for sale (General Accounting Office, 1988:8).

Extended use of cocaine is dangerous. Approximately 1.4 grams of cocaine is lethal in a 150-pound person; heavy cocaine users exhibit irritability, suspicion paranoia, nervousness, unrelieved fatigue, lapses of attention, inability to concentrate, and hallucinations (Ray, 1983:301). Cocaine also increases the "heart rate and blood flow while simultaneously constricting blood vessels, thus increasing the risk of blood vessel damage and stroke" (Currie, 1993:334). Consumers spend approximately $18 billion a year for cocaine (Lyman and Potter, 1997).

Heroin is produced from opium. For maximum effect it is usually "mainlined"—injected directly into a vein. It is a narcotic that, like cocaine, produces a euphoric reaction. Heroin is highly addictive; one quickly develops a craving for the drug, which can eventually lead to physical dependence. The drug has been found to suppress both respiratory and cardiovascular activity, and a high level of heroin ingestion can produce coma, shock, respiratory arrest, and even death (Inciardi, 1986:52). However, although the drug itself produces "little direct or permanent physiological damage," the dangers of heroin are chiefly related to amounts ingested and to users' disregard for standard practices of good health (for example, poor eating habits and lack of personal hygiene) (pp. 64–65). Not surprisingly, both hepatitis and AIDS (acquired immunodeficiency syndrome) are associated with the sharing of needles by addicts. As Inciardi reported with regard to AIDS, "since this invariably fatal disease was first described in June 1981, intravenous drug users have emerged as its second highest 'at-risk' category. In late 1985, they represented some 17% of the 11,919 known cases. In New York City, heroin users accounted for some 33% of the reported AIDS victims" (1986:65). Consumers spend approximately $12 billion a year for heroin (Lyman and Potter, 1997).

Finally, *marijuana*—the most widely used illegal drug in the United States—is derived from the dried leaves and flowering tops of the *cannabis sativa* plant. The dried parts are crushed and rolled into joints or packed in pipes for smoking. Marijuana does not appear to be addictive, nor are there tolerance or withdrawal symptoms associated with the drug. Moreover, the lethal dose is not known and no human fatalities have been linked to marijuana (Goode, 1984). Of course, this does not mean that adverse effects are not linked to smoking marijuana. Although the drug is not yet fully understood, research indicates that marijuana (1) can injure mucosal tissue, (2) may be more carcinogenic that tobacco, and (3) hinders attention, long-term memory, and psychomotor skill associated with such ac-

---

BOX 11.1   THE DRUG-CRIME CONNECTION

Approximately 60 percent of people arrested for crime test positive for recent drug use (National Institute of Justice, 1998). In some cities, such as Atlanta, Chicago, New York, St. Louis, and San Diego, the number is 70 percent or higher (pp. 15–60). Thus, there seems to be a relationship between drugs and crime. What is that relationship? First, *drugs affect crime* through "drug-defined offenses," such as engaging in various forms of larceny (e.g., robbery, burglary, and auto theft) to obtain cash to purchase illicit drugs. Second, *crime affects drug use.* For example, some individuals may use drugs to eliminate fear of engaging in crime (Walters, 1994). Third, there is a complicated relationship between *addiction* to certain drugs, such as heroin, and crime. Because of the illegal status of, and substantial demand for, addicting drugs, their cost is extreme. Accordingly, this can "push individuals toward crime in order to support their habit (drug-related offenses). Nevertheless, most criminologists argue that this does not mean drug addiction *causes* crime among relatively law-abiding people or that most heroin addicts, for example, engage in crime only after becoming addicted. On the contrary, most men and women who eventually become heroin addicts commit crime "proportionally in excess of their numbers in the population before becoming involved with narcotics" (Goode, 1984:256). Indeed, study after study shows that drug use and crime begin "more or less *independently* without one clearly causing the other" (Currie 1993:170). Nevertheless, arrest rates and self-report studies also show that highest crime rates occur when narcotic users become addicted and that substantially lower crime rates occur prior to addiction, or after addiction has ceased (Currie 1993; Collins, Hubbard, and Rachal, 1985; Gropper, 1985). Moreover, an important study by James Inciardi (1986:122–132) compared narcotic users (primarily heroin) with non-narcotic users (alcohol, sedatives, marijuana, and/or cocaine) for frequency, diversity, and severity of crime committed. His findings showed that the narcotic users "committed more crimes, engaged in a greater diversity of offenses, and significantly larger proportions committed the more serious crimes of robbery and burglary" (p. 129). The overall conclusion, then, of the addiction-crime connection is that drugs do not cause criminality. As Currie stated, "both crime and drug abuse tend to be spawned by the same set of unfavorable social circumstances, and they interact with one another in much more complex ways than the simple addiction-leads-to-crime view proposes" (1993:179). What the evidence does suggest is that *addiction to narcotics like heroin clearly escalates criminal involvement.* It is not addiction per se, however, but addiction to a highly expensive and illegal commodity that escalates criminal involvement.

---

tivities as driving an automobile (Murray, 1986:23–55). Consumers spend approximately $9 billion a year for marijuana (Lyman and Potter, 1997).

Decriminalization/Legalization

The study by Inciardi (1986), cited in Box 11.1, also found that most narcotic users are never arrested. The 573 narcotic addicts committed a total of 215,105 offenses, yet only 609 (0.3 percent) offenses resulted in an arrest—one arrest for every 353 crimes committed. Inciardi concluded that "drug-related crime is out of control, with law enforcement

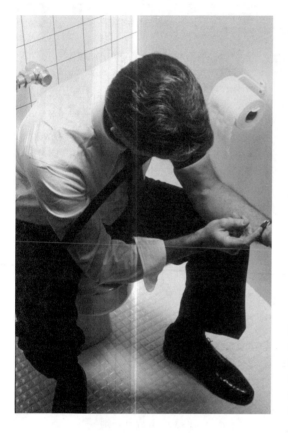

Decriminalization or legalization: A narcotics user "shoots up." Since the criminal justice system seems unable to control illegal drug use, many criminologists suggest decriminalization or legalization as alternatives to prohibitive drug laws.

and the administration of justice incapable of managing it. Since less than 1% of the crimes committed result in arrest, it would appear that the efficient control of drug-related crime is well beyond the scope of contemporary policing" (p. 131).

Others, as well, argue that the criminal justice system has dismally failed in its effort to control illegal drug use. Not only have increased law-and-order policies gone bankrupt—leaving no measurable impact on the drug problem—but according to an American Bar Association report, such policies have "instead distorted and overwhelmed the criminal justice system, crowding dockets and jails, and deluding law enforcement and judicial efforts to deal with the major criminal cases" (cited in Gravley, 1988:3). As Meier and Geis stated after reviewing the evidence: "Not only is the war on drugs not being won, it has not even achieved a stalemate" (1997:103).

Because of the inability of the state to deal adequately with the growing drug abuse problem, many argue that the only alternative is **decriminalization**—the minimization, or actual removal of, criminal prohibitions for illegal drugs while still *regulating* their use. For instance, Edwin Schur argued twenty years ago:

One might believe, for example, that "drug addiction is immoral" or at least highly undesirable and, nonetheless, also conclude that on balance and in actual operation restrictive narcotics laws make a bad situation worse rather than better. If the basic concern is to develop policies that work to minimize the overall social harm associated with a given problem, then using the criminal law merely to express moral disapproval when the actual result of such use will be an exacerbation of the disapproved conditions readily becomes counterproductive. (1979:460)

Decriminalization of marijuana actually has already occurred. Back in 1973, Oregon began to treat marijuana possession of less than one ounce as a misdemeanor, with only a small monetary fine as a sanction. By 1984, ten other states followed Oregon's lead, decriminalizing the possession of small quantities of marijuana (Goode, 1984:viii). In 1986 the Oregon Marijuana Initiative successfully placed a proposition on the state ballot that would have legalized the home growing of marijuana. Although defeated, the proposition received 27 percent of the vote (Gravley, 1988:10). Moreover, in 1996 the Baltimore police commissioner announced that his department would de-emphasize arrests for possessing small quantities of illegal drugs and focus their energy on gun possession and gun-violence (Meier and Geis, 1997).

In the late 1980s several conservatives joined forces with libertarians and called for **legalization** of all drugs and complete removal of all criminal sanctions for drug use, without subsequent regulation. Libertarians assert that the United States should abandon its attempt to "run other people's lives," stop imposing its beliefs on others, and realize that "there is all the difference in the world between deciding that you don't want to do something and trying to force other people to live your way" (Sowell, 1988:19). In other words, libertarians argue that people should be able to ingest whatever they choose as long as they do not violate the rights of others.

Conservatives, such as William F. Buckley and Milton Friedman, argue that prohibitive drug laws are really no match for the laws of supply and demand (Gravley, 1988:3). Not only does there continue to be a large demand for illegal drugs in the United States, but because of the demand, many people become suppliers. This supply operation is so widespread and extensive—contributing substantially to the profits of criminal syndicates—that it is impossible to stop (see Chapter 13.2). Legalization is therefore the only answer for these conservatives.

Others also have argued for the legalization of drugs, especially heroin. Jeffrey Reiman (1995:31–35), for example, has cited the fact that heroin is a relatively safe drug, especially when compared with such legal drugs as tobacco (nicotine) and alcohol. As Reiman stated:

There is no evidence conclusively establishing a link between heroin and disease or tissue degeneration such as that which has been established for tobacco and alcohol. . . . On the basis of the scientific evidence available, there is every reason to suspect that we do our bodies more damage, more *irreversible* damage, by smoking cigarettes and drinking liquor. (p. 27)

Indeed, each year tobacco and alcohol, both of which are addicting, are responsible for 320,000 and 200,000 deaths, respectively. The use of all illegal drugs combined—cocaine, heroin, marijuana, LSD, and so on—accounts for only approximately 3,600 deaths each year. What this means is that deaths resulting from tobacco and alcohol consumption are 150 times larger than all the deaths related to illegal drug consumption (Kappeler, Blumberg, and Potter, 1996).

In addition, Reiman (1995) argued that the illegal status of heroin creates additional harms to society. For example, because suppliers take serious risks, they charge outrageously high prices for addictive drugs. Because addicts need the drug to avoid withdrawal pains, they pay the high prices. What this creates is not merely users of heroin but many users who deal in drugs as well in order to obtain the required money to satisfy their habit. Addicts, therefore constantly look for new people to "turn on," which simply increases the market of heroin addicts.

Finally, Barbara Ehrenreich (1988:21) has argued that drug prohibition has become even more dangerous than drug abuse, causing approximately 7,000 deaths each year through drug-related crime, AIDS, and poisoned drugs—and an $80 billion-a-year economic loss to society. Without some type of legalization, Ehrenreich has argued, we will continue to "feed our legal addictions" while maintaining a large subculture of addicts "who steal for heroin or kill for crack" (p. 21).

11.2   ABORTION

The 1973 Supreme Court decision in the case of *Roe v. Wade* established that women have the constitutional right to choose an **abortion** to end a pregnancy. In this decision the Court established that state laws restricting abortion "only as a *life-saving* procedure on behalf of the mother, without regard to pregnancy stage and without recognition of the other interests involved," are unconstitutional (Goldstein, 1988:347). The Court went on to argue that in the first trimester of pregnancy women have the right to choose abortion without interference from the state. During the second trimester the state cannot prohibit abortion but may regulate abortion procedures in order to ensure the health of the mother. Finally, in the third trimester, abortion can be performed only to preserve the life or health of the mother (p. 347).

Support for Abortion

The public seems to have two related but distinct attitudes regarding support for abortion (Cook, Jelen, and Wilcox, 1992). On the one hand, support for abortion exists in circumstances of physical *trauma:* where the mother's health is in danger, where the fetus is seriously defective, and where the pregnancy results from rape. On the other hand, support for abortion exists for *elective* circumstances: poverty, when an unmarried woman does not want to marry the father, and when a married couple wants no more children.

Most abortions, however, are done for elective reasons. Surveys of abortion patients indicate that only seven percent list one of the three traumatic circumstances (noted above) as their primary reason for seeking an abortion (Cook, Jelen, and Wilcox, 1992:35). The vast majority of abortion patients obtain an abortion because of financial problems, to avoid raising a child outside marriage, or their belief that they are too immature to raise a child (p. 35).

Although most abortion patients obtain an abortion for "elective" reasons, the majority of the public supports abortion for "traumatic" reasons. As Cook, Jelen, and Wilcox (1992:35) pointed out:

- Seventy-six percent support abortion under all three traumatic circumstances, whereas only 7 percent oppose abortion in all three traumatic circumstances.
- Forty-seven percent oppose abortion in all three elective circumstances, whereas 37 percent support abortion under all three elective circumstances.
- Thirty percent favor abortion in all six circumstances, whereas 8 percent oppose abortion in all six circumstances.

An interesting study that investigated the relationship between support for abortion and support for the death penalty is Kimberly Cook's (1998) *Divided Passions: Public Opinions on Abortion and the Death Penalty.* Through in-depth interviews with thirty adult males and females in Mississippi and Maine, Cook found that punitive mentalities tend to underlie their positions. First, the pro-choice and anti-death penalty interviewees were classified as "anti-punitive" because they expressed an interest in curtailing the state's jurisdiction to punish. They were keenly interested in preserving the protection of personal privacy in the abortion decision and expressed a desire to abolish capital punishment altogether while advocating more alternatives to traditional forms of punishment. Second, the pro-choice and pro-death penalty interviewees were classified as "punitive" in a retributive sense. They felt that the state should have the right to punish individuals for offending behaviors and advocated the extension of the state's punitive authority. Irresponsibility in the form of unwanted pregnancy can be legitimately resolved through legal abortions, but women who choose to continue pregnancies should financially support their own children rather than rely on public aid. They felt that punitive sanctions for welfare recipients should be expanded and that the death penalty should also be expanded to all those convicted of killing others, including drug dealers. Third, the anti-abortion and anti-death penalty interviewees were classified as "non-punitive" because they did not offer a clearly articulated sanction toward those who engage in abortion and also did not subscribe to the punitive justifications for capital punishment. Their "sanctity of life" argument extended to those who are condemned as well as to "unborn children." Although they believed that abortion should be illegal, they were more concerned about creating social change so that the common justifications for abortion would no longer appeal to women facing this choice. Fourth, the anti-abortion and pro-death penalty interviewees were classified as "highly punitive" and were motivated by a feeling of vengeance. Stemming from the belief that life begins at conception, abortion becomes equivalent to first-degree murder worthy of capital punishment, and these interviewees advocated complex punishments for abortion and expansion of the death penalty.

In addition, young and unmarried women—especially those in the 15–24 age-group—are more likely than other women to have an abortion (*Statistical Abstract of the U.S.,* 1997:74). Approximately 60 percent of all women undergoing abortions each year since 1973 have been between the ages of fifteen and twenty-four. Moreover, since 1980 slightly more than 50 percent of all abortions were performed at nine or fewer weeks of gestation, and 90 percent were performed at twelve weeks or earlier (p. 74). It appears that for large numbers of

The right to abortion: Demonstrations continue around the country to maintain the legal right to abortion because the availability of safe and reliable abortion is one of the most important factors in the decline of infant and maternal mortality since the 1970s.

young women, abortion has been legitimized in U.S. society. However, fewer women now are obtaining an abortion. For example, in 1994 there were approximately 1.2 million abortions, down 2 percent from the previous year and down substantially from the 1990 figure of approximately 1.5 million (Meier and Geis, 1997).

Nevertheless, abortion rights have gradually eroded since *Roe v. Wade.* The 1976 Hyde Amendment—upheld by the Supreme Court in 1980—eliminates federal Medicaid funds for abortion except in cases of rape and incestuous assault. Insurance coverage of abortion has been eliminated for members of the Peace Corps, Department of Defense, and residents of public hospitals and prisons (Herman, 1984:i). In 1985 all federal funding was cut to international family planning organizations that either counseled or offered abortion (Glen, 1986). Moreover, two major Supreme Court decisions since *Roe v. Wade* have limited abortion rights. In the 1989 *Webster v. Reproductive Health Service* opinion, the Court prohibited the use of public facilities and public funds for both abortions and abortion counseling (Meier and Geis, 1997). And in the 1992 *Planned Parenthood v. Casey* decision, the Supreme Court upheld a Pennsylvania law that requires all women seeking an abortion to hear a lecture by a doctor or watch a video (covering such topics as alternatives to abortion and the medical risks to abortion) and then wait a day before having the abortion (p. 157).

Finally, at least twenty-four states require that young women obtain the consent of one or two parents to proceed with an abortion (Clarke et al., 1993). As Margaret Andersen pointed out, this is especially troubling once we consider the research on teenage sexuality, contraception, and parental relationships:

> Procrastination is the teenager's most frequent reason for delay in initiating contraceptive use; the second most frequent reason is fear that parents will find out. One-third of all teenagers delay going to a clinic because they fear their parents will find out. Regulations that limit the options available to young girls (or anyone else) seem unlikely, then, to solve the problems associated with teenage pregnancy. (1993:195–196)

In Chapter 9 we addressed the issue of child abuse. Here we add the unfortunate given that parental consent legislation actually may lead to physical abuse, and even death, of children. Indeed, parental notification of pregnancy "often precipitates a family crisis, characterized by severe parental anger and rejection of the minor," and therefore "it is reasonable to believe that some minors justifiably fear that they would be treated violently by one or both parents if they had to disclose their pregnancy to their parents" (Clarke et al., 1993:83). Consequently, to avoid parents "finding out," young women in parental consent states may be compelled to seek imprudent measures to maintain the confidentiality of their pregnancy. The case of Becky Bell of Indiana is illustrative. Indiana requires girls under eighteen to obtain the consent of one parent before they can have an abortion. However, not surprisingly, Becky Bell could not bring herself to tell either parent that she was pregnant. Consequently, "she died, the victim of an illegal abortion, an abortion doctors believe she may have given herself" (Halpern, 1990:43). The desire to maintain secrecy has been one of the leading reasons for illegal abortion deaths since the *Roe v. Wade* decision in 1973 (Clarke et al., 1993:83).

History of Abortion

Abortion did not become an issue in the United States until the late 1800s. Between 1800 and 1820 there were no laws related to abortion, and women commonly used either midwives or relatively safe "home remedies" to induce abortion. Women were not considered pregnant until "quickening" occurred—the point at which the fetus could be felt moving—and throughout the entire pregnancy the fetus was not considered a live human being. The first laws on abortion were enacted in the 1820s but concentrated on outlawing certain unsafe methods of inducing abortion rather than abortion itself (Mohr, 1978:3–46). As more and more women began practicing abortion and

> as the practice changed from being invisible to being visible, from being quantitatively insignificant to being a systematic practice that terminated a substantial number of pregnancies after 1840, and from being almost entirely a recourse of the desperate and the socially marginal to being a commonly employed procedure among the middle and upper classes of American society, state legislators decided to reassess their policies toward the practice. (Mohr, 1978:117–118)

This policy reassessment was largely in response to agitation by male physicians, who fought strongly for anti-abortion laws upon several grounds. First, they criticized

BOX 11.2   HARASSMENT AND VIOLENCE AGAINST ABORTION PROVIDERS

The premises of abortion providers have been the object of increasing harassment and violence. Consider three cases from the early 1990s (Meier and Geis, 1997:173–174):

- In 1993 Paul Hill killed a doctor in front of an abortion clinic in Pensacola, Florida. One year later, the doctor who had taken over the job in Pensacola was murdered along with his bodyguard.
- In 1993 Rachelle Shannon shot but did not seriously wound a doctor performing abortions in Kansas.
- In a two-day 1994 rampage in Massachusetts and Virginia, John Salvi III
    1. shot the receptionist and sprayed the waiting room with gunfire at the Brookline Planned Parenthood;
    2. killed the receptionist and wounded five other people at the Preterm Health Service Clinic;
    3. shot out the glass door of the Hillcrest Clinic where he was finally arrested.

As a result of this increasing violence, the Freedom of Access to Clinic Entrances Act, which criminalizes any interference with the entrance or exit to abortion clinics, became law in 1994 (Meier and Geis, 1997:173). As Meier and Geis argued, this law may have contributed to a decline in abortion harassment by the mid-1990s: "A [1995] survey of 310 clinics reported that blockades had all but disappeared and that there were fewer death threats. The number of clinics that suffered acts of vandalism had also dropped from 35% in 1994 to 25% in 1995" (p. 174).

midwives as incompetent to perform such medical procedures. During this period of time there existed a "popular health movement" whose backbone consisted of women healers who instructed audiences around the country in anatomy and personal hygiene—emphasizing preventive care that included such practices as frequent bathing, wearing loose-fitting clothing, and eating whole-grain cereals (Ehrenreich and English, 1973:25). These women were quite knowledgeable about abortion and birth processes, presiding over what was then a successful, female-centered activity (Dye, 1980:98–99). However, male physicians, obtaining economic support from the newly created Rockefeller and Carnegie Foundations, attacked the popular health movement and midwives as incompetent "quacks." Their economic support effectively created medical schools that were closed to midwives. Thus, by the 1860s the white, male, upper-middle-class physicians were regarded as *the* medical profession (p. 100; Ehrenreich and English, 1973:30–33).

Second, the statistics on falling birthrates and rising abortion rates in the United States communicated to these physicians that women who utilized abortion must be engaging in sexual intercourse without intending to procreate—simply having sex "for its own sake." And in nineteenth-century Victorian U.S. society—which defined women's place as in the home to nurture and care for children and husband and to engage in sexual intercourse only to have children—this was deemed threatening (Petchesky, 1984:78–84). As Mohr argued, "to many doctors the chief purpose of women was to produce children; anything that interfered with that purpose, or allowed women to 'indulge' themselves in less important activities, threatened marriage, the family, and the future of society itself" (1978:169).

Thus, sexual conservatism motivated male physicians to demand anti-abortion laws. They argued vociferously against "respectable" women engaging in sex or controlling their sexuality. These physicians attacked abortion among upper-middle-class "native" women while simultaneously supporting eugenic arguments to limit propagation of "lower-class," "unfit," immigrant women (p. 168). As Petchesky writes, "just as the Yankee woman was duty-bound to 'propagate the race' and 'defend the home,' the immigrant, poor, or black woman, regarded as a carrier of disease and a breeder of 'bad stock,' was admonished to avoid reproducing" (1984:79).

Consequently, the male physicians' response to abortion was shaped further by class and racial biases. If respectable women engaged in abortion, physicians argued, they would find themselves outbred by unfit members of society—the poor, foreign born, and racial minorities. Abortion was, in effect, seen as contributing to "race suicide" (Petchesky, 1984:82; Mohr, 1978:167).

For these reasons, then, male physicians strenuously lobbied state legislatures. From 1860 on, state after state enacted laws making abortion a crime for both the physician (or whoever performed the abortion) and the woman (Mohr, 1978:171–200). These laws remained in force until the 1960s. Nevertheless, these laws did not stop abortions from occurring; prior to decriminalization in the mid-1960s, approximately one in three married women underwent an illegal abortion (Meier and Geis, 1997).

Both Linda Gordon (1981) and Rosalind Petchesky (1984) have written about the changing conception of abortion in the 1960s and why abortion was eventually decriminalized in 1973. Gordon (1981:84–85) has argued that the drive for legal abortion in the late 1960s and early 1970s was a response to three factors that developed during the period 1920–1960. First, there was an increase in teenage sexual activity without an accompanying increase in contraceptive use. Thus, "it was not technology that increased sexual activity but the behavior that increased the demand" for contraception and abortion (p. 84). Second, during this time there was a substantial increase in female-headed households as well as in families dependent on two incomes. Without adequate child care facilities, this economic reality made it increasingly impossible for mothers to remain at home caring for an unplanned baby and led to an increased demand for abortion. Finally, Gordon has argued that the lack of safe and effective contraception helped create the movement for legal abortion.

Petchesky (1984:101–132) added to Gordon's explanation, arguing that in the late 1960s and early 1970s certain social conditions merged with a growing feminist movement. This merger created the foundation necessary for the development of legal abortion. Social conditions during the 1960s and the 1970s were such that women in the United States witnessed dramatic changes in their lives, including the following:

1.   later marriage and childbearing among younger women
2.   increasing levels of college attendance among women
3.   rising labor-force participation by women

4. rising divorce rates and increased numbers of female-headed households
5. women's continued primary responsibility for children
6. continued lack of government-funded social services, such as child care
7. women's need to avoid unwanted pregnancy for health reasons, to control their sexuality, and for overall social self-actualization (pp. 103–104)

According to Petchesky, these social conditions in the United States led to falling birthrates and to "a greater need for safe, reliable methods of fertility control among diverse groups of women" (p. 104).

These social conditions helped spawn a number of movements calling for legalization of abortion. One such movement was the emerging second wave of the feminist movement in the 1960s, which championed the ideas of "abortion on demand" and "a woman's right to control over her body." Feminists demanded the unconditional right to abortion. They vehemently opposed simply *reforming* the law through legalization of, for instance, "therapeutic abortions" or abortions only when a woman's health was in danger. Such reforms, feminists argued, would not give reproductive control to women. On the contrary, it simply would transfer control from the police to those who determined whether such medical conditions exist—namely, the male-dominated medical profession. Feminists argued further that this type of reform "implicitly suggested that women were incompetent to act as moral agents on their own behalf" (p. 126). Repeal, however, would abolish all restrictions that might be discriminatory and would not hinder a woman from obtaining an abortion. Repeal would give women the control, capacity, and right to make reproductive decisions, rather than allowing male physicians to control women's reproductive responsibility and, therefore, to act as the sole "moral gatekeepers" of society. Consequently, from 1968 to 1973 feminists directly pressured the medical profession, politicians, and the consciousness of society at large to repeal existing abortion laws. This feminist activism, Petchesky concluded, was critical in the establishment of legal abortion in the United States. It was, in essence, the coming together of the social conditions just discussed and, in particular, the feminist movement generated by those conditions that, Petchesky and Gordon argued, laid the groundwork for the *Roe v. Wade* decision in 1973.

Notwithstanding, feminists are not completely satisfied with the *Roe v. Wade* decision; many believe it does not go far enough. For most feminists, the state must provide uniform, funded, and high-quality abortion services to all women—thus making abortion a "public responsibility" (Petchesky, 1984:384). Moreover, most feminists agree that legal abortion is both minimal and indispensable for women because although it does not create total reproductive freedom for women, it does help minimize certain negative aspects of their responsibility for pregnancy, and although it does not empower women or liberate their sexuality, it does allow women "the space to move from one point in [their] life to the next" (p. 385).

11.3   PROSTITUTION AND PORNOGRAPHY

In the United States, as in most industrialized societies, there is a hierarchical system of sexual value. In other words, some forms of sexuality are defined as "normal" and "natural"; others are deemed "deviant." Marital, reproductive heterosexuals are at the top of the sexual hierarchy, followed closely by unmarried heterosexuals. Further down are those who prefer solitary sexuality, lesbians and gay males, prostitutes, transvestites, and sadomasochists (Rubin, 1984:279). Heterosexuals are rewarded with certified mental health, respectability, legality, social and physical mobility, institutional support, and material benefits. Those below heterosexuals in the hierarchy are often presumed to be mentally ill, disreputable, and criminal; their social and physical mobility is restricted; they have no institutional support; and they face economic sanctions (p. 279). In other words, U.S. culture emphasizes that "there is one best way to do it, and that everyone should do it that way" (p. 283).

Figure 11.1 depicts the sexual hierarchy in the United States. In the final two sections we examine two types of sexuality that are part of the "outer limits" in the figure, prostitution (for money) and pornography.

Prostitution

Most people commonly think of prostitution simply as accepting payment for sexual services. However, this definition is so broad that some monogamous relationships (such as marriage) could be defined as prostitution. Indeed, some define *all* marriages as a form of prostitution. As one radical feminist states, "We have long held that all women sell themselves: that the only available role of a woman—wife, secretary, girlfriend—all demand the selling of herself to one or more men" (cited in Jaggar, 1983:264). We agree that *some* women (and men) may marry for money and that *some* spouses may sexually service their husband/wife in order to receive some type of remuneration. However, we focus our definition of **prostitution** on the consensual grant of *illegal* and *nonmonogamous* sexual services to clients for payment. Although both males and females may become prostitutes, most sociological research has concentrated on female prostitution. Following a brief discussion of male prostitution, the remainder of this section addresses female prostitution.

In terms of numbers, males are clearly the more involved gender in prostitution. This is true for several reasons. First, the transaction in female prostitution entails one female providing sexual services to a number of "johns," or male clients. Second, female prostitutes often work for, and support, a male (namely, a pimp). And third, male prostitutes are probably "as numerous as female prostitutes" (Allen, 1980:399). Consequently, males are the most common actors in prostitution.

According to David Luckenbill (1986:285–286) there exist several types of male prostitutes. First, male prostitutes can be categorized in terms of "sex identification" (whether the prostitute is a heterosexual or homosexual "hustler"), "sex role" (whether or not the prostitute adopts a masculine or feminine role during the transaction), and "sexual services" (the type of service[s] provided—fellatio, sadomasochism, and so on). In addition, Luckenbill identified three major "modes of operation"—street hustler, bar hustler, and escort service:

> The street hustler stands around particular avenues, parks, bus stations, or bookstore entrances, attracts a customer from the passers-by, quickly arranges a sexual sale with him, and then moves to a private setting, to perform a brief sexual exchange.

The charmed circle:
good, normal, natural,
blessed sexuality
Heterosexual
Married
Monogamous
Procreative
Noncommercial
In pairs
In a relationship
Same generation
In private
No pornography
Bodies only
Vanilla

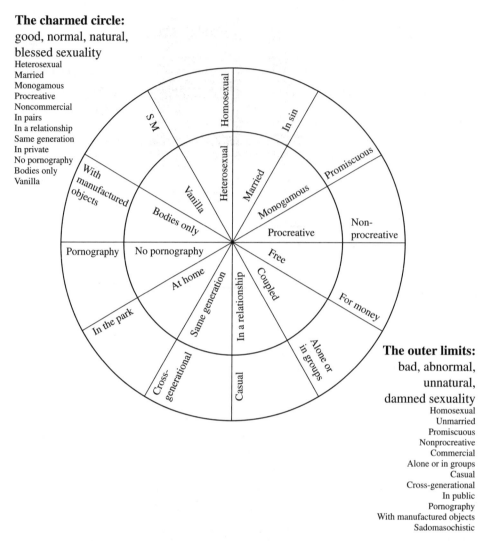

The outer limits:
bad, abnormal,
unnatural,
damned sexuality
Homosexual
Unmarried
Promiscuous
Nonprocreative
Commercial
Alone or in groups
Casual
Cross-generational
In public
Pornography
With manufactured objects
Sadomasochistic

FIGURE 11.1   The Sex Hierarchy

SOURCE: *Rubin,* 1984, p. 281.

The bar hustler frequents particular gay bars or discos, attracts a customer from the patrons, socializes with him for a time, arranges a sale, and moves to a private place for sex. The escort operates through an escort or modeling agency; a customer contacts the agency and requests a "date," the agency operator and customer agree on the terms of the date, and the escort takes the job, contacting the customer at his residence and engaging in sex and other agreed upon activities, such as having dinner. (p. 285)

In the mid-1980s, street hustlers earned approximately $10 to $25 per "trick," bar hustlers from $50 to $70, and escorts between $90 and $140. Accordingly, escort male prostitutes are more likely to attract the higher-paying customers. Because they solicit and operate in a private setting, they are also more likely to minimize risks of operation—such as arrest (p. 286).

A study of male prostitution in London expands on Luckenbill's conclusions. Donald J. West and Buz de Villiers (1993) interviewed fifty "street hustlers" and twenty-five "bar hustlers" and reported in their book *Male Prostitution* that most of these teenage boys describe themselves as gay or bisexual. The vast majority initially resorted to prostitution when they were "either very short or, more often, desperately short of money, sometimes to the extent of having no access otherwise to food or shelter" (p. 161). Prostitution transactions most commonly emerged in their later teens, when youths are expected to begin providing for themselves. For many, lack of family support and education, as well as limited employment options, made prostitution a deceptively easy option, especially for those describing themselves as gay or bisexual. As West and de Villiers concluded, street and bar hustling is not the result of sexual abuse as a young child (as some have suggested) but rather develops from an "urgent need of money as their prime motive for entry into prostitution" (1993:78).

There are approximately 250,000 full-time female prostitutes in the United States, serving 1.5 million customers per week (Miethe and McCorkle, 1998). The female prostitution business has a gross annual income of approximately $7–9 billion (p. 219).

Female prostitution, throughout the 1800s, was condemned in the United States but was not classified as a criminal offense. In the early 1800s, community gangs engaged in the infamous "whorehouse riots," demolishing houses of female prostitution and battling female prostitutes in the streets. These riots did not end female prostitution but helped segregate it within the "red-light districts" of the growing urban slums (Rosen, 1982:4–5). As a result, in the 1860s and 1870s a reform movement emerged that concentrated on regulation of female prostitution. These "regulationists" argued for medical control, maintaining that such control would contribute to overall public health. During this period men were thought to possess an excessive sexual "drive"; women were considered to be asexual. Regulated female prostitution would therefore serve as an "outlet" for those men who could not control their alleged special "drive." Regulation involving both police and medical supervision was seen by its supporters as being in the best interests of both society and the prostitutes. Compulsory medical examinations for female prostitutes rather than the complete suppression of prostitution itself was viewed by regulationists as the answer to prostitution (Messerschmidt, 1987:244).

However, not everyone agreed with the regulationists. Women involved in the late nineteenth- and early twentieth-century feminist movement opposed regulation. Feminists argued that regulation forced female prostitutes into vaginal examinations and licensing, thus providing men with the freedom to engage in sex with female prostitutes without acquiring venereal disease. They further showed that by not inspecting the men, regulation failed to regulate those men who were carriers of venereal disease—therefore not really protecting anyone. According to feminists, then, regulation actually served the interests of the men (customers) rather than the women (prostitutes) (p. 244). In the end, the movement *against* regulation in the United States proved so strong and successful that only one city (St. Louis) ever tried it, and the experiment there lasted for only four years (p. 245).

In spite of the "regulation" victory, feminists united with the conservative social purity movement of the time (a movement to reform sexual mores) to press for the actual *abolition* of female prostitution itself. This motley group consolidated into an abolitionist movement that embraced a program of social purity measures. Feminists argued that the alleged male "excessive drive" had to be eliminated. The abolition of female prostitution would contribute to this end by forcing men to control their "drive" and thereby raising men to the level of purity of women (pp. 246–247).

Subsequently, in the early 1900s state legislatures began enacting laws aimed at closing down red-light districts. Iowa enacted the first law in 1909—the Red-Light Abatement Act—making it illegal to maintain a building for "immoral purposes." By 1917 thirty-one states had enacted similar laws (Rosen, 1982:28–29). However, these laws failed to reduce female prostitution. On the contrary, because female prostitutes could not find "respectable work," new forms of prostitution emerged. As Rosen reported:

> Since brothels and parlor houses could no longer advertise their wares, rooming houses, flats, hotels, and massage parlors became the predominant sites for prostitution. To avoid detection, madams and prostitutes who had once catered to a wealthy clientele began to rely on the "call girl" system of prostitution, in which customers call to see a particular prostitute. In this way, connections could be made secretly without danger of police harassment. . . . For the majority of poor women, however, the closing of the houses meant increased streetwalking, which was immediately noticed in most American cities. Without recognized districts or brothels, prostitutes could no longer receive customers in the semiprotected environment of the brothel or district. Instead, they had to search for business in public places—hotels, restaurants, cabarets, or on the street. (p. 32)

This search for customers in public places made female prostitutes vulnerable to violent clients and police harassment. Consequently, control of female prostitution began to change hands. Because of the new conditions resulting from the abolitionist movement, female prostitutes turned to male pimps to help them ward off dangers, provide legal assistance, and offer some additional support. Eventually, the overall female prostitute/male "john" transaction became dominated by individual pimp entrepreneurs or male-dominated criminal syndicates (Rosen, 1982:33). Today, female prostitutes continue to search for customers in such public places as streets, bars, and hotels, and they work in a variety of private settings, such as massage parlors or brothels.

Women who work the streets often participate in prostitution subcultures, where they work together and rely on each other for safety and support. Within the subcultures they are emotionally and financially interdependent (Rosenblum, 1975:180). Moreover, many women who work the streets "laugh at the notion of having a pimp and say they only use men to give them back-up protection" (Andersen, 1988:258). However, Miller (1986:35–43) reported, in her in-depth examination of street women in Milwaukee, that most female prostitution is conducted in the context of "deviant street networks," or groups of individuals mobilized to carry out a variety of illegal behaviors, such as prostitution, larceny, check and credit-card fraud, auto theft, drug traffic, burglary, and robbery. Thus, although the women in Miller's study were involved in prostitution, there was also some diversity in their "hustling" activity.

Miller (p. 36) also reported that men clearly dominate the deviant street networks in Milwaukee. Commonly referred to as pimps, these men (while engaging in some property crime themselves) live off the earnings of the female prostitute and act as her agent and/or companion. The pimp usually controls two to three women, who are referred to on the streets as "wives-in-law" (pp. 37–38). In return for their earnings, the pimp may provide companionship, someone to live and be with. One female prostitute defined her relationship with her pimp as "just knowing that you have somebody there all the time, not just for protection, just someone you can go to" (James, 1982:304).

The pimp is not the only type of deviant street network "manager." Another type, referred to as the "man," works together with a single female prostitute, rather than two or three women. The "man," usually a husband or lover, not only shares the proceeds but is always close by, protecting his "woman" and supervising on-the-spot transactions (Cohen, 1980:56). As Cohen (p. 56) pointed out, the difference between the pimp and the man is that the prostitute works *for* a pimp but *with* a man.

The relationship between a female prostitute and pimp or man is not always conflict-free and can result in forced prostitution. That is, if the female prostitute attempts to depart the relationship, she may find that her pimp or man becomes violent and brutal. Thus, many prostitutes are physically victimized by their "partner" and customers (Miller and Schwartz, 1994).

Many "street walkers" today are teenage girls who have runaway from abusive homes (Chesney-Lind, 1997). As Meda Chesney-Lind has pointed out, "it is no accident that girls on the run from abusive homes or on the streets because of profound poverty get involved in criminal activities that exploit their sexual object status. American society has defined youthful, physically perfect women as desirable" (p. 29). Thus, girls on the street exchange their bodies for economic survival.

Moreover, the mid-1980s emergence of crack cocaine on the streets of the United States led to research interest in the relation between crack and participation in prostitution. Some criminologists argue that selling crack now provides a new opportunity for women on the street, generating a larger share of street women's income than in the past and, simultaneously, decreasing women's reliance on prostitution (Inciardi, Lockwood, and Pottieger, 1993; Fagan, 1994; Mieczkowski, 1994). As Fagan has argued, "the expansion of drug markets in the cocaine economy has provided new ways for women to escape their limited roles, statuses and incomes" (1994:210).

However, other research challenges this "new opportunity" perspective, arguing that not much has changed for street-level prostitutes (Maher and Daly, 1996; Maher and Curtis, 1992; Maher, 1997). Although in theory we might expect that an expansion of the cocaine market would provide more opportunities for street women to earn money, the real world of gender inequality suggests this is not the case—it is men who control the selling of crack on the street. As Maher and Daly (1996), Maher and Curtis (1992), and Maher (1997) have shown in studies of street women in New York City, the only consistent economic option for women on the street is prostitution. What has changed, then, is not "new opportunities" to move out of prostitution if they desired but, rather, increased adverse effects on their working lives from widespread crack consumption in poverty-ridden neighborhoods: "The market became flooded with novice sex workers, the going rates for sexual transactions decreased, and 'deviant' sexual expectations by dates increased, as did the levels of violence and victimization" (Maher and Daly, 1996:484).

Female prostitutes also work in settings other than "the streets." Two common private settings for female prostitution are massage parlors and brothels. The massage parlor prostitute usually, but not always, works for a male parlor manager who hires the masseuses, collects the clients' fees, keeps the books, and pays the masseuses. However, some massage parlors form "sisterhoods" to operate the parlor, sharing management duties and supporting one another. Most massage parlors in the United States are, of course, fronts for prostitution, in which the prostitute provides a massage and a variety of sexual services as well (Simon and Witte, 1982:244–246). The madam of a brothel operates somewhat like the massage parlor manager by hiring, firing, keeping records, and paying salaries. A typical brothel employs from two to four female prostitutes. But the brothel differs from the massage parlor in one important respect—it does not provide a legitimate service (such as a massage) and does not, therefore, have a legitimate front (p. 246). Probably the most well-known madam is Heidi Fleiss, who maintained an exclusive brothel in Los Angeles. Fleiss's "girls" made as much as $50,000 per month catering sexual services to politicians, film personalities, and businessmen. Fleiss was eventually convicted of pandering, conspiracy, income-tax evasion, and money laundering and was sentenced to three years in prison (Meier and Geis, 1997).

Finally, some female prostitutes work for the manager of a bar or hotel, who pays the women a 40 to 50 percent commission. Prostitutes working in bars may also be part- or full-time barmaids, waitresses, or strippers (Simon and Witte, 1982:246); the "high-class" female prostitutes working in hotels are known as "call girls." Not all call girls work in hotels, however; some simply work solo out of their home or apartment.

It is estimated that streetwalkers compose approximately 20 percent of all female prostitutes, call girls 15 percent, and that 65 percent work in an establishment of some type—25 percent in massage parlors, 15 percent in brothels, 15 percent in bars, and 10 percent in hotels (Simon and Witte, 1982:253). Moreover, the buyers of prostitution are less likely to be criminalized by the criminal justice system even though their behavior is likewise illegal. Prostitutes are arrested nearly twice as often for prostitution as are "johns" (Miethe and McCorkle, 1998:221). Yet as Lynn Chancer (1998) pointed out, prostitution entails a buyer-seller interaction in which the buyer is essential to the transaction. "The sexual demands (and economic resources) of a primarily male clientele could even be said to be more important to the system than prostitutes entering this profession on the side of supply: men's desire precedes, and functions as a necessary condition for sustaining, prostitution's existence" (p. 181).

Only one state in the United States has legalized prostitution. In 1971 the Nevada state legislature legalized regulated prostitution within licensed brothels (Chapkis, 1997). Only smaller counties in Nevada (rather than the large tourist cities, such as Reno, Las Vegas, and Lake Tahoe) were authorized to license brothels. However, this did not eliminate prostitution in the tourist areas: "Illegal prostitutes continue to far out-

The Hollywood madam: Probably the most well-known brothel madam is Heidi Fleiss, who maintained an exclusive brothel in Los Angeles. Fleiss's "girls" made as much as $50,000 per month catering sexual services to politicians, film personalities, and businessmen. Fleiss was eventually convicted of pandering, conspiracy, income-tax evasion, and money laundering; she was sentenced to three years in prison.

number those working legally in the state's licensed brothels" (p. 62). Moreover, the working conditions at Nevada's brothels are oppressive (pp. 163–164):

- The prostitutes are defined as "independent contractors" with no claim to health benefits, vacation pay, or retirement benefits.
- The prostitutes are required to live on premises while working and must register with the police.
- A standard shift runs 12–14 hours a day, seven days a week, for 21 days.
- Half of prostitutes' earned income goes to brothel management, and women's incomes are additionally reduced through brothel fees for room, board, and supplies (including condoms).
- Prostitutes cannot refuse customers unless management agrees.

As with other public-order crimes, differing opinions exist regarding prostitution. Some maintain that the female prostitute is clearly the victim of prostitution, being exploited and treated simply as a sexual object by the pimp and customer alike. Kathleen Barry has gone so far as to refer to female prostitution as "female sexual slavery":

> Because it is invisible to social perception and because of the clandestine nature of its practices, it is presently impossible to statistically measure the incidence of female sexual slavery. But considering the arrested sexual development that is understood to be normal in the male population and considering the numbers of men who are pimps, procurers, members of syndicate and freelance slavery gangs, operators of brothels and massage parlors, connected with sexual exploitation entertainment, pornography purveyors, wife beaters, child molesters, incest perpetrators, johns (tricks) and rapists, one cannot help but be momentarily stunned by the enormous male population participating in female sexual slavery. The huge number of men engaged in these practices should be cause for a declaration of a national and international emergency, a crisis in sexual violence. But what should be cause for alarm is instead accepted as normal social intercourse. (1979:220)

Thus, some people argue that society should find a way for female prostitutes to "escape their plight" (Cole, 1987:35).

However, some respond by arguing that prostitutes are not helpless victims who must be "saved." In her book *Live Sex Acts: Women Performing Erotic Labor,* Wendy Chapkis (1997) has documented, through the words of prostitutes themselves, the oppressive conditions they face in their everyday working lives. Yet these prostitutes do not criticize prostitution per se but, rather, they attribute their plight to the poor working conditions experienced and the illegal nature of their "profession." Thus, rather than criminalizing sex workers through the legal system, Chapkis has called for guaranteed full workers' rights and benefits for all prostitutes and the decriminalization of this consensual sexual activity.

Similarly, Margo St. James (1987:86), founder of Call Off Your Old Tired Ethics (COYOTE)—a female prostitute union that provides such legal services as bail and counseling for arrestees, as well as child care services for prostitutes—has said that the view of the female prostitute as "victim" and "sexual slave" is patronizing and condescending. St. James has argued that "in private the whore has power. She is in charge, setting the terms for the sexual exchange and the financial exchange. In public, of course, she has absolutely no rights—no civil rights, no human rights. Prostitution laws are how women are controlled in this society" (p. 82).

Moreover, regarding their relationship with pimps and their man, three female prostitutes have stated that those who oppose prostitution "use the pimp issue and the abuse issue as a way out, always pointing to him and pointing to the way we have to work as being very corrupt, when in fact these laws were the result of prostitutes being ostracized by society in general and specifically feminists" (Scott, Miller, and Hotchkiss, 1987:205).

Another female prostitute responded:

> I'm not condoning the men who do work several women, who are brutal—of course I'm not condoning that—but I would like to suggest to you that as adult women we have the right to choose a good man, a bad man. I don't want the culture telling me what man I can live with. I don't like knowing that the police can come and take my

man away at any moment. I could go home now and find him gone. The inferiority with which we are regarded is directed as well at the clients and the pimps. (Cited in Bell, 1987:119)

Finally, female prostitutes have argued that a democratic morality should be used to judge all sexual acts. Female prostitutes do not see themselves as sexual objects but rather as engaging in a specific type of sexuality that is stigmatized in this society. As Scott, Miller, and Hotchkiss have put it:

And we think the real thing is what works for the individual, and let's allow that individual to have that choice of what is the real thing for them. We don't want anyone telling us what kind of sex we can have, whether it's for money or not. And we certainly wouldn't tell anybody else what kind of sex they could have. We wouldn't go into a meeting of lesbians and say, "Well, we don't think that this kind of sex is right." Or we wouldn't go into a meeting at church and say, "Well, this kind of sex, if you're married and madly in love is not all right." (1987:208)

Increasingly, other sociologists are supporting many of these views held by female prostitutes. Although opposing gender inequality and, therefore, the male-dominated nature of the female prostitution "business" (just as they oppose gender inequality in other areas of society), these sociologists do not argue for the dissolution of commercial sex because it does not benefit the women involved. Rather, they emphasize the need for society to provide all women with equal opportunities to enter any type of employment they wish (Jaggar, 1983:180–181). As Lynn Chancer recently argued, society should concentrate on "guaranteed jobs and income support for all women (including health and child care, and family allowances where applicable). Under such conditions, women would never have to become sex workers out of necessity rather than interest" (1998:196). Moreover, rather than viewing female prostitution as degrading and the prostitute as a passive victim, more and more people regard female prostitution as a legitimate form of sexuality. Accordingly, they argue that we should work to empower women within the sex industry itself.

Pornography

Another sexually related topic under debate is **pornography**, which is usually defined as sexually explicit acts and depictions that have little or no artistic merit. Today, pornography is widely available through magazines, videos, cable television, CD-ROM, the Internet, and strip clubs. Indeed, the "porno industry" receives widespread support as U.S. citizens spend approximately $2.5 billion annually on pornography (Miethe and McCorkle, 1998).

In one of the earliest discussions of pornography by a criminologist, Ernest van den Haag (1969), attempted to answer the question, Is pornography a cause of crime? Not only did van den Haag answer in the affirmative—arguing that pornography "can contribute to the formation of dispositions" or pornography can "precipitate the action, once the disposition has been formed for whatever reasons"—but he also maintained that it was important to censor pornography (p. 841). As van den Haag suggested, "if we indulge pornography, and do not allow censorship to restrict it, our society at best will become ever more coarse, brutal, anxious, indifferent, de-individualized, hedonistic; at worst its ethos will disintegrate altogether" (p. 845).

One year later, the 1970 Commission on Obscenity and Pornography disagreed with van den Haag's position, concluding in its report that it had "found no evidence that exposure to explicit sexual materials plays a significant role in the causation of delinquent or criminal behavior among youth or adults" (Commission, 1970:27). In addition, the commission pointed out that explicit sexual imagery may in fact increase "the frequency and variety of coital performance . . . and conversation about sexual matters" (p. 25). The commission concluded that censorship was unwarranted.

In the 1980s pornography once again became an issue of governmental concern. The Attorney General's Commission on Pornography, headed by Edwin Meese, was formed in 1985 and released its report in July 1986. The commission membership clearly reflected the attorney general's political agenda. The panel was chaired by Henry Hudson, an anti-vice prosecutor from Arlington, Virginia, who was commended by President Reagan for "closing down every adult bookstore in his district" (Vance, 1986:76). Moreover, prior to being selected, seven of the eleven panel members had each indicated publicly their opposition to pornography and the importance of controlling it (p. 76).

The Meese Commission identified four types of sexual imagery: (1) sexually violent material; (2) nonviolent material depicting degradation, subordination, and humiliation; (3) nonviolent and nondegrading material; and (4) nudity. Not surprisingly, the commission concluded that all sexual imagery is in some way harmful but that the first two types are the most dangerous. Sexually violent material—defined as "actual or simulated violence presented in sexually explicit fashion with a predominant focus on the sexually explicit violence" (Meese Commission, 1986:323)—includes material depicting sadomasochistic themes, rape, and sexually motivated murder. After analyzing experimental laboratory research, the Meese Commission concluded that there is "a causal relationship between exposure to material of this type and aggressive behavior toward women" (p. 324). Regarding nonviolent material depicting degradation, subordination, and humiliation, the Meese Commission includes sexual imagery depicting women as (1) "existing solely for the sexual satisfaction of others," (2) "in decidedly subordinate roles in their sexual relations with others," or (3) "engaged in sexual practices that would to most people be considered humiliating" (p. 331). The Meese Commission concluded that experimental laboratory research indicates that substantial exposure to material of this type is "likely to increase the extent to which those exposed will view rape or other forms of sexual violence as less serious than they otherwise would have, will view the victims of rape and other forms of sexual violence as significantly more responsible, and will view the offenders as significantly less responsible" (p. 332). Thus, according to the Meese Commission, pornography causes males to be violent toward females.

Evidence for the alleged harmful effects of pornography was gathered primarily from the experimental laboratory research of two psychologists, Neil Malamuth and Edward Donnerstein. Although the Meese Commission accepted the findings of these researchers, it completely ignored the criticisms of this type of research made by other so-

Does pornography cause violence against women? Studies have been unable to show that pornography causes violence against women. Whereas some criminologists argue that pornography subordinates women and sexually objectifies them, others argue that pornography often benefits women by advocating sexual adventure for pleasure.

cial scientists, as well as the psychologists' own admonition that care must be exercised in interpreting their findings. Caution, the psychologists argued, must be exercised because the duration of the effects of exposure to pornography in the laboratory (for instance, the attitudinal changes could disappear immediately upon leaving the lab) is unknown, and although pornography may reinforce and strengthen already existing beliefs and values, there is no evidence it causes predispositions toward violence (Donnerstein and Linz, 1986:56–59). Moreover, there are other problems associated with this research. For instance, what people *tell* researchers they believe and what people *think* they will do might differ from what they *actually* do. In other words, we cannot generalize from controlled laboratory situations to situations outside the laboratory: If people do one thing in the lab, this does not necessarily mean they will do it outside the lab. In contrast to the Meese Commission, Thelma McCormack, in an exhaustive review of research on pornography, found "no systematic evidence to link either directly or indirectly the use of pornography with rape" (1985:192). In a more recent examination of research on pornography and violence against women, Michael Kimmel concluded:

In aggregate studies and in the laboratories, researchers have not been able to isolate pornography as the cause of violence against women. The pervasiveness of rape and violence, even in the absence of a single causal mechanism, means that we have a larger and more diffuse constellation of masculine attitudes to confront. (1993:8)

In addition to its remarkable acceptance of the experimental laboratory research without probing its weaknesses, the Meese Commission was also criticized for its simplistic definitions. For example, the commission included sadomasochistic (S/M) material as "violent pornography," yet it

called no witnesses to discuss the nature of S/M, either professional experts or typical participants. They ignored a small but increasing body of literature that documents important features of S/M sexual behavior, namely consent and safety. Typically, the conventions we use to decipher ordinary images are suspended when it comes to S/M images. When we see war movies, for example, we do not leave the theatre believing that the carnage we saw was real or that the performers were injured making the films. But the commissioners assumed that images of domination and submission were both real and coerced. (Vance, 1986:81)

Moreover, it is circular reasoning to define "humiliating sexual practices" as those "that would to most people be considered humiliating." It also implicitly assumes that there is somewhat of a consensus about the nature of humiliating sexual practices. Yet, no evidence suggests such a consensus exists. In fact, the evidence suggests that one person's humiliating sexual practice is another person's sexuality. Nevertheless, the Meese Commission concluded that pornography is harmful and that it should be controlled through the vigorous enforcement of obscenity laws.

Nevertheless, Schwartz and DeKeseredy's examination of woman abuse in dating relationships reported research showing that approximately 8–10 percent of college women state that they had been upset by their college dating partners "trying to get them to do what they had seen in pornographic media" (1997:86). Moreover, of those college women who had been forced into sexual acts since leaving high school, "22.3 percent had also been upset by attempts to get them to imitate pornographic scenarios" (p. 86). Despite this evidence, Schwartz and Dekeseredy concluded that pornography most likely does not cause violence against women because

the same factors that cause a man to abuse women [may] also cause him to purchase pornography. So, for example, if there is a factor such as an identified group of men with exceptionally anti-female attitudes on campus, it is possible that these anti-female attitudes cause them to attack women, and the same anti-female attitudes cause them to purchase pornographic materials. . . . [Thus] getting rid of all pornography would not change anything at all. The anti-female attitudes would still cause the sexual assault of women. (p. 88)

The U.S. Supreme Court has consistently ruled that pornography is not protected by the First Amendment of the Constitution, which prohibits any law from impending freedom of speech and press. In 1957 the Court ruled in *Roth v. U.S.* that if "the dominant theme" of any sexual imagery appeals to the "prurient interests" of the average person in a community, such material is deemed obscene (*Roth v. U.S.*, 354 U.S. 476 [1957]). Obviously, this decision has its problems. For example, it can be difficult to determine a dominant theme. Can we agree on the nature of "prurient interests"? What is the "average person"? Recognizing these problems, the Supreme Court attempted to be more precise in *Miller v. California* (1973). According to *Miller,* material is obscene if

1. the average person, applying contemporary community standards, would find that the work, taken as a whole, appeals to prurient interests;
2. the work depicts or describes, in a patently offensive way, sexual conduct;
3. the work, taken as a whole, lacks serious literary, artistic, political, or scientific value (*Miller v. California,* 413 U.S. 15 [1973]).

However, some oppose pornography because of an alleged harm against women. Pornography is seen as maintaining gender inequality by legitimizing violence against, and objectifying and dehumanizing, women. Therefore, pornography (MacKinnon, 1984:321–329)

1. subordinates women through sex, harming women openly, publicly, and with social legitimacy;
2. commodifies and objectifies women as possessions, to be controlled by men and used by men as men please;
3. promotes violence toward women as pleasing, pleasurable, and enjoyable by *both* men and women.

As such, numerous researchers assert that pornography institutionalizes the second-class citizenship of *all* women, hampers the sexual equality of women, and helps maintain male control in all spheres of society—employment, education, politics, media, courts, and in the home (see the various articles in Lederer, 1980).

In 1983, Catharine MacKinnon and Andrea Dworkin attempted to outlaw pornography—and thereby move beyond obscenity laws—by declaring, in the now famous "Minneapolis Ordinance," that pornography is a form of sex discrimination and a violation of women's rights. The ordinance was enacted by the Minneapolis city council but was vetoed by the mayor. A similar law was enacted in Indianapolis but was subsequently declared unconstitutional by a federal judge. The Minneapolis Ordinance defined pornography as "the sexually explicit subordination of women, graphically depicted, whether in pictures or in words" that includes one or more of nine categories of sexual imagery. If the ordinance had been enacted, it would have permitted individual women to initiate civil lawsuits against pornographers who cause harm by trafficking in pornography, coercing people into pornographic performances, forcing pornography on a person, or assaulting or physically attacking someone due to pornography.

MacKinnon offered the case of Linda Marchiano ("Linda Lovelace" in the movie *Deep Throat*) as an example of the type of pornography covered by the law. If the law were implemented, that movie would be actionable on two counts: coercion into pornographic performance (because Marchiano alleges she was coerced into making the movie) and trafficking in pornography (because the movie allegedly presents women as sexual objects). As MacKinnon stated, the film "subordinates women by using women . . . sexually, specifically as eager servicing receptacles for male genitalia and ejaculate. The majority of the film represents 'Linda Lovelace' in, minimally, postures of sexual submission and/or servility" (cited in Duggan, Hunter, and Vance, 1985:138).

MacKinnon (1984:335–340) argued further that the Minneapolis Ordinance does not abridge the freedom of speech of pornographers but promotes the freedom of speech of women. In a gender-unequal society, MacKinnon stated, the speech of the powerful (men) becomes dominant and, therefore, pornography (as "male speech") "invents women because it has the power to make its vision into reality, which then passes, objectively, for truth" (p. 337). Consequently, for MacKinnon, a law like the Minneapolis Ordinance provides women a means with which to obtain access to speech (p. 340).

Recognizing that pornography is embedded in a gender inegalitarian society, some nevertheless assert that we can likewise uncover progressive forces in pornography. Zillah Eisenstein has argued that in pornography "females are displayed as subjugated, objectified women. Pornography's scope, however, is broader than this; it includes fantasy and rebellion as well. Multiple meanings coexist within pornography, and they crisscross the realms of real and ideal" (1988:163).

Duggan, Hunter, and Vance (1985:145) likewise argued that pornography serves a number of social functions that benefit women, such as ridiculing conventional sexual mores and advocating sexual adventure, sex outside marriage, sex for no reason other than pleasure, casual sex, anonymous sex, group sex, voyeuristic sex, illegal sex, and public sex. Finally, Paula Webster has pointed out that pornography contains important messages for women because "it does not tie women's sexuality to reproduction or to the domesticated couple or exclusively to men" (1981:50). Indeed, Duggan, Hunter, and Vance have explained, using the example of *Deep Throat,* how this is accomplished: "In it, the main female character is shown both actively seeking her own pleasure and as trying to please men; a secondary female character is shown as actually directing encounters with multiple male partners" (1985:138–139).

These same authors have argued that the Minneapolis Ordinance never explicitly defined what was meant by "the sexually explicit subordination of women." This deficit exemplified a reality touched on earlier: One person's subordination can easily be another person's sexuality. As Duggan, Hunter, and Vance went on to point out:

> To some, *any* graphic sexual act violates women's dignity and therefore subordinates them. To others, consensual heterosexual lovemaking within the boundaries of procreation and marriage is acceptable, but heterosexual acts that do not have reproduction as their aim lower women's status and hence subordinate them. Still others accept a wide range of nonprocreative, perhaps even nonmarital, heterosexuality but draw the line at lesbian sex, which they view as degrading. (p. 140)

Duggan, Hunter, and Vance (pp. 144–146) argued that people should oppose this type of legislation because sexual imagery does not cause more harm to women than do other aspects of a sexist culture, and pornography, even in a sexist society, does serve some positive functions for women. However, these authors (pp. 146–151) went beyond this argument, correctly reasoning that passage of such laws would impede rather than enhance women's goals—that is, such laws would (1) do nothing to improve the material conditions of women's lives, (2) divert attention from support for other laws that would enhance women's condition, and (3) force pornography underground (rather than eliminate it), worsening the working conditions in the available sex industry.

REVIEW

This chapter examined four types of public-order "crimes"—drug use, abortion, prostitution, and pornography. There is considerable debate as to whether these behaviors should be criminalized by the state. Nevertheless, it is clear that the state selectively enforces public-order laws.

Drug Use

1. The criminal law itself contributes to the creation of an illegal drug market and subculture.

2. The most widely used illegal drugs are cocaine, heroin, and marijuana, whose dangers are attributed primarily to their illegal status.

3. Drugs do not cause crime, yet addiction to narcotics such as heroin clearly escalates criminal involvement.

4. Some argue that drug-related crime is so out of control, and the distribution of illegal drugs sufficiently unstoppable, that the only answer is to decriminalize, or even legalize, the drugs that are presently illegal.

Abortion

1. In *Roe v. Wade* (1973), the Supreme Court established that women have a constitutional right to abortion.

2. The public overwhelmingly supports the *Roe v. Wade* decision.

3. The history of abortion in the United States shows that it first became illegal after 1860 because of pressure from the male-dominated medical profession.

4. Certain social conditions in the 1960s and 1970s, as well as the second wave of the feminist movement, led to the decriminalization of abortion in 1973.

Pornography and Prostitution

1. Prostitution and pornography are within the "outer limits" of the sexual hierarchy.

2. Both males and females are involved in prostitution, men more frequently than women.

3. The major types of male prostitution are street hustler, bar hustler, and escort service.

4. The abolitionist movement of the early 1900s led to the control of prostitution by pimps and male-dominated criminal syndicates.

5. Contemporary female prostitutes search for customers in such public and private settings as the streets, bars, hotels, massage parlors, and brothels.

6. The debate continues as to whether prostitution is a "victimless" crime.

7. In 1970 the Commission on Obscenity and Pornography concluded that pornography was harmless; in 1986 the Attorney General's Commission on Pornography argued the opposite.

8. Researchers have pointed out several shortcomings in the latter commission's methodology.

QUESTIONS FOR CLASS DISCUSSION

1. Discuss whether the terms "victimless" or "complaintless" crimes adequately describe the nature of public-order "crimes."

2. We identified certain means by which the state selectively enforces morality. Can you identify any others? What impact does such selective enforcement have on the notion of public-order "crimes"?

3. Should heroin, cocaine, and marijuana be decriminalized, legalized, or more seriously controlled?

4. Should prostitution be legalized in all states?

5. Does "pornography" oppress women?

6. Of the theories presented in Part Two, which one best addresses the issues surrounding public-order crime?

FOR FURTHER STUDY

Readings

Cook, Kimberly. 1998. *Divided Passions: Public Opinions on Abortion and the Death Penalty.* Boston: Northeastern University Press.

Currie, Elliot. 1993. *Reckoning: Drugs, the Cities, and the American Future.* New York: Hill and Wang.

Meier, Robert F., and Gilbert Geis. 1997. *Victimless Crimes? Prostitution, Drugs, Homosexuality, Abortion.* Los Angeles: Roxbury.

Websites

1. <http://lindesmith.org/lindesmith/home.html>: The Lindesmith Center and its director Ethan Nadelman is a major source of reliable and useful information regarding the status and use of illegal drugs in the United States. This site provides databases for searching and on-line materials.

2. <http://www.december.com/cmc/mag/1996/cavalier.html>: This is an article by Robert Cavalier discussing the ethical issues surrounding pornography and feminism. Many important debates are summarized in this article.

3. <http://www.prevent-abuse-now.com/help10e.html>: This site is devoted to ending child pornography and abuse, including child pornography distributed on the Internet.
4. <http://www.agi-usa.org/abortion>: The Alan Guttmacher Institute is the leading source of reliable information regarding abortion rates and abortion laws in the United States. Readers can find up-to-date statistics and access barriers to legal abortion.
5. <http://www.bayswan.org/additional.html>: This is the URL for the Prostitutes' Education Network. It provides useful information for those who are researching the sex industry, from the perspective of the sex workers.

12.1 A History of Syndicated Crime

"Mafia" in Sicily

Syndicated Crime in the United States, 1800–1930

A National Crime Syndicate?

12.2 Syndicated Crime Today

Patron–Client Relationships

12.3 Principal Forms of Syndicated Crime

Syndicates and Illegal Goods and Services

Syndicates and Legitimate Businesses

Syndicates and the State

Preview

Chapter 12 introduces:
- the history of syndicated crime in the United States
- the structure and extent of syndicated crime in the United States today
- the principal forms of syndicated crime and their social costs

Key Terms

bookmaking	mafia
criminal syndicate	money laundering
labor racketeering	numbers
loan sharking	

The core of syndicated crime (commonly referred to as "organized crime") is the provision of illegal goods and services in a society that displays a continued and considerable demand for such goods and services. Syndicated crime has developed a structure that makes it possible to provide such goods and services on a regular basis. This structure can best be understood as a variety of **criminal syndicates**—associations of individuals such as businesspeople, police, politicians, and criminals—formed to conduct specific illegal enterprises for the purpose of making a profit. These enterprises include illegal gambling, illegal drug distribution, loan sharking, and such other illegal activities as money laundering, labor racketeering, and prostitution. However, the specific structure of a syndicate depends on its specific illegal activity. Thus, although criminal syndicates are highly organized, a syndicate engaged in the distribution of illegal drugs, for example, is structured differently than one engaged in illegal gambling.

In this chapter we examine three major aspects of syndicated crime: its history, its structure, and its principal activities today. We begin with a history of syndicated crime.

12.1   A HISTORY OF SYNDICATED CRIME

When we commonly think of "organized crime" (what we call syndicated crime), usually the first term that comes to mind is "the Mafia." However, we rarely ask ourselves where this term originated or whether it is appropriate to use such a term to describe syndicated crime in the United States. In this section we attempt to answer these two questions.

"Mafia" in Sicily

The word "mafia" is not found in Italian or Sicilian writings until the nineteenth century, and even then it designated a *method* rather than an *organization* (Albini, 1971:83–152). To understand this method, we must look at Sicily during the 1800s. During feudalism in the nineteenth century (1812–1833), Sicilian peasantry lived on land controlled by absentee landlords. The centralized Italian state attempted to curb the power of feudal landlords and emancipate its peasantry from traditional feudal obligations (Blok, 1974:10). Not surprisingly, the landlords did not cooperate with the centralized power in Italy and sought to maintain control over both the feudal estates and the peasantry. To accomplish this the landlords worked with a group of ambitious middle-class persons—the *gabelloti*—who paid the "absentee feudal owners a lump-sum rent for the whole estate" and then "sublet it at a profit to the peasantry" (Hobsbawn, 1959:38). The *gabelloti* ensured continued payment to the landlords while providing protection over the estates. In this way they served as mediators between the landlords and the peasantry. Moreover, because of their geographic location vis-à-vis the peasantry and landlords, the remoteness of a centralized power (in Italy), and the rural character of feudal Sicily, the *gabelloti* were the only authoritative "organ" for local law and order. In short, they controlled and monopolized the links between peasant, landlord, and a remote centralized government. As Eric Hobsbawn pointed out in his important work *Primitive Rebels,* the *gabelloti* provided a parallel machine of law and organized power; indeed, so far as the citizen in the areas under its influence was concerned, the only effective law and power. In a society such as Sicily, in which the official government could not or would not exercise effective sway, the appearance of such a system was as inevitable as the appearance of gang-rule, or its alternative, private posses and vigilantes in certain parts of *laissez-faire* America. (p. 35)

The *gabelloti* in Sicily then played an important role as an organ of social control—in the absence of official bodies—and in fact enjoyed a high degree of social acceptance within Sicilian communities. Consequently, a *method* of patronage developed whereby the *gabelloti* held sufficient power to maintain law and order and to control feudal estates, whereas the peasantry (in return) offered services and loyalty to the *gabelloti*. As Albini explained, a *gabelloti* "entrenched himself in a patronage system which continues today. As a client to his landowner in return for certain favors he promised continued suppression of the peasant. As a patron to the peasant he promised work and the continuation of contracts" (1971:133). It was this method of patronage that came to be identified as "mafia," and the role of the *gabelloti* as "mafioso." Because it represents a system of patron-client relationships, **mafia** is a method, not an organization (pp. 135, 140). As Dwight Smith noted:

Events in Sicily that we have subsequently called Mafia were essentially localized patron-client relationships . . . to which the word "Mafia" was generally applied. It existed in the absence of a strong governmental presence. The mafioso person served to mediate, in a heavily stratified economy, between absent landlords and landless peasants; inevitably, men of a mafioso character obtained influence that extended also into political affairs. The system was dependent upon patronage and upon the ability of a "man of respect" to utilize violence when necessary, to maintain his authority as middleman. (1976:82–83)

Other historical research supports this conclusion (see, for example, Blok, 1974; Hess, 1973).

Syndicated Crime in the United States, 1800–1930

Thus, mafia evolved from certain political, economic, and social conditions. Not being an organization per se, it was not "imported" to the United States. Yet, this does not mean that syndicated crime was not an important phenomenon in the United States during the 1800s and early 1900s. In fact, crime was clearly organized in the various vice districts of the growing urban centers. As Samuel Walker argued: "There was a large demand for liquor (regardless of the day or hour), gambling, and prostitution. To meet this demand vice districts flourished in every major city" (1980:107). Syndicates providing these illegal goods and services blossomed everywhere. They were well organized and run primarily by Irish, Jewish, and Italian working-class entrepreneurs.

Policy gambling provides an example. Policy gambling is based on the illegal drawing of numbers—usually around twelve—upon which players place bets, hoping that from one to four numbers of their choosing will be among the twelve drawn. This form of illegal gambling was a well-organized part of criminal syndicates early in U.S. history. For instance, at about the time of the Civil War, a number of politicians, gamblers, and businesspeople in New York City accumulated $1 million to organize policy shops in that city (Haller, 1976:105). Moreover, by 1900 other large cities (like Chicago) had policy writers in a sizable number of stores, saloons, and barbershops; policy writers collected bets and delivered the money twice daily to a headquarters where the winning numbers were then "drawn" by means of a wheel (p.105). During this time, criminal syndicates made substantial profits from policy gambling, and "the policy runners or writers operating on commission could be assured of a steady income" (p. 105).

Similarly, the cocaine trade was organized and coordinated by a variety of criminal syndicates. As a trade it was decentralized into importers, wholesalers, and retailers "who formed, re-formed, split, and came together again as opportunity arose and when they were able" (Block, 1979:94). Criminal careers in the cocaine trade were not structured in one centralized and particular organization but rather in an increasing network of small but efficient criminal syndicates. Some of these syndicate members had interests in other drug-related illegal syndicates as well as in other types of syndicates, such as gambling. The cocaine trade was not structured along ethnic lines; Block (p. 94) found substantial evidence of interethnic cooperation between cocaine importers, wholesalers, and retailers.

The vice districts, and subsequently syndicated crime, flourished because corruption pervaded city government and everyone involved benefited: Citizens had their liquor, gambling, sex, and drugs; ethnic groups had a means of social mobility; police and city officials benefited through financial gain (Walker, 1980:107). Thus, from the Civil War onward (perhaps even earlier), provision of illegal goods and services was *syndicated,* having well-established political and police connections. In fact, as time went on, the boundary between politician and syndicated criminal became more and more obscure as "ward bosses were in a good position to engage in racketeering, and racketeers and their nominees could move into political positions" (McIntosh, 1973:56). As Haller has shown concerning gambling during this period:

> It was not simply that gambling syndicates influenced political organizations, but that gambling syndicates sometimes were the local political organizations. Local bookmakers or policy writers served as precinct captains, and the leaders of syndicates became ward leaders and often won election as alderman or state representatives. By the early twentieth century it would not be possible to understand the structure of local politics without a knowledge of the structure of gambling syndicates. (1976:106)

In short: "The operations of the early criminal syndicates were carefully coordinated with, and often even controlled by, local machine politicians and police" (Nelli, 1987:16–17).

Enactment of the Volstead Act in 1919 made it illegal to produce, distribute, or sell alcoholic beverages. With law enforcement effectively neutralized and the demand for alcohol continuing unabated, Prohibition (1920–1933) provided the context for the rapid development of a new illegal enterprise: importing, manufacturing, bottling, wholesaling, distributing, and retailing illegal alcoholic beverages. Initially, bootlegging was chaotic and uncoordinated. By the middle of the 1920s, however, syndicates grew in strength and

Bootlegging: With the passage of the Volstead Act in 1919, the U.S. government attempted to limit the production and distribution of alcoholic beverages. With continued widespread demand for such beverages, however, "bootlegging" became a major activity for criminal syndicates. One of the largest illegal distilleries ever found in the United States during Prohibition is shown above.

increasingly coordinated the bootlegging activities. In fact, bootlegging, like the cocaine trade, became regional, national, and international.

To supply the large urban markets, bootlegging syndicates required improved coordination and organization. For example, Max Hassel—an owner of breweries in Reading, Pennsylvania, and Camden and Atlantic City, New Jersey—provided beer throughout the Delaware Valley and Philadelphia (Haller 1976:115). Similarly, in a single four-month period in 1926 and 1927, "Boo Boo" Max Hoff's bootlegging syndicate produced and diverted 350,000 gallons of pure alcohol throughout the Northeast and Midwest (p. 115). The Mill Creek Distillery, established in Cuba in 1929, further illustrates the national and international ties of bootlegging syndicates:

> Investors in the distillery included Leon Gleckman, perhaps the leading bootlegger in Minneapolis; representatives of Ansonia Copper and Iron Works of Cincinnati, a manufacturer of stills and other apparatus for making alcohol; G. L. Bevan of Montreal, through whom there were ties with major Canadian distilleries that exported for the American market; Charles Haim of New York, who may also have been a partner in "Boo Boo" Hoff's enterprises in Philadelphia. Mill Creek manufactured both

Scotch and rye whiskey. To transport the liquor into the United States, Mill Creek owned or chartered ships to take the liquor off ports such as New Orleans, from which contact boats carried the liquor to shore. Mill Creek also exported liquor directly to ports such as New York in cartons labeled ink or canned fruit. And Mill Creek sold liquor to George Gough of Belize, British Honduras. . . . Thus, the investments in Mill Creek were part of a complex set of relationships that linked New Orleans, Minneapolis, and New York bootleggers with Canadian and West Indian smugglers. (p. 116)

During Prohibition (1920–1933), criminal syndicates grew into larger organizations involving more participants than any other criminal grouping. They also developed a much more complex division of labor. As depicted by Mary McIntosh, criminal syndicates developed "the form that any organization theorist would suggest was most appropriate to their kind of business, that is, to coordinate and control one or a series of complex but routinized and continuous activities" (1973:42).

This does not mean that criminal syndicates became highly centralized into one organization, under the direction of an alleged Italian mafia. All evidence indicates the contrary. In fact, data on individuals considered to be the leading syndicate criminals during Prohibition indicate that they included a variety of ethnic groups—from Jews and Italians to the Irish and Polish (Haller, 1976; Block, 1983; Nelli, 1987).

Some criminologists argue, however, that toward the end of Prohibition syndicated crime became extremely centralized and controlled chiefly by Italians. According to this view, a national crime syndicate controlled by a small group of Italians was the "final product of a series of 'ganglord wars' in which an alliance of Italians and Sicilians first conquered other groups and then fought each other" (Cressey, 1969:9). It is to the validity of this argument that we now turn.

A National Crime Syndicate?

Donald Cressey (1969) argued in his classic book *Theft of the Nation* that a nationwide, centralized control of illegal goods and services came into existence in 1931. As a result of the so-called Castellammarese War, "in 1931 leaders of Sicilian-Italian organized crime units across the United States rationally decided to form monopolistic corporations, and to link these corporations together in a monopolistic cartel" (p. 35).

Basing his account "principally on the memoirs of one soldier, Joseph Valachi," Cressey (pp. 37–45) has presented the following argument. In 1929, Giuseppe Masseria controlled Sicilian-Italian syndicated crime in New York City. A group called the "Castellammarese" (named after a specific geographical area in Sicily) rebelled against this control, Salvatore Maranzano becoming the leader of the rebels. Throughout 1929 and 1930 a series of feuds and assassinations occurred between the two groups, Masseria declaring war against the Castellammarese on November 5, 1930. Within five months Masseria's "soldiers" realized they were outnumbered, and some of his "key men"—including Charles "Lucky" Luciano—secretly surrendered to Maranzano. To demonstrate their new loyalty, these men successfully arranged to have Masseria executed in April 1931.

According to Cressey, Maranzano immediately appointed himself the "Boss of Bosses" ("Godfather") and "established the notion that there would be bosses beneath him, each with an underboss and a '*caporegima,*' or 'lieutenant,' who, in turn, would have 'soldiers' working for him" (p. 42). Luciano was allegedly rewarded with a position as a boss, Vito Genovese becoming Luciano's underboss. However, within five months, so the argument goes, Luciano and Genovese grew disenchanted with Maranzano's demands for unquestionable allegiance, eventually aligning themselves with "four Jews"—Louis Buchalter, Meyer Lansky, Benjamin "Bugsy" Siegel, and Jake Shapiro—as well as Al Capone from Chicago. On September 11, 1931, Maranzano was assassinated, this day becoming the so-called Mafia Purge Day because, as Cressey has argued:

> On that day and two days immediately following, some forty Italian-Sicilian gang leaders across the country lost their lives in battle. Most, if not all, of those killed on the infamous day occupied positions we would now characterize as "boss," "underboss," or "lieutenant." Perhaps it is for that reason that the "purge day" terminology emerged. (p. 44)

Luciano then substituted the "Boss of Bosses" position with the "*consigliere* of six," which consisted of the six most influential syndicated criminals in the United States. Thus, what had previously been, according to Cressey, a local alliance of gangsters in the major U.S. cities became, in 1931, a nationally organized network under the control of an exclusive Italian "board of directors."

In 1951 this conspiracy theory was officially recognized by the U.S. government when it was crystallized in the infamous Kefauver Committee (1951) report, which examined the possibility of a national crime syndicate in the United States. Even though *all* the syndicated criminals testifying before the committee denied membership in, or knowledge of, a "mafia" (Albanese, 1985:31), the committee concluded that there "is a nationwide crime syndicate known as the Mafia, whose tentacles are found in many large cities"; it centralizes and controls syndicated crime in the United States, and its leadership is found in "a group rather than in a single individual" (Kefauver Committee, 1951:150).

In 1963, Joseph Valachi testified before the Senate Subcommittee on Investigations and outlined the Mafia Purge Day story (related above) to the committee. In addition, Valachi gave his view of the structure of syndicated crime at that time, arguing that it was centrally controlled by an Italian organization, "Cosa Nostra."

Cressey (1969:x–xi) echoed Valachi, arguing that "the Mafia" was superseded by Cosa Nostra (our thing) and structured as follows:

1. A nationwide alliance of at least twenty-four tightly knit "families" of criminals exists in the United States. (Because the "families" are fictive, in the sense that members are not all related, references to them are within quotation marks.)
2. Members of these "families" are all Italians and Sicilians, or of Italian and Sicilian descent; those on the Eastern Seaboard, especially, call the entire system "Cosa Nostra." Each participant thinks of himself as a "member" of a specific "family" and of Cosa Nostra (or some equivalent term).

3. The "families" are linked to each other, and to non–Cosa Nostra syndicates, by understandings, agreements, and "treaties," and by mutual deference to a "Commission" made up of the leaders of the most powerful "families."
4. The "boss" of each "family" directs the activities, especially the illegal activities, of the members of his "family."

Most recently, the President's Commission on Organized Crime (1986a:35–58), although recognizing the existence of a wide variety of criminal syndicates, simply echoed Cressey—and thereby Valachi—by arguing (without evidence to support it) that an alleged "Cosa Nostra" is the largest and most influential criminal group in the United States.

However, several criminologists question these conclusions. Alan Block (1983), for instance, has criticized Cressey for relying on the testimony of *one* gangster, Valachi. Also, he has reinvestigated the so-called Mafia Purge Day story. Block therefore went beyond simply questioning the competence of Cressey's source, investigating whether the event actually took place. Block surveyed newspapers in eight cities—New York, Los Angeles, Philadelphia, Detroit, New Orleans, Boston, Buffalo, and Newark—for any stories (two weeks before and two weeks after Maranzano's death) of gangland murders "remotely connected" to the Maranzano assassination. Block (p. 6) found various accounts of the Maranzano murder but could find only three murders of "gangsters" that might have been connected to the Maranzano killing. Thus, Block concluded that the killing of three gangsters did not constitute a purge, and he is perplexed as to the origin of Cressey's figure of forty killings. Additionally, in newspaper stories reporting the killing of Maranzano, it was disclosed that Maranzano was killed for simply *informing* on fellow gangsters for illegally importing aliens, not to rid the "Boss of Bosses" of power (pp. 7–8). Similarly, research by Nelli (1981:179–218) uncovered no evidence to support the Mafia Purge Day thesis.

Beyond questioning evidence on the so-called Mafia Purge Day, Block also analyzed syndicated crime in New York City between 1930 and 1950. These two decades are critical because this is the period between the alleged purge of "the Mafia" and the rise of the so-called Cosa Nostra (1930s) on the one hand, and the Kefauver Committee's endorsement of the centralization thesis (1950), on the other hand. What did Block find?

First, although clear that some criminal syndicates became increasingly centralized and hierarchically controlled between 1930 and 1950, Block found *no* evidence indicating the emergence of a national crime syndicate in the sense of Cosa Nostra. Instead, two types of criminal syndicates operating in New York City during this time period were uncovered: *enterprise* syndicates and *power* syndicates (p. 13). Enterprise syndicates are groups of people organized into illegal enterprises; power syndicates are "loosely structured, extraordinarily flexible associations centered around violence and deeply involved in the production and distribution of informal power" (p. 13). Enterprise syndicates organize the production and distribution of illegal goods and services, such as narcotics and gambling. These syndicates tend to be large, with a complex division of labor, a centralization of authority, and a hierarchy of command. In contrast, power syndicates have no clear division of labor, for their specific purpose is to maintain power over others through extortion—obtaining control through the use or threat of violence. Block (pp. 129–199) has demonstrated that certain of the more energetic power syndicates—controlled by such people as Charles "Lucky" Luciano, Arthur "Dutch Schultz" Flegenheimer, and Louis "Lepke"

Charles "Lucky" Luciano (1897–1962): Lucky Luciano was one of the most powerful syndicate criminals in New York City during the 1920s and 1930s. In 1936, he was found guilty of compulsory prostitution and was sentenced to thirty to fifty years in prison.

Buchalter—attempted to exploit enterprise syndicates for extortionary purposes. However, rather than resulting in a centralized Cosa Nostra, this move by the power syndicates was *disruptive,* creating the conditions for the gangsters' eventual downfall. The case of "Lucky" Luciano is illustrative.

Prior to 1933 in New York City, prostitution was well organized and centralized in enterprise syndicates. There were approximately six "bookers" (individuals who organized the prostitution business and "booked" prostitutes into brothels) who had numerous brothels—and the madams and prostitutes who staffed them—under their control. Luciano's power syndicate "conspired to carry this centralization to an extreme," attempting to control the entire operations of "bonding" (providing bail for arrestees) and "booking."

A prostitute made approximately $85 for a week's labor. However, a prostitute had to pay $10 each week to a bonder, who would then guarantee bail if she were arrested. In 1933, Luciano forced the bonders out of business, and his organization took control. The elimination of the bonders led to centralization and control of the bookers. As Block pointed out, Luciano's power syndicate used extortion, such as terrorizing

booker Dave Miller with threats of murder unless he paid $10,000. . . . Pete Harris was similarly threatened and told he must pay $250 a week to "a 'mob' being formed to 'protect' the bookers." Harris settled his problem by paying $100 a week to stay in business. The other major bookers including Weiner, Charlie Spinach, and Montana

were also "taken over." . . . By the end of 1933 . . . the bonders had been totally replaced and the bookers were now employees of the Luciano syndicate. (1983:144)

Once in control, however, Luciano's power syndicate became rapacious. For instance,
with regard to posting bond the syndicate decided to put up only one-half of the bond, the
other one-half coming from the particular madam affected. When the defendant (prostitute) appeared at trial—and the bond money was returned—the syndicate kept the entire
amount, returning nothing to the madam. This "exploitation of madams was one of the key
disruptive issues under the new syndicate" (Block, 1983:147). As time passed, madams
were less and less likely to cooperate (bookers joined them) and attempted to conceal
brothels from the syndicate. This rebellion by madams and bookers was so strong that by
1935 Luciano reportedly wanted out of the prostitution business because the profit was not
worth the trouble. Indeed, Luciano's power base was reduced considerably, and in February 1936 he was prosecuted successfully by Thomas Dewey for compulsory prostitution.
Luciano received a sentence of 30 to 50 years (pp. 68–69). As Block concluded, the
Luciano power syndicate

> took a fairly centralized operation, the booking system, and subjected it to intense
> pressures which threatened to disrupt the entire trade. It turned on the key personnel
> in the trade with the exception of the prostitute herself who was already cruelly ex-
> ploited, and initiated various methods of financially squeezing both bookers and
> madams who resorted to cheating and ultimately to testifying against their bosses. . . .
> It was clearly an effort at extreme centralization that attacked what was already a sta-
> ble system of organized prostitution. . . . As neither the price structure nor the volume
> of trade changed under the Luciano syndicate, profits for the entrepreneurs of vio-
> lence could only come from the pockets of the formerly independent syndicate lead-
> ers and madams. Indeed, one might want to argue that without substantial changes in
> the economics of organized prostitution, it had about all the centralization it could
> take by 1933. (pp. 147–148)

Syndicated prostitution continued, "but never under the centralized direction of a power
syndicate" (p. 148). Overall, Block found no evidence of the emergence of a national
crime syndicate in New York between 1930 and 1950.

Frank Pearce's (1976:124–131) important examination of the legendary Al Capone provides yet another example of historical inaccuracy. Although it is clear that Capone was a
central figure in such illegal activities as bootlegging and labor racketeering, there is no
evidence that he became a "boss" in an alleged national crime syndicate in the early
1930s. In fact, Pearce has shown that syndicated crime's involvement in corruption and,
therefore, its close relationship with the police and politicians, undermined "legitimate"
business endeavors at the time. It was this phenomenon that actually led to Capone's
downfall. As Pearce wrote:

> Many businessmen had begun to feel that City Hall could no longer be relied upon to
> provide the "rational legal" form of administration that they required to run their
> businesses. Chicago's judges were corrupt, her administration was inefficient, civic

Al Capone (1899–1947): Al Capone is probably the most famous syndicate criminal in the United States. He was a central figure in the bootlegging activities in the Chicago area during Prohibition. In 1932, Capone was convicted of tax evasion and sentenced to ten years in Alcatraz.

contracts were awarded to the highest briber; the infrastructure was starting to break down. The true magnitude of the city's crisis became clear in 1930 when it was found to be $300 million in debt. (pp. 128–129)

In addition to a corrupt and bankrupt state, businesspeople were also concerned about Prohibition and supported its repeal. Legal alcohol, they argued, would relieve social tensions, lessen class hatred, and provide tax revenues for the state. Thus, businesspeople appealed to the federal government to intervene in Chicago, and in 1929 federal proceedings began against Capone for tax evasion (Eliot Ness and his Justice Department Raiders soon destroyed his breweries). Three years later—in 1932—Capone was sentenced to ten years in Alcatraz; in 1933, Prohibition was repealed.

As with New York then, Pearce found no evidence of leading syndicate criminals in Chicago becoming involved in a national crime syndicate. Moreover, with the downfall of Capone—as with Luciano—criminal syndicates were not even bruised, continuing to operate such activities as extortion, loan sharking, gambling, drugs, and labor racketeering.

Given that it is highly unlikely that a national crime syndicate emerged between 1930 and 1950, most criminologists have also argued that it is doubtful such a syndicate emerged after 1950. Numerous scholars—such as William Moore (1974), Joseph Albini (1971), and Daniel Bell (1961)—found no evidence of a national crime syndicate in the

1950s, arguing that the Kefauver Committee's "Mafia" conclusion was based simply on assumptions and conjecture, not empirical evidence. Moreover, from Kefauver to the present, no reliable evidence indicates the existence of a national crime syndicate. For such to exist, one criminal syndicate would have to retain monopoly control of all syndicated criminal activity—from illegal gambling to the illegal drug trade, from labor racketeering to the illegal disposal of hazardous wastes. Although there is evidence of some large-scale syndicates—some of which are dominated by Italians and call themselves "Mafia" (there are also syndicates other than Italians that use this designation, such as the "Black Mafia" and "Mexican Mafia")—no such monopoly exists (Block, 1991; Lyman and Potter, 1997). As Jay Albanese concluded after an exhaustive review of research on syndicated crime: "It is difficult to understand, therefore, the continuing belief in a nationwide criminal conspiracy when no one has been able to produce reliable evidence of it" (1985:64).

12.2   SYNDICATED CRIME TODAY

The endless contemporary demand for illegal goods and services in the United States creates perfect conditions for criminal syndicates to flourish and prosper. These syndicates are not controlled by an Italian-dominated national crime syndicate. Rather, they are diverse and autonomous. For example, the President's Commission on Organized Crime (1986a:75–128) found the following racial and ethnic membership in syndicated crime: Chinese, blacks, Mexicans, Italians, Vietnamese, Japanese, Cubans, Colombians, Irish, Russians, Canadians, and a variety of others. Thus, there is no specific ethnic stereotype synonymous with syndicated crime (Nelli, 1987:27). Several sociological studies help us further understand the structure of syndicated crime in the United States today. We briefly summarize their conclusions.

Patron-Client Relationships

Albini (1971:263–304) has argued that syndicated crime in the United States is characterized by patron-client relationships. Syndicated criminals differ in the kinds of relationships they establish among themselves, between themselves, and with those who protect them. For Albini, no rigid formal structure is prevalent; syndicated criminals simply make use of whatever resources or persons are necessary to accomplish their goals. Moreover, every criminal syndicate has several powerful individuals who serve as "patrons" to the criminal clientele; patrons wield force and deliver favors. Yet, as Albini further argued:

> A powerful syndicate leader in the west at a particular time may be influential in his area because he has excellent protection in his city and because he provides funds for a multitude of new criminal enterprises, giving other syndicated criminals continued sources of revenue. Yet he may have no power whatsoever over other syndicated criminals in other parts of the country. (p. 265)

In addition, powerful syndicate figures may serve as "clients" to others more powerful, especially those with legal power to offer protection in return for payoffs. In other word,

the "entire system involves various levels of patron-client relationships" that are constantly permeated with conflict, cooperation, and accommodation (Albini, 1971:265).
Syndicated crime therefore is never formally or rigidly bureaucratized; rather, it maintains
numerous and complex criminal and noncriminal patron-client relationships. As Albini
concluded, syndicated criminal enterprises

> are generated at all levels of patron-client relationships and they are primarily held
> together by the fact that each participant is basically motivated by his own self-inter-
> est. Power within the system depends upon the individual's rise in the number of sig-
> nificant patron-client relationships he is able to establish. (p. 300)

Albini's perspective on the structure of syndicated crime is supported by other research
that employs a variety of methodologies, such as participant observation, interviews with
informants, and analysis of the government's syndicated crime files (Bynum, 1987:7).

12.3   PRINCIPAL FORMS OF SYNDICATED CRIME

In this section, we consider the principal forms of syndicated crime. Specifically, we examine the following:

1. three types of illegal sale and distribution of goods and services—illegal gambling, illegal drugs, and loan sharking
2. syndicated crime's involvement in legitimate business through direct investment, racketeering, and money laundering
3. syndicated crime's involvement with the state, such as corruption and performing political favors

Syndicates and Illegal Goods and Services

The first type of illegal sale and distribution of goods and services is gambling. It is estimated that the income generated by syndicated crime through illegal gambling is somewhere between $29 billion and $33 billion each year in the United States (President's
Commission on Organized Crime, 1986b). There are two major types of illegal gambling:
numbers and bookmaking. **Numbers** is a form of lottery in which the customer (bettor)
places a bet by choosing a three-digit number between 000 and 999. The customer usually
bets from $1 to $10, receiving from a "numbers runner" a receipt with the chosen number
and the amount of the bet written on it. The runner, who has several copies of the receipt,
passes one to the "pickup," who then carries it to the "bank" or to the accounting room of
the numbers operation. The customer, if a winner (that is, if she or he predicted correctly
the three numbers in their chosen order), is paid a fixed multiple (such as 500 to 1) of the
amount bet. A common procedure for determining the winning number is the "Brooklyn"
method, which is based on the last three digits of the total amount of money a particular
racetrack handles on a specific day. Another method calculates the three-digit number

BOX 12.1   CRIME NETWORKS

In his book *On the Take,* Chambliss (1988) has extended Albini's thesis a little further. He has documented how businesspeople, politicians, and members of the criminal justice system are involved in "the subterranean, often invisible" industry built upon, for example, illegal gambling, drugs, loan sharking, business fraud, and prostitution (p. 2). As shown in Figure 12.1 Chambliss studied syndicated crime in Seattle, finding that the vice district was prospering and controlled *not* by "Cosa Nostra" but by "a loose affiliation of businessmen, politicians, union leaders, and law-enforcement officials who cooperate to coordinate the production and distribution of illegal goods and services, for which there is a substantial demand" (p. 151).

Thus, financiers (who finance the operations) and middle-level organizers (who supervise the racketeers) unite in a loosely structured "crime network" for the purpose of financial gain. Rather than the existence of a highly centralized "Cosa Nostra," Chambliss's research

Financiers

Jewelers	Attorneys
Realtors	Businessmen
Contractors	Industrialists

Bankers

Organizers

Businessmen	**Politicians**	**Law-Enforcement Officers**
Restaurant owners	City councilmen	Chief of police
Cardroom owners	Mayors	Assistant chief of police
Pinball-machine license	Governors	Sheriff
holders	State legislators	Undersheriff
Bingo parlor owners	Board of supervisors	County prosecutor
Cabaret and hotel owners	members	Assistant prosecutor
Club owners	Licensing bureau chief	Patrol division commanders
Receivers of stolen property		Vice-squad commanders
Pawnshop owners		Narcotics officers
		Patrolmen
		Police lieutenants, captains,
		and sergeants

Racketeers

Gamblers Pimps Prostitutes Drug distributors Usurers Bookmakers

FIGURE 12.1   Seattle's Crime Network

SOURCE: *Chambliss,* 1988, p. 74.

(continues)

> **BOX 12.1** *(continued)*
>
> indicates that criminal syndicates are organized by those who primarily benefit from the criminal activities—those "legitimate" members of society who hold business, political, and criminal justice positions.
>
> More recently, Gary Potter (1994) investigated syndicated crime in "Morrisburg" (a pseudonym for a city in a Mid-Atlantic state). In this town of approximately 95,000 residents, one major syndicate and two smaller syndicates dominate the illegal distribution of goods and services, such as illegal gambling, illicit drugs, fencing and loan sharking, and illicit sexual services (prostitution, pornography, and sex clubs). None of the syndicates possess a monopoly on these illegal activities and none could exist without the close cooperation of "legitimate" members of the community. As Potter stated, "the overt connections between the leaders of the political parties, officeholders of both parties, and the organized crime network is the central theme in 'Morrisburg's' organized crime. The system of political payoffs and the active connivance of local business people add the final elements needed to organize crime" (p. 105). Indeed, "Morrisburg's" syndicates have extensive holdings in legitimate businesses, such as vending companies, the garment industry, and the coal industry. As Potter concluded, "crime, politics, and finance all clearly form part of a peculiar milieu. They are not separate activities, they are not distinct from one another—they are only different areas of a single economic spectrum" (p. 114).
>
> The importance of Albini's, Chambliss's, and Potter's research, then, is that it shows that the overall structure of syndicated crime has changed little since the 1800s. Syndicated crime is not centrally organized in a national crime syndicate, and "upright" businesspeople and public officials continue to play a regular and significant role in the organization and perpetuation of criminal syndicates.

from the winning dollar amounts paid on a $2 wager on the first, fifth, and seventh races at a particular racetrack (Reuter, 1983:45–54).

The structure of a numbers syndicate is not especially complex. At the bottom, of course, are the customers who make wagers with either "mobile runners" (those who travel over a territory to accept bets) or "stationary runners" (those who accept bets at their place of business—such as a bar, newsstand, or small business). Runners are usually paid a commission of 25 percent of their receipts (because they have the highest risk of apprehension) and also receive tips of, on the average, 10 percent of the winning payoffs. The pickup operates as an area manager, tabulates daily collections, maintains records of runners, and makes payoffs from the bank. The pickups receive between 5 and 10 percent of total receipts. Finally, the pickup transfers the day's receipts to the bank, which is the main organizer and manager of the numbers game. The banker usually employs a staff to audit the games and arranges payoffs to the police, bail bondsmen, and lawyers. For a game that pays 500 to 1, bankers earn a profit of approximately 14.5 percent (Simon and Witte, 1982:212–214).

Bookmaking, the second major type of illegal gambling, is the organized illegal betting on horse racing and sporting events. The major source of syndicated crime's bookmaking income is the latter category—primarily football (college and professional), basketball

Illegal gambling: Bookmaking syndicates often organize illegal betting on college and professional sporting events.

(college and professional), and baseball (professional only). Reuter provides an example of how sports betting works:

> Most sports bets are on the outcome of a single game. For basketball or football, one team is usually given a handicap of a certain number of points, called the "spread." Assume the Los Angeles Rams are handicapped by 8 points in their game against the Chicago Bears. This means that the person who wishes to bet on the Rams wins his bet only if the Rams win by more than 8 points. If the Bears win or lose by less than 8 points, bets on the Bears are paid. If the Rams win by exactly 8 points, all bets are returned to the bettors; to avoid this return, the spread is frequently a half-point value, such as 7. (1983:17)

The four major players in a bookmaking syndicate are the customer (bettor), runner, clerk, and bookmaker ("bookie"). The runner transfers money from the customers to the bookmaker; the clerk transcribes and records transactions. The bookie is the controlling figure, "setting the terms of the bets and the limits on the size of bets. He also provides capital to cover expenses and losses" (Reuter, 1983:20). Furthermore, the bookie may have others working in the syndicate in addition to a clerk and several runners. For instance, some bookies have what is referred to as a "tabber" who keeps "tabs" on the bets and changes the spreads when necessary (Simon and Witte, 1982:216). For both numbers and bookmaking, the best available evidence indicates that these illegal gambling syndicates operate autonomously and are not centrally controlled under the exclusive direction of one organization (Reuter, 1983).

In the "Morrisburg" study, Potter reported that numbers betting is "open and quite apparent," taking place in small bars, lunch counters, and newsstands (1994:73). In addition, "bets are placed in tobacco shops or other retail establishments doubling as bookmaking parlors" (p. 73).

A second type of illegal sale and distribution of goods and services is the illegal drug business (primarily heroin, cocaine, and marijuana), which reaps tremendous profits for syndicated crime. Take heroin, for example. According to Block and Chambliss (1981:33), annual gross sales of heroin alone exceed $30 billion. Overall, the illegal drug industry operates like importing, wholesaling, and retailing businesses. It is organized and coordinated by a variety of criminal syndicates—not one exclusive criminal elite. As a former police commissioner of New York City stated:

> The illegal drug industry today can more accurately be compared structurally to the garment industry. Many sources of raw materials exist. Many organizations, large and small, buy and process the raw materials, import the product into this country, where it is sold to and processed and distributed at retail by a host of outlets, some large and small, chain and owner-operated. . . . Organization in the drug business is largely spontaneous, with anybody free to enter it at any level if he has the money, the supplier, and the ability to escape arrest or robbery. (Cited in Block and Chambliss, 1981:57)

Simon and Witte (1982:128–134) have examined the structure of the heroin, cocaine, and marijuana distribution systems. Heroin seems to be the most organized of the three, with a few criminal syndicates sharing in monopolizing *importation* of heroin into the United States. Simon and Witte found the heroin industry inside the United States comprised a variety of small syndicates, thus creating a long vertical distributional structure. As they pointed out, small syndicates ("distribution units," they call them) serve somewhere between five and twenty customers and enjoy certain advantages over large monopolies because

> they require just a small number of transactions, they discourage information leaks, they facilitate supervision and discipline of customers, and they allow for quick and efficient adjustments in behavior. Furthermore, these distributional units will be well isolated from one another so that each dealer can limit information on his activities to just a few trusted customers, both for his own protection and to exploit some of his monopoly advantages. (p. 130)

Even though these distribution units are small, they nevertheless maintain different levels between production and sales, each level relatively insulated from other levels. At the top (as stated earlier) are the heroin *importers,* who coordinate large shipments of heroin into the United States. Importers have high operating costs because success is somewhat based on employing skilled smugglers. Importers almost never see or touch the actual heroin; they simply coordinate the shipment of uncut and undiluted heroin to a criminal syndicate in the United States, which then distributes it to a variety of *wholesalers.* The wholesalers dilute the purity of the heroin—usually with quinine, mannite, and/or lactose—thereby doubling the volume and weight of the heroin mixture. Eventually the heroin is reduced in purity to approximately 25 percent, and then divided into "street-ounce" sizes (a little less than one full ounce). These packages are then sold to a variety of what may be called "street syndicates," who also dilute the purity, reducing it to approximately 10–15 percent heroin, selling "half-ounces" or "bundles" to users.

Mieczkowski's (1986) work on heroin street sales indicated that there are three major players in street syndicates, all of whom are not heroin users: "runners," "guns," and "crew bosses." Runners are given allocations of heroin from the crew boss to sell on the street at a variety of locations. Runners maintain a specific "selling position" on the sidewalk or in an alley and sell their heroin to customers (p. 651). Guns are armed members of the syndicate who station themselves close to the sales areas to provide security for runners. As Mieczkowski stated: "Guns observe and monitor the street transactions. Should anything go awry, guns are expected to intervene" (p. 652). The crew boss manages the street syndicate, distributes the heroin to runners, and collects funds obtained by runners. Crew bosses either go "into the field" to collect the money or runners report to crew bosses at specific locations. The average "wage" of a runner is approximately $800 per week (if the runner works a five-day week); crew bosses average almost $1,500 per week. The crew bosses in Mieczkowski's study were approximately eighteen to nineteen years of age, the runners were several years younger. It is also the job of crew bosses to obtain quantities of heroin on a regular basis. This requires coming into contact with wholesalers, who either require payment for the heroin "up front" or after the street sales are completed.

Overall, Simon and Witte's and Mieczkowski's research is important because it reveals that the overall structure of the heroin distribution system is based on patron-client relationships. The runner requires the patronage of a crew boss and the crew boss the patronage of a supplier (p. 661); in turn, the supplier (or wholesaler) requires the patronage of an importer.

According to Simon and Witte (1982:158, 171–174), cocaine and marijuana distribution systems in the United States are very similar to the heroin system in that they maintain a long vertical distribution system with well-insulated syndicates, each servicing a small number of customers—or clients—below them. For cocaine, each participant dilutes the drug, thereby increasing its volume and price. By the time the mixture reaches the street, it is rarely over 5–10 percent pure. Marijuana is seldom diluted but is repackaged into smaller parcels as it passes from one level to the next.

In "Morrisburg," Potter (1994:79–90) found that the largest syndicate imports drugs from Toronto, Canada, and then supplies approximately twenty wholesalers, who in turn, sell the drugs to about two hundred street dealers. The "Morrisburg" drug operation, as Potter observed,

The drug economy: For many people in the inner city, participation in the drug economy is their only means of livelihood. Billy, Marie, and their six-month-old daughter survive on drug dealing. Billy—a "runner"—is notified of incoming drug shipments through a beeper.

is set up in such a way as to minimize contact between layers of the operation. Street-level pushers have no information on the activities of wholesalers. Dealers have no knowledge of financing and or sources of supply. In addition, on a horizontal axis, people performing similar functions often do not have contact with each other. A built-in system of compartmentalization separates operatives. (p. 87)

The vast majority of heroin, cocaine, and marijuana sold in the United States comes from foreign countries. The major heroin producers are the countries of the "Golden Crescent" area of Southwest Asia (Afghanistan, Iran, and Pakistan), Mexico, and Colombia, and the "Golden Triangle" area of Southeast Asia (Laos, Burma, and Thailand). The major cocaine producers are Bolivia, Colombia, and Peru, and of marijuana, Colombia and Mexico (Lyman and Potter, 1997).

Syndicates in these (and in other) countries work with a variety of syndicates in the United States to organize importation of the specific drug into this country. For example, in the late 1980s a major Colombian syndicate—commonly referred to as the "Medellin Cartel"—supplied approximately 75 percent of the cocaine used in the United States. It is alleged that this Colombian cocaine usually passes through Panama on its way to the United States. In fact, according to a U.S. Justice Department indictment of General Manuel Noriega—former ruler of Panama—Noriega allegedly worked closely with this Colombian syndicate, providing it with secure airstrips, allowing syndicate fugitives to remain in Panama if they were sought by law enforcement officials in other countries, and transforming certain Panamanian banks into "money laundering centers" for the syndicate.

Loan sharking is a third type of illegal sale and distribution of goods and services. For many individuals and small businesses in urgent need of money, legitimate sources of obtaining that money—such as relatives and banks—are not possible. Consequently, in times of financial crisis many such people must turn to loan sharks, who loan money at extremely high interest rates and who require rapid repayment of all loans. Larger loans seem to have lower interest rates than smaller ones. For instance, Reuter (1983:96–97) reported that a $1,000 loan usually requires repayment in twelve weekly sums of $100, or 20 percent interest per week; however, the interest rate for a $20,000 loan may be as low as 1 percent per week. Large borrowers are usually small businesses, speculators or promoters, and gamblers (Simon and Witte, 1982:229).

Most loan sharks also require some type of collateral—such as the ownership documents to the borrower's automobile—which lessens the need for engaging in violence to obtain repayment (Reuter, 1983:98–99). Loan sharks usually attempt to avoid violence, inasmuch as violence is likely to attract an official response. A more common strategy for a loan sharking criminal syndicate is loaning money to a legitimate business with the understanding that if repayment is not forthcoming, the syndicate simply takes over the business.

Loan sharking may be directed by syndicates involved in a variety of criminal activities. Or it may simply involve individuals with large quantities of cash—from either legitimate or illegitimate ventures—available for use in further moneymaking endeavors, such as creating their own loan sharking syndicate. For the latter type, loan sharking becomes a means of "moonlighting," whereby they employ a variety of individuals in their syndicate: attorneys, accountants, enforcers, runners (who contact borrowers), law enforcement officials, and so forth. For example, Simon and Witte (1982:230–231) reported that one loan shark in New York City employed nineteen runners (all held legitimate full-time jobs as well) and five bookkeepers (each kept records on three or four runners).

In the "Morrisburg" study, Potter (1994:79) described a fence who is also an "individual loan shark" (he works alone) who loans money to small businesspeople and gamblers with large debts. He does not use enforcers because he rarely has trouble collecting—he will not loan money without proper collateral, such as interest in a business or a mortgage. Finally, this loan shark loans money for up to three months and receives a return of 15 to 20 percent depending upon the risk involved.

Syndicates and Legitimate Businesses

In addition to illegal sale and distribution of goods and services, criminal syndicates work with legitimate businesses. There are three major means by which syndicated crime effects this involvement: direct investment, money laundering, and racketeering.

Criminal syndicates often reinvest their profits from the illegal sale and distribution of goods and services in legitimate enterprises. The President's Commission on Organized Crime (1986b:424) reported syndicate investments in (1) construction; (2) waste removal; (3) garments; (4) food processing, distribution, and retailing; (5) legal gambling; (6) hotels; (7) bars; (8) liquor retailing and wholesaling; (9) entertainment; (10) business and personal services; (11) motor vehicle sales and repair; (12) real estate; (13) banking; and (14) various other wholesale and retail businesses. The advantages of investing in legitimate businesses include less risk than expanding an illegal operation, opportunities for concealing illegal activities, and avenues for paying income taxes.

In addition to investing in legitimate businesses, legitimate businesspeople sometimes become involved in working relationships with syndicate-owned businesses. In the "Morrisburg" study, Potter (1994) found that syndicated crime and legitimate businesses were "cozy partners" in illegal transactions—businesses provided the sites for illegal gambling bets, illicit pornographic film distribution, and fencing and loan sharking operations.

Much of what is earned by criminal syndicates from the illegal sale and distribution of goods and services is in cash, and usually in small bills. Before this "dirty" money (illegally earned) can be spent or invested in legitimate businesses, it must be turned into "clean" money. Criminal syndicates accomplish this by engaging in **money laundering**. This is the process "by which one conceals the existence, illegal source, or illegal application of income and then disguises that income to make it appear legitimate" (President's Commission on Organized Crime, 1984:7). Those engaged in money laundering range from the small individual drug dealer who wishes to exchange smaller-denomination bills for larger ones to the large criminal syndicate that obtains enormous sums of money from numerous illegal activities.

Under the Bank Secrecy Act, financial institutions must report all currency transactions of $10,000 or more. When a financial institution fails to do this, it is engaging in money laundering. Syndicated crime's involvement in the illegal flow of drugs provides an excellent example of how money laundering occurs, benefiting both financial institutions and criminal syndicates. For example, in one case, certain New York City heroin dealers deposited tens of millions of dollars in cash at banks in New York City. The New York banks then transferred the funds to a variety of banks in other countries, such as Switzerland. From these foreign banks the money was channeled to various narcotic sources to pay for conversion of opium to heroin, to finance additional "drug" laboratories, and to support and profit the overall network of heroin trafficking. By transferring the funds around the world, the process of money laundering is considerably more difficult to detect.

One of the couriers, Franco Delle Torre, deposited almost $5 million (in $5, $10, $20 bills)—over a six-week period—in an account at the brokerage firm Merrill Lynch Pierce Fenner and Smith. The deposits apparently were so important to the brokerage firm that Merrill Lynch's "security employees determined that Delle Torre's funds could not be afforded proper security, and arrangements were made to escort the money from Delle Torre's hotel directly to Bankers Trust, where Merrill Lynch maintained accounts" (President's Commission on Organized Crime, 1984:33).

Eventually, however, Merrill Lynch closed the account, and Delle Torre simply moved his laundering operation to the Manhattan offices of the brokerage firm E. F. Hutton and Company. Delle Torre made eighteen different cash deposits totaling $13.5 million in a Hutton account. Security personnel at Hutton similarly provided Delle Torre protection from his hotel room to the depository institution.

This case reveals not only the close relationship between syndicated crime and legitimate businesses but also the *international* nature and context of this relationship. Approximately

$5–15 billion of the $50–75 billion in illegal drug money generated in the United States each year quite likely moves into international financial channels. As the President's Commission on Organized Crime (1984:13) found:

- More than two-thirds of the $5–15 billion is moved on behalf of foreign traffickers bringing drugs to the United States, as well as on behalf of Colombians and Mexicans involved in distributing cocaine and heroin in the United States. The remainder comes from funds earned by U.S. drug dealers and distributors.
- About one-third of the illegal drug money moves overseas in the form of currency, and much of the remainder is wired abroad after being deposited in the U.S. banking system.
- More than two-thirds of the $5–15 billion probably passes through Colombia, or the offshore banking centers of the Caribbean Basin, mainly Panama, the Bahamas, and the Cayman Islands.

In addition to direct investment and money laundering, criminal syndicates are also involved with legitimate businesses through **labor racketeering**, "the infiltration, domination, and use of a union for personal benefit by illegal, violent, and fraudulent means"

BOX 12.2   THE BCCI SYNDICATE

The case of the Bank of Credit and Commerce International (BCCI) illustrates the international networking of drugs and money laundering. BCCI was the seventh-largest privately held financial institution in the world, operating 400 branches in 73 countries. Some eighty-five people in seven U.S. cities allegedly laundered $14 million in narcotic funds, mostly serving Colombian criminal syndicates involved in the cocaine trade. The money laundering scheme involved shifting money around the world in order to make it difficult to trace. Once the money was deposited, BCCI wired it to a variety of foreign banks in France, Britain, Luxembourg, Uruguay, Panama, and the Bahamas, placing the money in certificates of deposit (CDs). The CDs were used as a basis for setting up phony loans to syndicated crime figures for slightly smaller amounts than the CDs. BCCI then "collected the CDs as 'payment' for the loans, pocketing the difference in the face amounts as a commission" (Castro, 1988:66). In this way syndicate crime obtained "clean" money and BCCI made a substantial cost-free profit. In 1991, the Federal Reserve Board fined BCCI $200 million for its illegal laundering activities (Simon, 1999).

Moreover, in that same year, it was revealed that BCCI had a clandestine division in the bank known as the "black network" (Beaty and Gwynne, 1991). This network functioned as a global intelligence and enforcement squad for the bank, while simultaneously operating a lucrative illegal arms trade and drug transport business. The network attracted deposits from drug syndicates, tax evaders, corrupt government officials, and frequently worked with governmental intelligence agencies, including the CIA. For example, BCCI kept secret CIA accounts so that the CIA could finance covert aid to the U.S.-backed contras in Nicaragua and the Mujahedin rebels in Afghanistan. In turn, the CIA acquiesced to BCCI's involvement in the heroin trade in Pakistan and the cocaine trade in Central America.

(President's Commission on Organized Crime, 1986b:9). Traditional forms of racketeering that continue to proliferate include (1) entering into "sweetheart contracts" with employers, (2) looting workers' benefit funds, and (3) extorting "strike insurance" payments from businesses. In addition to these traditional forms of racketeering, criminal syndicates wield "union power to facilitate marketplace corruption and to give businesses an advantage in the marketplace" (President's Commission on Organized Crime, 1986b:10). We briefly summarize the evidence from the President's Commission on Organized Crime on each racketeering form (1986b:12–23).

A "sweetheart contract" results from a criminal syndicate's extensive infiltration of a union, ensuring it the opportunity to control the union and consequently to collude with management, permitting employers to violate collective bargaining provisions. In return for payoffs to syndicate figures who negotiate such contracts, the employers have, for example, the privilege of using nonunion labor, a guarantee that workers will not be organized by specifically unwelcome unions, and the right to select union representatives with whom to negotiate. These sweetheart contracts seem to be flourishing in such industries as construction, trucking, and garments (p. 18).

Concerning workers' benefit funds (which cover pension, health, and welfare benefits for retired, disabled, and needy workers), infiltration of unions by criminal syndicates has resulted in the systematic looting of these funds to provide syndicate figures and their friends with such perks as "no show" jobs, homes, automobiles, travel expenses, stocks and bonds, and capital for legitimate investment. The International Brotherhood of Teamsters (IBT)—which has a long history of benefit-fund abuse—provides a shocking example (pp. 99–166). In the early 1960s, Jimmy Hoffa (then president of the Teamsters Union) shared pension-fund kickbacks with Allen Dorfman, a former asset manager and service provider to the Teamsters Central States Pension Fund. Hoffa was convicted of jury tampering in 1964. Prior to beginning his prison sentence, according to the President's Commission on Organized Crime, Hoffa

> convened a meeting of the Fund trustees to state, unequivocally, that Allen Dorfman was his spokesman while he, Hoffa, served time in jail. Hoffa and Dorfman were the moving forces behind the Central States Pension Fund's entry into speculative real-estate loans in Las Vegas, an action that eventually robbed the Teamsters of millions of pension fund dollars and resulted in the government's decision to place the Fund in receivership. (p. 99)

Other presidents of the Teamsters Union—such as Roy Williams and Jackie Presser—in association with criminal syndicates, have similarly looted the Teamsters pension fund. For example, Jackie Presser placed his uncle, Allen Friedman, on the union payroll at a $1,000 weekly salary, even though Friedman did not work for the union. In addition, Presser arranged to pay a syndicate-controlled firm—Hoover-Gorin and Associates—$1.3 million per year and a $350,000 yearly retainer to do advertising and public relations work that seems never to have been performed (pp. 107–108). Even before assuming the Teamsters' presidency, "Jackie Presser had compiled an extensive record" of syndicate crime associations, benefiting "from their support in his elevation to the IBT Presidency in 1983" (p. 90).

Teamster syndicates: Jackie Presser was one of numerous International Brotherhood of Teamsters presidents to have close connections to syndicated crime.

Criminal syndicates may also extort "strike insurance" from employers in return for the promise to keep the business "running as usual" (namely, free from labor strife). In other words, the employer pays a criminal syndicate a fee to keep labor peace. For example, syndicate figures in the past "created and owned a series of labor-leasing companies throughout the country" (pp. 110–111). These companies provided workers and labor peace to the corporations that hired them. Criminal syndicates received contractual payments, and the corporations minimized their labor costs. If a corporation did not voluntarily hire one of these syndicate companies, corrupt union officials created labor disputes to suggest the need for labor peace and, therefore, syndicated crime's leased labor.

As a union member one has the right to nominate candidates, vote in elections and on different referenda, attend membership meetings, participate in deliberations, and meet and assemble freely with other union members. However, the President's Commission on Organized Crime found that syndicate-influenced unions, such as the Teamsters

rely on fear and violence to deny these rights to members. The violence takes many forms, literally ranging from verbal harassment to murder, to quell all forms of dissent, criticism, and opposition. Violence need not be an everyday occurrence. Occasional "examples" are often sufficient to persuade members that any opposition may create a substantial risk of injury or death. (1986b:114)

When criminal syndicates control a union, they also have the power to participate in market corruption schemes. The construction industry of New York City provides a prime example of how this type of corruption occurs:

> New York construction businesses cooperating with organized crime have formed a cartel, and the union is the enforcing agent. General contractors are told what suppliers to use and who the subcontractors will be. If a contractor does not comply, either he will never get the job (having been purposely underbid by the cooperating companies) or he will get the job but never be able to complete it. Construction contractors have told Commission representatives that they simply cannot go into the New York market because they are underbid or cannot get work done when they get a bid. (p. 21)

In the 1980s several criminal syndicates imposed a 2 percent "tax" on New York City contractors who poured concrete for structures exceeding $2 million. These criminal syndicates in fact operated a cartel that not only rigged bids for supplying the concrete but also decided in advance which company would offer the winning bid; other "participating" companies were forced to place extremely high bids. The 2 percent tax alone produced $3.5 million in profits on 72 construction jobs. These criminal syndicates made over $71 million from 10 big construction jobs, including the luxurious apartment building in Manhattan known as Trump Plaza (Rowan, 1986:28).

Syndicates and the State

Finally, criminal syndicates are involved with the state in two essential ways: providing political favors for the state and colluding with state officials (such as the police and politicians). We consider each of these.

The use of syndicate figures to perform political favors for the state goes back to the time of "Lucky" Luciano. As David Simon pointed out, this began

> during World War II when the underworld figures in control of the New York docks were contracted by navy intelligence officials in order to ensure that German submarines or foreign agents did not infiltrate the area. It was thought that the waterfront pimps and prostitutes could act as a sort of counterintelligence corps. The man whose aid was sought for this purpose was Lucky Luciano, and he was reportedly quite successful in preventing sabotage or any other outbreaks of trouble on the New York docks during the war. In 1954, Luciano was granted parole and exiled for life in exchange for the aid he provided during the war. (1999:84)

Other historical examples abound (Pearce, 1976:148–152; Church Committee, 1975:40–41; McCoy, 1972:263; Hinckle and Turner, 1981:34–38):

- In France, in 1950, the CIA recruited syndicate figures to create a "criminal terror squad" to force recalcitrant Marseilles dockers to load ships with arms for use in Vietnam. For their assistance to the state, these syndicate figures were "allowed" to continue refining heroin in Marseilles and then export it to the United States.

• In the 1960s the CIA recruited anti-Castro, right-wing, syndicate figures to assassinate Fidel Castro. Such notables as John Roselli, Sam Giancana, and Santo Trafficante Jr., as well as Rafael "Chi Chi" Quintero, Felix Rodriguez, Frank Sturgis, and E. Howard Hunt were all involved in the assassination plans.

• In the middle to late 1960s syndicate figures worked together with the CIA to develop the Golden Triangle area as a major source for growing opium. In return for fighting the Pathet Lao opposition forces, the Meo tribespeople of the area were compensated by the CIA's own airline—Air America—which helped to transport the opium to heroin laboratories, and ultimately into the arms of GIs in Vietnam and users in the United States.

The overall viability and profitability of criminal syndicates have been based historically on a symbiotic relationship between syndicate figures and state officials. Earlier in the chapter we discussed this close relationship during the 1800s and early 1900s. Since then this relationship has continued, as a variety of governmental commissions and academic researchers have uncovered widespread corruption between state officials and criminal syndicates. For example, in 1931 the National Commission on Law Observance and Enforcement found that "nearly all of the large cities suffer from an alliance between politicians and criminals" (cited in Chambliss and Seidman, 1982:278). John Gardiner's (1970) study of Reading, Pennsylvania, found that for decades criminal syndicates in that city systematically worked closely with mayors, city council members, police officers and chiefs, and judges. After an investigation of police corruption in New York City, the Knapp Commission concluded:

> We found corruption to be widespread. . . . In the five plainclothes divisions where our investigation was concentrated we found a strikingly standardized pattern of corruption. Plainclothesmen, participating in what is known in police parlance as a "pad," collected regular bi-weekly or monthly payments amounting to as much as $3,500 from each of the gambling establishments in the area under their jurisdiction, and divided the take in equal shares. The monthly share per man . . . ranged from $300 and $400 in midtown Manhattan to $1,500 in Harlem. When supervisors were involved they received a share and a half. . . . Evidence before us led us to the conclusion that the same pattern existed in the remaining divisions we did not investigate. . . . Corruption in narcotics enforcement lacked the organization of the gambling pads, but individual payments . . . were commonly received and could be staggering in amount. . . . Corrupt officers customarily collected scores in substantial amounts from narcotic violators. . . . They ranged from minor shake-downs to payments of many thousands of dollars, the largest narcotics payoff uncovered in our investigations having been $80,000. . . . The size of this score was by no means unique. (1972:22)

Chambliss's (1988) study of Seattle demonstrated that syndicated crime in that city flourished with the support and cooperation of a number of state officials. Block and

Chambliss (1981:112) showed that criminal syndicates have been linked with leading political and legal figures in Detroit, Chicago, Denver, Columbus and Cleveland, Ohio, Miami, Boston, and a hoard of other cities. Finally, in the "Morrisburg" study, Potter found that collusion "extends from the cop on the beat to the most senior political officials" (1994:101–102).

This intimate and symbiotic relationship may even reach the White House. Some researchers have argued that since at least the 1940s, former President Richard Nixon socialized with and was involved in business endeavors with a number of syndicate members (Block et al., 1972:12).

Nixon, however, is not the only president implicated by researchers and journalists as a "friend" of shady individuals and dealing. Former President Ronald Reagan has had certain associations with people reportedly connected to syndicated crime. As Lyman and Potter have argued, syndicated crime

> played a major role in putting Ronald Reagan in the White House. Not only did he receive support from organized crime but his administration reciprocated that support and gave organized crime's representatives seats on the highest councils of the U.S. government. Persons with clear and compelling connections to organized crime were appointed to important governmental positions. (1997:371)

Moreover, Reagan has had an intimate relationship with Walter Annenberg, son of Moses Annenberg, the previously powerful and economically successful publisher of the Nationwide News Service that, in the 1920s, catered to bookies (Haller, 1976:122–123). In 1939, Moses and Walter were indicted for federal tax evasion and for selling pornography illegally through the mail. Moses eventually agreed to divest control of the "news" wire, settle his tax liabilities by paying $8 million, and go to prison for three years (p. 123). Moses' son, Walter, became publisher of the *Philadelphia Inquirer, Seventeen,* and *TV Guide* and was appointed ambassador to Britain by Richard Nixon (Block et al., 1972:13). In addition, when he was president, Ronald Reagan spent almost every January 1st at Walter Annenberg's Palm Springs estate to celebrate the New Year (Scott, 1988:2).

Finally, Reagan's close associate and friend, as well as past chair of both the Republican National Committee and the 1984 Reagan-Bush re-election committee—former Senator Paul Laxalt of Nevada—allegedly has had certain close associations with syndicate figures. As Robert Friedman (1984:32–39) reported, Morris "Moe" Dalitz (named by the Kefauver Committee as being involved in syndicate activities), Al Sachs (alleged to be involved in illegal casino profiteering operations), and Rudy Kolod (convicted in an extortion-murder plot) all contributed generously to Laxalt's campaigns for governor and senator. When governor, Laxalt allegedly helped Howard Hughes—whose corporation collaborated with criminal syndicates in several casino and resort speculations in Las Vegas and the Caribbean (Simon and Eitzen, 1986:65)—"become the largest landowner and casino operator in Clark County, Nevada," and "Governor Laxalt's Gaming Control Board waived investigations of Hughes' finances required by the state gaming and control board" (Friedman, 1984:36). Finally, Laxalt had a close relationship with Allen Dorfman, "the man who had supervised the use of the Teamsters' Central States Pension Fund as a private bank for organized crime figures" (Lyman and Potter, 1997:371).

White House crimes: Numerous U.S. presidents have been involved in illegal and/or unethical behavior. President Ronald Reagan is the most recent example of a president who had certain associations with people allegedly connected to syndicated crime.

REVIEW

This chapter examined the nature, extent, types, and costs of syndicated crime in the United States. The first section outlined a brief history of syndicated crime. The second section discussed the structure of syndicated crime in the United States today. The third described in greater depth the structure of various syndicates, examining this structure in light of the principal activities of syndicated crime. Some of the more important points of this chapter follow.

A History of Syndicated Crime

1. The term "mafia" originally described a method rather than an organization.

2. Syndicated crime can best be conceptualized as a variety of criminal syndicates, or associations of people (from all walks of life), formed to conduct specific illegal enterprises.

3. Early in U.S. history criminal syndicates were local in scope, primarily involved in such illegal enterprises as gambling and prostitution, and worked in a symbiotic relationship with state officials.

4. The passage of the Volstead Act in 1919 provided the context for the rapid development, increased size, and more complex division of labor of criminal syndicates.

5. It is quite unlikely that a national crime syndicate has ever existed in the United States.

Syndicated Crime Today

1. The work of sociologists—such as Joseph Albini, William Chambliss, and Gary Potter—reveals that criminal syndicates flourish and prosper today and that businesspeople and state officials continue to play a regular and significant role in them.

2. Albini argues that syndicated crime in the United States today is characterized by "patron-client" relationships. Chambliss and Potter document how numerous businesspeople, politicians, and members of the criminal justice system are involved in crime networks.

Principal Forms of Syndicated Crime

1. There are two major types of illegal gambling: numbers and bookmaking.

2. The illegal drug industry (heroin, cocaine, and marijuana) operates like importing, wholesaling, and retailing businesses.

3. Loan sharking is usually directed by small, locally organized syndicates.

4. Criminal syndicates directly invest some of their profits in legitimate businesses.

5. Criminal syndicates are also extensively involved in labor racketeering and money laundering.

6. Criminal syndicates provide political favors for the state and continue to maintain a symbiotic relationship with state officials.

QUESTIONS FOR CLASS DISCUSSION

1. How did the term "mafia" originate? Is it applicable today?

2. Summarize Cressey's argument concerning the national crime syndicate, and then outline the major criticisms of his position. Explain which position you support and why.

3. We presented evidence on the structure of syndicated crime in the United States today. Why do you think such a structure exists?

4. In the media, locate examples of syndicated crime, and then compare these to our analysis here. How are they similar? Different?

5. Discuss how general strain theory and routine activities theory—both discussed in Part Two—would explain syndicated crime.

FOR FURTHER STUDY

Readings

Chambliss, William J. 1988. *On the Take: From Petty Crooks to Presidents*. Bloomington: Indiana University Press.

Lyman, Michael D., and Gary W. Potter. 1997. *Organized Crime.* Upper Saddle River, N.J.: Prentice Hall.

Potter, Gary. 1994. *Criminal Organizations: Vice, Racketeering, and Politics in an American City.* Prospect Heights, Ill.: Waveland Press.

Websites

1. <http://www.yorku.ca/nathanson/default.htm>: This is the home page for York University's Nathanson Center for the Study of Organized Crime and Corruption. It provides readers with current bibliographies on syndicated crime and links to other related websites.
2. <http://www.laundryman.u-net.com>: This site is titled "Billy's Money Laundering Information Website" and is managed by Billy Steele, who is an attorney with a keen interest in studying the extent and techniques of money laundering.

White-Collar Crime

Preview

Chapter 13 introduces:
- what sociologists mean by white-collar crime
- the different types of white-collar crime
- the nature, extent, and costs of white-collar crime
- how white-collar crimes differ from other crimes

Key Terms

collective embezzlement
corporate crimes
corporate theft
corporate violence
deceptive advertising
embezzlement
employee theft
financial fraud

insider trading
occupational crimes
occupational fraud
occupational theft
physician fraud
price-fixing
transnational corporate crimes
white-collar crime

When we think of crime, we usually focus on the types of crimes already discussed—interpersonal crimes of violence, property crime, public-order offenses, and syndicate crime. This is natural because official agencies of social control (police and courts) concentrate on these behaviors (thus attracting media attention) and because these crimes are the most frequently studied by sociologists and criminologists. However, although the crimes discussed in Chapters 9 and 10 generate considerable fear and suffering in society, the white-collar crimes discussed in this chapter are clearly more harmful not only to U.S. society but also to other societies.

Edwin Sutherland (see also Chapter 5.4) was the first sociologist in the United States to conceptualize the problem of **white-collar crime**. Given the contemptuous attitude toward the law and business ethics displayed by the "robber barons" (such as Daniel Drew and John D. Rockefeller) in the late 1800s and the widespread and publicized fraud of the 1920s and 1930s, Sutherland focused his classic study on "crime committed by a person of respectability and high social status in the course of his occupation" (1983:2). Demonstrating that white-collar crime was widespread and endemic to U.S. business, Sutherland's findings led him to concentrate almost exclusively on one type of white-collar crime: corporate crime. However, later, sociologists and criminologists expanded the definition of white-collar crime to include not only corporate crimes but also occupational crimes and transnational corporate crimes (Clinard and Quinney, 1973).

Occupational crimes are committed by individuals in the course of their occupations for direct personal gain. These crimes are usually committed against an employer. Embezzlement is an example of an occupational crime.

Corporate crimes differ from occupational crimes in that they are not committed for direct personal gain—although certain individuals may benefit indirectly from the act. Rather, these crimes primarily benefit the corporation. We define corporate crimes as illegal and/or socially injurious acts of intent or indifference that occur for the purpose of furthering corporate goals and that physically and/or economically abuse individuals in the United States and/or abroad. Collusion of top executives of utility corporations to fix prices is an example of corporate crime.

Transnational corporate crimes constitute the third type of white-collar crime. Many corporations maintain operations in more than one country. Consequently, this transnational character of U.S. corporations sometimes results in crimes perpetrated on the people of other societies, ranging from bribery to export of hazardous products to dangerous working conditions.

These three types of white-collar crime are both similar and different from the crimes already discussed in Chapters 9 and 10. Like other crimes, white-collar crimes involve theft and violence. That is, commission of white-collar crimes results in loss of property and/or physical injury and death. But white-collar crimes differ from other crimes in two important ways. First, white-collar crimes entail far more victimization—in terms of economic loss and lives injured and lost—than do the crimes discussed earlier. Second, victimization resulting from white-collar crimes is less apparent—although once again, far more severe—than the one-on-one type of victimization resulting from, for example, interpersonal crimes of violence. Indeed, most of us who suffer the pains of white-collar crimes—corporate crimes in particular—are unaware of our own victimization.

13.1   OCCUPATIONAL CRIME

Occupational crime occurs in the workplace and is motivated by direct personal gain; it consists primarily of occupational theft and occupational fraud. **Occupational theft** stems from an abuse of trust between the employee and employer. We examine two types of occupational theft: employee theft and embezzlement. Both types affect consumers by increasing the cost of commodities; they also affect some businesses negatively. **Occupational fraud** is a deliberate workplace deception practiced for the purpose of obtaining personal financial gain. This type of fraud is ubiquitous; we explore the major aspects of occupational fraud through examples from the fields of medicine and securities.

Occupational Theft

In preindustrialized societies—such as feudal England in the seventeenth century—people had common rights to such necessities as the gathering of wood, the killing of game, and the grazing of animals. But with the transition from feudalism to capitalism, these "rights" were translated into "property." As Jason Ditton stated: The "annexation of common rights . . . naturally culminated in the simultaneous creation of 'property,' and the propertied classes, and the ultimate criminalization of customary practices" (1977b:41). As land previously open to everyone's use became the private property of a few, wood gathering became wood theft, game rights became poaching, and grazing rights became trespassing (p. 44). In addition, this privatization, as Ditton explained,

> released into urban life a working population not only used to receiving part of their "wages" in kind . . . but also one still stinging from the effects of the abrupt and cruel negation of those practices in the countryside. As one might expect, and empirical evidence supports this, a major source of irritation to factory owners who took on such "idle" rural laborers was their penchant for making off with parts of the workplace or the fruits of their labor there, in addition to their wages. (p. 43)

Indeed, the preindustrial cultural tradition of common rights was carried over into industrialized society. Workers expected "wages-in-kind"—extras to supplement their actual earnings. In eighteenth-century England, for instance, workers in manufacturing industries "constantly borrowed, bartered, and sold small quantities of materials among themselves," a good portion of which was stolen from the workplace (Henry, 1987:142). As Stuart Henry argued, "criminalization of the consumption of a part of one's daily labor was re-defined in conjunction with capitalist development of the factory to become employee theft and embezzlement; the trading of embezzled goods came to constitute a hidden econ-omy" (p. 142). In other words, accompanying the rise of capitalism was the emergence of two major forms of occupational theft: employee theft and embezzlement. We consider each form and its relation to the trade in stolen goods discussed in Chapter 10.1.

Employee theft—stealing merchandise and job-related items from one's workplace—is one of the most pervasive and costly crimes in the United States. Self-report studies suggest that 75 percent of employees *admit* to some sort of theft from the workplace (Greenberg, 1997).

The cost of employee theft is enormous. Most employees steal minor items; yet when these items are multiplied for many workers, the cost becomes substantial. "Inventory shrinkage" (loss from employee theft, shoplifting, poor paperwork, and vendor theft) adds approximately 15 percent to the price of all retail goods. Most of this loss is attributable to employee theft. According to Lloyd W. Klemke (1992:10), 40 to 50 percent of inventory shrinkage is attributable to employee theft, 31 percent to shoplifting, and 15 to 30 percent to accounting errors. Overall, researchers estimate that employee theft costs $200 billion (Greenberg, 1997). A survey of 9,000 employees in retail, hospital, and manufacturing sectors of the economy revealed that the primary forms of theft were for retail, misusing the discount privilege, for hospital, stealing supplies, and for manufacturing, stealing pro-duction material (Hollinger, 1986).

It is convenient to assume that employee theft is primarily a problem of lower-level em-ployees. This is not the case. A 1974 investigation of employee crime attributed 62 percent of losses to thefts by company supervisors (Jaspan, 1974:v). Comer reported that "the most dangerous" thefts "are those which occur at higher management levels" (1985:5). Hollinger and Clarke found in their study that one group of "high-theft" employees were "high-status engineering and technical employees," whereas low-status assembly-line workers tended to commit low levels of employee theft (1983:75). In 1987, Baker and Westin (1987:10) found that petty employee theft (loss of small amounts of office sup-plies, tools, and so on) tends to be committed by all employees; however, at least 38 per-cent of management or senior staff are the principal sources of major employee theft (loss of thousands of dollars in raw materials and components, supplies, tools, products, and so on).

Two classic studies by Ditton (1977a) and Mars (1983) enhance our understanding of the relationship between employee theft and occupation. Ditton considered employee theft a form of what he called "part-time crime." However, part-time crime is not simply a mat-ter of time commitment inasmuch as a part-time criminal may well "spend more hours and minutes breaking the law than somebody involved full-time in crime. The crucial distinc-tion is that whereas the full-time criminal's legitimate occupation is perceived by him [or her] to be merely nominal, the part-time criminal sees his [or her] illegitimate activities in the same way, as nominal" (p. 91). In other words, part-time criminals may spend more hours planning and executing their crime than full-time criminals, but this activity is *per-ceived* by them as inconsequential to their full-time legitimate activity at work.

In a participant observation study of bread salesmen at Wellbread Bakery, Ditton (pp. 92–113) found that part-time employee theft entailed three activities: fiddling, stealing, and dealing. "Fiddling" is the practice by salesmen (those who sell and deliver bakery goods) of overcharging customers by either increasing the price or reducing the number of items for the standard price. Ditton found that fiddling was tolerated—even overtly recommended—by management because the loser is the customer rather than the company. "Stealing" is theft from the company itself. Although production workers have "pilfering rights" to a daily loaf of bread, salesmen are excluded from this dubious privilege. As Ditton explained:

> It is assumed that production staff have no outlet other than domestic consumption of pilfered loaves, and that this empirical feature of the practice will de facto limit the amount of bread that they will take. Salesmen, on the other hand, are assumed to have guaranteed occupational access to facilities (a round of customers) which would encourage them systematically to escalate their thefts beyond tolerable levels. Thus, for salesmen at Wellbread's, we may define a successful steal as the removal of some sort of asset skillfully, unobserved, and without permission. Salesmen steal both convertible consumer goods, for resale to their customers, and nonconvertible assets, such as plastic bags and clipboards, which, as tools of the trade, make occupational life easier. (p. 101)

"Dealing"—the third employee theft activity identified by Ditton—is the clandestine unofficial "distribution of other people's goods to the mutual interest and profit of those covertly involved" (p. 106). Dealing involves the collusion of salesmen and other employee staff in arranging a profit-making venture. For example, the bread dispatcher may provide extra trays of bread to a salesman without "booking it." Subsequent to the sale of the extra trays, both the salesman and the dispatcher share the profits (pp. 107–113). Dealing involves the amateur trade (or fencing) in stolen goods from the workplace.

Ditton's book relates how crime can provide an outlet for creativity in monotonous and alienated work environments, as well as challenge the "official" view of crime as being predominantly a lower-class, nonoccupational phenomenon.

Mars's most important contribution distinguishes between types of employee theft and links these to types of jobs. Mars divided workers into four different types (hawks, donkeys, wolves, and vultures) distinguished by such elements as the amount of job autonomy, extent of isolation from others, and the degree of control over one's labor power. Mars (pp. 26–28) also examined the amount of collectiveness in the workplace, which varies according to how a workplace prioritizes the interests of the group over the individual and is distinguished by such elements as the frequency with which people interact with others, whether contacts occur within a mutually interconnecting network, and the scope of group social life outside the workplace.

"Hawks" are professionals, executives, and small business persons who maintain individuality, autonomy, and control over their labor power but have infrequent contact with others. Therefore, it is much easier for hawks to "bend the rules" to their personal advantage. Work-related expenses provide an example. A journalist, for instance, may claim first-class travel but actually go second class, or falsify costs of entertainment and meals as business expenses. More extremely, one journalist said: "It's not uncommon for you to say you're dashing . . . somewhere for a story. You look up fares plus a few beers for fictitious informants and a taxi or two and bang it in for expenses" (cited in Mars, 1983:47).

"Donkeys" have little autonomy, are not isolated from others, and have no control over their labor power. Moreover, donkeys do not work within a group setting with frequent interaction. Supermarket cashiers and workers "on long and noisy mass-production belts" are examples of donkeys. Because of the structured nature of these jobs, employee theft is more restricted than it is for hawks. Supermarket cashiers, for instance, are limited to undercharging—or not charging at all—friends and family who frequent the store where they work, or simply "taking from the till." As one cashier expressed to Mars: A theft may occur "when your mother or friend comes in. Then they get away with a load of stuff and you put hardly anything through the till" (p. 66).

"Wolves" are similar to donkeys in the sense of having little autonomy and lacking control over their labor power; but they are different in that their jobs require a group of workers. For both hawks and donkeys, control over theft belongs to the individual. For wolves, however, theft is under group control. Airport baggage handlers and longshoremen are examples of wolves. If dockworkers, for example, want to steal cargo, to do so they need the support of the group. This is so both because they work as a group and because they must divide their labor so that some workers steal cargo while others distract supervisors. As Mars explained:

> Theoretically, all these men can pilfer cargo. Yet supervision of unloading by the ships' officers at one end and the shed superintendent at the other greatly reduces *individual* opportunities. Those with *access* therefore need the *support* of those who do not have access, to distract the attention of the supervisors, to provide cover, to "clear" documents and to enable the swift removal and distribution of goods once they have been pilfered. (p. 103)

Finally, "vultures" have considerable individual autonomy, yet that autonomy operates within a loosely structured work group setting. Waiters, truck drivers, and hotel workers are examples of vultures. Such occupations enjoy a degree of independence yet rely on support from coworkers. For example, Mars (p. 112) found a coordinated group of truck drivers who arranged the "private delivery" of stolen company goods on company time.

Overall, Mars's work identifies how type of occupation and workplace setting help determine type of occupational theft. Indeed, his classification of hawks, donkeys, wolves, and vultures involves a combination of employee theft and embezzlement.

As with conventional property theft, much of employee theft involves trade in stolen goods. Friends, relatives, and workmates form "trading networks" in which goods are stolen and subsequently sold (Henry, 1978:17–41). For example, the cashier "donkey" referred to earlier may, once store detectives are out of view, signal "a friend who is buying various goods. The cashier rings up some of the items but lets the rest through. The extra goods obtained in this way may be shared out later between the cashier and her friend, or they may be passed on to a friend's friend for sale in a local office or factory" (p. 18).

Thus, the overall amateur trade in stolen goods involves a variety of theft-related techniques—from conventional property theft discussed in Chapter 5.1 to the stealing and dealing of stolen goods among "ordinary people in honest jobs" (Henry, 1978:20). Indeed, sometimes these techniques overlap. Henry (pp. 26–27) described a plumber who contracted out his labor to a variety of industrial firms. Coming into contact with a large number of people, he could "fence" or "deal" stolen goods provided to him by a shoplifter friend. Consequently, type of job not only determines the nature of employee theft—as Mars pointed out—but also creates opportunities for dealing stolen goods. The amateur trade in stolen goods—whether the stolen goods originate from conventional property theft or employee theft—creates a hidden economy governed primarily by social relationships rather than economic gain (Henry and Mars, 1978:245–251). This hidden economy is discussed more thoroughly in Chapter 15.1.

Embezzlement, like employee theft, involves a violation of employer/employee trust. However, embezzlement differs from employee theft in that it involves taking money—rather than merchandise and job-related items—for one's personal use. The supermarket cashier "donkey," for example, has the opportunity to steal both merchandise (employee theft) and money (embezzlement).

Embezzlement ranges from simply "taking from the till" to "manipulating the books," but people in certain occupations can embezzle more than those in others. Individuals who occupy top business or bank positions—such as loan officers, accountants, computer operators, and vice-presidents—have a much greater opportunity for embezzling large sums of money than do cashiers, bank tellers, sales clerks, or other lower-level employees. Consequently, individuals in the position to embezzle, and who actually do embezzle large sums of money, frequently are viewed by employers as some of the most important people in the company.

Much embezzlement results from the use of computers: The technology makes it easier to manipulate books because it is so difficult to detect and trace. Moreover, only about 15 percent of computer embezzlements are ever reported. Thus, like other embezzlements, we must rely on estimates to determine the magnitude of this crime. According to one estimate, the average computer crime nets approximately $500,000, and most computer embezzlement is committed by authorized users, trusted insiders, and skilled employees (Rosoff, Pontell, and Tillman, 1998). The most common method of computer embezzlement is to divert cash into fraudulent accounts. A variation of this method is called "salami slicing," where many small amounts of numerous private accounts are "sliced off" and diverted to the fraudulent account (p. 372).

Examples of computer embezzlement are wide-ranging. A bank teller at New York's Union Dime Savings Bank embezzled approximately $1.4 million over three years by manipulating hundreds of accounts and putting inaccurate information into the computer (p. 371).

Occupational Fraud

In Chapter 10.2 we discussed different types of fraud committed against the government and through the use of checks and credit cards. We now discuss two types of occupational fraud—physician fraud and insider trading—committed for direct personal gain in the course of one's occupation.

BOX 13.1 COLLECTIVE EMBEZZLEMENT

The above discussion identified embezzlement as a crime committed by employees *against* the company. However, a new type of embezzlement emerged from the savings and loan scandal, what Kitty Calavita, Henry Pontell, and Robert Tillman (1997) have termed **collective embezzlement**. This type of embezzlement entails the theft of funds from savings and loan institutions for personal gain, at the expense of the institutions and with the approval of management. In other words, like traditional embezzlement, collective embezzlement is a crime against the company. Yet collective embezzlement differs from traditional embezzlement in that it is endorsed, approved, and accomplished by management itself. It is, in short, "crime *by* the corporation *against* the corporation" (p. 63).

The savings and loan scandal is the most expensive white-collar crime in U.S. history and will most likely cost the U.S. government between $300 and $500 billion (Waldman, 1990:4). Ultimately, however, U.S. taxpayers are the victims of this crime because the money embezzled did not belong to the embezzlers. As Michael Waldman pointed out, "it was *ours,* because we, as taxpayers, insured the deposits in their banks. The result is an unprecedented government bailout, with an estimated cost of up to $15,000 per taxpayer" (p. 3).

In 1980, Congress increased the amount for which the Federal Savings and Loan Insurance Corporation (FSLIC) would insure S&L accounts from a maximum of $40,000 to $100,000 per deposit. Additionally, Congress phased out controls on interest rates. Subsequently, S&Ls raised their interest rates, thus attracting wealthy depositors who did not face any risk of loss; should an S&L fail, the U.S. government (and therefore taxpayers) would reimburse depositors up to $100,000 per deposit. This new opportunity, when combined with the Reagan administration's deregulation policies of "getting government off our backs," created the perfect conditions for this new form of occupational crime.

According to U.S. government reports, crime or misconduct played a crucial role in 70 to 80 percent of the S&Ls bailed (Calavita, Pontell, and Tillman, 1997:29). The vast majority of these bailouts were the result of embezzlement. The case of Erwin "Erv" Hansen's "shopping spree," or embezzling S&L funds to finance a lavish lifestyle, is one example of collective embezzlement. Hansen, president of Centennial Savings and Loan in northern California, embezzled S&L funds to purchase such things as antique furniture ($130,000), a penthouse in San Francisco ($773,487), a Mercedes limousine ($77,000), five cars for his family ($90,000), and a $137,000 Rolls-Royce for himself. In 1983, Hansen threw a Christmas party for his friends, described by Pizzo, Fricker, and Muolo as the most lavish Christmas party anyone could recall. "Elegant Renaissance Faire" was the theme. Couples gasped as jesters proclaimed their entry into the hall, now transformed into an Elizabethan forest of 300 living trees sparkling with 75,000 tiny white lights. Candlelight shimmered through piped-in fog that simulated the moors and woods of Nottingham. Oriental rugs covered the floor.

Once seated among the trees, the 500 guests were entertained by a hundred roving Robin Hoods, fiddlers, jugglers, jesters, and pantomimes. Waiters and waitresses, one for every two guests, wore Elizabethan costumes—swagger-plumed hats, ruffled laced bodices, yards of velvet. They rolled the ten-course, three-hour meal into the hall on flaming carts, meats crackling on open spits, each course heralded by twelve trumpeters.

(continues)

> **BOX 13.1** *(continued)*
>
> Men and women visiting the restroom were attended by shoeshine boys for the men and maids-in-waiting with an array of makeup and perfumes for the women. Dancing continued until three o'clock in the morning, and to this day many say it was the most romantic evening of their lives. (1989:25–26)
>
> Because of the outright looting (collective embezzlement), Centennial eventually became insolvent, costing the FSLIC an estimated $160 million (Calavita, Pontell, and Tillman, 1997:24).
>
> Other types of collective embezzlement include such group behavior as "land flips," "nominee loans," "reciprocal lending," and "linked financing." A land flip is described as follows:
>
>> A sells a parcel of real estate to B for $1 million, its approximate market value. B finances the sale with a bank loan. . . . B sells the property back to A for $2 million. A finances the sale with a bank loan, with the bank relying on a fraudulent appraisal. B repays his original loan and takes $1 million in "profit" off the table, which he shares with A. A defaults on the loan, leaving the bank with a $1 million loss. (Cited in Calavita, Pontell, and Tillman, 1997:49).
>
> Thus, this type of collective embezzlement requires three participants: two people to "flip" the money and a corrupt appraiser.
>
> In the case of nominee loans, the owner/officer of an S&L will extend a loan to a "straw borrower" (someone indirectly connected to the S&L) who receives a kickback for obtaining the loan and then returns the remaining money to the lender. One such owner/officer, Don Dixon (owner of all the stock of Vernon S&L in Texas), put together "an intricate network of at least 30 subsidiary companies for the express purpose of making illegal loans to himself," and overall, the Vernon collective embezzlement cost taxpayers approximately $1.3 billion (Calavita, Pontell, and Tillman 1997).
>
> Reciprocal lending refers to executives from at least two different S&Ls making loans to each other. One investigation in Wyoming revealed a chain of reciprocal loans among four S&Ls that resulted in a $26 million loss to taxpayers (Calavita, Pontell, and Tillman, 1997:54).
>
> Finally, linked financing involves someone depositing money in an S&L (which is insured by the FSLIC) under the condition that they receive a loan in return. Subsequently, the loan is defaulted on, the S&L becomes insolvent, and the federal government pays back the deposit because it was insured. Thus, both the depositor and the owner of the S&L make money.

According to a past president of the Federation of State Medical Boards, at least one of every twenty physicians is a severe disciplinary problem and one of nine is repeatedly guilty of practices unworthy of the profession (Jesilow, Pontell, and Geis, 1985:154). Most physicians are honest; some, however, commit **physician fraud** through unnecessary prescription of pharmaceutical drugs, unnecessary surgical procedures, and overtreatment of Medicare and Medicaid patients.

Approximately 22 percent of all antibiotic prescriptions in U.S. hospitals are prescribed unnecessarily, and some physicians even perform unnecessary surgeries (Coleman, 1994).

The white-collar crime of the century: The greatest heist in the history of the United States occurred in the savings and loan system during the 1980s. Many individuals who deposited money in a savings and loan lost it to these white-collar fraudsters. In the above scene, people line up, waiting for word as to the future of their money.

Unnecessary surgeries cost the people of the United States approximately $4 billion annually, and it is estimated that 10 percent of all surgeries performed in the United States are unnecessary (Jesilow, Pontell, and Geis, 1993:19). Moreover, estimated deaths each year from unnecessary surgeries range from 12,000 to 16,000 (Reiman, 1995; Coleman, 1994).

Scully's (1980a, 1980b) important study of surgical residents shed light on the issue of unnecessary surgeries. She found that a prerequisite of successful surgical residency "was the ability to find patients and persuade them that surgery was in their best interest" (1980a:90). Performing unnecessary hysterectomies was one of the most common forms of surgical residency abuse—for example, a hysterectomy to remove small, benign uterine fibroids that often disappear without surgery or remain intact without symptomology. Scully asked surgical residents how they would treat a nine- to ten-week asymptomatic uterine fibroid. The following is a representative answer:

> I don't think it would be right to say you have a horrible disease or you have cancer or anything like that, so I have to do this surgery. I would explain to her that she has fibroids that are nine- to ten-week size, that she isn't going to have a family any more, she doesn't want a family any more, that these fibroids may sometime in the future grow bigger, may get symptoms, may cause her trouble, she may need surgery at

some point in time, and if she would like to have surgery done now, it can be easy surgery, vaginally. As a consequence she won't have any more children, but she won't have any fibroids and she won't have any potential for disease. (Cited in 1980a:90–93)

Moreover, studies indicate a relationship between hysterectomy surgery, physician fraud, and racist sterilization. Contemporary findings show that the hysterectomy rate among never-married black women is three to four times higher than the rate for never-married white women and that the South has the highest hysterectomy rate in the country (Andersen, 1993:206–207). Clinical reports further suggest that although physicians often recommend this surgery to their patients, they also provide them with incorrect information about the overall effects of the surgery. Thus physician fraud seems to occur more often with minority and poor clients, resulting in the following statistics (pp. 191, 206):

- Approximately 43 percent of women living in East Harlem have had either a tubal ligation or a hysterectomy.
- Approximately 50 percent of welfare mothers have been sterilized, representing one-third more sterilizations than for other women.
- Among women of childbearing years, 36 percent of black women, 24 percent of Native American women, and 21 percent of white women have been sterilized.

Finally, physician fraud also occurs in Medicaid (for the poor) and Medicare (for the elderly) programs, costing an estimated $61 billion a year (Jesilow, Pontell, and Geis, 1993:12). When physicians know that medical costs will be paid for the poor and elderly, "there is a great deal to be gained by doing as much work as possible, needed or not, and doing it at a minimum cost" (Jesilow, Pontell, and Geis, 1985:159). A shocking example of Medicaid fraud is the case of a California ophthalmologist found guilty of performing unnecessary cataract surgery on the poor to obtain Medicaid fees. For the affluent the surgery was performed skillfully and successfully; for the poor it was performed in "slipshod fashion." For example, in one case the physician totally blinded a 57-year-old woman when he performed unnecessary surgery on her one *sighted* eye (Jesilow, Pontell, and Geis, 1993:19–20).

Paul Jesilow, Henry Pontell, and Gilbert Geis (1993) investigated specifically Medicaid fraud. For their book *Prescription for Profit*, they drew on case file material from California and New York (the two states with the largest number of violators) and found four primary categories of crimes committed by physicians caught violating Medicaid programs:

(1) billing schemes, which include billing for services not rendered, charging for nonexistent office visits, or receiving or giving kickbacks; (2) poor quality of care, which includes unnecessary tests, treatments, and surgeries as well as inadequate record keeping; (3) illegal distribution of controlled substances, which include drug prescriptions and sales; and (4) sex with patients whereby physicians under the guise of "therapy" received payments for sexual liaisons with their patients. (p. 105)

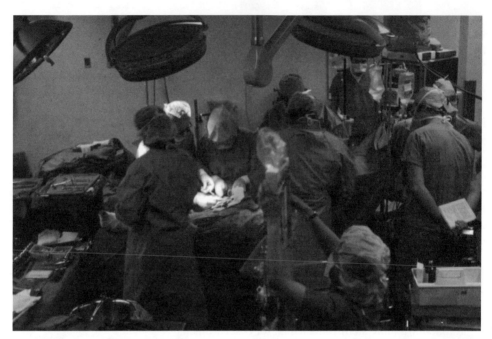

Unnecessary surgery kills: Surrounded by nurses and assistants, a surgeon performs a hysterectomy. Many such operations are not medically necessary, and unnecessary surgeries result overall in 10,000 deaths each year.

Psychiatrists constitute a disproportionate share (in relation to other medical specialists) of Medicare and Medicaid fraud. Examples of physician fraud by psychiatrists include charging patients for individual therapy when patients are actually involved in group therapy, charging a fee for "treatment" that is in reality sexual relations between psychiatrist and "patient," and charging for therapy that simply constitutes the prescription of pharmaceutical drugs (Jesilow, Pontell, and Geis, 1993:133). Moreover, psychiatrists represent approximately 8 percent of all physicians but about 20 percent of all physicians suspended from Medicaid for fraud (Rosoff, Pontell, and Tillman, 1998).

A second type of occupational fraud is insider trading, a form of securities fraud. **Insider trading** occurs when one uses "inside information" (information unavailable to the public) to gain a personal advantage over others in the buying and selling of stock. Individuals obtain such inside information because of their occupational position. For example, if one company plans to take over another, a large number of people are usually involved in the decisionmaking (lawyers, corporate executives, and others). All these people know that if the takeover occurs, the value of each company's stock will change. Thus, prior to takeover, some of these people may take advantage of their "inside information," using it to buy and/or sell stock prior to public disclosure. This is illegal.

One of the earliest insider trading cases involved the Texas Gulf Sulfur Company. In 1963 large deposits of copper and zinc were discovered by company engineers. Employees with access to this information (prior to public disclosure) abused that privilege to profit personally by buying considerable amounts of the company's stock. The employees were convicted of insider trading, the court concluding that all potential investors should have equal access to this type of information and that company employees—"insiders"— should not have an advantage over the public at large (Bequai, 1978:26).

In the 1980s and 1990s, numerous insider trading cases came to public attention, including the following (Green and Berry, 1985; Rosoff, Pontell, and Tillman, 1998):

- Paul Thayer, official of LTV Corporation and former deputy secretary of defense, admitted committing insider trading in 1985.
- Thomas Reed, former Reagan national security aide, used inside information to convert a $3,000 stock option into a $427,000 gain in two days.
- Dennis Levine, managing director of Drexel Burnham Lambert (an investment banking firm), and Ivan Boesky, Wall Street's most successful arbitrageur—two of the major actors in an informal 1986 network—exchanged information on mergers, takeovers, and corporate restructurings in order to execute trades prior to public disclosure. It is alleged that Boesky profited more than $50 million and Levine almost $13 million from this insider trading network.
- Part of the Levine/Boesky network was Martin A. Siegel, who sold takeover information to Boesky from August 1982 until February 1986.
- In 1987 it was uncovered that Timothy Tabor (ex-vice-president of Kidder, Peabody), Richard Wigton (Kidder vice-president), and Robert M. Freeman (head of arbitrage at Goldman, Sachs) were also involved in the network, exchanging takeover information that allegedly earned its participants millions of dollars.
- In 1994 it was shown an investor paid a Keystone mutual fund analyst $700,000 for insider information on the fund's future investments.
- In 1995, a Time Warner employee had advance information that company stock was about to fall in value. Subsequently, this employee sold 20,000 shares of Time Warner stock and avoided $413,700 in losses.

Overall, it is estimated that about one-half the stock market reaction to forthcoming takeovers occurs prior to announcement date, and therefore insider trading continues to be a frequent crime (Green and Berry, 1985:273). Indeed, corporate takeovers totaled $339 billion in 1994, breaking the previous record set in 1988, and a record number of insider trading cases (forty-five) were prosecuted that same year (Rosoff, Pontell, and Tillman, 1998).

13.2 CORPORATE CRIME

We define "corporate crime" as (1) illegal and/or socially injurious acts of intent or indifference (2) that occur for the purpose of furthering the goals of a corporation and (3) that physically and/or economically abuse individuals in the United States and/or abroad. Thus, corporate crime includes not only illegal acts but also socially injurious acts that lie outside the jurisdiction of criminal or regulatory law. Moreover, corporate crime includes harmful acts that result from indifference to the consequences of certain actions as well as from the deliberate intent to harm. By including "indifference," we follow Box, who explained that if

> a person intends doing *someone* harm, it cannot be assumed that s/he displays a disdain towards humanity, although it is clearly directed towards the particular intended victim. However, if indifference characterizes the attitude a person has toward the consequences of his/her action, then s/he is indifferent as to who suffers—it could literally be anybody—and this does display disdain for humanity in general. In this sense, the intent to harm someone may be less immoral (or at least no more immoral) than to be indifferent as to whom is harmed. (1983:21)

Finally, our definition notes that corporations perpetrate violence and theft on members of U.S. society and sometimes on other societies as well. Corporate crime victimizes large numbers of people throughout the world, and it is considerably more harmful and dangerous than the crimes we have already discussed in this and other chapters.

We are not alone in our concern about corporate crime. U.S. residents—according to opinion polls and studies—seem to believe that corporate crime is widespread and not something to be taken lightly (Cullen, Maakestad, and Cavender, 1987:43). The most comprehensive study to date on corporate crime, by Marshall Clinard and Peter Yeager (1980), substantiated these concerns. Clinard and Yeager analyzed federal, administrative, civil, and criminal actions either initiated or completed by twenty-five federal agencies against the 447 largest publicly owned manufacturing corporations in the United States. In addition, these sociologists conducted a smaller study of the 105 largest wholesale, retail, and service corporations, for a total of 552 corporations studied (p. 110). Clinard and Yeager limited their investigations to *actions initiated* against corporations for violations (roughly equivalent to arrests or prosecutions) and *actions completed* (equivalent to convictions). Although they uncovered only "the tip of the iceberg of total violations" (p. 111), Clinard and Yeager found considerable corporate crime. Of the corporations, 60 percent had at least one action initiated against them, 42 percent were multiple offenders, and the most frequent violators averaged 23.5 violations per corporation (p. 116). In short, corporate crime is, indeed, widespread.

We turn now to certain specific types of corporate crime.

Corporate Violence

In this section we examine **corporate violence** against workers, consumers, and the general public. We begin with workers.

Every year approximately 100,000 U.S. workers die from work-related diseases, approximately 11,000 workers die and 1.8 million are disabled from work-related accidents, and approximately 390,000 workers contract new cases of job-related diseases (Friedrichs, 1996).

Some criminologists have argued that workers are injured and die on the job not because of their own carelessness (although this does occur) but, rather, because of the conditions under which workers must labor, such as production quotas (Reiman, 1995). The organization of the workplace, then, primarily determines possible worker negligence and carelessness. In addition, Schraeger and Short (1978:413) reported in the late 1970s that approximately 30 percent of all industrial accidents were the result of safety violations and another 20 percent were caused by unsafe, yet legal, working conditions. In the mid-1980s, Messerschmidt (1986:100) reviewed studies on corporate violence against workers and found that between 35 and 57 percent of job-related accidents occurred because of safety violations. However, all the preceding figures are based primarily on company reports. Because a company's insurance rating and costs are related to the frequency of injuries, illnesses, and deaths in the workplace, corporations have an incentive to hide accidents. Indeed, studies show that many do (p. 101; Berman, 1978:108). Consequently, the preceding figures most likely understate the seriousness of corporate violence. Even so, the figures clearly indicate that corporate violence in the workplace exceeds the amount of interpersonal violence in U.S. society. We pointed out in Chapter 9 that we are actually safer in the street than indoors; the evidence presented here suggests that we are safer almost anywhere than the workplace.

An example of corporate violence caused by the intentional violation of safety standards is the case of Film Recovery Systems, Inc. (Frank, 1985; see also Frank and Lynch, 1992). Workers at the Film Recovery plant who worked around cyanide—poisonous if swallowed, inhaled, or absorbed through the skin—were not protected with adequate equipment (gloves, boots, aprons, and so on) and effective ventilation. In fact, the plant air was thick with an odorous "yellow haze" of cyanide fumes (p. 22). On February 10, 1985, Stephen Golab, a worker at the plant, collapsed on the plant floor and died. During the autopsy of Golab, when the "medical examiner made the first incision, a strong almond-like smell came out of the body, indicating cyanide poisoning. Subsequent blood tests revealed that Golab had a blood cyanide level of 3.45 micrograms per milliliter, a lethal dose" (p. 22).

Three executives of Film Recovery were eventually convicted of murder and fourteen counts of reckless conduct (p. 23). As Frank pointed out, the judge in the case

> found that the three convicted defendants were "totally knowledgeable" of the hazards of cyanide. Judge Banks reiterated the evidence substantiating his findings that each of the three executives knew the dangers of cyanide and understood that their failure to provide proper protective equipment created a strong probability of death or great bodily harm. (p. 24)

The conviction of the Film Recovery executives was the first of its kind in this country. Moreover, state courts have upheld the principle that employers can be criminally prosecuted for unsafe working conditions (Friedrichs, 1996).

Nevertheless, corporations continue to expose workers to dangers, such as the "silent killers." Workers are sometimes victims of corporate violence simply because they hold a job with a company that does not adequately protect them from such dangerous substances as chemical compounds, asbestos fibers, and cotton dust. Asbestos, for example, was a suspected "silent killer" as early as 1918 when a number of life insurance companies disallowed policies to asbestos workers because of their high death rate (Epstein, 1978:83). In the 1950s a connection between asbestos and lung cancer was found by British epidemiologist Richard Doll (p. 84). The asbestos industry funded eleven studies in an attempt to rebut this link; however, fifty-two independent studies found asbestos to pose a major threat to human health (Coleman, 1994). In the late 1980s, the National Institute for Occupational Safety and Health (NIOSH) reported that 10 to 18 percent of the 12 million U.S. citizens exposed to asbestos will die from the lung disease asbestosis, 11 percent of workers exposed to asbestos will most likely develop cancerous tumors, and approximately 6,000 asbestos-related lung cancers will occur every year (Cullen, Maakestad, and Cavender, 1987:69). As sociologist James Coleman stated: "Such evidence suggests that the asbestos industry knowingly perpetrated a massive fraud on its workers and the public" (1994:79). Finally, in 1995 three asbestos companies—Queens Corning, Pittsburgh Corning, and Falker-Austin Insulation—were found liable for $42.6 million in damages for causing disease and death of eleven workers (Rosoff, Pontell, and Tillman, 1998).

Since at least the 1960s medical studies have shown that byssinosis (or brown lung disease) is a severe health problem for textile workers; yet the textile industry remains insensitive to its effect on worker health (some 85,000 textile workers suffer impaired breathing due to acute byssinosis) (Mokhiber, 1988:4). By the late 1980s and into the 1990s textile workers continued to offer detailed testimony on the extreme levels of cotton dust that fills the mills (Guarasci, 1987; Friedrichs, 1996).

As noted earlier in this chapter, women of color and poor women have been especially victimized by physician fraud, high percentages having been forced to undergo sterilization. Similarly, in business today many working-class women, to survive economically, are forced into sterilization. Unlike men—who seldom are forced to make this choice—women are often required to surrender their right to produce children in order to work (Messerschmidt, 1986:103). For instance, five women who worked for American Cyanamid Corporation were forced to undergo sterilization or lose their jobs (p. 103). Rather than making the workplace safe, the company simply excluded the women. Moreover, American Cyanamid is not unique. In the 1980s "a number of corporations, such as General Motors, B. F. Goodrich, St. Joe's Minerals, Allied Chemical, and Olin, had policies that banned women, but not men, from certain jobs unless they could prove they were sterile" (p. 103).

Men also have been forced into sterilization because of the working conditions they endure. For example, in 1961, when Dow Chemical marketed DBCP (a soil fumigant), research at that time indicated that the pesticide was a sterility hazard. However, Dow failed to inform workers of this danger, and as a result, in 1977 many workers (approximately 3,000) who had worked with DBCP became sterile in plants from California to Arkansas to Alabama (Castleman, 1979:590). Mokhiber reported that DBCP workers

> stood upon platforms over 1,000-gallon containers known as batch tanks so that they could monitor the mixing of DBCP with diluting chemicals. To the side of the tanks, other workers would measure the finished DBCP product as it poured into cans for sale. There was no ventilation system to disperse the fumes from the chemicals. (1988:140)

Eventually the three largest chemical companies stopped producing DBCP, but a smaller company, Amvac, saw this as a profitable opportunity (Seager, 1993:73–74). As their annual report for 1977 stated, because of the extensive "publicity and notoriety surrounding DBCP, it was [our] opinion that a vacuum existed in the marketplace that we could temporarily occupy. . . . [We] further believed that with the addition of DBCP, sales might be sufficient to reach a profitable level" (p. 74).

As consumers, we also are subject to victimization from corporate violence. According to the National Commission on Product Safety, 20 million U.S. citizens have suffered injuries from using unsafe products in which 110,000 are permanently disabled and 30,000 die from the injuries (Rosoff, Pontell, and Tillman, 1998).

The case of the Dalkon Shield, an IUD, is a telling example. The Dalkon Shield was manufactured, promoted, and marketed in the face of company files containing several hundred negative reports from physicians and others about its safety. Although these reports represented firm evidence linking the Dalkon Shield with seventy-five cases of uterine perforation, ectopic pregnancies, and at least seventeen deaths, they were never made public (Braithwaite, 1984:258). Approximately 2.86 million Dalkon Shields were distributed in the United States, and the vast majority of women who used this IUD developed the dangerous infection known as pelvic inflammatory disease (Mintz, 1985:20).

Myriad products—from hazardous toys to dangerous automobiles—have been found harmful to consumers. A horrific example of corporate violence against youthful consumers is the drug thalidomide that was marketed as a safe treatment for "morning sickness" during the early stages of pregnancy. Approximately 8,000 pregnant women who took the prescription drug gave birth to terribly deformed babies. The corporation that patented and distributed the drug deliberately falsified test data and concealed the facts about the drug's serious side effects (Box, 1983:24). Two victims of this case of corporate violence are described below:

Terry was born without arms or legs, had a protruding eye that had to be surgically removed, and at the age of sixteen was only two feet tall.

Alex was born with a deformed and shortened arm; one hand did not have a thumb but the other hand had an extra finger. His palate had a hole in it; his face was paralyzed on one side; he had only one ear, and it was terribly deformed; his brain was damaged, and he was deaf and mute. (Jackall, 1980:357; Mokhiber, 1988:408)

Production of an unsafe automobile, the Ford Pinto, is a notorious illustration of corporate violence against consumers. As Simon and Eitzen pointed out: "Ford knew that this car had a defective gasoline tank that would ignite even in low-speed rear-end collisions, yet the company continued its sales. Ironically and tragically Ford continued to sell this defective and dangerous car even though the problem could have been solved for a cost of $11 per vehicle" (1986:4). It is reported that as many as 900 burn deaths occurred as a result of the exploding Pinto (Dowie, 1977:20).

In the early 1970s the Firestone 500 steel-belted radial tire was produced and sold, and throughout that decade the company continued to receive evidence of its danger to motorists. The tire was plagued with sudden blowouts and the separation of its tread from the steel-belted inner layer. Although the tire had been linked to thousands of automobile accidents and at least forty-one deaths, Firestone was fined $50,000 (Rosoff, Pontell, and Tillman, 1998).

Business as usual: Corporate violence routinely impacts our daily lives. Home is supposed to be a "haven in a heartless world," yet for many people—especially those of the working class—corporate violence invades their shelter.

Another example of the occasional dangers of automobile transportation concerns documents revealing that prior to production, internal General Motors' records repeatedly warned company executives that the rear-wheel brakes of its 1980 X-cars had a tendency to lock prematurely, causing the cars to spin out of control. As Hills pointed out, despite "more than 1,700 complaints, and at least 71 known injuries and 15 deaths, GM . . . bitterly fought the government's attempt to force a recall to repair, without any charge to the owners, of over one million 1980 X-cars" (1987:7). In the 1990s, Ford was accused of legal responsibility for deaths resulting from "rollovers" by their Bronco II's, and General Motors was found liable for gas tank defects in some of their pickup trucks (Friedrichs, 1996).

In the early 1990s, Bard Company of Murray Hill, New Jersey, *deliberately* sold faulty surgical devices to consumers and used unsuspecting heart patients as "guinea pigs" to test

BOX 13.2   BIG TOBACCO CORPORATE VIOLENCE

The violence of corporate crime recently was revealed in the fraud perpetrated by the tobacco industry (Rosoff, Pontell, and Tillman, 1998:59):

- For years tobacco companies hid unfavorable research indicating that nicotine is an
  addicting drug.
- Since at least the 1960s tobacco companies knew from their own studies that smoking causes lung cancer and heart disease, yet these studies were never made public
  until they were "leaked" in the 1990s.
- Tobacco companies manipulated the nicotine level in cigarettes to make sure each
  "smoke" had enough nicotine to keep smokers hooked.
- Tobacco companies created covert campaigns to addict teenagers to nicotine in order to create lifetime smokers. The percentage of high school students who smoke
  now exceeds the percentage of smokers in the adult population.

new products not approved by the Food and Drug Administration. The devices injured
dozens of patients and killed at least one (*Portland Press Herald,* 1993).

We turn now to a discussion of violence against the general public, not only specific
consumers. Corporate pollution provides an easy first illustration of this type of corporate
crime. The case of Love Canal is no doubt the most familiar. From the late 1930s until
1953, Hooker Chemical Company dumped hundreds of tons of toxic waste into the abandoned Love Canal, near Niagara Falls, New York (Tallmer, 1987:113). In 1953, Hooker
sold the dump site to the local school board, which in turn sold it to a private developer.
The canal was filled in, and eventually houses were built on top of the chemical dump.
Some twenty years later, "as leaching wastes began to be linked to miscarriages, birth defects, and other ailments, more than 200 families fled their homes" (p. 113).

U.S. corporations produce approximately 292 million tons of toxic waste each year, and
the Environmental Protection Agency (EPA) estimates that 90 percent of it is disposed of
improperly (Coleman, 1994). Thus, Love Canal is not unique. In Times Beach, Missouri,
the EPA found dioxin levels 100 times those considered safe, forcing the federal government to purchase the entire town and move the people out (p. 39).

Probably the worst hazardous waste condition in the United States—more serious than
Love Canal and Times Beach—is, as Russell (1988) reported, the chemical contamination
of a small Arkansas community, Jacksonville, referred to by local residents as "Dioxinville." Approximately twenty chemicals have been found in Jacksonville's air, twelve of
which were also found in the Love Canal area. But the major problem in Jacksonville is
dioxin, one of the most lethal substances ever produced. Dioxin has been found to cause
cancer and fetus-malforming effects in animals at concentrations as low as 10 to 100 parts
per trillion; the EPA considers dioxin dangerous to humans when it measures one part per
billion. As Russell pointed out, just "one part per million is therefore 1,000 times more
toxic. In Jacksonville, dioxin was measured . . . at concentrations as high as 111 parts per
million," or 111,000 times as toxic as the EPA danger level (p. 9).

Jacksonville is contaminated with at least 30,000 barrels containing dioxin waste. From 1946 to 1957, Reasor-Hill Chemical Corporation buried drums of chemical waste in an open field near its plant in Jacksonville. In 1961 the plant was acquired by the Hercules Chemical Corporation, which continued to bury drums of chemical waste and began discharging processed wastewater—from production of chlordane and Agent Orange™— into a nearby creek. By 1979 it became publicly known that the plant and surrounding area were contaminated with dioxin. Today, dangerous levels of dioxin (higher than one part per billion) have been found in soil samples (taken from residents' yards), as well as in the air, the city sewer system and lagoons, the sediments of the nearby floodplain, and in fish and wood ducks (Russell, 1988:9).

This disaster could have been avoided. Dow Chemical Company knew as far back as 1965 about the dangers of dioxin. As Green and Berry reported:

> One memorandum from Dow's toxicology director warned then (1965) that the chemical could be "exceptionally toxic"; the company's medical director said that dioxin-related "fatalities have been reported in the literature." Dow's response was to discuss these problems with its competitors at a March meeting, but *not* to inform the government or public because the situation might "explode" and spur more federal regulation of the chemical industry. (1985:263)

Dow's cover-up contributed to the violence at Love Canal, Times Beach, and Jacksonville. Yet the story of hazardous waste does not end here. More and more often we find our drinking water contaminated by hazardous toxic waste sites. Little wonder that in the 1980s one of every five public water systems was found to be contaminated to some extent, mainly because of toxic chemicals seeping from waste dumps (Shavelson, 1988). More recently, it has been estimated that approximately 30,000 waste sites pose significant health problems related to water contamination, and in Ponca City, Oklahoma, families were paid $40,000 to evacuate the town because of water contamination (Rosoff, Pontell, and Tillman, 1998).

Contaminated drinking water is only a tip of the corporate violence iceberg. As Jodi Seager noted:

> American chemical companies admitted that they annually leak or vent 196 "extremely hazardous" compounds into the air. The U.S. Environmental Protection Agency (EPA) cautiously estimates that as few as 15 to 45 of the hundreds of released air toxins directly cause up to 1,700 cases of cancer each year. American industry alone generates annually 280 million tons of lethal garbage and 10.3 billion pounds of toxic chemicals that are spewed each year into the air, discharged into public waters, and flushed into the sewers—enough to fill 8,000 Love Canals. (1993:72)

Corporate Theft

Corporate theft is similar to other forms of theft—in the sense that property is taken from people—yet it is significantly different, primarily because it does not entail a face-to-face confrontation and it is not easily apparent that a crime has been committed. Three of the most costly and prevalent forms of corporate theft are deceptive advertising, financial fraud, and price-fixing. We look briefly at each.

According to the Federal Trade Commission Act, **deceptive advertising** occurs when advertisements are "misleading in a material respect" (Coleman, 1994:23). This means that advertising can in fact be false, as long as it is not deceptive. In other words, it is illegal for advertising to be both false and deceptive, or just simply deceptive. When Jello™ claims that "every kid in America loves Jello brand gelatin," they are clearly making a false statement. However, "exaggerated claims" (hype) such as this have been interpreted by the courts as not deceptive because it is believed that no reasonable person would take the statement seriously (p. 16). Nevertheless, many corporations have simultaneously lied and deceived for decades. For example, Anacin™ was found to be the subject of deceptive advertising in that its manufacturer claimed that Anacin (Simon and Eitzen, 1986:88)

- relieved nervousness, tension, stress, fatigue, and depression
- was stronger than aspirin
- brought relief within 22 seconds
- was highly recommended over aspirin by physicians
- was more effective for relieving pain than any other analgesic available without prescription

Moreover, corporations have also violated the law by engaging in deception without outright lying. For example, the bottom of a bowl of Campbell's "chunky style" soup used in a TV commercial was lined with marbles, creating the illusion that the soup was much thicker and chunkier than it actually was (Coleman, 1994).

More recent 1990s cases include the following (Rosoff, Pontell, and Tillman, 1998:42–43):

- The Federal Trade Commission accused Exxon of deceptively advertising that its 93 Supreme premium gasoline could reduce automobile maintenance costs.
- The manufacturer of No Nonsense Pantyhose was penalized for wrongly claiming that its hosiery was virtually indestructible.
- The Federal Trade Commission ruled that Stouffer Lean Cuisine had deceptively asserted in a $3 million advertising campaign that its foods were "low sodium."
- The Sara Lee Corporation was fined $130,000 for wrongly claiming that several of its products were low in fat.

Corporate executives can engage in a form of fraud that serves the interests of the corporation, **financial fraud**. Such was the case with the firm E. F. Hutton and Company. Hutton officials pleaded guilty in 1985 to defrauding some 400 banks by writing checks in excess of amounts it had on deposit. Hutton officials then moved funds—to cover these amounts—from one bank to another, thereby avoiding overdrafts. In effect, what Hutton officials did was simply provide the company with interest-free loans (Nash, 1985:5; Claybrook, 1986:35). As Cullen, Maakestad, and Cavender pointed out, the entire "operation involved nearly $10 billion; on some days the company enjoyed $250 million in illegal 'loans'" (1987:56).

In 1988, E. F. Hutton pleaded guilty to two felony counts of laundering hundreds of thousands of dollars for criminal syndicate figures and businesspeople seeking to evade payment of taxes. According to the *Washington Post,* investigators found that "customers would bring suitcases full of cash to Hutton brokers," who would then transfer the money to secret overseas bank accounts (Kurtz, 1988:A3).

Both financial institutions and criminal syndicates profit from money laundering. It is against the law not to report cash transactions in excess of $10,000. Financial institutions evade this required federal disclosure by fraudulently converting large amounts of cash (sometimes provided by criminal syndicates) into bonds worth $9,999 or less, or they secretly launder it in foreign bank accounts. Financial institutions are attracted to obtaining money from criminal syndicates because large sums of money can be used for future investments and/or interest-earning loans. As pointed out in Chapter 12, criminal syndicates benefit from money laundering because, in essence, this process changes "dirty" money into "clean" money.

Price-fixing is probably the most expensive form of corporate theft. The basic purpose of antitrust laws is to impede corporations from colluding to fix prices (price-fixing) by ensuring that competition keeps prices as low as possible. Profits above those that would be produced in a competitive industry are illegal (Messerschmidt, 1986). Probably the most famous price-fixing incident is the case of Heavy Electrical Equipment, in which twenty-nine corporations—such as General Electric and Westinghouse—conspired to fix prices, primarily on government contracts (Pearce, 1976; Green, Moore, and Wasserstein, 1972). The illegal costs paid by purchasers of the electrical equipment in this case alone totaled $1.75 billion per year for seven years (Hills, 1987). Recent cases of price-fixing indicate that this crime is widespread, occurring in such diverse industries as steel, glass, natural gas, infant formula, commercial explosives, athletic shoes, residential doors, scouring pads, plastic dinnerware, video games, white bread, and Passover matzo (Rosoff, Pontell, and Tillman, 1998).

13.3 TRANSNATIONAL CORPORATE CRIME

Transnationals—large corporations that maintain business operations in more than one country—are clearly the worst corporate offenders. The Clinard and Yeager (1980:119) study discussed earlier found that small corporations (annual sales of $300–499 million) accounted for only 10 percent of violations, medium-sized corporations (annual sales of $500–999 million) for 20 percent, but large corporations (annual sales of $1 billion or more) for almost 75 percent of all violations. Moreover, large corporations accounted for 72.1 percent of the serious and 62.8 percent of the moderately serious violations (p. 119).

Of the fifteen largest corporations in the world in 1978 (the time of Clinard and Yeager's study), three were car manufacturers, eight were oil companies, and one was a chemical producer (Box, 1983:76). The largest corporations, then, are the worst offenders in

view of Clinard and Yeager's finding that "the oil, pharmaceutical, and motor vehicle industries" are the "most likely" to commit transnational corporate crime (p. 119).

Large corporations invest heavily outside the United States. As Michalowski and
Kramer reported:

> Three-fourths of all U.S. companies with sales over 100 million dollars had manu-
> facturing facilities in other countries by 1975. By 1977 developing nations had sur-
> passed developed ones in dollar value as locations for manufacturing by U.S. indus-
> tries. Re-importation of overseas assembly by U.S. companies increased five-fold
> between 1969 and 1983, and in the textiles and electronics industries more than half
> of all current sales by U.S. corporations are now assembled abroad. (1987:35)

Bribery

This transnational nature of U.S. corporations has resulted in considerable Third World corporate crime, ranging from bribery to export of hazardous products to dangerous working
conditions. Regarding bribery, one study of thirty-four U.S. transnational corporations that
admitted paying overseas bribes found that the bribes totaled $93.7 million and the result-
ing sales revenues amounted to $679 billion (Coleman, 1994). As Coleman pointed out,
"the bribe money constituted only 0.014 percent of the sales of those companies" (p. 42).

Because of the enormous volume of bribery, in 1977 Congress enacted the Foreign Corrupt Practices Act, which attempts to prevent such conduct. Yet transnational bribery continues. For example, in 1984 the Justice Department investigated the Bechtel Group for
bid rigging and for illegal payments to a South Korean utility company that was awarding
contracts for nuclear plant construction, and in the 1990s the media continued to report violations of the Foreign Corrupt Practices Act (Green and Berry, 1985:266; *Wall Street
Journal,* 1993).

Bribery is clearly profitable for transnationals and the political elites in Third World
countries, yet it perpetrates serious harm on a good portion of the rest of the people in
these countries. Braithwaite convincingly argued that transnational bribery is one of the
most destructive and injurious crimes today because of its unequal and antidemocratic
consequences:

> When a government official in a Third World country recommends (under the influ-
> ence of a bribe) that his country purchase the more expensive but less adequate of
> two types of aircraft, then the extra millions of dollars will be found from the taxes
> sweated out of the country's impoverished citizens. For a mass consumer product, the
> million dollar bribe to the civil servant will be passed on in higher prices to the con-
> suming public. Although it is conceivable that bribes can be used to secure the sale
> of a better and cheaper product, the more general effect is to shift the balance of busi-
> ness away from the most efficient producer and in favor of the most corrupt producer.
> The whole purpose of business-government bribes is, after all, the inegalitarian pur-
> pose of enticing governments to act against the public interest and in the interest of
> the transnational. (1979:126)

Dumping

Transnational corporations are also involved in "dumping" on other countries certain hazardous products banned or not approved for sale in the United States (Messerschmidt, 1986:112). U.S.-based transnationals frequently sell to other nations defective medical devices, lethal drugs, known carcinogens, toxic pesticides, contaminated foods, and other products ruled unfit for use and/or consumption in the United States (Dowie, 1987:47). For example, the contraceptive Depo-Provera—banned in the United States because of its severe side effects—was dumped in seventy foreign countries, especially in the Third World (pp. 51–52).

A. H. Robbins dumped approximately 1.71 million Dalkon Shields in forty foreign countries (Mintz, 1985:21), and the Agency for International Development (AID) purchased approximately 700,000 Dalkon Shields for distribution in the Third World (Mintz, 1986:2). These IUDs were sold by Robbins to the Agency for International Development at a 48 percent discount and were packaged *unsterilized* (Braithwaite, 1984:258). They were then distributed by AID to a variety of countries in Africa, Asia, the Middle East, the Caribbean, and Central and South America, where medical techniques are underdeveloped and consumer protection laws are practically nonexistent. Obviously, tens of thousands of women worldwide have been victimized by this corporate crime (Messerschmidt, 1986:113).

Corporations also dump chemicals, such as pesticides, on foreign markets. For example, DDT—a pesticide banned in the United States—in the mid-1980s was being sold particularly in Central and South America, only to return home on such imported food as bananas and coffee (Asinoff, 1985:3). Earlier in this chapter we discussed the effects of the pesticide DBCP on workers in the United States. Although eventually banned for sale in the United States, law permits the export of DBCP to other countries. As a result, some 20,000 plantation workers in Latin America have died from working around DBCP, and thousands have experienced sterility, breathing problems, convulsions, nerve damage, and blindness (Simon, 1999). Overall, more than 150 million pounds of "blacklisted" products worth up to $800 million are dumped each year, representing approximately 25 percent of U.S. pesticide production (p. 185). According to Russell Mokhiber:

> U.S. chemical companies ship overseas at least 150 million pounds a year of pesticides that are totally prohibited, severely restricted, or never registered for use in this country. Although data on the effects of this practice are incomplete, evidence indicates a problem of major proportions. The World Health Organization estimated in 1973 that 250,000 pesticide poisonings, 6,700 of which are fatal, occur each year in the Third World. The Oxford Committee on Famine Relief estimated in 1982 that the toll had risen to 375,000 poisonings with a resulting 10,000 deaths each year. (1988:185)

Dangerous Working Conditions

Transnationals have also—in addition to bribery, corruption, and dumping—relocated dangerous working conditions to other countries. Transnationals search for areas of the

The runaway hazardous shop: Many businesses relocate from the United States to Mexico, where pollution controls are minimal. This particular U.S.-owned plant employs Mexican workers and is situated in the "maquiladores zone," where working conditions are extremely dangerous.

world where pollution controls and worker safety regulations are minimal or nonexistent. As Barry Castleman has pointed out: "Runaway hazardous shops" have been leaving the United States for those areas of the world where illegal actions in home countries are permissible (1979:570). For example, in the United States, it is now illegal to expose workers to carcinogenic agents, such as asbestos. However, in Mexico, the "law merely provides a light fine ($45 to $90) for the failure to warn workers that they are working around a health hazard" (Simon, 1999:186) Consequently, U.S. asbestos makers have increasingly relocated plants in Mexico and other Third World countries where there exists little control over workplace hazards (p. 186).

Additionally, Mexico provides a prime example of the consequences from relocating dangerous polluting plants. Indeed, the U.S.–Mexico border has become "a two-thousand mile Love Canal":

These plants have filled the sky and water with a staggering amount of chemical pollution. With this contamination have come all the accompanying human miseries. A disturbing pattern of deformities and mental retardation has been observed among children of this area. Their mothers had all worked in the *maquiladoras* zone [border area where U.S. companies invest] and had been exposed to toxic chemicals. (Rosoff, Pontell, and Tillman, 1998:98)

Indeed, economists have argued that the North American Free Trade Agreement (NAFTA), signed by Canada, the United States, and Mexico in 1993, has accelerated the trend toward expansion of the Mexican maquiladora industrial sector. Whereas the U.S. economy has lost approximately 450,000 jobs since the signing of NAFTA, foreign direct investment rose 64 percent in 1994, the first year after NAFTA's activation. This resulted in approximately 750,000 Mexican workers employed in some 2,500 export maquiladora plants (Burgoon, 1996).

REVIEW

This chapter examined different types of white-collar crime—occupational crime, corporate crime, and transnational corporate crime. These crimes are similar to crimes previously discussed because they also entail theft and violence. However, they differ from other crimes because (1) they cause far greater victimization and (2) their type of victimization is less apparent. The more important points of this chapter are outlined as follows.

Occupational Crime

1. There are two major types of occupational crime: theft and fraud. Occupational theft includes employee theft and embezzlement, which differ in what is stolen—merchandise and job-related items or money, respectively.

2. Employee theft and embezzlement—two of the most costly crimes in the United States—occur in different ways depending upon the type of job and range from simply stealing merchandise to "taking from the till" and "manipulating the books" to collective embezzlement.

3. Two types of occupational fraud are physician fraud and insider trading. The former occurs through prescription of pharmaceutical drugs, surgical procedures, and treating Medicare and Medicaid patients. Insider trading results when "insiders" gain special advantage in the buying and selling of stock.

Corporate Crime

1. Corporate violence causes considerable worker illness, injury, and death; corporations perpetrate violence on consumers and the general public.

2. Three of the most costly and prevalent forms of corporate theft are deceptive advertising, financial fraud, and price-fixing.

Transnational Corporate Crime

1. Transnational corporations are the worst corporate offenders.

2. Three of the most costly and prevalent forms of transnational corporate crime are bribery, dumping, and relocating dangerous working conditions.

QUESTIONS FOR CLASS DISCUSSION

1. Why is it valuable to study white-collar crime?

2. How do various types of work help determine specific types of occupational theft? How does the thesis advanced by Ditton and Mars relate to your own job? Your parents' jobs?

3. Describe how corporate violence and theft differ from the types of violence and theft discussed in Chapters 9 and 10.

4. Discuss the differences and similarities between transnational corporate crime and the other types of white-collar crime examined in this chapter.

5. Are there other forms of white-collar crime not covered in this chapter? Would these forms fit one of the three types identified here?

6. Explain how self-control and differential association theories differ on their explanation of white-collar crime.

FOR FURTHER STUDY

Readings

Friedrichs, David O. 1996. *Trusted Criminals: White-Collar Crime in Contemporary Society.* Belmont, Calif.: Wadsworth.

Pearce, Frank, and Laureen Snider, eds. 1995. *Corporate Crime: Contemporary Debates.* Toronto: University of Toronto Press.

Rosoff, Stephen M., Henry N. Pontell, and Robert Tillman. 1998. *Profit Without Honor: White-Collar Crime and the Looting of America.* Upper Saddle River, N.J.: Prentice Hall.

Websites

1. <http://www.chubb.com/library/crtoc.html>: This site offers suggestions for companies to prevent loss due to employee and customer theft. Of particular interest are those sections describing cases of white-collar criminals.

2. <http://www.osha.gov/oshstats/work.html>: From the Occupational Safety and Health Administration, this site provides current statistics on workplace deaths and injuries. It should be kept in mind that these are conservative estimates from the Bureau of Labor Statistics.

3. <http://www.natlconsumersleague.org>: The National Consumers League compiles recent information on consumer fraud.

4. <http://www.pirg.org>: Public Interest Research Groups are nonprofit organizations that monitor the safety of consumer products. This site offers PIRG reports on child deaths from unsafe toys as well as some deadly consequences of illegal dumping of toxic chemicals. Readers may be interested to find out the contact information for the PIRG in their own state.

Political Crime

Preview

Chapter 14 introduces:
- what sociologists mean by "political crime"
- the extent, nature, and costs of political crime
- the various types of political crime, including crimes against the state and crimes by the state

Key Terms

civil disobedience	political crime
corrupt campaign practices	political kickbacks
election fraud	political repression
international law	state corruption
political bribery	terrorism

Criminologists rarely recognize the category "political crime." When they do, however, they usually conceptualize political crime as crime committed against the state. However, as we show in this chapter, the state, and its representatives, often *initiate* illegal attacks upon legally functioning—albeit politically challenging—subordinate groups. Moreover, criminologists' failure to label this conduct as harmful serves to obscure the real nature of such actions. As we assert in the following argument, the state's political actions not infrequently result in violations of domestic and international law.

Accordingly, our definition of **political crime** is threefold, entailing not only crimes *against* the state (violations of law for the purpose of modifying or changing social conditions) but also crimes *by* the state, both domestic (violations of law and unethical acts by state officials and agencies whose victimization occurs inside the United States) and international (violations of domestic and international law by state officials and agencies whose victimization occurs outside the United States).

14.1   POLITICAL CRIMES AGAINST THE STATE

Political crimes against the state are carried out for the purpose of changing or modifying existing social conditions. When individuals and/or groups believe a particular social condition (or overall social structure) is problematic in some important way, they may attempt to modify the social order, or alter it entirely, by means that violate criminal law. Political crimes against the state differ from other crimes discussed in this book in that they are not engaged in for personal gain. Rather, they are committed in behalf of a specific group (class, race, gender, political party, for example). Moreover, political crimes against the state are usually intentionally overt and public, rather than covert and secret.

Political crimes against the state, then, involve intentional violations of criminal law for political purposes, as well as various acts criminalized by the state for the purpose of curbing political dissent. Political crimes against the state may also be violent or nonviolent in nature. We consider first some examples of violent political crimes against the state.

Violent Political Crimes Against the State

Social groups have turned to violence in a bid to modify or change the social order throughout U.S. history. In fact, the United States was born of politically violent crimes against the British government. For example, by encouraging, and then engaging in, the Revolutionary War (1775–1783), colonists violated the British law of treason, which made it illegal to levy war against the king (Maier, 1972:19).

Native Americans in the United States have likewise resorted to violence to oppose state policies and to change social conditions. Although the examples are legion, consider briefly the case involving the Lakota Sioux and General George Armstrong Custer. In 1868 the U.S. government signed the Fort Laramie Treaty with the Lakota, guaranteeing the Lakota tribal sovereignty and assuring them perpetual control over "unceded Indian territory from which whites are excluded, stretching from the Missouri River west to the Powder River hunting grounds into the Wyoming Big Horn Mountains and from the Canadian border South into Nebraska" (Garitty, 1980:262).

The Battle of the Little Big Horn: Violations of treaty rights by the U.S. government led to the battle of the Little Big Horn in 1876. Today, Native Americans continue to struggle for control of their land, culture, and treaty rights.

However, the treaty was repeatedly broken by the U.S. government. In 1874 Custer trespassed onto Lakota land to confirm the existence of gold in the Black Hills of South Dakota. Gold was indeed found, and Custer's cavalry allowed thousands of "gold-hungry miners" to scrape the Black Hills clean (Johansen and Maestas, 1979:125). As a result, in 1876 the Lakota, Cheyenne, and Arapaho assembled at Little Big Horn in Montana. This gathering has been reported to be "the largest gathering of native peoples ever to have taken place in the hemisphere" (Garitty, 1980:263). Led by Gall, Two Moons, Dull Knife, and Crazy Horse, the Native Americans responded to the trespassers by killing Custer and 204 of his men because they had "violated the sanctity of the Black Hills" (Johansen and Maestas, 1979:29). This did not stop the U.S. government from violating the treaty; they continued to do so until 1889, when the Great Sioux Nation was reduced, in violation of the treaty, to five small reservations in western South Dakota (Ortiz, 1977:92).

Overall, between 1776 and 1871 the U.S. government ratified 371 treaties with native Indian nations (Weyler, 1982:65). Figure 14.1 traces the results of U.S. government violations of those treaties. The Lakota example is important not only for indicating the use of violence to change social conditions and to oppose state policy but also for understanding that groups often resort to violence *in response* to state violence and/or criminality.

Similarly, farmers in the United States have engaged in violence to change existing conditions. Prior to 1800, farmers were involved in numerous rebellions, the Shays' Rebellion being one of the most famous. In the late 1700s many farmers experienced severe social and economic problems, forcing many to borrow money at extremely high interest rates to

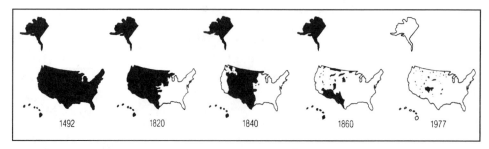

FIGURE 14.1   Native-American Land within the United States
SOURCE: *Weyler,* 1981, p. 65.

survive. Moreover, in order to meet their growing debts "they mortgaged their future crops and went still deeper into debt" (Parenti, 1983:63). And, as Parenti pointed out:

> Among the people there grew the feeling that the revolution against the English crown had been fought for naught. Angry armed crowds in several states began blocking foreclosures and forcibly freeing debtors from jail. They gathered at county towns to prevent courts from sentencing honest men to jail for being unable to pay mountainous debts and ruinous taxes. Disorders of a violent but organized kind occurred in a number of states. In the winter of 1787, debtor farmers in western Massachusetts led by Daniel Shays took up arms. But their rebellion was forcibly put down by the state militia after skirmishes that left eleven men dead and scores wounded. (p. 64)

Workers also have historically engaged in violence to change certain working conditions. The extraordinarily unsafe, lengthy, and alienating working conditions in the 1800s and early 1900s led many workers to turn to labor violence in order to make their grievances effective. A good example was the 1886 struggle for the eight-hour day that resulted in substantial violence between striking workers and the police. In May of that year a major rally was held at Haymarket Square in Chicago; when the last speaker had finished, a bomb exploded among the police, killing one and wounding many others. The police responded by firing into the crowd. The labor movement in the late 1800s and early 1900s—for the eight-hour day and other job demands—resulted in many long and bloody battles (Brecher, 1980:36–47; Lens, 1973:55–65).

Women also have engaged in violence at times in an attempt to change social conditions. For example, during the U.S. suffrage movement (to give women the right to vote) a number of feminist marches turned to mob violence between the demonstrators and outside agitators (O'Neil, 1969:76–81). However, the suffrage movement in the United States was clearly not as militant as it was in England. The British suffragettes (the Women's Social and Political Union) engaged in a specific strategy of violence—such as breaking windows, arson, and vandalism—to achieve political ends; their motto was "Deeds not Words" (Heidensohn, 1985:23–24).

More recent violent political crimes against the state abound. For instance, many of the African American urban rebellions in the 1960s and 1970s were motivated by political concerns for civil rights. During the same period, groups such as the Weather Underground—an organization that broke off in 1969 from the Students for a Democratic Society—turned to violence as a means for political change. The Underground announced the following in 1969: "Kids know that the lines are drawn; revolution is touching all of our lives. Tens of thousands have learned that protest and marches don't do it. Revolutionary violence is the only way" (cited in Evans, 1983:255).

Certain feminist groups in the United States have engaged in such violent acts as setting afire, or bombing, shops selling pornographic materials. For example, in 1980 in Seattle, women's antipornography groups stink-bombed several pornography bookstores, and in that same year in New York City, "three porn movie houses were firebombed" (Morgan, 1980:138). In 1986, six members of the United Freedom Front were convicted of violent, politically motivated crimes. According to the *New York Times,* the six were found guilty of bombing (unoccupied) military centers and corporate buildings that were either defense contractors or companies doing business in South Africa (Buder, 1986:B3).

Nonviolent Political Crimes Against the State

Most political crime against the state is not violent. Individuals and groups in the United States historically have engaged in such actions as civil disobedience and demonstrations of a nonviolent nature, which sometimes result in criminalization by the state. Consider a few examples.

The efforts of Martin Luther King Jr. and the civil rights movement of the early 1960s to end racial segregation in the United States were based on an explicitly nonviolent strategy. Dr. King's major weapon was **civil disobedience**, or refusing to obey certain laws because they are considered unjust. In his famous "Letter from Birmingham Jail," King put forth his arguments for such actions:

> There are two types of laws: there are *just* and there are *unjust* laws. I would agree with St. Augustine that "An unjust law is no law at all." Now what is the difference between the two? How does one determine when a law is just or unjust? . . . Any law that uplifts human personality is just. Any law that degrades human personality is unjust. All segregation statutes are unjust because segregation distorts the soul and damages the personality. It gives the segregator a false sense of superiority, and the segregated a false sense of inferiority. . . . So segregation is not only politically, economically, and sociologically unsound, but it is morally wrong and sinful. . . . So I can urge men to disobey segregation ordinances because they are morally wrong. . . . I hope you can see the distinction I am trying to point out. In no sense do I advocate evading or defying the law as the rabid segregationist would do. This would lead to anarchy. One who breaks an unjust law must do it *openly, lovingly,* and with a willingness to accept the penalty. I submit that an individual who breaks a law that conscience tells him is unjust, and willingly accepts the penalty by staying in jail to arouse the conscience of the community over its injustice, is in reality expressing the very highest respect for law. (Cited in Washington, 1986:293–294)

BOX 14.1   TERRORISM

Terrorism is generally defined as the use of violence or the threat of violence to coerce for political purposes. Thus, in addition to what previously was discussed, individuals sometimes assassinate members of the state for political reasons. Some of the more well-known political assassins are John Wilkes Booth, Leon Czolgosz, Oscar Collazo and Griselio Torresola, and Sirhan Sirhan (Hagan, 1997). John Wilkes Booth murdered President Lincoln in 1865 in support of slavery and the Confederacy; Czolgosz murdered President McKinley in 1901 as part of an anarchist revolt; Collazo and Torresola's assassination attempt of President Truman in 1950 was in support of Puerto Rican independence; and Sirhan felt the assassination of Robert Kennedy in 1969 would help the Palestinian cause. Probably the most well-known political assassination is that of President John F. Kennedy. However, as David Simon pointed out, that assassination remains unsolved and is marked by considerable controversy (1999:3–4, 261, 305–306):

- After the assassination, President Johnson, Assistant Attorney General Katzenbach, and FBI Director Hoover ordered a cover-up of the investigation. All three agreed that the public must be convinced that Lee Harvey Oswald was the lone killer.
- The House Special Committee on Assassinations found that President Kennedy's assassination most likely resulted from a conspiracy, not one individual. The committee pointed to syndicated crime as having the "means, motive, and opportunity" to assassinate the president, and/or anti-Castro Cubans killed the president because he did not support the Bay of Pigs invasion with air cover.
- Others have argued that the CIA killed President Kennedy because he was about to make peace with the Soviet Union, end the Cold War, and withdraw military personnel from Vietnam. Moreover, the CIA was allegedly upset because the Kennedy administration canceled covert operations against Cuba.

On April 19, 1995, the worst act of terrorism against the United States was committed by Timothy McVeigh and Terry Nichols. As members of antigovernment paramilitary right-wing militia groups (approximately 850 such groups currently operate in 49 states), these two conspired and carried out the bombing of the Alfred P. Murray Federal Building in Oklahoma City, killing 168 people and injuring more than 500. McVeigh was found guilty of murder, conspiracy, and using a weapon of mass destruction; Nichols was convicted of conspiracy and involuntary manslaughter in the bombing. Some 4,000 pounds of homemade explosives were packed inside a rented truck and detonated in front of the federal building. A large number of those killed were federal employees as well as 15 children under the age of five who were attending a day-care center in the building. According to the FBI (1997:16), the rise of the militia movement and recent increases in its activities pose a serious security threat to the United States.

All of the above examples of terrorism were committed by citizens of the United States. However, sometimes these violent political crimes are committed by citizens of other countries but directed toward the U.S. government. The bombing of the World Trade Center building in New York City—which killed six people, injured over 1,000, and caused more than $500 million in damage—is a prime example. On November 12, 1997, Ramzi Yousef and Eyad Najim were convicted of the 1993 bombing. Yousef directed and helped to carry out the bombing while Najim drove the truck that carried the bomb. Four others previously had also been convicted of the bombing. These men allegedly bombed the World Trade Center building in order to punish the United States for its continued support of Israel.

Individuals can also engage in civil disobedience not for the purpose of changing the law being broken but rather to protest—and hopefully put a stop to—particular state policies. For example, in 1976 members of the Clamshell Alliance engaged in civil disobedience by organizing a "sit-in" at the construction site of the Seabrook, New Hampshire, nuclear power plant. On May 1 of that year, 1,414 people occupied the construction site (for the purpose of halting construction of the plant) and were arrested for trespassing, more than half refusing bond and spending about two weeks in National Guard armories. The resulting publicity inspired other groups around the country, and a massive antinuclear movement eventually emerged (Dwyer, 1983:153–154).

Another example of this type of civil disobedience involved student and community demonstrators at the University of Massachusetts in the fall of 1986. The demonstrators—who included former President Carter's daughter, Amy, and ex-"yippie" leader Abbie Hoffman—engaged in a sit-in at a campus building used to recruit agents for the Central Intelligence Agency (CIA). Carter, Hoffman, and others, arrested for trespassing and disorderly conduct, were tried in April 1987. Although the demonstrators admitted at trial that they had trespassed on university property, they were nevertheless allowed by the judge to assert the criminal defense of necessity and won acquittal. This affirmative defense can be used to prove that a defendant's "illegal" acts were justified—in this case to stop a more dangerous crime: the recruiting of CIA agents who would, according to the demonstrators, most likely engage in significantly more heinous and illegal activities. After presenting the testimony of various experts on CIA criminality around the globe, the jury acquitted the demonstrators (Tushnet, 1988:2).

Individuals and groups may also engage in nonviolent protests and demonstrations against state policies that are not specifically directed at violating any law. Yet, because the state regards such behavior as threatening, it enforces certain laws chosen for the purpose of curbing the dissent. For example, the trial of the Chicago Eight—which grew out of nonviolent demonstrations against the Vietnam War conducted at the 1968 Democratic convention—resulted in the demonstrators being charged with "conspiracy." The state does not have to prove that an activity was actually planned, only that the conspirators communicated in some way (Clinard and Quinney, 1973:156). All Chicago Eight defendants were acquitted of conspiracy but received numerous contempt citations because of their behavior during the course of the trial. As Clinard and Quinney noted, "whether or not the defendants are convicted, the conspiracy law is an effective form of political harassment whereby those who threaten the system can be detained for long periods of time at great personal expense" (p. 156).

A final example of nonviolent political crime against the state is spying. There exist different types of political spies, which, Hagan (1997:124–131) argued, can be classified according to motivation. For example, there are "mercenary spies," which are the most common and provide intelligence secrets to a foreign government for monetary gain; "ideological spies," which provide secrets to foreign governments because of strong political or ideological beliefs; "alienated/egocentric spies," who provide secrets to a foreign government because they want to "get even" with the U.S. government or government agency; and finally, the "buccaneer spy," who provides secrets to a foreign government for adventure and for excitement.

Probably the most well-known recent case of illegal spying is that of Aldrich Ames, a thirty-two-year veteran of the Central Intelligence Agency (CIA). Beginning in 1985 and continuing until 1994, Ames stole intelligence secrets and sold them to the Soviet Union. Ames is probably the highest-paid known Soviet spy, earning between $1.5 and $2.5 million. He most likely got caught because of his lavish lifestyle—he paid $540,000 in cash for a home in Arlington, Virginia, bought two new cars (including a Jaguar), bought stock worth $165,000, and charged $455,000 on credit cards. Ames was sentenced to life in prison (Hagan, 1997:119).

"Computer spying" emerged as a growing security issue in the 1990s. Consider the following examples (Rosoff, Pontell, and Tillman, 1998:386):

- A twenty-two-year-old former Harvard student allegedly used stolen university passwords to break into military computers.
- Two "hackers" penetrated seven computer systems, gaining access to all information at Griffis Air Base in New York. The spies copied files—including sensitive battlefield simulations—and installed devices to read the passwords of everyone entering the systems.
- Five members of the Chaos Computer Club broke into computers at NASA, the Pentagon, the White Sands Missile Range, and the Redstone Missile Base. They sold classified computer data to the Russians.

14.2   DOMESTIC POLITICAL CRIMES BY THE STATE

Domestic political crimes by the state are violations of law and unethical conduct by state officials or agencies whose victimization occurs within the boundaries of the United States. We discuss two types: **state corruption** and **political repression**. State corruption is illegal or unethical use of state authority for personal or political gain (Benson, 1978:xiii); political repression is illegal or unethical conduct by state officials or agencies for purposes of repressing domestic political dissent.

State Corruption

State corruption exists at city, state, and national levels and consists of a wide range of state-directed activities—such as purchasing goods and services, use of public funds and property, tax assessment and collection, regulation of commercial activity, zoning and land use, law enforcement, and so on (Simon and Eitzen, 1986:170–177). We focus on four types of state corruption: political bribery, political kickbacks, election fraud, and corrupt campaign practices.

Political bribery is the acceptance of money or property by state officials in return for favors (Simon and Eitzen, 1986:169). Politicians, for example, have myriad opportunities for involvement in bribery, accepting money for such services as introducing special forms of legislation, voting a specific way on already introduced legislation, and voting in favor of a government contract. Probably the best-known recent case of bribery of politicians is the ABSCAM case. This FBI "sting" operation, which took place in the early 1980s, resulted in the conviction of seven members of Congress for accepting bribes from undercover FBI agents posing as Arab sheiks. The "sheiks" met the members of Congress in hotel rooms, offering them substantial amounts of money or stock for favorable legislation on business ventures. Only one of the eight politicians present refused the bribe (p. 214).

State officials, other than politicians, are also in a position to accept bribes. The police, for example, have a long history of involvement in corruption. From at least the 1890s, a legion of investigative committees has consistently unearthed substantial and wide-ranging forms of police bribery (Coleman, 1994). In the 1980s bribery in law enforcement once again came to national attention. In 1988, for example, seven Boston police detectives were convicted on fifty-seven counts of bribery totaling $18,000 over an eight-year period (*Boston Herald,* 1988:26). Moreover, over 100 law-enforcement drug-related bribery cases come before state and federal courts each year (Shenon, 1988a:A12).

Judges and lawyers have similarly been found to be involved in bribery. An investigation of the Circuit Court of Cook County, Illinois, for example, revealed that judges were found to provide specific dispositions or consideration to a case in exchange for money or other things of value and "lawyers would pay off judges for permission to 'hustle' clients in large volume criminal courtrooms" (Valukas and Raphaelson, 1988:4). In one particular court

> a corrupt chief judge assigned other judges to the "big rooms" (courts where driving under the influence cases were heard) based on their willingness to accommodate the corrupt defense lawyers who practiced there. These defense lawyers were called "miracle workers" because they never lost a case. These same lawyers got their results by paying judges, often through middlemen, for favorable disposition of their clients' drunk driving cases. Often the arresting police officer was also paid to testify in a way that created a reasonable doubt. The weakened evidence gave the corrupt judge "something to hang his hat on" in finding the defendant not guilty. (p. 4)

Most recently, several Dade County, Florida, judges were found guilty taking bribes from drug-trafficking defendants totaling $266,000, and a federal district judge in Louisiana was convicted of accepting $16,500 from a convicted drug dealer to obtain a lighter sentence (Rosoff, Pontell, and Tillman, 1998).

State officials may also participate in **political kickbacks** (that is, payment for help in obtaining a government contract). A good example of this type of corruption involved former vice president Spiro Agnew, who began receiving kickbacks from contractors, architects, and engineers when he was Baltimore County Executive in 1962. The kickbacks continued when he became governor of Maryland, and "as late as 1971, when Agnew was vice president, he received a payment in the basement of the White House" (Simon, 1999:208).

Many politicians have also been involved in **election fraud**—such as illegal voting, false registration, stuffing ballot boxes, and the like—which had its beginning in the heyday of political machines in the late 1800s. Some presidential examples include the following (Weld, 1988:187–188; Douglas, 1977:115):

- Harry Truman likely would not have been elected senator from Missouri if he had not received 50,000 fraudulent votes provided by the "Pendergast Machine" in Kansas City.

- John Kennedy was assured victory in 1960 when Chicago Mayor Richard Daley and his machine stuffed ballot boxes with Kennedy votes.
- Lyndon Johnson won his 1948 Senate race in Texas by 202 fraudulently obtained votes.
- Approximately $5,000 was allegedly used to purchase black votes for Jimmy Carter in the 1976 California primary.

Finally, **corrupt campaign practices** appear to be relatively widespread in the United States. For example, politicians tend to be extremely loyal to those who contribute to their campaign. In 1981, Senator Robert Dole, chair of the Senate Finance Committee, would not support tax loopholes for 333 Chicago commodity traders. Yet when these same traders contributed over $70,000 to Dole's 1984 campaign, he reversed himself and won the traders their loopholes (Judis, 1988). Moreover, all congressional members who received $30,000 or more in campaign contributions from the dairy industry lobby voted for dairy subsidies, and 97 percent of those members receiving $20,000 to $30,000 supported the bill (p. 7).

In addition to the foregoing, in June 1972 a group of ex-CIA Bay of Pigs operatives was caught breaking into the Democratic Party's national headquarters in the Watergate Building in Washington, D.C. Subsequent investigations revealed that the burglary was only part of an extensive campaign of political corruption "involving political espionage, electoral sabotage, wiretapping, theft of private records, and illegal use of campaign funds—planned and directed by members of Nixon's campaign staff and White House staff" (Parenti, 1983:173). In August 1974, in order to avoid an impeachment trial, Nixon resigned from office and eventually was pardoned of all crimes associated with Watergate by President Gerald Ford.

Corrupt campaign practices may also have been part of the 1980 Reagan-Bush campaign for the presidency. On November 4, 1979, the U.S. embassy in Tehran was taken over by pro-Khomeini forces. Sixty-six U.S. citizens were held captive until, mysteriously, January 20, 1981. Only two hours after President Reagan's inauguration on that day—the 444th day of captivity—the hostages were released. Why were the hostages released at that particular time? Abbie Hoffman and Jonathan Silvers (1988) think they know why. Fearing in the final weeks of the 1980 presidential campaign that President Carter would come up with an "October Surprise"—somehow bring home the hostages, thus almost guaranteeing his re-election—the Reagan-Bush campaign, Hoffman and Silvers argued, quite possibly managed to stop such an event from occurring. What follows is a summary of Hoffman and Silvers's argument.

In May 1984 the House Subcommittee on Human Resources, investigating "Unauthorized Transfers of Nonpublic Information during the 1980 Presidential Election," concluded in its report that what began as a simple inquiry into the alleged theft of Carter's debate briefing book unearthed an immense quantity of unethical—if not illegal—behavior by the Reagan-Bush campaign. For example, the subcommittee found that by October 1980, senior Reagan advisors had informants at the CIA, the Defense Intelligence Agency, the National Security Council, the White House Situation Room, and at military bases around the country for purposes of reporting any aircraft movements related to the hostages in any way. In short, by "the fall of 1980, the Carter White House was riddled with moles, spies, and informers" for the Reagan-Bush campaign (p. 151).

In addition to monitoring the possibility of a Carter "October Surprise," Reagan-Bush campaign officials may also have attempted to deal directly with the Iranians themselves. Basing their argument on anecdotal evidence, Hoffman and Silvers contend that in September 1980 Richard Allen (who would become Reagan's first National Security Adviser), Robert McFarlane (then a consultant on Iran for the Senate Armed Services Committee), and campaign adviser Laurence Silberman met a representative of the Iranian government at the L'Enfant Plaza Hotel in Washington, D.C. According to Hoffman and Silvers, Allen and Silberman admitted that this meeting did take place, yet asserted that they specifically *rejected* an offer by the Iranian that Iran could obtain release of the hostages to the Reagan-Bush campaign prior to the election. In any event, it seems neither Silberman nor Allen reported the meeting to the Carter White House.

Moreover, others, according to Hoffman and Silvers, disagreed with these Reagan-Bush officials, arguing that a deal had indeed been made with Iran. For example, Bassar Abu Sharif, Yasir Arafat's chief spokesperson, is on record saying that "Reagan people" contacted him during the first (1980) campaign, requesting "the PLO to use its influence to delay the release of the American hostages from the embassy in Tehran until after the election" (p. 152). Further, Barbara Honegger, a former policy analyst in the Reagan White House, has stated that Allen "cut a deal" with the Iranians on the hostages in Iran prior to the election. And former president of Iran, Abolhassan Bani-Sadr (exiled in France), stated that those at the Washington meeting "agreed in principle that the hostages would be liberated after the election, and that, if elected, Reagan would provide significantly more arms than Carter was offering" (p. 153). In other words, prior even to taking office, Reagan-Bush campaign officials may have attempted to guarantee victory by "cutting a deal" with Iran. In exchange for keeping the hostages until Inauguration Day, Hoffman and Silvers argued, Reagan-Bush officials pledged that Iran would receive U.S. military arms and supplies.

Others have supported Hoffman and Silvers's argument (Honegger, 1989; Sick, 1991). In particular, Gary Sick (1991) added that William Casey, Reagan's campaign manager, met with Iranian arms dealer Cyrus Hashemi in Madrid and Paris on July 26 and 27, 1980, to hammer out the deal.

The "October Surprise" argument is not without substance. The hostages were released on Inauguration Day, and that same year, on July 24, Israel contracted with Iran to sell them more than $100 million worth of U.S. arms (Marshall, Scott, and Hunter, 1987:172). Moreover, McFarlane, Casey, and Israel played important roles in the initial phases of the arms-for-hostages deal that eventually erupted as the Iran-Contra scandal.

Nevertheless, the above allegations prompted investigations by both the U.S. Senate and House. Neither inquiry found credible evidence of a secret deal. In fact, according to Lee H. Hamilton, chair of the House October Surprise Task Force, "there was virtually no credible evidence to support the accusations. Specifically, we found little or no credible evidence of communications between the 1980 Reagan campaign and the Government of Iran and no credible evidence that the campaign tried to delay the hostages' release" (1993:17).

Yet Sick (1993:17) responded to the House report by arguing that William Casey's activities were not adequately substantiated. For example, Sick has claimed that "the report says Mr. Casey could not have attended a Madrid meeting the weekend of July 26–27 because he was at the Bohemian Grove outside San Francisco. Yet the committee's own evidence places him at the Grove the following weekend, from Aug. 1 to Aug. 3" (p. 17). Casey's passport mysteriously vanished—therefore not available to the task force—and crucial pages were missing from his loose-leaf calendar. Thus, Sick concluded that questions remained, and he hoped "the task force will open its files to outside independent investigators to the maximum extent permissible by law" (p. 17).

State Political Repression

Federal agencies such as the FBI and the CIA have been involved in numerous illegal activities, many of which relate to political repression. For instance, although legally the CIA has no domestic security or law-enforcement functions, it has (1) opened and photographed the mail of over one million private citizens for twenty years, (2) broken into homes and offices, stealing documents and installing illegal surveillance devices, and (3) equipped, trained, and supported local police forces (Parenti, 1983:170–171). Similarly, since its inception in 1938, the FBI has been involved in a variety of illegal activities related to the repression of political dissent.

Historically, one of the first responsibilities of the FBI was to investigate "subversion," which was entirely unrelated to the enforcement of federal criminal laws (Church Committee, 1976:30). In 1938, for instance, the FBI *illegally* investigated subversion in (1) the maritime, steel, coal, clothing, garment, fur, automobile, and newspaper industries, (2) educational institutions, (3) organized labor, (4) youth groups, (5) African American groups, (6) government affairs, and (7) the military (p. 32). Explicit illegality included wiretapping, bugging, mail-openings, and breaking and entering. Through such illegal behavior the FBI gathered information on "radical" individuals and groups and forwarded it directly to the White House (pp. 36–38).

The major thrust of the FBI since at least 1941, however, has been its counterintelligence program, more commonly known as COINTELPRO. Although the FBI's counterintelligence function is restricted by law to "hostile foreign governments, foreign organizations, and individuals connected to them" (Churchill and Vander Wall, 1988:37), the FBI clearly went beyond that mandate to include not only intelligence gathering but also strategies and tactics for the purpose of disrupting and "neutralizing" organizations that the FBI felt were threatening to the social order. As William C. Sullivan, former head of the FBI Counterintelligence Division, stated in the mid-1970s (cited in Church Committee, 1976:66): "We were engaged in COINTELPRO tactics, to divide, conquer, weaken, in diverse ways, an organization. We were engaged in that when I entered the Bureau in 1941."

Between 1940 and the early 1960s, COINTELPRO activities were primarily directed at the U.S. Communist Party and the Socialist Workers Party (Church Committee, 1976:67). In the 1960s and early 1970s the FBI investigated new groups, implementing some 2,370 separate COINTELPRO actions (Kunstler, 1978:721). Some of the groups embraced by COINTELPRO activities were the Puerto Rican independence movement, the civil rights

The FBI and Dr. Martin Luther King Jr.: In the 1960s, the FBI attempted to "neutralize" Dr. Martin Luther King Jr. as one of the most important leaders of the civil rights movement. In the depiction above, King receives the Nobel Peace Prize in Stockholm, Sweden.

movement, Students for a Democratic Society, and the Black Liberation movement. Because of space limitation, it is impossible to discuss the effects of COINTELPRO on each of these movements. Therefore, we focus on one particular case, the FBI's campaign against Martin Luther King Jr.

In 1962 the FBI claimed that Dr. King and the civil rights movement had been duped by the Communists. This claim was eventually proved false (Garrow, 1981:59–60). Nevertheless, in December 1963—four months after the famous civil rights march on Washington and King's "I Have a Dream" speech—a nine-hour meeting was convened at FBI headquarters to discuss various "avenues of approach aimed at neutralizing King as an effective Negro leader" (Church Committee, 1976:220). Agents throughout the country were instructed to continue gathering information on King's personal life "in order that we may consider using this information at an opportune time in a counterintelligence move to discredit him" (p. 220). According to David Garrow (1981:115), the FBI went through the Southern Christian Leadership Conference's (SCLC) trash in hope of finding incriminating evidence against that organization and King. The FBI investigated Dr. King's bank and charge accounts, instituted electronic surveillance of King's apartment and his office, attempted to win cooperation with the bureau from certain SCLC employees, sent threatening forged letters in King's name to SCLC contributors, and attempted to intensify the well-known mutual dislike between King and NAACP head Roy Wilkins. However, the FBI was unable to produce any incriminating evidence against the SCLC or King himself.

BOX 14.2 THE CASE OF LEONARD PELTIER

Although COINTELPRO was allegedly abolished in 1971, FBI illegalities continued. The case of Leonard Peltier is extraordinary in this regard. Leonard Peltier is, and was in the 1970s, a member of the American Indian Movement (AIM), a national movement of Native Americans striving to restore their traditional culture and reclaim the rights guaranteed them by treaties entered into over a period of one hundred years. In 1975, Peltier was living at the Pine Ridge Indian Reservation in South Dakota (along with approximately thirty other AIM members and supporters) when, on the morning of June 26, two armed FBI agents entered the reservation allegedly in search of a young Native American accused of stealing a pair of cowboy boots. A firefight occurred between members of AIM and the FBI. Shortly thereafter, both agents and an AIM member were dead. There was never an investigation of the killing of the AIM member, yet four Native Americans were charged with the murder of the two agents. Only one, Leonard Peltier, was convicted. The charges against one of the original defendants were dropped allegedly due to a lack of evidence; the other two were brought to trial in Cedar Rapids, Iowa, in the summer of 1976. Both were eventually acquitted amid controversy concerning FBI misconduct in the prosecution of their case (Messerschmidt, 1986a:38–41).

Prior to the Cedar Rapids trial, Peltier sought political asylum in Canada, where he was apprehended by the Royal Canadian Mounted Police at the request of the FBI. He petitioned the Canadian government to grant him status as a political refugee, contending that it would be impossible for him to receive a fair trial in the United States because of his political beliefs and activities. The FBI's response to Peltier's petition was to provide the Canadian authorities with two fabricated "eyewitness" affidavits signed by a Lakota woman, Myrtle Poor Bear. It was later revealed at Peltier's trial, but out of the presence of the jury, that Myrtle Poor Bear never knew Leonard Peltier, had never seen him before, was more than fifty miles away from the crime scene on the day of the firefight, and was most likely coerced by FBI agents to sign the affidavits (pp. 78–87). The Canadian government honored the U.S. extradition request.

Unhappy with the acquittal in Cedar Rapids, and thus the "performance" of the federal judge in that case, the federal government obtained a change of venue to Fargo, North Dakota. Here the FBI found the judge they wanted. Virtually the entire defense, which had justified an acquittal in Cedar Rapids, was ruled inadmissible by the judge in Fargo. But more importantly, according to a detailed examination of the trial record (pp. 37–128), the prosecution enjoyed free rein to manipulate highly inconsistent and contradictory circumstantial evidence, and the entire trial was saturated with the suppression of evidence, the coercion of testimony and, quite possibly, judicial impropriety. It was under these circumstances that Leonard Peltier was convicted and sentenced to serve two consecutive life terms for the murder of two FBI agents.

Peltier appealed the conviction to the Eighth U.S. Circuit Court of Appeals in St. Louis. Although noting, for example, that the Myrtle Poor Bear affair was "disturbing," the court upheld his conviction. Several more appeals were heard, each fruitless. In the final appeal to the Eighth Circuit, the judges stated the following in their decision: "We recognize that there is evidence in this record of improper conduct on the part of some FBI agents, but we are reluctant to impute even further improprieties to them" (cited in Churchill and Vander Wall, 1988:326). As Churchill and Vander Wall responded, "thus, it was deemed more

(continues)

BOX 14.2   *(continued)*

appropriate that Leonard Peltier remain locked away in a maximum security cell rather than expose the FBI to further scrutiny concerning the way in which it had obtained its conviction, even *after* a clear pattern of Bureau misconduct had been demonstrated" (p. 326).

Because of the foregoing, many people worldwide believe that Peltier's arrest, prosecution, and continued confinement are the result of his political activities as a leader of AIM. Although Peltier remains behind bars, (1) he was selected to receive the International Human Rights Prize by the Human Rights Commission of Spain, (2) over fifty members of Congress have twice signed "Friend of the Court" briefs supporting Peltier's right to a new trial, (3) over fifty members of the Canadian Parliament signed a petition asking the U.S. government to order a new trial (six of the Canadian endorsers held cabinet posts at the time of Peltier's extradition), (4) human rights organizations, such as Amnesty International, have supported Peltier's request for a retrial and have recommended that an independent Commission of Inquiry be established to look into the case, and (5) over 14 million people worldwide have signed petitions demanding a new trial for Peltier.

Undaunted, on January 5, 1964, FBI agents planted a microphone in King's bedroom at the Willard Hotel in Washington, D.C. Over the next two years the FBI installed at least fourteen additional bugs in King's hotel rooms across the country, sometimes accompanied by physical and photographic surveillance (Church Committee, 1976:220). Alleging that the resulting tapes revealed "meetings" with prostitutes, the FBI then fabricated an anonymous letter to King, enclosing a copy of one of the tapes, and sent them to King on the eve of his receiving the Nobel Peace Prize (pp. 220–221). The letter, in part, reads as follows (cited in Garrow, 1981:125–126):

> King,
>   In view of your low grade . . . I will not dignify your name with either a Mr. or a Reverend or a Dr. . . . No person can overcome facts, not even a fraud like yourself . . . I repeat—no person can successfully argue against facts. You are finished . . .
>   King, there is only one thing left for you to do. . . . You are done. There is but one way out for you. You better take it before your filthy, abnormal fraudulent self is bared to the nation.

When this effort by the FBI failed to force King to commit suicide—as he himself allegedly interpreted the purpose of the message (Church Committee, 1976:221)—the FBI "leaked" the tapes and photographs to a number of leading newspapers in the United States (Wise, 1976; Bray, 1980).

Unhindered by the FBI's virulent attacks and efforts to halt his political movement, King traveled to Sweden to receive the Nobel Peace Prize. During his stay in Europe, and upon his return to the United States, the bureau continued its activities (Church Committee, 1976:221–222). The "neutralization" program actually continued until King's death.

As late as March 1968, FBI agents were instructed to neutralize King because he might, according to the bureau, become a "messiah" who could "unify and electrify the militant black nationalist movement" (p. 223). Moreover, as Churchill and Vander Wall pointed out: "Given the nature of the Bureau's campaign to neutralize King, there remain serious questions—unresolved by subsequent congressional investigations—as to the FBI's role in King's assassination in Memphis on March 31, 1968" (1988:57). Indeed, the FBI had long previously (1964) determined that New York attorney Samuel R. Pierce (an extreme conservative) should be King's successor; he would be, according to one FBI document, the "'right kind' of leader" (p. 395).

Most methods employed by the FBI under COINTELPRO were, according to the Church Committee investigating FBI illegalities, "secret programs . . . which used unlawful or improper acts" to carry out desired goals (Church Committee, 1976:137). Beyond falsification of information and documents and illegal surveillance, the FBI conducted hundreds of illegal burglaries against "threatening" individuals and organizations, stealing private files and documents. Moreover, through COINTELPRO the FBI conducted disinformation campaigns, used "agent provocateurs" to disrupt political (primarily leftist) organizations, and was implicated in the assassination of such dissident political group leaders as Fred Hampton of the Black Panther Party (Churchill and Vander Wall, 1988:64–77).

In the 1980s, the FBI was involved in intelligence gathering and overall monitoring of the Committee in Solidarity with the People of El Salvador (CISPES). Through the Freedom of Information Act, the Center for Constitutional Rights in New York obtained FBI files on CISPES, documenting political intelligence gathering and political harassment of individuals and groups associated with CISPES and working to change U.S. foreign policy in Central America. The files also reveal that fifty-two of the fifty-nine FBI field offices were involved in the massive investigation. Initially the FBI attempted to substantiate that CISPES was an agent of a foreign government and, therefore, in violation of the Foreign Agents Registration Act. When this failed, the FBI—with approval from then-Attorney General William French Smith—mounted a new investigation on the premise that CISPES was probably a "terrorist" organization. The FBI, however, never found any evidence to support this thesis either. In fact, field reports came into FBI headquarters indicating that those involved in CISPES and related organizations were "legitimate" and "respectable" people involved in such activities as demonstrations, lobbying, protests, rallies, newsletters, and occasionally conducting nonviolent civil disobedience—all protected by the First Amendment.

The FBI, however, did not stop there but went on to develop two rationales that allowed the investigation to continue. Ann Buitrago summarizes the rationales:

The "Covert Programs" Rationale: To explain away its negative results, the FBI reasoned that all the peaceful legal activities on which CISPES' broad support was based merely represented an *overt* program designed to cover a sinister *covert* program of which most CISPES members were unaware.

The "Front Groups" Rationale: The old concept of "front groups" was dredged up to enable the investigation to expand beyond CISPES chapters and affiliates to any of the hundreds of organizations whose work brought them in touch with CISPES or its members. The usefulness to the FBI of the notion of "front groups" was that even though a given group was clearly not involved in terrorism but only in public education and/or protest, it could continue to be investigated because it might be a CISPES "front." (1988:3)

These rationales had the effect of driving the investigation further and deeper. Under the guise of looking for "fronts" and "covert terrorists," the FBI employed the following techniques to investigate CISPES (pp. 7–8):

1. FBI informers infiltrated organizations and were sent to meetings and demonstrations.
2. Record checks were made of FBI files, other police records, school records, phone books, and student-faculty directories.
3. Frequent physical surveillance of people, residences, meeting places, offices, and demonstrations took place, often accompanied by photographic surveillance.
4. CISPES-related literature was collected and reviewed.
5. Radio programs were monitored.
6. License plate numbers of vehicles at or near demonstrations, public events, and conferences were traced, and the names of owners were investigated.
7. FBI interviews were attempted of CISPES leaders, members, former members, and members of other groups "knowledgeable" of CISPES.

In addition, the FBI worked closely with several right-wing groups, helping to develop further the privatization of intelligence gathering. For instance, right-wing groups—such as the Young Americans for Freedom (YAF) and CARP (followers of Sun Yung Moon)—would routinely gather "intelligence" and pass it on to the FBI. In one case a YAF document on the CISPES National Convention was sent to FBI headquarters, where it was disseminated to thirty-two field offices (Center for Constitutional Rights, 1988:3).

Ironically, the only "covert program" uncovered during this operation was conducted by right-wing groups and the FBI. In fact, the FBI's "terrorist" investigation was viewed by those investigating the case as simply a cover for conducting domestic security programs aimed at disrupting organizations critical of U.S. foreign policy. According to Buitrago, hostility toward CISPES "pours out of these documents" (1988:4–5). For example, the field office at "Dallas wrote frequently about the need to devise investigative activity '*against* this organization'; New Orleans fired off a tirade against CISPES and individuals who 'display contempt against the U.S. government,' calling for them to be deported or denied reentry if they ever left the country" (pp. 4–5).

At least one FBI agent refused to go along with this investigation. In January 1988, Jack Ryan, an FBI agent for twenty-two years, was fired because he refused to investigate peace groups opposed to U.S. policy in Central America. As Ryan stated: "Investigating this as domestic terrorism or domestic violence is absurd. . . . What our Government's doing is wrong in Central America. I don't want to be a part of it" (cited in Hopkins, 1988:14). Ryan was fired just ten months before his retirement.

14.3   INTERNATIONAL POLITICAL CRIMES BY THE STATE

In 1947, President Harry Truman signed into law the National Security Act, providing not only for the Central Intelligence Agency (CIA) but the National Security Council (NSC) as well. The primary responsibility of the CIA, according to this act, is to gather foreign intelligence and transmit it directly to the White House; the NSC was set up ostensibly as a civilian advisory group to the president on domestic, foreign, and military policies related to national security. However, both the CIA and the NSC have used their respective powers to go beyond their legislative mandates, engaging in a variety of covert operations almost from their inception. These covert operations have, at times, violated U.S. laws—such as the Neutrality Act, which makes it a crime to prepare a means for, or to furnish weapons for, military expeditions against any foreign country with which the U.S. is at peace (Tushnet, 1988:3).

In addition, both the CIA and the NSC have, at times, violated international law. **International law** embodies "various treaties, agreements, customary law principles, and general legal principles that serve to judge the actions and behavior of various nation-states that have agreed to them" (Frappier, 1984:3). The United Nations Charter, which most nations signed after World War II, is an essential part of international law. In particular, Article 2(4) of the UN Charter—which states that no country has the right to intervene in the internal affairs of another country—has been violated continually by the CIA and, most recently, by the NSC.

In this final section we present examples of violations of both domestic and international law by the CIA. Following this we turn to CIA and NSC violations of domestic and international laws during the Iran-contra affair. Both cases represent international political crimes by the state because although they may violate both domestic and international law, the resulting victimization occurs outside of the United States.

International Crimes by the CIA

In 1953 the CIA engaged in its first extensive operation to overthrow a democratically elected foreign leader. This occurred in Iran, where the legitimately elected and reform-minded prime minister, Mohammed Mossadegh, was toppled by the CIA. Mossadegh nationalized several large foreign-owned oil companies, thus challenging U.S. interests in the region (Prados, 1986:92–98). Even though Mossadegh offered compensation, Secretary of State John Foster Dulles, and his brother Allen Welsh Dulles (then director of the CIA), supported President Eisenhower's decision to reinstate the Shah as head of Iran. Once in power, the Shah—Reza Pahlavi—was considerably more favorable to U.S. economic interests. For example, he allowed U.S. oil companies to take over almost 50 percent of Iran's oil production, and U.S. arms merchants (such as Richard Secord, who would emerge as a leading figure in the Iran-Contra scandal in the 1980s) negotiated more than $18 billion in weapon sales over the next twenty years (Moyers, 1988:9).

In 1957 the CIA helped set up the Iranian secret police (SAVAK), which stalked Iranian dissidents and earned a worldwide reputation for extreme sadism and frequent use of torture. From its inception, SAVAK agents "received special training at the Marine base in

Quantico, Virginia, and attended orientation programs at CIA headquarters in Langley, Virginia" (Chomsky and Herman, 1979:49). While the Shah was in power, close to 1,500 people were arrested *monthly,* and on only one day, June 5, 1963, SAVAK and the Shah's army allegedly killed as many as 6,000 citizens (Simon and Eitzen, 1986:158). As noted earlier, future Iran-Contra operative Richard Secord (working with Albert Hakim) was chief of the U.S. Air Force's Military Advisory Assistance Group in Iran in 1975, which represented U.S. defense contractors selling the technology of control to the Shah (Sheehan, 1988:212). Secord proved an excellent representative. In 1977 alone, Iran purchased $4.2 billion worth of arms, "making Iran the largest foreign buyer of U.S. arms"; in the entire decade, the Shah purchased more than $17 billion worth of military equipment (Marshall, Scott, Hunter, 1987:152).

In addition, political prisoners (arrested and incarcerated because they disagreed with government policy) numbered as high as 100,000 each year in Reza Pahlavi's Iran. Amnesty International, the human rights organization, reported twenty years after the coup (the Shah still in power) that Iran "has the highest rate of death penalties in the world, no valid system of civilian courts, and a history of torture which is beyond belief. No country in the world has a worse record in human rights than Iran" (cited in Chomsky and Herman, 1979:13).

The Iranian people rebelled against the Shah in 1979, shouting such slogans during demonstrations as "Death to the Shah" and "Death to the American Satan" (Moyers, 1988:9). Historically, the emergence of the Shah's outrageous repression, the subsequent rise of Khomeini, the hostage crisis, and the subsequent Iran-contra scandal can all be seen as direct outcomes of the 1953 CIA policy in Iran (p. 9).

In 1954 the CIA turned its attention to Guatemala, overthrowing its president, Jacobo Arbenz, who received 65 percent of the vote in a democratic election (Herman, 1982:176). Not only did Arbenz maintain democratic institutions—such as allowing workers the right to unionize—he also launched a massive land reform program. Given that less than 3 percent of the landowners held more than 70 percent of the land when Arbenz was elected, he nationalized more than 1.5 million acres—including land owned by his own family—and turned it over to peasants (Moyers, 1988:9).

A considerable portion of this land belonged to a U.S.-based corporation, United Fruit Company, which immediately worked with the Dulles brothers in Washington to remove Arbenz from office (Herman, 1982:10). The CIA organized a contingent of "rebels," led by Castillo Armas, who crossed over the Honduras border on June 18, 1954. Although Arbenz's military attempted to hold off the rebels, it was unable to defend against CIA B-26 and P-47 air raids on Guatemala City (McClintock, 1985:28). Arbenz fled the country, and on July 8, 1954, was replaced by Armas, who immediately overturned the reformist policies of the Arbenz government, returning the land to United Fruit and other landowners. Virtually all beneficiaries of the agrarian reform movement under Arbenz were dispossessed, entire cooperatives dissolved, literacy programs suspended, teachers fired, and "subversive" books burned (p. 29). As Moyers pointed out, the CIA's "Operation Success" entailed even more:

> The CIA had called its covert action against Guatemala, "Operation Success." Military dictators ruled the country for the next 30 years. The United States provided

them with weapons and trained their officers. . . . Peasants were slaughtered, political opponents were tortured, suspected insurgents shot, stabbed, burned alive or strangled. There were so many deaths at one point that coroners complained they couldn't keep up with the workload. "Operation Success." (1988:10)

Approximately five years after Operation Success, the CIA began planning another covert action, this time in Cuba. As noted in Chapter 12, prior to 1959, syndicate figures—in particular, Santo Trafficante Jr.—were heavily invested in narcotics trafficking, gambling, and prostitution in Cuba. Fulgencio Batista, then dictator of Cuba, profited substantially from these syndicate ventures (Kruger, 1980). On January 1, 1959, however, Fidel Castro's revolution forced Batista, and much of syndicated crime, out of Cuba. Immediately the CIA moved to overthrow the Castro government, recruiting right-wing anti-Castro Cubans who had fled the country to do the dirty work (Hinckle and Turner, 1981). Under the title "Operation 40," this group organized by the CIA carried out terrorist acts against Cuba and conspired to assassinate various leaders in the Cuban government. Part of the program involved hiring Robert Maheu—an associate of Howard Hughes and a private investigator who worked for the CIA—to recruit syndicate figures John Roselli, Sam Giancana, and Santo Trafficante Jr. to orchestrate the assassination of Castro for $150,000 (Wyden, 1979). Also involved in Operation 40 were people later identified with the Iran-Contra scandal, such as Rafael "Chi Chi" Quintero and Felix Rodriguez (both anti-Castro Cubans working for the CIA) (Marshall, Scott, Hunter, 1987). Thus, Operation 40 consisted of a well-organized sabotage, invasion, and assassination force, later known as Brigade 2506, which was based and trained by the CIA in both the United States and Guatemala.

In mid-April 1961 a major invasion of the Bay of Pigs in Cuba took place, but was unsuccessful (Hinckle and Turner, 1981). At the last minute President John Kennedy—fearing the attack would be identified as a U.S. operation if air cover were provided to the anti-Castro Cubans—halted the air strike, leaving Brigade 2506 defenseless upon landing at the Bay of Pigs (Ranelagh, 1987). Nevertheless, the plan to assassinate Castro continued.

The assassination operation became known as JM/WAVE, was based in Miami, and consisted of some 300 agents and 4,000–6,000 Cuban exile operatives (Kruger, 1980). In addition to at least eight attempted assassinations of Castro, this CIA-directed unit was involved in *daily violations* of the law—from the National Security Act to the Neutrality Act—as well as statutes involving firearms possession and perjury (Prados, 1986). JM/WAVE involved terrorist attacks against Cuban infrastructure—such as railroads, oil and sugar refineries, and factories—as well as, for example, contaminating exported Cuban sugar with chemicals at San Juan, Puerto Rico, and at other ports, and sabotaging shipments of machinery and spare parts en route to Cuba (p. 212). Raids against Cuban targets continued until 1965 (pp. 215–217).

When JM/WAVE was dismantled in 1965, the CIA left behind "a highly trained army of 6,000 fanatically anticommunist Cubans allied to organized crime," who eventually merged into terrorist organizations such as Alpha 66 and Omega 7 (Kruger, 1980). These organizations ultimately became known as the "Cuban Refugee Terrorist Network," involving overlapping memberships in the different groups. According to Edward Herman

1982:65–66) in his examination of terrorism, this network was responsible for a substantial number of terrorist acts in the Western Hemisphere. Trained by the CIA in the "arts of bomb construction, demolition, and efficient murder as part of the secret war against Cuba," the network was found to be responsible for twenty-five to thirty bombings in Dade County, Florida, in 1975 alone (pp. 65–66). In addition, Herman has argued that this network has assassinated diplomats in Lisbon, Mexico City, New York City, and Washington, D.C.

Ironically, certain Bay of Pigs veterans in this network financed their underground terrorist operations through involvement in the illegal drug trade. Indeed, according to Kruger, a primary reason JM/WAVE was closed down was "because one of its aircraft was caught smuggling narcotics into the United States" (1980:146). Criminologist Howard Abadinsky has added that certain of these anti-Castro Cubans "imported only enough cocaine to satisfy members of their own community, but by the mid-1960s, the market began to expand, and they began to import the substance in greater quantities" (1989:209). And, as Marshall, Scott, and Hunter have asserted:

> America's drug problem today is arguably, in large measure, an out-growth of the "secret war" against Fidel Castro begun under Presidents Eisenhower and Kennedy. . . . The connection isn't fanciful. Over the years, federal and local law enforcement officials have found CIA-trained Cuban exiles at the center of some of this nation's biggest drug rings. They had the clandestine skills, the Latin connections, the political protection and the requisite lack of scruples to become champion traffickers. (1987:134)

In 1965 many of those involved in the Miami JM/WAVE operation were transferred to Laos, where the CIA organized its secret Meo tribe army (Kruger, 1980:146). CIA offices were set up in Vientiane and Long Tieng, both cities becoming new centers of the heroin trade. During this time, one of the most active heroin laboratories was in Vientiane and was under the direction of Huu Tim Heng, who also built a Pepsi-Cola bottling plant on the outskirts of the city (McCoy, 1972:186). This plant, however, never bottled a single Pepsi but rather served as a front for the purchase of chemicals vital to the processing of heroin (pp. 186–187). Moreover, one Vang Pao, head of the Meo secret army, was extensively involved in heroin production, operating a heroin plant at Long Tieng, in Laos (pp. 248–249).

As noted in Chapter 12, the CIA used the Meo tribespeople to combat leftist Pathet Lao forces in Laos. The only air transport in the area was the CIA's Air America. These planes ensured an adequate food supply to the Meo tribespeople through regular rice drops, thus allowing the Meo to "devote all their energies to opium production (McCoy, 1972:283). The opium was purchased by Vang Pao's officers and flown to heroin plants in Long Tieng and Vientiane by Air America. Ultimately, the heroin was distributed to GIs in Vietnam and users in the United States (p. 263). Indeed, syndicate figures invaded Southeast Asia, helping create the then-major producer and exporter of heroin around the world—the Golden Triangle (pp. 210–217; Kruger, 1980:147–149). (See Figure 14.2.) It is estimated that approximately 20 percent of U.S. troops were addicted to heroin during their tour of duty in Vietnam (Stanton, 1976:557). Moreover, as Bellis has argued:

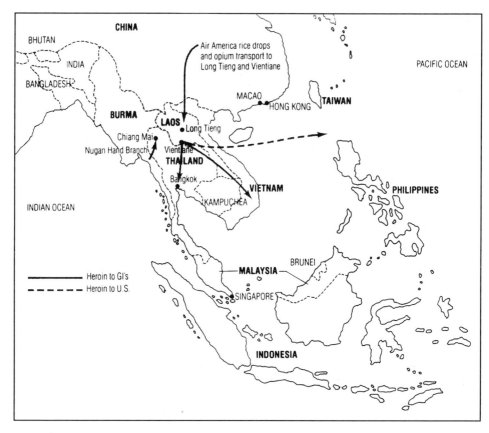

FIGURE 14.2   CIA-Meo Tribe Rice-Heroin Connection in the Golden Triangle
SOURCE: Adapted from *McCoy*, 1972, pp. 249–281.

Between 1965 and 1970 the estimated number of active heroin addicts in the United
States grew from about 68,000 to some 500,000. Extremely high and rapidly
spreading incidence and prevalence were taken as indicators of "epidemic" heroin
abuse, which grew to peak rates in American cities between 1969 and 1972.
(1981:19)

It has been alleged further by Sheehan (1988:18–24) that much of the money generated by
this drug trade was laundered through the Nugan Hand Bank. Nugan Hand operated a branch
in Chiang Mai, Thailand (in the Golden Triangle), and several of the bank's officials—such
as former CIA director William Colby—worked for the U.S. government at one time.

In 1968, "Operation Phoenix" (in Vietnam) was orchestrated by William Colby, who at
the time was working for the CIA (Branfman, 1978:112). Although "Phoenix" was originally formed to incarcerate and assassinate members of the Vietcong—the National Liberation Front—it engaged in the massive roundup, incarceration, murder, and torture of
thousands of Vietnamese citizens. Colby, according to Branfman, established "quotas for
the number of Vietnamese to be 'neutralized' each month" (p. 113). In the end, over

40,000 enemy civilians were murdered in a three-year period, 1968–1971, and thousands more tortured (Chomsky and Herman, 1979:322–328).

By 1972 the CIA had moved its covert operations to Chile, for the purpose of overthrowing the democratically elected socialist, Salvadore Allende. In the late 1960s the CIA had worked closely with International Telephone and Telegraph (ITT)—because of ITT's heavy investments in Chile—to prevent Salvador Allende from being elected president; if elected, Allende had pledged to nationalize ITT. When this failed and Allende was elected in 1970, the CIA, working with the State Department, did all it could to destabilize the Chilean economy through such practices as reducing U.S. aid to Chile (while increasing aid to the Chilean military); eliminating loans from U.S. banks and encouraging international financial institutions, such as the World Bank, to do the same; cutting supplies of and parts for U.S.-made machinery in Chile; and organizing a worldwide boycott of all Chilean products (Coleman, 1994:71). In addition to destabilizing its economy, the CIA worked with high officials in the Chilean military to overthrow Allende, which it did in 1973, resulting in the death of President Allende himself (p. 75). A military dictatorship under the direction of Augusto Pinochet subsequently came to power. Immediately, the nationalization policies of Allende were overthrown, many democratic institutions were dismantled, and repression by the Pinochet regime grew rampant. Between 1973 and 1976, for example, over 100,000 people were detained for political reasons in Chile—over 20,000 of them eventually killed during incarceration, and an even larger number tortured (Herman, 1982:115). According to Amnesty International's *Report on Torture, 1975–1976* in Chile under Pinochet:

> The most common forms of physical torture have been prolonged beating (with truncheons, fists or bags of moist material), electricity to all parts of the body, and burning with cigarettes or acid. Such physical tortures have been accompanied by the deprivation of food, drink and sleep. More primitive and brutal methods have continued to be used. On 19 December, one prisoner was found dead, his testicles burned off. He had also been subjected to intensive beating and electricity. One day later another prisoner who died from torture had the marks of severe burns on the genital organs. (Amnesty International, 1976:113)

During Pinochet's active and brutal repression of dissent in Chile, Congress approved George Bush, in 1976, to head the CIA (Maas, 1986:8–9). Under Bush's control, the agency continued its involvement in shady, covert operations, a few of which are listed below (Corn, 1988:157–160):

- The CIA secretly provided weapons and money to "our side of the Angolan war," much of the money never reaching the rebels but, rather, pocketed by President Mobutu Sese Seko of Zaire.
- The CIA secretly worked to destabilize the "democratic-socialist" Jamaican government of Michael Manly, spending an estimated $10 million trying to overthrow the prime minister.
- Bush allegedly met, and kept on the CIA payroll, General Manuel Noriega of Panama, even though the United States possessed evidence linking Noriega to drug dealing and other criminal activities.

Perhaps most disturbing of all is the CIA's possible connection to "Operation Condor" while Bush was at its helm. In 1976, six Latin American states—Argentina, Bolivia, Brazil, Chile, Paraguay, and Uruguay—"entered into a system for the joint monitoring and assassinating of dissident refugees in member countries" (Herman, 1982:69). The program was sponsored and organized by Pinochet's secret police, DINA, which provided the initial funding and centralized coordination for the operation. Herman illustrates how Condor initially worked in Uruguay and Argentina:

> Under Operation Condor, political refugees who leave Uruguay and go to Argentina will be identified and kept under surveillance by Argentinian "security" forces, who will inform Uruguayan "security" forces of the presence of these individuals. If the Uruguayan security forces wish to murder these refugees in order to preserve western values, Argentine forces will cooperate. They will keep the Uruguayans informed of the whereabouts of the refugees; they will allow them to enter and freely move around in Argentina and to take the refugees into custody, torture and murder them; and the Argentinians will then claim no knowledge of these events. (p. 70)

Hundreds of Latin Americans were abducted and subsequently murdered under Operation Condor.

Finally, the CIA's latest "secret" war also is possibly financed through the heroin trade. In the 1970s most of the heroin in the United States, as pointed out, came from the Golden Triangle geographical region. At that time, Afghanistan and northwestern Pakistan were virtually untapped opium areas, and heroin use was practically unknown in these countries (Lamour and Lamberti, 1974; Lifschultz, 1988). However, CIA support for Afghan rebels involved the Golden Crescent region (see Figure 14.3), which became one of the major heroin-producing areas of the world. The CIA arms pipeline from Karachi in the south through Pakistan to the Afghan mujahedeen in the north, according to the *Nation,* was "also one of the principal routes for the transport of heroin to Karachi for shipment to Europe and the United States" (Lifschultz, 1988:495). Moreover, the *New York Times* reported that a great deal of the poppy crop grew in areas controlled by Afghan rebels or in areas where they had influence (Sciolino, 1988:10). As Bellis reported in the early 1980s, "not surprisingly, the unleashing of this opium flow from Afghanistan coincided perfectly with the arrival of the CIA on the Afghan-Pakistan border—to support and arm the tribes who were both producing opium and fighting the Russian invaders" (1981:86).

Indeed, according to a General Accounting Office (1988:13) 1980s status report on drug abuse and drug trade, in the first six months of 1986, of the heroin in the United States, 19 percent came from the Golden Triangle and 40 percent from the Golden Crescent. In other words, as the CIA moved its operations from Southeast Asia to Southwest Asia, so, it seems, did the heroin trade.

The Iran-Contra Scandal

In February 1979 the U.S. State Department, under President Jimmy Carter, recalled more than half its officials from Nicaragua and suspended all new economic and military aid to that country. In July of that year a revolution occurred in Nicaragua, whereby the dictator

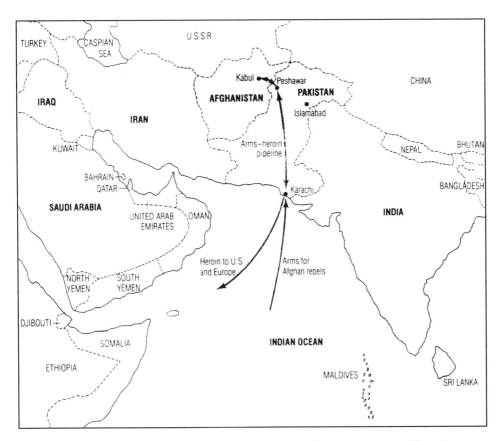

FIGURE 14.3   Probable CIA-Supported Arms-Heroin Pipeline in the Golden Crescent
SOURCE: Adapted from *Lifschultz,* 1988, pp. 495–496; *Sciolino,* 1988, p. 110; *Bellis,* 1981, p. 86.

Anastasio Somoza was ousted and the Sandinista National Liberation Front (FSLN) assumed power (Black, 1981).

In early March 1981, President Ronald Reagan, according to the *Washington Post,* authorized covert CIA activities against Nicaragua (Oberdorfer and Tyler, 1983). CIA Director William Casey then met with Argentina junta members, who subsequently supplied approximately 100 military officials to train the first Nicaraguan opposition forces—approximately 500 strong—in urban terrorist tactics and guerrilla war (Marshall, Scott, and Hunter, 1987). The CIA worked with the Argentinians and other governments in Central America to build a paramilitary force against Nicaragua (Oberdorfer and Tyler, 1983; Emerson, 1988). That same year (1981), Reagan authorized $19.95 million for this paramilitary force, which at the time was composed primarily of the former National Guard members and other loyalists of Somoza. Eventually, this creation of the White House and the CIA became the Nicaraguan Democratic Front (FDN), or the first of several Contra groups.

Toward the end of 1981, debate in Congress and throughout the country led to widespread criticism, and increasing scrutiny, of White House intentions in Central America, especially in Nicaragua. By December 21, 1982, Congress was so skeptical that it enacted the first Boland Amendment to the Defense Appropriations Act, terminating the use of any public money for the purpose of toppling or destabilizing the Nicaraguan government (Scheffer, 1987). Nevertheless, the Reagan administration chose to ignore the Boland Amendment by *secretly* seeking new ways to train and arm the contras.

One such way was "Operation Elephant Herd" (Emerson, 1988), wherein the CIA clandestinely obtained, on September 22, 1983, $12 million worth of military equipment (for deployment against Nicaragua) from the U.S. military. At least forty attacks employing Elephant Herd equipment against Nicaraguan targets occurred in 1984, the most well known occurring on March 7 and consisting of speedboats armed with Bushmaster 25-millimeter cannon-guns firing on and destroying numerous oil facilities and storage tanks at various Nicaraguan ports. Moreover, during this time the CIA also engaged in the mining of Nicaraguan harbors, resulting in the following:

> Two small fishing boats at the Caribbean port of El Bluff were the first to detonate the mines and sank on February 25. . . . A Dutch dredger was seriously damaged at Corinto on the Pacific coast on March 1, a week later a Panamanian freighter detonated a mine. On March 20, a Soviet oil tanker reported damage at Puerto Sandino on the Pacific coast. (Gutman, 1988:198–199)

In addition, the CIA prepared and distributed to the contras an "assassination manual" in direct variance with Executive Order 12333 signed by President Reagan in 1981, which specifically prohibited political assassinations, directly or indirectly, by intelligence agencies or entities of the U.S. government. The manual instructed the contras in the "selective use of violence" to "neutralize carefully selected and planned targets such as court judges, police, and state security officials" and to "kidnap all officials or agents of the Sandinista government." Moreover, the manual stated that "if possible, professional criminals will be hired to carry out selective 'jobs'" (cited in Woodward, 1988:388–389).

In June 1986 the World Court (the United Nations International Court of Justice) ruled that these actions by the U.S. government violated international law. U.S. aid to the contras, its support of attacks on Nicaraguan oil installations and ports, and the mining of Nicaragua's harbors constituted, according to the World Court, "force against another state." By organizing and supporting the contras, the United States had violated Nicaraguan sovereignty, amounting "to an intervention of one state in the internal affairs of another." Finally, the World Court ordered the United States "to cease and to refrain" from violating international law, and held further that the United States was obligated to pay reparations to Nicaragua. The United States simply ignored the rulings (Pfost, 1987:75).

Largely because of the foregoing crimes, in August 1984 Congress enacted a stronger Boland Amendment, which prohibited any administrative agency or entity involved in "intelligence activities" from "supporting, directly or indirectly, military or paramilitary operations in Nicaragua by any Nation, group, organization or individual" (cited in Scheffer, 1987:714). Congress also halted all military aid to the contras (Gutman, 1988:18).

The contras, however, were not without funds. In fact, considerable anecdotal evidence suggests that the contras were involved from the beginning in the illegal drug trade to support their cause (Marshall, Scott, and Hunter, 1987:134–139). In April 1988, for example,

Senator John Kerry's Senate Subcommittee on Terrorism, Narcotics, and International Operations began exploring Contra drug ties throughout the 1980s. One year later, the subcommittee—in its report *Drugs, Law Enforcement, and Foreign Policy*—concluded the following: "It is clear that individuals who provided support for the *contras* were involved in drug trafficking, the supply network of the *contras* was used by drug trafficking organizations, and elements of the *contras* themselves knowingly received financial and material assistance from drug traffickers" (U.S. Senate, 1989:36).

It has also been alleged that the "Medellin Cartel" contributed at least $10 million to the Contra cause between 1982 and 1985 (Cockburn, 1987). Thus, it is unlikely that the contras were "hurting" financially.

Nevertheless, according to the *Washington Post,* Oliver North (NSC liaison to the CIA), who claimed that the Boland Amendments did not apply to the NSC, proposed to Robert McFarlane (national security advisor) in early 1984 (he subsequently accepted) that they build a private funding and supply network for the contras (Ignatius, 1986:D1). The project initially entailed North "criss-crossing the globe" in 1984 and 1985, obtaining funds from private individuals in the United States and wealthy right-wing leaders in other countries (Marshall, Scott, and Hunter, 1987). For example, the Saudi royal family reportedly gave at least $32 million to the contras; the Sultan of Brunei reportedly deposited $10 million in a Swiss bank account controlled by North; both Israel and South Korea gave "generously to the contras" in terms of finances and arms; with the help of the World Anti-Communist League (WACL)—an organization with a strong right-wing and Nazi component (Anderson and Anderson, 1986)—and its leader, John Singlaub, Taiwan contributed at least $2 million to North's Swiss bank account (Marshall, Scott, and Hunter, 1987; Sheehan, 1988). North also solicited funds from wealthy people in the United States, such as Joseph Coors and Ellen Garwood, the latter contributing over $2,500,000 in 1986 for the purchase of weapons and ammunition (Moyers, 1988).

In the spring of 1984 a number of U.S. citizens were taken hostage in Lebanon, CIA Beirut station chief William Buckley receiving the most publicity (Sheehan, 1988). Inasmuch as Buckley was kidnapped by members of the pro-Khomeini Lebanese faction of the Hizbollah, the U.S. State Department imposed heavy restrictions on the export of aircraft, aircraft spare parts, and other military goods and technology to Iran (p. 177). Accordingly, the combination of U.S. hostages in Lebanon and Iran's need for U.S. arms and spare parts (the Shah had relied extensively on U.S. military hardware) created an alternative method with which to attract finances and arms for the contras.

Two arms shipments—coordinated with Iranian "moderates" by Manucher Ghorbanifar (former SAVAK commander and Iranian arms dealer)—were delivered to Iran on August 19 and September 14; the Reverend Benjamin Weir was released from captivity on the latter date. Another shipment of arms was to follow in November, but this delivery ran into logistical problems when (to avoid public exposure) the arms were sent from Israel to Portugal for transfer to Iran. Portugal denied air clearance because the delivery was contrary to stated U.S. policy. Thus, because no arms were received, no hostages were released (Sheehan, 1988).

Frustrated, on November 18, 1985, North asked Richard Secord (who had organized the secret war in Laos and coordinated the sale of U.S. arms to the Shah of Iran) to take over management of the arms shipments to Iran. North also arranged for transfer of $1 million from a well-known Israeli arms dealer to a Swiss bank account controlled by Secord and Albert Hakim (a business partner of Secord who, earlier in his career, sold surveillance equipment to the Shah for use by his secret police, SAVAK) (Sheehan, 1988:181). Approximately $150,000 of this money was used to purchase arms for Iran; the remaining $850,000 went to the contras, and to Secord and Hakim in the form of profit (p. 183).

On December 11, 1985, McFarlane resigned his office, and John Poindexter was appointed new national security adviser (Marshall, Scott, and Hunter, 1987). Subsequently, Poindexter, CIA Director William Casey, North, Secord, and Hakim worked closely with Israel in shipping arms to Iran with the hope of obtaining the hostages' release and simultaneously generating sufficient profits to help support the contras in Nicaragua. In early 1986, Poindexter and North arranged for Secord and Hakim—posing as agents of the U.S. government—to receive funds in payment for weapons to be shipped to Iran, to transmit those funds to the CIA, and then to transport replacement weapons from the United States to Israel. This arrangement permitted Secord and Hakim expanded control over the proceeds from the sale of arms in order to divert substantial amounts of money not only to the contras but to their own pockets as well.

An example of the foregoing arrangement occurred in January 1986 (Sheehan, 1988:186–188). North and Secord decided to transfer arms (TOW missiles) from a domestic storage facility to Kelly Air Force Base in Texas. Secord would travel to Texas, accept the missiles, and arrange their transportation via Southern Air Transport (a CIA-owned airline) to Israel; from Israel the missiles would go to Iran. Manucher Ghorbanifar agreed to purchase the missiles for $10,500 each. Initially, Iran bought $10 million worth, or approximately 1,000 missiles, the money being deposited in a Swiss bank account. Secord and Hakim, however, paid the U.S. government only $3,469 per missile, less than half the regular price. This amounted to approximately $3.7 million. The profit generated by *underpaying* the U.S. government and *overcharging* the Iranians ($6.3 million) went to the contras (in the form of weapons and supplies) and to Secord and Hakim (in the form of personal enrichment).

Throughout the remainder of 1986, Secord, North, and Hakim arranged additional shipments and diversions of funds to the contras. As a result, on July 26, 1986, Reverend Lawrence Jenco and, on November 2, 1986, David Jacobsen were released by their Lebanese captors. On the following day the entire arms network was exposed by the Lebanese magazine, *Al-Shiraa* (Sheehan, 1988:192).

The supply operation in Central America was managed by Robert Owen, North's "man in the field," who worked to coordinate contacts with the contras and the private aid network. The arms were apparently shipped to the Ilopango and Aguacate military bases in El Salvador and Honduras, respectively, as well as to a large ranch in Costa Rica (Sheehan, 1988). Rafael "Chi Chi" Quintero ran the Aguacate base and Felix Rodriguez the Ilopango base (Calonius, 1987:27; Cockburn, 1987:154). From these drop-off points, pilots and "kickers" (cargo handlers) made air drops to contras both inside and outside Nicaragua (Calonius, 1987). From April to October 1986, for example, at least twenty-five arms drops were made inside Nicaragua (p. 28).

Many of these planes may also have been involved in several drug runs (Marshall, Scott, and Hunter, 1987). Anecdotal evidence suggests that often supply planes utilized a drug trafficking connection on return flights to the United States (pp. 136–139; Sheehan,

1988; Cockburn, 1987). Moreover, anti-Castro Cuban veterans of the 2506 Brigade—who participated in the 1961 Bay of Pigs invasion—may also have been involved in the drug trade, operating from the ranch in Costa Rica (Marshall, Scott, and Hunter, 1987; Sheehan, 1988). In addition, the Subcommittee on Terrorism, Narcotics, and International Operations (U.S. Senate, 1989:36) found that the contra-drug links included the following:

- Involvement in narcotics trafficking by individuals associated with the contra movement.
- Participation of narcotics traffickers in contra supply operations through business relationships with contra organizations.
- Provision of assistance to the contras by narcotics traffickers—including cash, weapons, planes, pilots, air-supply services, and other materials—on a voluntary basis.
- Payments by the U.S. State Department to drug traffickers of funds authorized by Congress for humanitarian assistance to the contras, in some cases after traffickers had been indicted by federal law enforcement agencies on drug charges and in others while traffickers were under active investigation by these same agencies.

Regarding payments to traffickers, the State Department actually selected four companies owned and operated by narcotics traffickers to supply humanitarian assistance to the contras (U.S. Senate, 1989:43):

- SETCO Air: established by Honduran drug trafficker Ramon Matta Ballesteros.
- DIACSA: Miami-based air transport company operated as the headquarters of a drug trafficking enterprise for convicted drug traffickers Floyd Carlton and Alfredo Caballero.
- Frigorificos de Puntaremas: owned and operated by Cuban-American drug traffickers.
- Vortex: air service and supply company partly owned by admitted drug trafficker Michael Palmer.

Each company was under contract to the State Department in spite of the fact that federal law enforcement agencies knew the individuals controlling the companies were involved in the narcotics trade (p. 43). A portion of the profits realized from the overall drug smuggling operation into the United States and elsewhere was used to purchase additional weapons for the contras (p. 43; Moyers, 1988). Indeed, in its conclusion, the subcommittee argued: "The U.S. government failed to address the drug problem because to do so might have interfered with the war in Nicaragua" (p. 136).

In other words, just as with the heroin secret war connections in the Golden Triangle and possibly the Golden Crescent areas, it seems that the CIA and the NSC were quite possibly involved in a cocaine-contra connection in Central America. We do know that cocaine became "the most serious problem drug of the 1980s"; the number of U.S. citizens over the age of twelve who were current cocaine users between 1982 and 1985 increased 38 percent. Moreover, the use of "crack," a highly potent and addictive form of cocaine, became widely practiced in 1985 and 1986 (General Accounting Office, 1988). Interestingly, it was exactly during the height of the alleged contra arms-for-drugs trade in Central America that cocaine use peaked in the United States—and most of the cocaine coming into the United States during this period came from Colombia (see Figures 14.4 and 14.5).

Most distressing of all, of course, is the fact that as profits were secured in a variety of ways (such as illegally selling arms and drugs), many people were killed and lives destroyed in the process. On the one hand, the eight-year Iran–Iraq war—in which Iran made use of the weapons it received from the United States—resulted in the deaths of millions of Iraqi soldiers and citizens. On the other hand, in Nicaragua the contras conducted a campaign of terror. Certain organizations—from Witness for Peace (a religious group that

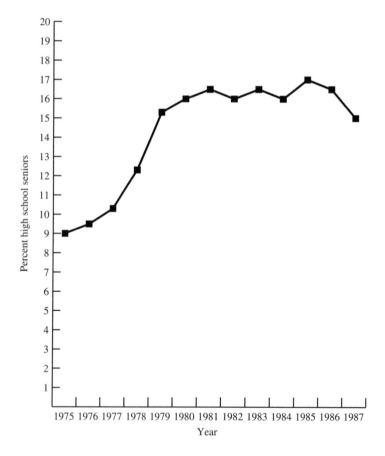

FIGURE 14.4   Trends in Lifetime Cocaine Use Among High School Seniors, 1975–1987

SOURCE: *General Accounting Office,* 1988, p. 5; *National Institute on Drug Abuse,* 1987, p. 47.

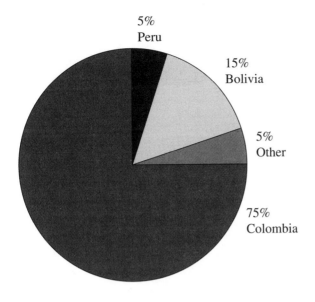

5%
Peru

15%
Bolivia

5%
Other

75%
Colombia

FIGURE 14.5 Probable Sources of Cocaine Available in the United States, 1985–1986

"Other" countries include Argentina, Brazil, and Ecuador.

SOURCE: *General Accounting Office*, 1988, p. 9.

maintained a permanent presence along the Nicaraguan border to monitor contra-Nicaragua activity) to America's Watch and Amnesty International (two human rights organizations)—have documented atrocities committed by the contras against Nicaraguan civilians.

Moreover, former assistant attorney general of the state of New York Reed Brody (1985) headed a fact-finding mission to Nicaragua in 1984 and 1985, which obtained testimony from victims and eyewitnesses of contra attacks against civilians. His report concluded that contra activity often included the following:

- attacks on purely civilian targets that resulted in the killing of unarmed men, women, children, and elderly
- premeditated acts of brutality including rape, beatings, mutilation, and torture
- individual and mass kidnapping of civilians . . . for the purpose of forced recruitment into the contra forces and for the creation of a hostage-refugee population in Honduras
- assaults on such economic and social targets as farms, cooperatives, food storage facilities, and health centers, including a particular effort to disrupt the coffee harvests through attacks on coffee cooperatives and on vehicles carrying volunteer coffee harvesters
- intimidation of civilians who participated or cooperated in government or community programs such as distribution of subsidized food products, rural cooperatives, education, and local self-defense militias
- kidnapping, intimidation, and even murder of religious leaders who supported the government, including priests and clergy-trained lay pastors

Thus, although the Iran-contra affair was a covert operation hidden from the people of the United States, it was clearly not secret to its victims.

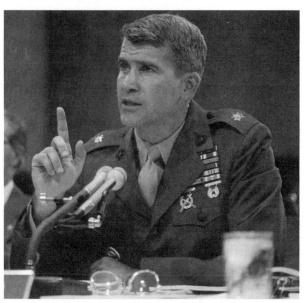

The "gang of four"—clockwise from top left: John Poindexter, Richard Secord, Albert Hakim, and Oliver North. These four men worked together to support the contras despite a congressional ban on such aid.

The diversionary plan was revealed on November 25, 1986, by Attorney General Edwin Meese. In time, Oliver North was fired and John Poindexter resigned. On March 11, 1988, Robert McFarlane pleaded guilty to four misdemeanor counts of withholding information from Congress about the Reagan administration's contra supply efforts (but was eventually pardoned by President George Bush) and agreed to serve as a prosecution witness in the criminal investigation of the Iran-contra affair (Shenon, 1988b:A1). On March 16 of that same year Poindexter, North, Secord, and Hakim were indicted, jointly accused of conspiracy to defraud the United States, of stealing government property, and of wire fraud (Shenon, 1988c:A1). These co-conspirators engaged in the foregoing crimes, according to the indictment, because they "deceitfully and without legal authorization" organized a program to support the contras despite a congressional ban on such aid, as set forth in the Boland Amendments (p. D27). The prosecution elected to try each co-conspirator separately. Albert Hakim eventually pleaded guilty to a misdemeanor, and John Poindexter was convicted on five counts of lying to Congress and obstructing congressional investigations. After conspiracy and fraud charges were dismissed. North was eventually convicted of only three charges: aiding and abetting the obstruction of Congress, destroying documents, and accepting an illegal gratuity. Richard Secord pleaded guilty to one felony count of making false statements to Congress. Secord was sentenced to two years probation, and both Poindexter's and North's convictions were overturned on appeal because their testimony to the Iran-contra Congressional Committee was allegedly unfairly used against them at their trials.

However, we believe the Iran-contra scandal involved numerous other violations of domestic and international law not covered by either the indictment or North's and Secord's trials. Domestically (in addition to the Boland Amendments), through the sale of arms to Iran the co-conspirators likely violated the Arms Export Control Act, which prohibits the export of arms to states supporting terrorism (Scheffer, 1987). Indeed, Secretary of State George Shultz stated on January 23, 1984, "that Iran is a country which has repeatedly provided support for acts of international terrorism" (pp. 699–700). Moreover, with regard to military assistance to the contras, the co-conspirators likely violated the U.S. Neutrality Act, which (as explained earlier) prohibits any U.S. citizen, whether in public office or not (including the president), from supporting (initiating, organizing, and/or funding) hostile expeditions against other nations with which the United States is at peace (Pfost, 1987:76–77). Internationally, the UN Charter was also likely violated. In 1965 the United Nations adopted its "Declaration of the Inadmissibility of Intervention in the Domestic Affairs of States and the Protection of Their Independence and Sovereignty." The declaration prohibits in part (Pfost, 1987:71):

- any State from intervening, directly or indirectly, for any reason whatsoever, in the internal or external affairs of any other State;
- the use of economic, political, or any other type of measure to coerce another State in order to obtain from it the subordination of the exercise of its sovereign rights or to secure from it advantages of any kind;
- efforts to organize, assist, foment, finance, incite, or tolerate subversive, terrorist, or armed activities directed toward the violent overthrow of the regime of another State.

REVIEW

This chapter examined the nature, extent, types, and costs of political crime in the United States in terms of (1) political crimes against the state (violations of the law for the purpose of modifying or changing social conditions), (2) domestic political crimes by the state (violations of the law by state officials and/or agencies whose victimization occurs *inside* the United States), and (3) international political crimes by the state (violations of domestic and international law by state officials and/or agencies whose victimization occurs *outside* the United States).

Political Crimes Against the State

1. Political crimes against the state involve intentional violations of criminal law for political purposes, as well as various acts criminalized by the state for the purpose of curbing political dissent.

2. Political crimes against the state may be violent or nonviolent.

3. From the Revolutionary War onward, various groups in the United States have used violence in an attempt to modify or change the social order.

4. Historically, various groups in the United States also have been engaged in such nonviolent actions as civil disobedience and demonstrations, involvement that sometimes results in their criminalization.

Domestic Political Crimes by the State

1. Domestic political crimes by the state are violations of law by state officials and/or agencies whose victimization occurs inside the boundaries of the United States.

2. Two major types of domestic political crimes by the state are corruption (political bribery, political kickbacks, election fraud, and corrupt campaign practices) and political repression (illegal repression of dissent).

International Political Crimes by the State

1. International political crimes by the state are violations of domestic and international law by state officials and/or agencies whose victimization occurs outside the boundaries of the United States.

2. Historically, both the CIA and the NSC have been involved in international political crimes—from illegally intervening in the affairs of other nations to sabotage to assassinations.

QUESTIONS FOR CLASS DISCUSSION

1. Should the concept of political crime encompass crimes *against* the state and crimes *by* the state? Why?

2. Explain the difference between violent and nonviolent political crimes against the state. Discuss why you believe the state may be interested in criminalizing each.

3. Choose two examples from each category of political crime by the state (domestic and international) and explain why you think they occur in U.S. society. Which theory discussed in Part Two of the text seems especially suited to helping you answer this question? Explain.

FOR FURTHER STUDY

Readings

Hagan, Frank E. 1997. *Political Crime: Ideology and Criminality.* Boston: Allyn and Bacon.

Marshall, Jonathan, Peter Dale Scott, and Jan Hunter. 1987. *The Iran-contra Connection: Secret Teams and Covert Operations in the Reagan Era.* Boston: South End Press.

Tunnell, Kenneth D. 1993. *Political Crime in Contemporary America.* New York: Garland.

Websites

1. <http://members.xoom.com/freepeltier/index.html>: This site updates readers on Leonard Peltier's case. It also offers links to e-mail discussion groups and to the FBI files on Peltier.

2. <http://www.actupny.org/documents/CDdocuments/CDindex.html>: From ACT UP! AIDS Coalition to Unleash Power, this site provides some basic information regarding the tactics and philosophy of nonviolent civil disobedience. Readers can learn about the typical scenario after arrests have been made and the many ways to practice nonviolent protest.

3. <http://www.jericho98.com/cointelpro.html>: From Jericho '98, a group dedicated to working on behalf of political prisoners in the United States, this site offers a history and current status of COINTELPRO, an operation of the FBI. Links to other activist organizations are provided.

Synthesis

Inequality, Crime, and Victimization

Preview

Chapter 15 introduces:
- social inequality and its relation to crime
- how social position both permits and prevents criminal opportunity
- patterns of crime and victimization in the United States

Key Terms

age	race
class	social inequality
gender	social position

In Part 3 we discussed the extent, nature, types, and costs of a variety of crimes—from interpersonal violence to political crimes. To understand the variety of crimes it is essential to establish their sociological context—how crime is shaped by the social factors of society. Accordingly, in Chapter 15 we discuss the considerable sociological research that is necessary to grasp the patterns of crime in the United States.

The chief social factor underlying crime is structured **social inequality**. All industrialized societies are marked by social inequalities. Critical aspects of life—such as economic benefits, life chances, social privileges, and political power—are intimately connected to the social inequalities that structure society. Inequality is a sociological question, a product of human history.

There are four major forms of inequality that influence crime: class, gender, race, and age. These inequalities create different life experiences for people, depending upon their class, gender, race, and age characteristics, and they also shape patterns of crime and victimization. In other words, criminal opportunities and victimization are intimately related to social position in the class, gender, race, and age hierarchies of society. **Social position** thus refers to one's individual location in society based on the social characteristics of class, gender, race, and age.

Some scholars, especially psychologists, attempt to explain why one individual commits crime and another individual in the same social position does not. Although this is an intriguing question, our focus is upon explaining sociological patterns of crime. Why do members of one class disproportionately commit a certain type of crime? Why do men commit more crimes than women? To answer such questions we must analyze those inequalities in social structures that shape our lives. Social position—in terms of class, gender, race, and age—influences, limits, and structures human behavior, whether that behavior is legal or illegal, harmful or safe. Social position permits and precludes criminal opportunities. The patterns of crime therefore reflect the broader inequalities embedded in society.

In this chapter, for analytical purposes, we discuss class, gender, race, and age separately. However, in the real world, social inequities are actually interrelated. As participating members of society, each of us has simultaneously a class, gender, race, and age social position. All four positions interact to structure society and its accompanying patterns of crime and victimization. Unfortunately, in an introductory textbook it is impossible to provide a complete picture of the relationship between social inequality and crime. Thus our discussion is limited to an examination of why and how general patterns of crime and victimization occur in the United States.

15.1 CLASS AND CRIME

In the United States there exist sharp class divisions, and inequalities structure the patterns of crime and victimization. Although class position is associated with level of income, occupation, and education, it is determined chiefly by the way in which the production system of a society is organized. Historically, societies have organized production in different ways, and this in turn created different types of social classes. Class, then, is an important sociological concept for understanding patterns of crime. We define a **social class** as a group of people who share the same position in the same economic system. Class structures both economic relationships and inequalities, as well as the *type* and *seriousness* of crime.

Patterns of Crime and Victimization

Uniform Crime Reports does not rank the crime rates of different social classes. However, John Braithwaite reviewed a significant number of studies that employed official statistics to generate data on the relationship between class and crime and concluded that they all "showed lower-class juveniles to have substantially higher offense rates than middle-class juveniles. Among adults, all . . . studies found lower-class people to have higher crime rates" (1981:38). Moreover, Braithwaite's earlier review (1979b:62) of nearly 300 studies based on official statistics *and* self-reports concluded:

1. Lower-class adults commit those types of crime handled by the police (conventional crimes) at a higher rate than do middle-class adults.
2. Adults living in lower-class areas commit those types of crime handled by the police at a higher rate than do adults living in middle-class areas.
3. Lower-class juveniles commit crime at a higher rate than do middle-class juveniles.
4. Juveniles living in lower-class areas commit crime at a higher rate than do juveniles living in middle-class areas.

Regarding specific offense types, self-report studies indicate that class differences exist for both serious property crime and interpersonal crimes of violence (Currie, 1985; Farnworth et al., 1994). A delinquency study by Elliott and Huizinga (1983) is of particular importance because it analyzed both the percentage of a social class committing certain offenses at a specific time (prevalence) and the frequency with which these class members commit crimes (incidence). For status offenses and general delinquency, class differentials in prevalence were practically nonexistent. Elliott and Huizinga did, however, find significant class differentials for youth in the serious conventional crimes: Middle-class youth were far less likely to report committing such crimes than were lower- and working-class youth. Regarding incidence, the same pattern held: Both male and female middle-class youth were much less likely than were other youth to report committing serious crimes.

But conventional crimes are only one aspect of the entire range of crimes. Unfortunately, criminological studies of class and crime have concentrated on class differences in conventional crimes, ignoring white-collar and political crimes. Although poor and working-class people may commit the more serious conventional crimes handled by the police, members of the professional-managerial class (traditionally seen as the middle class) have greater opportunities to commit white-collar and political crimes. In fact, when we consider this class/crime link, it is clear the vast bulk of avoidable harm and economic loss originates from the professional-managerial class. Consequently, the *type* and *seriousness* of crime are associated with social class position: Conventional crimes tend to be committed more often by the poor and working classes; white-collar and political crimes tend to be committed more often by the professional-managerial class.

The *National Crime Victimization Survey* provides information on victimization and aids in the formulation of conclusions about the *intra-* and *interclass* nature of conventional crimes. As Table 15.1 shows, for rape, robbery, assault, and purse snatching/pocket-picking, the lower the family income the greater the chance of victimization. The most frequent victims of such crimes are those with an annual family income of less than $15,000. We can conclude that such crimes tend to be *intra-class:* Both the *offenders* and the *victims* are usually members of the same class.

Table 15.2 shows victimization rates for the category termed "property" (household burglary, theft [which includes "personal larceny without contact" and "household larceny"], and motor vehicle theft). Each crime shows a different pattern: Household burglary victimization declines with annual family income; motor vehicle theft victimization remains relatively stable throughout incomes of $25,000 and above; and theft increases with annual family income.

With the exception of theft and motor vehicle theft, conventional crime victimization is therefore an intra-class phenomenon. In other words, the poor tend to victimize the poor, but they are *also* more susceptible to syndicated, corporate, and political crime victimization. Consequently, the poor face crime from all directions. With this information in mind, we now consider theory and research on class and crime.

Class and Varieties of Crime

Class inequalities have not always been the norm in all societies. Through societal evolution from gathering-hunting to industrialized capitalist societies, the class structure has changed. In industrial-capitalist societies such as the United States (which has evolved over the last 200 years), class and economic inequalities persist.

The unequal class relationships in society help explain the class patterns of crime and victimization. Regarding conventional crimes handled by the police, research has shown that economic conditions associated with the poor and working classes—in particular, unemployment, income inequality, and quality of job—play a significant role in the perpetuation of these crimes. Notwithstanding the inconsistencies in research on the relationship between unemployment and conventional crime, the majority of studies report a link between the two. M. Harvey Brenner's (1976) pioneering work in the 1970s, for instance, found that when the unemployment rate increased 1 percentage point, there was a corresponding 4 percent increase in homicides and a 6 percent increase in robberies. In the 1980s, research again uncovered a link between unemployment and conventional crime. James DeFronzo's study of thirty-nine U.S. metropolitan areas found that "unemployment rates had statistically significant positive effects on rape, burglary, and larceny" (1983:128). Thornberry and Christenson investigated the employment history of 1,000 boys born in 1945 and related this to the boys' involvement in conventional criminality. They concluded that "unemployment has significant instantaneous effects on crime" (1984:408). In other words, crime seems to follow the onset of unemployment.

Cook and Zarkin (1985) investigated the business cycle and its relationship to conventional crime from 1933 to 1980. They concluded that "an increase in the unemployment rate from, say, 7 percent to 8 percent will result in a 2.3 percent increase in the robbery rate and a 1.6 percent increase in the burglary rate" (p. 126). Finally, a number of studies have

TABLE 15.1 Personal Crimes, 1997: Victimization Rates for Persons Age 12 and Over, by Type of Crime and Annual Family Income of Victims

	Rate per 1,000 Persons Age 12 and Over						
	Less than $7,500	$7,500–$14,999	$15,000–$24,999	$25,000–$34,999	$35,000–$49,999	$50,000–$74,999	$75,000 or more
All personal crimes	73.7	83.1	41.9	41.7	40.1	35.5	32.2
Crimes of violence	71.0	51.2	40.1	40.2	38.7	33.9	30.7
Completed violence	27.9	19.3	13.1	11.9	11.0	8.0	9.2
Attempted/threatened violence	43.1	31.9	27.0	28.3	27.7	25.9	21.6
Rape/sexual assault	5.2	2.2	1.5	1.5	0.6[c]	0.7[c]	1.1
Rape/attempted rape	3.2	1.2	1.3	0.7[c]	0.4[c]	0.5[c]	0.6[c]
Rape	1.8[c]	0.6[c]	0.9[c]	0.2[c]	0.4[c]	0.3[c]	0.4[c]
Attempted rape[a]	1.8[c]	0.6[c]	0.4[c]	0.5[c]	0.0[c]	0.2[c]	0.2[c]
Sexual assault[b]	2.0[c]	1.0[c]	0.2[c]	0.8[c]	0.2[c]	0.1[c]	0.5[c]
Robbery	10.1	7.0	4.6	4.2	2.9	3.1	3.7
Completed/property taken	6.7	5.1	3.0	2.3	1.7	2.1	2.4
With injury	3.4	2.2	1.1	0.5[c]	1.0	0.9	0.6[c]
Without injury	3.3	2.9	1.9	1.9	0.7[c]	1.2	1.8
Attempted to take property	3.4	1.9	1.7	1.9	1.2	1.1	1.2
With injury	0.8[c]	0.7[c]	0.5[c]	0.0[c]	0.4[c]	0.3[c]	0.2[c]
Without injury	2.8	1.2	1.2	1.9	0.8	0.8[c]	1.1
Assault	55.6	42.0	34.0	34.6	35.2	30.1	26.0
Aggravated	13.6	11.8	10.4	8.2	8.6	7.2	4.7
With injury	5.2	4.8	3.5	2.4	2.4	2.1	1.3
Threatened with weapon	8.5	7.0	6.9	5.8	6.2	5.1	3.3
Simple	42.0	30.3	23.6	26.4	26.8	22.8	21.4
With minor injury	12.7	7.9	5.7	6.4	6.3	3.4	4.5
Without injury	29.3	22.4	17.9	20.1	20.3	19.5	16.9
Purse snatching/pocket picking	2.7	2.0	1.7	1.5	1.4	1.6	1.4
Population age 12 and over	13,085,420	23,275,460	30,729,010	28,817,790	34,712,640	32,446,570	26,884,180

NOTE: Detail may not add to total shown because of rounding.
[a] Includes verbal threats of rape.
[b] Includes threats.
[c] Excludes data on persons whose family income level was not ascertained.
SOURCE: Department of Justice, 1999.

TABLE 15.2   Property Crimes, 1997: Victimization Rates by Type of Crime and Annual Family Income

	Rate per 1,000 Households						
	Less than $7,500	$7,500–$14,999	$15,000–$24,999	$25,000–$34,999	$35,000–$49,999	$50,000–$74,999	$75,000 or more
Property crimes	258.8	236.3	242.4	260.3	271.7	270.9	292.5
Household burglary	79.5	53.9	47.2	42.4	39.8	35.0	42.4
Completed	70.9	45.5	38.7	34.9	32.8	29.8	35.9
Forcible entry	26.5	19.7	13.5	13.4	13.9	12.4	11.3
Unlawful entry without force	44.4	26.8	25.2	21.5	18.9	17.4	24.6
Attempted forcible entry	8.6	8.3	8.4	7.5	7.0	5.2	6.5
Motor vehicle theft	10.0	9.1	14.1	15.8	17.2	11.7	16.3
Completed	7.2	8.1	10.4	11.6	11.1	7.0	11.2
Attempted	2.8[b]	3.0	3.7	4.2	6.1	4.7	5.1
Theft[a]	169.3	173.3	181.2	202.0	214.6	224.2	234.1
Completed	183.7	187.9	174.3	193.5	204.3	216.5	223.9
Less than $50	80.4	67.9	67.6	76.7	77.4	84.8	81.3
$50–$249	54.9	60.4	62.5	65.0	71.4	76.2	81.2
$250 or more	34.6	29.1	33.7	38.9	45.0	46.8	51.4
Amount not available	13.8	10.5	10.2	12.8	10.6	8.8	10.1
Attempted	5.6	5.4	8.9	8.5	10.2	7.7	10.2
Total number of households	8,343,820	12,848,520	15,237,980	13,430,070	14,967,560	13,033,070	10,728,660

NOTE: Detail may not add to total shown because of rounding.
[a] Theft includes crimes previously classified as "personal larceny without contact" and "household larceny."
[b] Excludes data on families whose income level was not ascertained.
SOURCE: Department of Justice, 1999.

shown a positive and significant relationship between unemployment and property crime (Hagan, 1994; Land, Cantor, and Russell, 1995). Consequently, when large numbers of people are unemployed, there appears to be an increase in the conventional crime rate.

Given a correlation between unemployment and conventional crime, we cannot forget that other characteristics—such as gender and age—play an equally significant role in the patterning of conventional crime. Indeed, as noted later in this chapter, both the elderly and women have high unemployment rates yet do not commit conventional crimes at the rate, for instance, that young males do. Consequently, gender and age mediate the unemployment/crime association.

In addition to unemployment, income inequality significantly affects conventional crime. Braithwaite's study of 193 U.S. metropolitan areas found "strong and consistent support for the hypothesis that cities in which there is a wide income gap between poor and average-income families have high rates for all types of crime" (1979b:216). Jacobs (1981) studied property crimes and income inequality in some 200 cities and established a strong relationship between economic inequality and the crimes of burglary and larceny. Jacobs' study is important because it helps us understand why high rates of property crime victimization occur in higher income groups. As Jacobs points out:

When there are large differences in resources in a metropolitan area, those with little to lose and much to gain will find that potential victims with more to steal are located only a limited distance away. . . . The less successful can readily observe the fruits of affluence in unequal metropolitan areas. It follows that in a society where there is a great cultural emphasis placed on economic success, pronounced differences in resources seem to result in more property crimes. (pp. 22–23)

In other words, relative class deprivation and inequality seem conducive to higher rates of conventional property crime. This notion of relative deprivation helps explain the high theft and motor vehicle theft victimization rates for high income groups.

Other research demonstrates that income inequality directly affects both the rate of property crimes (Carrol and Jackson, 1983) and the rate of violent crimes (Blau and Blau, 1982). Blau and Blau's (1982) study found that in the 125 largest metropolitan areas, high rates of interpersonal violence result largely from economic inequalities. Income inequalities in cities promote interpersonal violence because "in a society founded on the principle 'that all men are created equal,' economic inequalities rooted in ascribed positions violate the spirit of democracy and are likely to create alienation, despair and conflict" (p. 26). Other studies have made similar conclusions about violent crime. For instance, Stack and Kanavy investigated the relationship between economic conditions and rape, reporting strong support "for an economic theory of crime based on unemployment as well as income inequality. Both variables exert positive, independent effects on rape" (1983:71–72). More recent work by Bursik and Grasmick (1993), Hagan (1994), Messner and Rosenfeld (1994), Sampson and Wilson (1995), and Shover (1996) showed a relationship between neighborhood poverty, relative deprivation, and violent crime.

Finally, the quality of occupation available seems to be highly associated with conventional crime. When jobs are low paying, unstable, and menial, and offer little opportunity for advancement, conventional property crime becomes significantly more attractive. In

Unemployment and crime: Historically, criminological research has found a correlation between unemployment and street crime. Despite the economic "boom" of the 1990s, many U.S. citizens lack access to the legitimate labor market.

his important book *Confronting Crime* (1985), Elliot Currie reviewed the literature on the relationship between the secondary labor market and conventional crime and concluded that not only unemployment and income inequality affect the conventional crime rate; another consistent influence is

> the *quality* of work—its stability, its level of pay, its capacity to give the worker a sense of dignity and participation, the esteem of peers and community. In our society these fundamental needs are virtually impossible to satisfy without a job—but they are all too often difficult even *with* a job, and nearly impossible in many of the kinds of jobs available in America today, especially to the disadvantaged young. (p. 117)

In a class society, those at the bottom are more likely to experience such economic conditions as unemployment, lower relative incomes, and the degradation and alienation associated with low-paying jobs. Consequently, they are also more likely to turn to conventional crime. Indeed, the reason working-class people are more likely than middle-class people to *persist* at street crime is that the former are "the least likely to find close at hand the resources needed to construct and maintain successful lives legitimately" (Shover, 1996:42).

These unequal economic conditions are also associated with crimes of the *hidden economy*—those economic transactions that are unreported and often illegal. For instance, baby-sitting for a friend is a *legal* part of the hidden economy. Illegal transactions of the hidden economy consist of conventional property crimes—from robbery to fencing—and also of such crimes as illegal drug distribution, gambling, prostitution, and employee theft. The hidden economy entails large numbers of people participating in economic activity—working, buying, selling—outside the view and control of the state (Mattera, 1985:1). Employee theft and the amateur trade in stolen goods are examples of activities within this hidden economy. Moreover, as Stuart Henry (1987:144) and others have suggested: "Modern capitalist industrial society encourages such economies by creating structural inequalities based on class." When the legitimate labor market offers few attractive alternatives, illicit work—selling drugs, running numbers rackets, engaging in prostitution, and organizing criminal syndicates—becomes relatively inviting. For example, some poor and working-class women elect prostitution not only for economic survival but also for the independence it offers.

Eleanor Miller (1986:140) reported in her work on deviant street networks that prostitutes, in their own way, have a degree of independence, excitement, and autonomy that similarly qualified persons in the world of legal work rarely enjoy. As noted, most jobs available to the poor and working class are routine, confining, and seriously alienating. One prostitute put it this way: "You don't have certain hours you have to work. You can go to work when you want, leave when you want. . . . You don't have a boss hanging over you, you're independent" (James, 1982:302).

However, conventional crimes of the hidden economy are not found solely on the street. Indeed, most crime occurs in the workplace. As Box (1987:34) showed, economic conditions such as inflation can affect the working class by pushing people into higher tax brackets and reducing the overall purchasing power of their remaining income. The result is that those who experience reduced standards of living and are not prepared to endure it sometimes turn to tax evasion, embezzlement, fraud, and other forms of occupational crime and off-the-books income.

However, occupational crimes cannot be explained solely by economic deprivation. Closer examination of crimes such as employee theft reveals that the *internal* structure of the workplace is equally important. Hollinger and Clark's study of employee theft in three different industries concluded that this crime "is best understood within the social context of the work environment that includes perceived job dissatisfaction as a principal component" (1983:86). Dissatisfaction includes not only job quality, as discussed, but also such issues as *perceived inequality*. Many workers, when belittled by employers and thus reminded of the inequality in the workplace, turn to employee theft to "get back" at the boss or company. Altheide and his colleagues provide an example:

> After a clean-up boy was lectured on the correct way to mop floors, the boy took several books to show the manager he was not to be belittled. Now the books were not made known to the manager, but were shown to friends with a story of how he showed the manager. . . . These types of thefts also occurred when the employees felt they had been screwed out of something. For instance, one employee took a shirt

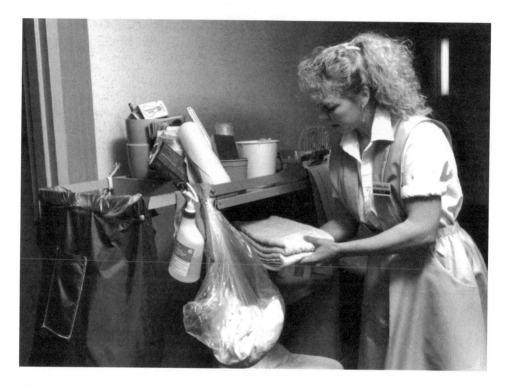

Quality of work and crime: Even those who do find work may turn to crime. The quality of work available in lower- and working-class communities is a consistent influence on the street crime rate.

from men's wear because he didn't get time and a half for working a Sunday. (1978:103)

Jerald Greenberg has called employee theft "the motive to even the score" (1997:94). In other words, employee theft is designed to bring harm to employers who are believed to have harmed employees. Thus employee theft is used to establish equity in an unequal relationship. Indeed, in a series of studies, Greenberg (1990, 1993a, 1993b) demonstrated that the more inequality in the workplace between employer and employee, the greater the likelihood of employee theft. Moreover, the *amount* of employee theft depends upon the nature of interpersonal treatment: Inequality is "magnified by the insult of insensitive treatment" by employers to employees (Greenberg, 1997:96).

The unequal relationships within the workplace and the workers' resentment of that inequality often trigger employee theft. Moreover, according to Henry (1987:145–146), employers often tolerate a certain amount of employee theft as a "hidden arm of control"; workplace thefts thus simply become "cheap symbolic concessions" to overall class inequality.

Thus far we have explored both crimes largely associated with the poor and working classes and how social position permits and precludes opportunities for committing conventional crimes. However, with the development of large corporations, financial institutions, and the state, a corresponding consolidation of a professional-managerial class has emerged. Members of this class can of course commit conventional crimes, but their structural position also provides the opportunity to engage in corporate and political crimes. The remainder of this section is devoted to a brief discussion of each.

Corporations in a capitalist economy endure only if they make a profit; yet profit making is not simply a matter of individual corporate greed. Rather, the pressure to make profits is created and enforced by the competitive structure of capitalism as an economic system. Corporations that do not continually reinvest their capital are likely to be "eaten up" by those that do. This pressure for profits drives many corporate executives to engage in corporate crime. As Stuart Hills argued in his book *Corporate Violence:*

> In a capitalist economy, profit-seeking firms must often compete in an uncertain and unpredictable environment. Competitive market pressures, fluctuating sales, increasing costs for safety and health measures, consumer and environmental concerns, governmental regulations, and other constraints may limit the ability of the business firm to achieve its profit goals through legitimate opportunities. Thus, some corporations may evade and violate the law or engage in practices that many Americans would consider unethical, endangering the well-being of workers, consumers, and citizens. (1987:190)

In other words, in the pursuit of profit, corporate executives must overcome several obstacles, such as minimizing costs and creating demand, to succeed at profit making. Corporate executives can increase profits by keeping down costs. The lower the cost to the corporation for labor, tools, machinery, and so on, the higher the profits. Many corporate executives secure profits by minimizing the costs of worker, consumer, and environmental safety. The pressure to minimize costs helps create the conditions for corporate crimes (such as unsafe working conditions, unsafe products, environmental pollution, sub-minimum wages) and transnational corporate crimes (such as dumping unsafe products and moving unsafe working conditions to more favorable environments).

A corporation has difficulty making a profit if it fails to sell what it produces. Thus in addition to minimizing costs, corporate executives must create a demand for their product. This necessity is conducive to corporate deception in marketing, especially when demand for the product is erratic and variable. Corporate executives thus may conquer this obstacle by engaging in such corporate crimes as consumer fraud, false advertising, and other deceptive practices (Messerschmidt, 1986b; Box, 1983).

In sum, then, although every corporation is not criminal, in a profit-driven society corporations are inherently criminogenic because of the intrinsic aspects of profit making and the obstacles a corporation must overcome to achieve its primary goal. Because of such corporate priorities, incentives exist that make corporate crime the logical outcome. In fact, sociological studies have shown that when corporate profits decline, corporate crime occurs more often (Clinard and Yeager, 1980; Box, 1987; Simpson, 1986, 1987). Thus the structural position of corporate executives in the professional-managerial class and the necessity of profit making help us understand corporate crime.

This constant requirement for profit making is also related to the corporate association with criminal syndicates (traditionally known as "organized crime"). Profits from the illegal sale and distribution of goods and services often are laundered in large financial institutions, providing profits for both the syndicate and these corporations. There is, then, a close relationship between the hidden economy and the formal economy. Through labor racketeering, criminal syndicates also serve corporate interests by providing a means for preventing unionization and for controlling labor organizing, which helps minimize costs. In short, the symbiotic relationship between criminal syndicates and legitimate businesses serves both interests by helping them achieve their common goal of profit making.

Members of the professional-managerial class serving in the political arena can use their position for personal ends. For instance, politicians can gain financially by engaging in a variety of corrupt practices such as bribery and the misuse of state funds. Political crimes for personal economic gain provide another example of how class position patterns the type of crime.

Finally, the state operates in certain ways to serve the economic interests of corporations. Although the managers of the state have historically come from the capitalist and the professional-managerial classes, the state is not simply an *instrument* of any class. In a capitalist economy the state operates to protect and support a corporate-dominated economy. As noted in Chapter 1.3, the state came into being with the development of social classes in agricultural societies; since then the economically dominant class has usually been the most politically powerful class. However, this does not mean the state operates in a monolithic manner. Rather, state actions result from political conflicts among classes and also within the capitalist class (Beirne, 1979). Nevertheless, these conflicts are embedded in an overall state policy of maintaining a viable capitalist economy.

Inasmuch as the major corporations (Fortune 500) dominate the U.S. economy, the state has a particular interest in their viability. This intimate relationship between the state and the economy often leads to political crime. For example, those who manage the state are interested in bolstering a healthy capitalist economy, not only for generating state revenues but also for their own continued political futures. Consequently, state managers take actions that facilitate corporate investment.

Corporations base their foreign investment decisions on such things as the cost of labor and raw materials, the size of the market, and the political climate (stability) of the society receiving the capital. Is the working class under control? Will the state raise taxes? Does the state support business freedom? If the answers to such questions are negative, it is unlikely that corporations will invest. Consequently, U.S. foreign policy has supported practices that permit the greatest opportunity for corporations to invest in other countries. Revolutionary movements in Africa and Central and Latin America, for example, that challenge the status quo also threaten corporate profits. The result is that the U.S. government has supported reactionary and oppressive regimes to quell such movements—as in Iran under the Shah and in Chile under Pinochet—and the CIA and National Security Council have moved to overthrow democratically elected governments. In other words, the state sometimes engages in international political crimes because of its inherent need to protect and maintain a capitalist economy.

The preceding discussion has provided selected examples of the relationship between class inequality, social position, and the types and seriousness of crime. Class position and inequality, however, provide only a partial understanding of how the patterns of crime and victimization occur in the United States. We now turn to a second, although equally important, sociological factor—gender inequality and crime.

15.2 GENDER AND CRIME

Sex and gender are not synonymous. Sex refers to the biological and physiological differences between men and women. **Gender** refers to historically and culturally developed behavior resulting from relationships between males/males, females/females, and males/females. Gender relations have developed sociologically into unequal relationships between males and females. This inequality has profound consequences for patterns of crime and victimization. In fact, gender is probably the best predictor of crime and victimization.

Patterns of Crime and Victimization

Arrest data, self-report studies, and victimization surveys help us form a picture of which gender commits the greatest number of conventional crimes and what *types* of conventional crimes are associated most often with each gender. Consider arrest data. According to the *Uniform Crime Reports (UCR),* males clearly outnumber females in terms of arrest numbers. Men compose the overwhelming majority of those arrested for the eight major felonies. Indeed, in every case except larceny, men account for 81 percent or more of the arrests. The most significant crimes committed by females, according to the arrest data, are larceny (35 percent), forgery and counterfeiting (39 percent), fraud (46 percent), embezzlement (47 percent), and prostitution and commercialized vice (60 percent) (Federal Bureau of Investigation, 1998:239).

Numerous researchers have employed self-report studies to generate data on gender and crime. Although we cannot discuss all aspects of this work here, Douglas Smith and Christy Visher (1980:693) reduced a large portion of this research (forty-four studies) to a single data base from which they determined the magnitude of the relationship between gender and crime. Smith and Visher concluded that the findings of the self-report studies were remarkably similar to arrest data. Thus males reported much more involvement in conventional crimes, especially in serious felonies. Moreover, in number and type, the female contribution to conventional crimes was found to be quite similar to the arrest data. However, Smith and Visher (p. 698) established that the arrest data underreport women's involvement in non-serious property crimes such as shoplifting and fraud, particularly for female youth. In other words, according to self-report studies, adult involvement in conventional crimes seems more male dominated than is youth crime, especially for property crimes. Subsequent discussions of data on gender and crime have reached similar conclusions (Steffensmeier and Allan, 1995a; Broidy and Agnew, 1997).

Thus arrest, self-report, and victimization data all suggest that both male adults and youth commit more conventional crimes and more serious types of conventional crimes than do female adults and youth. When women commit conventional crimes, they are primarily less serious offenses against property. In other words: "the profile of the typical female offender is much the same as it was 20 years ago—a minor property offender" (Morris, 1987:69). Women are most likely to commit larceny, fraud, and embezzlement (Belknap, 1996; Chesney-Lind, 1997). Males disproportionately commit interpersonal crimes of violence and property crimes, especially the more serious ones. Moreover, males have a virtual monopoly on the commission of syndicated, corporate, and political crime. Thus males commit the greatest number of crimes and the most serious types of them.

As Table 15.3 shows, males also have the highest rate of victimization for interpersonal crimes of violence (except rape and purse snatching/pocket picking). Consequently, for interpersonal crimes of violence, the highest victimization rate is *intragender:* males victimizing males. Nevertheless, there is substantial *intergender* victimization: males violating women through such offenses as rape and violence against women in the family.

Gender and Varieties of Crime

The patterns of crime and victimization identified above reflect broad social inequalities between men and women. Unequal relations between men and women are evident most clearly in the fact that men control the institutional structures of society and, therefore, women as well. Patterns of crime and victimization in contemporary U.S. society reflect these unequal gender relations. We consider first how these gender relations are structured and then relate that structure theoretically to the empirical evidence on gender and crime.

As industrialization has developed, women have been drawn out of the home and into the labor market in increasing numbers. More women today work in the labor market than ever before. For example, in 1970, 32 percent of all women sixteen years and older were in the labor force; by 1996 this figure had risen to 59.3 percent (*Statistical Abstract of the U.S., 1997*). Yet, as women enter the labor market they are segregated into certain "feminine" occupations. Most women are concentrated in service, retail, and clerical jobs (Renzetti and Curran, 1995). As Renzetti and Curran have noted, these occupations are among the lowest-paid positions in the labor market and provide little opportunity for advancement (1995). Women make up 93 percent of nurses; 98 percent of pre-kindergarten and kindergarten teachers; 78 percent of cashiers; 98 percent of secretaries, stenographers, and typists; 89 percent of clerks; 90 percent of bank tellers; 97 percent of child-care workers; and 78 percent of waiters and waitresses. At the other end of the job hierarchy, women make up only 8.5 percent of engineers; 14 percent of dentists; 26 percent of physicians; and 29 percent of lawyers and judges (*Statistical Abstract of the U.S., 1997*).

Women's position in this unequal, gendered labor market helps explain their patterns of crime. For example, as women experience economic pressure from increasing inflation and low pay, they are more likely to engage in crimes such as embezzlement. Moreover, the gender division of labor identified above determines the type of embezzlement women are most likely to commit. Although women make up slightly more than one-third of all embezzlers, they are primarily petty embezzlers (Chesney-Lind, 1997). The gendered

TABLE 15.3   Personal Crimes, 1997: Number of Victimizations and Victimization Rates for Persons Age 12 and Over, by Type of Crime and Sex of Victims

	Both sexes		Male		Female	
	Number	*Rate*	*Number*	*Rate*	*Number*	*Rate*
All personal crimes	8,970,600	40.8	5,044,250	47.3	3,926,350	34.7
Crimes of violence	8,614,070	39.2	4,877,390	45.8	3,738,680	33.0
Completed violence	2,879,080	12.2	1,428,930	13.4	1,250,150	11.0
Attempted/threatened violence	5,934,990	27.0	3,448,480	32.3	2,486,540	22.0
Rape/sexual assault	311,110	1.4	31,160	0.3	279,950	2.5
Rape/attempted rape	193,790	0.9	18,360[c]	0.2[c]	175,430	1.5
Rape	115,120	0.5	13,800[c]	0.1[c]	101,320	0.9
Attempted rape[a]	78,670	0.4	4,580[c]	0.0[c]	74,110	0.7
Sexual assault[b]	117,310	0.5	12,790[c]	0.1[c]	104,520	0.9
Robbery	943,940	4.3	650,820	6.1	293,120	2.6
Completed/property taken	606,860	2.8	411,190	3.9	195,460	1.7
With injury	243,220	1.1	168,020	1.6	75,200	0.7
Without injury	383,440	1.7	243,170	2.3	120,280	1.1
Attempted to take property	337,280	1.5	239,630	2.2	97,850	0.9
With injury	72,680	0.3	52,690	0.5	19,990[c]	0.2[c]
Without injury	264,610	1.2	186,940	1.8	77,670	0.7
Assault	7,359,030	33.6	4,195,410	39.4	3,163,620	27.9
Aggravated	1,883,110	6.6	1,163,250	10.9	719,860	6.4
With injury	594,900	2.7	360,500	3.4	234,390	2.1
Threatened with weapon	1,288,210	5.9	802,750	7.5	485,460	4.3
Simple	5,475,920	24.9	3,032,160	28.4	2,443,760	21.6
With minor injury	1,257,530	5.7	832,380	5.9	625,150	5.5
Without injury	4,218,390	19.2	2,399,770	22.5	1,818,610	16.1
Purse snatching/pocket picking	358,630	1.6	165,880	1.6	189,870	1.7
Population age 12 and over	219,839,110		106,598,660		113,240,440	

NOTE: Detail may not add to total shown because of rounding.
[a] Includes verbal threats of rape.
[b] Includes threats.
[c] Estimate is based on about ten or fewer sample cases.
SOURCE: Department of Justice, 1999.

Women and crime: Petty forms of property crime are the crimes committed most frequently by women. One such crime is embezzlement from institutions such as banks—a crime often committed to help solve unexpected financial problems arising in the family.

nature of embezzlement relates to women's subordinate position in the gender division of labor. As is clear from the foregoing evidence, the occupations in which women are employed today are not positions that handle large quantities of money. Kathleen Daly reported in her research on gender and white-collar crime that with regard to bank embezzlement "women are more likely than men to take cash from the till, and men are more likely to manipulate documents" because women are more likely to be bank tellers and men bank officers (1989:781).

In addition, women's motivation to engage in embezzlement seems to differ from that of men. Males embezzle because they experience a nonshareable financial problem they bring on themselves, such as gambling losses or "spending money foolishly"; they tend to rationalize their illegal behavior as simply "borrowing" (Cressey, 1971:80–105). Women embezzle because of unexpected financial problems and the impact these problems have on others. As Dorothy Zietz documented in her research on embezzlement, women embezzlers "consciously sacrifice their positions of trust in an effort to meet responsibilities associated with the role of wife and mother. Their behavior seemed to have a Joan of Arc quality, a willingness to be burned at the stake to obtain for a loved one the medical care needed or some service essential to his welfare" (1981:80).

In other words, women tend to embezzle because their social positions are predominantly those of homemakers and caretakers—even though they work outside the home. Rather than viewing their embezzlement as borrowing, the women in Zietz's study felt that any conduct—even embezzlement—was justified when it seemed the only solution to a problem affecting the welfare of a marriage or the potential loss of a child or lover (pp. 80–81). Daly's (1989:777) study also records that family need is one of the most frequent reasons women give for engaging in embezzlement.

Women's position in the gender division of labor also helps explain their involvement in other property crimes, such as larceny and fraud. The literature on the *feminization of poverty* indicates that "the fastest growing population living in poverty today is made up of women and children" (Sidel, 1987:25). The increasing impoverishment of women is caused by such factors as (1) rising divorce rates and the attendant rapid development of female-headed households; (2) the gender division of labor, which continues to discriminate against women; (3) the lack of adequate child care; and (4) a welfare system that maintains its recipients below the poverty line (p. 15). Not surprisingly, most female offenders are either unemployed or working in low-paying, menial jobs (Miller, 1986; Maher, 1997). Research has confirmed this relationship between the feminization of poverty and women's property crimes. For instance, Steven Box and Chris Hale reported: "As women become economically worse off, largely through unemployment and inadequate compensatory levels of welfare benefits, so they are less able and willing to resist the temptations to engage in property offenses as a way of helping solve their financial difficulties" (1983:199).

After reviewing close to fifty studies on economic conditions and crime, Box concluded that "the most plausible reason" for women's increasing involvement in property crimes "is that more women have become economically marginalized" (1987:43). Gender inequality, interacting with class inequality, structures women's social position and, therefore, female crime in U.S. society as well.

Although segregation into the "pink-collar ghetto" structures women's conventional criminality, women are largely absent from the major professions. Given that more women have become corporate managers in recent years, women managers are still systematically segregated into such lower-status managerial positions as personnel, research, affirmative action, and equal employment (Hymowitz and Schellhardt, 1986). These jobs do not lead to decisionmaking positions within the corporation. Rather, they are recommending bodies, where "*women do the work* to find out what is needed—make recommendations, and then *men decide* what is to be done with regard to these recommendations" (Sokoloff, 1980:243). In other words, the gender division of labor within the corporate managerial structure effectively segregates women from, but places men in, positions of power where corporate crimes are contrived. This process has been referred to as the *old-boy network,* a sponsorship system that recruits junior male executives into the upper ranks of the managerial divisions of the corporation (Messerschmidt, 1993). Consequently, corporate crime is a male-dominated activity. In the sample referred to above, Daly (1989:776) found that men committed 98 percent of Securities and Exchange Commission violations, 99.5 percent of antitrust violations, and 95 percent of bribery violations. She also identified a clear gender difference in white-collar crime motivation: Women's white-collar crimes are more often motivated from a need to make personal and familial ends meet, whereas men's white-collar crimes are more frequently associated with a need to make business ends meet (pp. 786–787). Thus the respective occupational crimes of males and females reflect different social positions in the gender division of labor.

BOX 15.1 SEXED WORK

Lisa Maher's study *Sexed Work: Gender, Race, and Resistance in a Brooklyn Drug Market* (1997) provided considerable support for the links between gender, race, and class inequality. Maher undertook an ethnographic study of homeless women drug users and their relation to the street-level drug economy of the Bushwick section of Brooklyn, New York. She examined three major options for women's survival in this poverty-ridden section of New York City: "drug-business hustles," "non-drug hustles," and "sexwork." Drug-business hustles include the provision of goods and services necessary for the distribution and consumption of illicit drugs. Non-drug hustles are acts of income generation not directly related to distributing and selling drugs, such as robbery, burglary, and larceny. Sexwork is confined to prostitution at the street level.

Maher found that men dominated at the highest levels of drug dealing and of all non-drug hustles; women were limited to the lowest positions of street-level drug sales and sexwork. Since women were viewed by men as unreliable, untrustworthy, and incapable of demonstrating an effective capacity for violence, they were used primarily as "informal steerers," which involved recommending to drug buyers a particular drug "in return for 'change,' usually a dollar or so" (pp. 88–89). As Maher stated, it is institutionalized sexism of the street culture that is "the most powerful element shaping women's experiences in the drug economy: it inhibited their access to drug-business work roles and effectively foreclosed their participation as higher-level distributors" (p. 106).

Consequently, sexwork was the only survival activity consistently available to homeless women drug users in Bushwick. However, this street-level prostitution was far from financially lucrative. Because prostitution was the only consistently available option for these women to survive, a flood of female sexworkers led to the lowering of the going rate for sex transactions, "encouraged 'deviant' sexual expectations on the part of dates, engendered relations of competition and hostility, and promoted the atomization and social isolation of women drug users" (p. 130).

One of the most interesting findings of Maher's research was the interrelation between gender and race. Maher found that this intersection positioned women differentially with respect to opportunities for income generation in the street culture. For example, being white and a woman proved to be advantageous in one aspect of the culture but a disadvantage in another. Indeed, white women had the least opportunity to participate in drug dealing because they would "stand out like a sore thumb" in relation to the Latino and African American women and thus would have a much greater chance of drawing police attention. However, regarding sexwork, white women had the advantage. As Maher put it, "European American women retain a relative advantage in that their skin colour allows them to cater to the racial prejudices of clients which devalue the sexual services of minority women" (p. 186). Thus opportunities to survive economically in Bushwick were both race-bound and gender-bound.

In the political arena, the gender division of labor likewise guarantees that political crime is dominated by men. There has never been a female president or vice president; only ten women have served in presidential administrations; and only 56 of the 435 representatives in Congress and 9 of the 100 senators currently are women (Neal, 1998).

Thus, women constitute more than 50 percent of the U.S. population yet hold approximately 12 percent of the seats in Congress. This absence of women from top governmental positions also results from an old-boy network. The gender division of labor within mainstream political parties—the Democratic and Republican parties in the United States—makes it extremely difficult for women either to reach positions of party responsibility or to be supported as candidates by parties. As Varda Burstyn has shown the major positionsin mainstream political parties "go to the people who control the funds and make political policy and alliances, people who are almost always men freed from much of the organizational nitty-gritty by the women's support work. . . . Thus in the mixed gatherings of party life where political policy, strategy, and selection of candidates is formally decided, the men predominate and dominate" (1983:73–74). The result is that men fill the ranks of those positions that are the chief source of political crime.

An old-boy network also functions in criminal syndicates and street gangs. Steffensmeier (1983) has shown that women are excluded or underrepresented in criminal syndicates and, if present, are allocated less-valued roles. Criminal syndicates are masculine dominated because of what Steffensmeier termed "homosocial reproduction," "sex-typing," and the "task environment of crime" (pp. 1012–1016).

"Homosocial reproduction" refers to the ways in which those in powerful positions fill positions with men like themselves. Because men dominate (control and populate) criminal syndicates, they prefer to work, associate, and do business with other men. This homosocial reproduction works in tandem with sex-typing. According to Steffensmeier, males in criminal syndicates stereotype women and criminal work in certain ways that effectively discriminate against women. Males in criminal syndicates, for example, see their work as (1) too hard, heavy, and dangerous for women and (2) too degrading and cheapening for women, leading to a loss of women's dignity. Steffensmeier added that men view "women as not as *capable,* or not as skilled, or not as stable; and believe that, while women *take orders* from men, men do not take orders from any woman" (p. 1013). Finally, the "task environment of crime" refers to the fact that to survive in the world of crime, a criminal syndicate must deal with the threat of arrest and imprisonment as well as threats from other criminal groups. Consequently, because both *secrecy* and *violence* are inextricable aspects of criminal syndicates, they recruit people who the leaders feel certain can help satisfy these needs. As Steffensmeier stated:

> A premium is placed on attributes such as trust and reliability and on physical characteristics such as strength and "muscle"—the capacity for force or violence. These characteristics have not been the prerogative of females. Furthermore, there is an almost inexhaustible pool of males to fill openings in crime groups; there are few empty places left for females. (p. 1014)

The three factors identified by Steffensmeier show that the structure of criminal syndicates tends to reflect the broader gender inequalities of society.

All this does not mean, of course, that women are never involved in important roles within professional and syndicated crime. Clearly, throughout history some women have been involved in such criminal activities (Block, 1977, 1980; Carlen, 1988). The important point is that these activities are highly dominated by men, a phenomenon that is socially determined by gender relations in the broader society.

Not surprisingly, males also dominate street gangs. Within a culture based on gender inequality, parents tend to control the spare time of young females more closely than that of males, leaving males freer to explore the outside world and to come into contact with one another (Hagan, Simpson, and Gillis, 1979). Young male criminality is therefore much more likely than female criminality to be collective in nature. And as Box has pointed out, women are seen by male gang members as emotional, unreliable, illogical, and untrustworthy—"not the type of person you want along on an armed robbery" (1983:182). Thus the old-boy network also infiltrates street gangs. When women are members of street gangs, they usually inhabit powerless positions and are pushed to the periphery of social activity. As Anne Campbell reported in her book *Girls in the Gang:*

> Females must accept the range of roles within the gang that might be available to them in society at large. The traditional structure of the nuclear family is firmly duplicated in the gang. In straight society the central, pivotal figure is the male. His status in the world of societal and material success is the critical factor, while the woman supports, nurtures, and sustains him. The gang parodies this state of affairs, without even the economic infrastructure to sustain it, for the male rarely works and often it is the female who receives a more stable income through welfare. Nevertheless, the males constitute the true gang! Gang feuds are begun and continued by males; females take part as a token of their allegiance to the men. (1991:242–243)

Finally, interpersonal violence against women is also closely associated with gender inequalities. Although some rapists actually may be psychopathic, research indicates that the vast majority are not emotionally disturbed. For example, comparisons of males convicted of rape with control groups of males not convicted indicate that the two groups are "indistinguishable in both their sexual behavior and other characteristics" (Morris, 1987:178). Moreover, most assumptions about rape held by the public—such as rape is impossible; women want to be raped; "no" means "yes"; and rape is a sexual act—have been disproven by research (see Morris, 1987:166–178 for a review). Most criminologists therefore view rape as the result of the structural subordination of women in contemporary society.

The United States actually has been described as a rape-prone society. In her research of 186 tribal societies, social anthropologist Peggy Sanday (1981) found that high rape rates occur in societies that are dominated by males and that feature male violence. Rape-prone societies, then, are those in which males dominate politically, economically, and ideologically and that glorify male violence. Rape-free societies, Sanday found, are marked by relative gender equality, the belief that the sexes are complementary, and a low level of interpersonal violence overall. Thus Sanday's work helps us understand why the United States can be considered a rape-prone society. Not only is U.S. society dominated politically, economically, and ideologically by males but it also glorifies male violence in the street, in sports, in the state, and so on.

Indeed, the assertion of dominance enables rape (Morris, 1987:178). As Messerschmidt has put it:

The rapist uses sex as a violent attack on the integrity of the woman as a person. In a rape, what is normally understood as an act of affection becomes an act of hate. This act destroys the woman's integrity by denying the victim her own will to engage, or not to engage, in sexuality as she pleases. By prohibiting this freedom, the rapist creates conditions of dominance and subordination. (1986b:135)

Rape reflects the dominance/subordination gender relationships in society. This was clearly evident in a study by Philippe Bourgois (1996) of inner city Puerto Rican men. Because of economic marginalization, these men were unable to become "head of the household" like their grandfathers' generation. Consequently, Bourgois found that many of these men took "refuge" in a drug economy that celebrated misogyny and in a predatory street culture that normalized gang rape. As Bourgois stated, "Marginalized men lash out against the women and children they can no longer support economically nor control patriarchally" (p. 412).

Like rape, violence by men in the family (wife rape, wife battering, and child sexual abuse) reflects gender power and inequality. The structure of the traditional nuclear family encourages the husband/father to view "his" wife and children as under his control. Violence in the family is intimately linked to our cultural expectation that males are authority figures within monogamous relationships. Some men therefore feel they have the right to dominate and control their wives; and wife battering serves to ensure continued compliance with their commands. If a wife questions such authority in any way, a violent husband turns to force simply to "get his way" (Ptacek, 1998).

Women's subordinate social position reinforces masculine dominance and violence in the family. If a wife is unemployed or works in a low-paying job, as is all too typical nowadays, it is easier for a husband to control her. In this type of society a husband usually has the economic power and the wife is dependent, often even if she works outside the home. Such conditions make it very difficult for her to leave a violent relationship, especially if she has children.

Economic dependency and powerlessness in the family also affect the likelihood of wife rape. Because of this unequal economic familial relationship, wife rape may not be physically violent in nature. If she is unwilling to "oblige" him, a husband can obtain access to "his" wife's body by threatening a beating or loss of affection or economically supportive relationship (Box, 1983:124). The wife may thus conclude that unwanted sexual intercourse is not as harmful as the alternative—economic poverty and distress. This situation is exacerbated for women with children and/or without skills.

In addition to the above, gender inequality is related to wife killing. For example, Bailey and Peterson (1995) found that the rate of women being killed by their husbands is significantly higher in cities where the college education gap between males and females is greater, where women experience higher levels of unemployment than men, and where a positive association exists with male-female inequality in income. As Bailey and Peterson concluded, "The overall pattern of findings for wife killings suggests that gender inequality breeds violence against wives" (p. 202).

Similarly, child sexual abuse results from the powerlessness of children (especially young girls) in the family and their economic and emotional dependence. Children are essentially a captive population; they are economically and emotionally dependent upon parents. Particularly at young ages, children do what is necessary to maintain a supportive relationship with their parents, even to the extent of keeping the assault secret. Consequently, this dependency and powerlessness makes child sexual abuse highly exploitative and nonconsensual. In other words, to understand child sexual abuse it is essential to understand power within the family. This type of abuse primarily entails a father as perpetrator and his daughter as victim. The power and authority claimed by the father structures the offender/victim relationship. Believing that women's role is to serve the needs of men—including their sexual needs—the male authority figure uses his power to assault his daughter incestuously.

Our discussion points to the fact that analysis of gender inequality adds considerably to our understanding of the patterns of crime and victimization in U.S. society. As with class position, gender position structures the opportunities for engaging in crime and the possibilities of being victimized by crime. In addition to class and gender, racial inequality also structures patterns of crime and victimization.

15.3   RACE AND CRIME

Genetic differences in skin color assume social significance when they are used to justify unequal treatment of one race by another. **Race** relations, like class and gender relations, have developed into unequal relations in which one race (white) uses skin color to legitimate domination and control of other races. Simultaneously, this inequality has important consequences for the patterns of crime and victimization in the United States.

Although whites continue to dominate several racial and ethnic groups in the United States—such as Native Americans, Asians, Mexican Americans, and African Americans—we focus on the inequality between whites and African Americans and the relationship of that inequality to crime and victimization. We concentrate on these two groups because, unfortunately, criminologists generally have ignored other racial and ethnic groups; therefore, there are insufficient data with which to make comparisons. We begin with a discussion of racial patterns of crime and victimization and then turn to a discussion of race and varieties of crime.

Patterns of Crime and Victimization

The *UCR* indicates that whites account for approximately 67 percent of all arrests; African Americans account for 30 percent; and the remainder of arrests are of other races (Federal Bureau of Investigation, 1998:222). Racial arrest disparities are evident when we take population into account. African Americans constitute only 12.8 percent of the U.S. population (Current Population Reports, 1997), yet they account for 41 percent of violent crime arrests and for over 32 percent of property crime arrests (Federal Bureau of Investigation, 1998:240).

Although arrest data show striking differences in rates for adults, self-report studies show that African American and white youth report similar involvement in youth crime (Hagan and Peterson, 1995). When specific offenses are analyzed, however, it appears that African American adults and youth report more involvement in the most serious conven-

Racism and the criminal justice system: For the same crime, young, lower- and working-class, racial minority males are more likely than other males to be arrested, prosecuted, convicted, and sentenced to prison for longer terms.

tional crimes, especially crimes of interpersonal violence (p. 22). Moreover, Hindelang's widely cited analysis of victim data—in which victims report such characteristics of offenders as race, approximate age, and so on—showed that African American male youths were more often reported as offenders in crimes of interpersonal violence and in property crimes committed against a person such as robbery (1981:464–469).

Summing up their analysis of arrest, self-report, and victimization data on race and crime, Hagan and Peterson stated the following: "These data reflect a crucial aspect of crime and race in America: not only are rates of offending and arrest high in African American communities, but so too are rates of victimization. That is, crime is predominantly intraracial" (1995:23).

Thus the higher *arrest* rate for African Americans is probably the result of *both* the criminal justice system's selection bias and a greater involvement of African Americans in conventional crimes. Criminologists have known for quite some time that when individuals of different social classes and races come into contact with the criminal justice system *for the same crime,* young, lower-class, minority males are more likely to be arrested, prosecuted, convicted, and sentenced to prison for longer terms (Reiman, 1995). Nevertheless, to argue that the higher arrest rate for African Americans is *solely* the result of a racist criminal justice system and that in reality the crime rate for all racial groups is otherwise the same is "tantamount to the suggestion that the black community does not in reality suffer any additional ill-effects from racial discrimination" (Lea and Young, 1984:111). Because of racial inequality in U.S. society, African Americans indeed suffer considerable discriminatory and oppressive conditions that whites do not. It is this disadvantageous social position that most likely results in a higher crime rate by African Americans than otherwise would be expected for their population size.

African Americans are also more often the victims of violent crime. As Table 15.4 shows, African Americans are victimized at a greater rate for all personal crimes—in particular, for robbery and assault. Moreover, as Table 15.5 shows, African Americans are victimized at a higher rate than whites for all household property crimes—in particular, for both household burglary and motor vehicle theft. Thus we can conclude that conventional crimes—especially crimes of interpersonal violence and property crimes—are *intraracial.* Nevertheless, there seems to be an increasing rate of *interracial* violence directed by whites *against* African Americans (see Chapter 9.1)

Conventional crimes are only one aspect of criminality, and, unfortunately, criminologists have concentrated their analysis of race and crime only on racial differences in rates of conventional crimes. However, whites clearly dominate in corporate and political positions where corporate and political crimes are committed (Staples, 1987). Therefore, although conventional crimes may be committed more often by African Americans than by whites, the more harmful and economically damaging white-collar and political crimes are disproportionately committed by whites.

Race and Varieties of Crime

As we pointed out in our discussion of "hate crimes" (see Chapter 9.1), African Americans are among the most frequent victims of interracial violence. However, they are also the primary victims of conventional crime. Discrimination continues to augment the disadvantages African Americans already suffer, creating conditions for high rates of intraracial crime. Obstacles experienced by the white working class are greater for African Americans because of racial discrimination. As Hagan and Peterson have pointed out, numerous studies have shown that racial discrimination, segregation, and concentrated poverty produce "pervasive family and community disadvantages as well as educational and employment difficulties, which in turn cause delinquent and criminal behavior among young minority males" (1995:16):

- Overall, African Americans account for one-third of all arrests and one-half of all incarcerations in the United States.
- About one-fifth of all sixteen- to thirty-four-year-old black males are under justice system supervision.
- One-half of all African American school dropouts, and three-quarters of dropouts who are between twenty-five and thirty-four years old, are under justice system supervision.

TABLE 15.4   Personal Crimes, 1997: Number of Victimizations and Victimization Rates for Persons Age 12 and Over, by Type of Crime and Race of Victims

| | Rate per 1,000 Persons Age 12 and Over | | | |
| | White | | African American | |
	Number	Rate	Number	Rate
All personal crimes	7,331,440	39.7	1,394,020	52.2
Crimes of violence	7,088,590	38.3	1,306,810	49.0
Completed violence	2,113,000	11.4	485,460	17.4
Attempted/threatened violence	4,955,590	26.8	841,350	31.5
Rape/sexual assault	257,710	1.4	43,890	1.6
Rape/attempted rape	168,950	0.9	18,280[c]	0.7[c]
Rape	96,260	0.5	12,310[c]	0.5[c]
Attempted rape[a]	72,690	0.4	5,980[c]	0.2[c]
Sexual assault[b]	88,760	0.5	25,610[c]	1.0[c]
Robbery	703,740	3.8	197,640	7.4
Completed/property taken	442,170	2.4	134,000	5.0
With injury	183,500	1.0	41,590	1.6
Without injury	258,660	1.4	92,410	3.5
Attempted to take property	261,570	1.4	63,640	2.4
With injury	55,400	0.3	12,360[c]	0.5[c]
Without injury	206,170	1.1	51,290	1.9
Assault	6,107,140	33.1	1,065,290	39.9
Aggravated	1,504,590	8.2	326,640	12.2
With injury	456,640	2.6	121,140	4.5
Threatened with weapon	1,048,050	5.7	205,500	7.7
Simple	4,802,450	24.9	738,640	27.7
With minor injury	1,041,610	5.6	172,410	6.5
Without injury	3,560,380	19.3	566,230	21.2
Purse snatching/pocket picking	282,860	1.4	57,200	3.3
Population age 12 and over	184,817,470		26,683,380	

NOTE: Detail may not add to total shown because of rounding.
[a] Includes verbal threats of rape.
[b] Includes threats.
[c] Estimate is based on about ten or fewer sample cases.
SOURCE: Department of Justice, 1999.

- Three-quarters of all black prison inmates have less than twelve years of schooling.
- African American prisoners between twenty-five and thirty-four years of age report pre-prison incomes that average $11,368, compared with $20,175 for this age group in the general population.
- Homicide is the leading cause of death among African American youth.

The relationship between unemployment and crime discussed in the class and crime section above is especially helpful in understanding the high crime rates of African American

TABLE 15.5 Property, Crimes, 1997: Number of Victimizations and Victimization Rates, by Type of Crime and Race of Head of Household

| | Rate per 1,000 Households | | | | | |
| | All Races | | White | | Black | |
	Number	Rate	Number	Rate	Number	Rate
All property crimes	25,817,140	248.3	21,245,940	242.3	3,743,430	292.0
Household burglary	4,634,920	44.6	3,707,090	42.3	801,610	62.5
Completed	3,892,970	37.4	3,115,540	35.5	666,000	51.9
Forcible entry	1,497,370	14.4	1,079,240	12.3	353,550	27.6
Unlawful entry without force	2,395,600	23.0	2,036,300	23.2	312,450	24.4
Attempted forcible entry	741,960	7.1	591,550	6.7	135,820	10.6
Motor vehicle theft	1,433,370	13.8	1,042,710	11.9	309,410	24.1
Completed	1,006,960	9.7	719,910	8.2	235,480	18.4
Attempted	426,410	4.1	322,800	3.7	73,950	5.6
Theft[a]	19,748,840	189.9	16,498,140	188.1	2,632,400	205.3
Completed	18,960,020	182.3	16,817,970	180.4	2,561,830	199.8
Less than $50	7,218,020	69.4	6,014,320	68.6	948,880	73.9
$50–$249	6,680,070	84.2	5,567,660	63.5	936,530	73.0
$250 or more	3,955,010	38.0	3,365,710	38.4	481,340	37.5
Amount not available	1,106,910	10.6	870,280	9.9	196,980	15.4
Attempted	788,820	7.6	678,170	7.7	70,680	5.5
Total number of households	103,988,670		87,880,170		12,821,410	

NOTE: Detail may not add to total shown because of rounding.
[a] Theft includes crimes previously classified as "personal larceny without contact" and "household larceny."

BOX 15.2   WHITE VIOLENCE AGAINST NATIVE AMERICANS

Although the vast majority of interpersonal violence is intraracial, an interesting study released by the Justice Department found that Native Americans are the victims of violent crimes at a rate more than twice the national average and that the perpetrators are mostly whites (Butterfield, 1999). Additional facts reported in this study included the following:

- The rate of murders committed by Native Americans in 1996 was 4.0 per 100,000 Native Americans, well below the national average of 7.9 per 100,000 and less than the white rate of 4.9 per 100,000.
- Native Americans, unlike whites and African Americans, are most likely to be victims of violent crimes committed by members of a race other than their own.
- Native Americans are more likely to be victims of violent crimes than members of any other racial group.
- The rate of violent crimes against Native American women is nearly 50 percent higher than that of African American men.
- 60 percent of those committing violent crimes against Native Americans from 1992–1996 were white, whereas 29 percent were Native American and 10 percent were African American.
- The annual rate at which Native Americans were victims of crime between 1992–1996 (124 crimes per 1,000 people ages 12 and older) is approximately two and a half times the national average of 50 crimes per 1,000 people.

male and female youth. Research has shown consistently that the overrepresentation of African American adults and youth in conventional crime statistics is the result of racial economic inequality (Sampson and Wilson, 1995). Indeed, the 1954 official unemployment rates of African American and white sixteen–nineteen-year-olds were almost identical: 15.4 and 14.0 percent, respectively (Duster, 1987). By 1998, however, 30 percent of African American sixteen–nineteen-year-olds and 13 percent of white sixteen–nineteen-year-olds were officially unemployed (Department of Labor, 1998). In other words, increasing economic inequality between white and African American youth has occurred since the mid-1950s.

The high rate of property crimes committed by African American youths has thus stemmed from their deteriorating economic situation. Other research supports this argument. Good and Pirog-Good analyzed the relationship between employment, property crime, and African American youth and found "a vicious circle for blacks in which lower employability increases their criminality which further lowers their employability" (1987:122). As African American employment increases, it "subsequently lowers their criminality, having the effect of further enhancing their employability" (p. 123). Similarly, Phillips and Votey (1987) used data of the National Longitudinal Survey of Young Americans to examine a variety of relationships, including the impact of legitimate labor market activity on participation in property crime. Their findings confirmed the hypothesis that "black and white differences in criminal participation . . . reflect differences in economic opportunity" (p. 129). Finally, an extensive study of the relationship between labor market conditions, inner-city African American youth, and crime reported similar results. For African American youth

> crime serves an economic function by providing many with a substantial income source. . . . A fundamental influence on criminal behavior is the role of economic factors, such as labor market status. Respondents who were in school or employed were much less likely to engage in crime. . . . Respondents who were not employed or in school were much more strongly driven by economic incentives to commit crime. (Viscusi, 1986:343)

Viscusi also found a relationship between crime and quality of job, especially the low paying jobs available to African American youth. Viscusi concluded that "if youth can make more money from crime than from labor market earnings, they will be more likely to engage in crime" (p. 343).

One increasingly profitable crime is selling drugs. However, though dealing drugs may be financially rewarding, it has a dangerous, negative side: "To many poor black kids living in a run-down housing project, the thriving drug business looks a lot more accessible and promising than school or a traditional job, despite the obvious down side: violence, murder and possibly their own death" (Moore, 1988:53).

Those involved in the drug trade are clearly more likely to be both the perpetrators and the victims of violence. Yet violence, as we have seen earlier, is related to such structural conditions as income inequality. Although most studies on this topic have concentrated on class and crime, a study by Blau and Blau (1982) related income inequality to race. As noted above, in their study of the 125 largest metropolitan areas in the United States, Blau and Blau found that the greater the gap between incomes in a metropolitan area, the higher the rate of criminal violence (p. 121). When they controlled for class, Blau and Blau found that socioeconomic inequality between African Americans and whites has a positive and direct effect on criminal violence. In other words, inequalities rooted in ascribed racial positions create alienation and despair and have a profound impact on the generation of criminal violence. This helps us understand the high violent crime rates of *both* African American females and African American males.

Indeed, as Currie added, after reviewing the literature on homicide and race: "Homicide is the leading cause of death for blacks of both sexes between the ages of fifteen and twenty-four: 39% of black men and 25% of black women who die at these early ages are murdered. At this age, homicide death rates are five times higher for blacks than whites among men and four times higher for women" (1985:153).

Thus although the African American female violent crime rate is high, within the African American community the vast majority of criminal violence is committed *by* African American men *against* African American men. For African American men ages 15–44, homicide is the leading cause of death, and African American men are eight times more likely to die by murder than are white males (p. 154).

The work of Bruce, Roscigno, and McCall (1998) has likewise shown the relationship between racial inequality and violence by African Americans. Specifically, they demonstrated that there exists a link between structural racial disadvantage and the perpetuation of interpersonal violence in inner-city African American communities. Growing up in dis-

Inequality, race, and crime: Despite the prospering economy of the 1990s, many African Americans continue to live in poverty-ridden communities. The socioeconomic and racial inequality between African Americans and whites has a direct effect on criminal violence.

advantaged communities, African Americans become aware of the structural constraints of their existence—such as the lack of educational and job opportunities. Bruce and his colleagues argued that this "barrage of indicators which signify their powerlessness shape social and psychological well-being and certainly may lead to anger, frustration, and despair" (p. 44).

Moreover, because of the lack of legitimate economic opportunities, many poor inner-city African Americans participate in the informal economy of drugs and weapons trafficking. The combination of illegal activities and the availability of weapons increases the potential for gun use to solve conflicts. The result is the "transformation of peaceful neighborhoods into tense areas gripped by the ever-present threat of violent confrontation" (p. 44). Such a threat of danger can result in interactional rituals that lead to violence:

The reality of living in an area where individuals have to depend on illegitimate activities for survival can have negative consequences for social psychological processes which, in turn, may increase the potential for violence. . . . Because gang members hold such grim prospects for life, minor incidents such as accidentally bumping into someone or wearing a particular color create the possibility that an individual will be attacked. (p. 44)

Thus these authors have shown how violence among African Americans results from the intersection of structural disadvantage, local context, and individual social action.

In summary, racial inequality structures conventional crime, both interracial and intraracial. Interracial violence results from extreme racist beliefs in a racially segregated and unequal society. Crime by African Americans is the product of their positions in class and racial hierarchies, which are, of course, mediated by gender.

As argued earlier, combined class, gender, and racial inequality also determine who can engage in white-collar and political crimes. African Americans hold only 4.7 percent of executive, administrative, and managerial positions and only 6.4 percent of professional positions (*Statistical Abstract of the U.S.,* 1997). Moreover, there has never been an African American president or vice president; and currently African Americans do not hold any seats in the U.S. Senate, and they hold only 9 percent of the seats in the House (Neal, 1998). Thus racial inequality determines that whites hold more of those positions in which the most serious and harmful crimes—white-collar and political crimes—occur. Racial inequality—as with class and gender inequality—governs social position in society and, therefore, criminal opportunities.

15.4   AGE AND CRIME

Economic benefits, social privileges, and political power are based not only on class, gender, and race but also on **age**. Even such basic rights as sexual activity, voting, and drinking alcohol are conferred by age. Thus age inequality and age discrimination exist in U.S. society; these phenomena are most pronounced for youth but also affect the elderly. Unequal generational divisions between young and old are prevalent, and social behavior—including crime—is linked to the aging process. One's position in the age hierarchy permits or precludes opportunity for engaging in crime. Consider the patterns of crime and victimization based on age.

Patterns of Crime and Victimization

According to arrest data in the *UCR* (Federal Bureau of Investigation, 1998: 232), participation in conventional crime rises with age, peaks in the teenage and early adulthood years, and then declines. Two important age patterns for conventional property and violent crimes emerge. Property crime arrest rates peak between the ages of thirteen and seventeen and then decline rather quickly. For violent crimes the rate peaks at around the ages of eighteen and nineteen and declines much more slowly with age.

Some criminologists have questioned arrest data on age. For example, because youth tend to commit conventional crimes in groups, they are allegedly more visible to the police and thus more likely to be arrested. Also, some criminologists argue that youth are less skilled than are adults in committing crime and, therefore, more likely to be arrested. It may be, then, that arrest statistics on age are biased; this would explain the overrepresentation of youth in *UCR* data. However, self-report studies report very similar age patterns for conventional crimes, and an empirical examination of such possible biases (using both self-report and victimization surveys) "suggests that the biases do not account for the relation between age and crime" (Hirschi and Gottfredson, 1983:552). We conclude therefore that arrest data are reliable evidence of the age distribution of conventional crime.

Tables 15.6 and 15.7 show victimization rates for conventional crimes by age. For crimes of violence, young persons ages twelve–nineteen have the highest rates of victimization. For victims over the age of nineteen, violent crimes decline with age, so that those age sixty-five and older have the lowest victimization rates for violent crimes. Moreover, as Table 15.7 shows, property crime victimization rates are highest for the youngest heads of household and decline with age. For conventional crimes, then, the highest victimization rates are *intra-age*.

Age and Varieties of Crime

We begin with a discussion of age differences. David Greenberg (1977) has shown that during the transition from childhood to adolescence, the links between children and parents decrease (yet economic dependence remains) while receptivity to peers and peer evaluation increases. Being popular and connected with the "right" groups becomes critically important for most youth. The partial disengagement of youth from family and the heightened closeness to peers, combined with advertising directed toward the teenage market, have created the conditions for youthful involvement in pleasure-seeking, consumption-oriented social lives. Indeed, participation in this teenage social life requires money for buying the "right stuff": clothing, cosmetics, cigarettes, alcoholic beverages, narcotics, CDs, CD players, gasoline for cars and motorcycles, tickets to films and concerts, and meals in restaurants. However, because teenage labor force participation has declined drastically, youths are finding it more and more difficult economically to support their participation in teen life. Thus the high rate of property crimes for youth ages twelve–nineteen is, according to Greenberg, "a response to the disjunction between the desire to participate in social activities with peers and the absence of legitimate sources of funds needed to finance this participation" (p. 197). Because of teenage social position, youth property crimes increasingly serve as an alternative to work.

When youth leave high school—and when their social position changes accordingly—peer evaluation decreases and opportunities for becoming financially self-sufficient expand. This situation reduces teenage motivation to engage in property crimes, and their involvement in property crimes drops off rapidly at post-high school ages. As Greenberg stated: "Employment, leaving school, military enlistment, and marriage eliminate major sources of criminogenic frustration, and at the same time supply informal social control" (1983:33).

Steffensmeier and Allan (1995b:102–103) expanded on Greenberg's thesis, arguing that five major changes mark the transition from late adolescence to early adulthood:

TABLE 15.6 Personal Crimes, 1997: Victimization Rates for Persons Age 12 and Over, by Type of Crime and Age of Victims

	Rate per 1,000 Persons in Each Age Group						
	12–15	16–19	20–24	25–34	35–49	50–64	65 and Over
All personal crimes	90.7	99.7	69.6	48.0	33.8	15.7	5.7
Crimes of violence	87.9	96.2	87.8	46.9	32.2	14.6	4.4
Completed violence	30.2	30.7	25.5	13.7	9.1	3.2	1.4
Attempted/threatened violence	57.7	65.6	42.2	33.1	23.1	11.3	3.0
Rape/sexual assault	2.5	5.6	2.4	2.3	0.6	0.2[c]	0.2[c]
Rape/attempted rape	2.3	3.4	1.8	1.2	0.3[c]	0.1[c]	0.1[c]
Rape	1.5[c]	1.6[c]	1.5[c]	0.6[c]	0.2[c]	0.1[c]	0.0
Attempted rape[a]	0.7[c]	1.9	0.3[c]	0.6[c]	0.1[c]	0.1[c]	0.1[c]
Sexual assault[b]	0.3[c]	2.2	0.6[c]	1.1	0.3[c]	0.1[c]	0.1[c]
Robbery	6.2	10.2	7.4	4.7	3.7	2.2	0.9
Completed/property taken	5.8	6.4	5.1	2.7	2.3	1.5	0.7[c]
With injury	2.6	2.4	2.4	0.9	0.9	0.6[c]	0.3[c]
Without injury	3.2	4.1	2.7	1.8	1.3	0.9	0.5[c]
Attempted to take property	2.4	3.8	2.3	2.0	1.5	0.6[c]	0.1[c]
With injury	0.3[c]	0.3[c]	0.7[c]	0.5[c]	0.4[c]	0.2[c]	0.0[c]
Without injury	2.1	3.4	1.6	1.5	1.1	0.4[c]	0.1[c]
Assault	77.1	80.4	57.9	39.9	27.9	12.2	3.4
Aggravated	15.1	24.6	17.0	9.5	7.4	2.8	0.6[c]
With injury	6.1	7.1	6.1	3.1	2.2	0.5[c]	0.2[c]
Threatened with weapon	9.0	17.4	10.9	5.5	5.3	2.3	0.4[c]
Simple	62.0	55.8	40.9	30.4	20.4	9.4	2.8
With minor injury	16.6	13.6	12.2	6.4	4.3	1.1	0.4[c]
Without injury	45.4	42.4	28.7	23.9	16.2	5.3	2.4
Purse snatching/pocket picking	2.8	3.5	1.8	1.1	1.6	1.1	1.2
Population in each age group	16,701,280	15,244,130	17,648,850	40,162,600	62,604,840	38,488,320	31,991,100

NOTE: Detail may not add to total shown because of rounding.
[a] Includes verbal threats of rape.
[b] Includes threats.
[c] Estimate is based on about ten or fewer sample cases.
SOURCE: Department of Justice, 1999.

TABLE 15.7   Property Crimes, 1997: Victimization Rates by Type of Crime and Age of Head of Household

	Rate per 1,000 Households				
	12–19	*20–34*	*35–49*	*50–64*	*65 and Over*
All property crimes	600.6	324.3	304.4	206.2	96.5
Household burglary	125.6	59.6	48.8	39.0	22.5
Completed	108.5	50.3	40.7	32.9	18.8
Forcible entry	23.2[b]	22.0	14.8	12.2	6.7
Unlawful entry without force	85.4	28.3	25.9	20.7	12.1
Attempted forcible entry	17.1[b]	9.3	8.1	6.1	3.7
Motor vehicle theft	20.5[b]	21.3	15.2	10.6	5.6
Completed	14.2[b]	15.1	10.6	7.6	3.7
Attempted	5.2[b]	6.2	4.6	3.0	1.9
Theft[a]	454.5	243.4	240.4	156.6	68.5
Completed	447.0	232.2	231.2	151.4	65.3
Less than $50	167.0	77.3	94.5	56.6	28.8
$50–$249	167.4	84.8	81.2	54.8	18.1
$250 or more	88.1	58.1	43.4	29.9	11.9
Amount not available	24.4[b]	12.1	12.1	10.1	8.5
Attempted	7.6[b]	11.1	9.2	5.2	3.1
Total number of households	850,880	25,399,880	34,599,260	21,653,380	21,485,500

NOTE: Detail may not add to total shown because of rounding.
[a] Theft includes crimes previously classified as "personal larceny without contact."
[b] Estimate is based on about ten or fewer sample cases.
SOURCE: Department of Justice, 1999.

1. greater access to legitimate sources of material goods and excitement: jobs, credit, alcohol, sex, and so forth
2. age-graded norms: externally, increased expectation of maturity and responsibility; internally, anticipation of assuming adult roles, coupled with reduced subjective acceptance of deviant roles and the threat they pose to entering adult status
3. peer associations and lifestyle: reduced orientation to same-age/same-sex peers and increased orientation toward persons of the opposite sex and/or persons who are older or more mature
4. increased legal and social costs for deviant behavior
5. patterns of illegitimate opportunities: with the assumption of adult roles, opportunities increasing for crimes (for example, gambling, fraud, and employee theft) that are less risky, more lucrative, and/or less likely to be reflected in official statistics

Greenberg also attempted to explain the high rates of interpersonal violence committed by youth and young adults. As discussed earlier in this chapter, interpersonal crimes of violence are committed primarily by males. Traditional gender ideology calls for males to work outside the home and support a family. However, lower- and working-class males have less of a chance than other males of fulfilling these activities. This situation, Greenberg reasoned, generates a masculine status anxiety in which such men "may attempt to alleviate their anxiety by exaggerating those traditionally male traits that *can* be expressed. Attempts to dominate women (including rape) and patterns of interpersonal violence can be seen in these terms. In other words, crime can . . . provide a sense of potency that is expected and desired but not achieved in other spheres of life" (1977:207).

Greenberg pointed out that arrest rates for interpersonal crimes of violence peak in the immediate post–high school age brackets when primarily lower- and working-class males—who do not attend college—anticipate or actively seek full-time work. He argued that masculine status anxiety helps us understand not only age variations in interpersonal crimes of violence but class, gender, and race as well. Greenberg concluded that the variable relationship between age and crime depends on historical, cultural, and economic factors. Patterns of crime in the United States therefore reflect the particular development of age segregation and of the social position of youth in U.S. society.

Not everyone agrees that age is an important factor in explaining patterns of crime. Hirschi and Gottfredson, for example, have agreed that the age distribution of crime depicted in the *UCR* is accurate and that it "represents one of the brute facts of criminology" (1983:552). But, whereas Greenberg argued that the age distribution of crime varies with social conditions, Hirschi and Gottfredson have contended that the age distribution of crime is *invariant* across all social and cultural conditions. For them the shape and form of the age distribution remains "virtually unchanged" from time to time and place to place (pp. 554–562). Criminological theory and research therefore need not consider age as an important variable in explaining crime.

Greenberg (1985) has countered this argument with considerable historical and cross-cultural evidence. Greenberg has shown that today there is less adult crime relative to juvenile crime in the United States than there used to be. Similarly, an analysis of other societies—both industrial and preindustrial—displays a noticeable shift toward younger ages involved in criminality once industrialization occurs. For example, in contemporary Norway, the age distribution of crime is similar to that in the United States. Yet as criminologist Nils Christie pointed out, speaking of Norway: "Police statistics for 1870 showed no peak for teenagers. They did not exist at that time. A hundred years ago, the peak was somewhere in the middle twenties and with a *slow decrease* in criminal activity among the older groups" (cited in Greenberg, 1985:12, emphasis added).

For the Banyoro and Basoga (two preindustrialized Bantu-speaking peoples of Uganda), the peak age of those who commit homicide is thirty-five, and rarely are homicides committed by teenagers (Greenberg, 1985:13). Consequently, Greenberg's theory of the age distribution of conventional crime remains the most sound, and empirical research supports his conclusions. In particular, Steffensmeier and his colleagues (1989) examined arrest data on age in the United States for three time periods: 1940, 1960, and 1980. They found that a considerable change in the age of offenders occurred from 1940 to 1980: The "most significant change has been the progressive concentration of offending among the young; this suggests increasing discontinuity in the transition from adolescence to adulthood in modern times" (p. 803).

Despite the soundness of his theory about the age distribution of conventional crime, we should note that Greenberg is mistaken when he implies that age is the single most important variable for explaining crime. Greenberg argued that "in modern capitalist societies, children of all classes share, for a limited period, a common relationship to the means of production (namely exclusion) which is distinct from that of most adults, and they respond to their common structural position in fairly similar ways" (1977:212). Greenberg thus suggested that youth have developed into their own social class; this suggestion seems to reduce the importance of other social divisions and characteristics.

Yet age is not a simple or homogeneous category; it is divided not only by class but also by gender and race. Distinct youth subcultures—based on such categories as race and class—develop within a broader youth culture; these youth subcultures differ from one another, and they can become hostile and antagonistic toward each other (Schwendinger and Schwendinger, 1985). Mungham and Pearson went so far as to argue that working-class, skinhead subcultures developed in reaction to the middle-class hippy subculture of the 1960s and early 1970s. The result was a distinct *style* that is "both a caricature and a reassertion of solid male working-class toughness" (1976:7). Greenberg's theory downplays this subcultural differentiation and conflict. Although age structures patterns of crime and victimization, it is not a uniform entity.

Moreover, race and class can affect an individual's ability to move out of crime; that is, race and class inequality limit access to legitimate resources—such as college attendance or employment at adequate wages—that allow "maturation" out of crime. Steffensmeier and Allan provided one example: "For black inner-city youths, the high level of youth inequality that characterizes modern societies is compounded by the problems of living in a racist society, and they are less able to leave behind the inequality of youth status. As they move into young adulthood they continue to experience limited access to the adult labor market" (1995b:103–104). In a similar vein, Hagan (1991) has shown that crime rates for working-class youth decline less slowly than rates for middle-class youth.

The segregation and subordination of youth in society as a whole—and the accompanying adolescent subcultures—are not the only factors that generate specific patterns of crime. The subordination of youth within specific institutions also plays a role. Unequal relationships between parents and children can set the stage for generational conflict and at least three types of crime: child physical abuse, child sexual abuse, and youth crime. Child abuse results from power relations across generations and the accompanying ideology that children should at all times be subordinate to parents. A thin line separates authoritarian, punitive, and harsh forms of discipline, on the one hand, and child abuse on the other; indeed, they seem to coexist.

Moreover, research reveals a strong relationship between child sexual abuse and future delinquency. The vast majority of victims of child sexual abuse (both girls and boys) report severe forms of trauma, leading many to run away from home. In particular, girls on the street report high rates of physical abuse and sexual abuse (Chesney-Lind, 1997). Running away from sexual abuse and a violent home, these young women and men turn to crime to survive. After reviewing the literature on young women, Meda Chesney-Lind pointed out that sexually abused female runaways are "significantly more likely than their

From home to street: Many homeless girls have run away from physical and sexual abuse at home. Once on the street, they turn to a variety of crimes to survive. These two girls have become street prostitutes.

non-abused counterparts to engage in delinquent or criminal activities, such as substance abuse, petty theft, and prostitution" (p. 27).

Consequently, the powerlessness of children in the home and the extreme results of that subordination (child physical abuse, child sexual abuse, and neglect—along with the lack of community social services for homeless youth) contribute to crime both quantitatively and qualitatively. These findings demonstrate the important ties between social position, victimization, and subsequent crime.

Although the social position of youth presents young people with opportunities for committing certain crimes, it also precludes them from committing others. Systematically denied access to the labor market, youth are effectively segregated from positions where workplace-related crimes—such as embezzlement and corporate crimes—and political crimes occur.

For corporate and political crimes, the ages 30–60 clearly dominate; these are the prime ages of employment, and individuals of these ages make up the most powerful age-group in society. As Steffensmeier and Allan have argued, this connection of middle age with white-collar crime "reflects age-related opportunities for criminal behavior that emerge as a result of one's position within a firm that, either directly or indirectly, encourages shady business practices" (1995b: 109).

BOX 15.3   YOUTH CRIME AND HOMELESSNESS

John Hagan and Bill McCarthy used observational, survey, and interview data obtained in two Canadian cities, Toronto and Vancouver, to examine the family and school histories, the living conditions, and the criminality of youth who live on the streets. In their book *Mean Streets: Youth Crime and Homelessness* (1997), Hagan and McCarthy documented that the vast majority of street youth who engage in crime have recently run away from explosive, sexually and physically violent parents; as a result these youth are not committed to school and schoolwork. Once on the street they experience the day-to-day problems of finding food, shelter, and work. Not surprisingly, Hagan and McCarthy's data provided consistent evidence of a relationship between the involvement of these youth in street crime and their lack of food, shelter, and work.

Interestingly, there is an important difference between Toronto and Vancouver regarding street youth involvement in theft, prostitution, and the drug trade. According to Hagan and McCarthy Toronto has a social welfare orientation toward street youth, whereas Vancouver provides few social support services for the homeless. The result is more crime by street youth in Vancouver than by the street youth in Toronto: "The implication is that an absence of social capital in the form of services and support in Vancouver encourages street youth to capitalize on opportunities that they encounter to become involved in theft, prostitution and the drug trade" (p. 232). Moreover, for street youth in both cities who eventually were able to find employment, they were much more likely than non-employed street youth to move away from the street and, thus, crime: "They spent less time hanging out, panhandling, searching for food and shelter, using drugs, stealing with other youth, or pursuing other kinds of criminal activities" (p. 234).

As we stated earlier, the elderly are also increasingly segregated and subordinated in the United States. Not surprisingly, in the 1980s criminologists became interested in the topic "crime and the elderly" (Goetting, 1983; Wilbanks and Kim, 1984; Newman, Newman, and Gewirtz, 1984; McCarthy and Langworthy, 1988). An important article by Cullen, Wozniak, and Frank (1985:155) concluded that the majority (78 percent) of elderly arrests are for larceny, which is almost six times higher than the next highest category, aggravated assault. Elderly males and females seem to commit larceny in equal proportions (Feinberg, 1984). Moreover, the elderly tend to steal household and personal necessities of low value—such as toothpaste, cigarettes, and tools (Curran, 1984). It should be noted, however, that although larceny seems to be the most frequent crime committed by the elderly, they are much less likely to commit larceny than any other age group (Klemke, 1992:43–44).

As would be expected from our earlier analysis, elderly property crime rates are correlated with adverse economic conditions. In fact, those above the age of 55, and especially 65, have an economic situation similar to that of youth. The labor force participation rate for people 55 and older has decreased since 1980: In particular, for males ages 55–64 it fell from 72.1 in 1980 to 67.0 in 1996; for ages 65 and over it fell from 19.0 to 16.9 (*Statistical Abstract of the United States,* 1997). This decreasing labor force participation rate for males may help explain the high rate of larceny by males over 65. Bachand and Chressanthis

(1988) investigated the relationships between inflation, unemployment, labor force participation rates, and elderly crime. They concluded that as each of these economic factors worsens, so, too, does the property crime rate of the elderly.

REVIEW

This chapter discussed considerable empirical research to help explain the patterns of crime and victimization in the United States. Of primary importance is structured inequality: Class, gender, race, and age hierarchies determine social position and thus criminal opportunities.

Class and Crime

1. Arrest data, self-report studies, and victimization surveys all show that conventional crimes by adults and youth are disproportionately concentrated in the lower and working classes.

2. White-collar and political crimes are disproportionately committed by members of the professional-managerial class.

3. Victimization data show that all conventional crimes—except personal larceny without contact and motor vehicle theft—are likely to be intra-class.

4. Unemployment, income inequality, and job quality are associated both with conventional crimes and with nonoccupational crimes of the hidden economy.

5. Both economic conditions such as inflation and job quality and perceived inequality within the workplace itself are conducive to occupational crimes such as employee theft.

6. Corporate crimes are caused chiefly by the desire of corporate executives to overcome obstacles to profit making.

7. Because of their position within the state, politicians have opportunities to gain financially by engaging in a variety of corrupt practices.

8. The close association between the state and the economy creates conditions for systematic state crimes—such as international political crimes.

Gender and Crime

1. Arrest data, self-report studies, and victimization surveys show that male adults and youth are the chief perpetrators of all forms of conventional crime.

2. Males have a virtual monopoly on the commission of syndicated, corporate, and political crimes.

3. When females commit crime, they engage mostly in petty forms of theft like shoplifting, fraud, and minor embezzlement, and in prostitution.

4. Victimization data on conventional crimes suggest that males victimize other males.

5. Women's subordinate position in the gender division of labor structures the type of embezzlement women commit.

6. The feminization of poverty is associated with female fraud, shoplifting, and other forms of petty theft.

7. Males dominate in syndicated, corporate, and political crimes because of their power to exclude women systematically from positions where these crimes originate.

8. Male violence toward women derives from gender inequality, the structural subordination of women, and the power and dominance accorded men in U.S. society.

Race and Crime

1. Data on race and crime suggest that African American adults and youth commit a disproportionate amount of conventional crimes—especially interpersonal crimes of violence.

2. Whites clearly dominate the more harmful and economically damaging white-collar and political crimes.

3. Victimization data show that conventional crimes are intraracial in nature (e.g., African Americans typically victimize African Americans and whites typically victimize whites).

4. Because racial oppression multiplies African Americans' disadvantages, they experience a disproportionate number of economic and social obstacles.

5. Overrepresentation of African American adults and youth in conventional crime statistics—both property crimes and interpersonal crimes of violence—is the result of racial economic inequality.

6. The racial hierarchy results in white domination of the positions where white-collar and political crimes occur.

Age and Crime

1. Conventional crime arrest rates vary with age. Property crimes peak between 13 and 17 years of age and decline rapidly with age; violent crimes peak around 18 and 19 years of age and decline much more slowly.

2. Victimization rates for conventional crimes show that young persons ages 12–24 have the highest rates of conventional crime victimization.

3. The high rate of property crime for youth results from their desire to participate in youth social activities and from a lack of adequate funds to pay for them.

4. Not all criminologists agree that age is an important factor in crime.

5. Power and inequality within the family can create social positions leading to the victimization of youth. This victimization has implications for future involvement in crime.

6. White-collar and political crimes are committed by the most powerful age group, those 30–60 years of age.

7. Elderly crime consists mostly of petty forms of theft, such as shoplifting, and is caused by their decreasing participation in the labor market.

QUESTIONS FOR CLASS DISCUSSION

1. Choose several crimes. Then explain how social position permits and prevents opportunities for their commission.

2. Discuss how the interaction of class, gender, race, and age affects criminal opportunities. Cite several examples.

3. How does our discussion of the varieties of crime differ from those offered by the media?

4. Choose three theories presented in Part Two and then examine how they would explain the class, gender, race, and age patterns of crime and victimization.

FOR FURTHER STUDY

Readings

Hagan, John, and Bill McCarthy. 1997. *Mean Streets: Youth Crime and Homelessness.* New York: Cambridge University Press

Hagan, John, and Ruth D. Peterson, eds. 1995. *Crime and Inequality.* Stanford, Calif.: Stanford University Press.

Maher, Lisa. 1997. *Sexed Work: Gender, Race, and Resistance in a Brooklyn Drug Market.* New York: Clarendon Press.

Mann, Coramae Richey, and Marjorie S. Zatz, eds. 1998. *Images of Color, Images of Crime: Readings.* Los Angeles: Roxbury Publishing.

Websites

1. <http://www.americanhumane.org/cpwho.html>: The American Humane Association operates this website and provides reliable information on child abuse and neglect. It also provides information on the abuse of animals.
2. <http://www2.bitstream.net/~alpropes/mav/index.html>: This site is titled "Men Against Violence Webring" and offers some action-oriented solutions to male violence. Useful links are provided, with a goal for men to take greater responsibility for violence.
3. <http://www.fbi.gov/ucr/hatecm.htm>: This is a report from the U.S. Department of Justice on hate crimes reported to the police. Victimization patterns are race and gender specific, and this report provides recent victimization and offender characteristics.

Preview

Chapter 16 introduces:
- the importance of comparative criminology to the understanding of crime in the United States
- the chief sources of cross-national crime data
- the problem of cultural relativism
- cross-national generalizations about crime and crime rates
- the punitive nature of criminal justice in the United States when viewed in comparative perspective

Key Terms

comparative criminology	ethnocentrism
cultural relativism	methodological relativism
epistemological relativism	modernization thesis

Some of the chapters in this book have already been illustrated with information about crime in different societies. In this chapter we are now concerned with explicitly comparing crime and crime rates in the United States with the same phenomena in other parts of the world.

The majority of theories regarding the causes of crime have been fashioned in the sociocultural context of criminology in the United States. Few such theories have been tested against the empirical and theoretical evidence of other societies. But just as scientific theories must be scrutinized under conditions that are as diverse as possible, so too must theories regarding the causes of crime. Undertaken in a sensitive way, comparative analysis can remedy **ethnocentrism**, namely, the view that generalizations derived from any given society (e.g., the United States) apply necessarily to crime in all other parts of the globe. Moreover, as the renowned anthropologist Margaret Mead reflected in her book *Coming of Age in Samoa,* "as the traveler who has once been from home is wiser than he who has never left his doorstep, so a knowledge of one other culture should sharpen our ability to scrutinize more steadily, to appreciate more lovingly, our own."

We believe that **comparative criminology** can sharpen our understanding of a number of key questions that confront criminologists. For example, it should help us to understand why penal policies in the United States have continually failed to control crime. Indeed, one reason why the United States has experienced such relatively high crime rates is that policymakers have relied on limited parochial theories regarding the causes of crime.

We begin by noting the interesting position of the United States in cross-national homicide data and then move to a general outline of the sources of cross-national crime data.

16.1   CROSS-NATIONAL CRIME AND VICTIMIZATION DATA

According to police-based data, the United States has by far the highest rate of homicide among all industrialized countries. From the data in Table 16.1 we can see, in comparative terms, the extent of homicide in the United States. The chance of being murdered was 3.5 times greater in the United States in 1997 than in Canada or Australia, 4.2 times greater than in France, 4.7 times greater than in England and Wales, and 6.6 times greater than in Japan.

These data force us to raise a number of difficult questions. How much trust can actually be invested in data such as these? Are homicide rates really higher in the United States than in other comparable societies? If so, why? How do we draw valid comparisons between crime rates in the United States and those in other parts of the world? We learned in Chapter 2 how hard it is to measure crime rates meaningfully in the United States; now we will learn that it is even harder to make intelligible or reliable comparisons between U.S. crime rates and those elsewhere.

TABLE 16.1 Homicide Rates in Selected Industrialized Countries, 1995–1997

	Number of Homicides			Rate/100,000 Population
	1995	*1996*	*1997*	
United States	21,606	19,645	18,209	6.8
Czech Republic	277	267	291	2.82
Finland	146	153	142	2.76
Northern Ireland	24	39	42	2.51
New Zealand	50	63	89	2.37
Poland	854	873	807	2.09
Australia	356	348	360	1.93
Greece	151	169	203	1.93
Canada	588	635	581	1.91
Scotland	137	135	95	1.85
Austria	176	176	147	1.82
Sweden	179	199	157	1.77
Netherlands	273	273	–	1.75
Italy	1,047	1,010	928	1.61
France	1,336	1,171	963	1.60
Germany	1,373	1,249	1,178	1.44
Belgium	142	118	145	1.44
England and Wales	745	679	739	1.42
Portugal	123	116	131	1.32
Switzerland	82	83	87	1.22
Ireland (Eire)	43	42	38	1.08
Japan	1,281	1,218	1,282	1.02
Norway	43	43	38	0.87

SOURCE: Adapted from "Criminal Statistics," *Home Office Research Development Statistics,* December, 1998, Table 10.

We begin this task with an outline of the sources of cross-national crime data for comparative criminology.

Cross-National Crime Data

Perhaps one of the greatest obstacles to comparative criminology is the lack of reliable and meaningful cross-national crime data. Most gatherers of cross-national crime data tend to ignore national differences in the legal definitions of crime as well as the variety of ways in which crimes are reported by the public and accepted and recorded by the police. Such problems plague the cross-national crime data of organizations like the United Nations, the World Health Organization, Interpol, the World Crime Survey, and Amnesty International. Accordingly, much of these data are inadequate for the purpose of rigorous cross-national comparison.

Scholars acknowledge that the best sort of cross-national crime data available are the police-based data provided by the United Nations and by Dane Archer and Rosemary Gartner (1984) in their *Violence and Crime in Cross-National Perspective*. We examine each in turn.

United Nations. The United Nations has collected and analyzed comparative statistical data on crime since 1946. Although the UN's original concern was limited to a rather simplistic notion of the prevention of crime and the treatment of offenders, it now adopts a much broader policy toward crime. This larger view is clearly stated in Article 55 of the United Nations Charter (United Nations, 1983:iii):

> With a view to the creation of conditions of stability and well-being which are necessary for peaceful and friendly relations among nations based on respect for the principle of equal rights and self-determination of peoples, the United Nations shall promote:
>
> A. higher standards of living, full employment, and conditions of economic and social progress and development;
> B. solutions of international economic, social, health, and related problems; and international cultural and educational cooperation; and
> C. universal respect for, and observance of, human rights and fundamental freedoms for all without distinction as to race, sex, language or religion.

This extension of the scope of the UN to encompass human rights resulted largely from the exposure of Nazi atrocities at the end of World War II. The perspective was extended first to war crimes and genocide and then to the widespread use of cruel, inhumane, or degrading treatment of political dissidents. It now includes the violation of human rights, political and economic abuses of colonial and institutional terrorism, and crime resulting from abuses of economic and political power by transnational enterprises. The complex organizational machinery (based in Geneva, Vienna, and New York City) of UN criminal policy includes the General Assembly, the Secretariat, the International Court of Justice, the Committee on Crime Prevention and Control, the Commission for Social Development, and various specialist bodies such as the Crime Prevention and Criminal Justice Branch, the Commission of Human Rights, and the Fund for Drug Abuse Control.

The UN has wrestled often with the need to provide adequate sets of international criminal statistics but has never succeeded. It has tried to collect and disseminate data in two ways. First, since 1955, UN congresses on crime prevention—during which researchers report on crime in their own countries—have been held every five years. Some of these reports appear in the UN publication *Crime Prevention and Criminal Justice* and include such diverse topics as human rights, capital punishment, and torture; prison labor, aftercare, parole, and recidivism; economic development, crime, and colonialism; juvenile delinquency; and ethical standards in criminal justice. Many UN reports contain data on crime rates, but few provide useful data for comparative criminology: The vast majority concern data in only one country. Strictly, then, they are not even comparative in nature.

Second, the UN publishes in its annual *Demographic Yearbook* a limited amount of data concerning rates of homicide and personal injury in selected countries. These data almost entirely omit African and Asian countries, whose inhabitants represent two-thirds of the world's population. Moreover, the *Yearbook*'s homicide data are calculated from each country's unique system of national crime statistics, each of which defines homicide differently. The *Yearbook*'s homicide rates are thus of dubious value for comparative criminology.

It is difficult to understand why the UN has not managed to do a better job concerning data collection on crime. Because crime data are politically sensitive materials, perhaps the UN is reluctant to publish them for fear of embarrassing some of its members.

Comparative Crime Data File.   The most ambitious set of data is provided by Dane Archer and Rosemary Gartner's *Comparative Crime Data File (CCDF)* (1984:171–328). The *CCDF* appears to offer several advantages over UN data. Most impressively, the *CCDF* is perhaps as comprehensive in its scope as is possible. After lengthy correspondence with national and metropolitan governments throughout the world, and after a search of existing statistical documents of many national and international agencies, Archer and Gartner managed to obtain crime data on 110 countries and 44 large cities. The *CCDF* also:

- lists both the raw number of offenses and the offense rate (per 100,000) for murder, manslaughter, homicide, rape, assault, robbery, and theft. It tabulates the data under the legal labels with which they arrive, adding explanatory footnotes where appropriate
- lists categories for offenses known and convictions
- combines multiple definitions of the same event into a single entry (such as murder)

In preparing the *CCDF,* the authors (pp. 22–28) sensitively identified several key methodological problems that arise when one translates national crime data into a comprehensive international data set. Because these problems apply to any attempt to construct comparable transnational crime data, they are worth summarizing:

- Different countries record offenses in different ways. For example, some countries use a single national item termed "murder and manslaughter," whereas others distinguish between them. The *CCDF* tabulates the data under the label with which it arrives, with explanatory footnotes when appropriate.
- Some homicide data are based on offenses known to the police, others on convictions. The *CCDF* lists both categories.
- Some countries' definitions of homicide are unique, such as Scotland's "culpable homicide."
- Some countries' definitions of homicide have several subdivisions; for example, France uses the following: *meurtre, assassinat, parricide,* and *empoisonnement.* The *CCDF* combines these into a single entry (murder).

- For certain countries with small populations (such as New Zealand, where homicides from 1946–1947 increased from two to four), a modest change in the number of offenses produces a dramatic change in the crime rate. The *CCDF* usefully lists both the raw number of offenses and the offense rate.
- The size of a country's population cannot always be estimated accurately, especially if censuses are undertaken only every ten years and with varying degrees of thoroughness.
- Methods for measuring crime rates sometimes change. Until 1926, for example, Finland based its crime statistics on convictions; after 1927 it changed its base to offenses known to the police.
- Political events can create problems with longitudinal analyses of crime rates. It is almost impossible to study changing crime rates in "Germany" from 1900 to the present, for example, because in 1946 Germany was divided into the Federal Republic of Germany and the German Democratic Republic. Prior to the political reunification of Germany in 1989–1990, each country had its own legal system with wide variations in definitions of crimes.
- There is variation in the quality of crime data collected and published by different countries. Certain countries, such as those in central Africa, do not even collect crime statistics. Other countries, such as the former Soviet Union, did not freely publish their crime statistics because they had been regarded as classified data.

Cross-National Victimization Surveys

As discussed in Chapter 2.1, victimization surveys offer a more reliable indicator of crime trends in the United States than do police-based statistics such as the *Uniform Crime Reports (UCR)*. Besides the *National Crime Victimization Survey* in the United States (see Chapter 2.1), national victimization surveys also have been conducted in Canada, Holland, West Germany, England, Scotland, Ireland, Switzerland, and elsewhere. At first glance, the growth of these surveys offers a good source of information on comparative crime trends. Common sense tells us that if victims of crime are more willing to report their victimization to survey interviewers than to police officers, then victimization surveys reveal more about the incidence of crime than do police statistics.

Consider, for example, what we can learn from the comparative findings of victimization surveys conducted, respectively, in the United States and in England and Wales (see Figure 16.1). We can see that, contrary to most popular opinion and media claims about where the United States stands in the league tables of crime, according to 1995 victimization surveys, the rates of robbery, assault, burglary, and motor vehicle theft were all higher in England and Wales than in the United States (Langan and Farrington, 1998). We should add that these perhaps surprising comparative findings from victimization surveys tend to be confirmed by police statistics. Indeed, it appears to be true that compared with the rate in England and Wales, the homicide rate in the United States is the only exception to this trend in serious crimes (see Table 16.1). Moreover, even the difference in the homicide rate has been narrowing: Whereas during the 1980s the homicide rate in the United States

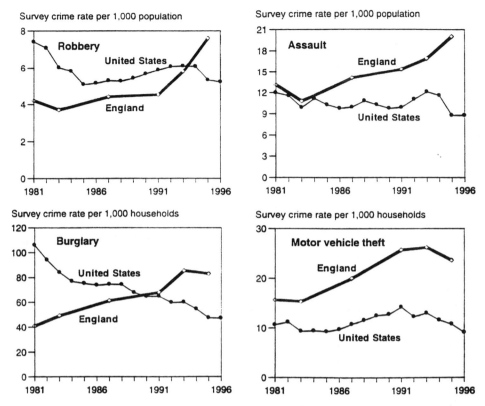

FIGURE 16.1   Victim Surveys of Selected Crimes in the United States Compared with England and Wales, 1981–1996

SOURCE: Bureau of Justice Statistics, 1998.

was about ten times that of England and Wales, by the late 1990s it had become "only" five times higher.

Yet victimization surveys have their own peculiar methodological limitations that complicate their use in comparative analysis. Most surveys outside the United States, for example, have been very small, though it is possible that these small samples are as representative of the levels of victimization of their national populations as the large samples in the U.S. *National Crime Victimization Survey.* Furthermore, in some countries (such as the United States), victimization rates are calculated with households as the data base; in other countries (for instance, Holland), rates are based on per capita victimizations. This difference casts some doubt on the validity of some comparative studies of victimization. Because household size tends to decline with affluence, different databases tend to obscure differences in the opportunity for crime that arise from variations in population size and household composition. Further problems arise from the wording of survey questions— these reflect legal definitions of crime, which vary from one country to another. Thus in their analysis of U.S., Irish, and Dutch victimization surveys, Breen and Rottman concluded that comparisons based on U.S. and Irish surveys were accurate only for burglary and vehicle thefts and that comparisons based on Dutch surveys were even more approximate in nature (1985:55–67).

Some of these problems appear to have been overcome in the three sweeps of the *International Crime Survey (ICS)*, held respectively in 1989, 1992, and 1996 (Van Dijk and Mayhew, 1993; Mayhew and Van Dijk, 1997). Five countries took part in all three sweeps (Canada, England/Wales, Finland, the Netherlands, and the United States); another three took part in both 1989 and 1992 (Australia, Belgium, and Japan); another seven in 1989 (West Germany, France, Northern Ireland, Norway, Scotland, Spain, and Switzerland); and another five in 1992 (Italy, New Zealand, Sweden, Czechoslovakia [now the Czech Republic and the Slovak Republic] and Poland).

Though there is little new in the format and methodology of the survey itself, the *ICS* is unique in its consistent attempt to apply standardized questionnaires, sampling methods, and data analyses to a large number of countries. In each country, 500–2,500 subjects are selected by random digit dialing telephone interviews. Subjects are questioned about eleven main forms of "ordinary" victimization, divided into "household property crimes" and "personal crimes." The former include theft of, theft from, and vandalism to cars; theft of motorcycles; theft of bicycles; burglary with entry; attempted burglary; and break-ins to outbuildings. The latter include robbery; theft of personal property, pickpocketing, and noncontact personal thefts; sexual incidents, sexual assaults, and offensive sexual behavior; and assaults/threats, assaults with force, and threats without force. If the subjects indicate that they had been victimized, more detailed questions are then asked about the event(s). Subjects also are asked a number of questions reflecting fear of crime and attitudes toward police. Prior to presentation in the *ICS* report, interview data are weighted for gender, regional population distribution, age, and household composition, so as to make the samples as representative as possible of actual national populations age sixteen or higher.

For countries participating in both the 1989 and 1992 surveys, the overall victimization rates (for eleven crimes) were highest (27.5–30.0 percent) in New Zealand, the Netherlands, Australia, Canada, and the United States. In terms of specific forms of victimization—both personal and property—the United States was consistently among the five highest nations. However, with the exception of attempted burglary, it was not the industrial world's leader. New Zealand and Australia vied for this dubious title. Both countries exhibited relatively high rates of victimization with respect to property crimes like car theft (2.7 percent) and attempted burglary (Australia 2.8 percent, New Zealand 2.5 percent). Canada, too, was positioned quite prominently among high-crime nations and was a high-risk nation in terms of theft from, and vandalism of, cars; burglary; personal theft; sexual incidents and assaults; and assault with threat and assault with force.

The most striking observation, and confirmation of existing police-based data, is that Switzerland and Japan were among the nations with the lowest overall victimization rates (15.0–17.4 percent and under 12.4 percent, respectively); also at low levels were Norway (15.0–17.4 percent) and Northern Ireland (12.5–14.9 percent). According to the *ICS*, not one Swiss resident was the victim of car theft; only 0.1 percent of Japanese subjects had been victims of robbery; and only 0.2 percent of respondents in Japan and Switzerland reported attempted burglary. Contrast these data with the highest reported figures: a 2.8 percent car theft rate in England and Wales; a 2.9 percent robbery rate in Spain; and a 4.6 percent attempted burglary rate in the United States. In terms of relative risk, then, Switzerland and Japan appear to be the safest of the nations surveyed.

The 1996 sweep of the *ICS* revealed that the United States had an overall victimization rate surpassed only by the Netherlands and by England/Wales (see Figure 16.2). However, it also pointed out that rates of recorded crime and victimization in the United States continued to fall during the 1990s. By way of conclusion about the condition of the United States, the *ICS* summed up:

> The level of crime in the USA has declined since 1988 according to both the ICVS and police figures. The current moderately high crime rates are more in line with rather average levels of urbanisation and economic strain than the much higher rates measured in 1988. . . . Levels of contact crime [are] high, and the USA [is] unusual in the extent to which guns are mentioned in assaults and robberies. (Mayhew and Van Djik, 1997:67)

As interesting as the *ICS* data are, it must be stressed that they cannot be accepted at face value (Beirne and Perry, 1994). As we already know (see Chapter 2.1), peculiar methodological problems are associated with all victimization surveys. Thus there is no

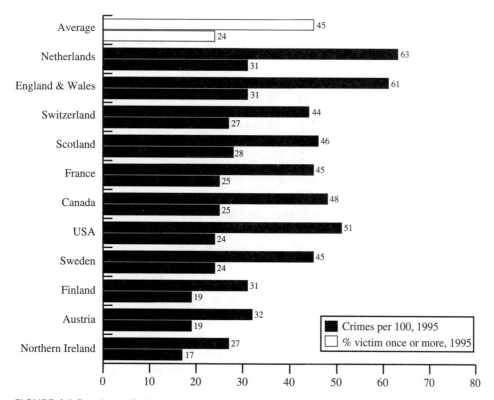

FIGURE 16.2   Overall Victimization Rates in Eleven Countries, 1995

SOURCE: Pat Mayhew and Philip White (1997), "The 1996 International Crime Victimization Survey," *Research Findings,* Home Office Research and Statistics Directorate, no. 57, p. 4.

reason to suppose that the rate of underreporting to survey interviewers is the same in each country. Quite the contrary. Consider, for example, the finding that the prevalence of victimization was 24 percent in the United States, compared with 31 percent in the Netherlands (Mayhew and Van Dijk, 1997:29). Does the surprisingly high figure in the Netherlands derive from the fact that more persons are victimized there? Or are the Dutch simply more likely to report victimization? We believe that it is likely that when compared with the U.S. rate the Dutch victimization rate is greatly exaggerated because the population is more sensitive to violence and far more likely to report it.

We therefore have good reason to be cautious about the present usefulness of victimization surveys in comparative criminology. Let us now explore various comparative generalizations about crime in the wider context of certain analytical problems that apply to all comparative studies. These problems derive from a set of issues associated with **cultural relativism**.

16.2   CULTURAL RELATIVISM AND COMPARATIVE CRIMINOLOGY

Cultural relativism has two forms: epistemological and methodological (Beirne, 1983a:377–385). **Epistemological relativism** involves the extraordinary claim that one can understand another culture only through the prism of one's own culturally determined system of values. Therefore, it implies the impossibility of meaningful comparative generalizations other than comparisons that stem from ethnocentrism. Thus if our concepts of crime differ from those of another culture, it is meaningless to say that an action does or does not seem criminal to the other culture in our terms. Although this conclusion has some logical and philosophical merit, it is so pessimistic that for practical purposes it can only be noted and then—not entirely with satisfaction—ignored.

Methodological relativism, on the other hand, is a strategy that operates as a sensitizing device to variation in the definition and meaning of crime in other cultures. It is a slogan system requiring the criminologist to "maximize his understanding of alien cultures by honest-to-God fieldwork, moral charity, intellectual humility and a determination of the taken-for-granted assumptions of both his own and others' cultural milieu" (Dixon, 1977:76). Methodological relativism, therefore, operates as a warning to potential comparativists about certain methodological difficulties peculiar to comparative analysis.

The difficult issues of relativism can be better understood if we examine the methods and findings of a classic case study in the literature of comparative anthropology: Julia Brown's (1952) comparative study of deviations from sexual mores.

A Case Study of Comparative Sexual Deviance

In her study, Brown proposed that every known society has a range of approved sexual practices and another range of practices subject to taboo. Those members of a society who faithfully follow the approved sexual customs are rewarded; those who deviate from such customs are punished. Brown (p. 135) focused on the following three problems: (1) the relative frequency with which specific types of sexual practices are considered deviant by different societies, where frequency is defined as the percentage of societies that forbids such practices; (2) the relative severity with which various deviant sexual practices are punished; and (3) the degree of correlation between the frequency and the severity of punishments. Addressing the first two problems, Brown analyzed data in Yale University's Human Relations Area File, gleaning information about the sexual practices punished by 110 "simple" societies in Africa, North America, South America, Eurasia, and Oceania (pp. 135–136). (We do not agree with Brown's characterization of technologically undeveloped societies as "simple" because in many ways, especially in the realm of certain social relationships, such societies are actually quite "advanced.") Brown's findings are summarized in Table 16.2.

Brown next determined a punishment scale for deviant sexual practices. Her scale of ratings was based on a combination of the percentage of societies that forbade a specific practice and the intensity (mild, moderate, severe, very severe) of the punishment inflicted for each sexual deviation. The scale is summarized in Table 16.3.

Tables 16.2 and 16.3 contain at least two important findings. Examining the data in Table 16.2, we learn that the sexual practices most often forbidden in Brown's sample are incest, abduction, and rape. Those practices least often forbidden are premarital affairs and

TABLE 16.2   Percentages of Societies Punishing Specific Sexual Practices

Number of Societies	% Punishing	Practice and Person Punished
54	100	Incest
82	100	Abduction of married woman
84	99	Rape of married woman
55	95	Rape of unmarried woman
43	95	Sex during postpartum period
15	93	Bestiality by adult
73	92	Sex during menstruation
88	89	Adultery (paramour punished)
93	87	Adultery (wife punished)
22	86	Sex during lactation period
57	86	Infidelity of fiancée
52	85	Seduction of another man's fiancée
74	85	Illegitimate impregnation (woman punished)
62	84	Illegitimate impregnation (man punished)
30	77	Seduction of prenubile girl (man punished)
44	68	Male homosexuality
49	67	Sex during pregnancy
16	44	Masturbation
97	44	Premarital relations (woman punished)
93	41	Premarital relations (man punished)
12	33	Female homosexuality
67	10	Sex with one's betrothed

SOURCE: Brown, 1952: p. 138, abridged.

TABLE 16.3   Mean Severity Values of Specific Punishments

Mean Severity Value	Specific Punishment
1.0	Small fine
1.2	Fistfight
1.4	Quarreling within family
1.5	Parental reproof
1.8	Beating by family member
2.1	Duel
2.2	Public ridicule and disgrace
2.2	Enforced marriage
2.2	Illness
2.2	Bad luck
2.3	Danger to near kin
2.4	Ceremonial penance
2.4	Lowered bride-price
2.4	Knifing
2.5	Temporary exile
2.5	Humiliation at wedding
2.5	Heavy fine
2.5	Enslavement of relative
2.5	Divorce, and return of bride-price
2.5	Public flagging
2.6	Difficulty in acquiring a husband
2.6	Failure of hunting or fishing
2.6	Desertion of spouse
2.7	Puniness of offspring, injury to child
2.9	Divorce with disgrace, no remarriage allowed
2.9	Facial mutilation
2.9	Multiple mutilation
2.9	Madness
3.0	Spearing of legs
3.1	Repudiation of bride by groom
3.1	Sorcery to injure or kill
3.3	Loss of virility
3.4	Public raping
3.4	Enslavement
3.4	Destruction of major property
3.5	Barrenness
3.6	Permanent exile
3.7	Life imprisonment
3.7	Torture, possibly resulting in death
3.7	Enforced suicide
3.9	Death

SOURCE: Brown, 1952: p. 137, abridged.

intercourse with one's fiancée. Second, from the data recorded in Table 16.3 and from a series of correlational analyses, Brown inferred that the more often a given sexual practice is forbidden, the more severely and the more often it is punished. Assuming that severity of punishment reflects the seriousness of an offense, as Brown (p. 138) did, we can infer that incest, abduction, and rape are generally viewed across cultures as the most serious offenses. However, Brown went beyond this inference: "The fact that these correlations exist is of interest since it tends to support the view that there may be generalized attitudes of permissiveness and punitiveness toward sexual activity" (p. 139).

How justified was Brown in her finding that different cultures have common attitudes toward sexual deviation? There are at least two problems with the method Brown used to arrive at this generalization: One problem involves the definition of certain behavior as criminal; the other involves the seriousness attached to such behavior.

Brown's assumption that all 110 societies criminalize sexual practices similarly is most implausible. Consider incest. It is true that anthropologists have not discovered any place, past or present, where incest is tolerated in an entire society. But there are documented cases where some cultures regard incest—however defined—as a necessary and obligatory social practice. For example, what we regard as incest seems to have been obligatory for members of royal families in Inca Peru, in Hawaii, and in ancient Egypt, where Cleopatra was the offspring of a brother–sister union (Guttmacher, 1951:16). In Bali fraternal twins of the opposite sex have been permitted to marry because they had already been completely familiar *in utero*. Moreover, the Gusii of southwestern Kenya will not proclaim it a sexual taboo if, during the ceremony of "taking by stealth," sexual intercourse occurs between kin as close as brother and sister (Mayer, 1953:31).

How do such counterexamples affect Brown's generalization about sexual practices in similar "simple" societies? As formulated—there are "generalized attitudes of permissiveness or punitiveness toward sexual activity"—Brown's generalization can be neither falsified nor confirmed by counterexamples. It cannot clearly be falsified because conditional clauses (of the sort "No society exerts incest taboos during the rainy season") could in principle account for any number of counterfactual cases. This limitation is shared by all scientific and sociological attempts to generalize.

Additionally, Brown's generalization cannot be confirmed. One of the necessary criteria for an intelligible generalization is that there must be an identity between the practices within its scope. But there is no way of knowing from Brown's research, or from much data lodged in the Human Relations Area File, whether the sexual practices defined as incestuous are the same practices in the societies observed: Are they perhaps seen as similar only by the observer's own methodology? The sexual practices defined as incestuous by the Western observer inclined to generalizations, by the Sambia tribe in the highlands of New Guinea, and by travelers in North America may in fact all be quite different.

The problem of the identity of social practices is probably acute for comparisons between "simple" societies. There is good reason to suppose that the problem is even more acute for comparisons between "simple" and modern societies, and even for comparisons between modern societies with similar legal cultures and traditions. Suppose, for example, that we wished to compare incest rates between England and the United States. Under the Sexual Offenses Act of 1956, it is an offense for a male in England to have sexual intercourse with a female whom he knows to be his granddaughter, daughter, sister, or mother. But in the United States, statutory incest refers to an additional range of behavior not prohibited by English law: sexual relations between males and their grandmothers, nieces, and aunts. Moreover, marriage between first cousins is not an uncommon practice in England; in the United States it is illegal in nearly half the states.

A second difficulty with Brown's generalization is the assumption that a rank order of punishment can be applied meaningfully across cultures. How items are entered in cross-cultural rankings in part depends on the values of those doing the ranking. How is an objective order of punishment to be devised? And by whom? Brown devised her rank order on the advice of "judges conversant with anthropological phenomena" (p. 137). Yet consider the item "death" as the most serious punishment in her scale. There are many cases recorded (in the Homeric myths, the Icelandic sagas, and others) where banishment or permanent exile is seen as a far more serious punishment than death. Moreover, in some modern cultures (for example, among the top levels of the Japanese military), enforced suicide is not a punishment but an honorable recourse to defeat in war. And in some cultures (for instance, in England among men of gentle birth and fashion until 1850 [Andrew, 1980]), a duel is not a punishment (as in Brown's scale) but the normal form of asserting honor or reputation following insult.

Let us return to the idea of exile to illustrate another point. Exactly how much of a punishment is exile? The effect of exile partly determines the answer to this question. Exile is culturally and subjectively variable; for example, to an Orpheus exiled to Hades (the Greek underworld), to Alexander Solzhenitsyn exiled from Russia to Vermont, and to Yasir Arafat exiled from his Palestinian homeland, expulsion certainly has very different effects. The seriousness of expulsion depends partly "on how easy it is to attach oneself to another community and to what extent one is a second-class citizen in that community" (Moore, 1978:124): Does the exile become a refugee, a hero, an outlaw, or a welfare immigrant? The number of such complicating items can of course be multiplied greatly. But their message is a simple one: The severity of punishment attached to practices in a given society cannot simply be wrenched from its specific cultural context and inserted artificially into a rank order. Following the claims of epistemological relativism, we must initially understand punishment in its own cultural milieu, within its own system of meaning.

Let us summarize the discussion so far. The aim of comparative criminology is the construction of cross-cultural generalizations on crime. Three initial problems confront comparativists. The first is variation in the type of society. At present it seems that only societies with common sociological and structural features are appropriate as units of comparison, which sharply curtails the range of societies for which generalizations can be made legitimately. The second problem concerns cultural variation in the definition of illegal practices. If legal definitions differ, what range of behavior is actually compared? Finally, there is cultural variation in the meaning of the seriousness of crime. If an offense is regarded with different degrees of seriousness in different countries, then it is quite possibly meaningless to compare the rates of that offense in different countries.

How, then, should the comparative criminologist proceed? Do cross-cultural generalizations on crime necessarily ignore cultural diversity? Consider now one attempt to resolve these questions.

Toward Uniform Cross-National Crime Statistics?

One of the most influential strategies of methodological relativism in criminology was suggested by Marvin Wolfgang (1967). The major comparative problem identified by Wolfgang is the adequacy and reliability of international criminal statistics. He noted correctly that statistical data produced by agents such as Interpol are based on an unwarranted assumption: that such crimes as homicide, robbery, and rape, for example, are regarded with the same degree of seriousness by all countries. This error is aggravated by wide cultural variation in legal definitions of crime and by differing attitudes toward the sanctity of life and property.

Wolfgang made several proposals to remedy this situation. The first relates to such official administrative policies as police efficiency; quality of criminal records; and discrepancies among countries for reported crimes, trials, and convictions. According to Wolfgang (1967:66), national police data must be standardized. These data could easily be made more reliable because "a team of experts from an international organization could, like the field representatives of the Department of Justice in the United States, help individual countries to set up and promote reliable reporting systems" (p. 66).

Wolfgang's second proposal is even more unconventional: the elimination of legal definitions of crime for purposes of comparative measurement of crime rates. The legal components of homicide, robbery, rape, and so forth would be replaced by requests for information about the type and extent of physical injury in violent crimes and/or the monetary value of property stolen or damaged. Thereby, Wolfgang argued, specific legal definitions of crime in national data would be eliminated but cultural integrity would be maintained.

Finally, Wolfgang proposed the use of a psychophysical weighting scale. A weighted crime for each participating country could thus be had by obtaining for each country the sum of the frequency of each measured crime, multiplying by its weight, and then dividing by a constant population unit.

Would such a scale really permit a comparativist to assess the relative seriousness of crimes in different countries? We think not. Wolfgang's strategy contains a serious problem. Wolfgang's major proposal for comparative research is the elimination of legal definitions of crime. Behind this proposal lurks what should be the central theoretical problem of criminology as a discipline: If criminological generalizations are based solely on legal definitions, then criminology depends exclusively on the values enshrined in criminal law (see Chapter 1.2). But no criminologist enjoys the license to study solely the practices prohibited by criminal law.

Assume that the primary goal of criminology is the construction of sociological generalizations regarding the distribution and causes of antisocial practices. Some, but not all, of such practices will be forbidden by criminal law. If this is true, then the unqualified acceptance of legal definitions of crime makes criminology a parasitic affair at the very outset. On the other hand, if legal definitions of crime are eliminated from comparative criminology (as Wolfgang would have it), then much of what is most interesting and important about different cultures—why certain cultures define certain practices and not others as illegal, cultural variation in notions of right and justice, and different penal practices, to mention but a few—is wished away by fiat.

Wolfgang's strategy is not unlike that of students of religious practices who, in attempting to compare the extent of religious sentiments in different cultures, base their analyses exclusively on official statistics of baptisms, church attendance, and marriages. Perhaps such practices aid in understanding what people do but not necessarily in understanding why people do them or what they mean. Indeed, the replacement of legal definitions of crime by such "neutral" indicators as the assessment of bodily and monetary damages still results in a criminology based on definitions of criminal justice agencies because these assessments are provided by lawful national authorities. By no stretch of sociological imagination can such indicators be termed "neutral." Additionally, if the legal definition of crime is abandoned entirely as the initial object of study, we risk describing social practices and relations not as they in fact are but only as we would like them to be.

How, then, should comparative criminology proceed? What crimes can be compared cross-culturally? How should comparative generalizations regarding crime be tested?

16.3   CROSS-NATIONAL GENERALIZATIONS REGARDING CRIME

Among criminologists, the most popular procedural guidelines for constructing comparative generalizations regarding crime are those offered by Clinard and Abbott (1973). They offered this procedural advice:

> The goal of a comparative criminology should be to develop concepts and generalizations at a level that distinguishes between universals applicable to all societies and unique characteristics representative of one or a small set of societies. . . . Research should proceed . . . first in a single culture at one point in time, . . . second in societies generally alike, . . . and third in completely dissimilar societies. (p. 2)

In other words, comparative criminology must proceed in three stages. Any generalization must be tested (1) in one culture at a single point in time, (2) across two cultures that share some common sociological feature—such as a similar level of technological development or a common type of political culture, and (3) across cultures that are completely dissimilar. Because this advice follows the course often used for testing generalizations in the natural sciences, it has much to recommend it. Clearly it is easier to generalize about the United States and England, for example, than about the United States and Japan.

But the third stage of testing is difficult to conduct. What criteria allow us to identify cultures that are completely dissimilar? Such criteria are increasingly rare in the modern world, whose outermost reaches have been penetrated by the routine operations of transnational corporations and the global culture of commercialism.

Assume that what Clinard and Abbott actually meant was not "completely dissimilar societies" but societies as different as possible. What sociological properties would such societies have? No doubt these properties would include major differences in religious or scientific beliefs, economic systems, political structures, and the degree of technological development. The greater the difference between any two cultures along such axes, one presumes, the more entitled we are to term them "dissimilar." But this assumption is not

> **BOX 16.1   CONSTRUCTING CROSS-CULTURAL GENERALIZATIONS REGARDING CRIME**
>
> We suggest there must be a minimum of five rules for the construction of cross-cultural generalizations regarding crime:
>
> 1. Crime in different cultures can be compared only if the definition and meaning of criminal behavior in these cultures is the same.
> 2. An event p (e.g., urbanization) is not the cause of rising crime rates if it occurs when rising crime rates do not occur.
> 3. p is not the cause of rising crime rates if p does not occur when rising crime rates do occur.
> 4. p is not necessarily the cause of rising crime rates if one or more other variables (a, or $a, b \ldots n$) are present in the same circumstances as p.
> 5. For the generalization "p causes rising crime rates" to be intelligible, it must be explained by a theory.

without difficulty. The more two cultures differ, the less likely it is that they have common items to compare, and the less likely it is that verifiable generalizations can be made about them.

Let us now examine the strengths and weaknesses of two recent generalizations in comparative criminology. The two generalizations that we examine have been visible in criminology for about two decades, though our discussion of them begins with their presence in the *1996 International Crime Victims Survey* (Mayhew and van Dijk, 1997). In the course of the presentation of the findings of this survey, the lead authors, Pat Mayhew and Jan Van Jijk, ventured the claim that for a range of industrialized and less developed countries "the three main determinants of crime" might be (1) the degree of modernization, (2) the degree of urbanization, and (3) the level of economic strain (pp. 60–69). Since we have already dealt extensively with the third factor (e.g., see Chapters 7.4, 8.3), we will confine our attention to the importance of modernization and urbanization.

The Modernization (or Convergence) Thesis

Since the early 1960s, sociologists have often argued that the mere fact of technological development produces common effects that tend, irrespective of different or even antagonistic political systems, to make all societies increasingly similar. In this scenario, technology itself is seen as a factor that inevitably determines that all modern societies eventually converge to a common industrial model. This industrial model, also termed the **modernization thesis**, has eight characteristics (Lane, 1996:146–149; 1970:184–185):

1. Populations grow rapidly, family size falls, women are emancipated, relationships between spouses become more equal.

2. Knowledge, wealth, political power, and human rights become more available to the entire population.
3. The division of labor is highly developed, and education and occupation determine individual positions in the social hierarchy.
4. Ideological differences are minimized and a premium is placed on hard work and economic productivity.
5. Legal systems apply a more-or-less common law to individuals of all social ranks.
6. Although political ideologies can be quite different, the central government organizes all of society.
7. Human relationships tend to be specific and achievement oriented rather than diffuse and ascribed.
8. Large-scale urbanism ensures that social relationships are impersonal, superficial, and differentiated.

The industrial convergence theory has exerted great influence in comparative criminology (see, for example, Shelley, 1981a; Heiner, 1996; Beirne and Nelken, 1997). Yet one of the basic problems with existing modernization theory is that there is a wide range of crime rates—both interpersonal and property—among modern societies. Moreover, crime patterns in the Third World are not likely to repeat patterns of criminality in the more technologically advanced nations of the world. Criminality in the Third World is not simply a replay of the histories of more modernized nations. Indeed, many crimes committed in Third World countries actually originate in the First World in the form of transnational crime (see Chapter 13.2).

Consider, for example, the worst industrial accident of record, which occurred when toxic gas leaked from a Union Carbide insecticide plant early on the morning of December 3, 1984, in the central Indian town of Bhopal (see Chapter 13.2):

> Witnesses said thousands of people had been taken to hospitals gasping for breath, many frothing at the mouth, their eyes inflamed. The streets were littered with the corpses of dogs, cats, water buffalo, cows and birds killed by the gas, methyl isocyanate, which is widely used in the preparation of insecticides. Doctors from neighboring towns and the Indian Army were rushed to the city of 900,000, where hospitals were said to be overflowing with the injured. Most of the victims were children and old people who were overwhelmed by the gas and suffocated, Indian press reports said. (*New York Times*, December 4, 1989)

The Bhopal chemical leak has resulted in the deaths of an unknown number of Indian residents—estimates range from 4,000 to 15,000—and injuries to several hundred thousand others; 600,00 people have injury claims outstanding in injury compensation courts (G. Cohen, 1998). Despite extradition orders pending since 1992, the Indian government has so far failed to bring Union Carbide CEO Warren Anderson to trial. The implications of the Bhopal tragedy of course extend far beyond the borders of India. As Gary Cohen wrote:

> What is most frightening about Bhopal is that it is not unusual in the New World Order. It is the way people are routinely treated by corporations in the world today. Can-

"The Apocalypse of Grime," the painter Lowry's own term to convey all the bleakness of the industrial scene.

cer-causing pesticides banned in the West are freely sold to farmers in Latin America, Eastern Europe and Asia. Native American nations are bribed to accept nuclear waste on their sacred lands. Malaysian hill people are killed or run off their land so Japanese companies can cut down the forests to make chopsticks. Leaded gasoline, banned in the West because of its devastating health effects on children, is sold to Thailand, Mexico and India. This kind of corporate violence is repeated in every corner of the Earth. (1998:3)

What tragedies such as the Bhopal disaster imply, in other words, is that societies "modernize" not according to some inner benevolent logic but, rather, according to the dictates of economic and political power within a global capitalist system. Many patterns of crime and many large-scale acts of social harm cannot be understood if societies are viewed in isolation from each other.

Urbanization and Homicide

Another example of existing comparative generalizations on crime derives from another aspect of the modernization thesis. As discussed often in this book, criminologists believe urbanism is a bedrock cause of the growth of impersonal, violent, and predatory crime. In the

United States this causal relationship is clearly documented by cross-sectional data in the *UCR*. Recall two points made in Chapter 9.1. First, there is a strong positive correlation between city size and homicide rates: the larger the city population, the higher the homicide rate. Second, rural areas tend to have higher homicide rates than very small cities.

For comparative criminology, then, two important questions await answers. Does the same correlation between city size and homicide rates also exist in countries other than the United States? Do rural areas of other countries also have higher homicide rates than their very small cities? Archer and Gartner (1984:98–117) considered these questions and drew four conclusions:

1. The absolute size of a city does not correspond directly with its homicide rate. In other words, all cities around the world with a population between 500,000 and 999,999 do not have a homicide rate of (or even near, in many cases) 18 per 100,000. Comparatively, cities of the same size show great variation in their homicide rates.

2. The finding in (1) suggests "the intriguing possibility that large cities have homicide rates which are unusually high *only in terms of the overall homicide rates of their societies*" (p. 107). For variations in homicide rates, therefore, it is not absolute city size that is important but the size of a city relative to its national population. Extending their analysis, Archer and Gartner (pp. 105–108) reported that of the primary cities of twenty-three countries, seventeen had homicide rates higher than their national homicide average. Five of six exceptions to this tendency were in Third World countries; the sixth was Tokyo, the primary city of Japan.

3. The five exceptions in the Third World suggest in turn that the factors that produce high homicide rates in large cities of developed countries are not present, or are not present in the same circumstances, in large cities of underdeveloped countries. As Archer and Gartner hypothesized: It might be that primary cities weaken kinship and community ties in developed societies but not in developing societies. Perhaps developing societies have lower rates of mobility, or perhaps people moving to cities in developing societies move with their families rather than alone. Developed societies might also have greater controls over rural homicides—for example, decentralized law enforcement, which reduces blood feuds, marauding gangs, etc.

4. A city's homicide rate does not necessarily increase as its population expands. Longitudinal data (Archer and Gartner, 1984:108–114) reveal that of thirty-four international primary cities, the homicide rates of seventeen declined with city growth and those of seventeen have increased. Thus these data suggest no discernible correlation between city growth and homicide rates.

These conclusions concerning a lack of correlation between city size and homicide rates are reinforced to a certain extent by studies of homicide that offer an alternative explanation of cross-national variations in homicide rates. The most common alternative explanation of variation in homicide rates in industrialized societies can be found in studies that point to the importance of social and economic inequality, especially where this is accompanied by strain and a popular sense of injustice. One avenue of research found that in thirty-four industrialized countries high homicide rates tended to be accompanied by high levels of income inequality and concentrated poverty (Rosenfeld and Messner, 1991; Neapolitan, 1997:89–103; Currie, 1998:125–126); this correlation holds even when controlling for variations in gross national product, population size, population density, and degree of urbanization. As Elliott Currie has stressed:

> The links between extreme deprivation, delinquency, and violence . . . are strong, consistent, and compelling. The effects are compounded by the absence of public supports to buffer economic insecurity and deprivation, and they are even more potent when racial subordination is added to the mix. And this—rather than "prosperity"—helps us begin to understand why the United States suffers more serious violent crime than other industrial democracies, and why violence has remained stubbornly high in the face of our unprecedented efforts at repressive control. (1998:131)

Countries with Low Crime Rates

One of the most interesting sets of questions for comparative criminology concerns the nature of countries with low crime rates. Why do some countries consistently have low crime rates? What, if anything, do these countries have in common? What can we learn from their experience? Let us briefly examine two countries where low crime rates are renowned.

For much of the twentieth century Japan has had persistently low, stable, and occasionally declining crime rates. For example, in 1997 the Japanese homicide rate was 1:500,000 (or about one-eighth of the U.S. rate). When criminologists attempt to explain Japanese crime rates, they usually refer to the strong elements of social control in Japanese life, which tend to produce—from a Western perspective—a crushing conformity in social relationships. For example, Freda Adler has noted that in Japan "regulation and control characterize daily life, where the individual is strongly committed to the group" (1983:123). Such control, this explanation continues, is manifest in certain vital areas: the patriarchal nature of the family, the quality of formal education, the power of religion, and the surrogate family provided by businesses in urbanized areas. In such ways Japanese life is controlled to such an extent that, to many citizens, crime and deviance are actually unthinkable. These ordered features of Japanese life are themselves supplemented by an efficient police force that has an excellent rapport with the Japanese public (Bayley, 1991; Currie, 1998:181–182).

Moreover, while pointing to the extremely harsh treatment meted out to deviants of all sorts in Japan—which Western commentators often do not see—the Japanese criminologist Setsuo Miyazawa (1993; and see Komiya, 1999) stressed that the push to conformity begins at a very early age for Japanese children. This push toward conformity is then nourished through the combined power of education, work, family, religion, and ancestor worship. Miyazawa stressed how different the routines of Japanese childhood are compared with the daily lives of children in other parts of the world. He wrote:

The value of conformity is first taught at schools. For children, school epitomizes the conventional world. Japanese school children are among the busiest children in the world. A survey conducted by the Japanese government indicates that they do homework more than anyone else, play for a relatively short time, and sleep the least. ... Japanese junior high school students spend six hours in the classroom each day and more than three hours in extracurricular activities and homework. (p. 98)

Before arguing for the relevance of the Japanese experience to understanding crime in the United States, we note our disagreement with the emphasis of the foregoing explanations. Two points, in particular, need to be made here. First, it is one thing to dispute the reasons why Japan has relatively low rates of interpersonal crime, but it is quite another thing to do so at the expense of examining other forms of crime. It is quite possible that rates of white-collar crime, for example, are higher in Japan than in most other industrialized societies. Thus, as some researchers have already pointed out, although the rate of individualistic forms of white-collar crime like embezzlement may be quite low in Japan, white-collar crimes motivated for "the good of the company" may be very high there (Kerbo and Inoue, 1990).

Second, the Japanese experience reflects the fact that high crime rates are by no means an inevitable feature of modernized societies. However, we believe that explanations of low Japanese crime rates inappropriately focus on the element of control in Japanese life. Two decades of failed get-tough conservative crime policies in the United States should tell us that control, as such, explains neither low nor high crime rates. In Japan's case the emphasis on control as an explanation of low crime neglects the ways in which Japanese society is more supportive of its citizenry than is the United States in terms of providing social and welfare services. As many commentators on Japanese culture have pointed out, this supportive network is apparent in the relative absence in Japan of an underclass, in the fact of egalitarianism in income distribution, in very few slums, and in a complete absence of urban ghettos. Let us see which, if any, of these sociological characteristics are also evident in another country with a relatively low crime rate, namely, the Republic of Ireland.

Throughout the 1950s and early 1960s, the Republic of Ireland had exceptionally low and stable crime rates (McCullagh, 1996:chap. 1; and see Wilbanks, 1996). However, by 1975 there were five times as many recorded "shopbreakings," six times as many "housebreakings," and twenty-nine times as many robberies as had been recorded in 1951. A substantial increase was also recorded for offenses against the person, with indictable assaults rising seven times over the same twenty-five years (Rottman, 1980:3–4). In the 1950s the average annual number of homicides was 7.2; in the 1960s it was 10.1; and from 1970 to 1975 it was 20.8. By 1997 the annual number of homicides had risen to 38 (see Figure 16.1), though compared with the industrialized countries the rate of homicide was still very low at 1.08.

These dramatic changes suggest that Ireland both conforms to major strands of the modernization thesis and yet differs from it in significant ways. During the 1940s the rapid decline of Irish agriculture—a decline that was not relieved but exacerbated by intensive industrialization during the early 1960s—created serious among the Irish working class. This unemployment, in turn, led to enormous intrafamilial conflict and to other forms of dislocation, such as emigration. Rottman (1980:117–140) analyzed the changing Irish homicide patterns immediately after these great economic and social upheavals. He showed that after the early 1960s there occurred in Ireland a diminishing incidence of family homicide, an increasing proportion of homicides involving strangers, and a greater incidence of homicides in which females killed males. In these respects Ireland appears to conform to the modernization thesis.

But in other respects Ireland contradicts the modernization thesis. For example, after the industrialization of the 1960s, crime rates did not increase more in urban areas than in rural areas: The increase was diffuse rather than concentrated in cities (Rottman, 1980:116). Also, even though we are dealing with a small number of homicides, the rising percentage of men murdered by women—a 41.3 percent increase between the 1950s and the 1970s—is probably not typical of other modernized countries. Moreover, Irish rates of violent crime may actually have declined since 1986. As three Irish sociologists have remarked concerning perceptions of crime in Ireland: "We have been encouraged to worry about a surge in crime, the appearance of which may have more to do with the growth of private insurance policies (and the need to report break-ins to the police before making a claim), than with any dramatic increase in criminal activity as such" (Tomlinson, Varley, and McCullagh, 1988:14).

It is fair to say, therefore, that Ireland is a real exception to the view that rising crime rates accompany modernization. Although there is as yet no sustained explanation of Ireland's persistently low crime rates, we note especially the powerful influence of Roman Catholicism in government, education, and family (McCullagh, 1996: 57). An additional factor is undoubtedly the relationship between the Irish citizenry and the Garda, the Irish police force. According to the *Irish Value Survey* (cited in McCullagh, 1996:156), 85 percent of the Irish population has "a great deal" or "quite a lot" of confidence in the Irish police—more confidence, in fact, than in any other Irish institution. Moreover, similar levels of confidence in the police are exhibited by a remarkable 84.5 percent of Irish skilled and unskilled manual workers (p. 169).

One of the few attempts to identify common features among countries with low crime rates is Freda Adler's book *Nations Not Obsessed with Crime* (1983). Adler isolated five diverse "regions" in the world (European capitalist, European socialist, Latin America, Islam, and Asia) and then selected from each region two countries (respectively: Switzerland/Eire, Bulgaria/German Democratic Republic (GDR), Costa Rica/Peru, Algeria/Saudi Arabia, and Japan/Nepal) with the lowest, or among the lowest, crime rates in its region. Adler's strategy was twofold.

First, she attempted to determine for each country the statistical correlations existing between their arrest rates (as a reasonable index of crime rates) and forty-seven socioeconomic variables, including such factors as age and occupational structures, national income, education, and patterns of consumer expenditure. Adler inferred from her statistical analysis that these ten countries had no truly significant socioeconomic or cultural factors in common. Even after analyzing the variables by comparing each of the low crime rate countries with the mean of its region, no specific common factors emerged. However, Adler managed to identify various broad trends among the ten countries:

Most low crime countries have in common lower than average population densities, lower than average urban populations, . . . lower than average population numbers which are economically active, a lower than average number of radio receivers and telephones, a higher than average population in agriculture, . . . and a higher than average crude death rate. (p. 10)

In spite of these common trends, the broad sociocultural differences among these countries were quite startling. The ten countries had a variety of state structures, including people's republic, military government, parliamentary democracy, popular democracy, absolute monarchy, and constitutional monarchy. Their economies ranged from subsistence agriculture (Nepal, Peru) to extensive industrialization (GDR, Switzerland, Japan). Some had urbanized slowly (Ireland, Switzerland), others quickly (Saudi Arabia, Japan). In some (Peru), unemployment rates were high; in others (GDR, Bulgaria, Japan, Switzerland) they were low. Some of the countries contained homogeneous populations, others were heterogeneous. As Adler concluded: "These countries represent a broad spectrum of socioeconomic and politico-cultural systems" (p. 130).

Adler's second qualitative strategy was an analysis of the formal and informal mechanisms of social control in each of the ten countries. At first glance, Adler suggested (pp. 124–126), the countries appeared to have various systems of law, politics, and criminal justice. Each had differing levels of success in solving reported crimes, ranging from high (Japan, Saudi Arabia) to low ("probably among some of the countries whose figures are not available") (p. 125). It was difficult to measure their actual support for human rights. Five countries retained the use of capital punishment; although, with the exception of Japan, executions were quite rare.

Nevertheless, Adler did find a common aspect among countries with low crime rates: the element of popular involvement in, or popularity of, the criminal justice system. Six of the ten countries—four highly industrialized (Japan, Switzerland, Bulgaria, and the GDR) and two underdeveloped (Nepal and Peru)—were "marked by an extraordinarily high degree of popular participation in crime control" (p. 128). Moreover, Saudi Arabia, Algeria, and Ireland had succeeded, despite foreign intervention, in maintaining the integrity of their indigenous systems of social control. Costa Rica (which has no standing army) had fostered local self-government and was actively popularizing its criminal justice system.

A second common factor in the arena of social control was that all ten countries seemed to have strong elements of social control outside the criminal justice system. According to Adler, these elements did not exercise control by formal constraint; rather, "they transmit and maintain values by providing for a sharing of norms and by ensuring cohesiveness" (p. 130). First and foremost, her argument continued, was the survival of the power of the family, even during modernization. In each case the family, often patriarchal in nature, remained a closely woven unit that exerted a powerful influence on its members. In societies where employment levels were high—with women composing a large segment of the labor force—strong efforts had been made to provide for children during work hours in day care facilities and kindergartens. The retention of traditional family values was itself reinforced by a second system of control: religious, moral, or secular values. In all ten countries—whether Islamic, Christian, or socialist—such values exhorted the citizenry to act for the common good; they "solidify the moral obligations of the community to reaffirm in common their common sentiments" (p. 132).

There is much of value in Adler's analysis. Quite remarkably, hers is the only study to date that addresses the immensely important question of what distinguishes countries with high and low crime rates, respectively. However, we note two difficulties with Adler's analysis. First, her study was so brief that she avoided all thorny methodological and relativist problems of comparative research. Indeed, Adler condensed her observations on each country's demography, history, law, economy, family, and polity into a mere eight pages. It is quite likely that, on closer inspection, countries with low rates of crime will be found to have large structural differences. Second, when examining countries whose native tongue is not English, Adler was forced to rely either on statements by government officials or on secondary English-language commentaries. Interviewing government officials about such things as the popularity of the criminal justice system, for example, is not a very reliable way to gather objective information on other cultures. And because she was reliant on secondary sources, Adler was necessarily unable to determine either the accuracy of their analyses or the range of opinions they reflected.

16.4   U.S. CRIME IN COMPARATIVE PERSPECTIVE

Five Causes of High U.S. Crime Rates

Our chief focus in this chapter has been to supply a comparative dimension to comparative criminology. We have examined some of the major issues involved in actually doing comparative studies and have outlined some of the most common comparative generalizations on crime.

Students often ask: "*Why* does the United States have one of the highest crime rates in the world?" Because we stress how difficult it is to offer good answers to this question, our only answer is, "We really don't know." However, if pressed to respond with a simple answer, we would reply that at least five factors distinguish the social structure of the United States from other "comparable societies" and that these factors contribute to its high crime rate:

1. The United States has had one of the highest rates of structural unemployment since 1945.
2. The United States has the largest underclass of persons economically, socially, and politically discriminated against because of race and ethnic background.
3. The United States has inferior support systems of welfare, social security, health, and education.
4. The extreme commercialism of U.S. capitalism provides incentives and motivations to circumvent acceptable (namely, legal) means of achievement.
5. The U.S. criminal justice system is one of the most punitive control mechanisms in the world.

We conclude this chapter with a brief outline of number 5, reviewing comparative evidence of the relationship between punitive penal policies and crime rates in the United States.

Punitive Penal Policies

The comparatively high rates of personal and property crimes in the United States have been explained in numerous ways, but in recent times criminologists have tended to focus on the general climate of tolerance and permissiveness (whose roots go back to the turbulent liberalism of the 1960s) in the United States. It was not accidental, this explanation continues, that the turbulence and permissiveness of the 1960s coincided with unprecedented increases in the rates of violent crime. This permissiveness has become a favorite target of conservatives, and as an explanation of crime it surfaces in two major forms.

Both explanations of permissiveness focus on the consequences of the apparent weakening of social control in U.S. society. One explanation focuses on weakened control in such crucial socializing agencies as families, schools, and neighborhoods. For some people, therefore, the rise of permissiveness derives from liberal or weak-minded child-rearing practices within families that are, in their turn, paralleled and reinforced by lax discipline in high schools. The other explanation refers to the loss of control, or the lack of punitiveness, in the criminal justice system and, specifically, to the mild or lax punishment apparently meted out to convicted criminals.

We firmly reject the foregoing explanations because the evidence simply does not support them.

Regarding the first explanation, it is very difficult to support the argument that U.S. society has somehow become more permissive (and what, precisely, does this vague term mean?) in its child-rearing practices since the 1960s. Take only the example of corporal punishment of children. In Chapter 9.2 we outlined the extraordinary amount of physical child abuse in the United States, which is no doubt caused partly by the positive relationship demonstrated between the development of aggression in children and the use of corporal punishment (Straus, 1996; Straus and Stewart, 1999). For us the corporal punishment of children is a form of child abuse. About 75 percent of the U.S. public believes that physical punishment of children is acceptable behavior, and as many as 98 percent of parents in the United States sometimes "spank" their children. These figures contrast with Sweden, where the same belief is held by only about 25 percent of parents. As Currie has pointed out:

> In Sweden, where corporal punishment was outlawed in 1979, even when inflicted by parents, rates of serious violent crime are much lower than in Finland, where corporal punishment is more widely accepted. But the Finns are less violent than we Americans, whose support for punishment is among the highest in the industrial world. Even higher rates of criminal violence are found in some Caribbean countries, where corporal punishment—especially in low-income families—is applied on a scale and with a severity that might shock even Americans. (1985:42)

Evidence is also easy to provide against the argument that the U.S. criminal justice system is insufficiently firm with its target populations. Indeed, the United States and Turkey are the only Western countries that retain and use the death penalty! Comparative evidence consistently reveals that the United States incarcerates a greater proportion of its population than other Western countries, counting both the number of those incarcerated and the number of convicts on parole and probation. In 1995 there were 5.4 million persons in the United States either in prison or under the supervision of the prison system, accounting for 5 percent of men age eighteen and over and for one in five African American males (Wacquant, 1998: 8). In 1997 the number of inmates in state and federal prisons and in local jails in the United States had soared to 1,725,842, up from 1,100,000 in 1990 (Currie, 1998:12–23). During the period 1990–1997 the incarceration rate in state and federal prisons increased from 292 per 100,000 in 1990 to 445 per 100,000 in 1997. Other industrial democracies have far lower incarceration rates than those in the United States, with most countries clustering around 55–120 per 100,000 and with some countries, such as Japan, lower still at 36 per 100,000.

Moreover, the gap between the U.S. incarceration rate and the rates of other countries may well be increasing. According to longitudinal data the U.S. incarceration rate has grown consistently since 1925, with reductions occurring only during World War II and the Vietnam era. During the entire period 1925–1985, the average annual growth rate of the prison population was 2.8 percent (Bureau of Justice Statistics, 1986b). By 1992 the U.S. incarceration rate was the highest ever recorded, as was the number of individuals incarcerated; by the late 1990s the growth rate was nearly 6 percent per year.

We suggest that there is no evidence that the punitive nature of U.S. penal sanctions reduces the crime rate significantly. On the contrary: punitive penal policies are a violent part of the very problem they are apparently designed to solve. Instead of pursuing ever-harsher penal policies, we should pursue reductions in the crime rate through social policies applied to the class structure itself. Certain societies in Western Europe have reported great success with a host of practical social policies. In conclusion, we can do no better than to recommend Currie's summary of these policies:

- exploration and development of intensive rehabilitation programs for youthful offenders, preferably in the local community or in a supportive institutional milieu
- community-based, comprehensive family support programs, emphasizing local participation and respect for cultural diversity
- improved family planning services and support for teenage parents
- paid work leaves and more accessible child care for parents with young children, to ease the conflicts between child rearing and work
- high-quality early education programs for disadvantaged children
- expanded community dispute-resolution programs
- comprehensive, locally based services for domestic violence victims
- intensive job training, perhaps modeled along the lines of supported work, designed to prepare the young and the displaced for stable careers
- strong support for equity in pay and working conditions, aimed at upgrading the quality of low-paying jobs
- substantial permanent public or public–private job creation in local communities, at wages sufficient to support a family breadwinner, especially in such areas of clear and pressing social need as public safety, rehabilitation, child care, and family support
- universal—and generous—income support for families headed by individuals outside the paid labor force (1985:275–276; see also 1998:149–161; and Savelsberg, 1998/1999)

REVIEW

This chapter has taught the importance of testing theories under conditions as diverse as possible, and, therefore, it has explored the crucial role of comparative studies for the theoretical development of criminology in the United States. The major task of this chapter has been to outline the key concepts, data, and findings of comparative criminology.

Cross-National Crime and Victimization Data

1. Until very recently there was no systematic comparative criminology in the sense of analyses that systematically compare crime in two or more cultures. The ideal goal of comparative criminology is to test generalizations regarding crime in three stages: (1) in similar societies, (2) in societies largely similar but different in some respects, and (3) in societies as different as they possibly can be. This goal is unlikely to be met.

2. There are various sources of cross-national crime data, including those of the United Nations and other international agencies, the *Comparative Crime Data File,* and victimization surveys. For comparative purposes, using these sources entails the difficulty that societies both define certain practices as crimes in different ways and also differ in the degree of seriousness that they attach to them.

Cultural Relativism and Comparative Criminology

1. We explored the foregoing difficulty in the context of a set of issues raised by cultural relativism. Epistemological relativism—which we were forced to recognize but then ignore—holds that because we can never understand the beliefs of cultures different from our own, we cannot compare our culture with such cultures. Methodological relativism is a strategy for comparing different cultures that, at the same time, attempts to respect the facts of cultural diversity.

2. The precise difficulties presented by cultural relativism were illustrated by Brown's (1952) classic study of sexual deviance.

3. We examined Wolfgang's (1967) methodological strategy to reformulate crime statistics in order to overcome the difficulties raised by Brown's attempt to construct cross-national generalizations regarding sexual deviance.

Cross-National Generalizations Regarding Crime

1. In this section several cross-national generalizations regarding crime were outlined. Each has its own respective merits and its own conceptual and relativist problems.

2. The crime and modernization thesis suggests that generalizations can be made about the way in which industrialization and urbanization affect crime rates in all societies. The major problems with generalizations derived from this thesis are that (1) they ignore relativist issues regarding differences in legal definitions of crime; (2) they are often contradicted by empirical evidence; (3) they wrongly assume that criminality in Third World societies is a replay of the history of criminality in technologically advanced societies; and

(4) they often ignore the repressive colonial influence of First World countries and transnational corporations on the patterns of crime in the Third World.

3. We examined, and largely agreed with, the generalization that homicide rates are likely to be higher in societies with high degrees of social and economic inequality. The correlation between homicide rates and urbanization, however, was determined to be problematic.

4. Little research has been completed on the sociological nature of societies with low crime rates. We outlined the available research, applied it especially to the cases of Japan and Ireland, and could offer only provisional answers.

U.S. Crime in Comparative Perspective

1. We believe that there are many reasons why the United States has one of the highest crime rates in the world. Our reasons, as with those of other criminologists, remain tentative and as yet unsubstantiated.

2. One of the many reasons for the high U.S. crime rates is that U.S. society, including its criminal justice system, is one of the most punitive in the world. Punitive penal policies are a violent part of the very problem they are apparently designed to solve.

3. To address the causes of high rates of crime, one must look beyond penal policies to fundamental changes in society itself.

QUESTIONS FOR CLASS DISCUSSION

1. Twenty-five hundred years ago, the Greek historian Herodotus (quoted in Feyerabend, 1987:42) recorded the following story:

When Darius was king of Persia, he summoned the Greeks who happened to be present at his court, and asked them what they would take to eat the dead bodies of their fathers. They replied they would not do it for any money in the world. Later, in the presence of the Greeks, and through an interpreter, so that they could understand what was said, he asked some Indians, of the tribe called Callatiae, who do in fact eat their parents' dead bodies, what they would take to burn them. They uttered a cry of horror and forbade him to mention such a dreadful thing.

What does this story tell us about the problem of cultural relativism?

2. Do crime rates in the Third World tend to repeat the patterns of recorded crime in countries such as the United States?

3. What lessons, if any, can U.S. policymakers derive from the incidence of crime in other countries?

4. Why are the rates of violent crime in the United States so high in comparison with other modern industrialized countries?

FOR FURTHER STUDY

Readings

Beirne, Piers, and David Nelken, eds. 1997. *Issues in Comparative Criminology*. International Library of Criminology and Criminal Justice. Aldershot: Dartmouth.

McDonald, William F. 1997. Crime and Justice in the Global Village: Towards Global Criminology. In *Crime and Law Enforcement in the Global Village,* edited by William F. McDonald, 3–21. Cincinnati, Ohio: Anderson.

Neapolitan, Jerome L. 1997. *Cross-National Crime: A Research Review and Sourcebook*. Westport, Conn.: Greenwood Press.

Websites

1. <http://www.ccurecweb.com/les/res/resour4.htm>: This website has links to a collection of numerous national and international criminal justice and law websites.
2. <http://www.hrw.org>: This is the website of the humanitarian organization Human Rights Watch. It monitors human rights, prison conditions, and prison abuses in some seventy countries worldwide.
3. <http://www.ifs.univie.ac.at/^uncjin/uncjin.html>: This is the homepage of the United Nations Crime and Justice Information Network. It provides a mass of information regarding crime and justice on the national and international levels.

Glossary

A

abortion   The removal of an embryo or fetus from the uterus to end a pregnancy; it became a constitutional right in the Supreme Court decision *Roe v. Wade.*

age   The length of time for which a human has existed. Economic benefits, social privileges, and political power are often based on age.

aggravated assault   An unlawful attack by one person upon another for the purpose of inflicting severe or aggravated bodily injury.

animal abuse   Any act that contributes to the physical, psychological, or emotional pain, suffering, or death of an animal, or that otherwise threatens its welfare. The act may involve active maltreatment or passive neglect or omission, and may be direct or indirect, intentional or unintentional.

anomie   A condition of normlessness; a breakdown in the social order. A concept favored by Merton in his explanation of the high rate of crime and deviance in the United States.

armed robbery   The display of a deadly weapon to carry out a robbery.

arson   The willful or malicious burning of a house, public building, motor vehicle, aircraft, or other property of another.

automobile theft   The unlawful taking of, or the attempt to take, an automobile.

B

battering   Slapping, shoving, pushing, and other violent acts that result in injury to the victim; typically occurs for years.

bookmaking   Organized illegal betting on horse racing and other sporting events.

born criminality   Cesare Lombroso's theory that physical attributes are associated with, or even cause, criminal behavior.

burglary   The unlawful entry into a house, business, or other structure with the intent to commit a felony.

C

carjacking   The use of direct physical force to steal a motor vehicle from a driver.

check fraud   Deliberate deception for personal gain by the use of a counterfeit or forged check.

Chicago school of criminology   Part of the post–Progressive Era social science movement that evolved in Chicago between 1915 and the early 1940s.

child abuse   Those intentional acts of a parent, relative, or guardian that result, or are likely to result, in physical, mental, or emotional injury or impairment of a child. Child abuse has four forms—physical abuse, sexual abuse, emotional abuse, and child neglect.

civil disobedience   A nonviolent action against the state or a refusal to obey certain laws considered unjust.

class (or social class)   A group of people who share the same position in the same production system.

classical criminology   A criminology based on both free will and determinism and whose chief aim was to deter crime. It was part of the humanist reaction during the Enlightenment to the barbarities and inequities characteristic of feudal systems of justice. It was popularized by classical theorists Cesare Beccaria and Jeremy Bentham.

collective embezzlement   Theft of funds from a savings and loan institution for personal gain, at the expense of the institution and with the approval of management.

communism   A theory advocating the elimination of private property. Its proponents tentatively believe that with the abolition of private property and with the disappearance of the class nature of the state, crime will almost disappear under communism.

comparative criminology   The systematic comparison of crime in two or more cultures.

complaintless crimes   Public-order crimes in which those directly involved do not feel harmed or victimized and so do not report the behavior to police.

concepts   Ideas that describe a property of an empirical datum or a relation among empirical data. They are usually a smaller part of a theory that is used to generate hypotheses.

conduct norms   Rules of behavior that embody the values of some powerful group in society.

conflict theory   An ancient theory that, when used in criminology, suggests that crime, criminalization, and criminal law must be seen in the overriding context of social, economic, and political inequality.

constitutive criminology   The most thoroughgoing postmodern perspective in criminology, it is a political perspective that seeks to lay bare the rhetoric and mystification that enters public discourse about crime.

containment theory   A theory suggesting that variation in the crime rates of different social groups is caused by variations in the ability to contain norm-violating behavior in the face of social change and cultural conflict.

control balance   A theory claiming that the amount of control to which an individual is subject, relative to the amount of control s/he can exercise, determines the probability of deviance occurring as well as the likely type of deviance.

control deficit   In Tittle's theory of control balance, if one is subject to control more than one controls, then one has a control deficit.

control surplus   In Tittle's theory of control balance, if one controls more than one is subject to control, then one has a control surplus.

control theory   A theory arguing that to find the factors leading to delinquency one must look for the causes of conformity; delinquency turns out to be merely an absence of the causes of conformity.

corporate crimes   Illegal or socially injurious acts of intent or indifference that are committed in order to further corporate goals and that physically and/or economically harm individuals in the United States and/or abroad.

corporate theft   Differs from other forms of theft in that it does not entail face-to-face confrontation; it is not always readily apparent that a theft has occurred; and it serves the interest of the corporation.

corporate violence   Acts of violence committed by corporations against workers, consumers, or the public.

corrupt campaign practices   Various forms of illegal or unethical behaviors used to obtain political office, ultimately for the purpose of influencing state policy.

credit-card fraud   The use of stolen credit cards to purchase goods.

crime   In criminal law, crime is an action or omission that is prohibited by law, that is voluntary, and that coincides with a defendant's mental state. This book uses an eclectic and more sociological approach to crime, however; this approach views crime as a dynamic outcome of the relationship between the state and the social relations embedded in gender, race, age, and class. Crime can be seen as a violation of conduct norms, as a social harm, as a violation of human rights, and as a form of deviance.

crime rate   The prevalence of crime relative to the population.

criminalization   The process whereby criminal law is selectively applied to social behavior. It involves the enactment of legislation that outlaws certain types of behavior and provides for surveillance and policing of that behavior and, if the behavior is detected, for punishment.

criminal justice system   An elaborate system used to deal with those who violate criminal laws.

criminal law   Rules enacted by legislatures or that result from judicial decisions that protect members of the public from state definitions of wrongdoing.

criminal syndicate   An association, which can include businesspeople, police, politicians, and criminals, formed to conduct specific illegal enterprises for profit.

cultural relativism   The philosophical and sociological claim that beliefs and practices in one culture may translate only roughly, or not at all, into those of another culture.

D

dangerous classes   A derogatory nineteenth-century term applied by law-abiding citizens to describe those members of the working classes, the unemployed, and the unemployable who seemed to pose a threat to law and order.

deceptive advertising   Occurs when advertisements are misleading in a material respect; advertisers can make false statements so long as they are not deceptive.

decriminalization   The removal of criminal prohibitions for certain behaviors while still regulating them.

deviance   Any social behavior or social characteristic that departs from the conventional norms and standards of a community or society and for which the deviant is sanctioned.

differential association   A theory that attempts to explain both the process by which a person learns to engage in crime and also the content of what is learned.

drift   The lack of commitment to either the subculture of delinquency or conventional culture.

E

election fraud   A form of state corruption that includes illegal voting, false voter registration, and stuffing ballot boxes.

embezzlement   The taking of money from the workplace for one's personal use.

employee theft   Stealing merchandise or job-related items from the workplace.

Enlightenment   A philosophical and humanist eighteenth-century movement professing that reason and experience, rather than faith and superstition, must replace the excesses and corruption of feudal societies. It opposed cruel and inhumane punishments and challenged the prevailing views of the time concerning the relation between crime and punishment.

epistemological relativism   Involves the extraordinary claim that one can understand another culture only through the prism of one's own culturally determined system of values.

ethnocentrism   The view that concepts and generalizations about one society necessarily apply to crime in other societies.

F

feminism   A critical perspective that maintains that women are discriminated against because of their gender and that seeks to use social change to end women's resulting subordination.

fencing   Buying, selling, or dealing in stolen goods.

financial fraud   A form of fraud that serves the interests of the corporation.

G

gender   Historically and culturally developed patterns of behavior resulting from relationships between males/males, females/females, and males/females.

general theory   A theory that is constructed according to the logic of the natural sciences and that seeks at once to be both as simple and as general as possible.

H

hate crimes   Violence committed against people because of their race, ethnicity, disability, religion, or sexual orientation.

human rights   Natural and inalienable rights accorded to all human beings, such as the right to life, liberty, and happiness. They also may include rights essential to a dignified human existence, such as freedom of movement, free speech, a good education, employment, and so on.

I

ideology   Any set of structured beliefs, values, and ideas that can at once reflect social reality and distort it.

imitation   Gabriel Tarde reasoned that crime was influenced by the processes of imitation and that thereby people are socialized into criminality.

income-tax fraud   Cheating on one's income tax by, for example, underreporting wages.

insider trading   Occurs when information unavailable to the public is used to gain an advantage over others in the buying and selling of stock.

integrated theory   A theory that combines some of the assumptions and propositions of two or more other theories into an explanatory framework with a broader scope.

international law   Various treaties, agreements, customary law principles, and general legal principles that serve to judge the actions and behavior of nation states assenting to them.

interpersonal coercion   Occurs when a woman has sex with her husband or employer in the face of nonviolent threats.

L

labeling   A perspective suggesting that crime and deviance exist in the eye of the beholder.

labor racketeering   The infiltration, domination, and use of a union for personal benefit by illegal, violent, and fraudulent means.

larceny   The unlawful taking of property from the possession of someone other than one's employer.

left idealism   A type of critical criminology that focuses almost exclusively on the harms of the ruling class and that ignores the development of a coherent program for curbing conventional crime.

left realism   The view that conventional crime is driven by relative deprivation and by reactionary, selfish, and individualistic attitudes.

legalization   Complete removal of all criminal sanctions for certain behaviors without subsequent regulation.

liberal feminism   The view that women's subordinate status in society stems from socialization processes and from unequal opportunities and rights for women.

loan sharking   Financial loans at extremely high interest rates with rapid repayment required and violence as a potential sanction for nonpayment.

M

mafia   A method or system of patron–client relationships; in Sicily it was a system dependent upon patronage and the ability of a man of respect to utilize violence when necessary.

manslaughter   The killing of another person through gross negligence or without specific intent.

Marxist feminism   The view that class and gender divisions of labor together determine the social position of women and men in any society and that the gender division of labor derives from the class division of labor.

mass murder   This crime is committed when an individual kills a number of people at once, rather than singly over time.

methodological relativism   A strategy that operates as a sensitizing device to variation in the definition and meaning of crime in other cultures.

methodology   Techniques of measurement used to collect and manipulate empirical data.

middle-class measuring rod   Prevailing middle-class standards by which, in A. K. Cohen's theory of the origin of delinquent gangs, all adolescents are evaluated.

mode of production   A Marxist concept denoting the means of production and the social relations of production.

modernization thesis   The view that technological development produces common effects that tend to make all societies increasingly similar, irrespective of different or even antagonistic political systems.

money laundering   The process by which one conceals the existence, illegal source, or illegal application of income and then disguises that income to make it appear legitimate.

motor vehicle theft   The unlawful taking of or the attempt to take a motor vehicle such as an automobile, van, truck or motorcycle.

murder   The willful killing of one human being by another, usually with premeditation.

N

neoclassical criminology   The doctrinal and procedural compromise between classicism and positivism, devised roughly between 1890 and 1910, that has become the basis of criminal responsibility and punishment in most Western societies.

numbers   An illegal form of lottery in which the customer (or bettor) places a bet by choosing three numbers between 000 and 999.

O

occupational crimes   Crimes committed by individuals in the course of their occupations for direct personal gain.

occupational fraud   A deliberate workplace deception practiced for personal financial gain.

occupational theft   An offense that stems from an abuse of trust between employee and employer; it includes employee theft and embezzlement.

official crime data   Data collected by the government and its official agencies.

P

patriarchy   Male control of the labor power and sexuality of women.

peacemaking criminology   A critical perspective that examines the essence of the person charged with a crime and emphasizes cooperation, compassion, and respect for all species.

physician fraud   A type of occupational fraud that involves writing pharmaceutical prescriptions, performing unnecessary surgical procedures, or overtreating Medicaid and Medicare patients.

political bribery   The giving of money or property to state officials in return for favors.

political crime   Includes crimes against the state (violations of law for the purpose of modifying or changing social conditions) and crimes by the state, both domestic (violations of law and unethical acts by state officials and agencies where victimization occurs inside the United States) and international (violations of domestic and international law by state officials or agencies where victimization occurs outside the United States).

political kickbacks   The illegal or unethical use of state authority for personal or political gain.

political repression   Illegal or unethical conduct by state officials or agencies for purposes of repressing political dissent.

pornography   Sexually explicit acts and depictions that have little or no artistic merit.

positivism   The belief that crime can be observed directly by using the procedures and explanatory logic of the natural sciences.

positivist criminology   The second great theoretical movement in modern criminology, its method of analysis is based on the collection of observable scientific facts, and its aim is to uncover, to explain, and to predict the ways in which the observable facts of crime occur in uniform patterns.

postmodernism   This theoretical movement challenges all truth claims, emphasizing alternative discourses, meaning, and subjectivist accounts.

price-fixing   Violates antitrust laws through collusion to ensure profits above those that would be produced in a competitive industry.

primary deviance   An original act of crime or deviance that may derive from a wide variety of social, cultural, psychological, and physiological events.

professional murder   This crime takes place when one individual kills another for profit.

prostitution   The consensual grant of nonmonogamous sexual services to clients for payments.

R

race   Genetic differences in skin color only assume social significance when they are used to justify unequal treatment of one race by another.

radical feminism   Views masculine power and privilege as the root of all social relations in any society; all other relations (such as class) are secondary and derive from gender relations.

rape   As traditionally defined in the criminal law, the carnal knowledge of a female forcibly and against her will, though an expanded definition is used in this book.

rational choice   Alleged basis of all calculated human action, including crime, that operates in some of the same ways as free will in theology.

reaction formation   A process of adjustment whereby, for example, the academic success typically denied working-class boys is contemptuously redefined as sissy and whereby street knowledge is regarded as superior.

reinforcement   A key concept in social learning theory, which states that crime is largely a response to reinforcing stimuli. If individuals are rewarded for committing crimes, they are more likely to commit them again.

repressive law   In Durkheim's sociology this type of law is religious in its origin and is associated chiefly with societies of mechanical solidarity. Its most common form is criminal law; its violation invites punishment.

restitutive law   In Durkheim's sociology this type of law is associated chiefly with societies of organic solidarity. Its most common form is contract law; its violation invokes a demand to enforce the terms of a prior agreement.

robbery   The unlawful taking of, or the attempt to take, something of value from another person or persons by using violence or the threat of violence.

routine activities theory   A theory claiming that patterns of crime and victimization are the result of the everyday interaction of likely offenders, suitable targets, and guardians.

S

secondary deviance   Society's reaction to some of those who engage in primary deviance, often causing them to accept their identity as a deviant.

self-control theory   The view that claims that individual differences in criminal behavior derive from differences in self-control.

serial murder   This crime occurs when an individual kills a number of people over a period of time.

sexual harassment   An offense that occurs when the submission to or rejection of sexual advances affects one's employment, or when it affects an individual's work performance by creating an environment that is intimidating, hostile, and offensive.

shoplifting   A type of larceny that entails the theft of property from a retail store by customers.

social coercion   An offense that occurs when women feel that they should have sex with their husbands even if they do not want to because of social pressures—their wifely duty.

social control   Occurring in both public and private realms, this control has ideological and repressive forms, including primary socialization within the family and secondary socialization within peer groups, the educational system, and the media.

social disorganization   A lack of fit between culturally prescribed aspirations and socially structured avenues for achieving them.

social ecology   A type of research that examines different geographical areas within cities, communities, and neighborhoods as well as the area concentrations, regularities, and patterns of social life in such fields as work/leisure, health/sickness, and conformity/deviance.

social inequality   The fact that critical aspects of life such as economic benefits, life chances, social privileges, and political power are unequally distributed in society.

socialist feminism   The view that argues that the relationship of class and gender structures crime in society.

social mechanics   A nineteenth-century discourse based on the belief that the same law-like regularity existing in the heavens and in nature also exists in society.

social position   One's individual location in society based on such social characteristics as class, gender, race, and age.

social problem   A social condition that is perceived as having harmful effects; opinions about whether a condition is a social problem vary among groups and depend upon how and by whom the condition is defined and perceived in society.

social solidarity　Social order that is abstract and internal to consciousness and that is observable via other, more visible aspects of social life.

societal reaction　Part of the process of deviance by which society labels primary deviants, thus giving them an identity that leads them to act in expected ways, causing secondary deviance.

sociological problem　A sociological explanation of how patterns of crime arise from the interplay of political, economic, social, and ideological structures in society.

state, the　The central political institution of a given society, whose major apparatuses are the government, the legal system, the military, and a variety of public bureaucracies.

state corruption　The illegal or unethical use of state authority for personal or political gain.

statistics　A set of techniques for the reduction of quantitative data to a limited number of more convenient and easily communicated descriptive terms.

status frustration　The lack of status in middle-class life, which causes negative feelings and the search for status in delinquent subcultures.

stigma　A sign of disgrace imposed on an individual.

strain　In Mertonian anomie theory, *strain* refers to the many forms of response that one might have to the lack of fit between socially acceptable means and socially desirable goals.

strong-arm robbery　A robbery in which the offender does not use a weapon.

subculture　Applied to delinquency, it is a set of beliefs, values, codes, tastes, and prejudices that differs somehow from the main or dominant culture.

T

techniques of neutralization　The process by which potential delinquents are freed from conventional social and moral controls and because of which they are then able to engage in delinquency.

terrorism　The use of violence or the threat of violence to coerce for political purposes.

theories　Sets of assumptions, mediated by concepts, that guide the interpretation of data and that try to explain both regularities and irregularities in data.

transnational corporate crimes　Illegal behaviors of U.S.-based corporations that conduct business in more than one country and that harm members of other societies; these crimes range from bribery to the export of hazardous products to dangerous working conditions.

U

unofficial crime data　Nongovernmental data usually collected by private or independent agencies and researchers.

utilitarianism　The doctrine of free will that holds that all men rationally and freely choose to engage in the social contract and that those who challenge this contract, break its rules, or pursue harmful pleasures or wickedness are liable to be punished.

V

victimization surveys　Surveys of representative samples of a general population that try to uncover what crimes have been experienced in a given period.

victimless crimes　Crimes created by the attempt to ban through criminal legislation the exchange of strongly desired goods and services between willing partners.

victim precipitation　Cited as a defense to a crime when the victim is said to be a direct, positive precipitator in the crime.

W

white-collar crime   The term first coined by Edwin Sutherland to describe a crime committed by a person of respectability and high social status in the course of his or her occupation. It typically takes an economic form and is stimulated by economic cycles.

wife rape   Differs from rape in that women are raped only by a husband or an ex-husband.

References

Abadinsky, Howard. 1983. *The Criminal Elite: Professional and Organized Crime.* Westport, Conn.: Greenwood.

_____. 1989. *Drug Abuse: An Introduction.* Chicago: Nelson-Hall.

Abt, Vicki, and Douglas J. McDowell. 1987. Does the Press Cover Gambling Issues Poorly? *Social Science Research* 71 (3): 193–197.

Adamson, Christopher. 1998. Tribute, Turf, Honor, and the American Street Gang. *Theoretical Criminology* 2 (1): 57–84.

Adler, Freda. 1975. *Sisters in Crime: The Rise of the New Female Offender.* New York: McGraw-Hill.

_____. 1977. The Interaction Between Women's Emancipation and Female Criminality: A Cross-Cultural Perspective. *International Journal of Criminology and Penology* 5 (1): 101–112.

_____. 1983. *Nations Not Obsessed with Crime.* Littleton, Colo.: Fred B. Rothman.

Adler, Jeffrey S. 1989. A Historical Analysis of the Law of Vagrancy. *Criminology* 27 (2): 209–229.

Adler, Patricia A., and Peter Adler. 1998. Foreword to *Ethnography at the Edge,* edited by Jeff Ferrell and Mark S. Hamm, xii–xvi. Boston: Northeastern University Press.

Ageton, Suzanne, and Delbert S. Elliott. 1974. The Effects of Legal Processing on Self-Concept. *Social Problems* 22 (1): 87–100.

Agnew, Robert. 1985. Social Control Theory and Delinquency: A Longitudinal Test. *Criminology* 23 (1): 47–61.

_____. 1992. Foundation for a General Strain Theory of Crime and Delinquency. *Criminology* 30 (1): 47–87.

_____. 1995. Strain and Subcultural Theories of Criminality. In *Criminology: A Contemporary Handbook,* edited by Joseph F. Sheley, 305–327. Belmont, Calif.: Wadsworth.

_____. 1998. The Causes of Animal Abuse: A Social-Psychological Analysis. *Theoretical Criminology* 2 (2): 177–209.

Agnew, Robert, Francis T. Cullen, Velmer S. Burton, T. David Evans, and R. Gregory Dunaway. 1996. A New Test of Classic Strain Theory. *Justice Quarterly* 13 (4): 681–704.

Akers, Ronald L. 1973. *Deviant Behavior.* Belmont, Calif.: Wadsworth.

_____. 1997. *Criminological Theories.* Los Angeles: Roxbury.

_____. 1998. *Social Learning and Social Structure: A General Theory of Crime and Deviance.* Boston: Northeastern University Press.

Akers, Ronald L., Marvin D. Krohn, Lonn Lanza-Kaduce, and Marcia Radosevich. 1979. Social Learning and Deviant Behavior: A Specific Test of a General Theory. *American Sociological Review* 44 (4): 636–655.

Albanese, Jay. 1985. *Organized Crime in America.* Cincinnati: Anderson.

Albini, Joseph L. 1971. *The American Mafia: Genesis of a Legend.* New York: Appleton-Century-Crofts.

Alexander, Herbert E. 1985. Organized Crime and Politics. In *The Politics and Economics of Organized Crime,* edited by Herbert E. Alexander and Gerald E. Caiden, 89–98. Lexington, Mass.: Lexington Books.

Allen, Donald M. 1980. Young Male Prostitutes: A Psychological Study. *Archives of Sexual Behavior* 9 (5): 399–426.

Altheide, David L., Patricia A. Adler, Peter Adler, and Duane A. Altheide. 1978. The Social Meanings of Employee Theft. In *Crime at the Top,* edited by John Johnson and Jack Douglas, 90–124. New York: Lippincott.

Amir, Menachim. 1967. Victim-Precipitated Forcible Rape. *Journal of Criminal Law, Criminology, and Police Science* 58 (4): 493–502.

———. 1971. *Patterns in Forcible Rape.* Chicago: University of Chicago Press.

Amnesty International. 1976. *Report on Torture, 1975–1976.* New York: Farrar, Straus, Giroux.

———. 1998. *USA—Rights for All.* London: Amnesty International Secretariat.

Andersen, Margaret L. [1988] 1993. *Thinking About Women: Sociological Perspectives on Sex and Gender.* New York: Macmillan.

Anderson, Scott, and Jon Lee Anderson. 1986. *Inside the League.* New York: Dodd, Mead and Company.

Anderson, Tammy L., and Richard R. Bennett. 1996. "Development, Gender, and Crime: The Scope of the Routine Activities Approach. *Justice Quarterly* 13 (1): 31–56.

Andrew, D. T. 1980. The Code of Honour and Its Critics: The Opposition to Duelling in England, 1700–1850. *Social History* 5 (3): 409–434.

Archer, Dane, and Rosemary Gartner. 1984. *Violence and Crime in Cross-National Perspective.* New Haven: Yale University Press.

Ascione, Frank. 1998. Battered Women's Reports of Their Partners' and Their Children's Cruelty to Animals. *Journal of Emotional Abuse* 11: 120–133.

Asinoff, Robert. 1985. India Accident Raises Questions of Corporate Responsibility. *In These Times,* December 19–January 8, 10.

Bachand, Donald J., and George A. Chressanthis. 1988. Property Crime and the Elderly Offender: A Theoretical and Empirical Analysis, 1964–1984. In *Older Offenders,* edited by Belinda McCarthy and Robert Longworthy, 76–103. New York: Praeger.

Bachman, Ronet. 1994. *Violence and Theft in the Workplace.* Washington, D.C.: Bureau of Justice Statistics.

Baer, Justin, and William J. Chambliss. 1997. Generating Fear: The Politics of Crime Reporting. *Crime, Law, and Social Change* 27 (2): 87–107.

Bailey, William C., and Ruth D. Peterson. 1987. Police Killings and Capital Punishment: The Post-Furman Period. *Criminology* 25 (1): 1–25.

———. 1995. Gender Inequality and Violence Against Women: The Case of Murder. In *Crime and Inequality,* edited by John Hagan and Ruth D. Peterson, 174–205. Stanford, Calif.: Stanford University Press.

———. 1997. Murder, Capital Punishment, and Deterrence: A Review of the Literature. In *The Death Penalty in America: Current Controversies,* edited by Hugo Adam Bedau. New York: Oxford University Press.

Baker, James C. 1985. The International Infant Formula Controversy: A Dilemma in Corporate Social Responsibility. *Journal of Business Ethics* 4 (3): 181–190.

Baker, Michael, and Alan F. Westin. 1987. *Employer Perceptions of Workplace Crime.* Washington, D.C.: U.S. Department of Justice.

Balkan, Sheila, Ronald Berger, and Janet Schmidt. 1980. *Crime and Deviance in America: A Critical Approach.* Monterey, Calif.: Wadsworth.

Ball, Richard A. 1966. An Empirical Exploration of Neutralization Theory. *Criminology* 4 (2): 22–32.

Bandura, Albert. 1973. *Aggression: A Social Learning Analysis.* Englewood Cliffs, N.J.: Prentice-Hall.

Barak, Gregg. 1988. Newsmaking Criminology: Reflections on the Media, Intellectuals, and Crime. *Justice Quarterly* 5 (4): 565–587.

———. 1998. *Integrating Criminologies.* Boston: Allyn and Bacon.

Barlow, Melissa Hickman. 1998. Race and the Problem of Crime in *Time* and *Newsweek* Cover Stories, 1946 to 1995. *Social Justice* 25 (2): 149–183.

Barry, Kathleen. 1979. *Female Sexual Slavery.* Englewood Cliffs, N.J.: Prentice-Hall.

Baumer, Terry L., and Dennis P. Rosenbaum. 1984. *Combating Retail Theft: Programs and Strategies.* Boston: Butterworth.

Bayley, David H. 1976a. Learning About Crime: The Japanese Experience. *Public Interest* 44 (Summer): 55–68.

_____. 1976b. *Forces of Order: Police Behavior in Japan and the United States.* Berkeley: University of California Press.

_____. 1991. *Forces of Order: Policing Modern Japan.* Berkeley: University of California Press.

Beaty, Jonathan, and S. C. Gwynne. 1991. The Dirtiest Bank of All. *Time,* July 29, 42–47.

Beccaria, Cesare. [1764] 1963. *Of Crimes and Punishments.* Translated by Henry Paolucci. Indianapolis: Bobbs-Merrill.

Becker, Howard S. 1963. *Outsiders: Studies in the Sociology of Deviance.* New York: Free Press.

Beirne, Piers. 1979. Empiricism and the Critique of Marxism on Law and Crime. *Social Problems* 26 (4): 373–385.

_____. 1983a. Generalization and Its Discontents: The Comparative Study of Crime. In *Comparative Criminology,* edited by Israel Barak-Glantz and Elmer Johnson, 19–38. Beverly Hills, Calif.: Sage.

_____. 1983b. Cultural Relativism and Comparative Criminology. *Contemporary Crises* 7 (4): 371–391.

_____. 1987a Adolphe Quetelet and the Origins of Positivist Criminology. *American Journal of Sociology* 92 (5): 1140–1169.

_____. 1987b. Between Classicism and Positivism: Crime and Penality in the Writings of Gabriel Tarde. *Criminology* 25 (4): 785–819.

_____. 1988. Heredity Versus Environment: A Reconsideration of Charles Goring's *The English Convict* (1913). *British Journal of Criminology* 28 (3): 315–339.

_____. 1993. *Inventing Criminology: Essays on the Rise of* Homo Criminalis. Albany: State University of New York Press.

_____. 1994. The Law Is an Ass: Reading E. P. Evans, *The Medieval Prosecution and Capital Punishment of Animals. Society and Animals* 2 (1): 27–46.

_____. 1995. The Use and Abuse of Animals in Criminology: A Brief History and Current Review. *Social Justice* 22 (1): 5–31.

_____. 1999. For a Nonspeciesist Criminology: Animal Abuse as an Object of Study. *Criminology* 37 (1): 117–148.

Beirne, Piers, and Alan Hunt. 1989. Law and the Constitution of Soviet Society: The Case of Comrade Lenin. *Law and Society Review* 22 (3): 575–614.

Beirne, Piers, and Barbara Perry. 1994. Criminal Victimization in the Industrialized World. *Crime, Law, and Social Change* 21 (2): 155–165.

Beirne, Piers, and David Nelken, eds. 1997. *Issues in Comparative Criminology.* International Library of Criminology and Criminal Justice. Aldershot: Dartmouth.

Belknap, Joanne. 1996. *The Invisible Woman: Gender, Crime, and Justice.* Belmont, Calif.: Wadsworth.

Bell, Daniel. 1961. *The End of Ideology.* New York: Collier.

Bell, Laurie, ed. 1987. *Good Girls/Bad Girls: Feminists and Sex Trade Workers Face to Face.* Seattle: Seal Press.

Bellis, David J. 1981. *Heroin and Politicians: The Failure of Public Policy to Control Addiction in America.* Westport, Conn.: Greenwood.

Benedict, Jeffrey, and Alan Klein. 1998. Arrest and Conviction Rates for Athletes Accused of Sexual Assault. In *Issues in Intimate Violence,* edited by Raquel Kennedy Bergen, 169–179. Thousand Oaks, Calif.: Sage.

Bennett, James. 1981. *Oral History and Delinquency: The Rhetoric of Criminology.* Chicago: University of Chicago Press.

Bennett, Richard R., and Jeanne M. Flavin. 1994. Determinants of Fear of Crime: The Effect of Cultural Setting. *Justice Quarterly* 11 (3): 357–381.

Bennett, Trevor, and Richard Wright. 1984. *Burglars on Burglary.* Brookfield, Vt.: Gower.

Benson, Donna J., and Gregg E. Thompson. 1982. Sexual Harassment on a University Campus: The Confluence of Authority Relation, Sexual Interest, and Gender Stratification. *Social Problems* 29 (3): 236–251.

Benson, George C. S. 1978. *Political Corruption in America.* Lexington. Mass.: Lexington Books.

_____. 1971. *Panopticon: Or, The Inspection-House.* 1787. 3 Vols. Reprinted and sold by T. Payne.

Bentham, Jeremy. [1780] 1973. *An Introduction to the Principles of Morals and Legislation.* New York: Hafner Press.

Bequai, August. 1978. *White-Collar Crime: A 20th-Century Crisis.* Lexington. Mass.: Lexington Books.

Bergen, Raquel Kennedy, ed. 1998. *Issues in Intimate Violence.* Thousand Oaks, Calif.: Sage.

Berman, Daniel. 1978. *Death on the Job.* New York: Monthly Review Press.

Bernard, Thomas J. 1983. *The Consensus-Conflict Debate: Form and Content in Social Theories.* New York: Columbia University Press.

_____. 1987. Structure and Control: Reconsidering Hirschi's Concept of Commitment. *Justice Quarterly* 4 (3): 409–424.

Bernard, Thomas J., and Jeffrey B. Snipes. 1996. Theoretical Integration in Criminology. In *Crime and Justice: A Review of Research,* edited by Michael Tonry, 20:301–348. Chicago: University of Chicago Press.

Berrill, Kevin T. 1992. Anti-Gay Violence and Victimization in the United States: An Overview. In *Hate Crimes: Confronting Violence Against Lesbians and Gay Men,* edited by Gregory M. Herek and Kevin T. Berrill, 19–45. Newbury Park, Calif.: Sage.

Berry, Steve. 1998. Special Report: Time-Honored Oath to "Whole Truth" May Be Losing Aura. *Los Angeles Times,* August 9.

Best, Joel. 1990. *Threatened Children: Rhetoric and Concern About Child Victims.* Chicago: University of Chicago Press.

Bianchi, Herman, and Rene Van Swaaningen, eds. 1986. *Abolitionism: Towards a Nonrepressive Approach to Crime.* Amsterdam: Free University Press.

Biderman, Albert D., Louise Johnson, Jennie McIntyre, and Adrianne Weir. 1967. *Report on a Pilot Study in the District of Columbia on Victimization and Attitudes to Law Enforcement.* U.S. Presidents Commission on Law Enforcement and Administration of Justice, Field Surveys 1. Washington, D.C.: U.S. Government Printing Office.

Black, Donald. 1970. Production of Crime Rates. *American Sociological Review* 35 (4): 733–748.

_____. 1976. *The Behavior of Law.* New York: Academic Press.

_____. 1989. *Sociological Justice.* New York: Oxford University Press.

Black, George. 1981. *Triumph of the People: The Sandinistas Revolution in Nicaragua.* London: Zed Press.

Blau, Judith R., and Peter M. Blau. 1982. The Cost of Inequality: Metropolitan Structure and Violent Crime. *American Sociological Review* 47 (1): 114–129.

Block, Alan. 1977. Aw Your Mothers in the Mafia: Women Criminals in Progressive New York. *Contemporary Crises* 1 (1): 5–22.

_____. 1979. The Snowman Cometh: Coke in Progressive New York. *Criminology* 17 (1): 75–99.

_____. 1980. Searching for Women in Organized Crime. In *Women, Crime, and Justice,* edited by Susan K. Datesman and Frank R. Scarpitti, 192–213. New York: Oxford University Press.

_____. 1983. *East Side, West Side: Organizing Crime in New York, 1930–1950.* New Brunswick, N.J.: Transaction.

Block, Alan A., ed. 1991. *The Business of Crime: A Documentary Study of Organized Crime in the American Economy.* Boulder, Colo.: Westview Press.

Block, Alan, and William J. Chambliss. 1981. *Organizing Crime.* New York: Elsevier.

Block, Maggie, Rosa Bernstein, Penny Ciancanelli, Gay Ferguson, Alan Howard, Kathy Huenemann, Marta Sanchez, Bob Seltzer, Julio Velazquez, and Sol Yurick. 1972. Nixon and Organized Crime. *North American Congress on Latin America (NACLA)* 6: 3–17.

Blok, Anton. 1974. *The Mafia of a Sicilian Village. 1860–1960.* New York: Harper and Row.

Blumer, Herbert. 1971. Social Problems as Collective Behavior. *Social Problems* 18 (3): 298–306.

Bohm, Robert M. 1993. Social Relationships That Arguably Should Be Criminal Although They Are Not: On the Political Economy of Crime. In *Political Crime in Contemporary America,* edited by Kenneth D. Tunnell, 3–29. New York: Garland.

Boostrom, Ronald L. 1974. The Personalization of Evil: The Emergence of American Criminology, 1865–1910. Ph.D. diss. University of California, Berkeley.

Boston Herald. 1988. 7 Cops Guilty in Racketeering Case. September 4, 10.

Boswell, A. Ayres, and Joan Z. Spade. 1996. Fraternities and Collegiate Rape Culture: Why Are Some Fraternities More Dangerous Places for Women? *Gender and Society* 10 (2): 133–147.

Bourgois, Philippe. 1996. In Search of Masculinity: Violence, Respect, and Sexuality Among Puerto Rican Crack Dealers in East Harlem. *British Journal of Criminology* 36 (3): 412–427.

Box, Steven. 1983. *Power and Mystification.* New York: Tavistock.

_____. 1987. *Recession, Crime, and Punishment.* London: Macmillan.

Box, Steven, and Chris Hale. 1983. Liberation and Female Criminality in England and Wales Revisited. *British Journal of Criminology* 22 (3): 35–49.

Brady, James P. 1983. Arson, Urban Economy, and Organized Crime: The Case of Boston. *Social Problems* 31 (1): 127.

Braithwaite, John. 1979a. Transnational Corporations and Corruption: Towards Some International Solutions. *International Journal of the Sociology of Law* 7 (2): 125–142.

_____. 1979b. *Inequality, Crime, and Public Policy.* Boston: Routledge and Kegan Paul.

_____. 1981. The Myth of Social Class and Criminality Reconsidered. *American Sociological Review* 46 (1): 36–57.

_____. 1984. *Corporate Crime in the Pharmaceutical Industry.* Boston: Routledge and Kegan Paul.

_____. 1989. *Crime, Shame, and Reintegration.* Cambridge: Cambridge University Press.

_____. 1997. Charles Tittle's *Control Balance* and Criminological Theory. *Theoretical Criminology* 1 (1): 77–97.

Braithwaite, John, and Philip Pettit. 1990. *Not Just Deserts: A Republican Theory of Criminal Justice.* Oxford: Oxford University Press.

Brake, Mike. 1980. *The Sociology of Youth Culture and Youth Subcultures.* Boston: Routledge and Kegan Paul.

Branfman, Frank. 1978. South Vietnam's Police and Prison System: The U.S. Connection. In *Uncloaking the CIA,* edited by Howard Frazier, 110–127. New York: Free Press.

Brantingham, Paul, and Patricia Brantingham. 1984. *Patterns in Crime.* New York: Macmillan.

Bray, Howard. 1980. *Pillars of the Post.* New York: W. W. Norton.

Breacher, Edward M. 1972. *Licit and Illicit Drugs.* Boston: Little, Brown.

Brecher, Jeremy. 1980. *Strike!* Boston: South End Press.

Breen, Richard, and David B. Rottman. 1985. *Crime Victimisation in the Republic of Ireland.* Paper no. 121. Dublin: The Economic and Social Research Institute.

Breines, Wini, and Linda Gordon. 1983. The New Scholarship on Family Violence. *Signs* 8 (3): 490–531.

Brenner, M. Harvey. 1976. *Estimating the Social Costs of National Economic Policy.* Joint Economic Committee of the U.S. Congress. Washington, D.C.: U.S. Government Printing Office.

Brezina, Timothy. 1996. Adapting to Strain: An Examination of Delinquent Coping Responses. *Criminology* 34 (1): 39–60.

Bridges, George S., and Robert D. Crutchfield. 1988. Law, Social Standing, and Racial Disparities in Imprisonment. *Social Forces* 66 (3): 699–724

Brody, Reed. 1985. *Contra Terror in Nicaragua: Report of a Fact-finding Mission, September 1984–January 1985.* Boston: South End Press.

Broidy, Lisa, and Robert Agnew. 1997. Gender and Crime: A General Strain Theory Perspective. *Journal of Research in Crime and Delinquency* 34 (3): 275–306.

Brown, Julia S. 1952. A Comparative Study of Deviations from Sexual Mores. *American Sociological Review* 17 (2): 135–146.

Browne, Angela. 1987. *When Battered Women Kill.* New York: Free Press.

_____. 1995. Fear and Perception of Alternatives: Asking "Why Battered Women Don't Leave" Is the Wrong Question. In *The Criminal Justice System and Women*, edited by Barbara Raffel Price and Natalie J. Sokoloff, 228–245. New York: McGraw-Hill.

Brownmiller, Susan. 1975. *Against Our Will: Men, Women, and Rape.* New York: Simon and Schuster.

Bruce, Marino A., Vincent J. Roscigno, and Patricia L. McCall. 1998. Structure, Context, and Agency in the Reproduction of Black-on-Black Violence. *Theoretical Criminology* 2 (1): 29-55.

Buder, Leonard. 1986. In Partial Verdict, U.S. Jury Finds 6 Radicals Guilty of 2 Bombings. *New York Times,* March 5, B3.

Buikhuisen, Wouter, and Fokke P. H. Dijksterhuis. 1971. Delinquency and Stigmatisation. *British Journal of Criminology* 11 (2): 185–187.

Buitrago, Ann Mari. 1988. *Report on CISPES Files Maintained by FBI Headquarters and Released under the Freedom of Information Act.* New York: Fund for Open Information and Accountability, Inc.

Bulmer, Martin. 1984. *The Chicago School of Sociology: Institutionalization, Diversity, and the Rise of Sociological Research.* Chicago: University of Chicago Press.

Bureau of Justice Statistics. 1984. *Bank Robbery.* Report NCJ–94463. Washington, D.C.: U.S. Department of Justice.

_____. 1985. *The Crime of Rape.* Report NCJ–96777. Washington, D.C.: U.S. Department of Justice.

_____. 1986a. *Jail Inmates, 1986.* Report NCJ–107123. Washington, D.C.: U.S. Department of Justice.

_____. 1986b. *State and Federal Prisoners, 1925—1985.* Report NCJ–102494. Washington, D.C.: U.S. Department of Justice.

_____. 1987a. *Violent Crime Trends.* Report NCJ–107217. Washington, D.C.: U.S. Department of Justice.

_____. 1987b. *Imprisonment in Four Countries.* Report NCJ–103967. Washington, D.C.: U.S. Department of Justice.

_____. 1988a. *Prisoners in 1987.* Report NCJ–110331. Washington, D.C.: U.S. Department of Justice.

_____. 1988b. *Proceedings of the Third Workshop on Law and Justice Statistics.* Report NCJ–112230. Washington, D.C.: U.S. Department of Justice.

_____. 1988c. *Criminal Victimization 1987.* Report NCJ–113587. Washington, D.C.: U.S. Department of Justice.

_____. 1988d. *Lifetime Likelihood of Victimization.* Report NCJ–104274. Washington, D.C.: U.S. Department of Justice.

_____. 1988e. *Households Touched by Crime, 1987.* Report NCJ–111240. Washington, D.C.: U.S. Department of Justice.

_____. 1989a. *New Directions for the National Crime Survey.* Report NCJ–115571. Washington, D.C.: U.S. Department of Justice.

_____. 1989b. *BJS Data Report, 1988.* Report NCJ–116262. Washington, D.C.: U.S. Department of Justice.

_____. 1993a. *Highlights from 20 Years of Surveying Crime Victims.* Report NCJ–144–525. Washington, D.C.: Department of Justice.

_____. 1993b. *Prisoners in 1992.* Report NCJ–141874. Washington, D.C.: U.S. Department of Justice.

_____. 1994. *Murder in Families.* Report NCJ–143498. Washington, D.C.: U.S. Department of Justice.

_____. 1997a. *Criminal Victimization, 1973–95.* Report NCJ–163069. Washington, D.C.: U.S. Department of Justice.

_____. 1997b. *Criminal Victimization 1996.* Report NCJ–165812. Washington, D.C.: U.S. Department of Justice.

_____. 1997c. *Criminal Victimization 1996: Changes 1995–1996, With Trends 1993–1996.* Washington, D.C.: U.S. Department of Justice.

_____. 1998. *Crime and Justice in the United States and in England and Wales, 1981–1996.* Report NCJ–173402. Washington, D.C.: U.S. Department of Justice.

Burgess, Ann W., and Linda L. Holmstrom. 1983. *The Victim of Rape.* New Brunswick, N.J.: Transaction Books.

Burgess, E. W. 1925. The Growth of the City: An Introduction to a Research Project. In *The City,* edited by Robert E. Park and E. W. Burgess, 47–62. Chicago: University of Chicago Press.

Burgess, Robert L., and Ronald L. Akers. 1966. A Differential Association-Reinforcement Theory of Criminal Behavior. *Social Problems* 14 (2): 128–147.

Burgoon, Brian. 1996. Job-Destroying Villain: Is It NAFTA or the Mexican Currency Crisis? In *Real World International*, edited by Marc Breslow, David Levy, and Abby Scher, 14–18. Somerville, Mass.: Dollars and Sense.

Bursik, Robert J. 1984. Urban Dynamics and Ecological Studies of Delinquency. *Social Forces* 63 (2): 393–413.

Bursik, Robert J., and Harold G. Grasmick. 1993. Economic Deprivation and Neighborhood Crime Rates, 1960–1980. *Law and Society Review* 27 (2): 263–283.

Burstyn, Varda. 1983. Masculine Dominance and the State. In *The Socialist Register,* edited by Ralph Miliband and John Saville, 45–89. London: Merlin Press.

Burton, Velmer S., Francis T. Cullen, T. David Evans, Leanne Fiftal Alarid, and R. Gregory Dunaway. 1998. Gender, Self-Control, and Crime. *Journal of Research in Crime and Delinquency* 35 (2): 123–147.

Butterfield, Fox. 1996. Survey Finds That Crimes Cost $450 Billion a Year. *New York Times,* A8.

———. 1999. Indians Are Crime Victims at Rate Above U.S. Average. *New York Times,* February 15, A12

Bynum, Timothy. 1987. Controversies in the Study of Organized Crime. In *Organized Crime in America: Concepts and Controversies,* edited by Timothy Bynum, 3–11. Monsey, N.Y.: Willow Tree Press.

Byrne, James M., and Robert J. Sampson, eds. 1986. *The Social Ecology of Crime.* New York: Springer-Verlag.

Cahill, Tom A. 1985. Rape Behind Bars. *The Progressive* 49 (11): 12–19.

Cain, Maureen, and Alan Hunt. 1979. *Marx and Engels on Law.* London: Academic Press.

Calavita, Kitty, Henry N. Pontell, and Robert H. Tillman. 1997. *Big Money Crime: Fraud and Politics in the Savings and Loan Crisis.* Berkeley: University of California Press.

Calonius, Erik, with Tom Morganthau. 1987. The Secret Warriors Tell Their Story. *Newsweek,* February 9, 26–28.

Cameron, Mary Owen. 1964. *The Booster and the Snitch.* New York: Free Press.

Camic, Charles, and Yu Xie. 1994. The Statistical Turn in American Social Science: Columbia University, 1890 to 1915. *American Sociological Review* 59 (5): 773–805.

Caminer, Brian F. 1985. Credit Card Fraud: The Neglected Crime. *Journal of Criminal Law and Criminology* 76 (Fall): 746–763.

Campbell, Anne. 1991. *The Girls in the Gang: A Report from New York City.* London: Basil Blackwell.

Carlen, Pat. 1988. *Women, Crime, and Poverty.* Philadelphia: Open University Press.

Carlen, Pat, and Tony Jefferson, eds. 1996. *Masculinities and Crime.* Special Issue of the *British Journal of Criminology* 33 (6).

Carroll, Leo, and Pamela Irving Jackson. 1983. Inequality, Opportunity, and Crime Rates in Central Cites. *Criminology* 21 (2): 170–194.

Carson, W. G. 1979. The Conventionalization of Early Factory Crime. *International Journal of the Sociology of Law* 7 (1): 37–60.

Castleman, Barry. 1979. The Export of Hazardous Factories to Developing Nations. *International Journal of Health Services* 9 (4): 569–606.

Castro, Janice. 1988. The Cash Cleaners. *Time,* October 24, 65–66.

Caulfield, Susan L., and Angela R. Evans. 1997. Peacemaking Criminology: A Path to Understanding and a Model for Methodology. In *Thinking Critically About Crime*, edited by Brian D. MacLean and Dragan Milovanovic, 102–108. Vancouver, B.C.: Collective Press.

Cavan, Ruth Shonle, and Jordan Ture Cavan. 1968. *Delinquency and Crime: Cross-Cultural Perspectives.* Philadelphia: J. J. Lippincott.

Cavender, Gray. 1998. In "The Shadow of Shadows": Television Reality Crime Programming. In *Entertaining Crime: Television Reality Programs,* edited by Mark Fishman and Gray Cavender, 79–94. New York: Aldine de Gruyter.

Cavender, Gray, and Lisa Bond-Maupin. 1993. Fear and Loathing on Reality Television: An Analysis of *America's Most Wanted* and *Unsolved Mysteries. Sociological Inquiry* 63 (3): 305–317.

Center for Constitutional Rights. 1988. Political Spying and the Central America Movement. *Movement Support Network News* 4: 13.

Cernkovich, Stephen A. 1978. Evaluating Two Models of Delinquency Causation. *Criminology* 16 (3): 335–352.

Cernkovich, Stephen A., and Peggy C. Giordano. 1987. Family Relationships and Delinquency. *Sociological Quarterly* 20 (2): 131–145.

Chambliss, William J. 1964. A Sociological Analysis of the Law of Vagrancy. *Social Problems* 12 (1): 67–77.

_____. 1975. Toward a Political Economy of Crime. *Theory and Society* 2 (Summer): 149–170.

_____. 1976. Functional and Conflict Theories of Crime. In *Whose Law? What Order? A Conflict Approach to Criminology,* edited by William J. Chambliss and Milton Mankoff, 1–28. New York: John Wiley.

_____. 1988a. *On the Take: From Petty Crooks to Presidents.* Bloomington: Indiana University Press.

_____. 1988b. *Exploring Criminology.* New York: Macmillan.

Chambliss, William J., and Robert B. Seidman. 1982. *Law, Order, and Power.* Reading, Mass.: Addison-Wesley.

Chancer, Lynn S. 1998. *Reconcilable Differences: Confronting Beauty, Pornography, and the Future of Feminism.* Berkeley: University of California Press.

Chapkis, Wendy. 1997. *Live Sex Acts: Women Performing Erotic Labor.* New York: Routledge.

Chermak, Steven. 1994. Body Count News: How Crime Is Presented in the News Media. *Justice Quarterly* 11 (4): 561–582.

Chesney-Lind, Meda. 1978. Chivalry Reexamined: Women and the Criminal Justice System. In *Women, Crime, and the Criminal Justice System,* edited by Lee Bowker, 335–366. Lexington, Mass.: Lexington Books.

_____. 1986. Women and Crime: The Female Offender. *Signs* 12 (1): 78–96.

_____. 1989. Girl's Crime and Woman's Place: Toward a Feminist Model of Female Delinquency. *Crime and Delinquency* 35 (1): 5–29.

_____. 1995. Girls, Delinquency, and Juvenile Justice: Toward a Feminist Theory of Young Women's Crime. In the *Criminal Justice System and Women,* edited by Barbara Raffel Price and Natalie J. Sokoloff, 71–88. New York: McGraw-Hill.

_____. 1997. *The Female Offender.* Thousand Oaks, Calif.: Sage.

Chesney-Lind, Meda, and Noelie Rodriguez. 1983. Women Under Lock and Key: A View Inside. *The Prison Journal* 63 (Summer/Autumn): 47–65.

Chevalier, Louis. 1973. *Laboring Classes and Dangerous Classes in Paris During the First Half of the Nineteenth Century.* Translated by Frank Jellinek. Princeton: Princeton University Press.

Chiricos, Ted, Sarah Eschholz, and Marc Gertz. 1997. Crime, News, and Fear of Crime: Toward an Identification of Audience Effects. *Social Problems* 44 (3): 342–357.

Chiricos, Theodore G., and Gordon P. Waldo. 1975. Socioeconomic Status and Criminal Sentencing. *American Sociological Review* 40 (6): 753–772.

Chomsky, Noam, and Edward S. Herman. 1977. The United States Versus Human Rights in the Third World. *Monthly Review* 29 (July–August): 22–45.

_____. 1979. *The Washington Connection and Third World Fascism.* Boston: South End Press.

Church Committee. 1975. Select Committee to Study Governmental Operations with Respect to Intelligence Activities. *Alleged Assassination Plots Involving Foreign Leaders.* Washington, D.C.: U.S. Government Printing Office.

_____. 1976. Select Committee to Study Governmental Operations with Respect to Intelligence Activities. *Intelligence Activities and the Rights of Americans.* Washington, D.C.: U.S. Government Printing Office.

Churchill, Ward, and Jim Vander Wall. 1988. *Agents of Repression.* Boston: South End Press.

Cicourel, Aaron V. 1968. *The Social Organization of Juvenile Justice.* New York: John Wiley.

Clark, Terry N. 1969. *Gabriel Tarde on Communication and Social Influence.* Chicago: University of Chicago Press.

Clarke, Oscar W., John Glasson, Alison M. August. John A. Barrasso, Charles H. Epps, Robert Mc-Quillan, Victoria N. Ruff, Charles W. Plows, George T. Wilkins, and David Orentticher. 1993. Mandatory Parental Consent to Abortion. *Journal of the American Medical Association* 269 (1): 81–86.

Clarke, Ronald V., and Patricia M. Harris. 1992. Auto Theft and Its Prevention. In *Crime and Justice: A Review of Research,* edited by Michael Tonry, 16: 1–54. Chicago: University of Chicago Press.

Claybrook, Joan. 1984. *Retreat from Safety.* New York: Pantheon.

_____. 1986. White-Collar Crime. *Trial,* April, 35–36.

Clinard, Marshall B. 1952. *The Black Market: A Study of White-Collar Crime.* New York: Rinehart.

_____. 1964. The Theoretical Implications of Anomie and Deviant Behavior. In *Anomie and Deviant Behavior,* edited by M. Clinard, 1–56. New York: Free Press.

_____. 1978a. Comparative Crime Victimization Surveys: Some Problems and Results. *International Journal of Criminology and Penology* 6 (3): 221–231.

_____. 1978b. *Cities with Little Crime: The Case of Switzerland.* Cambridge: Cambridge University Press.

Clinard, Marshall B., and Daniel J. Abbott. 1973. *Crime in Developing Countries: A Comparative Perspective.* New York: John Wiley.

Clinard, Marshall B., and Richard Quinney. 1973. *Criminal Behavior Systems.* New York: Holt, Rinehart and Winston.

Clinard, Marshall B., and Peter C. Yeager. 1980. *Corporate Crime.* New York: Free Press.

Cloward, Richard A., and Lloyd E. Ohlin. 1960. *Delinquency and Opportunity: A Theory of Delinquent Gangs.* New York: Free Press.

Cockburn, Leslie. 1987. *Out of Control.* New York: Atlantic Monthly Press.

Cohen, Albert K. 1955. *Delinquent Boys: The Culture of the Gang.* New York: Free Press.

_____. 1965. The Sociology of the Deviant Act: Anomie Theory and Beyond. *American Sociological Review* 30 (1): 5–14.

Cohen, Bernard. 1980. *Deviant Street Networks: Prostitution in New York.* Lexington, Mass.: Lexington Books.

Cohen, Gary. 1998. Bhopal and the New World Order. *Third World Network* <http://www.econet.apc.org/hotspots/bhopal/bhopal.html>.

Cohen, Lawrence E., and Marcus Felson. 1979. Social Change and Crime Rate Trends: A Routine Activity Approach. *American Sociological Review* 44 (4): 588–608.

Cohen, Lawrence E., and Richard Machalek. 1988. A General Theory of Expropriative Crime: An Evolutionary Ecological Approach. *American Journal of Sociology* 94 (3): 465–501.

Cohen, Stanley. [1972] 1980. *Folk Devils and Moral Panics: The Creation of the Mods and Rockers.* New York: St. Martins Press.

_____. 1982. Western Crime Control Models in the Third World. *Research in Law, Deviance, and Social Control* 4: 85–119.

_____. 1985. *Visions of Social Control.* Cambridge: Polity Press.

_____. 1986. Community Control: To Demystify or to Reaffirm? In *Abolitionism: Towards a Non-Repressive Approach to Crime,* edited by Herman Bianchi and Rene Van Swaaningen, 127–132. Amsterdam: Free University Press.

_____. 1988. The Object of Criminology: Reflections on the New Criminalization. In *Against Criminology,* 235–276. New Brunswick N.J.: Transaction.

_____. 1993. Human Rights and Crimes of the State: The Culture of Denial. *Australian and New Zealand Journal of Criminology* 26 (1): 87–115.

Cohen, Stanley, and Andrew Scull. 1983. Social Control in History and Sociology. In *Social Control and the State,* edited by Stanley Cohen and Andrew Scull, 1–14. Oxford: Martin Robertson.

Cole, Susan. 1987. Sexual Politics: Contradictions and Explosions. In *Good Girls/Bad Girls: Feminists and Sex Trade Workers Face to Face,* edited by Laurie Bell, 33–36. Seattle: Seal Press.

Coleman, James. 1994. *The Criminal Elite.* New York: St. Martins Press.

Collier, Richard. 1998. *Masculinities, Crime, and Criminology: Men, Heterosexuality, and the Criminal(ised) Other.* Thousand Oaks, Calif.: Sage

Collins, James J., Robert L. Hubbard, and J. Valley Rachal. 1985. Expensive Drug Use and Illegal Income: A Test of Explanatory Hypotheses. *Criminology* 23 (4): 743–764.

Comer, Michael J. 1985. *Corporate Fraud.* London: McGraw-Hill.

Commission on Obscenity and Pornography. 1970. *The Report of the Commission on Obscenity and Pornography.* Washington, D.C.: U.S. Government Printing Office.

Commission on the Review of the National Policy Toward Gambling. 1976. *Gambling in America, Final Report.* Washington, D.C.: U.S. Government Printing Office.

Congressional Quarterly. 1988. Record Number of Women, Blacks in Congress. November 12, 329–395.

Conklin, John. 1972. *Robbery and the Criminal Justice System.* New York: Lippincott.

_____. 1977. *Illegal but Not Criminal.* Englewood Cliffs, N.J.: Prentice-Hall.

Conway, Lucian G., and Joe A. Cox. 1987. Internal Business Shrinkage. *Baylor Business Review* (Summer): 8–11.

Cook, Elizabeth Adell, Ted G. Jelen, and Clyde Wilcox. 1992. *Between Two Absolutes: Public Opinion and the Politics of Abortion.* Boulder, Colo.: Westview Press.

Cook, Kimberly. 1998. *Divided Passions: Public Opinions on Abortion and the Death Penalty.* Boston: Northeastern University Press.

Cook, Philip J., and Gary A. Zarkin. 1985. Crime and the Business Cycle. *Journal of Legal Studies* 14 (1): 115–128.

Cooley, Charles H. 1930. *Sociological Theory and Social Research.* New York: Henry Holt.

Corn, David. 1988. Bush's CIA: The Same Old Dirty Tricks. *The Nation,* August 27–September 3, 157–160.

Cornish, Derek B., and Ronald V. Clarke. 1986. *The Reasoning Criminal: Rational Choice Perspectives on Offending.* New York: Springer-Verlag.

Costello, Barbara. 1997. On the Logical Adequacy of Cultural Deviance Theories. *Theoretical Criminology* 1 (4): 403–428.

Crawford, Susan. 1993. A Wink Here, a Leer There: It's Costly. *New York Times,* March 28, 17.

Cressey, Donald. 1969. *Theft of the Nation.* New York: Harper and Row.

_____. 1971. *Other People's Money.* New York: Free Press.

Crites, Laura, ed. 1976. *The Female Offender.* Lexington, Mass.: Lexington Books.

Cromwell, Paul F., ed. 1996. *In Their Own Words: Criminals on Crime.* Los Angeles, Calif.: Roxbury.

Cromwell, Paul F., James N. Olson, and D'Aunn Wester Avary. 1991. *Breaking and Entering: An Ethnographic Analysis of Burglary.* Newbury Park, Calif.: Sage.

Cromwell, Paul F., Roger Dunham, Ronald Akers, and Lonn Llanza-Kaduce. 1995. Routine Activities and Social Control in the Aftermath of a Natural Catastrophe. *European Journal on Criminal Policy and Research* 3: 56–69.

Cullen, Francis, John Wozniak, and James Frank. 1985. The Rise of the Elderly Offender: Will a New Criminal Be Invented? *Crime and Social Justice* 23: 151–165.

Cullen, Francis, William J. Maakestad, and Gray Cavender. 1987. *Corporate Crime Under Attack.* Cincinnati: Anderson.

Cullen, Francis T., and Robert Agnew, eds. 1999. *Criminological Theory, Past to Present: Essential Readings.* Los Angeles: Roxbury Publishing.

Curran, Debra. 1984. Characteristics of the Elderly Shoplifter and the Effect of Sanctions on Recidivism. In *Elderly Criminals,* edited by William Wilbanks and Paul Kim, 123–137. New York: University Press of America.

Current Population Reports. 1988. *Projections of the Population of the U.S. by Age, Sex, and Race: 1983 to 2080.* Washington, D.C.: U.S. Government Printing Office.

Current Population Reports. 1997. *The Black Population in the United States.* Washington, D.C.: Census Bureau.

Currie, Elliott. 1985. *Confronting Crime: An American Challenge.* New York: Pantheon.

_____. 1993. *Reckoning: Drugs, the Cities, and the American Future.* New York: Hill and Wang.

_____. 1997. Market, Crime, and Community. *Theoretical Criminology* 1 (2): 147–172.

_____. 1998. *Crime and Punishment in America.* New York: Metropolitan.

Daly. Kathleen. 1989. Gender and Varieties of White-Collar Crime. *Criminology* 27 (4): 769–793.

Daly, Kathleen, and Meda Chesney-Lind. 1988. Feminism and Criminology. *Justice Quarterly* 5 (4): 101–143.

Daly, Kathleen, and Lisa Maher, eds. 1998. *Criminology at the Crossroads: Feminist Readings in Crime and Justice.* New York: Oxford University Press.

Daly, Martin, and Margo Wilson. 1988. *Homicide.* Hawthorne, N.Y.: Aldine de Gruyter.

Davis, Nanette J. 1980. *Sociological Constructions of Deviance.* Dubuque, Iowa: Wm. C. Brown.

_____. 1988. Battered Women: Implications for Social Control. *Contemporary Crises* 12 (4): 345–372.

DeFronzo, James. 1983. Economic Assistance to Impoverished Americans. *Criminology* 21 (1): 119–136.

De Haan, Willem. 1990. *The Politics of Redress: Crime, Punishment, and Penal Abolition.* Boston: Unwin Hyman.

DeKeseredy, Walter, and Katheryn Kelly. 1993. The Incidence and Prevalence of Woman Abuse in Canadian University and College Dating Relationships. *Canadian Journal of Sociology* 18 (2): 137–159.

DeKeseredy, Walter S., and Ronald Hinch. 1991. *Woman Abuse: Sociological Perspectives.* Lewiston, N.Y.: Thompson Educational Publishers.

DeKeseredy, Walter S., and Martin D. Schwartz. 1991. British and U.S. Realism: A Critical Comparison. *International Journal of Offender Therapy and Comparative Criminology* 35 (3): 248–262.

Department of Justice. 1988. *United States Secret Service Investigative Activity.* Washington, D.C.: Treasury Department.

_____. 1999. *Criminal Victimization in the United States.* Washington, D.C.: U.S. Government Printing Office.

Department of Labor. 1988. *Labor Force Statistics Derived from the Current Population Survey, 1948–1987.* Washington, D.C.: U.S. Government Printing Office.

_____. 1998. *News.* Washington, D.C.: Bureau of Labor Statistics.

Diamond, Stanley. 1973. The Rule of Law Versus the Order of Custom. In *The Social Organization of Law,* edited by Donald Black and Maureen Mileski, 318–334. New York: Seminar Press.

Ditton, Jason. 1977a. *Part-Time Crime.* New York: Macmillan.

_____. 1977b. Perks, Pilferage, and the Fiddle: The Historical Structure of Invisible Wages. *Theory and Society* 4 (1): 39–71.

_____. 1979. *Contrology.* London: Macmillan.

Dixon, Keith. 1977. Is Cultural Relativism Self-Refuting? *British Journal of Sociology* 28 (1): 75–88.

Dobash, R. Emerson, and Russell P. Dobash. 1979. *Violence Against Wives.* New York: Free Press.

Dobash, Russell P., R. Emerson Dobash, Margo Wilson, and Martin Daly. 1992. The Myth of Sexual Symmetry in Marital Violence. *Social Problems* 39 (1): 71–91.

Donnerstein, Edward, and Daniel B. Linz. 1986. The Question of Pornography. *Psychology Today,* December, 56–59.

Donovan, Josephine. 1985. *Feminist Theory.* New York: Ungar.

Douglas, Jack D. 1977. Watergate: Harbinger of the American Prince. In *Official Deviance,* edited by Jack D. Douglas and John M. Johnson, 112–120. New York: Lippincott.

Douglas, Jack D., and Paul K. Rasmussen, with Carol Ann Flanagan. 1977. *The Nude Beach.* Beverly Hills: Sage.

Dowie, Mark. 1977. Pinto Madness. *Mother Jones* 2 (7): 18–19, 32.

_____. 1979. The Corporate Crime of the Century. *Mother Jones* 4 (9): 23–25, 37.

_____. 1987. The Dumping of Hazardous Products on Foreign Markets. In *Corporate Violence,* edited by Stuart Hills, 47–58. Totowa, N.J.: Rowman and Littlefield.

Dubowitz, Howard, Maureen Black, Raymond H. Starr Jr., and Susan Zuravin. 1993. A Conceptual Definition of Child Neglect. *Criminal Justice and Behavior* 20 (1): 8–26.

Duesterberg, Thomas J. 1979. Criminology and the Social Order in Nineteenth-Century France. Ph.D. diss., Indiana University.

Duggan, Lisa, Nan Hunter, and Carol S. Vance. 1985. False Promises: Feminist Anti-Pornography Legislation in the U.S. In *Women Against Censorship,* edited by Varda Burstyn, 130–151. Toronto: Douglas and McIntyre.

Dumm, Thomas L. 1987. *Democracy and Punishment: Disciplinary Origins of the United States.* Madison: University of Wisconsin Press.

Durkheim, Émile. 1948. *The Elementary Forms of Religious Life.* 1912. Translated by Joseph W. Swain. Glencoe, Ill.: Free Press.

_____. 1951. *Suicide: A Study in Sociology.* 1897. Translated by J. A. Spaulding and G. Simpson. New York: Free Press.

_____. 1958. *Professional Ethics and Civil Morals.* 1900. Translated by Cornelia Brookfield. Glencoe, Ill.: Free Press.

_____. 1982. *The Rules of Sociological Method.* 1894. Translated by W. D. Halls. London: Macmillan.

_____. [1901] 1983. Two Laws of Penal Evolution. In *Durkheim and the Law,* edited by Steven Lukes and Andrew Scull, 102–132. Translated by T. Anthony Jones and Andrew Scull. New York: St. Martin's Press.

_____. 1984. *The Division of Labor in Society.* 1893. Translated by W. D. Halls. New York: Free Press.

Duster, Troy. 1987. Crime, Youth Unemployment, and the Black Underclass. *Crime and Delinquency* 33 (2): 300–316.

Dwyer, Lynn E. 1983. Structure and Strategy in the Antinuclear Movement. In *Social Movements of the Sixties and Seventies,* edited by Jo Freeman, 148–161. New York: Longman.

Dye, Nancy Schrom. 1980. History of Childbirth in America. *Signs* 6 (1): 97–108.

Eaton, Mary. 1986. *Justice for Women? Family, Court, and Social Control.* Philadelphia: Open University Press.

Ehrenreich, Barbara. 1988. Drug Frenzy. *Ms.* 17 (5):20–21.

Ehrenreich, Barbara, and Deirdre English. 1973. *Witches, Midwives, and Nurses: A History of Women Healers.* Old Westbury, N.Y.: Feminist Press.

Einstadter, Werner, and Stuart Henry. 1995. *Criminological Theory.* Fort Worth: Harcourt Brace.

Eisenstein, Zillah R. 1988. *The Female Body and the Law.* Berkeley: University of California Press.

Elliott, Delbert S., and Suzanne S. Ageton. 1980. Reconciling Race and Class Differences in Self-Reported and Official Estimates of Delinquency. *American Sociological Review* 45 (1): 95–110.

Elliott, Delbert S., and David Huizinga. 1983. Social Class and Delinquent Behavior in a National Youth Panel: 1976–1980. *Criminology* 21 (2): 149–177.

Elliott, Delbert S., David Huizinga, and Suzanne S. Ageton. 1989. *Multiple Problem Youth: Delinquency, Substance Abuse, and Mental Health Problems.* New York: Springer-Verlag.

Emerson, Steven. 1988. *Secret Warriors: Inside the Covert Military Operations of the Reagan Era.* New York: G. P. Putnam.

Engels, Friedrich. [1884] 1970a. *The Origin of the Family, Private Property, and the State.* In *Karl Marx and Frederick Engels: Selected Works,* 3: 191–334. Moscow: Progress Publishers.

_____. [1886] 1970b. Ludwig Feuerbach and the End of Classical German Philosophy. In *Karl Marx and Frederick Engels: Selected Works,* 3: 337–376. Moscow: Progress Publishers.

_____. [1888] 1970c. The Role of Force in History. In *Karl Marx and Frederick Engels: Selected Works,* 3: 377–428. Moscow: Progress Publishers.

_____. [1893] 1970d. Letter to F. Mehring in Berlin. In *Karl Marx and Frederick Engels: Selected Works,* 3: 495–499. Moscow: Progress Publishers.

_____. [1843] 1975a. Outlines of a Critique of Political Economy. In *Karl Marx/Frederick Engels: Collected Works,* 3: 419–443. New York: International Publishers.

_____. [1845] 1975b. *The Condition of the Working Class in England.* In *Karl Marx/Frederick Engels: Collected Works,* 4: 295–583. New York: International Publishers.

_____. [1885] 1975c. *Anti-Dühring.* London: Lawrence and Wishart.

Epstein, Samuel. 1978. *The Politics of Cancer.* San Francisco: Sierra Club Books.

Ericson, Richard V., Patricia M. Baranek, and Janet B. L. Chan. 1980. *Visualizing Deviance.* Toronto, Ontario: University of Toronto Press.

_____. 1989. *Negotiating Control: A Study of News Sources.* Toronto, Ontario: University of Toronto Press.

_____. 1991. *Representing Order: Crime, Law, and Justice in the News Media.* Toronto, Ontario: University of Toronto Press.

Erikson, Kai T. 1966. *Wayward Puritans: A Study in the Sociology of Deviance.* New York: John Wiley.

Evans, Ernest. 1983. The Use of Terrorism by American Social Movements. In *Social Movements of the Sixties and Seventies,* edited by Jo Freeman, 252–261. New York: Longman.

Fagan, Jeffrey. 1994. Women and Drugs Revisited: Female Participation in the Cocaine Economy. *Journal of Drug Issues* 24 (2): 179–225.

Faris, Robert E. L. [1967] 1970. *Chicago Sociology, 1920–1932.* Chicago: University of Chicago Press.

Farley, Lin. 1978. *Sexual Shakedown.* New York: Warner Books.

Farley, Reynolds. 1980. Homicide Trends in the United States. *Demography* 17 (2): 177–188.

Farnworth, Margaret, Terence P. Thornberry, Marvin D. Krohn, and Alan J. Lizotte. 1994. Measurement in the Study of Class and Delinquency: Integrating Theory and Research. *Journal of Research in Crime and Delinquency* 31 (1): 32–61.

Farrell, Kathleen L., and John A. Ferrara. 1985. *Shoplifting.* New York: Praeger.

Farrington, David P. 1989. Self-reported and Official Offending from Adolescence to Adulthood. In *Cross-National Research in Self-reported Crime and Delinquency,* edited by Malcolm W. Klein. Dordrecht: Kluwer-Nijhoff.

Federal Bureau of Investigation. 1992. *Uniform Crime Reporting Handbook: NIBRS Edition.* Washington, D.C.: U.S. Government Printing Office.

_____. 1997. *Terrorism in the United States.* Washington, D.C.: Federal Bureau of Investigation.

_____. 1998. *Uniform Crime Reports, 1997.* Washington, D.C.: U.S. Government Printing Office.

Feeney, Floyd. 1986. Robbers as Decision-Makers. In *The Reasoning Criminal: Rational Choice Perspectives on Offending*, edited by Derek Cornish and Ronald Clarke, 53–71. New York: Springer-Verlag.

Feinberg, Gary. 1984. A Profile of the Elderly Shoplifter. In *Elderly Criminals,* edited by Evelyn Newman, Donald Newman, and Mindy Gewirtz, 35–50. Cambridge: Oelgeschlager, Gunn, and Hain.

Felson, Marcus. 1994. *Crime and Everyday Life.* Thousand Oaks, Calif.: Pine Forge Press.

_____. 1997. A "Routine Activity" Analysis of Recent Crime Reductions. *The Criminologist* 22 (6): 1–3.

_____. 1998. *Crime and Everyday Life.* 2d ed. Thousand Oaks, Calif.: Pine Forge Press.

Felson, Marcus, and Ronald V. Clarke. 1997. *Business and Crime Prevention.* Monsey, N.Y.: Willow Tree Press.

Felson, Richard, and Henry J. Steadman. 1983. Situational Factors in Disputes Leading to Criminal Violence. *Criminology* 21 (1): 59–74.

Felson, Richard B., and Steven Messner. 1998. Disentangling the Effects of Gender and Intimacy on Victim Precipitation in Homicide. *Criminology* 36 (2): 405–423.

Ferracuti, Franco, and Marvin E. Wolfgang, eds. 1983. *Criminological Diagnosis: An International Perspective.* 2 vols. Lexington, Mass.: Lexington Books.

Ferrell, Jeff. 1993. *Crimes of Style: Urban Graffiti and the Politics of Criminality.* Boston: Northeastern University Press.

———. 1997. Against the Law: Anarchist Criminology. In *Thinking Critically About Crime*, edited by Brian D. MacLean and Dragan Milovanovic, 146–154. Vancouver, B.C.: Collective Press.

Ferrell, Jeff, and Clinton R. Sanders, eds. 1995. *Cultural Criminology.* Boston: Northeastern University Press.

Ferrell, Jeff, and Mark S. Hamm, eds. 1998. *Ethnography at the Edge: Crime, Deviance, and Field Research.* Boston: Northeastern University Press.

Ferri, Enrico. [1884] 1917. *Criminal Sociology.* Translated by J. I. Kelly and J. Lisle. Boston: Little, Brown.

Feyerabend, Paul. 1987. *Farewell to Reason.* London: Verso.

Figueira-McDonough, Josephina, with Elaine Selo. 1980. A Reformulation of the Equal Opportunity Explanation of Female Delinquency. *Crime and Delinquency* 26 (3): 333–343.

Fink, Arthur E. 1938. *Causes of Crime: Biological Theories in the United States, 1800–1915.* Philadelphia: University of Pennsylvania Press.

Finkelhor, David, and Kersti Yllö. 1985. *License to Rape: Sexual Abuse of Wives.* New York: Holt, Rinehart and Winston.

Fisher, Joseph C. 1976. Homicide in Detroit: The Role of Firearms. *Criminology* 14 (November): 387–400.

Fishman, Mark. 1978. Crime Waves as Ideology. *Social Problems* 25 (5): 535–543.

Flanagan, William G., and Brigid McMenamin. 1992. Why Cybercrooks Love Cellular. *Forbes,* December 21, 189.

Fogarty, Michael, ed. 1984. *Irish Values and Attitudes: Report of the European Value Systems Survey.* Dublin: Dominican Publications.

Foucault, Michel. 1979. *Discipline and Punish: The Birth of the Prison.* Translated by Alan Sheridan. New York: Vintage Books.

———. 1980. *Power/Knowledge: Selected Interviews and Other Writings, 1972–1977.* Translated by Colin Gordon et al. New York: Pantheon.

Fox, James Alan, and Jack Levin. 1994. Firing Back: The Growing Threat of Workplace Homicide. *Annals, AAPSS* 536 (November): 16–30.

Frank, Nancy K. 1985. *Crimes Against Worker Health and Safety.* San Francisco: Sierra Club Books.

Frank, Nancy K., and Michael J. Lynch. 1992. *Corporate Crime, Corporate Violence.* Albany, N.Y.: Harrow and Heston.

Frappier, John. 1984. Above the Law: Violations of International Law by the U.S. Government from Truman to Reagan. *Crime and Social Justice* 21/22: 1–36.

Friedman, Robert I. 1984. Senator Paul Laxalt: The Man Who Runs the Reagan Campaign. *Mother Jones* 9 (7): 32–39.

Friedrichs, David O. 1996. *Trusted Criminals: White-Collar Crime in Contemporary America.* Belmont, Calif.: Wadsworth.

Fuller, Lon L. 1949. The Case of the Speluncean Explorers. *Harvard Law Review* 62 (4): 616–645.

Galliher, John F. 1980. The Study of the Social Origins of Criminal Law: An Inventory of Research Findings. *Research in Law and Sociology* 3: 301–319.

Galliher, John F., and John R. Cross. 1983. *Morals Legislation Without Morality: The Case of Nevada.* New Brunswick, N.J.: Rutgers University Press.

Gallup, George Jr. 1997. *The Gallup Poll: Public Opinion 1996.* Wilmington, Del.: Scholarly Resources.

Galton, Francis. 1869. *Hereditary Genius.* London: Macmillan.

———. 1889. *Natural Inheritance.* London: Macmillan.

Gardiner, John. 1970. *The Politics of Corruption: Organized Crime in an American City.* New York: Russell Sage.

Garitty, Michael. 1980. The U.S. Colonial Empire Is As Close As the Nearest Reservation. In *Trilateralism: The Trilateral Commission and Elite Planning for World Management,* edited by Holly Sklar, 238–688. Boston: South End Press.

Garland, David. 1983. Durkheim's Theory of Punishment: A Critique. In *The Power to Punish,* edited by David Garland and Peter Young, 37–61. London: Heinemann Educational Books.

_____. 1985. *Punishment and Welfare: A History of Penal Strategies.* Aldershot, U.K.: Gower.

_____. 1990. *Punishment and Modern Society.* Chicago: University of Chicago Press.

_____. 1997. "Governmentality" and the Problem of Crime: Foucault, Criminology, Sociology. *Theoretical Criminology* 1 (2): 173–214.

_____. 1999. The Commonplace and the Catastrophic. *Theoretical Criminology* 3 (3): 353–364.

Garofalo, Raffaele. 1885. *Criminologia.* Turin: Bocca.

Garrow. David. 1981. *The FBI and Martin Luther King Jr.* New York: Penguin.

Garry, Eileen M. 1997. *Juvenile Firesetting and Arson.* Washington, D.C.: Office of Juvenile Justice and Delinquency Prevention.

Gaylord, Mark S., and John F. Galliher. 1988. *The Criminology of Edwin Sutherland.* New Brunswick, N.J.: Transaction Books.

Geis, Gilbert. 1979. *Not the Law's Business: An Examination of Homosexuality, Abortion, Prostitution, Narcotics, and Gambling in the United States.* New York: Schocken Books.

Geis, Gilbert, and Colin Goff. 1983. Introduction to *White Collar Crime: The Uncut Version,* by Edwin H. Sutherland, ix–xxxiii. New Haven: Yale University Press.

Geis, Gilbert, Paul D. Jesilow, Henry N. Pontell, and Mary Jane O'Brien. 1985. Fraud and Abuse by Psychiatrists Against Government Medical Benefit Programs. *American Journal of Psychiatry* 142 (February): 231–234.

Geis, Gilbert, Henry N. Pontell, and Paul D. Jesilow. 1988. Medicaid Fraud. In *Controversial Issues in Crime and Justice,* edited by Joseph Scott and Travis Hirschi, 17–39. Beverly Hills: Sage.

Gelles, Richard J. 1977. Power, Sex, and Violence: The Case of Marital Rape. *The Family Coordinator* 26 (4): 339–347.

_____. 1998. The Youngest Victims: Violence Toward Children. In *Issues in Intimate Violence,* edited by Raquel Kennedy Bergen, 5–24. Thousand Oaks, Calif.: Sage.

Gelsthorpe, Loraine, and Allison Morris. 1988. Feminism and Criminology in Britain. *British Journal of Criminology* 28 (2): 93–110.

General Accounting Office. 1988. *Controlling Drug Abuse: A Status Report.* Washington, D.C.: GAO/GGD.

Gibbons, Don C. 1994. *Thinking About Crime and Criminals.* Englewood Cliffs, N.J.: Prentice-Hall.

Gibbs, John J., and Dennis Giever. 1995. Self-Control and Its Manifestations Among University Students. *Justice Quarterly* 12 (2): 231–255.

Gibbs, John J., Dennis Giever, and Jamie S. Martin. 1998. Parental Management and Self-Control: An Empirical Test of Gottfredson and Hirschi's General Theory. *Journal of Research in Crime and Delinquency* 35 (1): 40–70.

Giordano, Peggy C., and Stephen A. Cernkovich. 1979. On Complicating the Relationship Between Liberation and Delinquency. *Social Problems* 26 (4): 467–481.

Glaser, Daniel. 1956. Criminality Theories and Behavioral Images. *American Journal of Sociology* 61 (4): 433–444.

_____. 1960. Differential Association and Criminological Prediction. *Social Problems* 8 (1): 6–14.

Glen, Kristin B. 1986. Understanding the Abortion Debate: A Legal, Constitutional, and Political Framework. *Socialist Review* 16 (5): 51–69.

Goetting, Ann. 1983. The Elderly in Prison: Issues and Perspectives. *Journal of Research in Crime and Delinquency* 20 (3): 291–309.

Goffman, Erving. 1961. *Asylums.* New York: Anchor Books.

_____. 1963. *Stigma.* Englewood Cliffs, N.J.: Prentice-Hall.

_____. 1967. *Interaction Ritual: Essays on Face-to-Face Behavior.* Garden City, N.Y.: Doubleday.

Goldstein, Leslie Friedman. 1988. *The Constitutional Rights of Women.* Madison: University of Wisconsin Press.

Good, David H., and Maureen A. Pirog-Good. 1987. A Simultaneous Probit Model of Crime and Employment for Black and White Teenage Males. *The Review of Black Political Economy* 16 (12): 109–127.

Goode, Erich. 1984. *Drugs in American Society.* New York: Alfred A. Knopf.

Goodman, Ellen. 1993. Sex, Power, and the Establishment. *Boston Globe,* April 29, 15.

Gordon, Linda. 1976. *Woman's Body, Woman's Right: A Social History of Birth Control in America.* New York: Grossman.

_____. 1981. The Long Struggle for Reproductive Rights. *Radical America* 15 (1/2): 75–88.

Gordon, Michael R. 1993. Pentagon Report Tells of Aviators' Debauchery. *New York Times,* April 24, 1, 9.

Goring, Charles. 1913. *The English Convict: A Statistical Study.* London: M.M.S.O.

Gottfredson, Michael R., and Travis Hirschi. 1990. *A General Theory of Crime.* Stanford, Calif.: Stanford University Press.

Graber, Doris A. 1980. *Crime News and the Public.* New York: Praeger.

Graham, James M. 1975. Amphetamine Politics on Capitol Hill. In *Whose Law? What Order? A Conflict Approach to Criminology,* edited by William J. Chambliss and Milton Mankoff, 107–122. New York: John Wiley.

Gramsci, Antonio. [1926] 1978. Some Aspects of the Southern Question. In *Gramsci: Selections from Political Writings,* translated by Quintin Hoare, 44–162. New York: International Publishers.

Grauerholz, Elizabeth, and Amy King. 1997. Prime Time Sexual Harassment. *Violence Against Women* 3 (2): 129–148.

Gravley, Eric. 1988. Building the Case Against America's Narcotic Jihad. *In These Times,* December 14–20, 3, 10.

Greek, Cecil, and Deborah B. Henry. 1997. Criminal Justice Resources on the Internet. *Journal of Criminal Justice Education* 8 (1): 91–99.

Green, Gary S. 1987. Citizen Gun Ownership and Criminal Deterrence: Theory, Research, and Policy. *Criminology* 25 (2): 63–81.

Green, Mark, Beverly C. Moore, and Bruce Wasserstein. 1972. *The Closed Enterprise System.* New York: Bantam Books.

Green, Mark, and John Francis Berry. 1985a. *The Challenge of Hidden Profits.* New York: William Morrow.

_____. 1985b. White-Collar Crime Is Big Business: Corporate Crime 1. *The Nation,* June 8, 705–706.

Greenberg, David F. 1977. Delinquency and the Age Structure of Society. *Contemporary Crises* 1 (2): 189–224.

_____. 1983. Crime and Age. In *Encyclopedia of Crime and Justice,* edited by Sanford Kadish, 1: 30–35. New York: Macmillan.

_____. 1985. Age, Crime, and Social Explanation. *American Journal of Sociology* 91 (1): 1–21.

_____. 1988. *The Construction of Homosexuality.* Chicago: University of Chicago Press.

Greenberg, David F., ed. 1993. *Crime and Capitalism: Readings in Marxist Criminology.* 2d ed. Palo Alto, Calif.: Mayfield.

Greenberg, David, Douglas Wolf, and Jennifer Pfiester. 1986. *Using Computers to Combat Welfare Fraud.* Westport, Conn.: Greenwood Press.

Greenberg, Jerald. 1990. Employee Theft as a Reaction to Underpayment Inequity: The Hidden Cost of Pay Cuts. *Journal of Applied Psychology* 75 (5): 561–568.

_____. 1993a. The Social Side of Fairness: Interpersonal and Informational Classes of Organizational Justice. In *Justice in the Workplace,* edited by Robert Cropanzano, 79–103. Hillsdale, N.J.: Lawrence Erlbaum.

_____. 1993b. Stealing in the Name of Justice: Informational and Interpersonal Moderators of Theft Reactions to Underpayment Inequity. *Organizational Behavior and Human Decision Processes* 54 (2): 81–103.

_____. 1997. The STEAL Motive: Managing the Social Determinants of Employee Theft. In *Antisocial Behavior in Organizations*, edited by Robert A. Giacalone and Jerald Greenberg, 85–108. Thousand Oaks, Calif.: Sage.

Gropper, Bernard A. 1985. Probing the Links Between Drugs and Crime. *National Institute of Justice: Research in Brief.* Washington, D.C.: U.S. Department of Justice.

Guarasci, Richard. 1987. Death by Cotton Dust. In *Corporate Violence,* edited by Stuart Hills, 76–92. Totowa, N.J.: Rowman and Littlefield.

Gurr, Ted Robert, Peter N. Grabosky, and Richard C. Hula. 1977. *The Politics of Crime and Conflict.* Beverly Hills: Sage.

Gusfield, Joseph R. 1963. *Symbolic Crusade.* Urbana: University of Illinois Press.

Gutek, Barbara A., and Mary P. Koss. 1997. Changed Women and Changed Organizations: Consequences of and Coping with Sexual Harassment. In *Gender Violence: Interdisciplinary Perspectives*, edited by Laura L. O'Toole and Jessica R. Schiffman, 151–164. New York: New York University Press.

Gutman, Roy. 1988. *Banana Diplomacy: The Making of American Foreign Policy in Nicaragua, 1981–1987.* New York: Simon and Schuster.

Guttmacher, Manfred Schanfarber. 1951. *Sex Offenses.* New York: W. W. Norton.

Hacker, Andrew. 1988. Black Crime, White Racism. *New York Review of Books* 35 (3): 36–41.

Hacking, Ian. 1990. *The Taming of Chance.* Cambridge University Press.

Hagan, Frank E. 1997. *Political Crime: Ideology and Criminality.* Boston: Allyn and Bacon.

Hagan, John. 1974. Extra-Legal Attributes and Criminal Sentencing: An Assessment of a Sociological Viewpoint. *Law and Society Review* 8 (3): 357–383.

_____. 1980. The Legislation of Crime and Delinquency: A Review of Theory, Method, and Research. *Law and Society Review* 14 (3): 603–628.

_____. 1989. *Structural Criminology.* New Brunswick, N.J.: Rutgers University Press.

_____. 1991. Destiny and Drift: Subcultural Preferences, Status Attainments, and the Risks and Rewards of Youth. *American Sociological Review* 56 (5): 567–582.

_____. 1994. *Crime and Disrepute.* Thousand Oaks, Calif.: Pine Forge Press.

Hagan, John, John H. Simpson, and A. R. Gillis. 1979. The Sexual Stratification of Social Control: A Gender-Based Perspective on Crime and Delinquency. *British Journal of Sociology* 30 (1): 25–38.

_____. 1987. Class in the Household: A Power-Control Theory of Gender and Delinquency. *American Journal of Sociology* 92 (4): 788–816.

Hagan, John, and Alberto Palloni. 1990. The Social Reproduction of a Criminal Class in Working-Class London, circa 1950–1980. *American Journal of Sociology* 96 (2): 265–299.

Hagan, John, and Ruth D. Peterson, eds. 1995. *Crime and Inequality.* Stanford, Calif.: Stanford University Press.

Hagan, John, and Bill McCarthy. 1997. *Mean Streets: Youth Crime and Homelessness.* New York: Cambridge University Press.

Hall, Jerome. 1952. *Theft, Law, and Society.* New York: Bobbs-Merrill.

_____. 1969. Theft, Law, and Society: The Carriers Case. In *Crime and the Legal Process,* edited by William J. Chambliss, 32–51. New York: McGraw-Hill.

Hall, Stuart, and Tony Jefferson, eds. 1976. *Resistance Through Rituals.* London: Macmillan.

Haller, Mark. 1976. Bootleggers and American Gambling, 1920–1950. In *Gambling in America, Commission on Review of National Policy Toward Gambling,* 102–143. Washington, D.C.: U.S. Government Printing Office.

Halpern, Sue. 1990. Teen-Abortion Laws Turn Trauma to Tragedy. *Rolling Stone,* August 9, 43–44, 72.

Hamilton, Lee H. 1993. Case Closed. *New York Times,* January 24, 17.

Hamlin, John E. 1988. The Misplaced Role of Rational Choice in Neutralization Theory. *Criminology* 26 (3): 425–438.

Hamm, Mark S. 1993. *American Skinheads: The Criminology and Control of Hate Crime.* Westport, Conn.: Praeger.

Haran, James F., and John M. Martin. 1977. The Imprisonment of Bank Robbers: The Issue of Deterrence. *Federal Probation* 41 (3): 29–36.

_____. 1984. The Armed Urban Bank Robber: A Profile. *Federal Probation* 48 (4): 47–53.

Harlow, Caroline Wolf. 1987. *Robbery Victims.* Washington, D.C.: U.S. Department of Justice.

Hart, Barbara. 1986. Lesbian Battering: An Examination. In *Naming the Violence: Speaking Out About Lesbian Violence,* edited by Kerry Lobel, 173–189. Seattle: Seal Press.

Hay, Douglas. 1975. Property, Authority, and the Criminal Law. In *Albion's Fatal Tree,* edited by Douglas Hay, Peter Linebaugh, John G. Rule, E. P. Thompson, and Cal Winslow, 17–63. New York: Pantheon.

Heidensohn, Frances. 1985. *Women and Crime: The Life of the Female Offender.* New York: New York University Press.

Heiner, Robert, ed. 1996. *Criminology: A Cross-Cultural Perspective.* Minneapolis/St. Paul: West Publishing.

Helmer, John. 1975. *Drugs and Minority Oppression.* New York: Seabury Press.

Henderson, Charles Richmond. 1893. *Introduction to the Study of the Dependent, Defective, and Delinquent Classes.* Boston: D.C. Heath.

Henry, Stuart. 1976. The Other Side of the Fence. *Sociological Review* 24 (November): 793–806.

_____. 1977. On the Fence. *British Journal of Law and Society* 4 (1): 124–133.

_____. 1978. *The Hidden Economy.* London: Martin Robertson.

_____. 1987. The Political Economy of Informal Economies. *Annals of the American Academy of Political and Social Science* 493 (September): 137–153.

Henry, Stuart, and Gerald Mars. 1978. Crime at Work: The Social Construction of Amateur Property Theft. *Sociology* 12 (2): 245–263.

Henry, Stuart, and Dragan Milovanovic. 1991. Constitutive Criminology: The Maturation of Critical Criminology. *Criminology* 29 (2): 293–315.

_____. 1994. The Constitution of Constitutive Criminology: A Postmodern Approach to Criminological Theory. In *The Futures of Criminology.* Edited by David Nelken. London: Sage.

_____. 1996. *Constitutive Criminology: Beyond Postmodernism.* London: Sage.

Henry, Stuart, and Werner Einstadter, eds. 1998. *The Criminology Theory Reader.* New York: New York University Press.

Herbert, David. 1982. *The Geography of Urban Crime.* London: Longman.

Herman, Edward. 1982. *The Real Terror Network.* Boston: South End Press.

Herman, Ellen. 1984. Introduction to *Not an Easy Choice,* by Kathleen McDonnell, i–xv. Boston: South End Press.

Herman, Judith, and Lisa Hirschman. 1977. Father-Daughter Incest. *Signs* 2 (4): 735–756.

Hess, Henner. 1973. *Mafia and Mafioso: The Structure of Power.* Lexington, Mass.: D.C. Heath.

Hills, Stuart, ed. 1987. *Corporate Violence.* Totowa, N.J.: Rowman and Littlefield.

Hills, Stuart L., and Ron Santiago. 1992. *Tragic Magic: The Life and Crimes of a Heroin Addict.* Chicago: Nelson-Hall.

Hinckle, Warren, and William Turner. 1981. *The Fish Is Red: The Story of the Secret War Against Castro.* New York: Harper and Row.

Hindelang, Michael J. 1970. The Commitment of Delinquents to Their Misdeeds: Do Delinquents Drift? *Social Problems* 17 (4): 502–509.

_____. 1973. Causes of Delinquency: A Partial Replication and Extension. *Social Problems* 20 (4): 471–487.

_____. 1974. Moral Evaluations of Illegal Behaviors. *Social Problems* 21 (3): 370–385.

_____. 1976. *Criminal Victimization in Eight American Cities: A Descriptive Analysis of Common Theft and Assault.* Cambridge: Ballinger.

_____. 1979. Sex Differences in Criminal Activity. *Social Problems* 27 (2): 143–156.

_____. 1981. Variations in Sex-Race-Age-Specific Incidence Rates of Offending. *American Sociological Review* 46 (4): 461–474.

Hindelang, Michael J., Michael R. Gottfredson, and James Garofalo. 1978. *Victims of Personal Crime: An Empirical Foundation for a Theory of Personal Victimization.* Cambridge: Ballinger.

Hindelang, Michael J., Travis Hirschi, and Joseph Weis. 1979. Correlates of Delinquency: The Illusion of Discrepancy Between Self-Report and Official Measures. *American Sociological Review* 44 (6): 995–1014.

Hindess, Barry. 1973. *The Use of Official Statistics in Sociology.* London: Macmillan.

Hirschi, Travis. 1969. *Causes of Delinquency.* Berkeley: University of California Press.

_____. 1983. Crime and the Family. In *Crime and Public Policy,* edited by James Q. Wilson, 53–68. San Francisco: Institute for Contemporary Studies.

Hirschi, Travis, and Michael J. Hindelang. 1977. Intelligence and Delinquency: A Revisionist Review. *American Sociological Review* 42 (4): 571–587.

Hirschi, Travis, and Michael Gottfredson. 1983. Age and the Explanation of Crime. *American Journal of Sociology* 89 (3): 552–584.

_____. 1993. Commentary: Testing the General Theory of Crime. *Journal of Research in Crime and Delinquency* 30 (1): 47–54.

Hite, Shere. 1976. *The Hite Report on Female Sexuality.* New York: Knopf.

Hobsbawn, Eric. 1959. *Primitive Rebels.* New York: W. W. Norton.

Hoffman, Abbie, and Jonathan Silvers. 1988. An Election Held Hostage. *Playboy* 35 (10): 73–74.

Hoffman-Bustamante, Dale. 1973. The Nature of Female Criminality. *Issues in Criminology* 8 (2): 117–132.

Hofstadter, Richard, and Michael Wallace. 1970. *Violence: A Documentary History.* New York: Knopf.

Hollinger, Richard C. 1986. Acts Against the Workplace: Social Bonding and Employee Deviance. *Deviant Behavior* 7 (1): 53–75.

Hollinger, Richard C., and John P. Clark. 1983. *Theft by Employees.* Lexington, Mass.: Lexington Books.

Holmes, Ronald M., and James E. DeBurger. 1985. Profiles in Terror: The Serial Murderer. *Federal Probation* 49 (3): 29–34.

_____. 1988. *Serial Murder.* Beverly Hills: Sage.

Holmstrom, Lynda L., and Ann Burgess. 1983. *The Victim of Rape.* New Brunswick, N.J.: Transaction Books.

Honegger, Barbara. 1989. *October Surprise.* New York: Tudor Publishing.

Hooton, Ernest Albert. 1939. *Crime and the Man.* Cambridge, Mass.: Harvard University Press.

Hopkins, Elaine. 1988. A Matter of Conscience for a G-Man. *The Progressive* 52 (3):14.

Howe, Laura K. 1977. *Pink-Collar Ghetto.* New York: G. P. Putnam.

Hudson, Barbara. 1997. Punishment or Redress? Current Themes in European Abolitionist Criminology. In *Thinking Critically About Crime*, edited by Brian D. MacLean and Dragan Milovanovic, 131–138. Vancouver, B.C.: Collective Press.

Huizinga, David, and Delbert S. Elliott. 1987. Juvenile Offenders: Prevalence, Offender Incidence, and Arrest Rates by Race. *Crime and Delinquency* 33 (2): 206–223.

Humphreys, Laud. 1970. *Tearoom Trade: Impersonal Sex in Public Places.* Chicago: Aldine.

Hunt, Alan. 1978. *The Sociological Movement in Law.* London: Macmillan.

Hunt, Morton. 1979. Legal Rape. *Family Circle* 92 (1): 24, 37–38, 125.

Hymowitz, Carol, and Timothy D. Schellhardt. 1986. The Glass Ceiling. *Wall Street Journal,* March 24, 1D, 4D–5D.

Iadicola, Peter, and Anson Shupe. 1998. *Violence, Inequality, and Human Freedom.* Dix Hills, N.Y.: General Hall.

Ignatius, David. 1986. The Contrapreneurs: Skirting Congress and the Law for Years. *Washington Post,* December 7, D1, D2.

Inciardi, James A. 1986. *The War on Drugs: Heroin, Cocaine, Crime, and Public Policy.* Palo Alto, Calif.: Mayfield.

Inciardi, James A., Dorothy Lockwood, and Anne E. Pottieger. 1993. *Women and Crack Cocaine.* New York: Macmillan.

Ingrassia, Michele. 1993. Abused and Confused. *Newsweek,* October 25, 57–58.

Island, David, and Patrick Letellier, eds. 1991. *Men Who Beat the Men Who Love Them: Battered Gay Men and Domestic Violence.* New York: Harrington Park Press.

Jackall, Robert. 1980. Crime in the Suites. *Contemporary Sociology* 9 (3): 357–358.

Jackson, Bruce. 1964. *A Thief's Primer.* New York: Macmillan.

Jacobs, David. 1981. Inequality and Economic Crime. *Sociology and Social Research* 66 (1): 12–28.

Jacobs, David, and David Britt. 1979. Inequality and Police Use of Deadly Force: An Empirical Assessment of a Conflict Hypothesis. *Social Problems* 26 (4): 403–412.

Jacobson, Michael. 1985. *The Enigmatic Crime: A Study of Arson.* Ph.D. diss., City University of New York.

Jacobson, Michael, and Philip Kasinitz. 1986. Burning the Bronx for Profit. *The Nation,* November 15, 512–515.

Jaggar, Alison M. 1983. *Feminist Politics and Human Nature.* Totowa, N.J.: Rowman and Allanheld.

Jaggar, Alison M., and Paula Rothenberg, eds. 1984. *Feminist Frameworks.* New York: McGraw-Hill.

James, Jennifer. 1982. The Prostitute as Victim. In *The Criminal Justice System and Women,* edited by Barbara Raffel Price and Natalie J. Sokoloft, 291–315. New York: Clark Boardman.

James, Jennifer, and William Thornton. 1980. Women's Liberation and the Female Delinquent. *Journal of Research in Crime and Delinquency* 17 (3): 230–244.

Jamrozik, Adam, and Luisa Nocella. 1998. *The Sociology of Social Problems.* Cambridge: Cambridge University Press.

Jaspan, Norman. 1974. *Mind Your Own Business.* Englewood Cliffs, N.J.: Prentice-Hall.

Jeffery, Clarence Ray. 1965. Criminal Behavior and Learning Theory. *Journal of Criminal Law, Criminology, and Police Science* 56 (3): 294–300.

Jeffery, Clarence Ray, ed. 1979. *Biology and Crime.* Beverly Hills: Sage.

Jencks, Christopher. 1987. Genes and Crime. *New York Times Review of Books,* February 12, 33–34.

Jenkins, Philip. 1984. Varieties of Enlightenment Criminology. *British Journal of Criminology* 24 (2): 112–130.

———. 1988. Myth and Murder: The Serial Killer Panic of 1983–1985. *Criminal Justice Research Bulletin* 3 (11): 1–7.

———. 1994. *Using Murder: The Social Construction of Serial Homicide.* New York: Aldine de Gruyter.

Jensen, Gary F. 1972. Delinquency and Adolescent Self-Conceptions: A Study of the Personal Relevance of Infraction. *Social Problems* 20 (1): 84–102.

Jesilow, Paul D., Henry N. Pontell, and Gilbert Geis. 1985. Medical Criminals: Physicians and White-Collar Offenses. *Justice Quarterly* 2 (2): 149–165.

———. 1993. *Prescription for Profit: How Doctors Defraud Medicaid.* Berkeley: University of California Press.

Jessop, Bob. 1982. *The Capitalist State: Marxist Theories and Methods.* Oxford: Martin Robertson.

Joe, Karen A., and Meda Chesney-Lind. 1998. "Just Every Mother's Angel": An Analysis of Gender and Ethnic Variations in Youth Gang Membership. In *Criminology at the Crossroads: Feminist Readings in Crime and Justice,* edited by Kathleen Daly and Lisa Maher, 87–109. New York: Oxford University Press.

Johansen, Bruce, and Roberto Maestas. 1979. *Wasicbu: The Continuing Indian Wars.* New York: Monthly Review Press.

Judis, John. 1988. The Big Sleazy: A New Era of Government Corruption. *In These Times,* July 20–August 2, 7.

Junger-Tas, Josine. 1994. Delinquency in Thirteen Western Countries: Some Preliminary Conclusions. In *Delinquent Behavior Among Young People in the Western World: First Results of the International Self-report Delinquency Study,* edited by Josine Junger-Tas, Gert-Jan Terlouw, and Malcolm W. Klein, 370–385. Amsterdam: Kugler Publications.

Jurik, Nancy, and Peter Gregware. 1992. A Method for Murder: The Study of Homicides by Women. *Perspectives on Social Problems* 4 (2): 179–201.

Kalish, Carol B. 1988. *International Crime Rates.* Report NCJ–110776. Washington. D.C.: Bureau of Justice Statistics, U.S. Department of Justice.

Kania, Richard R., and Ruth E. Tanham. 1987. Rise and Fall of Television Crime. Paper presented at the American Society of Criminology annual meeting, Montreal, November.

Kappeler, Victor E., Mark Blumberg, and Gary W. Potter. 1996. *The Mythology of Crime and Criminal Justice.* Prospect Heights, Ill.: Waveland Press.

Katz, Jack. 1988. *The Seductions of Crime.* New York: Basic Books.

Keat, Russell, and John Urry. 1975. *Social Theory as Science.* London: Routledge and Kegan Paul.

Kefauver Committee. 1951. *Special Committee to Investigate Organized Crime in Interstate Commerce.* Washington, D.C.: U.S. Government Printing Office.

Kelling, George L., and Catherine M. Coles. 1996. *Fixing Broken Windows: Restoring Order and Reducing Crime in Our Communities.* New York: Martin Kessler Books.

Kellor, Frances A. 1899. Psychological and Environmental Study of Women Criminals. Parts 1 and 2. *American Journal of Sociology* 5 (4): 527–543; 5 (5): 67–182.

_____. 1901. *Experimental Sociology: Delinquents.* New York: Macmillan.

Kelly, Orr, and Ted Gest. 1982. Reagan Revolution Takes Firm Hold at Justice. *U.S. News and World Report,* April 26, 24–26.

Kendall-Tackett, Kathleen, and Roberta Marshall. 1998. Abuse. In *Issues in Intimate Violence*, edited by Raquel Kennedy Bergen, 47–63. Thousand Oaks, Calif.: Sage.

Kerbo, Harold, and Mariko Inoue. 1990. Japanese Social Structure and White-Collar Crime. *Deviant Behavior* 11 (2): 139–154.

Kimmel, Michael S. 1993. Does Pornography Cause Rape? *Violence Update* 3 (10): 18.

King, Harry, and William J. Chambliss. 1984. *Box Man: A Professional Thief's Journey.* New York: John Wiley.

Kitsuse, John I., and Aaron V. Cicourel. 1963. A Note on the Uses of Official Statistics. *Social Problems* 11 (2): 131–139.

Kitsuse, John I., and David C. Dietrick. 1959. Delinquent Boys: A Critique. *American Sociological Review* 24 (2): 208–215.

Klanwatch. 1989. *Intelligence Report: Special Report on Hate Crime in 1988.* Montgomery, Ala.: Southern Poverty Law Center.

Kleck, Gary. 1997. *Point Blank: Guns and Violence in America.* New York: Aldine de Gruyter.

Klein, Dorie. 1973. The Etiology of Female Crime: A Review of the Literature. *Issues in Criminology* 8 (2): 3–30.

_____. 1979. Can This Marriage Be Saved? Battery and Sheltering. *Crime and Social Justice* 12 (Winter): 19–33.

Klein, Malcolm W. 1995. *The American Street Gang: Its Nature, Prevalence, and Control.* New York: Oxford University Press.

Klemke, Lloyd W. 1992. *The Sociology of Shoplifting: Boosters and Snitches Today.* Westport, Conn.: Praeger.

Klinger, David A. 1994. Demeanor or Crime? Why "Hostile" Citizens Are More Likely to Be Arrested. *Criminology* 32 (3): 475–493.

Klockars, Carl B. 1974. *The Professional Fence.* New York: Free Press.

_____. 1979. The Contemporary Crises of Marxist Criminology. *Criminology* 16 (3): 477–515.

Knapp Commission. 1972. *Knapp Commission Report on Police Corruption.* New York: Braziller.

Komiya, Nobuo. 1999. A Cultural Study of the Low Crime Rate in Japan. *British Journal of Criminology* 30 (3): 369–390.

Koss, Mary P., T. E. Dinero, C. A. Seibel, and S. L. Cox. 1988. Stranger and Acquaintance Rape: Are There Differences in the Victim's Experience? *Psychology of Women Quarterly* 12 (1): 1–24.

Koss, Mary P., and Sarah L. Cook. 1998. Facing the Facts: Date and Acquaintance Rape Are Significant Problems for Women. In *Issues in Intimate Violence*, edited by Raquel Kennedy Bergen, 147–156. Thousand Oaks, Calif.: Sage.

Krohn, Marvin D., and James L. Massey. 1980. Social Control and Delinquent Behavior: An Examination of the Elements of the Social Bond. *Sociological Quarterly* 21 (4): 529–544.

Krohn, Marvin D., Lonn Lanza-Kaduce, and Ronald L. Akers. 1984. Community Context and Theories of Deviant Behavior: An Examination of Social Learning and Social Bonding Theories. *Sociological Quarterly* 25 (3): 353–371.

Kruger, Henrik. 1980. *The Great Heroin Coup.* Boston: South End Press.

Kruttschnitt, Candace. 1982. Women, Crime, and Dependency. *Criminology* 9 (4): 495–513.

Kunstler, William. 1978. FBI Letters: Writers of the Purple Rage. *The Nation,* December 30, 721–722.

Kunze, Michael. 1987. *Highroad to the Stake.* Translated by William E. Yuill. Chicago: University of Chicago Press.

Kurtz, Howard. 1988. E. F. Hutton to Plead Guilty. *Washington Post,* April 2, A3.

Lamour, Catherine, and Michael R. Lamberti. 1974. *The International Connection: Opium from Growers to Pushers.* New York: Pantheon Books.

Land, Kenneth C., David Cantor, and Stephen T. Russell. 1995. Unemployment and Crime Rate Fluctuations in the Post-World War II United States: Statistical Time-Series Properties and Alternate Models. In *Crime and Inequality,* edited by John Hagan and Ruth D. Peterson, 55–79. Stanford, Calif.: Stanford University Press.

Lander, Bernard. 1954. *Towards an Understanding of Juvenile Delinquency.* New York: Columbia University Press.

Lane, David. 1970. *Politics and Society in the USSR.* London: Weidenfeld and Nicolson.

_____. 1996. *The Rise and Fall of State Socialism.* Cambridge: Polity Press.

Langan, Patrick A., and David P. Farrington. 1998. Executive Summary to *Crime and Justice in the United States and England and Wales, 1981–96.* Report NCJ–173402. Washington D.C.: Bureau of Justice Statistics.

Lanier, Mark M., and Stuart Henry. 1998. *Essential Criminology.* Boulder, Colo.: Westview.

Lanza-Kaduce, Lonn. 1980. Deviance Among Professionals: The Case of Unnecessary Surgery. *Deviant Behavior* 1: 333–359.

Laub, John H. 1983. *Criminology in the Making: An Oral History.* Boston: Northeastern University Press.

Laub, John H., and Robert J. Sampson. 1988. Unraveling Families and Delinquency: A Reanalysis of the Gluecks Data. *Criminology* 26 (3): 355–380.

Lea, John, and Jock Young. 1984. *What Is to Be Done About Law and Order?* New York: Penguin.

_____. 1986. A Realistic Approach to Law and Order. In *The Political Economy of Crime: Readings for a Critical Criminology,* edited by Brian MacLean, 358–364. Englewood Cliffs, N.J.: Prentice-Hall.

Lederer, Laura, ed. 1980. *Take Back the Night: Women on Pornography.* New York: William Morrow.

Lemert, Edwin M. 1951. *Social Pathology: A Systematic Approach to the Theory of Sociopathic Behavior.* New York: McGraw-Hill.

_____. 1967. *Human Deviance, Social Problems, and Social Control.* Englewood Cliffs, N.J.: Prentice-Hall.

Lens, Sidney. 1973. *The Labor Wars: From the Molly Maguires to the Sitdowns.* New York: Doubleday.

Levi, Ken. 1981. Becoming a Hit Man: Neutralization in a Very Deviant Career. *Urban Life* 10 (April): 47–63.

Levin, Jack, and James A. Fox. 1988. *Elementary Statistics in Social Research.* New York: Harper and Row.

Levin, Jack, and Jack McDevitt. 1993. *Hate Crimes: The Rising Tide of Bigotry and Bloodshed.* New York: Plenum Press.

Liebert, Robert M., and Joyce Sprafkin. 1988. *The Early Window: Effects of Television on Children and Youth.* New York: Pergamon.

Lifschultz, Lawrence. 1988. Inside the Kingdom of Heroin. *The Nation,* November 14, 477, 492–496.

Lindesmith, Alfred R. 1947. *Opiate Addiction.* Bloomington, Ind.: Principia Press.

Linebaugh, Peter. 1976. Karl Marx, the Theft of Wood, and Working Class Composition. *Crime and Social Justice* 6 (Fall/Winter): 5–16.

Link, Bruce G., Francis T. Cullen, James Frank, and John F. Wozniak. 1987. The Social Rejection of Former Mental Patients: Understanding Why Labels Matter. *American Journal of Sociology* 92 (6): 1461–1500.

Lizotte, Alan J. 1978. Extra-Legal Factors in Chicago's Criminal Courts: Testing the Conflict Model of Criminal Justice. *Social Problems* 25 (5): 564–580.

Lobel, Kerry. 1986. Introduction to *Naming the Violence: Speaking Out About Lesbian Battering,* edited by Kerry Lobel, 1–8. Seattle: Seal Press.

Lockhart, Lettie L., Barbara W. White, Vicki Causby, and Alicia Isaac. 1995. Letting Out the Secret: Violence in Lesbian Relationships. *Journal of Interpersonal Violence* 9 (4): 469–492.

Lombroso, Cesare. 1876. *L'uomo delinquente* (Criminal man). Milan: Hoepli.

———. 1918. *Crime: Its Causes and Remedies.* 1902. Translated by Henry P. Horton. Boston: Little, Brown.

Lombroso, Cesare, and William Ferrero. 1895. *The Female Offender.* 1893. Reprint, London: T. Fisher Unwin.

Lombroso-Ferrero, Gina. [1911] 1972. *Lombroso's Criminal Man.* Montclair, N.J.: Patterson Smith.

Los, Maria. 1983. Economic Crimes in Communist Countries. In *Comparative Criminology,* edited by Israel Barak-Glantz and Elmer H. Johnson, 39–57. Beverly Hills: Sage.

Lott, Bernice, Mary E. Reilly, and Dale R. Howard. 1982. Sexual Assault and Harassment: A Campus Community Case Study. *Signs* 8 (Winter): 296–319.

Luckenbill, David F. 1977. Criminal Homicide as a Situated Transaction. *Social Problems* 25 (2): 176–186.

———. 1981. Generating Compliance: The Case of Robbery. *Urban Life* 10 (1): 25–46.

———. 1986. Deviant Career Mobility: The Case of Male Prostitutes. *Social Problems* 33 (4): 283–296.

Lyman, Michael D., and Gary W. Potter. 1997. *Organized Crime.* Upper Saddle River, N.J.: Prentice-Hall.

Lynd, Robert S. 1939. *Knowledge for What?* Princeton: Princeton University Press.

Maas, Peter. 1986. *Manhunt.* New York: Random House.

MacKinnon, Catharine A. 1979. *Sexual Harassment of Working Women.* New Haven, Conn.: Yale University Press.

———. 1984. Not a Moral Issue. *Yale Law and Policy Review* 2 (2): 32–145.

———. 1986. Pornography and Sex Discrimination. *Law and Inequality* 4 (1): 38–49.

MacIntyre, Alasdair. 1971. Is a Science of Comparative Politics Possible? In *Against the Self-Images of the Age,* 260–279. London: Duckworth.

———. 1981. *After Virtue.* Notre Dame: University of Notre Dame Press.

MacLean, Brian D., and Dragan Milovanovic, eds. 1998. *Thinking Critically About Crime.* Vancouver, B.C.: Collective Press.

Madriz, Esther. 1997. Latina Teenagers: Victimization, Identity, and Fear of Crime. *Social Justice* 24 (4): 39–55.

Maher, Lisa. 1997. *Sexed Work: Gender, Race, and Resistance in a Brooklyn Drug Market.* New York: Clarendon Press.

Maher, Lisa, and Richard Curtis. 1992. Women on the Edge of Crime: Crack Cocaine and the Changing Contexts of Street-Level Sex Work in New York City. *Crime, Law, and Social Change* 18 (2): 221–258.

Maher, Lisa, and Kathleen Daly. 1996. Women in the Street-Level Drug Economy: Continuity or Change? *Criminology* 34 (4): 465–491.

Maier, Pauline. 1972. *From Resistance to Revolution: Colonial Radicals and the Development of American Opposition to Britain,* 1765–1776. New York: Knopf.

Mann, Coramae Richey, and Marjorie S. Zatz, eds. 1998. *Images of Color, Images of Crime: Readings.* Los Angeles: Roxbury Publishing.

Marcuse, Herbert. 1964. *One Dimensional Man.* Boston: Beacon Press.

Mars, Gerald. 1983. *Cheats at Work.* Boston: Unwin.

Marshall, Johnathan, Peter Dale Scott, and Jane Hunter. 1987. *The Iran-Contra Connection.* Boston: South End Press.

Martin, Del. 1982. Battered Women: Society's Problem. In *The Criminal Justice System and Women,* edited by Barbara Raffel Price and Natalie J. Sokoloff, 263–290. New York: Clark Boardman.

Martin, Patricia Yancey, and Robert A. Hummer. 1998. Fraternities and Rape on Campus. In *Issues in Intimate Violence*, edited by Raquel Kennedy Bergen, 157–167. Thousand Oaks, Calif.: Sage.

Marx, Gary T. 1981. Ironies of Social Control: Authorities as Contributors to Deviance Through Escalation, Non-Enforcement, and Covert Facilitation. *Social Problems* 28 (3): 221–246.

Marx, Karl. 1859. Population, Crime, and Pauperism. *New York Daily Tribune,* September 16.

_____. 1956. Capital Punishment. 1853. In *Karl Marx: Selected Writings in Sociology and Social Philosophy,* edited by T. B. Bottomore and Maximilian Rubel, 228–230. New York: McGraw-Hill.

_____. [1868] 1967. *Capital.* 3 vols. New York: International Publishers.

_____. [1848] 1969a. The Communist Manifesto. In *Karl Marx and Frederick Engels: Selected Works,* 1: 108–137. Moscow: Progress Publishers.

_____. [1852] 1969b. The Eighteenth Brumaire of Louis Bonaparte. In *Karl Marx and Frederick Engels: Selected Works,* 1: 398–487. Moscow: Progress Publishers.

_____. [1859] 1969c. Preface to *A Contribution to the Critique of Political Economy.* In *Karl Marx and Frederick Engels: Selected Works,* 1: 502–506. Moscow: Progress Publishers.

_____. [1871] 1969d. The Civil War in France. In *Karl Marx and Frederick Engels: Selected Works,* 2: 190–244. Moscow: Progress Publishers.

_____. [1857–1858] 1973. *Grundrisse: Introduction to the Critique of Political Economy.* Translated and introduced by Martin Nicolaus. New York: Vintage.

_____. [1842] 1975a. Comments on the Latest Prussian Censorship Instruction. In *Karl Marx/Frederick Engels Collected Works,* 1: 109–131. London: Lawrence and Wishart.

_____. [1842] 1975b. Proceedings of the Sixth Rhine Province Assembly. Debates on the Law on Thefts of Wood. In *Karl Marx/Frederick Engels: Collected Works,* 1: 224–263. London: Lawrence and Wishart.

_____. [1845] 1975c. *The Holy Family.* In *Karl Marx and Frederick Engels: Collected Works,* 4: 92–111. New York: International Publishers.

Marx, Karl, and Friedrich Engels. [1845] 1976. *The German Ideology.* Moscow: Progress Publishers.

Mathiesen, Thomas. 1997. The Viewer Society: Michel Foucault's "Panopticon" Revisited. *Theoretical Criminology* 1 (2): 215–234.

Matsueda, Ross L. 1988. The Current State of Differential Association Theory. *Crime and Delinquency* 34 (3): 277–306.

_____. 1997. "Cultural Deviance Theory": The Remarkable Persistence of a Flawed Term. *Theoretical Criminology* 1 (4): 429–452.

Mattera, Philip. 1985. *Off the Books.* New York: St. Martin's Press.

Matthews, Roger. 1987. Taking Realist Criminology Seriously. *Contemporary Crises* 11 (4): 371–401.

Matza, David. 1964. *Delinquency and Drift.* New York: John Wiley.

_____. 1969. *Becoming Deviant.* Englewood Cliffs, N.J.: Prentice-Hall.

Matza, David, and Gresham M. Sykes. 1961. Juvenile Delinquency and Subterranean Values. *American Sociological Review* 26 (5): 712–719.

Mayer, P. 1953. Gusii Initiation Ceremonies. *Journal of the Royal Anthropological Institute* 83:9–36.

Mayhew, Pat, and Jan J. M. Van Dijk. 1997. *Criminal Victimisation in Eleven Industrialised Countries: Key Findings from the 1996 International Crime Victims Survey.* The Hague: Ministry of Justice and University of Leyden. No. 162.

Mayhew, Pat, and Philip White. 1997. The 1996 International Crime Victimisation Survey. *Research Findings,* London: Home Office Research and Statistics Directorate. No. 57.

McCaghy, Charles H., Peggy C. Giordano, and Trudy Knicely Henson. 1977. Auto Theft: Offender and Offense Characteristics. *Criminology* 15 (3): 367–385.

McCarthy, Belinda, and Robert Langworthy. 1988. *Older Offenders.* New York: Praeger.

McClennan Committee. 1963. *Organized Crime and Illicit Traffic in Narcotics.* Hearings Before the Permanent Subcommittee on Investigations. Washington, D.C.: U.S. Government Printing Office.

McClintock, Michael. 1985. *The American Connection: State Terror and Popular Resistance in Guatemala.* London: Zed Books.

McCormack, Thelma. 1985. Making Sense of Research on Pornography. In *Women Against Censorship,* edited by Varda Burstyn, 181–205. Toronto: Douglas and McIntyre.

McCoy, Alfred. 1972. The Politics of Heroin in Southeast Asia. New York: Harper and Row.

McCullagh, Ciaran. 1996. *Crime in Ireland: A Sociological Introduction.* Cork: Cork University Press.

McDevitt, Jack. 1989. The Study of the Implementation of the Massachusetts Civil Rights Act. Unpublished paper.

McDonald, William F. 1997. Crime and Justice in the Global Village: Towards Global Criminology. In *Crime and Law Enforcement in the Global Village,* edited by William F. McDonald, 3–21. Cincinnati, Ohio: Anderson.

McGarrell, Edmund F., and Thomas C. Castellano. 1991. An Integrative Conflict Model of the Criminal Law Formation Process. *Journal of Research in Crime and Delinquency* 28 (2): 174–196.

McIntosh, Mary. 1973. The Growth of Racketeering. *Economy and Society* 2 (1): 35–69.

_____. 1976. Thieves and Fences: Market and Power in Professional Crime. *British Journal of Criminology* 16 (3): 257–266.

Mead, Margaret. 1928. *Coming of Age in Samoa.* New York: Blue Ribbon Books.

Meese Commission. 1986. *Final Report.* Attorney General's Commission on Pornography. Washington, D.C.: U.S. Department of Justice.

Meier, Robert F. 1983. Shoplifting. In *Encyclopedia of Crime and Justice,* edited by Sanford H. Kadish, 4: 1497–1500. New York: Free Press.

Meier, Robert F., and Gilbert Geis. 1997. *Victimless Crime? Prostitution, Drugs, Homosexuality, Abortion.* Los Angeles, Calif.: Roxbury.

Merrill, Gregory S. 1998. Understanding Domestic Violence Among Gay and Bisexual Men. In *Issues in Intimate Violence,* edited by Raquel Kennedy Bergen, 129–141. Thousand Oaks, Calif.: Sage.

Merton, Robert K. [1938] 1969. Social Structure and Anomie. In *Delinquency, Crime, and Social Process,* edited by Donald R. Cressey and David A. Ward, 254–284. New York: Harper and Row.

Messerschmidt, James W. 1986a. *The Trial of Leonard Peltier.* Boston: South End Press.

_____. 1986b. *Capitalism, Patriarchy, and Crime: Toward a Socialist Feminist Criminology.* Totowa, N.J.: Rowman and Littlefield.

_____. 1987. Feminism, Criminology, and the Rise of the Female Sex Delinquent, 1880–1930. *Contemporary Crises* 11 (3): 243–263.

_____. 1988. From Marx to Bonger: Socialist Writings on Women, Gender, and Crime. *Sociological Inquiry* 58 (4): 378–392.

_____. 1993. *Masculinities and Crime: Critique and Reconceptualization of Theory.* Lanham, Md.: Rowman and Littlefield.

_____. 1997. *Crime as Structured Action: Gender, Race, Class, and Crime in the Making.* Thousand Oaks, Calif.: Sage.

Messner, Steven F. 1980. Income Inequality and Murder Rates. *Comparative Social Research* 3: 185–198.

Messner, Steven, and Kenneth Tardiff. 1985. The Social Ecology of Urban Homicide: An Application of the Routine Activities Approach. *Criminology* 23 (2): 241–267.

Messner, Steven F., and Richard Rosenfeld. 1994. *Crime and the American Dream*. Belmont, Calif.: Wadsworth.

————. 1998. *Crime and the American Dream*. 2d ed. Belmont, Calif.: Wadsworth.

Michael, Jerome, and Mortimer J. Adler. [1933] 1971. *Crime, Law, and Social Science*. Montclair, N.J.: Patterson Smith.

Michalowski, Raymond J. 1983. Crime Control in the 1980s: A Progressive Agenda. *Crime and Social Justice* 19 (Summer): 13–23.

————. 1985. *Order, Law, and Crime*. New York: Random House.

Michalowski, Raymond J., and Ed Bolander. 1976. Repression and Criminal Justice in Capitalist America. *Sociological Inquiry* 46 (2): 99–110.

Michalowski, Raymond J., and Ronald C. Kramer. 1987. The Space Between Laws: The Problem of Corporate Crime in a Transnational Context. *Social Problems* 34 (1): 34–53.

Mieczkowski, Thomas. 1986. Geeking Up and Throwing Down: Heroin Street Life in Detroit. *Criminology* 24 (4): 645–666.

————. 1994. The Experiences of Women Who Sell Crack: Some Descriptive Data from the Detroit Crack Ethnography Project. *Journal of Drug Issues* 24 (2): 227–248.

Miethe, Terance D., and Richard C. McCorkle. 1997. Gang Membership and Criminal Processing: A Test of the "Master Status" Concept. *Justice Quarterly* 14 (3): 407–427.

————. 1998. *Crime Profiles: The Anatomy of Dangerous Persons, Places, and Situations*. Los Angeles, Calif.: Roxbury.

Mill, John Stuart. [1851] 1970. *The Subjection of Women*. New York: Source Book Press.

Miller, Eleanor. 1983. International Trends in the Study of Female Criminality: An Essay Review. *Contemporary Crises* 7 (1): 59–70.

————. 1986. *Street Women*. Philadelphia: Temple University Press.

Miller, Jodi, and Martin Schwartz. 1994. Rape Myths and Violence Against Street Prostitutes. *Deviant Behavior* 16 (1): 1–23.

Miller, Ted R., Mark A. Cohen, and Brian Wiersma. 1996. *Victim Costs and Consequences: A New Look*. Report NCJ–155282. Washington D.C.: National Institute of Justice.

Miller, Walter B. 1958. Lower Class Culture as a Generating Milieu of Gang Delinquency. *Journal of Social Issues* 14 (3): 5–19.

Milovanovic, Dragan, and Stuart Henry. 1991. Constitutive Penology. *Social Justice* 18 (3): 204–224.

Mintz, Morton. 1985. At Any Cost: Corporate Greed, Women, and the Dalkon Shield. *The Progressive* 49 (11): 20–25.

————. 1986. A Crime Against Women: A. H. Robbins and the Dalkon Shield. *Multinational Monitor*, January 15, 17.

Miyazawa, Setsuo. 1993. The Enigma of Japan as a Testing Ground for Cross-Cultural Criminological Studies. *Annales Internationales de Criminologie* 32: 81–102.

Mohr, James C. 1978. *Abortion in America*. New York: Oxford University Press.

Mokhiber, Russell. 1988. *Corporate Crime and Violence*. San Francisco: Sierra Club.

Moore, Sally Falk. 1978. *Law as Process*. London: Routledge and Kegan Paul.

Moore, Thomas. 1988. The Black-on-Black Crime Plague. *U.S. News and World Report*, August 22, 49–55.

Moore, William. 1974. *The Kefauver Committee and the Politics of Crime, 1950–1952*. Columbia: University of Missouri Press.

Morgan, Robin. 1980. Theory and Practice: Pornography and Rape. In *Take Back the Night: Women on Pornography*, edited by Laura Lederer, 134–147. New York: William Morrow.

Morris, Allison. 1987. *Women, Crime, and Criminal Justice*. New York: Basil Blackwell.

Moyers, Bill. 1988. *The Secret Government: The Constitution in Crisis*. Washington, D.C.: Seven Locks Press.

Mungham, Geoff, and Geoff Pearson. 1976. *Working-Class Youth Culture*. London: Routledge and Kegan Paul.

Murray, John. 1986. Marijuana's Effects on Human Cognitive Functions, Psychomotor Functions, and Personality. *Journal of General Psychology* 113 (1): 23–55.

Musto, David F. 1973. *The American Disease: Origins of Narcotic Control.* New Haven, Conn.: Yale University Press.

Naffine, Ngaire. 1987. *Female Crime: The Construction of Women in Criminology.* Boston: Allen and Unwin.

Nagel, Ilene. 1981. Sex Differences in the Processing of Criminal Defendants. In *Women and Crime,* edited by Allison Morris, 44–62. Cambridge: Cambridge University Press.

Nagi, Saad Z. 1975. Child Abuse and Neglect Programs: A National Overview. *Children Today* 4 (May–June): 13–17.

Nash, Nathaniel. 1985. Capitalist Punishment. *The New Republic,* May 27, 56.

National Advisory Commission on Criminal Justice Standards and Goals. 1973. *A National Strategy to Reduce Crime.* Washington, D.C.: U.S. Government Printing Office.

National Center on Child Abuse and Neglect. 1993. *National Child Abuse and Neglect Data Systems Working Paper 2.* Washington, D.C.: U.S. Department of Health and Human Services.

National Church Arson Task Force. 1997. *First Year Report for the President.* Washington, D.C.: U.S. Government Printing Office.

National Coalition of Anti-violence Programs. 1998. *Anti-Lesbian, Gay, Bisexual, and Transgendered Violence in 1997.* New York: NCAVP.

National Coalition for Jail Reform. 1986. *Jail Is the Wrong Place to Be for Public Inebriates.* Washington, D.C.: National Coalition for Jail Reform.

National Commission on the Causes and Prevention of Violence. 1970. *Final Report: To Establish Justice, To Insure Domestic Tranquility.* New York: Bantam Books.

National Crime Survey. 1987. *Criminal Victimization in the U.S., 1985.* Washington, D.C.: U.S. Department of Justice.

National Institute of Justice. 1998. *Annual Report on Adult and Juvenile Arrestees.* Washington, D.C.: U.S. Department of Justice.

National Institute on Drug Abuse. 1987. *National Trends in Drug Use and Related Factors Among American High School Students and Young Adults, 1975–1986.* Washington, D.C.: U.S. Government Printing Office.

Neal, Terry. 1998. In 106th Congress, New Faces but Little Change in Diversity. *Washington Post,* November 8, A5.

Neapolitan, Jerome L. 1997. *Cross-National Crime: A Research Review and Sourcebook.* Westport, Conn.: Greenwood Press.

Nelli, Humbert S. 1981. *The Business of Crime.* Chicago: University of Chicago Press.

_____. 1987. A Brief History of American Syndicate Crime. In *Organized Crime in America: Concepts and Controversies,* edited by Timothy S. Bynum, 15–29. Monsey, New York: Willow Tree Press.

Nettler, Gwynn. 1978. *Explaining Crime.* New York: McGraw-Hill.

Neuman, Joel H., and Robert A. Baron. 1997. Aggression in the Workplace. In *Antisocial Behavior in Organizations*, edited by Robert A. Giacalone and Jerald Greenberg, 37–67. Thousand Oaks, Calif.: Sage.

Newburn, Tim, and Elizabeth A. Stanko. 1994. *Just Boys Doing Business? Men, Masculinities, and Crime.* New York: Routledge.

Newman, Evelyn, Donald Newman, and Mindy Gewirtz. 1984. *Elderly Criminals.* Cambridge: Delgeschlarger, Gunn, and Hain.

Newman, Oscar. 1973. *Defensible Space: Crime Prevention Through Urban Design.* London: Macmillan.

New York Times. 1987. Boesky and Levine Snared in Inquiry, January 2, D2.

Nye, F. Ivan. 1958. *Family Relationships and Delinquent Behavior.* New York: John Wiley.

Oakley, Ann. 1972. *Sex, Gender, and Society.* New York: Harper and Row.

Oberdorfer, Don, and Patrick E. Tyler. 1983. U.S.-Backed Nicaraguan Rebel Army Swells to 7,000 Men. *Washington Post,* May 8, A1, A10, A11.

O'Kelly, Charlotte G., and Larry S. Carney. 1986. *Women and Men in Society.* Belmont, Calif.: Wadsworth.

O'Neil, William L. 1969. *The Woman Movement: Feminism in the United States.* New York: Barnes and Noble.

Ortiz, Roxanne Dunbar. 1977. *The Great Sioux Nation.* Berkeley: Moon Books.

O'Toole, Laura L., and Jessica R. Schiffman. eds. 1997. *Gender Violence: Interdisciplinary Perspectives.* New York: New York University Press.

Paolucci, Henry. [1764] 1963. Translator's introduction to *On Crime and Punishments,* by Cesare Beccaria, ix–xxiii. Indianapolis: Bobbs-Merrill.

Parenti, Michael. 1983. *Democracy for the Few.* New York: St. Martin's.

Park, Robert E. 1915. The City: Suggestions for the Investigation of Human Behavior in the City. *American Journal of Sociology* 20 (5): 577–612.

Parker, Donn B. 1976. *Crime by Computer.* New York: Charles Scribner.

Parmalee, Maurice. 1918. *Criminology.* New York: Macmillan.

Passas, Nikos. 1990. Anomie and Corporate Deviance. *Contemporary Crises* 14 (2): 157–178.

Paternoster, Raymond, and Lee Ann Iovanni. 1989. The Labeling Perspective and Delinquency: An Elaboration of the Theory and an Assessment of the Evidence. *Justice Quarterly* 6 (3): 379–394.

Paternoster, Raymond, and Paul Mazerolle 1994. General Strain Theory and Delinquency: A Replication and Extension. *Journal of Research in Crime and Delinquency* 31 (3): 235–263.

Paternoster, Raymond, and Robert Brame. 1997. Multiple Routes to Delinquency? A Test of Developmental and General Theories of Crime. *Criminology* 35 (1): 49–80.

Peacock, Patricia. 1998. Marital Rape. In *Issues in Intimate Violence*, edited by Raquel Kennedy Bergen, 225–235. Thousand Oaks, Calif.: Sage.

Pear, Robert. 1980. Sexual Harassment at Work Outlawed. *New York Times,* April 12, 1, 20.

Pearce, Frank. 1976. *Crimes of the Powerful.* London: Pluto Press.

Pearce, Frank, and Laureen Snider. 1995. Regulating Capitalism. In *Corporate Crime: Contemporary Debates,* edited by Frank Pearce and Laureen Snider, 19–47. Toronto: University of Toronto Press.

Pearson, Geoffrey, and John Twohig. 1976. Ethnography Through the Looking-Glass. In *Resistance Through Rituals: Youth Subcultures in Post-War Britain,* edited by Stuart Hall and Tony Jefferson, 119–125. London: Hutchinson.

Pearson, Karl. 1919. Charles Goring and His Contribution to Criminology. In *The English Convict: A Statistical Study,* xv–xx. Abridged version. London: M.M.S.O.

Pepinsky, Hal. 1997. What Is Peacemaking? In *Thinking Critically About Crime,* edited by Brian D. MacLean and Dragan Milovanovic, 109–114. Vancouver, B.C.: Collective Press.

Pepinsky, Harold E. 1978. Communist Anarchism as an Alternative to the Rule of Criminal Law. *Contemporary Crises* 2 (3): 315–334.

Pepinsky, Harold E., and Richard Quinney, eds. 1991. *Criminology as Peacemaking.* Bloomington: Indiana University Press.

Perrot, Michelle. 1975. Délinquance et systéme pénitentaire en France au XIXe siécle. *Annales: Économies, société, civilisations* 30 (1): 67–91.

Perry, Barbara J. 1998. Defenders of the Faith: Hate Groups and Ideologies of Power in the United States. *Patterns of Prejudice* 32 (3): 32–54.

Petchesky, Rosalind Pollack. 1984. *Abortion and Woman's Choice: The State, Sexuality, and Reproductive Freedom.* Boston: Northeastern University Press.

Petit, Jacques G. 1984. The Birth and Reform of Prisons in France. In *The Emergence of Carceral Institutions: Prisons, Galleys, and Lunatic Asylums, 1550–1900,* edited by Pieter Spierenburg, 125–147. Rotterdam: Erasmus University.

_____. 1985. *Images of Deviance and Social Control.* New York: McGraw-Hill.

Pfost, Donald. 1987. Reagan's Nicaraguan Policy: A Case Study of Political Deviance and Crime. *Crime and Social Justice* 27/28: 66–87.

Phillips, Llad, and Harold Votey. 1987. Rational Choice Models of Crimes by Youth. *The Review of Black Political Economy* 16 (12): 129–187.

Phillipson, Coleman. [1923] 1975. *Three Criminal Law Reformers: Beccaria, Bentham, Romilly.* Montclair, N.J.: Patterson Smith.

Piquero, Alex, and Matthew Hickman. 1999. An Empirical Test of Tittle's Control Balance Theory. *Criminology* 37 (2): 319–341.

Pizzo, Stephen, Mary Fricker, and Paul Muolo. 1989. *Inside Job: The Looting of America's Savings and Loans.* New York: McGraw-Hill.

Platt, Tony. 1974. Prospects for a Radical Criminology in the United States. *Crime and Social Justice* 1 (Spring/Summer): 2–10.

Platt, Tony, and Paul Takagi. 1979. Biosocial Criminology: A Critique. *Crime and Social Justice* 11 (Spring/Summer): 5–13.

Polk, Kenneth. 1994. *When Men Kill: Scenarios of Masculine Violence.* New York: Cambridge University Press.

Polk, Kenneth, and William Schafer. 1972. *Schools and Delinquency.* Englewood Cliffs, N.J.: Prentice-Hall.

Pollak, Otto. 1961. *The Criminality of Women.* Philadelphia: University of Pennsylvania Press.

Pollock, John Crothers, and Arney Ellen Rosenblatt. 1984. Fear of Crime: Sources and Responses. In *Criminal Justice,* edited by John J. Sullivan and Joseph L. Victor, 34–36. Guildford, Conn.: Dushkin Publishing.

Polsky, Ned. 1967. *Hustlers, Beats, and Others.* Chicago: Aldine.

Porterfield, Austin L. 1946. Delinquency and Its Outcome in Court and College. *American Journal of Sociology* 49 (3): 199–208.

Portland Press Herald. 1993. Health Firm Fined $61 Million for Selling Faulty Heart Catheters. October 16, 1, 6.

Potter, Gary. 1994. *Criminal Organizations: Vice, Racketeering, and Politics in an American City.* Prospect Heights, Ill.: Waveland.

Prados, John. 1986. *President's Secret Wars.* New York: William Morrow.

President's Commission on Law Enforcement and the Administration of Justice. 1967a. *The Challenge of Crime in a Free Society.* Washington, D.C.: U.S. Government Printing Office.

———. 1967b. *Task Force Report: Organized Crime.* Washington, D.C.: U.S. Government Printing Office.

President's Commission on Organized Crime. 1984. *The Cash Connection: Organized Crime, Financial Institutions, and Money Laundering.* Washington, D.C.: U.S. Government Printing Office.

———. 1986a. *The Impact: Organized Crime Today.* Washington, D.C.: U.S. Government Printing Office.

———. 1986b. *The Edge: Organized Crime, Business, and Labor Unions.* Washington, D.C.: U.S. Government Printing Office.

Price, Barbara Raffel, and Natalie Sokoloff, eds. 1982. *The Criminal Justice System and Women.* New York: Clark Boardman.

Ptacek, James. 1998. Why Do Men Batter Their Wives? In *Issues in Intimate Violence*, edited by Raquel Kennedy Bergen, 181–195. Thousand Oaks, Calif.: Sage

Quetelet, Adolphe. 1842. *A Treatise on Man.* Translated by R. Knox and T. Smibert. Edinburgh: Chambers.

———. 1848. *Du systéme social et des lois qui le régissent.* Paris: Guillaumin.

———. 1826. Mémoire sur les lois des naissances et de la mortalit Bruxelles. *Nouveaux mémoires de l'académie royale des sciences et belles-lettres de Bruxelles* 3: 495–512.

———. [1831] 1984. *Research on the Propensity for Crime at Different Ages.* Translated by Sawyer Sylvester. Cincinnati: Anderson

Quinney, Richard. 1970. *The Social Reality of Crime.* Boston: Little, Brown.

———. 1973a. There's a Lot of Us Folks Grateful to the Lone Ranger: Some Notes on the Rise and Fall of American Criminology. *Insurgent Sociologist* 4 (Fall): 56–64.

———. 1973b. Crime Control in Capitalist Society: A Critical Philosophy of Legal Order. *Issues in Criminology* 8 (Spring): 75–79.

_____. 1977. *Class, State, and Crime*. New York: Longman.

_____. 1997. Socialist Humanism and Critical/Peacemaking Criminology: The Continuing Project. In *Thinking Critically About Crime*, edited by Brian D. MacLean and Dragan Milovanovic, 114–117. Vancouver, B.C.: Collective press.

Quinney, Richard, and John Wildeman. 1977. *The Problem of Crime*. New York: Harper and Row.

Rafter, Nicole Hahn. 1985. *Partial Justice: Women in State Prisons, 1800–1935*. Boston: Northeastern University Press.

Rafter, Nicole Hahn, ed. 1988. *White Trash: The Engenic Family Studies, 1877–1919*. Boston: Northeastern University Press.

Rafter, Nicole Hahn. 1992. Criminal Anthropology in the United States. *Criminology* 30 (4): 525–545.

_____. 1997. Psychopathy and the Evolution of Criminological Knowledge. *Theoretical Criminology* 1 (2): 235–259.

Rafter, Nicole Hahn, and Elizabeth A. Stanko, eds. 1982. *Judge, Lawyer, Victim, Thief*. Boston: Northeastern University Press.

Rand, Michael R. 1994. *Carjacking*. Washington, D.C.: Bureau of Justice Statistics.

Ranelagh, John. 1987. *The Agency: The Rise and Decline of the CIA*. New York: Simon and Schuster.

Ray, Oakley. 1983. *Drugs, Society, and Human Behavior*. St. Louis: C. V. Mosley.

Reasons, Charles. 1974. The Politics of Drugs: An Inquiry in the Sociology of Social Problems. *Sociological Quarterly* 15 (381): 40–44.

Reckless, Walter C. 1940. *Criminal Behavior*. New York: McGraw-Hill.

_____. 1961. *The Crime Problem*. New York: Appleton-Century-Crofts.

Reckless, Walter C., Simon Dinitz, and Ellen Murray. 1956. Self-Concept as an Insulator Against Delinquency. *American Sociological Review* 21 (6): 744–746.

Redburn, F. Stevens, and Terry E. Buss. 1986. *Responding to Americas Homeless: Public Policy Alternatives*. New York: Praeger.

Redhead, Steve. 1987. *Sing When You're Winning: The Last Football Book*. Manchester: Manchester University Press.

_____. 1997. *Subculture to Clubcultures: An Introduction to Popular Cultural Studies*. Oxford: Blackwell.

Reed, Gary E., and Peter Cleary Yeager. 1996. Organizational Offending and Neoclassical Offending: Challenging the Reach of a General Theory of Crime. *Criminology* 34 (3): 357–382.

Reiman, Jeffrey. 1995. *The Rich Get Richer and the Poor Get Prison*. Boston: Allyn and Bacon.

Reisner, Marc. 1991. *Game Wars: The Undercover Pursuit of Wildlife Poachers*. New York: Viking.

Reiss, Albert J., Jr. 1951. Delinquency as the Failure of Personal and Social Controls. *American Sociological Review* 16 (2): 196–207.

Reiss, Albert J., and Michael Tonry, eds. 1986. *Communities and Crime*. Chicago: University of Chicago Press.

Reiss, Albert, and John Roth, eds. 1993. *Understanding and Preventing Violence*. Washington, D.C.: National Academy Press.

Reiter, Rayna. 1975. *Toward an Anthropology of Women*. New York: Monthly Review Press.

Renzetti, Claire M. 1992. *Violent Betrayal: Partner Abuse in Lesbian Relationships*. Newbury Park, Calif.: Sage.

_____. 1998. Violence and Abuse in Lesbian Relationships: Theoretical and Empirical Issues. In *Issues in Intimate Violence*, edited by Raquel Kennedy Bergen, 117–127. Thousand Oaks, Calif.: Sage.

Renzetti, Claire M., and Daniel J. Curran. 1995. *Women, Men, and Society*. Boston: Allyn and Bacon.

Reuter, Peter. 1983. *Disorganized Crime*. Cambridge, Mass.: MIT Press.

Rich, Spencer. 1988. HHS Says 86 Welfare Errors Cost $1.1 Billion. *Washington Post*, April 30, A15.

Riedel, Marc, and Margaret A. Zahn. 1985. *The Nature and Patterns of American Homicide*. Washington, D.C.: U.S. Government Printing Office.

Ritchie, Robert C. 1986. *Captain Kidd and the War Against the Pirates*. Cambridge, Mass.: Harvard University Press.

Robin, Gerald D. 1963. Patterns of Department Store Shoplifting. *Crime and Delinquency* 9 (2): 163–172.

Roby, Pamela A. 1969. Politics and Criminal Law: Revision of the New York State Penal Law on Prostitution. *Social Problems* 17 (1): 83–109.

Rosen, Ruth. 1982. *The Lost Sisterhood: Prostitution in America, 1900–1918*. Baltimore: Johns Hopkins University Press.

Rosenblum, Karen. 1975. Female Deviance and the Female Sex Role: A Preliminary Investigation. *British Journal of Sociology* 25 (2): 169–185.

Rosenfeld, Richard, and Steven F. Messner. 1991. The Social Sources of Homicide in Different Types of Societies. *Sociological Forum* 6 (1): 51–70.

Rosoff, Stephen M., Henry N. Pontell, and Robert Tillman. 1998. *Profit Without Honor: White-Collar Crime and the Looting of America*. Upper Saddle River, N.J.: Prentice-Hall.

Ross, Dorothy. 1991. *The Origins of American Social Science*. Cambridge: Cambridge University Press.

———. 1992. *Confronting Drunk Driving: Social Policy for Saving Lives*. New Haven: Yale University Press.

Rossi, Peter, James D. Wright, Gene A. Fisher, and Georgianna Willis. 1987. The Urban Homeless: Estimating Composition and Size. *Science* 235: 133–641.

Rothman, David. 1971. *The Discovery of the Asylum: Social Order and Disorder in the New Republic*. Boston: Little, Brown.

Rottman, David. 1980. *Crime in the Republic of Ireland*. Paper no. 102. Dublin: Economic and Social Research Institute.

Rowan, Roy. 1986. Biggest Mafia Bosses. *Fortune,* November 10, 24, 38.

Rubin, Gayle. 1984. Thinking Sex: Notes for a Radical Theory of the Politics of Sexuality. In *Pleasure and Danger: Exploring Female Sexuality,* edited by Carol S. Vance, 267–319. Boston: Routledge and Kegan Paul.

Russell, Diana E. H. 1982. *Rape in Marriage*. New York: Macmillan.

———. 1986. *The Secret Trauma: Incest in the Lives of Girls and Women*. New York: Basic Books.

———. 1990. *Sexual Exploitation*. Beverly Hills: Sage.

———. 1998. The Making of a Whore. In *Issues in Intimate Violence*, edited by Raquel Kennedy Bergen, 65–77. Thousand Oaks, Calif.: Sage.

Russell, Dick. 1988. Welcome to Dioxinville, Arkansas. *In These Times,* March 9–15, 8–13.

Sabo, Donald. 1992. Understanding Men in Prison: The Relevance of Gender Studies. *Men's Studies Review* 9 (1): 4–9.

Saleilles, Raymond. 1911. *The Individualization of Punishment*. 1898. Translated by Rachel Szold Jastrow. Boston: Little, Brown.

Sampson, Robert J. 1987. Urban Black Violence: The Effect of Male Joblessness and Family Disruption. *American Journal of Sociology* 93 (2): 348–382.

Sampson, Robert J., and William Julius Wilson. 1995. Toward a Theory of Race, Crime, and Urban Inequality. In *Crime and Inequality,* edited by John Hagan and Ruth D. Peterson, 37–54. Stanford, Calif.: Stanford University Press.

Sanday, Peggy. 1981. The Socio-Cultural Context of Rape: A Cross-Cultural Study. *Journal of Social Issues* 37 (1): 5–27.

Sasson, Theodore. 1995. *Crime Talk: How Citizens Construct a Social Problem*. New York: Aldine de Gruyter.

Savelsberg, Joachim. 1998/1999. Controlling Violence: Criminal Justice, Society, and Lessons from the United States. *Crime, Law, and Social Change* 30 (2): 185–203.

Scacco, Anthony M. 1982. *Male Rape: A Casebook of Sexual Aggressions*. New York: AMS Press.

Schechter, Susan. 1982. *Women and Male Violence: The Visions and Struggles of the Battered Women's Movement.* Boston: South End Press.

Scheffer, David J. 1987. U.S. Law and the Iran-Contra Affair. *The American Journal of International Law* 81 (3): 696–723.

Schlossman, Steven, and Michael Sedlak. 1983. The Chicago Area Project Revisited. *Crime and Delinquency* 29 (3): 398–462.

Schmidhauser, John R. 1959. The Justices of the Supreme Court: A Collective Portrait. *Midwest Journal of Political Science* 3: 237, 409.

Schrag, Clarence. 1962. Delinquency and Opportunity: Analysis of a Theory. *Sociology and Social Research* 46 (2): 167–175.

Schrager, Laura Shill, and James F. Short. 1978. Toward a Sociology of Organizational Crime. *Social Problems* 25 (4): 407–419.

Schuessler, Karl. 1973. Introduction to *Edwin H. Sutherland on Analyzing Crime,* edited by Karl Schuessler, ix–xxxvi. Chicago: University of Chicago Press.

Schur, Edwin M. 1968. *Law and Society: A Sociological View.* New York: Random House.

———. 1974. A Sociologist's View: The Case for Abolition. In *Victimless Crimes: Two Sides of a Controversy,* edited by Edwin M. Schur and Hugo Adam Bedau, 3–52. Englewood Cliffs, N.J.: Prentice-Hall.

———. 1979. *Interpreting Deviance: A Sociological View.* New York: Harper and Row.

———. 1984. *Labeling Women Deviant: Gender, Stigma, and Social Control.* New York: Random House.

———. 1988. *The Americanization of Sex.* Philadelphia: Temple University Press.

Schwartz, Martin D. 1988. Ain't Got No Class: Universal Risk Theories of Battering. *Contemporary Crises* 12 (3): 373–392.

———. 1989. Asking the Right Questions: Battered Women Are Not All Passive. *Sociological Viewpoints* 5 (1): 46–61.

Schwartz, Martin D., and Victoria L. Pitts. 1995. Exploring a Feminist Routine Activities Approach to Explaining Sexual Assault. *Justice Quarterly* 12 (1): 9–31.

Schwartz, Martin D., and Walter S. DeKeseredy. 1997. *Sexual Assault on the College Campus: The Role of Male Peer Support.* Thousand Oaks, Calif.: Sage.

Schwartz, Martin D., and David O. Friedrichs. 1998. Postmodern Thought and Criminological Discontent: New Metaphors for Understanding Violence. In *The Criminology Theory Reader*, edited by Stuart Henry and Werner Einstadter, 419–435. New York: New York University Press.

Schwartz, Richard D., and Jerome C. Miller. 1964. Legal Evolution and Societal Complexity. *American Journal of Sociology* 70 (2): 159–169.

Schwartz, Richard D., and Jerome H. Skolnick. 1964. Two Studies of Legal Stigma. In *The Other Side,* edited by Howard S. Becker, 103–117. New York: Free Press.

Schwendinger, Julia, and Herman Schwendinger. 1971. Sociology's Founding Fathers: Sexists to the Man. *Journal of Marriage and the Family* 33 (4): 783–799.

———. 1974. *The Sociologists of the Chair: A Radical Analysis of the Formative Years of North American Sociology (1883–1922).* New York: Basic Books.

———. 1975. Defenders of Order or Guardians of Human Rights? In *Critical Criminology,* edited by Ian Taylor, Paul Walton, and Jock Young, 113–146. London: Routledge and Kegan Paul.

———. 1977. Social Class and the Definition of Crime. *Crime and Social Justice* 7 (Spring/Summer): 4–13.

———. 1983. *Rape and Inequality.* Beverly Hills: Sage.

———. 1985. *Adolescent Subcultures and Delinquency.* New York: Praeger.

Sciolino, Elaine. 1988. Fighting Narcotics: U.S. Is Urged to Shift Tactics. *New York Times,* April 10, A1, A10.

Scott, Valerie, Peggy Miller, and Ryan Hotchkiss. 1987. Realistic Feminists. In *Good Girls/Bad Girls: Feminists and Sex Trade Workers Face to Face,* edited by Laurie Bell, 204–217. Seattle: Seal Press.

Scott, Walter. 1988. Personality Parade. *Parade Magazine,* October 30, 2.

Scully, Diana. 1980a. How Residents Learn to Talk You into Unnecessary Surgery. *Ms.* 8 (11): 89–93.

———. 1980b. *Men Who Control Women's Health.* Boston: Houghton Mifflin.

Seager, Jodi. 1993. *Earth Follies: Coming to Feminist Terms with the Global Environmental Crisis.* New York: Routledge.

Sellin, Thorsten. 1938. *Culture Conflict and Crime.* New York: Social Science Research Council.

Shacklady-Smith, Leslie. 1978. Sexist Assumptions and Female Delinquency: An Empirical Investigation. In *Women, Sexuality, and Social Control,* edited by Carol Smart and Barry Smart, 74–86. Boston: Routledge and Kegan Paul.

Shavelson, Lonny. 1988. Tales of Troubled Waters. *Hippocrates,* March/April, 70–77.

Shaw, Clifford R. 1930. *The Jack-Roller: A Delinquent Boy's Own Story.* Chicago: University of Chicago Press.

———. 1939. *The Natural History of a Delinquent Career.* Chicago: University of Chicago Press.

Shaw, Clifford R., et al. 1929. *Delinquency Areas: A Study of the Geographic Distribution of School Truants, Juvenile Delinquents, and Adult Offenders in Chicago.* Chicago: University of Chicago Press.

Shaw, Clifford, Henry D. McKay, and James F. McDonald. 1938. *Brothers in Crime.* Chicago: University of Chicago Press.

Shaw, Clifford R., and Henry D. McKay. [1942] 1969. *Juvenile Delinquency and Urban Areas.* Chicago: University of Chicago Press.

Sheehan, Daniel. 1988. *Inside the Shadow Government.* Washington, D.C.: Christic Institute.

Shelley, Louise I. 1981a. *Crime and Modernization: The Impact of Industrialization and Modernization on Crime.* Carbondale: Southern Illinois University Press.

Shelley, Louise I., ed. 1981b. *Readings in Comparative Criminology.* Carbondale: Southern Illinois University Press.

Shenon, Philip. 1988a. Enemy Within: Drug Money Is Corrupting Enforcers. *New York Times,* April 11, A1, A2.

———. 1988b. McFarlane Admits Withholding Data on Aid to Contras. *New York Times,* March 12, A1, A6.

———. 1988c. North, Poindexter, and Two Others Indicted. New York Times, March 17, A1, D27.

Sherman, Lawrence W., Patrick R. Gartin, and Michael E. Bueger. 1989. Hot Spots of Predatory Crime: Routine Activities and the Criminology of Place. *Criminology* 27 (1): 27–55.

Short, James F. 1957. Differential Association and Delinquency. *Social Problems* 4 (3): 233–239.

———. 1958. Differential Association with Delinquent Friends and Delinquent Behavior. *Pacific Sociological Review* 1 (1): 20–25.

———. 1962. Gang Delinquency and Anomie. In *Anomie and Deviant Behavior,* edited by Marshall B. Clinard, 98–127. New York: Free Press.

———. 1969. Introduction to *Juvenile Delinquency and Urban Areas,* edited by Clifford R. Shaw and Henry D. McKay, xxv–liv. Rev. ed. Chicago: University of Chicago Press.

———. 1997. *Poverty, Ethnicity, and Violent Crime.* Boulder, Colo.: Westview.

Short, James F., and Fred L. Strodtbeck. 1965. *Group Process and Gang Delinquency.* Chicago: University of Chicago Press.

Shostak, Marjorie. 1983. *Nisa: The Life and Words of a !Kung Woman.* New York: Vintage Books.

Shover, Neal. 1972. Structures and Careers in Burglary. *The Journal of Criminal Law, Criminology, and Police Science* 64 (4): 540–549.

———. 1996. *Great Pretenders: Pursuits and Careers of Persistent Thieves.* Boulder, Colo.: Westview Press.

Sick, Gary. 1991. *October Surprise: Americas Hostages in Iran and the Election of Ronald Reagan.* New York: Times Books.

———. 1993. Missing Link. *New York Times,* January 24, 17.

Sidel, Ruth. 1987. *Women and Children Last.* New York: Penguin.

Simon, Carl P., and Ann D. Witte. 1982. *Beating the System: The Underground Economy.* Boston: Auburn House Publishing.

Simon, David R. 1999. *Elite Deviance*. Boston: Allyn and Bacon.

Simon, Rita. 1975. *Women and Crime*. Lexington, Mass.: D.C. Heath.

Simpson, A. W. Brian. 1984. *Cannibalism and the Common Law*. Chicago: University of Chicago Press.

Simpson, Sally. 1986. The Decomposition of Antitrust: Testing a Multi-Level Longitudinal Model of Profit-Squeeze. *American Sociological Review* 51 (6): 859–875.

_____. 1987. Cycles of Illegality: Antitrust Violations in Corporate America. *Social Forces* 65 (June): 943–963.

Singleton, Royce, Jr., Bruce C. Straits, Margaret M. Straits, and Ronald J. McAllister. 1988. *Approaches to Social Research*. New York: Oxford University Press.

Skinner, B. F. 1953. *Science and Human Behavior*. New York: Macmillan.

Sklar, Holly, and Robert Lawrence. 1981. *Who's Who in the Reagan Administration*. Boston: South End Press.

Skocpol, Theda, and Margaret Somers. 1980. The Uses of Comparative History in Macrosocial Inquiry. *Comparative Studies in Society and History* 22 (2): 174–197.

Smart, Carol. 1976. *Women, Crime, and Criminology: A Feminist Critique*. Boston: Routledge and Kegan Paul.

_____. 1979. The New Female Offender: Reality or Myth? *British Journal of Criminology* 19 (1): 50–59.

_____. 1998. The Woman of Legal Discourse. In *Criminology at the Crossroads: Feminist Readings in Crime and Justice*, edited by Kathleen Daly and Lisa Maher, 21–36. New York: Oxford University Press.

Smith, Douglas, and Christy A. Visher. 1980. Sex and Involvement in Deviance/Crime: A Quantitative Review of the Empirical Literature. *American Sociological Review* 45 (4): 691–701.

Smith, Dwight. 1976. *The Mafia Mystique*. New York: Basic Books.

Snodgrass, Jon. 1973. The Criminologist and His Criminal: The Case of Edwin H. Sutherland and Broadway Jones. *Issues in Criminology* 8 (1): 1–17.

_____. 1976. Clifford R. Shaw and Henry D. McKay: Chicago Criminologists. *British Journal of Criminology* 16 (1): 1–19.

Sokoloff, Natalie. 1980. *Between Money and Love*. New York: Praeger.

Sowell, Thomas. 1988. Let's Just Say No to Anti-Drug Laws. *Boston Herald,* August 20, 19.

Sparks, Richard F. 1981. Surveys of Victimization: An Optimistic Assessment. *Crime and Justice: An Annual Review of Research* 3: 1–60.

Spitzer, Steven. 1975. Toward a Marxian Theory of Deviance. *Social Problems* 22 (5): 638–651.

_____. 1980. Left-Wing Criminology: An Infantile Disorder. In *Radical Criminology: The Coming Crises,* edited by James A. Inciardi, 169–190. Beverly Hills: Sage.

_____. 1981. Beyond Crime: Seven Methods to Control Troublesome Rascals. In *Law and Deviance,* edited by H. Laurence Ross, 127–157. Beverly Hills: Sage.

Stack, Steven, and Mary Jeanne Kanavy. 1983. The Effect of Religion on Forcible Rape: A Structural Analysis. *Journal for the Scientific Study of Religion* 22 (1): 67–74.

Stanko, Elizabeth. 1985. *Intimate Intrusions: Women's Experience of Male Violence*. Boston: Routledge and Kegan Paul.

Stanton, Duncan. 1976. Drugs, Vietnam, and the Vietnam Veteran: An Overview. *American Journal of Drugs and Alcohol Abuse* 3: 557–570.

Staples, Robert. 1987. Black Male Genocide: A Final Solution to the Race Problem in America. *Black Scholar* 18 (May/June): 2–11.

Stark, Evan, and Anne Flitcraft. 1998. Women and Children at Risk: A Feminist Perspective on Child Abuse. In *Issues in Intimate Violence*, edited by Raquel Kennedy Bergen, 25–41. Thousand Oaks, Calif.: Sage.

Statistical Abstract of the United States. 1997. Washington, D.C.: U.S. Government Printing Office.

Stead, Philip John. 1983. *The Police of France*. London: Macmillan.

Steffensmeier, Darrell J. 1981. Crime and the Contemporary Woman: An Analysis of Changing Levels of Female Property Crimes, 1960–1975. In *Women and Crime in America,* edited by Lee Bowker, 39–59. New York: Macmillan.

_____. 1983. Organization Properties and Sex Segregation in the Underworld: Building a Sociological Theory of Sex Differences in Crime. *Social Forces* 61 (4): 1010–1032.

_____. 1986. *The Fence: In the Shadow of Two Worlds.* Totowa, N.J.: Rowman and Littlefield.

Steffensmeier, Darrell J., Emilie Andersen Allan, Miles D. Harer, and Cathy Streifel. 1989. Age and the Distribution of Crime. *American Journal of Sociology* 94 (4): 803–831.

Steffensmeier, Darrell, and Emilie Anderson Allan. 1995a. Criminal Behavior: Gender and Age. In *Criminology: A Contemporary Handbook*, edited by Joseph Sheley, 83–114. Belmont, Calif.: Wadsworth.

_____. 1995b. Age-Inequality and Property Crime: The Effects of Age-linked Stratification and Status-Attainment Processes on Patterns of Criminality Across the Life Course. In *Crime and Inequality*, edited by John Hagan and Ruth D. Peterson, 95–115. Stanford, Calif.: Stanford University Press.

Sterngold, James. 1987. Tangled Trail Ends Today for Levine. *New York Times,* February 20, D1, D4.

Stinchcombe, Arthur. 1963. Institutions of Privacy in the Determination of Police Administrative Practice. *American Journal of Sociology* 69 (2): 150–160.

_____. 1964. *Rebellion in a High School.* Chicago: Quadrangle.

St. James, Margo. 1987. The Reclamation of Whores. In *Good Girls/Bad Girls: Feminists and Sex Trade Workers Face to Face,* edited by Laurie Bell, 81–87. Seattle: Seal Press.

Straus, Murray A. 1977/1978. Wife Beating: How Common and Why? *Victimology* 2 (34): 443–457.

_____. 1996. Spanking and the Making of a Violent Society. *Pediatrics* 88 (4): 837–842.

Straus, Murray A., Richard J. Gelles, and Susan Steinmetz. 1980. *Behind Closed Doors.* New York: Doubleday.

Straus, Murray A., and Richard J. Gelles. 1988. How Violent Are American Families? Estimates from the National Family Violence Resurvey and Other Studies. In *Family Abuse and Its Consequences: New Directions in Research,* edited by Gerald T. Hotaling, David Finkelhor, John T. Kirkpatrick, and Murray Straus, 14–36. Newbury Park, Calif.: Sage.

Straus, Murray A., and Julie H. Stewart. 1999. Corporal Punishment by American Parents: National Data on Prevalence, Chronicity, Severity, and Duration in Relation to Child and Family Characteristics. *Clinical Child and Family Psychology Review*, in press.

Sumner. Colin. 1994. *The Sociology of Deviance: An Obituary.* New York: Continuum.

Surette, Ray, ed. 1984. *Justice and the Media.* Springfield, Ill.: Charles C. Thomas.

Surette, Ray. 1992. *Media, Crime, and Criminal Justice.* Pacific Grove, Calif.: Brooks/Cole.

_____. 1998. *Media, Crime, and Criminal Justice.* Belmont, Calif.: West/Wadsworth.

Sutherland, Edwin H. 1937. *The Professional Thief: By a Professional Thief.* Chicago: University of Chicago Press.

_____. [1924] 1947. *Criminology.* Philadelphia: J. B. Lippincott.

_____. [1942] 1956. Development of the Theory. In *The Sutherland Papers,* edited by Albert Cohen, Alfred Lindesmith, and Karl Schuessler, 13–29. Bloomington: Indiana University Press.

_____. [1949] 1983. *White Collar Crime.* New Haven, Conn.: Yale University Press.

Sutherland, Edwin H., and Donald R. Cressey. [1949] 1970. *Criminology.* Philadelphia: L. B. Lippincott.

Swaaningen, Rene Van. 1986. What Is Abolitionism? In *Abolitionism: Towards a Non-Repressive Approach to Crime,* edited by Herman Bianchi and Rene Van Swaaningen, 9–21. Amsterdam: Free University Press.

Swigert, Virginia. 1984. Public-Order Crime. In *Major Forms of Crime,* edited by Robert Meier, 95–117. Beverly Hills: Stage.

Sykes, Gresham M., and David Matza. 1957. Techniques of Neutralization: A Theory of Delinquency. *American Sociological Review* 22 (6): 664–670.

Tallmer, Matt. 1987. Chemical Dumping as a Corporate Way of Life. In *Corporate Violence,* edited by Stuart Hills, 111–120. Totowa, N.J.: Rowman and Littlefield.

Tannenbaum, Frank. 1938. *Crime and the Community.* Boston: Ginn.

Tappan, Paul W. 1947. Who Is the Criminal? *American Sociological Review* 12 (1): 96–102.

Tarde, Gabriel. 1884. Qu'est-ce qu'une société? *Revue philosophique* 18: 501.

_____. 1886. Problémes de penalité. In *La criminalité comparé,* 122–211. Paris: Alcan.

_____. 1892. Les crimes des foules. *Archives de l'anthropologie criminelle* 7: 353–386.

_____. 1893. Foules et sectes au point de rue criminal. *Revue des deux mondes* 120: 349–387.

_____. [1886] 1902. *La criminalité comparé.* Paris: Alcan.

_____. [1890] 1903. *The Laws of Imitation.* Translated by F. Parsons. New York: Henry Holt.

_____. 1912. *Penal Philosophy.* 1890. Translated by R. Howell. Boston: Little, Brown.

Taylor, Ian. 1983. *Crime, Capitalism, and Community: Three Essays in Socialist Criminology.* Toronto: Butterworths.

Taylor, Ian, Paul Walton, and Jock Young. 1973. *The New Criminology.* London: Routledge and Kegan Paul.

Taylor, Laurie. 1984. *In the Underworld.* Oxford: Basil Blackwell.

Thomas, William I. 1923. *The Unadjusted Girl: With Cases and Standpoints for Behavior Analysis.* Boston: Little, Brown.

Thomas, William I., and Florian Znaniecki. 1918–1920. *The Polish Peasant in Europe and America.* Chicago: University of Chicago Press.

Thornberry, Terence P. 1973. Race, Socio-Economic Status, and Sentencing in the Juvenile Justice System. *Journal of Criminal Law, Criminology, and Police Science* 64 (1): 90–98.

Thornberry, Terence, and Margaret Farnworth. 1982. Social Correlates of Criminal Involvement: Further Evidence on the Relationship between Social Status and Criminal Behavior. *American Sociological Review* 47 (4): 505–518.

Thornberry, Terence, and R. L. Christenson. 1984. Unemployment and Criminal Involvement: An Investigation of Reciprocal Causal Structures. *American Sociological Review* 49 (3): 398–411.

Thrasher, Frederic Milton. 1927. *The Gang: A Study of 1,313 Gangs in Chicago.* Chicago: University of Chicago Press.

Tifft, Larry, and Dennis Sullivan. 1980. *The Struggle to Be Human: Crime, Criminology, and Anarchism.* Orkney, U.K.: Cienfuegos Press.

Time. 1983. Wife Beating: The Silent Crime. September 5, 23.

Tittle, Charles R. 1975. Labeling and Crime: An Empirical Evaluation. In *The Labeling of Deviance,* edited by Walter R. Gove, 241–263. Beverly Hills: Sage.

_____. 1995. *Control Balance: Toward a General Theory of Deviance.* Boulder, Colo.: Westview.

_____. 1997. Thoughts Stimulated by Braithwaite's Analysis of Control Balance Theory. *Theoretical Criminology* 1 (1): 99–110.

_____. 1999. Continuing the Discussion of *Control Balance. Theoretical Criminology* 3 (3): 344–352.

Tittle, Charles R., Wayne J. Villemez, and Douglas A. Smith. 1978. The Myth of Social Class and Criminality: An Empirical Assessment of the Empirical Evidence. *American Sociological Review* 43 (5): 643–656.

Toby, Jackson. 1957. Social Disorganization and Stake in Conformity: Complementary Factors in the Predatory Behavior of Hoodlums. *Journal of Criminal Law, Criminology, and Police Science* 48 (1): 12–17.

_____. 1979. The New Criminology Is the Old Sentimentality. *Criminology* 16 (3): 516–526.

_____. 1983. Crime in the Schools. In *Crime and Public Policy,* edited by James Q. Wilson, 69–88. San Francisco: Institute for Contemporary Studies.

Tombs, Robert. 1980. Crime and the Security of the State: The Dangerous Classes and Insurrection in Nineteenth-Century Paris. In *Crime and the Law: The Social History of Crime in Western Europe Since 1500,* edited by V. A. C. Gatrell, Bruce Lenman, and Geoffrey Parker, 214–237. London: Europa.

Tomlinson, Mike, Tony Varley, and Ciaran McCullagh. 1988. Introduction to *Whose Law and Order? Aspects of Crime and Social Control in Irish Society,* edited by Mike Tomlinson et al., 9–20. Belfast: Sociological Association of Ireland.

Tremblay, Pierre. 1986. Designing Crime: The Short Life Expectancy and the Workings of a Recent Wave of Credit Card Bank Frauds. *British Journal of Criminology* 26 (3): 234–253.

Tunnell, Kenneth D. 1992. *Choosing Crime: The Criminal Calculus of Property Offenders.* Chicago: Nelson-Hall.

Turk, Austin. 1969. *Criminality and Legal Order.* Chicago: Rand McNally.

———. 1979. Analyzing Official Deviance: For a Nonpartisan Conflict Analysis in Criminology. *Criminology* 16 (3): 459–476.

Tushnet, Mark. 1988. *Central America and the Law: The Constitution, Civil Liberties, and the Courts.* Boston: South End Press.

UCLA. 1998. *The UCLA Television Violence Report, 1997.* Los Angeles: University of California–Los Angeles, UCLA Center for Communication Policy.

United Nations. 1983. *Human Rights: A Compilation of International Instruments.* Publication E.83.XIV.1. New York: United Nations.

———. 1986. *Demographic Yearbook, 1984.* New York: United Nations, Department of International Economic and Social Affairs, Statistical Office.

U.S. Department of Health and Human Services. 1997. *Preliminary Results from the 1996 National Household Survey on Drug Abuse.* Rockville, Md.: SAMHSA.

U.S. House Subcommittee on Crime. 1980. *Increasing Violence Against Minorities.* Washington, D.C.: U.S. Government Printing Office.

U.S. Senate Subcommittee on Terrorism, Narcotics, and International Operations. 1989. *Drugs, Law Enforcement, and Foreign Policy.* Washington, D.C.: U.S. Government Printing Office.

Valukas, Anton R., and Ira Raphaelson. 1988. Judicial Corruption. In *Prosecution of Public Corruption Cases,* edited by U.S. Department of Justice, 1–15. Washington, D.C.: Department of Justice.

Vance, Carol S. 1986. The Meese Commission on the Road. *The Nation,* August 2–9, 65, 76–82.

van den Haag, Ernest. 1969. Is Pornography a Cause of Crime? In *The Norton Reader,* edited by Arthur M. Eastman, 838–845. New York: W. W. Norton.

———. 1975. *Punishing Criminals: Concerning a Very Old and Painful Question.* New York: Basic Books.

Van Dijk, Jan J. M., and Patricia Mayhew. 1993. *Criminal Victimization in the Industrialized World: Key Findings of the 1989 and 1992 International Crime Surveys.* In *Understanding Crime: Experiences of Crime and Crime Control, 1–49.* Publication 49. Rome: United Nations.

Vaz, Edmund W., ed. 1967. *Middle-Class Juvenile Delinquency.* New York: Harper and Row.

Vila, Brian. 1994. A General Paradigm for Understanding Criminal Behavior. *Criminology* 32 (3): 311–360.

Viscusi, W. Kip. 1986. Market Incentives for Criminal Behavior. In *The Black Youth Employment Crisis,* edited by Richard B. Freeman and Harry J. Holzer, 301–346. Chicago: University of Chicago Press.

Vistica, Gregory L. 1996. Rape in the Ranks. *Newsweek,* November 25, 28–32.

Vitalis, André. 1998. Big Brother Is Watching You. *Manchester Guardian Weekly,* September 20, 15.

Vold, George B. 1958. *Theoretical Criminology.* New York: Oxford University Press.

Vold, George B., and Thomas J. Bernard. 1986. *Theoretical Criminology.* New York: Oxford University Press.

Vold, George B., Thomas J. Bernard, and Jeffrey B. Snipes. 1998. *Theoretical Criminology.* 4th ed. New York: Oxford University Press.

von Hirsch, Andrew. 1976. *Doing Justice: The Choice of Punishments.* New York: Hill and Wang.

Voorhis, Patricia Van, Francis T. Cullen, Richard A. Mathers, and Connie Chenoweth Garner. 1988. The Impact of Family Structure and Quality on Delinquency: A Comparative Assessment of Structural and Functional Factors. *Criminology* 26 (2): 235–261.

Wacquant, Loic. 1998. Imprisoning the American Poor. *Manchester Guardian Weekly* 159 (12): 8–9.

Waldman, Michael. 1990. *Who Robbed America?* New York: Random House.

Walker, Samuel. 1980. *Popular Justice: A History of American Criminal Justice.* New York: Oxford University Press.

Walklate, Sandra. 1998. *Understanding Criminology: Current Theoretical Debates.* Philadelphia: Open University Press.

Wall Street Journal. 1992a. Baxter Made Cut-Rate Deal with Syria to Escape Blacklist, U.S. Probe Finds. December 22, A3.

_____. 1992b. Foreign Job Bid by Southern Co. Probed by SEC. February 6, A4.

_____. 1993. Justice Department Probing for Possible Law Violations. May 20, A7.

Walsh, Dermot. 1986. *Heavy Business: Commercial Burglary and Robbery.* Boston: Routledge and Kegan Paul.

Walsh, Dermot, and Adrian Poole. 1983. *A Dictionary of Criminology.* Boston: Routledge and Kegan Paul.

Walsh, Marilyn E. 1977. *The Fence.* Westport, Conn.: Greenwood Press.

Walters, Glenn D. 1994. *Drugs and Crime in Lifestyle Perspective.* Thousand Oaks, Calif.: Sage.

Warchol, Greg. 1998. *Workplace Violence, 1992–1996.* Washington, D.C.: Bureau of Justice Statistics.

Washington, James Melvin, ed. 1986. *A Testament of Hope: The Essential Writings of Martin Luther King, Jr.* New York: Harper and Row.

Weber, Max. [1924] 1978. *Economy and Society.* Edited by Guenther Roth and Claus Wittich. Translated by Ephraim Fischoff et al. 2 vols. Berkeley: University of California Press.

Webster, Paula. 1981. Pornography and Pleasure. *Heresies* 3 (1): 48–51.

Weis, Joseph G. 1976. Liberation and Crime: The Invention of the New Female Criminal. *Crime and Social Justice* 6 (Fall): 17–27.

Welch, Michael, Melissa Fenwick, and Meredith Roberts. 1998. State Managers, Intellectuals, and the Media: A Content Analysis of Ideology in Experts' Quotes in Feature Newspaper Articles on Crime. *Justice Quarterly* 15 (1): 219–241.

Weld, William F. 1988. Introduction: Why Public Corruption Is Not a Victimless Crime. *Prosecution of Public Corruption Cases,* edited by U.S. Department of Justice, i–v. Washington, D.C.: Department of Justice.

Weldon, W. F. R. 1894–1895. An Attempt to Measure the Death-Rate Due to the Selective Destruction of Carcinus Moenas with Respect to a Particular Dimension. *Proceedings of the Royal Society of London* 57: 360–382.

Wells, L. Edward, and Joseph H. Rankin. 1988. Direct Parental Controls and Delinquency. *Criminology* 26 (2): 263–285.

West, Donald J., and Buz de Villiers. 1993. *Male Prostitution.* New York: Harrington Park Press.

Weyler, Rex. 1982. *Blood of the Land.* New York: Everest House.

Whyte, William Foote. 1943. *Streetcorner Society.* Chicago: University of Chicago Press.

Wilbanks, William. 1996. Homicide in Ireland. *International Journal of Comparative and Applied Criminal Justice* 20 (1): 59–75.

Wilbanks, William, and Paul Kim. 1984. *Elderly Criminals.* New York: University Press of America.

Wilkins, Leslie T. 1964. *Social Deviance: Social Policy, Action, and Research.* London: Tavistock.

Williams, Linda S. 1984. The Classic Rape: When Do Victims Report? *Social Problems* 31 (4): 459–467.

Wilson, James Q. 1985. *Thinking About Crime.* New York: Vintage.

Wilson, James Q., and Richard J. Herrnstein. 1985. *Crime and Human Nature.* New York: Simon and Schuster.

Wise, David. 1976. *The American Police State.* New York: Random House.

Wolf, Douglas, and David Greenberg. 1986. The Dynamics of Welfare Fraud. *Journal of Human Resources* 21 (4): 437–455.

Wolfe, David A. 1985. Child-Abusive Parents: An Empirical Review and Analysis. *Psychological Bulletin* 97 (3): 462–482.

Wolfgang, Marvin E. 1958. *Patterns in Criminal Homicide.* Philadelphia: University of Pennsylvania Press.

———. 1967. International Criminal Statistics: A Proposal. *Journal of Criminal Law, Criminology, and Police Science* 58 (1): 65–69.

Wolfgang, Marvin E., and Franco Ferracuti. 1967. *The Subculture of Violence.* London: Tavistock.

Wollstonecraft, Mary. [1792] 1975. *A Vindication of the Rights of Women.* New York: W. W. Norton.

Won, George, and George Yamamoto. 1968. Social Structure and Deviant Behavior: A Study of Shoplifting. *Sociology and Social Research* 53 (1): 44–55.

Wood, Peter B., Walter R. Gove, James A. Wilson, and John K. Cochran. 1997. Non-Social Reinforcement and Habitual Criminal Conduct: An Extension of Learning Theory. *Criminology* 35 (2): 335–366.

Woodward, Bob. 1988. *Veil: The Secret Wars of the CIA, 1981–1987.* New York: Simon and Schuster.

Wright, Gordon. 1983. *Between the Guillotine and Liberty: Two Centuries of the Crime Problem in France.* New York: Oxford University Press.

Wright, James, Peter H. Rossi, and Kathleen Daly. 1983. *Under the Gun: Weapons, Crime, and Violence in America.* New York: Aldine.

Wright, Richard T., and Scott H. Decker 1994. *Burglars on the Job: Streetlife and Residential Break-ins.* Boston: Northeastern University Press.

———. 1997. *Armed Robbers in Action: Stickups and Street Culture.* Boston: Northeastern University Press.

Wyden, Peter. 1979. *Bay of Pigs: The Untold Story.* New York: Simon and Schuster.

Yablonsky, Lewis. 1962. *The Violent Gang.* New York: Macmillan.

Yeager, Peter C. 1995. Law, Crime, and Inequality: The Regulatory State. In *Crime and Inequality,* edited by John Hagan and Ruth D. Peterson, 247–276. Stanford, Calif.: Stanford University Press.

Yin, Peter. 1985. *Victimization and the Aged.* Springfield, Ill.: Charles C. Thomas.

Young, Gary. 1978. Justice and Capitalist Production: Marx and Bourgeois Ideology. *Canadian Journal of Philosophy* 8 (3): 421–455.

Young, Jock. 1971. The Role of the Police as Amplifiers of Deviancy, Negotiators of Reality, and Translators of Fantasy. In *Images of Deviance,* edited by Stanley Cohen, 27–61. Harmondsworth, U.K.: Penguin.

———. 1986. The Failure of Criminology: The Need for a Radical Realism. In *Confronting Crime,* edited by Roger Matthews and Jock Young, 4–30. Beverly Hills: Sage.

———. 1997. Left Realist Criminology: Radical in Its Analysis, Realist in Its Policy. In *Oxford Handbook of Criminology*, edited by Mike Maguire, Rod Morgan, and Robert Reiner, 473–498. Oxford: Clarendon Press.

Zietz, Dorothy. 1981. *Women Who Embezzle or Defraud: A Study of Convicted Felons.* New York: Praeger.

Zimring, Franklin E., and Gordon Hawkins. 1997. *Crime Is Not the Problem: Lethal Violence in America.* New York: Oxford University Press.

Index

References to artwork are indicated with italic page numbers.

About the Authors

 **Piers Beirne** is professor and chair of criminology at the University of Southern Maine. Prior to working in Maine he taught law, sociology, and criminology in England, at the University of Wisconsin–Madison, and at the University of Connecticut–Storrs. He is the founding coeditor of the international journal *Theoretical Criminology*, and his recent books include *Inventing Criminology* (1993) and *Issues in Comparative Criminology* (1997, edited with David Nelken). His research has been published in numerous scholarly journals, including *American Journal of Sociology; British Journal of Criminology; Criminology; Journal of Criminal Justice; Journal of Crime, Law, and Social Change; Law and Society Review; Social Justice; Social Problems; Society and Animals;* and *Theoretical Criminology*.

 **James W. Messerschmidt** received his Ph.D. from the Criminology Institute in the Department of Sociology at the University of Stockholm, Sweden. He is a professor of sociology at the University of Southern Maine. His research interests focus on the interrelation of gender, race, class, and crime. In addition to numerous articles and book chapters, he is the author of *The Trial of Leonard Peltier* (South End Press, 1983); *Capitalism, Patriarchy, and Crime: Toward a Socialist Feminist Criminology* (Rowman and Littlefield, 1986); *Masculinities and Crime: Critique and Reconceptualization of Theory* (Rowman and Littlefield, 1993); *Crime as Structured Action: Gender, Race, Class, and Crime in the Making* (Sage, 1997), and *Nine Lives: Adolescent Masculinities, the Body, and Violence* (Westview, 2000).